The Islamic Secular

The Islamic Secular

SHERMAN A. JACKSON

OXFORD
UNIVERSITY PRESS

OXFORD
UNIVERSITY PRESS

Oxford University Press is a department of the University of Oxford. It furthers the University's objective of excellence in research, scholarship, and education by publishing worldwide. Oxford is a registered trade mark of Oxford University Press in the UK and certain other countries.

Published in the United States of America by Oxford University Press
198 Madison Avenue, New York, NY 10016, United States of America.

CIP data is on file at the Library of Congress
ISBN 978–0–19–766178–9

DOI: 10.1093/oso/9780197661789.001.0001

Printed by Sheridan Books, Inc., United States of America

To the memory of my parents,
who gave so much from so little.

وَقُل رَّبِّ أَدْخِلْنِي مُدْخَلَ
صِدْقٍ وَأَخْرِجْنِي مُخْرَجَ
صِدْقٍ وَاجْعَل لِّي مِن لَّدُنكَ
سُلْطَانًا نَّصِيرًا

Contents

Acknowledgments xi

Introduction 1
The Nemesis of Language 1
Divine Law and *Sharīʿah* 5
Islamic Studies 2.0 11
The Chapters 15

PART I: THE CONCEPTUAL LANDSCAPE

1. Secular, Religious, Islamic 27
Basic Lay of the Land 27
The Secular 27
The Secular in Historical Perspective 30
The Secular: Macro- and Micro-Modes 35
Differentiation 39
Between the Non-*Sharʿī* and the Non-Religious 42
The Religious 43
Religion As Subject and Object 43
Of Definitions and Usages 46
"Religion" and "*Dīn*" 48
The Islamic Secular's Religion 50
The Islamic 54
"Muslim" versus "Islamic" 54
"Islamic" and My Evolutionary Turn 54
Marshall Hodgson 59
Shahab Ahmed 63

2. Islam, *Fiqh*, the *Ḥukm Sharʿī*, and the Differentiated Realm 74
Between "Bad" and "Juristically Proscribed" 74
Beyond the *Ḥukm Sharʿī* 77
The Standard View 83
The Bounded *Ḥukm Sharʿī* 87
Islamic Law: *Sharīʿah, Fiqh, Madhhab* 89
Of Horizontal and Vertical Boundaries 90
Early Proponents of an Unbounded *Sharīʿah* 90
The Emergence of the Theoretical Foundations of a Bounded *Sharīʿah* 94
The Theoretical Consummation of a Bounded *Sharīʿah* 98

Modern Continuities and Discontinuities 107
Misrecognizing the Bounded Nature of *Sharīʿah* 108
Sharīʿah Minimalism and Maximalism 110
Ibn Ḥazm and the Ẓāhirī Project 110
The *Sharīʿah*-Maximalism of Ibn al-Qayyim and Ibn Taymīyah 112
Ibn al-Qayyim 112
Ibn Taymīyah 115

3. The Islamic Secular 121
Between Divine Sovereignty and Divine Communication 121
Islām Mā Warāʾ al-Ḥukm al-Sharʿī 124
Islamic Law Beyond *Sharīʿah* 127
The Dystopian Narrative of Islamic Law 127
Sharīʿah and "Islamic Law" 128
Siyāsah 134
Maẓālim 144
Ḥisbah 151
The Islamic Secular: "Beyond the Law" 156
Nomos and Plausibility Structure 156
Efficient Decision-Making 164
The Islamic Secular versus *Ijtihād* 169
The "Islamic" in the Islamic Secular 173
Coda: The Islamic Secular and the Challenge of Talal Asad 175
The Asadian Frame 176
The Asadian Challenge 177
The Islamic Secular's Response 179
Has Islam Become a Religion? 184

PART II: THE ISLAMIC SECULAR, MODERNITY, AND THE MODERN STATE

4. The Islamic Secular and the Impossible State 193
Basic Anatomy 193
The Impossible State 194
Avoiding Distortions and Straw Men 197
What Hallaq Is *Not* Saying 198
Hallaq and the Modern State 201
Provenance 203
Sovereignty and Law 204
Violence, Sacrifice, Bureaucracy, Culture 210
Sharīʿah between Hallaq and the Islamic Secular 216
Reason and Islamic Law 217
The Curse of Modernity 223
Al-Ḥusn wa al-Qubḥ al-ʿAqlīyān 224

Morality vs. *Shar‘* 228
Is vs. Ought 229
Back to Reason 232
The Islamic Secular and the Islamic State 235
Shar‘ī vs. Non-*Shar‘ī*: Law vs. Fact 235
Islamic Governance between Discretion and Juristic Law 237
The Promise and Threat of Discretionary Authority 240
The Authority of the Islamic Secular 243

5. The Islamic Secular and the Secular State 250
Basic Anatomy 250
The Islamic State, Secularism, and An-Na‘im's Secular State 251
The Basic Aim of the Present Analysis and Critique 254
Two Necessary Digressions 256
The Purity of Religiosity 257
Human Rights 262
The Na‘imian Secular State: Substantive Details 264
The Alchemy of the Secular 265
History 268
The Wages of Rational Certainty: *Khilāf*, *Sui Juris*, and "Decreed by God" 270
Undifferentiated Religion and An-Na‘im's Secular 276
The Nemesis of Neutrality 277
Non-Muslims: Islam-cum-*Sharī‘ah* between the Modern State and the Empire-State 279
Al-Shāfi‘ī, Mālik, Ḥanafīs, and the Early Period 282
The Post-Formative Scene 285
The Empire-State between *Sharī‘ah* and the Islamic Secular 287
The Secular State and the Islamic Secular 292

6. The Islamic Secular and Liberal Citizenship 304
Basic Anatomy 304
March's Framing and Its Implications 306
Rawls, March, and the Basic Question 313
Rawls 314
The Rawlsian March and the Marchian Rawls 317
The Marchian Challenge 317
Islam and Comprehensive Doctrines: Between March and Rawls 319
The Primacy of Public Reason 321
March's Response to the Challenge of Islam and Liberal Citizenship 323
Conjecture and Islam's Ostensible Default Position 324
Liberal Citizenship between March and the Islamic Secular 328
March on Islam's Response to His Four-Part Criterion 329
Residence 331
Loyalty 332
Pluralism and Solidarity 339

Islam, Liberalism, and American Democracy: An Alternate Approach 344
Standing Where I Sit 344
Race 345
Religion 354
Politics 358
The US Constitution between *Sharī'ah* and the Islamic Secular 360
Protecting the Protection 363

Conclusion 372

Notes 381
Bibliography 495
Index 519

Acknowledgments

From the time I completed my PhD dissertation on the seventh-/thirteenth-century Mālikī jurist Shihāb al-Dīn al-Qarāfī in the early 1990s, the idea of the limits or boundaries of Islamic law has informed my thinking about *sharīʿah* and its place in Islam. In this sense, the basic idea behind this book is not new. From another perspective, however, my move in 2011 from an Area Studies department at the University of Michigan, where I spent most of my career, to a Religious Studies department at the University of Southern California consummated my exposure to a different set of conversations and a different bibliography, which cumulatively suggested that the matter of *sharīʿah*'s boundaries might have significance beyond what I had been able to discern or contemplate theretofore. This proved particularly relevant to the interest I developed in the question of Islam's relationship with the "secular," as religion's presumed binary "Other." This book brings aspects of these two academic disciplines into conversation with each other around the topic of the secular (and by entailment the religious) against the backdrop of the modern encounter between Islam and the West, mediated through insights and arguments gleaned from the legacy of Islam's juristic (and theological) tradition.

Over the course of my thinking about and re-thinking Islam's relationship with the secular (and religious) countless individuals contributed to the ideational tributaries that flowed into this book. No one looms larger in my Area Studies background than my mentor, the late Professor George Makdisi, whose memory continues to guide, inspire, and discipline me. Meanwhile, I am deeply indebted to the late Professor Charles Long, a towering scholar of religion, who, for over two decades, albeit from a distance, provided kind and edifying tutelage. Similar thanks go to my colleagues at USC's School of Religion, who also helped me expand my gaze beyond Area Studies into the world of Religious Studies. I must also acknowledge the selfless instruction I received all those years ago in Egypt from Shaykh Ḥasan Salīm Ḥasan Ṣāliḥ of al-Azhar University and the profound impact it has had on my understanding of the Islamic juristic tradition.

Beyond these scholarly influences, many contributions came from non-scholarly quarters, for example, during some of my public speaking engagements or more casual social settings or even telephone-conversations. The queries, challenges, and suggestions I received were often indirect and open-ended, aimed at a still inchoate and imperceptibly evolving thesis whose concrete contours had not yet fully crystallized in my own mind. Yet, as serendipitous and indirect as these interventions often were, they continued to inform my thinking over the entire course of writing this book. The sheer number of these "unwitting" contributors (and the treachery of my memory) makes it impossible to name names today. But I want to acknowledge and thank all these interlocutors for what they so charitably and meaningfully contributed to this book.

More directly, several accomplished (and very busy) scholars were kind enough to share their intellectual capital with me. Ebrahim Moosa (a constant soundboard), Joseph Lowry, Intisar Rabb, and Ahmad Ahmad (also constantly engaged) were all gracious enough to read and comment on an earlier (and painful) draft of the entire manuscript. All of them went beyond the call of duty in demonstrating a kindness of candor that testifies not only to their big-heartedness as human beings but also to their integrity as scholars. While the final product shows that I did not always agree with their critiques or suggestions, I have not the words to express the deep gratitude and appreciation I feel towards them all. I can only hope that "Thank you" will suffice for the moment. My colleague at USC, David Albertson, dutifully read and provided useful comments and suggestions on an earlier draft of Chapter 1. My former teacher, Adel Allouche, agreed to "re-traumatize" me with a brief review of aspects of Mamlūk economics, discussed in Chapter 2. Jessica Marglin, Nomi Stolzenberg, Arjun Nair, Mohammad Fadel, Samy Ayoub, Ovamir Anjum, Asma Sayeed, Humaira Iqtidar, Michael Cooperson and Rushain Abbasi were valued interlocutors at various points along the way. I would also like to thank my graduate students at USC, especially Hadi Qazwini, Omar Qureshi, and Naseeha Hussain, all of whom suffered me through semesters on end of seeing the Islamic Secular around every corner and underneath every bed but who continued to engage me all the same. Of course, it goes without saying in connection with all these scholars that I alone am responsible for the views I express herein.

A distinct challenge I faced in writing this book sprang from the counter-intuitive, if not oxymoronic, ring of "Islamic Secular." Beyond their substantive intellectual contributions, several friends and colleagues (especially Ebrahim Moosa and Ahmad Ahmad) offered much needed encouragement to persevere and see this project through, despite what they (and I) recognized to be the formidable psychological barrier standing between readers—especially perhaps some Muslim readers—and their ability (initially at least) to reconcile the juxtaposition of "Islamic" with "Secular" or to avoid seeing any articulation of the "secular" in Islam as necessarily entailing "secularism" or "secularization." This encouragement proved critical to my ability to complete this book, and I would like to thank all those who offered it for so courageously and insistently doing so.

I would also like to thank the fine folks at Oxford University Press, especially Theo Calderara and Chelsea Hogue, for their professionalism and kind indulgence in seeing this book to production. I must also thank OUP's anonymous

Readers. Jubilee James and the team at Newgen also deserve recognition for their hard work and kind assistance. I am also grateful to Ursula DeYoung for her editorial support.

Last but not least, I would like to acknowledge the sacrifice, love, and support of my family, especially my wife, Dr. Heather Laird, and my dear departed mother, Mrs. Evelyn Crute, not only for continuing to believe in me and for encouraging and allowing me to stay the course but also for simply putting up with me—the often distracted husband, father, and son—throughout the vicissitudes that invariably accompany a project of this magnitude, import, and complexity. Thank you, family, for this and for all that you so graciously and consistently provide.

Introduction

The Nemesis of Language

In a lecture at the University of California, Berkeley, in 1979, the celebrated American writer James Baldwin (d. 1987) spoke of the nemesis of language: "What a writer is obliged at some point to realize is that he is involved in a language which he has to change." Applying this more specifically to Blackamerican[1] writers, Baldwin continued: "For a Black writer, especially in this country, to be born into the English language is to realize that the assumptions of the language, the assumptions on which the language operates, are his enemy."[2] Speaking of the dislocations visited by the Western lexicon on the Muslim East, the contemporary Arab philosopher Ṭaha ʿAbd al-Raḥmān strikes a similar chord: "The reality is that as long as Muslim society does not find its way to innovating new conceptual tools or reprocessing the conceptual tools of others to the point that they become as if they had been innovated originally by Muslims, there will be no hope of exiting the intellectual desert that has become the Muslim mind."[3] Both of these thinkers go to the heart of what it means to have to represent oneself in a language that has routinely been used, consciously or otherwise, to *mis*represent one—a language, alas, that modern reality will not permit one to ignore.

This book is an attempt to address this problem of language and the various assumptions, polarities, and obstructions it spawns, with specific reference to the term and concept(s) of the "secular." My basic argument is that, while the secular, as commonly understood in the contemporary West, connotes a fundamentally dichotomous relationship with the religious, the Islamic juristic tradition, particularly *uṣūl al-fiqh*, points to an alternate understanding of the construct. By "alternate understanding," I do not mean simply a different way of mapping the reigning Western meaning of "secular" onto Islam; nor am I referring to a different vocabulary by which Islam's *lingua franca* might express the standard Western understanding of the concept. I am arguing, rather, that, understood against the structural and ideational backdrop of Islam and its juristic tradition, "secular" acquires a different meaning altogether, one that does not render it the antithesis of religion. This alternate meaning is what I refer to in this book as the "Islamic Secular."

In his thoughtful summary of the history of Western studies of Islamic law, Baber Johansen provides insight into how, beginning in the nineteenth century, unquestioned presuppositions made their way into the scholarly literature,

The Islamic Secular. Sherman A. Jackson, Oxford University Press. © Oxford University Press 2024.
DOI: 10.1093/oso/9780197661789.003.0001

powered by Western hubris.[4] These presuppositions routinely denied Islamic law its own story and effectively assigned it a mere supporting role in that of the modern West. Accordingly, academic discussions of the secular in Islam rarely take Islam-cum-*sharīʿah* as their point of departure. This book is an attempt to remedy this failure, not by ignoring the West or assuming a zero-sum relationship between it and Islam, but by recognizing that, even where Islam and the West share vocabulary or concepts, taking the Western understanding as touchstone generates significant inaccuracies, dislocations, and blind spots. From the perspective of the Islamic juristic tradition, "secular" (as we will see) intimates what many in the modern West would consider a contradiction in terms, namely a "religious secular." This contradiction only exists, however, on the prior assumption of an oppositional relationship between the "secular" and the "religious" as one's point of departure. My point here is not that the West is wrong in holding its position; it is simply to question the universality of the West's position. For, Islam's secular—what this book terms the "Islamic Secular"—defies the paradigmatic assumption of secular/religious antipathy: the Islamic Secular is not "non-religious". Equally critical, as I detail in Chapter 3, the Islamic Secular cannot be translated into Arabic as simply *al-fikr al-ʿalmānī fī al-islām* or *al-ʿalmānī al-islāmī* or some other equivalent representing the wholesale grafting of the regnant Western understanding of "secular" onto Islam.

The basic assumption of the Islamic Secular is that, while the divine gaze of the God of Islam is universal and totalizing, God's concrete communiqué, in the form of *sharīʿah*, is bounded. As such, between the circumference of *sharīʿah* and that of Islam as a whole there exists a "space" within which Muslims do not and cannot rely solely on concrete divine dictates. Yet, while operating within this space, Muslims are neither removed from nor necessarily seek to remove themselves from a conscious awareness of the presence and adjudicative gaze of the God of Islam. When the great Ottoman architect Sinān (d. 996/1588) designed and built the buildings that became signatures of Islamic architecture, or when Ulugh Beg (Muḥammad Ṭaraghāy b. Shāhrukh b. Tīmūr (d. 853/1449) founded his famous observatory in Samarqand, neither was drawing on direct, concrete instructions from *sharīʿah* or its sources as the basis of his craft. Yet, it would be presumptuous to assume (especially given their time and place) that a conscious awareness of the divine gaze of the God of Islam did not inform their efforts. Just as Michelangelo painted "to the glory of God," so they designed, built, and studied to the same end. Their activity remained 'secular,' however, in that God's revelation contributed almost nothing to its concrete substance. But it was also "religious," in that it was carried out with sustained devotional intent. Moreover, in seeking a successful outcome to their efforts, their appeal to God (*istiʿānah*) would be as likely as it would be in connection with any properly religious act of worship (*ʿibādah*). Their efforts, in sum, fell within the province of the Islamic Secular.

This understanding of "secular"—plainly counterintuitive for contemporary Westerners (and those under their influence)—takes us back to the problem highlighted by Baldwin and 'Abd al-Raḥmān. If the word "secular" as commonly understood in the modern West implies a necessarily dichotomous relationship with "religion" while Islam-cum-*sharī'ah* assumes that the two concepts need not be dichotomous, then the present deployment of Western languages (my focus is English), through which Islam is studied and engaged, can neither produce nor accommodate an accurate depiction of the Faith. In other words, if Islam-cum-*sharī'ah* is to be understood on its own terms, this language, entrenched though it may be, must be changed, at least in its implications. This is what *The Islamic Secular* will attempt to do.

Part of the argument of this book is that neither Islam nor Islamic law can be adequately understood without fully appreciating the Islamic Secular. As a religion (i.e., *dīn*), Islam consists in not one but *two* distinct yet inextricably bound modes of religiosity: 1) a *shar'ī* mode, whose ground is *sharī'ah*, its sources, and dictates; and 2) a non-*shar'ī* mode—what I refer to as a "differentiated," 'secular mode'—whose concrete substance is not a dictate or derivative of *sharī'ah* or its sources. Adherence to the dictates of *sharī'ah* (i.e., the *shar'ī* mode) is readily recognized as both religious and Islamic; but culture-creation, technology-development, institution-building, mundane and everyday decision-making, and even various rational disciplines (e.g., medicine, astronomy, economics, dialectics [*adab al-baḥth*], geometry or algebra) are equally indigenous to Islam as *dīn*,even though hermeneutical engagement with *sharī'ah* or its sources does not, *mutatis mutandis*, determine the concrete substance of any of these pursuits. In this sense, while these pursuits are all 'secular,' in that their concrete substance falls outside the dictates of *sharī'ah* and its sources, they remain (at least potentially) "religious"—and, I argue, Islamic—in the sense of falling within the attention of Islam as religion.

To be sure, the idea that things do not have to be derived directly from scripture in order to be Islamic will strike some readers as "almost absurdly obvious." For this reason, in their view, the Islamic Secular is not saying anything new or important. Muslims, they argue, routinely greet such actions as "choosing the right color of flowers for a hospitalized friend" or "going to law school to fight police brutality" with "an instinctive *mā shā' Allāh*," enthusiastically praising such actions as Islamically constituted good deeds.[5] While this may be true, this perspective fails to capture the basic argument of this book. The meaning such observers impute to "Islamic" is overly broad, popular, untheorized, and breaks down fatally in application. If the mere fact that Muslims praise Pakistan's victory over India in cricket renders this victory Islamic, then Muslims exclaiming "*mā shā' Allah*" upon Brazil's beating Germany in soccer must render that victory equally Islamic.[6] Ultimately, "Islamic"—like "legal" or "constitutional," indeed, like "Islam"—is a technical term whose technical meaning and deployment must be distinguished from its popular usages, even as the latter are acknowledged as a matter of fact. More importantly, the praise in question tells us nothing about whether the acts in question are perceived as secular or as religious. The Islamic Secular, by contrast, includes definitions and usages of "secular," "religious," and "Islamic" as fully theorized technical terms that can be successfully applied across the board. Moreover—and here is where the view in question most crucially misapprehends my thesis—the Islamic Secular as a theory is not simply about how acts become Islamic but about how they can be Islamic *and* secular *and* religious at the same time.

Again, it is not my contention that the reigning definition of "secular" in the West is wrong. It is that this is not the only way that "secular" can be deployed. Words bear possibilities beyond their etymologies and even their dominant meanings. Often, a word's currency will stem not from its meaning or definition but from its usage and, as importantly, from the standing of the group whose usage counts most. This explains how in America the prevailing sense of "anti-Semitic" comes to be "anti-Jewish," that of "immigrant" (as in "immigration") to be "non-White," and that of "terrorism" to be "publicly directed violence committed by Muslims." Jeffrey Stout sheds useful light on the point I am trying to make here in his discussion of the history of "meaning" as a concept in the West. "Meaning," argues Stout (following Ian Hacking), makes its debut as a centerpiece of Western thought in the late nineteenth century.[7] Drawing on Wittgenstein, he notes that what is really at stake in debates over words is not the relative correctness of the sense or definition attributed to them but the frequency with which they are used in association with a particular meaning. The aim in such contests, in other words, is not to champion a specific *meaning* as the most technically or lexically correct; it is to inspire more frequent and uncontested *usage* of a word according to a particular meaning, even if other meanings of the word may be just as (or even more) historically or philologically correct.[8]

Stout's point is clearly reflected in the scholarly literature on the actual or ur-meaning of "secular." For example, Talal Asad cites the secular's roots in the Latin noun *saeculum* and notes how it evolved into a series of transfers first from monastic life to a life of cannons and then from Church proprietorship to private hands and ultimately the market.[9] Charles Taylor writes, "Secular, as we all know, comes from 'saeculum,' a century or age."[10] Craig Calhoun adds, "The root notion of the secular is a contrast not to religion but to eternity. It is derived from *saeculum*, a unit of time."[11] Timothy Fitzgerald confirms: "The term 'secular' did not mean 'non-religious.'"[12] And, according to Nikki Keddie, "secular" derived from the Latin adjective *saecularis* and came down through the French *seculer*, originally referring to "clergy who were not bound by the religious rules of a monastic order."[13] Yet, the technical accuracy of these attributions notwithstanding, little of this has much impact on the way the word "secular" is commonly used and understood today. Today, "secular" stands in contrast with "religious." And this is a function not of language or philology but of historical actors, intellectual interventions and civilizational authority-cum-prestige.

In sum, successfully anchoring a word or concept to a particular usage and connotation goes beyond the simple accuracy of the meaning attributed to it. The word or concept must also be paired with deeply felt needs, interests, perceptions or even vogues in a manner that secures these associations and ideally places them beyond critique. Such a process requires that those who wish to make such associations exercise enough agency to make them stick, as occurred, for example, with the term "Communism," originally excavated from the legacy of Christianity. According to Owen Chadwick, Marx and Engels simply "took an existing word, deconstructed it, and made it a name for a new system of social thought."[14] Rather than seeking to gain currency for an entirely unvetted neologism, they appropriated the authority and basic sense (or one of the senses) of an already existing term, the apparent ideological contradiction between Christianity and their theory of Communism notwithstanding. I will take a similar approach in this book.

I proceed, however, on the assumption that the West holds no copyright on the term "secular" and that Muslims can assume and exercise the same kind of agency that Marx and Engels used to imbue an old concept with new meanings, connotations, and usages. At the same time, I will demonstrate that, while the Islamic Secular participates in the same semantic field as the Western secular, a careful reading of the Islamic juristic tradition not only moves Islam's secular beyond the reigning Western meaning of the term but also renders it as Islamically authentic as the Islamic juristic discourse from which it derives. This authenticity, along with the concept's utility as a conceptual, analytical, and generative tool in the service of various academic and confessional interests, will be relied upon to sustain the legitimacy and naturalness of "Islamic Secular" as a term of art.

Divine Law and *Sharīʿah*

A key constituent of my thesis is the argument that *sharīʿah* is a bounded entity rather than the totalizing, all-encompassing construct it is commonly understood to be. Indeed, the bounded nature of *sharīʿah* is what establishes the possibility of the aforementioned "space" between its jurisdictional circumference and that of Islam as a whole, the space wherein the Islamic Secular resides. But I shall argue additionally that, on close examination, the assumption that *sharīʿah* is totalizing, in the sense of carrying universal jurisdiction and in that capacity constituting the only Islamically relevant metric of assessment, has no real basis in the Islamic juristic tradition, at least not as the dominant view. Yet the totalizing view of *sharīʿah* has endured for generations and has thoroughly informed the perception of Islam-cum-*sharīʿah* in the Western academy and beyond. This longstanding misimpression raises an important question: If this is not the view with which one emerges from an attentive reading of *uṣūl al-fiqh*—the ultimate theoretical basis of *sharīʿah*—why has this presumption endured for so long? What other interpretive prisms or presuppositions might explain this long-standing perspective on Islamic law?

The Dutch Orientalist Christiaan Snouck Hurgronje (d. 1936) was among the first continental European authorities on Islamic law, and his characterizations "left lasting traces in the occidental understanding of the subject."[15] Among these traces was the notion that *fiqh* was not a legal system but a "deontology," an undifferentiated collection of religious duties and dictates handed down from on-high by the God of Islam, essentially the Ten Commandments times ten thousand.[16] On this understanding, it was reasonable to assume that *sharīʿah*'s status as a "sacred law" (after Weber, who was also influenced by Hurgronje) implied all-encompassing jurisdiction, the Divine Itself being presumed to possess unbounded power and authority.[17] Thus, echoing Hurgronje, Joseph Schacht (d. 1969) wrote, "The sacred law of Islam is an all-embracing body of religious duties rather than a legal system proper. [18] Meanwhile, Hurgronje had claimed "*fiqh* was, from its very beginning, considered by its exponents as a divine doctrine which is complete and perfect."[19] But while Hurgronje effectively denied Islamic law's rationality, Schacht affirmed it. And in this way, mutually reinforcing notions of comprehensiveness, perfection, and completeness, underwritten by the possibility of infinite extension through reason, came to be associated with *sharīʿah*.

In her insightful book, *What's Divine About Divine Law?*, Christine Hayes looks at how the notion of divine law was understood "in the Mediterranean and Near Eastern world in the thousand-year period prior to the rise of Islam."[20] She notes that the Greek understanding of divine law differed dramatically from the Biblical conception of the Jewish rabbis. In much of Greek thought, what made a law divine was not that it issued from a god or gods but that it "expresses the profound structures of a permanent natural order,"[21] the ingrained laws that infuse the cosmos, including the physical world and our nature as humans in it. A law was divine, in other words, "*by virtue of such qualities inherent in it*, first and foremost its rationality, which entails its truth value, its universality, and its static unchanging character."[22] In this sense, divine law was as comprehensive in scope as the natural order of which it was assumed to be a reflection, whence its association with universal jurisdiction.

Anyone familiar with the early debates in Islam that pit the Muʿtazilites and their "moral objectivism" against their Rationalist and Traditionalist adversaries will recognize a similar fault line in early Islam. All of the major schools of Sunni theology lined up against the Muʿtazilite insinuation that God's law, that is, what God rewards and punishes, has a pre-existence in nature that ultimately dictates its status as law, implying that the law was simply "uncovered" (*kashf*) by reason or revelation.[23] The Sunnī counter-thesis was that divine law was not "uncovered," as a buried trove, but unilaterally stipulated (*waḍʿ*) by God, as a function of God's autonomous, unilateral will. In taking this position, Sunnīs were comparable to the pre-Islamic rabbis in their disagreement with Greek thought. What made Islam's divine law divine for Sunnīs was not its conformity to or reflection of a rationally constituted, pre-existing cosmic order but the fact that it issued from the Possessor of divine *authority*.

If a divine law is divine not because it is a reflection of an all-encompassing, ingrained, cosmic order but because it is the product of the Divine's unilateral will, such a will might intentionally limit its field of address. This need not mean that everything outside this field is beyond the Divine's interest, any more than a child, employee, or lover can assume that everything outside his parent's, employer's, or lover's explicit communications remains unregulated. Nor need we assume that analogy (*qiyās*) based on explicit instructions necessarily exhausts the demands of living in such a regulated space. The Sunnī understanding of divine law does suggest, however, that outside the Greek notion of divinity, there is nothing to compel the presumption that divine law is all-encompassing simply because it is divine. In seeing *sharīʿah* as bounded, the Islamic Secular simply privileges the Sunnī over the Greek perspective on the nature of the Divine, seeing the Divine as (*inter alia*) voluntary Issuer of Commands rather than Avatar of the Cosmos.

But there is another side to the issue. The Greek (and later Greco-Roman) understanding of divine law typically emphasized ontological realism as its point of departure. By this I do not mean that the law confronted rather than fled from socio-political reality; nor do I have in mind the "legal realism" championed by the likes of the legal scholars Jerome Frank (d. 1957) or Karl Llewelyn (d. 1962). By ontological realism, I mean that the structure of the law was assumed to be pegged to the extra-mental structure of the world, its prescriptions corresponding to the inherent nature of the universe. Murder, on this understanding, is evil and must incur punishment not because God said it must but because it is objectively evil in the same sense that fire is objectively hot and water objectively wet. From this perspective, no authority can make murder good or not deserving of punishment, any more than it can make fire cold.

By contrast, the nominalist approach, such as is found in the ancient Biblical and later Islamic traditions, tends to emphasize divine *fiat* as the basis of the law's authority, thus embracing the idea that things are good or evil (i.e., rewarded or punished) because God names them as such, which implies that God could have named them otherwise. In other words, it is neither the inherent nature of what God names as law nor its correspondence with an extra-mental index that renders it law; it is the fact that God names it as law.[24] Of course, as Hayes observes, "All legal systems appeal to nature and mind-independent reality in determining the law; what makes a system realist or nominalist is the *degree* to which such appeals are dispositive and uncontestable (more for the realist, less for the nominalist)."[25] The same holds for Islam: nominalists recognize any number of acts, for example, killing a prophet or accusing an innocent person, as plainly evil, while realists understand any number of things, such as the number of units in a prayer, along nominalist lines. Realists simply leave much less room for nominalism overall, while nominalists are palpably more sparing in their subscription to realist explanations.

The tendency to approach *sharīʿah* as a realist system (or a functional equivalent thereof) has become more explicit in recent years. We see it, for example, in certain appeals to "natural law" (often an iteration of realism) as the purported basis of Islamic law.[26] We see it as well, and perhaps more prominently, in the proposed bifurcation between *sharīʿah* and *fiqh*. This divide is often an attempt to loosen the grip of Islamic law and make room for more human deliberation. Muslim scholars tend to pursue this interest, however, not by limiting *sharīʿah*'s scope but by suggesting that even within *sharīʿah*'s jurisdiction what is claimed to be divine law is really only a human understanding thereof. *Fiqh*, in other words, while constituting a good-faith attempt to apprehend God's all-encompassing law, is not necessarily God's law and need not always be deferred to as such.[27]

At issue here, for my purposes at least, is not whether jurists always hit the ontological bull's-eye but whether their conclusions *must* correspond to an objective, extramental preexistent in order to qualify as God's law. If *sharīʿah* is ultimately a realist entity that is all-encompassing, transcendent, and unchanging, no Islamic Secular can exist. For, on such an understanding, *sharīʿah* is coterminous with Islam as God's will and correspondingly as expansive as God's creation. There can be no "space" between the circumference of Islam and that of *sharīʿah* and thus nothing within Islam that could be presumed to lie beyond *sharīʿah*'s scope (again, as described above). This, however, is precisely the presumption that the Islamic Secular calls into question.

By "functional equivalent" of *sharīʿah* as a realist bull's-eye, I am referring to the understanding of Islamic law that restricts it to a pure, unadulterated index that exists objectively not in nature but in 'the divine mind.' This appears to be the approach, for example, of Professor Khaled Abou El Fadl. In one of his descriptions of the classical juristic tradition, he writes: "Shariʿah, it was argued, is the Divine ideal, standing as if suspended in mid-air and uncorrupted by the vagaries of life. The *fiqh* is the human attempt to understand and apply the ideal. Therefore, Shariʿah is immutable, immaculate, and flawless—*fiqh* is not."[28] Much more recently, he wrote: "*Shariʿah* was considered to be the immutable, unchangeable and objectively perfect Divine truth. Human understanding of *Shari'ah*, however, was subjective, partial, subject to error and change. While *Shari'ah* is Divine, *fiqh* (the human understanding of *Shari'ah*) was recognized to be only potentially so."[29] Of course, assuming that he takes its locus to be 'the divine mind' Abou El Fadl's reference to an "objectively perfect" *sharī'ah* need not be understood in properly realist terms, that is, as ontologically pegged to nature. Where it becomes the functional equivalent thereof, however, is in its assertion that divine law is strictly limited to the perfect apprehension of an objectively identifiable pre-existing rule.

Let us consider this, however, from the perspective of the celebrated jurist-theologian Abū Ḥāmid al-Ghazālī (d. 505/1111). In his opus on *uṣūl al-fiqh*, in the context of discussing *ijtihād* (unmediated juristic interpretation of scripture), al-Ghazālī notes that not every issue is addressed by apodictic revelatory indicants (*adillah*/sg. *dalīl*). For many issues, there exists no more than "probable indicants" (*amārāt*/sg. *amārah*).[30] In these latter cases, according to al-Ghazālī, the assumption is that "God has no concrete, predetermined rule" (*laysa fīhā ḥukm*^{un} *mu'ayyan*^{un} *lillāhi ta'ālā*).[31] But this does not render the attainment of Divine pleasure, or the obligation to seek it, impossible or null and void. On the contrary, assuming due diligence, God's ruling, *ḥukm Allāh*, according to al-Ghazālī, is in such cases what the independent interpreter (*mujtahid*) concludes it to be. In effect, al-Ghazālī collapses the distinction between *fiqh*, or the human attempt to apprehend God's rule, and *sharī'ah*, or God's actual rule. Practically speaking, the two become identical. As Abou El Fadl himself summarizes this position, "sincerity of conviction, the search, and the process are in themselves the ultimate moral values."[32] As many if not most issues lack apodictic, revelatory indicants, much of the time, "God's ruling" must effectively become a human deduction ensnarled in the vagaries of life, as opposed to a pristine entity suspended in mid-air like a Platonic form.

Al-Ghazālī's view is grounded in the position of the so-called *muṣawwibah*, or those who believe that, assuming due diligence, every *mujtahid* is correct (*kullu mujtahid muṣīb*). As this group was opposed by the so-called *mukhaṭṭi'ah* (who argued that there is a specific, concrete view in each instance that represents the actual rule of God and that those who miss this mark are simply wrong), al-Ghazālī's position cannot be put forth as the sole view of Islam. But it was widely endorsed (differences in detail notwithstanding),[33] and even *mukhaṭṭi'ah* who opposed it neither generally attributed sin to *mujtahid*s who arrived at 'wrong' views nor insisted that these jurists could not profess or act upon those views in the name of *sharī'ah*.[34]

On a practical level, then, pursuing God's pleasure is not always a matter of apprehending a fixed and "flawless" *sharī'ah*, neither as an extramental, ontological preexistent nor as a pristine, pre-existing notation in the divine mind. Nor is the pursuit of divinely sanctioned human interests (i.e., *maṣāliḥ*/sg. *maṣlaḥah*), individually or collectively, necessarily a simple matter of apprehending God's pre-existing "flawless" *sharīʿah*. Both God's pleasure and humans' concrete, divinely sanctioned interests may lie beyond the objective, concrete revelatory indicants of *sharīʿah*, or *fiqh*. Yet—and this is the thesis of the Islamic Secular—this does not mean that Muslims must (or can) go outside of Islam altogether to pursue either God's pleasure or their own divinely sanctioned interests. For, neither "outside the dictates of *fiqh*" nor "outside the dictates of *sharīʿah*" necessarily means "outside the attention of Islam," in contradistinction to what a totalizing, especially a totalizing realist, understanding of *sharīʿah* would imply.

This is fundamental to my overall argument: the pursuit of divine pleasure, like the pursuit of divinely sanctioned human interest, is not strictly limited to the concrete dictates of *sharīʿah*. Nor is it limited to *fiqh* (which I argue in Chapter 3 is synonymous with *sharīʿah*[35]). And yet, such extra-*sharʿī* pursuits are also not necessarily any less religious or, I shall argue, any less Islamic, than those that are based directly on *sharʿī* indicants. For, not only is *fiqh/sharīʿah* not all-encompassing (in the sense that I argue), but it is also neither self-sustaining nor self-perpetuating; rather, it requires cultural, intellectual, and institutional support for which its sources provide no concrete directives or instruction. One thinks here of the role of pre-modern Islam's monied community, who established and maintained its educational and public welfare institutions, with no concrete *sharīʿah* directives and no instructions from scripture on how to do so. It is difficult to imagine the state of *sharīʿah* education (to take one example) including the relative independence of the *fuqahāʾ*, without the efforts of these men and women, whose roles have been almost entirely eclipsed by a singular focus on *sharʿīyāt* and their personnel as the sole presumed determinants of a healthy, functional Islam. Similar recognition must go to the entire field of "humanist *adab*"—grammar, rhetoric, poetry, history, and the epistolary arts, all of which were integral to Islam's success and self-understanding as a civilization and yet palpably distinct from *fiqh/sharīʿah*.[36] in a modern context, we might add such enterprises as editing and publishing important texts from Islam's vast repertoire of pre-modern Arab (and Persian and Turkish) manuscripts, as recently studied by Aḥmad El Shamsy.[37] For all of these reasons, we can hardly justify ignoring or discounting non-*sharʿī* contributions to Islam's health and stature as God-pleasing, religious, and, indeed, Islamic activity, even though they were (or are) not concretely dictated by *sharīʿah*.

In sum, I am proposing that the totalizing, absolutist vision of Islamic law, in whatever form, distorts the academic understanding of Islam-cum-*sharīʿah*, on the one hand, and impoverishes the Muslim attempt to instantiate Islam as praxis, on the other. By excluding the Islamic Secular from our interpretive prism as academics, we exclude extra-*sharʿī* contributions to the concrete instantiation of Islam-cum-*sharīʿah* in history. At the same time, by assuming that non-*sharʿī* activity is, by definition, non-religious, non-Islamic or, perhaps, contra-Islamic, we render *sharīʿah* itself the totalizing, coterminous equivalent of Islam, effectively excluding everything else from the designation "Islamic." Meanwhile, modern Muslims who do not recognize as religious non-*sharʿī* activity consciously pursued under the adjudicative gaze of the God of Islam will nurse a similarly dim estimate of its Islamic value. And given the centrality of non-*sharʿī*—"secular"—activity to everyday existence, this lack of recognition may well drive Muslims toward secularization in the modern Western sense, by limiting what they recognize as "religious" activity to *sharʿīyāt* and stigmatizing or discounting non-*sharʿī* activity (and those who undertake it) as "non-religious." The wages of such a perspective are clearly reflected in the words an Imām in Philadelphia once conveyed to me in explaining a group of Muslims' hostile indifference to a major economic development project by another group of Muslims in the city: "Ain't no *dīn* in it." Remedying such misrecognition is among the fundamental concerns of the Islamic Secular.

Islamic Studies 2.0

It should be clear by now that there is a confessional dimension to my thesis and its application. This should neither alarm nor surprise. As Talal Asad observes, "The question of secularism has emerged as an object of academic argument *and of practical* dispute."[38] Part of my aim in the present project is to reverse the effects of the Islamic Secular's exclusion not only from the interpretive prism through which the West has studied Islam but also from that of modern Muslims—an exclusion that has brought the latter to a similarly dichotomous understanding of the relationship between the religious and the secular, which ultimately sustains the power and primacy of the Western secular/religious divide in favor of the secular. The idea that an act is *either* religious/Islamic *or* secular/non-Islamic affects Muslims' perceptions not only of the quotidian efficacy of Islam but also of themselves whenever they engage in activities commonly deemed to be secular. This, as I explain in Chapter 1, can only promote civilizational failure or civilizational schizophrenia, both of which the Islamic Secular seeks to retard if not reverse.

To be sure, there are liabilities attending an approach to the academic study of Islam that includes confessional interests. First, if the aim is to proffer prescriptive articulations that contribute to the normative understanding of Islam, a scholar's identity as a Muslim can privilege his or her perspective over those of non-Muslims who neither have nor seek to represent any authority to speak in the name of Islam. This in turn can insulate Muslim views from non-Muslim scholarly critique, potentially lowering the standards of the scholarly enterprise and allowing all manner of bias, sloppiness, and unfounded claims to parade as scholarship. Second, as non-Muslims may have no interest in contributing to or debating the normative understanding of Islam, confessional approaches may leave non-Muslim scholars with no incentive to engage with such scholarship. This can ultimately reduce the latter to a Muslim echo-chamber, in which Muslim academics effectively sit around talking to themselves, unconsciously (or perhaps consciously) confirming each other's biases and blind spots and then wondering why the rest of the world looks on with apathy, if not quiet contempt.

Such is the explicit concern of Professor Aaron Hughes in his polemical book, *Islam and the Tyranny of Authenticity: An Inquiry into Disciplinary Apologetics and Self-Deception*.[39] Hughes expresses alarm at what he characterizes as an unhealthy co-mingling, indeed, a hopeless conflation, of "theology" with bona fide academic inquiry in the work of Muslim academics—particularly, according to him, "Muslim converts."[40] Hughes argues that, while pretending to be engaged in objective, critical analysis, these scholars are really playing a dangerous, ideological game of identity politics wherein they seek to manipulate the sources and tradition of Islam in an effort to confer upon their Faith the status of a "good religion." Their point of departure is the West's ideological reaction to the horrific attacks of September 11, 2001. They write thus not in the interest of scholarly truth but, according to Hughes, "in the service of correcting negative stereotypes and of self-aggrandizement."[41] They begin by imagining an Islam that is "liberal, inclusive, pluralistic, feminist, gay-friendly, and so on,"[42] and from there try to force the sources and tradition of Islam to validate this vision. According to Hughes, "Creating Islam as a religion of peace, if not *the* religion of peace, has now become the foundation of the subfield of Islam as taught within departments of religious studies in the United States."[43] In the place of critical research, he laments, "we instead witness the creation and dissemination of a liberal form of Islam to counter the version of the tradition linked with terrorism."[44]

Hughes explicitly states his belief that such attempts to determine or influence the normative understanding of Islam are *not* within the purview of what scholars may legitimately undertake in the secular, Western academy.[45] Rather, that enterprise must limit itself strictly to teaching *about* religion and avoid the teaching *of* religion.[46] In this light, he fleshes out the framing of his book with three seminal questions: (1) What happens when we use judgmental and reverential language in the classroom?; (2) What happens to an academic field when historical questions retreat into the background and instead become replaced with presentist concerns?; and (3) What role is there for the non-Muslim scholar of Islam in the contemporary period?[47]

The first of these questions is reminiscent of Bruce Lincoln's assertion that "Reverence is a religious, and not a scholarly, virtue."[48] One is also reminded, however, of Timothy Fitzgerald's retort, that this negative depiction of reverence is simply "an act of power," an attempt to reinscribe the primacy of the "secular" over the "religious."[49] In other words, we may, as Hughes does, speak reverentially about the secular without compromising our scholarly objectivity but not about the religious. Meanwhile, Hughes seems to imply that for a Muslim scholar in the Western academy to teach, for example, that Muʿtazilism or Khārijism was excluded from Sunnī orthodoxy is somehow to speak "reverentially" of the latter. But how would a non-Muslim scholar teach such facts? And what about the use of intentionally irreverent language in the classroom ("spurious *ḥadīth*," "blind following," "patriarchy," and the like)?

Regarding Hughes's second question, an exclusively presentist approach, with which, as we will see, I do not agree, is simply one approach to speaking normatively about Islam (or any other religious tradition), not the equivalent of speaking normatively about Islam per se. It is a part that should not be taken as the whole, as Hughes does, to discredit all approaches that speak normatively about religion. At any rate, these two questions reveal as much about Hughes's agenda as they do about that of the scholars he critiques. And I will leave interested readers to investigate this issue further for themselves. It is to the third of Hughes's questions, however, that I would like to speak more substantively.

Let me begin by noting that I do not see Hughes's attempt to intervene in the so-called insider/outsider problem in the study of religion as an entirely negative enterprise—though, again, it is telling that he does not see a similar problem with "insider" scholarly advocacy of the secular. Nor is it my contention that the criticisms he directs at the views he targets are always unfounded. Though I take issue with, *inter alia*, his mischaracterizations of scholars' views (including my own[50]), I agree with his insistence that discipline, honesty, and integrity are critical to the scholarly enterprise. As I recall Leonard Binder (d. 2015) stating decades ago, high standards are the only way to keep us all honest. But I do *not* agree that the Western academy should ban or even look askance upon attempts by Muslim academics to shape the normative understanding of Islam, any more than it does in the case of Black, gay, feminist, Marxist, Jewish, Critical Theory, Law-and-Economics scholars, or other academics who seek to influence the self-perception and/or broader image of their respective affiliations or even the broader intellectual or socio-political ecosystems in which these affiliations find themselves embedded.[51]

Nor, given the disparity in power as well as in cultural and intellectual authority between the West and "the rest," should the Western academy pretend that the "objective" scholarship of non-Muslim scholars does not exert (or intend to exert) any impact on the normative understanding of Islam. Does not

Schacht's thesis on the authenticity of *ḥadīth* imply something about how confidently Muslims should rely on this corpus? Does not Wansbrough's scholarship placing the date of the final fixing of the Qur'ānic text in the late second/eighth or early third/ninth century imply something about how Muslims should approach their Holy Book?[52] Non-Muslim scholars in Area Studies or Religious Studies should also not pretend that Muslim silence on presentist issues will be equated with the lofty objectivity or critical distance of their own. On the contrary, Muslim silence is often taken to imply not a justifiable, erudite neutrality but a functional inability on the part of Islam to speak effectively to modern issues, essentially reducing the Faith to a civilizational museum piece, what Khaled Abou El Fadl refers to as an "orphan of modernity."

And yet, *pace* Hughes, rather than entrapping ourselves in a zero-sum proposition that holds scholarship to be *either* objective *or* engaged, we might simply develop and insist on the appropriate standards to be applied to each. This would mean, from my perspective, that if Muslim (or non-Muslim) scholars want to argue that a view should be accepted as a normative expression of Islam, they must be prepared to do the hard work of principled validation, which entails painstaking excavation from the archives of the Muslim intellectual tradition and then placing the results of this effort in meaningful and honest conversation with the contemporary realities they wish to address.

Here I would like to introduce the concept of "Islamic Studies 2.0," as an approach to proffering normative understandings of Islam that neither defies the standards of serious scholarship nor excludes the contributions of non-Muslim scholars. Among the most important features of this approach is that it entails necessarily "Islamic Studies 1.0," by which I mean precisely the kinds of historical questions to which Hughes alludes—the kind of scholarship that is standard in the Area Studies/Islamic Studies curriculum, where scholars critically investigate, debate, and analyze the substance of the classical intellectual tradition, while being guided, challenged, and disciplined by the efforts of other (mostly) non-Muslim Western scholars engaged in the same enterprise. This kind of work is then enfolded into Islamic Studies 2.0, which deploys it in articulating a normative position on a given contemporary issue. Judging the validity of any view put forth as an expression of Islamic Studies 2.0 is thus a compound process consisting of two co-equal parts: (1) assessing the accuracy of the historical excavation; and (2) assessing the degree to which this is convincingly deployed in promoting the contemporary view one wants to promote.

While non-Muslim scholars may have no interest in the second part of Islamic Studies 2.0, their involvement in the first is highly valued if not indispensable. Who in the Western academy, for example, could make normative claims about Islamic law and theology without considering the excavations of Makdisi, Schacht, Coulson, Schimmel, Hourani, Goldziher, Van Ess, Watt, Hallaq, and countless others? Indeed, the 1.0 dimensions of any normative articulation would be assessed against the cumulative criteria set precisely by these scholars, a process in which non-Muslims would be equal to Muslims, that is, if they did not actually enjoy an advantage over the latter, given the general presumption that non-Muslims are more likely to approach the study of Islam with greater objectivity.

Pace Hughes, even non-Muslim scholars who have no direct interest in the normative aspects or aspirations of this book will not be condemned to spectatorial silence. Their critical engagement of its excavational aspects may lead to important if not critical insights or correctives. For example, in my book *Islam and the Problem of Black Suffering*, which sought to contribute to the normative understanding of Black Theodicy in both the academe and the Muslim community, I misidentified the tenth-/sixteenth-century jurist and theologian Kamal al-Dīn al-Maqdisī (d. 905/1499) as a Māturīdī, when in fact he was an Ash'arī,[53] and then with the Ḥanafī Kamal al-Dīn Ibn al-Humām (d. 861/1455), on whose work he was commenting, when he was actually a Shāfi'ī.[54] These mistakes did not undermine the argument in question, but they remain on formal grounds serious, embarrassing mistakes (the kind we relish in the work of our graduate students as "teachable moments"). For a non-Muslim scholar to point out such mistakes would constitute no less a duty and service to the field of Islamic Studies or Religious Studies than it would in the case of the kind of scholarship that Hughes considers to be objective, if for no other reason than to prevent future generations from repeating such infelicities. In a similar vein, non-Muslim scholars might see fit to interrogate any number of my views on Islamic law, theology, legal theory, or history, separate and distinct from the roles I assign to them in my overall thesis.

In sum, even for scholars who have no dog in the secular/religious fight at the heart of this book, there will be plenty to analyze, critique, and hopefully learn.

The Chapters

This book is divided into two parts. Part I, including Chapters 1 to 3, is dedicated to establishing, vindicating, and explaining the theoretical foundations of the Islamic Secular. Part II, including Chapters 4 to 6, are more practical in orientation, focusing on the relationship between Islam-cum-*sharī'ah* and the modern state. The choice of the modern state as interlocutor is neither gratuitous nor self-serving. The chief function of the secular in the modern world has been to regulate the public space and the proper role and authority of religion within it. In this capacity, the secular has been invoked as the Great Mediator in the relationship between religion, society, and the state, the state constituting *the* "immanent frame" or "*über*-context" within which all modern life takes shape. In this context, to speak about Islam in the modern world is of necessity to speak about its relationship not only to the secular but also to the modern state. In fact, here is where the Islamic Secular assumes perhaps its most prominent practical application. For, if Islam as religion is *not* identical to *sharīʿah*, that is, if *sharīʿah*'s jurisdiction is *not* coterminous with that of Islam, then any assessment of the normative relationship between Islam and the modern state will be incomplete, even misleading, absent the clue of the Islamic Secular. For this reason, in Part II, I place the Islamic Secular in conversation with three important works on Islam-cum-*sharīʿah* and the modern state: Wael Hallaq's *The Impossible State*, Abdullahi An-Naʿim's *Islam and the Secular State*, and Andrew March's *Islam and Liberal Citizenship*.

As a construct, the Islamic Secular entails three constituent concepts: (1) the secular; (2) the religious, as that against which the secular acquires meaning; and (3) the Islamic. Each of these concepts has a history of its own and remains a topic of debate, each functioning not merely as a lexical item but also as an ideological tool deployed to promote specific goals, interests, and points of view. In Chapter 1, I engage each of these concepts in historical context to clarify its meanings, associations, and the manner in which I deploy it as a constituent of the Islamic Secular. I should reiterate that, while my project is more about associations than meanings or definitions per se, the Islamic Secular's semantic relationship to the Western secular remains relevant. For, part of my aim is to challenge the global hegemony of the Western associations attaching to the concept. By shedding light on the historical contingency of these associations, I aim to highlight the possibility of alternate understandings. And yet, this kind of linguistic change-cum-appropriation—of which Baldwin and ʿAbd al-Raḥmān spoke—ultimately entails an element of internal critique, which can normalize novel deployments of a language from within and change the way that even native speakers use and hear words and concepts. This is what occurred, for example, with the term "Black" in America in the 1960s, when it was successfully converted from a term of disparagement into one of pride.[55] The Islamic Secular would not be able to execute this kind of internal critique-cum-appropriation if it positioned itself as an entirely alien construct.

Again, I will not attempt to conceal the confessional dimension of my arguments behind a cover of objectivity or transcendent, universal reason. Instead, I shall allow the ideological and imaginative elements of my argument to stand (or fall) on their own, to appeal (or not) to whom they may. This is not a nod to relativism, as a self-serving means of shielding my arguments from objective critique. It is more an effort to promote (and live with) greater transparency, as an alternative to feigned impartiality. One need not agree entirely with the Romantics to recognize that, beyond the powers of reason, those of imagination, affect, pre-commitment, intuition, and even the *Zeitgeist* play a role in the production and reception of ideas. As Richard Rorty (d. 2007) suggests, "speaking differently, rather than arguing well, is [or may be] the chief instrument of cultural change."[56] Reason, at any rate, will not always tell the whole story behind the production, success, or failure of an argument. Yet, it is precisely the whole story that we as scholars and intellectuals should be committed to telling.

The story of the Islamic Secular includes my engagement not only with "secular," but also with "religious" and, of course, "Islamic," particularly as these have evolved in and out of the Western tradition. After all, it is the power of these terms as part of that tradition that produces the aforementioned "nemesis of language" to begin with. As the Western tradition has not produced a consensus on the meaning or proper deployment of these terms, however, I will extract from, deploy, and assign priority to various arguments and interpretations that may or may not be a point of agreement in the West. An example of this is my use of "differentiation" as the conceptual core of the secular. While this is certainly a view upheld in the West, one could challenge the claim that it is the only or even the most widely recognized view.[57] But the Islamic Secular, like the modern Western secular itself, is ultimately a construct. And, as with constructs generally, I bring technical accuracy into synergistic alliance with functional utility en route to practical synthesis. Where I make interpretive or executive decisions in processing the Western tradition, I try to vindicate my choices in as transparent a manner as possible.

In Chapter 2, I turn to the task of demonstrating not only that *sharīʿah* is a bounded entity but also that the Islamic juristic tradition of *uṣūl al-fiqh* identifies it as such. In other words, the limits to *sharīʿah*'s jurisdiction are not imposed from without, as are the limits on religion in the modern West, but *self*-imposed by Islam's jurists. I make this point via a diachronic analysis of the juristic discussion of the *ḥukm sharʿī*, or "legal ruling," in the context of which jurists isolate and distinguish between what is *sharʿī*—that is, what can be determined based on the sources of *sharīʿah*—and what is not. This *sharʿī*/non-*sharʿī* distinction I identify with "differentiation," which Western scholars going back at least as far as Kant (d. 1804) associate with the separation of the religious from the non-religious, or secular. As I lay out in my discussion of "secular" in Chapter 1, however, there is an important difference between Western and Islamic differentiation: whereas the Western secular differentiates the "secular" from the "religious," the Islamic Secular differentiates the 'secular' non-*sharʿī* not from the "religious" but from the *sharʿī*, as that whose substance or validity is determined by the concrete sources of *sharīʿah*. Because, however, the *sharʿī* is not coterminous with Islam as religion, this allows for an entire realm that is non-*sharʿī*, or 'secular,' yet still within the parameters of Islam as religion.

Beginning in Chapter 2, the reader will notice the centrality to my thesis of the thought of the seventh-/thirteenth-century Mālikī jurist Shihāb al-Dīn al-Qarāfī (d. 684/1285). This reverts to al-Qarāfī's position in an evolutionary development in the tradition of speculative jurisprudence (*ṭarīqat al-mutakallimīn*) that begins with the Mālikī jurist Ibn al-Qaṣṣār (d. 397/1007) in the fourth/tenth century and runs through to the modern period, reaching its apogee in the sixth/twelfth to the seventh/thirteenth century with the famed Shāfiʿī jurist, theologian, and philosopher Fakhr al-Dīn al-Rāzī (d. 606/1210). Al-Rāzī's seminal contribution was his novel way of organizing the discourse on the *ḥukm sharʿī* such that it could be theorized in a manner unprecedented in the history of *uṣūl al-fiqh*. Al-Qarāfī, who wrote no less than three analyses/abridgements of al-Rāzī's work on *uṣūl al-fiqh*, captured the importance of al-Rāzī's innovation and pressed it into what would become (and perhaps remains) the clearest theorization of the *sharʿī*/non-*sharʿī* division in the history of Islamic law. He maps out the full implications of this distinction (along with the distinction between law and fact) with a boldness and clarity that I have not found in any other jurist. Given the centrality of the *sharʿī*/non-*sharʿī* distinction to the Islamic Secular, it stands to reason that al-Qarāfī plays a considerable role in my efforts at theorization.

Yet, while al-Rāzī's systematization was widely, if not unanimously, recognized among those writing in the "mode of the speculative theoreticians," it did not spread as evenly among those who thought in the traditional mode of the Ḥanafīs, that is, *ʿalā ṭarīqat al-fuqahāʾ*. While there were later Ḥanafīs, beginning in the seventh/thirteenth century, who recognized the *sharʿī*/non-*sharʿī* distinction, which seems to have become a trend across the schools as a whole, the division does not appear to have been a point of consensus nor a priority among them, at least not explicitly. Thus, while I am confident of a discernible trend toward this mode of thinking among later Ḥanafīs, I am less confident about the going position and its evolution in the Ḥanafī school overall. I welcome correction in this regard by those more learned in the Ḥanafī *uṣūl*-tradition.

I also confront in Chapter 2 two other potential challenges to my thesis from within the pre-modern juristic tradition. The first is the *sharīʿah*-minimalism represented by the Ẓāhirī approach to Islamic law. Because the Ẓāhirīs are explicit in their attempt to limit the jurisdictional reach of the sources of the law, for example, by denying analogy (*qiyās*), one might get the impression that the Islamic Secular also subscribes to *sharīʿah*-minimalism. In fact, however, the Islamic Secular does not seek to impose any particular limits on *sharīʿah*; nor does it care what the dimensions of those limits are. As we will see, even within the boundaries of *sharīʿah*'s jurisdiction, however widely or narrowly drawn, there are ways in which the law can only be properly instantiated by relying on non-*sharʿī*—Islamic Secular—deliberations. Moreover, rather than relying on mere assumption, the Islamic Secular, in contradistinction to Ẓāhirism, explicitly identifies activity that falls outside the dictates of *sharīʿah* as religious and potentially Islamic. In sum, Ẓāhirism and the Islamic Secular are two distinct programs, a fact that I hope this book's full argument will throw into relief.

The second challenge that I address in Chapter 2 comes from the likes of Ibn Taymīyah (d. 728/1328) and Ibn Qayyim al-Jawzīyah (d. 751/1350) in the form of *sharīʿah*-maximalism. These scholars question the definitiveness of the *sharʿī*/non-*sharʿī* divide promoted by the speculative theoreticians and strive instead to keep *sharīʿah*'s jurisdiction as broad as possible, the better to preempt the encroachment of other forms or bases of adjudication, for example, *ʿaql*, or various "systems of reason," or *siyāsah*, the discretionary authority of the state. Again, to the extent that the bounded nature of *sharīʿah* is called into question, so is the integrity of the Islamic Secular as a construct. In the end, however, I try to show that Ibn al-Qayyim's and Ibn Taymīyah's disagreement on this point is more one of degree than of kind.

Chapter 3 is where I concretize the Islamic Secular by describing its function both within *sharīʿah* and "beyond the law." I also put forth and vindicate my Arabic translation of "Islamic Secular," explicitly setting it apart from such Arabic terms as *ʿalmānīyah*, *ʿilmānīyah*, and *dunyawīyah*, as none of these, being essentially translations of the Western secular, capture the Islamic Secular's essence or thrust. I also point out the ways in which failure to recognize the Islamic Secular has affected the interpretation of Islamic legal sources and history. I show, for example, that, early on, the Islamic juristic tradition recognized—as a matter of principle and not as an anomaly or capitulation—the role and legitimacy of non-*sharʿī* deliberations and regulations, such that going outside the strictly *sharʿī* was not automatically perceived as going outside of Islam or Islamic law. In fact, I argue, "Islamic law" was not—and is not—limited to *sharīʿah*, and Muslim jurists have long recognized reglementary regimes that are "legal," in that they carry legitimately imposed sanctions, yet not *sharʿī*, in that their concrete substance is not derived directly from the sources of the *sharʿ*. *Siyāsah*, *maẓālim*, and *ḥisbah* are all examples of this. I then build on the argument that *sharīʿah* is not entirely self-sustaining in either its substance or its authority and suggest that its integrity in any given time and place will depend in part on non-*sharʿī* energies and non-*sharīʿah* personnel. I argue in this context that failure to recognize the Islamic Secular has led to a misdiagnosis of the challenges facing Islam-cum-*sharīʿah* in history, ultimately limiting the presumed solution to *ijtihād*. If, however, I suggest, Muslims are challenged not by others' superior legal systems or even by the purported failures of their own but by others' superior military, economic, intellectual, or cultural achievements, then *ijtihād sharʿī*, which can only produce legal rules (*aḥkām sharʿīyah*), will hardly make up the deficit. Islam-cum-*sharīʿah*'s efficacy does not rest and never has rested solely in the hands of the *fuqahāʾ*. Non-*sharʿī*, Islamic Secular activity by non-jurists always has been and always will be integral to the quotidian success (or failure) of Islam-cum-*sharīʿah*.

Having laid the theoretical foundations of the Islamic Secular, at the end of Chapter 3, I engage more directly with the thought of Talal Asad on Islam and the secular. The point here, except by entailment, is not to critique Asad's thesis per se; it is to control for the way that Asad's influential articulations might inform others' readings of *The Islamic Secular*. If, for example, Asad directs attention to ways in which modernity and its secular have forcibly imposed restrictions on *sharīʿah*'s public role and authority, this could impede readers' ability to recognize that the pre-modern Islamic juristic tradition voluntarily placed limits on *sharīʿah*'s jurisdiction and that the notion of a bounded *sharīʿah* is Islamically authentic and not a capitulation to modernity. Meanwhile, much of Asad's (and many others') focus is on the "secular" and "secularization" as decidedly political constructs that do decidedly political work. Following Asad, this is what the late Saba Mahmood (d. 1439/2018) referred to as "political secularism," that is, "the sovereign prerogative of the state to regulate religious life through a variety of disciplinary practices that are political as well as ethical."[58] This emphasis on the political entailments of the secular, beyond the "nemesis of language" as a theoretical challenge, sets the stage for my transition into the final three chapters of this book, which focus on what and how the Islamic Secular can contribute to our understanding of the relationship between Islam-cum-*sharīʿah* and the modern, secular, and liberal state—in effect, the relationship between Islam and modernity.

Chapter 4 is the portal to this practical frontier. It engages with Wael Hallaq and his provocative book, *The Impossible State*. My basic aim here is to examine how the fact that Hallaq does not consider the Islamic Secular informs his thesis and the overall question of how modern Muslims might organize themselves politically. This exploration includes a critical analysis of his understanding of Islamic law. Not only has Hallaq contributed significantly to the understanding of *sharīʿah* in the Western academy, but he has also shaped that understanding in a fairly major way. And of course, how one understands *sharīʿah* has direct implications for the Islamic Secular, since only on the understanding of *sharīʿah* as a bounded entity is it possible for an Islamic Secular to exist. This is the basis of my critical engagement with Hallaq on the nature and function of *sharīʿah*, especially regarding questions of *sharīʿah*'s scope, morality, and relationship to reason. Beyond this, Hallaq presents his own paradigmatic definition of the "state," which I also engage, more in its application than in its substance. Hallaq's basic conclusion is that the idea of an Islamic State, that is, a modern state that seeks to implement the substance and vision of *sharīʿah*, is a contradiction in terms, whence his notion of *The Impossible State*. I critically engage with all of this in light of the logic and calculus of the Islamic Secular.

Chapter 5 places the Islamic Secular in conversation with Abdullahi An-Naʿim's *Islam and the Secular State.* Unlike Hallaq, An-Naʿim's argument is not that an Islamic State is impossible but that it is undesirable because it cannot accommodate, *inter alia*, the separation between religion and the state. He rejects the Islamic State, however, not categorically but only as advocated by modern Islamists. In fact, An-Naʿim sees the secular state as a more accurate actualization of what a real Islamic state would look like. According to him, the normative function of the state for Muslims never was and never should be to apply *sharīʿah* as state-law but rather to separate *sharīʿah* from the machinery of government. Like American secularism, however, An-Naʿim advocates a secular *state*, as opposed to a secular *society*. Yet, as with Hallaq, he does not factor the Islamic Secular into any of his deliberations. And because he does not distinguish between the *sharʿī* and the non-*sharʿī*, he tends to conceive of Islam-cum-*sharīʿah* as an entirely *sharʿī* enterprise. On this understanding, the all-encompassing, undifferentiated *sharīʿah* becomes the entire problem, and the solution for An-Naʿim is located entirely in the domestication of *sharīʿah* and its complete separation from the state. I argue that the Islamic Secular holds out other possibilities, and Chapter 5 critically engages An-Naʿim in light of these.

Chapter 6 turns to Andrew March's *Islam and Liberal Citizenship.* Unlike Hallaq and An-Naʿim, March's ideational context is not the Muslim-majority states of the traditional Muslim world but the non-Muslim liberal democracies of the West, especially America, where Muslims are a religious minority far removed from the reins of power. His basic question is whether and how Muslims, assuming their ideological attachment to Islam-cum-*sharīʿah*, can embrace citizenship in a secular, liberal democracy. Citizenship, in his view, is mediated not by liberalism as an orientation or background culture but by liberalism as a concrete political theory, specifically that of John Rawls (though March adds his own touch). On his reading of Islam's '*juridical and ethical tradition*,' March argues in favor of doctrinally observant Muslims being able to embrace "liberal citizenship" in good conscience.

Like Hallaq and An-Naʿim, however, he proceeds on an understanding of Islamic law that does not include the Islamic Secular. Chapter 6 thus engages with March's understanding of Islam-cum-*sharīʿah* and how it relates to liberal citizenship in light of the logic and calculus of the Islamic Secular. My argument is not that March fails to prove that the Islamic juristic tradition renders it permissible according to *sharīʿah* for Muslims to embrace American liberal citizenship. I argue, rather, that, even if Islam-cum-*sharīʿah* renders it permissible (*mubāḥ*) for Muslims to embrace American liberal citizenship, as March defines it, his approach fails to consider—in fact, is incapable of considering—the kinds of material interests contemplated under the sign of the Islamic Secular that might lead Muslims not to embrace this arrangement or to embrace it with significant qualifications. I propose, first, that the Islamic Secular be included in the understanding of Islam-cum-*sharīʿah* through which Muslims negotiate their relationship with American citizenship and, second, that the US Constitution replace Rawlsian-cum-Marchian liberalism as Muslims' interlocutor. I also ask if liberalism, in its single-minded focus on *doctrinal* conflict, can speak to—and allow Islam to speak to—the most intractable sources of division in America, most prominently, the affective commitments that bind the country's racial, ethnic, religious, and cultural groups, and how the dictates and limitations of liberalism in this regard affect American Muslims.

In closing, I would like to register five quick points that I hope will inform the ideational backdrop against which the reader engages with this book. First, every book has its limitations, and I would like to call attention to three conspicuous limitations of the present effort. The first is that it does not address the tradition of Shīʿism. This is due mainly to the limits of my own expertise and my fear of imposing Sunnī meanings and presuppositions onto Shīʿism or of missing certain subtleties of the latter that a Sunnī interpretive prism might not allow me to see. I make no claims, however, one way or the other, about how the Islamic Secular would map onto Shīʿism, including, for example, Shīʿism's concept of *minṭaqat al-farāgh* (unaddressed region).[59]

The second limitation is my omission of the perspective of the great Spanish jurist Abū Isḥāq Ibrāhīm b. Mūsā al-Shāṭibī (d. 790/1388). Al-Shāṭibī was a major figure in post-formative Sunnī jurisprudence. But he goes against the grain of various aspects of Sunnī juristic theory. In particular, my understanding of his approach to the *ḥukm sharʿī*, which is at the heart of this study, suggested that it might be better not to include him in this book but to return to him, perhaps, in a later effort. Again, however, I make no claims one way or the other about how al-Shāṭibī's views would align or not with the thesis of *The Islamic Secular*.

The third omission is that, except for a few passing references, I do not discuss the Ottoman period, despite its close association with the extra-*sharʿī* reglementary regime of *siyāsah* (discretionary powers of the ruler). There are two reasons for this. The first is, again, the limits of my expertise: I am not an Ottomanist, and I feared that my failure to capture various details and subtleties of Ottoman history might compromise my argument. The second is that I wanted to highlight the fact that the Islamic juristic tradition's recognition of the Islamic Secular is not an early modern, reactionary phenomenon but, rather, has deep roots in the pre-modern classical and post-formative tradition. As we will see in Chapter 3, this raises some interesting questions about how we continue to study Islamic law.

The second overarching point I would like to make about this book relates to Thomas Kuhn's *The Structure of Scientific Revolutions*. Part of what I mean by this is that, just as Kuhn argued that all scientific theories are essentially paradigms that confront counterfactuals that these theories themselves cannot account for, there are bound to be counterfactuals confronting the theory of the Islamic Secular. My hope is that *The Islamic Secular* will be read as a new paradigm for conceptualizing Islamic thought. And as Kuhn argued in the case of scientific paradigms, the mere existence of counterfactuals is not automatically enough to doom a theory, given all the other important work it may do. In other words, a scientific theory is like a horseshoe, the space between the two ends being as wide as the number and magnitude of counterfactuals pushing back against the theory. But scientists typically treat the theory as if it were a fully closed circle, as if there was no space between the two ends in which counterfactuals reside.[60] My hope is that, instead of taking one or two counterfactuals as sufficient to damn my theory altogether, despite the other important work it may do, readers will be willing to explore the power and full potential of the Islamic Secular, even in the face of non-lethal counterfactuals.

The third point is that the "Islamic Secular" is my own neologized construct, which I have encountered nowhere else in the literature. While I believe that I have successfully made my case for its basis in the Islamic juristic tradition, the cumulative historical weight and cognitive mass of the word "secular" may be too immoveable for many to get past its non-religious or anti-religious connotations and accept its juxtaposition with "Islamic." Given this difficulty, I ask that the evidence I put forth simply be given a fair hearing, despite the counterintuitive thrust of my thesis. I am reminded in this context of a drawing entitled, "My Wife and My Mother-in-Law," published in 1915 by the cartoonist W. E. Hill. At first glance one sees either a beautiful young woman or an old crone; and were it not for the trust one placed in the title's suggestion, this would be all one would be able to see. With time and focus, however, one's perception shifts, and one is able to see the beautiful woman and the crone simultaneously. By analogy, the incumbent Western meanings of "secular" are so powerful and entrenched in our daily lives that it is difficult for many of us to see any other meanings in the word. But, as I hope *The Islamic Secular* will show, those meanings are there. And, as in the case of "My Wife and My Mother-in-Law," we simply need to look long enough to see them. This is what I am asking my reader to do: please, keep looking.

My fourth point is that this project should be distinguished from the intellectual movement among modern Muslims known as the "Islamization of Knowledge."[61] To be sure, there is overlap, for example, in the desire to address a certain intellectual dislocation among Muslims and the idea that the disciplines and achievements of non-Muslims might be "Islamicized." Beyond this, however, the two are separated by fundamental differences in outlook and approach. At the most basic level, the Islamization of Knowledge sees *sharīʿah* as unquestionably totalizing. As Ismāʿīl al-Fārūqī (d. 1406/1986), a leader in what is perhaps the most popular expression of the movement, once put it, "The will of

Islām to culture and civilization is comprehensive, as it must be if it is meant seriously. This comprehensiveness is at the foundation of the comprehensiveness of *sharī'ah*."[62] To be fair, al-Fārūqī hints at the need to engage with the world of culture and lifestyle *beyond* the dictates of *sharī'ah*; and he insists that the religious and the secular must be brought together.[63] But none of this is formally theorized. Moreover, when he affirms that "Every discipline must be recast so as to embody the principle of Islam in its methodology, in its strategy, in what it regards as its data, its problems, its objectives, and its aspirations,"[64] he intimates a misrecognition if not dismissal of the concept of differentiation that is at the heart of the Islamic Secular. There are other equally important differences that I do not have the space to go into here. Over the course of this book, however, it will become clear that the Islamization of Knowledge and the Islamic Secular are two distinct and different projects.

Finally, in presenting my arguments, I have found it necessary to characterize and critique the work of other scholars, at times pronouncing on the ideational roots and implications of their views. My efforts at civility and scholarly decorum notwithstanding, no amount of polite talk here will conceal or neutralize the polemical dimensions of this book. I hope, however, that it will be equally apparent that I have learned much and been greatly enriched by my engagement with the scholars I discuss. And in case it is not, let me express here, openly and unequivocally, my deep gratitude and sense of debt to them all. Throughout this endeavor, I have tried to be fair and respectful and to side with what I believe to be the truth, for or against myself. In the end, I can only hope—and this is my solemn prayer—that my pen did not get the better of me.

PART I
THE CONCEPTUAL LANDSCAPE

1
Secular, Religious, Islamic

Basic Lay of the Land

For all its ubiquity, few contemporary constructs generate the semantic ambiguity of the term "secular." This multivalence notwithstanding, all discussions of the concept in the contemporary West converge on a single trope: the secular's oppositional relationship with the religious.[1] Depending on who is defining or using it, "secular" can range from openly anti-religious to benignly non-religious. And the boundary between the two may be unstable,[2] open to mutual penetration,[3] or, being traversed back and forth.[4] In the end, however, an idea, activity, or institution is invariably conceived of as *either* secular *or* religious; and it is rarely if ever considered to be simultaneously both.[5] Emile Durkheim (d. 1917) consummated this modern Western *Weltanschauung* when he famously divided the world into the "sacred" and the "profane" (read: "religious" and "secular") and insisted that these have "always and everywhere been conceived by the human mind as separate genera, as two worlds that have nothing in common."[6] Today, even scholars who are unwilling to cast the secular and the religious as absolute opposites recognize them as each other's "Other."[7]

It is precisely this presumed binary relationship between the secular and the religious that the Islamic Secular calls into question. Doing so implies, of course, some novel usages of "secular," "religious," and, ultimately, "Islamic." In this chapter, my aim will be to explain and vindicate these usages, beginning with that of "secular."

The Secular

Over the past three hundred years of Western history, the authority of the secular has steadily expanded at the expense of religion, delivering Western civilization (and some argue the world[8]) into what Charles Taylor famously referred to as "a secular age." Part of the success of this secularization project has resided in its proponents' ability to conflate the secular's prescriptive with its descriptive element. Craig Calhoun captures this point when he observes that the secular has succeeded in preserving its commitment to excluding religion from the public sphere, while somehow maintaining its own status as neutral.[9] Talal Asad exposes

The Islamic Secular. Sherman A. Jackson, Oxford University Press. © Oxford University Press 2024.
DOI: 10.1093/oso/9780197661789.003.0002

the secular's pretensions to innocence and neutrality by pointing out the ways in which its proponents seek to discipline, control, and domesticate religion, by subjecting it to an evolving series of consciously developed cognitive oppositions (reason/myth, public/private, autonomy/submission), all of which signal and reinforce the primacy of the secular *over* the religious.[10] Timothy Fitzgerald notes that secular approaches habitually cast religious views and commitments as "objects of nostalgia, thus clearing a cognitive space . . . for value-free scientific facts,"[11] thereby destroying any legitimate relationship between religion and power.[12] In the end, part of the power of the modern Western secular is that it is routinely misrecognized as contributing nothing to the marginalization of religion, being seen instead as simply what remains, descriptively, after the weakness of religion's internal constitution catches up with it and results in its natural withering away. Yet, as one observer colorfully summarizes the matter, "The secular is not simply a remainder; it is a sum, created by addition, a product of intellectual multiplication."[13]

Beyond the academy, people who are religiously inclined tend to agree with those academic critics who see the secular as inherently predatory and expressive of an ideology that is not neutral but consciously committed to a particular ordering of the world. They tend to fear that, once the germ of the secular invades the prevailing cognitive or socio-political ecosystem, religion's viability will be mortally threatened. Muslims among this demographic might even dismiss a neologism such as the "Islamic Secular" as naive and misguided if not cynical, ultimately suspecting it of promoting the secular's predatory designs on Islam. This is understandable, given that the Western purchase on the meaning and connotations of "secular" is so complete, powerful, and pervasive that it is difficult to use the term in any affirmative sense without implying anti- or non-religious associations. And, unless the aim is actually to secularize Islam, many Muslims might think a better plan would be simply to avoid the term in association with Islam altogether.

But to abandon "secular" on that basis would endorse precisely the view that I want to challenge, namely, that the modern Western secular is the only secular and that the history that produced that secular can be universalized to the point of foisting upon anyone who uses the term in relation to Islam the wholesale mapping of the Western meaning of "secular" onto Islam. The conventional suppression of "Western" from academic and popular uses of "secular" should not blind us to its European origins nor obscure the possibility of authentic non-Western alternatives. As José Casanova observes, "[T]heories of secularization and modernization should be open to the possibility that other religions may also play some role in institutionalizing their own particular patterns of secularization."[14] Nikki Keddie confirms: "[T]he Western definition of secularism may not be fully applicable in all parts of the world, because of religious differences."[15]

The Islamic Secular is an alternative understanding of the secular viewed from the perspective of Islam and its juristic tradition.

Casanova and Keddie point to two important derivatives of the modern Western secular: "secularism" and "secularization." As with "secular" itself, there is no consensus on the meaning of either of these terms or even on whether they are primarily religious, social, political, or epistemological categories.[16] Generally speaking, however, secularism may be thought of as the ideological-cum-practical commitment to establishing and preserving the primacy of the secular over the religious by placing authority over public affairs entirely in human hands, with minimal if any pertinent recognition of God. I say "pertinent" because, depending on the mode of "secular" in question, "secularism" does not necessarily imply "atheism." One may believe in God, but with secularism, this belief is simply not relevant in the domain cordoned off as secular. As the seventeenth-century Dutch jurist Hugo Grotius explained, secularism entails a commitment to proceeding in certain areas "even if God didn't exist" (*etsi Deus non daretur*).[17] Secularization, on the other hand, refers both to the actual process by which secularism is pursued and to the state of affairs that obtains upon its realization, which invariably includes the privatization of religion and its removal from the state apparatus.[18] Both secularism and secularization flow naturally from the modern Western secular, as they are the means by which this view of the secular is institutionalized. As we will see, however, a major distinction between the modern Western secular and the Islamic Secular is that neither secularism nor secularization flows from the latter. The Islamic Secular does not seek to control, restrict, or discipline religion, nor to augment itself at religion's expense. In fact, a commitment to the Islamic Secular entails an unavoidable commitment to Islam *as* religion. For the Islamic Secular has no meaning outside this religious "immanent frame."

Given such differences, obvious questions arise: What relevant similarities remain between the modern Western secular and the Islamic Secular that might justify their continued membership in a single generic category? And, even if they remain in the same generic category, if the point is to establish the existence of an authentic non-Western secular, why not argue exclusively based on a non-Western vocabulary and dispense with that of the modern West altogether, including the term "secular"? Is it not possible to lay out the substance of Islam's non-Western secular without relying on the lexicon of the West? And what does the need to rely on a Western vocabulary say about the authenticity of any would-be non-Western alternative?

Let me try to address these pointed questions in somewhat reverse order. In Chapter 3, where I discuss the substance and function of the Islamic Secular, I will show how it is authentically expressed in Arabic, the *lingua franca* of Islam. But while that may be meaningful to those who know Arabic, it will be of little use for others, who will continue to rely on the global (read: Western) lexicon in thinking about and articulating their understanding of Islam as religion and its purported relationship with the non-religious. For most people, in other words, the term "secular" will remain unavoidable. And rather than reinforce the meaning of secular according to its dominant Western usage, I want to infuse it with alternative associations, polarities, and functions to enable it to accommodate Islam on Islam's own terms. Among the reasons for preferring this approach over abandoning the term altogether, beyond what has already been stated, is simply this: given the vast disparity between the West and "the rest" in terms of power, cultural and intellectual authority, not to mention the means of amplifying, popularizing, and disseminating ideas across the globe, the likelihood of successfully lifting the word secular from the global lexicon and replacing it with a globally recognized alternative that can safely convey related but distinct meanings relative to religion hovers around zero. And yet, as long as the word "secular" retains its global authority *and* the modern West retains its monopoly over its meanings and associations, it will continue to do the work it presently does, including that of forcing Muslims (and non-Muslims), both within and beyond the academy, into what I see as a false choice between the secular and the religious in their conceptualizations, practice, and articulations of Islam. Muslims will continue to see themselves and routinely be seen as engaging in activity that is *either* secular *or* religious, a perspective that translates into an inaccurate barometer for measuring how religious (or secular) they actually are and how much authority and relevance Islam as religion retains in the modern world, ultimately, to the ideological advantage of the secular over the religious.

To my mind, there is nothing necessarily unavoidable (or innocent) about the presumption of a zero-sum dichotomy between the secular and the religious. The possibility, however, of an alternative understanding that is authentic from both a Western and an Islamic perspective becomes easier to appreciate against a backdrop of how the term and modern concept of "secular" itself evolved in the West and from there spread to the lands of Islam.

The Secular in Historical Perspective

Even as religion's "Other," the secular is not an entirely modern invention. As Talal Asad notes, examples of people separating religious from secular institutions can be found in both medieval Christianity and Islam.[19] St. Augustine's (d. 439) "City of God" versus his "Earthly City" is already suggestive. But later Christianity would become even more explicit. According to José Casanova, medieval Christendom divided "this world" into a secular and a religious domain. This division was distinct, however, from a parallel separation between "this world" and "the next world." In other words, there were at least *two* distinct senses of the term "secular": one focused on the practical affairs of this world to the conscious exclusion of concern for the next; the other, without denying the importance of the next world, simply focused on the worldly or practical concerns *of this world*, as opposed to the religious concerns *of this world*, for example, whether there is food to eat versus whether there is a church in which to pray.[20]

Clearly, on this division, one could be secular in the second sense without being so in the first, that is, one could focus on this-worldly concerns without denying God or the Afterlife. And until the Enlightenment, this seems to be how most Westerners conceived of and indulged the secular. There was ambiguity, of course, and even conflict, regarding the boundary separating the "worldly secular" from the "worldly religious," as seen in the ongoing conflict over spiritual versus worldly authority among Christian kings, princes, popes, bishops, and other church officials.[21] But the Church would ultimately succeed in its claim to supreme and universal epistemological authority. And with this victory it not only established the superiority of the religious *over* the secular; it also promoted the diffusion of religion's authority throughout society.[22] In effect, all knowledge fell under the adjudicative gaze of the Church, an epistemological authority that later proponents of the modern "secular" would reject with a vengeance.[23]

In the meantime, the (this-worldly) secular would be effectively subsumed unto the (this-worldly) religious, to the point that the former nearly dissolved as an autonomous category. As Charles Taylor describes the West on the eve of modernity, "[Y]ou couldn't engage in any kind of public activity without 'encountering God.'"[24] Going back farther, he notes, "[T]he whole set of distinctions we make between the religious, political, economic, social, etc., aspects of our society ceases to make sense. . . . [R]eligion was 'everywhere,' was interwoven with everything else, and in no sense constituted a separate 'sphere' of its own."[25] Or, as Brent Nongbri puts it, "The very idea of 'being religious' requires a companion notion of what it would mean to be 'not-religious,' and this dichotomy was not part of the ancient world."[26]

Of course, the tables would eventually turn. And as they did, the line separating the religious from the secular once again blurred. This time, however, "this world" would constitute a complex but single domain wherein not the religious but the secular reigned dominant. As Casanova puts it, "If before, it was the religious realm which appeared to be the all-encompassing reality within which the secular found its proper place, now the secular sphere will be the all-encompassing reality, to which the religious sphere will have to adapt."[27] On this development, not only does the secular take over an authority and a large plot of real estate formerly under the proprietorship of religion, but also its gains are invariably viewed as religion's loss, even where this is ultimately understood to be in the interest of religion and the society it seeks to serve.

For our purposes, what is relevant in this development is the emergence of the possibility of being "non-religious," not simply in the sense of habitual non-compliance with religion's dictates but as an identity, a mode of being, a *Weltanschauung*. Pursuing secular interests in this new stage increasingly implied a conscious obliviousness to, if not a turning away from, religion. Conversely, remaining or becoming religious implied an attitude of conscious resistance to or devaluation of the secular.[28] As certain ideas and activities come to be seen as belonging more distinctly to one or the other domain, it became increasingly difficult to engage with the secular *and* remain religious. As Casanova points out, "The more the performance of the nonreligious roles becomes determined by autonomous 'secular' norms, the less plausible become the traditional global claims of religious norms."[29] Richard Tarnas is even more direct:

> The Christian dualistic stress on the supremacy of the spiritual and transcendent over the material and concrete was now largely inverted, with the physical world becoming the predominant focus for human activity. An enthusiastic embrace of this life as the stage for a full human drama now replaced the traditional dismissal of mundane existence as an unfortunate and temporary trial in preparation for eternal life. Human aspiration was now increasingly centered on secular fulfillment.[30]

Cumulatively, this development would breed a secular/religious dichotomy that proved increasingly difficult to reconcile into anything fully believable or livable, with the secular increasingly winning out over and displacing the religious as peoples' primary commitment in life.

Partly as a function of their colonial and post-colonial encounters, this is how many Muslims would come to experience the new world order, which increasingly called upon people to make a conscious choice between the secular and the religious. Theretofore, Muslims had never faced such a decision, at least not on the same terms.[31] Even in pre-modern times, there were people in the lands of Islam who failed to observe the proper norms of revealed religion, some even scoffing at the idea itself. Excepting the so-called *dahrīyūn* (/sg. *dahrī*), however, their skepticism and lax practice did not necessarily force them to choose between an "identity" that was *either* religious *or* secular, especially since religion was not synonymous with morality, as it would later become under the influence of Kant. Even figures who rejected revealed religion altogether, such as the erstwhile Muʿtazilite theologian Ibn al-Rāwandī (d. ca. 328/930) or the philosopher (*faylasūf*) Muḥammad b. Zakarīyah al-Rāzī (d. 313/925), did not reject the concept of God or even what many might consider a religious (i.e., God-centered) orientation.[32] Meanwhile, even the most debaucherous cultural figures of early Islam, for example, Abū Nuwās (d. 200/815) and his crew, reportedly "spent hours on end consumed by wine-drinking only to remember the prayer and promptly establish it, sometimes in that state."[33] Similarly, the legendary Umayyad lieutenant al-Ḥajjāj b. Yūsuf (d. 95/713), though notorious for the rivers of Muslim blood he caused to flow, played a pivotal role in fixing the orthography of the Qur'ān as we now have it.[34] Even the Prophet, while acknowledging that a man who repeatedly drank wine had violated the religious law, could say of him, "Do not curse him; for I have only known him to love God and God's Messenger."[35] Much later, after Islam had matured as a civilization and absorbed numerous peoples and cultures, Ibn Taymīyah, despite his reputation as a puritanical proponent of religious rectitude, would insist (against the Mu'tazilah and Khawārij) that "faith" (*īmān*) is not categorically contradicted by sin.[36]

As in the West, however, modern Muslims would increasingly feel pressured by the idea that the tension between the religious ideal and the human real can be resolved only by moving out of a religious and into a secular mode of being. But, unlike their counterparts in the West, religiously committed Muslims showed little interest in putting Islam's primacy up for negotiation. Rather, by the mid- to late nineteenth century, attempts to navigate the new zero-sum terrain would push them toward a totalizing vision of *sharī'ah—the* putative expression of Islam—which reached its apogee in the mid- to late twentieth century with the rise of Islamist movements. This new vision recognized no normative mode of human existence other than a strictly scripture-driven one, with no activities, concrete forms, or bases of knowledge or value other than those directly provided, implicated, or presided over by scripture.[37] Only on this "life-boat" understanding of religion,[38] so the assumption went, would Muslims be able to resist the secular deluge. And in this context, human frailty, will to power, libido, and everything not pristinely moral, devotional, or concretely scripture-driven became increasingly perceived as being fully and authentically at home only in the world of the non-religious secular. Whereas the Qur'ān could speak openly (however guardedly) of sex (*rafath*), money (*māl, khayr*), power (*quwwah*), and glory (*'izzah*) as features of a full and dignified human existence, these came increasingly to be viewed as religiously suspect, on the one hand, and as the tainted spoils of a "secular" approach to life, on the other.[39]

Ultimately, such a zero-sum perspective could only promote civilizational failure or civilizational schizophrenia: failure by denying Muslims legitimate access not only to Islam's restorative powers (e.g., *tawbah* (repentance), *kaffārah* (expiation), etc.) but also to critical non-revelatory knowledge, expertise, and creativity; schizophrenia by the fact that, while they might recognize the need for non-revelatory enterprises, Muslims, under the influence of this perspective, could hardly acknowledge (or perhaps even recognize) these enterprises as religious, let alone Islamic. This is especially problematic given the modern West's projection of a causal relationship between the "secular" and the "modern," the former being assumed to be the *sine qua non* of the latter (used here in the sense of developed, sophisticated, progressive). On this view, one could place little priority on being powerful, wealthy, or sexy if one was to be religious; for these were now perceived as distinctly "secular" pursuits. As Casanova suggests, the secularization of Europe might be better explained in terms of "the triumph of a knowledge regime," at the heart of which lay this teleological presumption. Europeans consider themselves irreligious, in other words, because they think they are supposed to be, and they think they are supposed to be because they are supposed to be modern.[40] The British anthropologist Mary Douglas (d. 2007) adds further clarity: "Progress means differentiation [read: secularization]. Thus, primitive means undifferentiated [read: indiscriminately religious]; modern means differentiated."[41] In other words, while the modern West may still have religion (domesticated, compartmentalized, rational, and safe), in the underdeveloped lands of the "modern ancestors," religion (still naively self-assured and untamed) has them. Such ideas are all a part of the positive connotation of "secular" and its far-reaching illocutionary influence. In such a context, simply ignoring this word as the marker and carrier of this knowledge regime and its teleological associations is not likely to neutralize or send it away.[42]

The impact of the causal assumptions carried by the new Western knowledge regime and its key conveyor, "secular," has been evident among elites in the modern Muslim world for some time. Writing in the 1970s, Bryan Turner noted that secularism did not evolve naturally in Muslim countries or succeed on the basis of the triumph of secular thought; it was imposed by secularizing elites who were trained in the West and sought to mimic what they took to be the basis of the West's success.[43] In a similar vein, Nikki Keddie observed that twentieth-century Muslim elites carried out secularization projects "as a concomitant to modernization."[44] Islam as religion had to be marginalized in this context in order to accommodate the needs of development, because development was perceived to be a secular enterprise that Islam as religion could only impede if not frustrate.[45] Beyond this, and also contributing to its positive connotations, the secular was associated with tolerance. As the Indian scholar Ashis Nandy observes, the association of "secular" with "tolerance" has become so natural that "anyone who is not secular becomes definitionally intolerant."[46]

By encouraging such associations, secularizing Muslim elites were, and still are, able to bolster their own legitimacy. The positive connotations of "secular" reposition "religion" as something from which society needs protection, presumably by a caring, paternalistic state. Meanwhile, to the extent that such practical endeavors as cultural production, technological development, administrative acumen, tolerance, and the like are conceived of as secular, religion is expected to contaminate if not stifle them. In such a context, religiously conscious Muslims can engage in such "secular" activities only with a nagging sense of DuBoisian double consciousness;[47] or they may simply leave these commitments to the secular West or "secularized Muslims" or, shall we say, Muslims who are seen and perhaps see themselves as secular because of their involvement in such activities? Or perhaps the religious scholars, whose learning, like the scope of *sharīʿah* itself, is assumed to be all-encompassing, will be called upon to step into the breach, in which case the Community will be held to the limits of whatever actual expertise happens to be in their possession.[48]

In sum, even in a Western context, "secular" has been an ideologically malleable construct that has evolved over time. At the same time, all the aforementioned effects presently contribute to its psychological and practical influence as part of the language and logic (and power) of modernity. Clearly, in such light, while the meaning of "secular" is not inalterably set, it is also not just another word whose mind-altering impact will disappear if we simply ignore or critically analyze it long enough. Nor is it likely to cede voluntarily any ground to an entirely foreign substitute. Without new meanings, associations, and possibilities successfully attaching to the word "secular," thereby challenging its regnant Western connotations and entailments, this word will continue to do the work it presently does. This is what justifies the approach I take in this book.

The Secular: Macro- and Micro-Modes

Regarding the generic relationship between the modern Western secular and the Islamic Secular, we must begin with an important distinction between two modes of the secular as it evolved in the West, which I shall call the "macro-" and "micro-" modes. The macro-mode targets religion as a whole, either actively seeking to extirpate it from human life or simply relying on the secularizing momentum of social, intellectual, historical or economic forces to usher it out of existence. Marxism, "the most powerful philosophy of secularization in the nineteenth century," is an expression of the macro-secular at work in this first sense.[49]

The second and more popular way in which the macro-secular obtains is through what thinkers such as Charles Taylor, Peter Berger, Marcel Gauchet, Max Weber (d. 1920), and others have in mind when they equate the secular with the rise of the mechanistic view of the universe, the so-called disenchantment of the world.[50] The idea here is that belief in God relies upon an experience or sense of the world as an entity infused with supernatural forces, magical agents, and spiritual presences that stir up religious energies and prime the religious imagination to seek the source of such phenomena or, perhaps, simply protection from them. The "secular" in this context is the result of a process by which the world is emptied of these forces, which is facilitated by such developments as modern science and the spread of logical positivism.[51] This emptying or "disenchantment" nullifies the search for the Originator of the charged worldly presence and ultimately undermines belief in God.[52] And of course, with no God, there can be no theistic religion. In sum, through disenchantment, the macro-secular displaces religion, normalizes unbelief, and ultimately promotes atheism.[53]

For its part, Islam never produced a macro-secular of its own, at least not as a consciously promoted ideological platform. Even Muslim *falāsifah* who scoffed at the religion of the masses—or even the religious establishment—preserved and continued to engage the idea of "God," belief in whose existence did not rely on an enchanted cosmos.[54] In fact, while he clearly did not wish to disabuse the Arabians of their belief in God, the Prophet's mission included a clear attempt to "disenchant" Arabia, in the sense of ridding its people of their surfeit of superstitions and habits of appealing to various sprites and "powers." But this did not mean emptying the world entirely of supernatural forces; for among these powers were positive energies that could be rightly indulged, for example, *barakah* (favor, augmentation, benediction), as well as other entities that were assumed to exist as a simple matter of fact, for example, *jinn*, angels, Satan, and even "devils" (*shayāṭīn*/sg. *shayṭān*). The reduction in supernatural forces did not entail a reduction in Arabian religiosity, which was obviously not Muḥammad's mission. Muḥammad's mission was simply to reorient the Arabians (and ultimately humanity) away from an overindulgence of superstition and to redirect their *sensus numinous* toward God, properly defined, as the ultimate supernatural power and source of everything else deemed to possess any.

As for God's existence, where the Qur'ān argues for it at all, it grounds its arguments not in the existence of autonomous supernatural forces but in the fact of human contingency in the contexts of both Nature and History, contexts the Qur'ān presumes the inborn human disposition (*fiṭrah*) is primordially calibrated to respond to religiously. It casts both the provisions of Nature and God's interventions in History as signs (*ayāt*/sg. *ayah*)—indeed, among the ultimate signs—that point to a personal Creator, whose non-contingency is the very source of the Creator's power to intervene. We see this in the repeated references to supernatural aid dispatched to Noah, Jesus, the Children of Israel, even Quraysh. Meanwhile, as Fazlur Rahman (d. 1408/1988) notes regarding the Qur'ān's depiction of Nature, "This plenitude of natural being is . . . itself 'supernaturally' miraculous and the greatest of all miracles."[55]

Ultimately, Muḥammad's message assumes that there is a God-backed, supernatural enterprise at work in all natural phenomena. This is very different, however, from the notion of "enchantment," or the world's being suffused with autonomous supernatural energies identified as the driving force behind religion. With Muḥammad, the supernatural element implied by Nature is not its inclusion of spiritual forces (though, again, these are not entirely denied) but the fact that, while humans remain fundamentally dependent upon Nature, something outside of Nature—something supra-natural—consistently and deliberately decides what Nature shall or shall not produce: no blue roses, no immortal humans, no pinstripe skies. Moreover, the Qur'ān depicts interruptions in the natural order (*kharq al-'ādah*) for the purpose of aiding particular groups or individuals as pointing to a willful agent from outside both Nature and human History. On this understanding, contrary to the basic belief alleged (or assumed) to underpin Western religious history, even a world emptied entirely of sprites and spirits would not necessarily undermine belief in the God of the Qur'ān. For, belief in this God is sustained not by a charged or supernaturally infused cosmos but by the supra-natural implications of Nature and History. Thus, the Prophet's mission might be rightly described as including an effort at disenchantment. But this "Islamic disenchantment" never resulted and was never intended to result in any decrease in belief in God or in religiosity.

Some might argue that we do find a form of the macro-secular in Islam in the radical separation between the affairs of this world and those of the Afterlife—"*al-dunyā*" versus "*al-ākhirah*"—some seeing the former as a God-free or non-religious domain. This *dunyā/ākhirah* distinction is abundantly referenced in the Qur'ān, and major figures such as al-Ghazālī are emphatic in confirming it. But such Qur'ānic references should not be so quickly identified with the macro-secular. For, even the most mundane worldly activities remain, according to the Qur'ān, part of a God-sponsored reality that should be engaged, acknowledged, and appreciated as such. This is clearly the thrust of in such verses as "*Do you not see that which you ejaculate? Is it you who created it, or are We its creator?*" [56:58–9] "*Do you see that which you cultivate? Is it you who brings forth its produce, or is it Us?*" [56:63–4]. As for al-Ghazālī, while he defines "*al-dunyā*" as "everything prior to death,"[56] this does not strip all worldly activities of religious value or significance; one can engage with *dunyā* or *dunyawī* activity *as* a religious act. In fact, many *dunyawī* activities are identified as necessary for a successful reckoning and tenure in the Afterlife. Al-Ghazālī thus equates *al-dunyā* with a "land to be tilled and harvested for the Afterlife" (*mazra'ah li al-ākhirah*).[57] In other words, engagement with *al-dunyā* does not preempt God's presence or adjudicative gaze; nor is it the categorical opposite of *dīn*, or religion.[58] In fact, on al-Ghazālī's rendering, "*al-dunyā*" represents not so much a category or domain of non-religious activity as much as it does an attitude or metric of valuation. He notes thus that even prayer or acquiring religious knowledge can be termed "*al-dunyā*," in the sense of occurring before death, but not in the sense of contradicting, frustrating, or negating religion.[59] Conversely, he insists that any activity, however worldly, evaluated and taken as a means to serving God (*'ibādah*) may be "*dunyā*" in the sense of "worldly" but not in the sense of "non-religious." In sum, *al-dunyā* is neither the categorical opposite of *dīn* nor an expression of the macro-secular.[60]

Due to the far-reaching influence of Taylor, Berger, Gauchet, Weber, Asad, and the like, the macro-secular remains the dominant understanding of "secular" today. This may cause some readers of this book, especially Muslims, to scoff at, if not recoil from, the notion of an "Islamic Secular," prompting them perhaps to dismiss it as a misguided, even offensive oxymoron, an ill-conceived attempt to graft an alien concept onto Islam. We should note, however, that this mode of the secular, that is, the macro-mode, is not the only mode, even in the West. The 'secular' element of the "Islamic Secular," therefore, need not be associated with the modern West's macro-secular. Enter micro-secular.

The micro-mode of the secular does not reject the presence of supernatural powers, question the existence of God, or challenge the propriety of religion per se. It focuses instead on the question of the extent to which humans are bound by what God *says*. The Indian sociologist Andre Béteille aptly summarizes the stakes of the secular/religious divide when he writes, "What causes the most anxiety to secular intellectuals is a conception of religion which demands that every aspect of every individual's life be brought under religious scrutiny and control." The critical question, he continues, is "how much space will be allowed within society by doctrinaire religion for the growth of secular ideas and institutions."[61] By "doctrinaire religion," Béteille is not speaking of religiosity or religious orientation in general; he is speaking of the concrete dictates and duties that religion imposes, what Muslim jurists refer to as "*taklīf*," that is, what humans are directed to do and not do, believe and not believe, based on God's revelation, God's speech (*kalām*, *khiṭāb*).[62] The micro-secular simply assumes that the jurisdictional scope of the revelatory sources from which this *taklīf* is derived is limited. And it sees the realm beyond this *taklīfī* jurisdiction as an iteration of Béteille's "space," in which "secular ideas and institutions" find their welcome, even as this "secular" space does not negate the existence of God, its own participation in a broader religious space, an overarching "sacred canopy," or the totalizing adjudicative gaze of the God of Islam.

A perhaps extreme instance of the micro-mode of the secular can be found in pre-Islamic Arabian religion. This religion neither recognized nor relied upon any notion of revelation or divine speech as the conduit through which God communicated concrete commands, prohibitions, likes, dislikes, or even facts about the world. In effect, God, was virtually mute. And this afforded the Arabians maximum space within which to fashion their own regime of right and wrong, virtue and flaw—what W. Montgomery Watt referred to as "tribal humanism."[63] Yet, the Arabians remained deeply religious, their *shirk* (associationism) being a thoroughly religious enterprise. Muḥammad's mission, again, was not so much to establish God's existence as it was to communicate concrete information about God, including God's concrete will, and to establish God as the only rightful object of humans' cosmic fear, hope, love, and worship. While his countrymen initially rejected him, this did not entail rejecting belief in God. Rather, the Arabians continued to acknowledge *Allāh* and, through their idols and rituals, continued to try to draw near to God. Virtually none of these attempts, however, was based on anything that God had directly *said*, in the form of "revelation." In fact, Muḥammad's claim to be God's Messenger was among the most difficult for the Arabians to accept. God existed and was even responded to; but God's concrete commands in the form of God's concrete communiqué were limited if not unknown, leaving the Arabians to fill the breach on their own (occasionally in God's name).

By contrast, the Western micro-secular does not denude God entirely of the power of speech. But it does restrict the authority or relevance of what God says to a deliberately circumscribed realm of human activity, again, without challenging the existence of God. This restriction marks the boundary between the Western "religious" and the Western "secular," or "non-religious": the two constitute two distinct and mutually exclusive realms, in contrast to what I shall argue to be the case in Islam.

Differentiation

In essence, restricting the application of God's concrete communiqué to a circumscribed realm amounts to what scholars of religion refer to as "differentiation," a concept as vital to the micro-secular as disenchantment is to the macro-secular. As José Casanova writes:

> [T]he core and the central thesis of the theory of secularization is the conceptualization of the process of societal modernization as a process of differentiation and emancipation of the secular spheres—primarily the state, the economy, and science—from the religious sphere and the concomitant differentiation and specialization of religion within its own newly found religious sphere.[64]

At bottom, differentiation revolves around the combined issues of jurisdiction and metrics. Specific disciplines or fields of endeavor are "differentiated" from others by the ideas and activities deemed proper to their domain, as well as the distinctive metrics of execution and assessment by which they produce and assess their final products. Casanova focused on those disciplines that were most symptomatic of the mood of the Enlightenment. But differentiation does not stop with these. Weber famously referred to the various differentiated realms as "spheres of value," identifying several—the economic, the political, the aesthetic, the intellectual, and so on—each possessing an "*internal and lawful autonomy*"[65] and each existing in tension with religion. This tension, according to Weber, was the result of a conflict between such traditional religious values as brotherly love, on the one hand, and the un-brotherly, un-loving, dispassionate conduct that was becoming the norm for the newly emergent *homo economicus* and *homo politicus*, on the other. To be economically efficient or politically expedient, in other words, now clashed categorically with the traditional values of religion.

It would be a mistake, however, to read our secularized present too seamlessly into this past. While the aforementioned developments ultimately contributed to the emergence of what Charles Taylor described as our "secular age," we should not see differentiation itself as necessarily implying hostility toward religion.[66] Well before Weber, Kant (d. 1804) had also embraced differentiation. In fact, according to Jeffrey Stout, "Kant . . . was the great philosopher of differentiation. He did more than anyone else to codify and legitimate a culture of separate compartments."[67] Yet, Kant (in his own way) was a religious man.[68] His aim was not to differentiate other domains from religion to raise them above religion; it was to affirm and protect religion's integrity as its own differentiated realm. This he did by arguing that religion was the distinctive domain of morality. For Kant, morality, not science, led to God.[69] His philosophy raised religion above the (atheistic) empiricism of Hume (d. 1776) and the pseudo-science of the Deists—both of which he perceived as threats to religion.[70] In the process, Kant secured morality as religion's exclusive "sphere of value" from which other domains could now be differentiated.[71]

For Kant, religion was no longer the all-encompassing category of categories.[72] Instead, "true religion" was expressed as morality, and true morality was both transcendent and differentiated. From an historical perspective, Kant might be seen as consummating a process that had long preceded him. According to Nomi Stolzenberg, as far back as his fellow German Martin Luther (d. 1546), a major impetus behind the embrace of a differentiated realm was that Europe's churchmen increasingly accepted the fact that "the divine law and sacred ideals of justice have to be violated in the temporal world."[73] Stolzenberg implies that separating or differentiating worldly pursuits from religion came to be seen as a way of protecting both. Religion could retain its purity, as its own distinct "sphere of value," while society could be spared the drawbacks of an over-extended conceptualization of religious authority.

Sheldon Wolin (d. 2015) summarized Luther's commitment to differentiation as follows: "[T]he world would be reduced to chaos if men tried to govern by the Gospel."[74] J.M. O'Sullivan (d. 1948?) adds (also representing Luther): "The State is a purely human and worldly institution—between it and the Church there can be no essential connection. . . . [T]he Gospel cannot and must not be misused as a legal code or political manual."[75] By contrast, *sharīʿah* has always been recognized for its relevance to the government of worldly affairs. Like the Gospels, however, it was not immune to the challenge of responding to the vagaries of everyday life. But until modern times, Muslims never responded by attempting to create a separate, *non-religious* space. In fact, the general impulse (with the exception of the now-extinct Ẓāhirī movement) was to *expand* the scope of God's commands and prohibitions via such instruments as analogy (*qiyās*) "equity" (*istiḥsān*), public utility (*maṣlaḥah*), adaptive legal precepts (*qawāʿid*), and inductive readings of scripture (*istiqrāʾ*), as part of an effort to negotiate between the moral and the practical, the ideal and the real. In this context, obedience to God's concrete will becomes a more protean construct. For example, while early Ḥanafīs condemned "provisional sales" (*bayʿ al-wafāʾ*) as a violation of *sharīʿah*, later Ḥanafīs sanctioned them, as dictated by need, declaring this sanctioning to be firmly within God's law.[76]

This tendency to expand *sharīʿah*'s reach while simultaneously adjusting it to the challenges of everyday life did not imply that *sharīʿah*'s jurisdiction was boundless, in the sense of constituting the only Islamically legitimate metric of assessment. Nor were non-*sharʿī* metrics necessarily deemed "non-religious." As we will see in Chapter 2, by the end of the fourth/tenth century, jurists were imputing explicit jurisdictional boundaries to *sharīʿah*. And while these boundaries placed numerous issues and pursuits outside *sharīʿah*'s proper scope or metrics of assessment, they did not place them outside the notice of Islam.

This simple act by Muslim jurists of acknowledging *sharīʿah*'s bounded nature and the existence of "spheres of value"—human endeavors whose concrete substance is neither determined nor adjudicated on the basis of the concrete indicants of revelation or their reasoned extension—amounts to differentiation. This is what preserves the Islamic Secular's mutual participation with the Western secular in a single generic category. In both cases, "secular" (and we are speaking here primarily of the micro-secular) refers to the domain of human activities whose concrete substance is neither dictated nor adjudicated by God's concrete communiqué. Whereas the Western *macro*-secular denies the authority of God's communiqué altogether, by effectively denying God's existence, the Western *micro*-secular simply demarcates the authority of God's divine address—without challenging God's existence or God's authority as a whole. The Islamic Secular is a species of micro-secular.

There is a critical difference, however, between the Islamic Secular and the Western micro-secular. As Casanova puts it, "The [Western micro-] secular has become a central modern category . . . to construct, codify, grasp, and experience a realm or reality differentiated from 'the religious.'"[77] By contrast, the Islamic Secular is differentiated not from religion, or *dīn*, but from God's concrete *sharʿī* directives, which are themselves *not* co-extensive with Islam. This allows for the existence of a realm that falls *outside* the circumference of *sharīʿah*'s concrete injunctions and metrics of assessment but *within* the circumference of Islam as religion. In this capacity, the Islamic Secular constitutes a "religious secular."

Given the global diffusion of the notion of the secular as disenchantment, some may see my focus on the secular as differentiation as an attempt at evasion, invoking a less authentic form of the secular out of convenience or desperation. In fact, however, the micro-secular has a credible claim to being the original form of the secular, even in the West, rendering not it but the macro-secular the aberration. Charles Taylor, for example, suggests that the latter, what he calls "the unbelief of the elite," was an eighteenth-century phenomenon that did not reach full tide until the twenty-first century.[78] Thus, even if one could argue that the idea of the secular as differentiation is less *popular* than the idea of the secular as disenchantment, one could not argue that the former is a less *authentic* expression of the secular, even in the West. Nor could it be argued that "secular" has always and everywhere implied "unbelief" or "anti-religion." On these facts, a construct such as the Islamic Secular, which does not imply absolute, mutual contradiction between the secular and the religious, cannot be deemed an ideological abuse of the historical record nor, as some modern secularists (or religionists) might suggest, a contradiction in terms.

Between the Non-*Sharʿī* and the Non-Religious

I should reiterate that my basic aim is not to *promote* the use of "secular" as a lexical item but to *infuse* it, as an already immoveable constituent of the modern lexicon, with alternate meanings, uses, and implications. This is necessitated in part by certain structural differences between Christianity and Islam that make it problematic to apply "secular" to the latter according to the meanings and uses it has acquired in the former. Chief among these differences is that, in differentiating itself from religion in the West, the secular—even the micro-secular—was understood to constitute a non-religious space. In Islam, by contrast, while there is a distinction between God's will communicated concretely in the form of *sharīʿah* and God's will discerned more generally from revelation through a God-conscious phronesis or religious imagination, both remain spheres of religious encounter. In other words, in differentiating itself from *sharīʿah*, the secular in Islam does not—and does not have to—differentiate itself from religion, which by contrast is the central point of differentiation in the West. Ultimately, however, this Islamic iteration of differentiation implies a novel understanding not only of "secular" but also of "religion" and "religious." It is thus to a discussion of religion that I shall now turn.

Before doing so, it may help those seeking to understand the difference between the way that certain constructs function in Islam and the way they function in the Christian (or perhaps "post-Christian") West to consider the concept of complementarity. "Complementarity" is the name I give to an ontological theory put forth by the great Traditionalist theologian Taqī al-Dīn Ibn Taymīyah (d. 728/1328). According to him, while everything in existence has an inherent nature and capacity instilled in it by God, this nature and capacity are not absolute. They function, rather, with one or another effect, depending on whether and how they come into contact with their complements. Fire, on this understanding, does not burn in the absolute; it merely burns in the presence of such complements as wood or paper. It does not burn in the presence of asbestos, magnesium oxide, or various metals.[79] In a similar fashion, Islam and the West may be thought of as different complements for such constructs as "secular" and "religious": as each interfaces with Islam or Christianity, it exerts different effects and performs different functions. Whereas the Catholic Church exercised an interpretive authority that was coterminous with religion, the authority of *sharī'ah* and thus of Muslim jurists (as we will see in Chapter 2) was not coterminous with Islam. Whereas the Protestant response to a totalizing Catholic authority was to create a secular, differentiated space that fell outside the reach of religion, Islam could simply recognize a differentiated, non-*shar'ī* space *within* the broader circumference of religion but outside the bounds of the interpretive authority of the religious establishment. Both moves—Christian and Muslim—amounted to micro-secular acts of differentiation. But the broader implications for Christianity differed significantly from those for Islam.[80]

The Religious

If the semantic ambiguity surrounding "secular" can be described as daunting, attempts to pin down the meaning of "religion" have proved no less bewildering. En route to modernity, practically every major Western thinker had something to say about religion. Today, many scholars hold the category to be a modern invention, certainly on its most common understanding and usage.[81] In the most extreme expression of this view, the late Jonathan Z. Smith (d. 2017) insisted that "Religion has no independent existence apart from the [modern] academy."[82] Others insist that "religion" is ancient and came down to us from the Romans.[83] There is confusion at times between the origins of the term and what it eventually came to mean. But, even when this is not the case, problems remain, especially regarding the proper way to study religion, including Islam.

Religion As Subject and Object

As late as the turn of the twentieth century, major European scholars such as Adolph von Harnack (d. 1930) were still insisting that Christianity was the only religion that mattered and that it should be recognized as the touchstone against which all other religions are compared. As he put it, "Whoever does not know this religion knows none, and whoever knows it and its history knows all."[84] This was partly a response to the rise in the latter half of the nineteenth century of *Religionswissenschaft* ("Science of Religion" in Europe, "History of Religions" in the US), championed by the German émigré to England F. Max Müller (d. 1900), which took as its central concern "the understanding of other religions," ostensibly on their own terms.[85] Of course, "other," even for Müller, ultimately meant non-European and, given the colonial reality of the times, invariably implied a power differential between subject and object. Power, moreover, was invariably indexed to race, as the religious other was routinely a racial other, and vice-versa. As Charles Long observes, the Enlightenment was more committed to relocating than to destroying the gods, "[a]nd one of the most powerful loci for the gods was in the cultures and among the peoples outside the West."[86] This patronizing attitude toward religion would intensify in the long nineteenth century, itself "famous for an explosion of unbelief."[87] During this era, alongside such religiously grounded scholars as Schleiermacher (d. 1834), Kierkegaard (d. 1855), Müller, and Otto (d. 1937) the secularizing pioneers of anthropology and sociology—Feuerbach (d. 1872), Marx (d. 1883), Durkheim, Weber (d. 1920), and Freud (d. 1939), came on the scene, all of whom implied that religion was more at home among the less developed.

Neither of these perspectives fully displaced the other; they coexisted, rather, in an awkward, unresolved tension. Mircea Eliade (d. 1986), for example, famously championed the concept of man as *homo religiosus*, who is naturally inclined to see himself in a sacralized world and to respond to it religiously.[88] Freud, on the other hand, saw religious belief as an illusion, a childhood fantasy or phase of neurosis.[89] Meanwhile, Ninian Smart (d. 2001) characterized Eliade as, "in a disguised form, a preacher."[90] Ultimately, these differences in perspective reflected a general though incomplete division between theological and anthropological or sociological approaches to the study of religion, between the ideals of what humans *should* believe and practice and the reality of what they actually *do* (or appear to) believe and practice.[91] There was a shift, in other words, from a focus on texts and questions of truth, piety, exegesis, and so on to an emphasis on peoples, myths, cultural practices, symbols, taboos, fetishes, the socio-political function of religion, and the like,[92] from "rational categories and concepts of religion to religious experience itself."[93] This would be further complicated in the case of Islam by the fact that Area Studies (Middle East, Near East Studies), which produced some of the most authoritative scholarship on Islam, approached its object as a constituent of a distinctly non-Western geography (religion's newly "relocated home") as much as it did—in fact, more, than it did—from the perspective of any scholarly discipline. In the end, at any rate,

Western Europe, Christianity, and the Enlightenment dominated scholars' interpretive prisms and points of departure. It was this heritage and its obsessions that informed the kinds of questions asked (and not asked), the database and methods relied upon for answers, and the language and concepts that mediated the discussion of all of this.

This historical backdrop raises important questions about how fruitfully we can apply the tropes, methods, obsessions, and language that inform the "scientific" study of religion as it developed in the West to Islam.[94] By "fruitfully" I mean how likely such methods are to reveal Islam on its own terms rather than merely mirroring back to the West reflections of its own mindset.[95] In a deeply thoughtful and courageous essay, "The History of Religions and the Study of Islam," Charles Adams (d. 2011), an Islamicist who studied with Joachim Wach at the University of Chicago, concluded that "the main thrust of scholarship in History of Religions in our day has little relevance, even little interest, for students of Islam."[96] He noted how unhelpful such staple Western categories as "myth," "ritual," "symbolism," and "sacral kingship" are for the study of Islam. Much of the difficulty, Adams argued, stems from the fact that Western scholars of religion tend to privilege archaic and "primitive" religion as the most faithful reflection of this purportedly universal phenomenon. The problem, however, from Adams's perspective, was that Islam, while clearly absorbing primitive elements, is *not* a primitive religion. "[N]or is it the connection with its 'primitive' roots that constitutes its historical significance."[97] Meanwhile, the excesses and inadequacies of Area Studies relative to the study of Islam have been extensively examined as part of the general critique of Orientalism.

Much has changed since the late 1960s, when Adams penned these words, and the late 1970s when Edward Said (d. 2003) wrote *Orientalism*. But it was precisely in this period that foundational presuppositions about "religion" and Islam were being reaffirmed in Western scholarship, including how the sacred/profane, secular/religious distinction mapped onto Islam. As Jonathan Z. Smith reminds us, "Religious studies came into being in its present ubiquitous form during the academic boom years of the 1960s through the 1970s."[98] Meanwhile, major representatives of Area Studies (e.g., Schacht, Coulson) made seminal contributions to the study of Islamic law as "the epitome of Islamic thought"[99] precisely during this period.[100] As a religion, Islam was perceived as representing the sacred/religious par excellence, a supremely totalizing, religious commitment that was profoundly agnostic in its relationship with the secular/profane. Meanwhile, the comparative ease with which Protestantism could compartmentalize life and religion signaled the modern West's superiority over Islam. In fact, today, and throughout its history, whenever Islam is seen as departing from its sacred-cum-religious profile, questions arise as to whether it is remaining true to its essence and constitution, simple change or the mere contemplation of material interests routinely being conflated with "deviation," "decline," or even "secularization."

Of Definitions and Usages

In his noted article, "Religion, Religions, Religious," Jonathan Z. Smith famously cited the psychological study by J. H. Leuba (d. 1946) in which Leuba lists more than fifty meanings for "religion."[101] This large number suggests that such factors as imagination, historical accident, ideology, vested interests, and even vogue all had their say in shaping the concept. It is in this context of the open recognition of the role of synthetic, non-essential, utilitarian factors in determining accepted meanings or deployments of "religion" that I will introduce my own use of the term.

The early-modern controversy over the definition and use of "religion" began with etymology.[102] One camp favored the testimony of the pre-Christian Roman scholar and statesman Cicero (d. 43 BCE), the other that of the early Christian author Lactantius (d. 320 CE). According to Cicero, the root of the Latin word *religio* (from which the English "religion" comes) was *relegere*, meaning "to go through or over again in reading, speech or thought."[103] Lactantius, on the other hand, traced the origin of *religio* to *religare*, "to bind."[104]

On Cicero's rendering, *religio* was a psychodynamic disposition—a sense of awe, anxiety, nervousness, care, and scruple regarding the proper worship of the gods. Such sentiments engendered a constant impulse to reflect upon, review, and correct one's relationship with traditional beliefs and practices. Cicero did not use *religio* to refer to specific beliefs about the gods or the practices of a particular cult or religious institution. Nor was *religio* apolitical, the equivalent of privatized belief. In fact, Cicero's interest in *religio* was quite political: he looked to "ceremonies which had some political importance and to cults supported by the state" as key ingredients in maintaining the pre-modern version of political community.[105] For him, *religio* was associated with *traditio*, which tied individuals to their respective ancestors—a perspective that admitted a plurality of different religions.[106] In this sense, religion was neither divisive nor intolerant but, normatively speaking, part of the apparatus of good civics and the maintenance of a healthy, pluralistic, political order. The opposite of *religio* for Cicero was not non-religion or anti-religion but *superstitio*, the overly instrumentalized, mechanized performance of worship, an unreasoning fear of the gods or the worship of gods not recognized by the Roman state.[107]

For Lactantius, by contrast, *religio* was not a disposition but a commitment to a specific set of beliefs about the gods, including God, and a regime of worship that together constituted the true religion. *Religio*, according to him, was "the just debt of service to the God who brings us into being, that we know Him alone, that we follow Him. We are fastened and bound to God by this bond of piety, whence religion itself takes its name."[108] While there is overlap with Cicero, in that both men see religion as the right thing to do, the distinction between them is patent and perhaps most clearly manifested in their different understandings of *superstitio*. According to Lactantius, "they are superstitious who worship many and false gods; but we, who supplicate the one true God, are religious."[109] For Lactantius, *religio* focused far more concretely on *what* and *how* one worships; and taking the wrong entity as the object of one's worship negated the latter's status as *bona fide* religion. For Cicero, by contrast, even the most explicit paganism could be authentically religious. In other words, for Lactantius, the concrete *substance* of worship was what determined its status as religion. For Cicero, it was the psychodynamic *energies and obsessions* that drove worship that constituted religion.

Lactantius's stance was clearly theological. For this reason, perhaps, it found favor in medieval Christianity. While the etymological controversy has never been resolved, Lactantius's position was later strengthened by the success of those who sought to have religion understood not as a human disposition but as a reified, extra-mental entity out in the world that could be concretely targeted and moved around as such. In the words of Wilfred Cantwell Smith (d. 2000), Europe's intellectual elites "took over our term to designate now that in which they were increasingly interested. They gave the name 'religion' to the system, first in general but increasingly to the system of ideals, in which men of faith were involved or with which men of potential faith were confronted."[110] In other words, "religion" came to apply primarily not to the "*faith*" of the "men of faith" but to the concrete *doctrines and practices* presumed to tie them to God and the sacred. These stood in clear and identifiable contrast to other kinds of doctrines and practices, such as those that could be described as social, political, or economic.[111] This reification facilitated the process of "liberating" these latter disciplines from religion-as-concrete-doctrine-and-practice and its presumed universal jurisdiction. By contrast, religion-as-psychodynamic-orientation posed no such challenge; moreover, given its amorphous nature, it could not be as successfully targeted in the same way. Yet, privileging religion-as-psychodynamic-orientation, duly privatized, could contribute to the resolution of Western Europe's religious problem by largely emptying the public space of religion-as-concrete-doctrine-and-practice and rendering it, practically speaking, a predominantly "secular" domain, without, however, entirely negating the value of religion in human life. In the end, the global discourse on religion that began in the early-modern West came to entail a palpable tension between the ostensibly zero-sum options of religion-as-concrete-doctrine-and-practice and religion as "faith," disposition, internalized belief, or psychodynamic orientation.

"Religion" and "*Dīn*"

For our purposes, the importance of these developments lies in what they contributed to the search for and understanding of "religion" in Islam. By the time the West took up the study of Islam in earnest, the tension between religion-as-psychodynamic-orientation and religion-as-concrete-doctrine-and-practice had already crystalized, with the latter eventually winning out as the prism through which Islam would be viewed. While there are several Arabic terms associated with "religion" (e.g., *millah, ummah, fiṭrah, ʿibādah*), Islam as "religion" came to be identified with "*dīn*." Meanwhile, Western scholars tended to associate *dīn* with the reified understanding of religion championed by Lactantius and the early-modern Europeans. Under the entry "*dīn*" in the *Encyclopedia of Islam*, for example, we read: "*Religio* evokes primarily that which binds man to God." *Dīn*, itself is identified, meanwhile, as "the corpus of obligatory prescriptions given by God" and, further, "the obligations which God imposes on His 'reasoning creatures.'"[112]

This Western association of *dīn* with Islam as a totalizing régime of religion-as-concrete-doctrine-and-practice, as opposed to religion-as-psychodynamic-orientation, is not always neutral or positive. It often signals Islam's "failure" (or inability) to privatize religion, separate it from the state, and thereby achieve the tolerance, peace, freedom, pluralism, and progress enjoyed by the West.[113] This is clearly the sentiment behind various Western readings of Jamāl al-Dīn al-Afghānī (d. 1314/1897), Muḥammad ʿAbduh (d. 1323/1905), or Rashīd Riḍā (d. 1354/1935), not to mention later figures such as Ḥasan al-Bannā (d. 1368/1949), Sayyid Quṭb (d. 1386/1966), or Abū al-Aʿlā al-Mawdūdī (d. 1399/1979). All of these men stress the centrality of *sharīʿah* (i.e., concrete doctrine and practice), to the *dīn* of Islam and in so doing cast Islam as, *inter alia*, a religiously grounded socio-political system. And this is partly what Western scholars such as Bernard Lewis (d. 2018) point to in explaining "what went wrong" in Islam. My point here is not that conceptualizing *dīn* as concrete-doctrine-and-practice is wrong or even unique to Western scholars.[114] It is to suggest that the triumph of Lactantius[115] and the early-modern (Protestant) West's presumption of a binary separation between religion-as-concrete-doctrine-and-practice and religion-as-psychodynamic-orientation, between bodily practices and mental-cum-"spiritual" states, led to the tendency to see *dīn* as either one *or* the other, rather than as encompassing both simultaneously as equally authentic and operative constituents of a polysemic whole. The traditional presumption in Western scholarship of a fundamental conflict between *sharīʿah* and Sufism is a prime example of this tendency.

In his informative treatment of "*dīn*," the Japanese scholar Toshihiko Izutsu (d. 1993) suggests that its association with religion-as-concrete-doctrine-and-practice probably dates back to its original meaning among the Arabs.[116] But

Izutsu also notes that, like *religio*, *dīn* can carry several meanings simultaneously, including "custom" and "requital," just as it can simultaneously connote other basic Qur'ānic concepts such as worship (*'ibādah*), "faith" (*īmān*), even *islām* itself. In fact, according to Izutsu, *dīn* belongs to that category of Arabic words known as "*aḍdād*," which simultaneously admit two opposite meanings.[117] Viewed from the perspective of humans interacting with God, *dīn* translates into "humble obedience" and "absolute obedience." But viewed from the perspective of God receiving God's due from humans, *dīn* amounts to "absolute rule" and "absolute *Sulṭān*" (sovereignty): "His is the *dīn* forever!" (*lahu al-dīn wāṣib*^{an}) [54:52].[118] In sum, *dīn* is a rich and multivalent term that is not limited to a single meaning. It can connote, simultaneously, meanings associated with religion-as-concrete-doctrine-and-practice *and* meanings associated with religion-as-psychodynamic-orientation, all as part and parcel of its authentic semantic reach and usage.

We find this polysemic understanding of *dīn* even among the staunchest proponents of the centrality of *sharī'ah* (read: concrete doctrine and practice) to Islam. Ibn Taymīyah, for example, stresses the psychodynamic, internalized dimension of *dīn* as a critical aspect of the Faith: "The *dīn* of Islam with which God is pleased and with which God sent God's messengers is ultimate submission to none other than God (*al-istislām lillāh waḥdah*). And its place is in the heart."[119] Before him, al-Ghazālī, while recognizing *dīn* as a system of socio-political organization, composed his classic *Revivification of the Religious Sciences* (*Iḥyā' 'Ulūm al-Dīn*) precisely for the purpose of restoring the balance between religion-as-concrete-doctrine-and-practice and religion-as-psychodynamic-orientation.[120] After him, al-Shāṭibī, whose commitment to Islam-as-concrete-doctrine-and-practice is beyond question, insisted that "faith (*al-īmān*) is among the actions of the heart" (*'amal*^{un} *min a'māl al-qulūb*).[121] In short, unlike what appears to have happened in the modern West, with "religion" being split between external practice and internalized belief, in Islam *dīn* did not imply a zero-sum or even a binary relationship between the two. Rather, *dīn* subsumed both aspects of religion simultaneously.[122] This explains the widespread assertion among the majority (*al-jūmhur*) of pre-modern Muslim theologians and jurists that, "*imān*," is "confirmation in the heart, affirmation with the tongue, and action via the limbs" (*al-taṣdīq bi al-qalb wa al-qawl bi al-lisān wa 'amal bi al-jawāriḥ*).

This is not to suggest that Muslim jurists and theologians deploy "*dīn*" only in this polysemic sense, such that its "religious" and "worldly" dimensions cannot be conceptually disaggregated; jurists frequently separate the two. For example, in speaking about the early controversy over the Caliphate between the *Anṣār* (Muslim natives of Medina) and the *Muhājirūn* (Muslim immigrants from Mecca) al-Qarāfī depicts this as a dispute over leadership, hierarchy, and authority. "This," he notes, that is, the question of who should be Caliph, "is a worldly (*dunyawī*) not a religious (*dīnī*) affair," clearly delineating the two spheres.[123] My argument is that *dunyawī* in such articulations is not a domain entirely outside or separate from *dīn*; rather, it is a distinct constituent of a broader "sacred canopy," if you will, which is itself ultimately identified *as dīnī*. In other words, the *dunyawī*, or "worldly," implicates the *dīnī*, or "religious," even if the reverse is not always the case, as, for example, with prayer. This is reminiscent of the situation described earlier by Casanova wherein pre-modern Europeans distinguished between the practical and religious concerns of this world while remaining consciously committed to God and the Afterlife.[124] That the distinction in question exists as part of a larger religious composite is confirmed by al-Qarāfī's explicit recognition of the "*dunyawī*" caliphate as a constituent of the fundamental "interests of religion" (*min maṣāliḥ al-dīn*), which is routinely treated in books on the "foundations of religion" (*uṣūl al-dīn*).[125]

The Islamic Secular's Religion

The Islamic Secular invests in the non-reified dimension of *dīn* as psychodynamic disposition or orientation, including the keen and conscious awareness of the ubiquitous gaze of the God of Islam, not as a replacement, however, for religion-as-concrete-doctrine-and-practice but as a normative and necessary complement to it. The primary driver of *dīn* in this iteration is not doctrine or rules but one of the most ubiquitous constructs in the Qur'ān, namely, *taqwā*, or "God-consciousness," leavened by the impulse toward *qurbah*, or performing acts that draw one near to God. Like aspects of Cicero's understanding of *relegere*, this side of *dīn* represents "a faculty or talent to be cultivated, a refined talent for listening, and the continual exercise of this talent: a life-long task . . . a mode of being in a state of attentive listening and acting accordingly."[126]

The late Charles Long (d. 2020) put forth a notion of religion as "orientation" that goes a long way toward capturing my intended meaning here.[127] Drawing on the thought of Rudolph Otto (and Otto's student Joachim Wach), Long locates the ground of this "orientation" in the *sensus numinous*, or "capacity for the experience of the sacred that has always been the same for every human being."[128] In more general terms, to "orient" oneself means "to use a given direction . . . in order to find the others—literally, to find the *sunrise*."[129] In other words, to know where the sun rises is to know all the other directions and thus to know one's own location. But this requires being first possessed of the innate sense by which one knows one's left from one's right. Precisely in this sense, *taqwā* is required for *dīn* to retain its ability to orient one toward and away from certain aims, actions, non-actions, sensibilities, and concerns, as a part of the pursuit and avoidance of divine pleasure and displeasure, respectively, even beyond what God concretely prescribes through revelation.

There is a pedigree here that runs from Long through Wach and Otto and ultimately back to the celebrated German theologian Friedrich Schleiermacher (d. 1834), "arguably the greatest [Christian] theologian of the nineteenth century, if not of the entire modern age."[130] It may be useful, as such, to say a word about how Schleiermacher's notion of religion as "intuition and feeling" compares and contrasts with the Islamic Secular's "*dīn*," especially given some of the details of Schleiermacher's definition and their interpretation by later scholars. On the one hand, as a response to Kant's reduction of God to a noetic postulate of practical reason, the ground of morality, and a consequence of our moral sensibilities,[131] Schleiermacher's "intuition and feeling" might be likened to the Qur'ānic concept of *fiṭrah*, or primordial faculty, which can apprehend extra-mental realities in the supersensible realm.[132] Through this "intuition and feeling," Schleiermacher argues, God can be known and responded to not simply as a noetic occurrence but as an actual, ontological, extra-mental existent.[133] This much is consistent with the Islamic Secular's "religion-as-psychodynamic-orientation." But the Islamic Secular also recognizes *dīn* as religion-as-concrete-doctrine-and-practice; and here it parts with Schleiermacher, for whom there was a "sharp opposition in which religion is found over against morals and metaphysics."[134] "Law," he argued, "must not even require ethical life . . . it must stand completely alone for itself."[135] This is because, according to Schleiermacher, "Religion's essence is neither thinking nor acting, but intuition and feeling."[136] By contrast, while the Islamic Secular's *dīn* is not limited to law, law also does not fall outside the circumference of its *dīn*. In sum, the Islamic Secular's *dīn* is broader and more inclusive than Schleiermacher's "intuition and feeling."

But there is another dimension of Long's "orientation" that is critical to the *dīn* of the Islamic Secular. Long's concept, which was developed in the context of describing Blackamerican religion, included the notion of "oppugnancy." Whereas Otto's famous *mysterium tremendum* expressed the ineffable awe and wonderment experienced upon encountering the Divine, Long pointed to a "spurious *mysterium tremendum*" that befell Blackamericans in the New World. In this spurious version, " 'The Other' of religious experience, with its impenetrable majesty, was replaced by the quixotic manipulations of a fascinating trickster whose rationality was only a veneer for control."[137] Oppugnancy emerges, thus, as a counter-energy that resists all attempts to substitute the "impenetrable majesty" of God, including God's ubiquitous gaze and presence, with that of anything else. Like Islam's *shahādah*, or "Testimony of Faith," its point of departure is negation, and in an unrefined state it can target everything other than God, not just false claimants to divine majesty. In the end, like Long's, the Islamic Secular's religious orientation goes beyond awe and wonderment to include a dogged vigilance against false pretenders. This distinguishes it from, say, Otto's *mysterium tremendum*, in that whatever feelings of "nothingness" might attach to one's "creature-consciousness,"[138] these can never neutralize the impulse to reconnoiter for fascinating tricksters. Nor will the Islamic Secular's oppugnancy drop its guard against the undue influence of the myriad sprites, spirits, and "powers" inhabiting Charles Taylor's "enchanted world," Mircea Eliade's "sacralized world," or Peter Berger's "sacred canopy."[139]

Meanwhile, the God of the Islamic Secular is not simply "a God who commands."[140] It is also a God whose perceived presence generates in humans a heightened consciousness, an elevated sense of expectation, and a desire to appease beyond the fulfillment of God's concrete commands. This is the ground of the impulse commonly referred to in classical literature as "*qurbah*," the attempt to "draw near" to God. In effect, this conscious awareness of the divine presence and gaze renders the whole of life religious. And from this perspective, there are no "areas free from religion."[141] Of course, Muslims can (and do) engage in acts that are secular in the modern Western sense of "non-religious"; but the non-religious nature of these acts stems from the Muslim state of mind, not from the acts themselves belonging to a separate realm cordoned off as "secular." This is clearly the point of the famous *ḥadīth*: "Actions are simply judged according to their intentions" (*innamā al-aʿmāl bi al-niyāt*).[142] Ultimately, *taqwā*, *qurbah* and awareness of the divine presence and gaze can convert *any* licit act (and possibly acts that are technically illicit) into a religious act, including acts that are not dictated by *sharīʿah*. In fact, it is the very throwing off or suppression of this awareness of the divine gaze that the Qur'ān condemns as an undue obsession with the immediacies of this world, *al-ḥayāt al-dunyā*, and occasionally as *kufr* (generally translated as "Unbelief"). One may get a sense of the workings of the divine presence and gaze in this context from another famous *ḥadīth* in the collections of al-Bukhārī and Muslim that speaks of worshipping God *as if* one sees God, knowing that even if one does not see God, God nevertheless sees one.[143] Obviously, merely "seeing" God would not generate any additional concrete commands. Yet, one's sense of commitment is heightened, and one's behavior is informed by an added sense of urgency and possibility fired by a religious imagination that is itself inspired (and haunted) by the Divine's omnipotent presence and omniscient gaze. All of this informs the *dīn*, or religious orientation, of the Islamic Secular.

At or near the conceptual core of all pre-modern Muslim understandings of *dīn* is the concept of *ṭāʿah*, generally translated as "obedience."[144] This also applies to the Islamic Secular's *dīn*, with one important adjustment: with the Islamic Secular, *ṭāʿah* is better understood as "obeisance." Whereas "obedience" is suggestive of a concrete command to be directly obeyed, "obeisance" implies a general desire to appease, meet unspoken expectations, and curry favor above and beyond what is concretely commanded. As in the relationship between religion-as-concrete-doctrine-and-practice and religion-as-psychodynamic-orientation, however, the Islamic Secular's obeisance does not *replace* obedience but simply complements it. Obedience is the response to God's concrete dictates in the form of *sharīʿah*; obeisance is a function of the non-*sharʿī* dictates of *taqwā*, informed by a conscious awareness of the divine presence and gaze. Ultimately, obeisance underscores the fact that neither divine guidance nor the full worship of God is exhausted by what God communicates concretely in the form of revelation. This is confirmed by no less a champion of religion-as-concrete-doctrine-and-practice than the redoubtable "*sharīʿah*-maximalist" Ibn Taymīyah:

> Even were we to assume that a person came to know every command and every prohibition in the Qur'ān and Sunna, the Qur'ān and Sunna would simply address matters of general, categorical import, as it is impossible to do other than this. They would not mention that which is specific to each and every individual. And for this reason, humanity has been commanded to ask for guidance (*hudā*) to the straight path.[145]

Beyond religion-as-concrete-doctrine-and-practice, then, I use the terms "religion" and "religious" to refer to a quotidian orientation that engages life via a conscious awareness of the divine presence and adjudicative gaze of the God of Islam. This in turn generates a whole universe of unspoken opportunities and expectations in relation to God, beyond what God communicates concretely via revelation. Religion, on this understanding, is not reducible to an interiorized belief separate from politics, economics, or public affairs; for all of these are ultimately implicated by the concept of obeisance (not to mention the extent to which they are addressed by religion-as-concrete-doctrine-and-practice, i.e., *sharīʿah*).[146] Nor, however, is the internal or private dimension of religion negated or even marginalized; for the heart (*qalb*) remains the site of religion-as-psychodynamic-orientation. Yet, pace Schleiermacher, religion cannot be reduced to "feeling and intuition." For law, or religion-as-concrete-doctrine-and-practice, remains a vital part of the *dīn* of Islam, a fact the Islamic Secular fully embraces. But, inasmuch as the Islamic Secular remains differentiated from *sharīʿah*, it stands in contradistinction to religion-as-concrete-doctrine-and-practice. Crucially, however, even in this capacity, that is, as a differentiated, "secular" domain or obsession, the Islamic Secular does *not* stand in contradistinction to "religion." Nor, as we shall see presently, does the Islamic Secular's non-*sharʿī* secularity stand in contradiction to the "Islamic."

The Islamic

"Muslim" versus "Islamic"

I must begin this section with a point of clarification and a reversal.

The clarification concerns the word "Muslim," as a possible adjectival equivalent of "Islamic," and the reason why I focus exclusively on the latter.[147] To be sure, there is overlap between these two terms, "Muslim theology," for example, being essentially synonymous with "Islamic theology." But there is also divergence: "Muslim law" is not necessarily the same as "Islamic law," as reflected in the legal landscape of the Muslim world today. While each term has both descriptive and prescriptive potential, "Islamic" is used prescriptively with far fewer problems than "Muslim," which in turn presents fewer problems as a descriptor. In other words, "Muslim" speaks more to the *Is* dimension of Muslim behavior, while "Islamic" is more suggestive of the *Ought*. This is why it is easier to speak of "Muslim adultery" or "Muslim murder" than it is to speak of "Islamic adultery" or "Islamic murder." Again, my point is not to deny the prescriptive potential of "Muslim" or the fact that the two terms, depending on context and subject matter, can be used interchangeably. But an act, according to the Islamic Secular, even a morally or practically good act, does not become Islamic merely by being performed by a Muslim; it becomes so by being grounded in obeisance, *qurbah*, and *taqwā*, as part of a commitment to pleasing the God of Islam. Obeisance is the *sine qua non* of the Islamic Secular.

The term "Islamic" in the "Islamic Secular" has a necessarily normative thrust and implies an orientation toward serving the God of Islam as a normative ideal, though such efforts may or may not hit the mark in every instance. "Muslim" (as an adjective), on the other hand, does not necessarily imply a normative commitment. A Muslim can engage in acts that are secular in the modern Western sense, and these "Muslim secular" acts may be converted into "Islamic Secular" acts, by means of *taqwā*, *qurbah*, and obeisance. But these acts may also not be converted. Rooting for Pakistan in a cricket match against India can be a simple expression of secular nationalism; but it can also be a means of supporting Islam's prestige and plausibility structure. And in the latter case it would fall within the Islamic Secular.[148] In sum, the "Muslim Secular" may amount to little more than the wholesale importation of the Western secular.[149] By contrast, the "Islamic Secular," by definition, departs fundamentally from the Western secular and does not admit it.

"Islamic" and My Evolutionary Turn

As for the reversal, in my earlier work, I articulated a position that was undeniably hostile toward the use of the adjective "Islamic." In *Islamic Law and the State*,

I wrote of "the hegemonic rise of the broad and imprecise Arabic neologism, '*islāmī*,' and its English equivalent, 'Islamic,' both of which impute religious provenance and authority to ideas and institutions of little to no relationship to the sources of Islam."[150] Later, in *Islam and the Blackamerican*, I described the use of "Islamic" as a hegemonic tool deployed to promote "false universals" by which the historically, socio-culturally, and even politically informed choices and preferences of the modern "Muslim world" (read: Middle East and South Asia) could be held up as normative for Muslims everywhere.[151] As one observer of the contemporary scene noted, "Some Muslim circles tend to imply that the process of Islamization should essentially lead to Arabization or Pakistanization, etc."[152] Against this use of "Islamic" and "Islamization," I noted that classical jurists assessed ideas and actions in accordance with one of the Five Juristic Categories, *al-aḥkām al-khamsah*, through a process of deliberation that was theoretically open to all, regardless of historical or socio-cultural background.[153] While some have understood my position to be a call to greater compliance with *sharīʿah*,[154] my real aim was to enshrine *sharīʿah* as a basis for levelling the playing field between Blackamerican and immigrant Muslims by denying the latter the ability to claim ownership over Islamic normativity and proffer positions from which, given their status as cultural and historical insiders, there could be no appeal.

But my critical posture toward "Islamic" was not merely a protest against Western Muslims being penalized or demoted because of their Western heritage. Already as an undergraduate, I had been exposed to Marshall Hodgson's (d. 1968) three-volume, posthumous opus, *The Venture of Islam*, wherein he limited the use of "Islamic" to "Islam *in the proper, the religious, sense*."[155] On this understanding, Islamic art and Islamic literature, for example, were not really "Islamic," because they were not properly "religious." Later, I read Janet Abu Lughod's (d. 2013) critique of the idea of the Islamic city, wherein she asks what could possibly be "Islamic" about the climate, technology, or pre-modern modes of social organization or transportation which any would-be "Islamic city" would have to take into account and of which it would be a by-product.[156] The answer, she implies, is nothing; for, again, none of these things are "religious" in the sense of deriving from hermeneutical engagement with the sources of Islam.[157]

Besides these academic influences, there were those extramural Salafī sensibilities that made their way to America (and especially my hometown of Philadelphia) with the mission of "purifying" Islam of all cultural and historical accretions that could not be traced to the Qur'ān and Sunna. These sensibilities were reinforced by the reform efforts of the influential Ismāʿīl al-Fārūqī, who joined Philadelphia's Temple University in 1968 and worked tirelessly both within and beyond the academy.[158] Not only did such teachings seem entirely reasonable to me at the time; they also sat well with my critique of the hegemonic deployment of "Islamic" and the fact that pre-modern Muslims seemed so conspicuously sparing in their use of the term.

Later, however, I came to see this position (both mine and theirs) as overly broad, naive, and shortsighted, not to mention its indebtedness to an overly narrow understanding of religion itself. The real problem began with the fact that "Islamic" was largely undertheorized, as a result of which immigrant Muslims could vest their cultural and other preferences with an unassailable religious authority that could be deployed as a silencing mechanism. A more disciplined approach, however, could avoid these problems and produce a definition of "Islamic" at once theoretically sound, historically grounded, and devoid of undue bias.

In his book *To Change the World*, James Davison Hunter asks why American Christians, despite their majority status, their newfound political power in such movements as the Moral Majority, and their representation in the highest echelons of business and all the major institutions in the US, have failed to reinstate their religion as the moral and ideological benchmark through which the nation might be saved from decline. In fact, they have lost almost every major battle—from school prayer to abortion to gay marriage. Unconvinced that Christians are simply not trying hard enough, Hunter locates a major part of the problem in the substance and polarity of America's dominant culture. For, it is here, he observes, that minds, hearts, and sensibilities are shaped and calibrated to see and feel about Christianity one way versus another. Yet, like the technology, social organization, and modes of transportation we saw in our discussion of Abū Lughod, little of what might constitute the cultural antidote to this situation would be directly traceable to the Bible or Church tradition; nor would it be counted "religious" by Hodgson or Abu Lughod; nor would it meet my or the Salafis' criterion of a direct genealogical relationship to religion's foundation documents.

Earlier, the late Peter Berger (d. 2017) had made a similar observation. In *The Sacred Canopy*, he argued that Christianity, indeed, religion as a whole, has fallen on difficult days in the modern world because its "plausibility structure" has been severely degraded if not destroyed. By "plausibility structure," Berger was referring to, *inter alia*, "the presence of social structures within which [a particular] reality is taken for granted and within which successive generations of individuals are socialized in such a way that this world is real to them."[159] Religion, in other words, is not self-sustaining. In the same way that living organisms require appropriate eco-systems to perpetuate their existence, religion requires an appropriate plausibility structure. And, "The firmer the plausibility structure is, the firmer will be the world that is 'based' upon it."[160] When a plausibility structure fades or is disrupted, however, the world it underwrites "begins to totter and its reality ceases to impose itself as self-evident truth."[161] Yet, religion is no more automatically productive of its own plausibility structure than are fish of the aquatic eco-systems upon which they rely. Ultimately, religion requires something that is *not* "religious" (in the strict sense in which I,

Hodgson, the Salafis, and Abu Lughod had conceptualized it) to ensure its viability. And without this added something, religion will be very much like a fish out of water.

Still earlier, H. Richard Niebuhr (d. 1962) framed his discussion in *Christ and Culture* around the fact that "the Christian church enduringly struggles with the problem of Christ and culture."[162] This struggle, according to him, produced five distinct general attitudes: (1) Christ Against Culture; (2) Christ of Culture; (3) Christ Above Culture; (4) Christ and Culture in Paradox; and (5) Christ the Transformer of Culture. Again, culture here, despite its status as essentially "non-religious," is clearly recognized as a central problem. Even Christ-Against-Culture Fundamentalists who attack Christ-of-Culture liberals routinely appeal to the cosmological and other assumptions embedded in some earlier culture.[163] Culture, in other words, is critical to the health, viability, and self-understanding of Christianity, or any religion, as a concrete, lived reality. Of course, "culture" in this context means something broader than leisure, sport, and entertainment. Perhaps Gramsci's notion of "hegemony" would be the appropriate analogue here.

At any rate, if the status of Christianity (or any religion) as a lived reality is significantly informed by its relationship with the prevailing culture, it is difficult—*pace* Hodgson, Abu Lughod, the Salafis, and my earlier view—to see how a deliberate, conscious, and sustained attempt to shape that culture to the explicit benefit of Christianity can constitute something other than a Christian/religious act, even if it does not take scripture as its concrete point of departure. Similarly, it is difficult to see Christianity itself—again as a lived reality, not as a transcendent ideal—at any given moment in time and space, as something other than (let alone less than) a composite of concrete doctrines and practices, religious orientation, *and* plausibility structure.

In sum, the relationship between religion and culture is not casual but essential; and it is not always amenable to disaggregation.[164] This is what the late-modern (re-)definition of religion, which I was educated, socialized, and calibrated to accept, tends to conceal. Secular modernity (as an ideology, not a time-period) cannot grant religion real purchase on the prevailing culture without jeopardizing the primacy of its own vision and authority. And if we are honest, we will recognize the call for a separation between religion and state precisely for what it is: a call for the domestication of religion vis-à-vis the secular culture sponsored and relied upon by the secular state. That this modern arrangement is more recent than commonly assumed can be gleaned from such views as that expressed by Ernst Troeltsch (d. 1923) and later echoed by H. Richard Niebuhr as late as the middle of the twentieth century: "Christianity and Western culture are so inextricably intertwined that a Christian can say little about his faith to members of other civilizations, and the latter in turn cannot encounter Christ save as a member of the Western world."[165] Leaving aside whatever exaggerations Troeltsch might be guilty of here, the basic point remains: no religion, as a lived, functioning reality, can separate itself from its socio-cultural plausibility structure and survive. For this reason, we can no more think or speak meaningfully of religion in isolation from its requisite socio-cultural, epistemological, and political eco-system than we can meaningfully think or speak of sustaining fish in isolation from water.

On this understanding, I came to see that the problem with the use of "Islamic" was not its entailment of the historically and socio-culturally informed choices and preferences settled upon in the modern (or pre-modern) Muslim world. There is no life outside of culture, and the conflation of culture with religion is precisely what all functioning religions' plausibility structures promote (and all successful ones actually achieve). To blame Muslim immigrants in the West for being carriers of successful plausibility structures is not only wrong but naive and shortsighted (which is not to suggest that attachment to plausibility structure alone explains all their prejudices). The problem, as I now see it, is twofold. First, failure to recognize the extent to which immigrant Muslims have sublated the prescriptive "Islamic" into the descriptive "Islamic" has too often raised their historically embedded preferences beyond critique, review, or modification, promoting a regime of domination wherein Western Muslims are routinely denied their own story and assigned a supporting role in that of their immigrant co-religionists. Second, and relatedly, the tendency to universalize the achievements of the traditional Muslim world as the sole possible plausibility structure for Islam stifles the emergence of what might prove (in an American context, at least) to be a more effective alternative.

In this light, I came to embrace the construct "Islamic" as inclusive of much more than the "religious" in the sense of what is derived concretely from the sources of religion. Domes, minarets, skull caps, calligraphy, and even bean pies may not be essential to Islam as products of the hermeneutical engagement of its sources; but without these things—or viable alternatives to fill their practical and semiotic roles—the plausibility structure of Islam will be palpably weakened. In this capacity, such things must be recognized as part of the composite "Islam" as a concretely lived reality in any given time and place. In short, they are "Islamic." And how could they not be, when they so obviously, consistently, and effectively announce and sustain the welcome presence and efficacy of Islam? This is almost certainly what the late Shaykh Yūsuf al-Qaraḍāwī (d. 1444/2022) had in mind when he wrote, "The 'Islamic culture' we have in mind is not simply 'religious culture,' as some people imagine it to be. Rather, what is 'Islamic' encompasses more than what is 'religious,' considering that Islam is religion and worldly affairs (*dīn wa dunyā*)."[166] As we shall see in Chapter 3, an important aspect of the Islamic Secular relates to the role of plausibility structure in the constitution and sustainability of Islam and the Islamic. And culture-production (broadly speaking and including, e.g., technology) is a major constituent of that enterprise.

As with "religion" and "secular," however, there are other definitions of "Islamic" whose popularity and influence might promote readings of my argument that distort or cloud its meaning. In such light, I will now try to clarify how my use of "Islamic" compares with what I take to be the two most influential definitions thereof to date: that of Marshall Hodgson and that of the late Shahab Ahmed (d. 2015).

Marshall Hodgson

I mentioned earlier that Hodgson equated "Islamic" with religion "*in the proper, the religious, sense.*" But Hodgson's thesis is actually broader, more sophisticated and, ultimately, more ambiguous than this excerpt suggests. His three-volume opus is an historical overview of Islam, and his most in-depth discussion of "Islamic" appears in a few densely packed pages in the Introduction, which aim to calibrate his readers' faculties to a proper construction of the rest of the book. At bottom, however, Hodgson appears to operate on the basis of *two* understandings of religion, one narrow, the other quite broad. This dual understanding results in a number of unresolved antinomies and makes it difficult to grasp with full confidence how Hodgson's understanding of "Islamic" relates to that of the Islamic Secular.

We saw Hodgson's narrow understanding of religion in his reference to "Islam *in the proper, the religious, sense.*" Hodgson renders this even narrower by an explicit distinction he draws between Christianity and Islam: "[F]or Christians, being based in revelation means being in response to redemptive love. . . . For Muslims, being based in revelation means being in response to total moral challenge."[167] Morality, in other words, is the properly religious, or "Islamic," concern of Islam. Given the clear Kantian underpinnings here, this implies that prudence and pragmatics are not the proper concern of Islam as religion—Kant conceiving of both as basically contradicting morality. On this understanding, there are "religious" ideas and activities that "express Islam as a faith,"[168] and there are "secular" ideas and activities that do not "express Islam as a faith," even if some of these secular ideas and activities are recognized as "contributing to the fully Islamic life."[169] That the secular for Hodgson is antonymous to the religious is also reflected in his assertion that religion aspires to shape all social patterns "without adulteration from . . . secular ideals."[170] Yet, the religious can neither obliterate the secular nor be sustained in its absence. Thus, in an attempt to explicate the relationship between the two, Hodgson developed his famous tripartite typology of "Islamic," "Islamdom," and "Islamicate."

"Islamic," for Hodgson, refers to ideas and practices arising from the hermeneutical engagement with Islam's scripture or religious law. This is religion proper, which "expresses Islam as a faith."[171] The remaining two terms, "Islamdom" and "Islamicate," are non-religious, or "secular." "Islamdom" refers to "the society in which the Muslims and their faith are recognized as prevalent and socially dominant."[172] "Islamicate" refers to the "*culture*, centered on a lettered tradition, which has been historically distinctive of Islamdom, the *society*, and which has been naturally shared in by both Muslims and non-Muslims."[173] Hodgson observes that "much of what Muslims have done as a part of the 'Islamic' civilization can only be described as 'un-Islamic.'"[174] It would be erroneous, therefore, to refer to this civilization as a whole as simply "Islamic." After all, non-Muslims (one thinks of the Ṣābi'ī families of Sabians in Baghdad[175] or the Christian administrators in Mamlūk Egypt) contributed handsomely to the culture of Islamdom. Thus, the culture that matured under the political and social dominance of Muslims can also not be properly described, at least not entirely, as "Islamic," "*in the proper, the religious, sense*." And yet, neither this culture, nor this society nor this civilization can be meaningfully dissociated from Islam. This is the point of Hodgson's "Islamdom" and "Islamicate."

The Islamic Secular recognizes the basic validity of Hodgson's conceptual troika. It too insists that not everything in Islam is an expression of religion-as-concrete-doctrine-and-practice. In contradistinction to Hodgson, however, the Islamic Secular aggregates these elements under a *single* designation, "Islamic." Whereas Hodgson sees some of the constituents of his typology as religious, *in the proper, the religious, sense*, and some not, the Islamic Secular subsumes *all* of them under the umbrella of religion, recognizing all of them as potentially "Islamic." The disagreement, then, is not with Hodgson's analysis per se but with his narrower understanding of "religion," on the basis of which the religious/secular antinomy persists in a manner that it does not under the Islamic Secular.[176] For Hodgson, "every sort of belles-lettres in prose and verse . . . written under the sign of Islam"[177] would be Islamicate and thus secular, because it falls outside "the realm of what are clearly points of Islamic religion."[178] This religion/secular divide is thrown into even bolder relief by his explicit reference to Muslims equating the "realm of Islamic religion" with what he terms "the Shar'ī Vision," noting that from the time this vision crystalized, "any public concern was either a matter of fulfilling God's will, or it was illegitimate frivolity."[179] Under the Islamic Secular, by contrast, non-*shar'ī*, 'secular,' belle-lettristic, and other activity can all qualify as religious and, ultimately, Islamic.

But there is another sense in which Hodgson's understanding of "religion" is narrower than that of the Islamic Secular. This appears in his notion that the properly religious is that which "expresses Islam as a faith."[180] My emphasis here is not on "Islam *as a faith*" but on the notion that religiosity resides strictly in acts of *expressing* faith. If what I said earlier about a religion's plausibility structure has any value, religiosity must reside not simply in acts that *express* Islam but also in acts that seek to *sustain* its integrity, viability, and relevance in the world. In such light, an act may be less valuable as an expression of the faith but more valuable as a sustainer of it. For example, in his *Fayṣal al-Tafriqa Bayna al-Islām wa al-Zandaqa*, al-Ghazālī is bitingly critical of speculative theology (*kalām*): "Were we ourselves to put aside all pretensions of deference and decorum, we would declare outright that delving into speculative theology, due to its many liabilities, is religiously forbidden (*ḥarām*)."[181] Yet, he draws two exceptions: (1) an individual who develops doubts that might be removed by speculative theology, and (2) one of superior intelligence who can treat people's doubts and beat back the spurious arguments of the enemies of Islam. In such cases, using speculative theology may even be religiously obligatory (*wājib*).[182] While *kalām* (on al-Ghazālī's depiction, at least) may be frowned upon as an *expression* of Islam, it is lauded as a means of *sustaining* it. From the perspective of the Islamic Secular, meanwhile, all of this activity—that which expresses Islam as well as that which sustains it—would be "religious," again, rendering the category "religion" significantly broader than it is in Hodgson's scheme.

I should note, incidentally, that Hodgson clearly recognizes the importance of plausibility structure (or something like it). As he puts it, "The determinacy of tradition is limited, in the long run, by the requirement that it be continuously relevant in current circumstances."[183] Despite this acknowledgment, however, he still restricts the properly religious to *moral* responses to revelation, a move that excludes the prudential and practical from religion's purview. In sum, while Hodgson recognizes the value of all sustentative acts as Islamicate, they remain in his understanding secular and thus not "properly" religious or Islamic. The Islamic Secular, by contrast, recognizes all such acts as religious and at least potentially Islamic.

Alongside this narrower understanding of religion, however, Hodgson has another articulation that seems to bring his conception of "Islamic" closer to that of the Islamic Secular. Prior to explaining Islam/Islamicate/Islamdom, Hodgson had not explicitly defined "religion." Later in the Introduction, however, he does, and his definition is strikingly broad:

> In a person's life, we may call "religious" in the most restricted sense (in the sense of "spiritual") his ultimate orientation and commitments and the ways in which he pays attention to them, privately or with others. Properly, we use the term "religious" for an ultimate orientation (rather than "philosophical" or "ideological"), so far as orientation is personally committing and is meaningful in terms of a cosmos, without further precision of what this may come to. In an Islamic context, this has meant, in effect, a sense of cosmic transcendence,

> and we may apply the word, more concretely, to efforts, practical or symbolical, to transcend the limits of the natural order of foreseeable life—that is, efforts based on hope from or struggle toward some sort of "supernatural" realm. Then we may call "religious" (extending the term a bit) those cultural traditions that have focused on such cosmic commitments: cumulative traditions of personal responses to presumed possibilities of transcending the natural order.[184]

In a footnote for this passage, Hodgson summarizes his point: "One can apply the term 'religious' to any life-orientational experience or behavior in the degree to which it is relatively most focused on the role of a *person in an environment felt as cosmos*."[185] This "orientational" focus has obvious resonances with the Islamic Secular and the aforementioned universe of opportunities and expectations engendered by a conscious awareness of the Divine presence and gaze. But if religion is an orientation that extends to such enterprises as cultural production and the like, it is difficult to see how Hodgson's "Islamic" can be so definitively set apart from his "Islamicate," and why the two cannot be *equally* religious, "*in the proper, the religious, sense*," as the result of religious orientation simply running its course. If "every sort of belles-lettres in prose and verse" can be "written under the sign of Islam"[186] and "[a]ll can, in some sense, be derived as consequent upon the initial posture of *islām*, of personal submission to God"[187] and, further, justified "as in some way contributing to the fully Islamic life,"[188] *all* would seem to qualify as both religious and Islamic. This is especially so, given Hodgson's recognition that "to separate religion from the rest of life is partly to falsify it."[189] Yet, he persists in maintaining that religion and culture are distinct, designating the latter as an essentially secular enterprise.[190] Indeed, he seems to see only the "unlearned Muslim" as likely to conflate the two, as when he expresses indirect criticism of the lay Indian Muslim who exchanges his European street clothes for an "old fashioned costume" before going to the mosque, "feeling the latter costume to be more 'Islamic,'" despite the fact that "*such a change is not prescribed by Islamic law*" and it "is not found in other Muslim lands."[191]

In sum, according to Hodgson's narrower definition of religion, his "Islamic" is at odds with that of the Islamic Secular, in that it explicitly perpetuates the religion/secular divide. Yet, his broader definition of religion appears to reverse this relationship and in so doing comes closer to the perspective of the Islamic Secular. Of the two, the narrower definition predominates in his overall presentation, maintaining the basic tension between his conception of "Islamic" as essentially religious "*in the proper, the religious, sense*," that is, derived from the sources of Islam, and that of the "Islamic Secular," which is differentiated from those sources, even as it remains within the scope of Islam as *dīn*.

To this I would add one final element: Hodgson's comment that the Indian Muslim's costume "is not found in other Muslim lands" could be read as implying that the "Islamic" in his view must be universal, holding whatever meaning or value it holds for all Muslims everywhere. To the extent that this a correct reading, this view would also stand in contrast to that of the Islamic Secular. For, as we shall see, in terms of concrete substance, neither permanence nor universality is a precondition of the Islamic Secular.

Shahab Ahmed

Hodgson's typology was the most imaginative and remains, in theory at least, the most influential of his generation, though in practice many have continued to use "Islamic" in loose and imprecise ways. Today, however, no serious discussion of "Islamic" can avoid engaging with the thesis of the late Shahab Ahmed as set forth in his posthumous book, *What Is Islam?: The Importance of Being Islamic.* Like Hodgson's, Ahmed's is a marvelously rich, highly innovative, expansively researched, and challenging work, layered with bold and intricate assertions, presuppositions, and mildly polemical "correctives." Moreover, his entire book is devoted to defining "Islam" and "Islamic." The main point of my engagement with Ahmed is not to respond to his work as a whole but simply to throw my own concept of "Islamic" into bolder relief, the better to minimize unwanted conflations. Given this limited purpose, much in his hefty tome will be passed over in silence.

One could easily get the impression from *What Is Islam?* that Ahmed, like Hodgson, sees an inherent contradiction between the religious and the secular. This would be the logical deduction from the fact that his "Islamic" vacates the religious in an explicit effort to avoid clashing with the secular. As he puts it, "I have proposed an epistemological agenda where one puts aside the concept of 'religion' when conceptualizing Islam/Islamic precisely because it forces us into the religion-secular binary that . . . in numerous ways defeats the conceptual purpose."[192] What seems closer to the truth, however, is that Ahmed is frustrated with the zero-sum tension between "religious" and "secular" as defined by modern, Enlightenment-drenched scholars and the way this forces Islam almost completely into the religion category while inexorably pushing it away from anything that might be defined as secular. In his view, there is value, meaning, and even truth in the realm of the putative secular, some of which Islam cannot dispense with without impoverishing itself. Ahmed's aim is thus to do away with this zero-sum, religion/secular binary by transcending it altogether. He speaks thus of the possibility of an idea, action, or artifact being "neither religious nor secular, but *Islamic*."[193] His "Islamic," in other words, transcends the religious/secular divide by effectively negating both.

By contrast, my conception of "religion" and "religious" does not negate but confirms the secular as its own entity possessed of an actual constitution.

Meanwhile, my concept of "Islamic" includes *both* the "secular," in the form of religious orientation differentiated from *sharīʿah, and sharīʿah*, in the form of religion-as-concrete-doctrine-and-practice. In other words, in contradistinction to Ahmed, whose Islamic is neither religious nor secular, on my thesis, an idea, action, or artifact can be *both* religious *and* secular, indeed, both secular and Islamic.

At or near the core of Ahmed's project is the desire to find a way around what he terms the "totalizing 'legal supremacist' conceptualization of Islam as *law*."[194] As Ahmed describes it, the entrenched, all-encompassing authority of Muslim jurists or, as he calls them, the "*fuqahā*ʾ-jurisprudents," closes off all alternate paths to Islamic Meaning and Truth, paths such as those taken by the Sufis, philosophers, litterateurs, and others. As with the religious/secular divide, Ahmed accepts as fact and at face value that the *fuqahā*ʾ-jurisprudents embraced the totalitarian vision that he imputes to them, if not as an ideal then certainly as a fact, which is too pervasive, long-standing, and deeply entrenched to ignore or approach agnostically. Ultimately, however, in responding to what he takes to be their perspective, he appears at times to internalize it, in which capacity it escapes more careful analysis.

For example, the *fuqahā*ʾ-jurisprudents' purported inability to see the distinction between *sharīʿah* and *dīn* informs Ahmed's interpretation of a provocative passage from the third-/ninth-century polymath Ibn Qutaybah (d. 276/889), who also served, incidentally, as a judge. According to Ahmed, the passage in question could be understood as asking, "What do they know of *dīn* who only *dīn* know?"[195] What Ibn Qutaybah was actually highlighting, however, was the importance of recognizing the need to go *beyond* "the Qurʾān, Sunnah, *ordinances* of religion (*sharāʾiʿ al-dīn*) and knowledge of what is permissible and impermissible" in order to provide everything Islam needs to survive, flourish, and perpetuate itself as a lived reality.[196] In other words, *dīn* was for Ibn Qutaybah, as I describe it above, much broader than religion-as-concrete-doctrine-and-practice (i.e., *sharīʿah*). And what he should really be interpreted as saying is, "What do they know of *dīn* who only *sharīʿah* know?" In his words:

> The path to God is not singular, and goodness is not confined to nightly prayers, daily fasting and knowledge of the permissible and impermissible (*ʿilm al-ḥalāl wa al-ḥarām*). Rather, there are many paths to God, and the gates of goodness are expansive. The quality of religion (*ṣalāḥ al-dīn*) depends on the quality of the temporal order; and the quality of the temporal order depends on the quality of those in authority (*ṣalāḥ al-sulṭān*); and the quality of those in authority obtains upon God's facilitation through the provision of guidance and penetrating insight.[197]

In other words, even as a member of the class of *fuqahā'*-jurisprudents, *sharī'ah* and *dīn* are not coterminous for judge Ibn Qutaybah; nor is the health and integrity of Islam—and the Islamic—viewed as being sustainable on the basis of *sharī'ah* alone. It seems, however, that the force of Ahmed's imputation of a totalitarian epistemology to the *fuqahā'*-jurisprudents occluded his ability to recognize the true import of Ibn Qutaybah's words. This oversight, in turn, both drives and is driven by Ahmed's perception of the *fuqahā'*-jurisprudents as denying (or at least questioning) the Islamic legitimacy, benefits, and authority of all other—that is, non-*shar'ī*—regimes of deliberation, a view that I shall show in Chapter 2 to be at odds with what emerges as the predominant opinion in the juristic tradition.

Over the course of his argument, Ahmed does not directly engage with the jurisprudential writings of the *fuqahā'*-jurisprudents; as a result, his depictions of Islamic law and jurisprudence are at times impressionistic if not caricatural. He appears to encounter nothing that might suggest to him the possibility of things being other than what he assumes. Of course, any presumed monopoly by the *fuqahā'*-jurisprudents over religious—and not just *shar'ī*—authority would, as Ahmed suggests, truncate and limit what could be considered Islamic. For, their position as the sole definers of a proper response to God and God's concrete communiqué would reduce everything "Islamic" to that which is faithful to the sources and interpretive methods upon which they rely and over which they preside as authorities. In such a context, as Ahmed puts it, "we would likely hesitate to think that a discourse on humour might somehow meaningfully be called 'Islamic' . . . by the same measure that we would likely *not* hesitate to classify, for instance, a treatise on the meaning of *jihad* as 'Islamic.'"[198] Certainly with regard to pre-modern Islam, however, this suggestion assumes rather than proves the totalitarian epistemology he imputes to the *fuqahā'*-jurisprudents, according to which *sharī'ah* and Islam are jurisdictionally coterminous.

As we will see more concretely in Chapter 2, the *fuqahā'*-jurisprudents were clear in distinguishing *shar'ī* from non-*shar'ī* domains of inquiry. And while a work on humor might not have been counted as *shar'ī*, this would not necessarily prevent the *fuqahā'*-jurisprudents from recognizing its value to *dīn*. In his humorous book on misers, for example, the Shāfi'ī jurist and *ḥadīth* expert al-Khaṭīb al-Baghdādī (d. 463/1071) states explicitly that among the aims of this work is to "lift the weight of seriousness from the hearts of scholars and relieve their minds from (the burdens of) constant study and mental exertion," clearly recognizing its service and value to *dīn*.[199] Meanwhile, the Ḥanbalī Ibn al-Jawzī (d. 597/1200) opens his book, *Akhbār al-Adhkiyā'* (*Annals of the Clever*), some of whose humor borders on the risqué,[200] with an explicit recognition of the value of reason as "the instrument through which one gains knowledge of God."[201]

Meanwhile, the basic structure and language of the book clearly point to the *fuqahā'*-jurisprudents as a major part of its primary audience. In a similar vein, Ṭaha Ḥusayn reports that the *fuqahā'*-jurisprudents were often enamored of the poetry of even the most unscrupulous poets, to the point of quoting some of this material in their own works. In fact, the staunch Traditionalist Sufyān al-Thawrī (d. 161/777) is reported to have referred to Abū Nuwās as "the most poetic of people" (*ash'ar al-nās*)![202]

While al-Thawrī would obviously not approve of all of Abū Nuwās's oeuvre, he almost certainly appreciated its contributions to the linguistic sensibilities of the Muslims, as well as to the development of a Muslim aesthetic, Muslim cultural literacy, and Muslim cultural self-reliance, with all that this implies for the plausibility structure (though he would not have called it that) of Islam. Yet, neither he nor any of the other jurists I have cited saw themselves as necessarily going outside of Islam in engaging with this literature, at least not those aspects of it of which they approved. They certainly did not see themselves as going outside of the divine gaze or as proceeding "*as if* God did not exist." If none of this literature was explicitly referred to as "Islamic," or "*islāmī*," this was probably because this adjective itself was not a very active part of the classical Muslim lexicon. After all, neither *fiqh* nor *kalām* nor *adab* nor Sufism nor art nor architecture nor any other pursuit was generally paired with the adjective "*islāmī*."

At any rate, Ahmed's response to this situation is not to pit the Sufis, philosophers, littérateurs, and others against the *fuqahā'*-jurisprudents directly. His solution, rather, is to dislocate the *fuqahā'*-jurisprudents' authority (and thus their alleged monopoly) by invoking a concept of revelation that includes aspects regarding whose interpretation the *fuqahā'*-jurisprudents' superiority cannot be assumed. According to Ahmed, the revelation from which "Islam" and "Islamic" derives is not limited to God's Text (i.e., the Qur'ān) but includes as well what he refers to as Revelation's "Pre-Text" and "Con-Text." The "Islamic," he argues, is the result of any serious engagement in Meaning-making or Truth-discovery on the basis of *any* of these "texts." As Ahmed puts it, "*something is Islamic to the extent that it is made meaningful in terms of hermeneutical engagement with Revelation to Muhammad as one or more of Pre-Text, Text, and Con-Text*."[203] This definition, in Ahmed's view, expands the possibilities of the "Islamic" well beyond what the *fuqahā'*-jurisprudents could imagine or produce. For, the sources of Islam and the Islamic are now much broader, richer, and multivalent than the limited regime upon which the *fuqahā'*-jurisprudents traditionally rely.

According to Ahmed, the Con-Text is simply "the whole lexicon of meanings that is the product and outcome of previous hermeneutical engagement with Revelation which are already present in the context of a given time and place as Islam."[204] It is "*the full historical vocabulary of Islam* at any given moment."[205]

Con-Text is constructed, "*ab initio*, first in the Text's interpretation of itself, second, in the re-constitution by and in the Text of pre-Islamic elements with new Islamic meaning, and, third, by the engagement of the speaker and audience of the Muhammadan revelation, the first hermeneutical community, with Pre-Text, Text, and Con-Text."[206] Whenever an individual engages in Meaning-making or Truth-discovery, relying on Ahmed's expanded notion of "revelation" and using vocabulary and terms of engagement historically recognized by Muslims consciously acting as Muslims, the result is Islamic.[207] Acknowledging (as did Hodgson) that the space that Muslims occupied in producing and passing on the Con-Text invariably included non-Muslims, Ahmed implodes what W. Montgomery Watt (d. 2006) once described as the myth of Muslim self-sufficiency.[208] He insists that non-Muslims contributed (and may still contribute) to Islam's Con-Text and thereby have informed the end product of what becomes Islamic. Even where the Text does not recognize them as a source for enhancing Muslims' hermeneutical insight or imagination, history on the ground undeniably does. As such, "That Aristotle and Plato were not *Muslims* is simply irrelevant to their meaningful designation as Islamic."[209]

I think there is something valuable here. After all, domes, minarets, and *atabeg*s are universally recognized as extra-scriptural, of non-Muslim provenance and yet Islamic. Similarly, the celebrated heresiologist al-Shahrastānī (d. 548/1153) places such non-Muslims as Ḥunayn b. Isḥāq (d. 260/873), Abū Bakr Thābit b. Qurah (d. 288/901), Yaḥyā b. ʿAdī (d. 364/974), and others under the rubric "Later Philosophers of Islam" (*al-mutaʾakhkhirūn min falāsifat al-islām*).[210] But there are two scores on which Ahmed's notion of Con-Text would clash with that of the Islamic Secular. First, he seems to impute to his Con-Text an authority that is equal (if not superior) to that of the Text, such that it can functionally override the Text. From the perspective of the Islamic Secular, however, the authority of any Con-Text would be provisional, secondary, and subject to expiration, whereas that of the Text is original, primary, and enduring.[211] Second, whereas Ahmed seems to be saying that non-Muslims can contribute directly to the Islamic, the Islamic Secular would see their contributions as necessarily mediated through a process of validation over which Muslims preside, as non-Muslims lack consciously cultivated obeisance to the God of Islam. This was certainly the case with Aristotle and Plato, the "Islamization" of whose ideas was clearly overseen and ratified by Muslims. To give a modern example, the company that makes Barbie dolls might introduce a model with a *ḥijāb,* in recognition of Muslim sensibilities or markets. But such a doll will only become an "Islamic doll" through a validation brought about by its acceptance and popularity among Muslims. Otherwise, it will likely fall flat as a hollow and possibly offensive caricature.

As for the Pre-Text, here is where Ahmed's innovative energies are most brightly displayed. It is also here, however, that his and my concepts of "Islamic" most radically part ways. According to Ahmed, the reality of the Pre-Text emerges out of the fact that the Text itself had to recline upon some pre-existing Truth of which it is only a partial representation. As he puts it, "Pre-Text is present *ab initio* because the Text comes from some Truth behind and beyond the Revelation."[212] On this understanding, Revelation is not the only portal to truth, not even divine Truth. The divine Truth expressed in Revelation is simply a part, a subset or narrower expression, of an infinitely broader Truth. As such, one can go beyond or around Revelation and gain unmediated access to Truth by engaging with the Pre-Text directly via the correct application of reason. For, again, "the Truth of the Pre-Text finds expression in the world of the cosmos beyond the Text."[213] Ahmed credits Sufis and especially philosophers with having recognized this fact and taken it as a means of accessing an alternate and "higher" Truth. As he puts it, "Through Reason, the philosophers produce Real-Truth directly from the Pre-Text rather than from the Text (the Qur'ān), the mediation of which latter is not necessary (or even necessarily useful) *for them* to access and know the Divine Truth (although it is necessary for the great masses of non-philosophers inexpert in Reason)."[214]

In Ahmed's view, when, through the proper use of reason, a Muslim engages with the Pre-Text through the machinery of the Con-Text in search of Truth and arrives at a conclusion that contradicts the Text, this conclusion is considered both Islamic and superior to Truth conventionally derived from the Text, despite this contradiction. And because it is superior, this Truth can override that of the Text. On such an approach, one can arrive at notions of Islamic justice or morality that contradict and take precedence over the justice or morality identified or implied by the Text, as authenticated by the *fuqahā'*-jurisprudents. In other words, through the hermeneutical engagement with the Pre-Text, an act such as wine-drinking can be "made meaningful . . . in terms of Islam" and thereby qualify as Islamic.[215] Ahmed sees this approach and its far-reaching implications as his singular achievement. As he puts it, "As far as I am aware, no modern reformer has attempted to play the philosophical card and to appeal explicitly to the categorical higher Truth-value of Pre-Text as trumping Text."[216]

It is difficult to miss or ignore the ontological-cum-moral realism coursing through Ahmed's notion of Pre-Text. The "Truth" he points to as pre-existing Revelation calls to mind not only Christine Hayes's Greeks but also what the late Stanley Tambiah (d. 2014) described as ancient pagan cosmology, which insists on "the existence of a primordial realm and primordial stuff anterior to, or parallel with, or even independent of the gods."[217] In this cosmology, "pagan gods do not transcend the universe but are rooted in it and bound by its laws."[218]

Pre-Textual Truth, in other words, is both sempiternally "present" and autonomous. For this reason, it can be invoked against the Truth of the gods or God. Like Hayes with the Greeks, Tambiah points out that this ancient pagan notion of pre-existing Truth ran afoul of ancient Judaism. I would argue that Islam finds it equally problematic.

The Qur'ān states unequivocally that God is ultimately the Creator of *everything* in existence, *khāliq kulli shay'* [6:102; 13:16], clearly implying God's prior existence to everything, without exception. *Ḥadīth* literature confirms this, as in the report wherein the Prophet is said to have responded to a group of Yemenīs who asked him about the beginning of things. He stated, "There was God and nothing else" (*kāna Allahu wa lam yakun shay'^un ghayruh*).[219] On this understanding, God's revealed Truth is not a subset of some larger, pre-existing backdrop of autonomous primordial stuff, and there is thus no Pre-Text that serves as its repository. Revelation does not emanate inexorably from a blind, sempiternal reality but is instead the deliberate proclamation of God as a willful and ultimate agent who addresses what God pleases to address in the way that God pleases to do so, a fact unchanged by reason's ability to apprehend Revelation's referents or its internal logic. Even identifying the Pre-Text with "nature," as Ahmed occasionally does, does not alter the situation.[220] For, as Tambiah notes, summarizing early Judaism's critique of ancient paganism, "[T]here is no natural bond between God and nature, for nature did not participate in any of God's substance or body (i.e., nature was not 'iconically'connected with God). There is no bridge between the God [*sic*] and the created universe."[221] In short, God precedes nature, not the other way around; and nature is simply God's creation—from nothing. It seems, however, that the ancient pagans did not like the idea of nothingness.[222]

The Islamic Secular assumes a cosmology that begins with God alone as its point of departure. It recognizes no transcendent, metaphysical, or cosmic sources antecedent to Revelation upon which to build a hermeneutical exercise that could violate the Text in the name of "higher" Truth or Meaning.[223] As we will see in Chapter 2, there are realities—created realities—to which Revelation does not speak directly. And whether the truths of these realities can contradict those of Revelation is an ongoing debate. But even were we to concede the possibility of contradiction between what God creates and what God commands, this would not automatically privilege creation's truth over that of Revelation. To say that truths discovered in creation automatically override the Truths of Revelation would be like saying that discovering that there is no actual human equality in nature must automatically override, as a "higher truth," our democratic commitment to equality. The Islamic Secular simply does not recognize any ontologically "higher truth" that can independently or automatically override scripture.[224]

In fact, not only is the Islamic Secular unmusical—to use Weber's term—to any "higher" Truth or Meaning than Revelation; it is not always necessarily about truth or meaning at all. Professor Ahmed seems to see the pursuit of truth and meaning as the raison d'être of any inquiry, hermeneutical or other. And this obsession seems at times to jeopardize his goal of expanding Muslims' horizons, by instead binding them to a concretely devotional mode of existence, wherein every thought and action must be in pursuit of some concrete Islamic Truth or Meaning. According to him, "That which holds no meaning for someone is of no consequence for him/her."[225] As handsome as this statement may be on its face, I tend to agree with Christopher Shannon when he writes, "The world of friendship—of drinking and talking, working and playing, loving and hating—may bring happiness, or it may not; in neither case does it bring 'meaning.' It is no less important for being, in a sense, 'meaningless.'"[226] This is not to mention the questionable relationship between meaning or truth and prudence, or the lethal blow that a single-minded obsession with meaning must deal to ritual.[227] I do not know the truth or meaning (certainly not in any ultimate sense) of an efficient economic policy or of Michael Jackson's inimitable "*whooo hooo*"; nor do I particularly care. Nor do I know the metaphysical truth or meaning behind the fact that Lebanese cuisine tastes so good or why the ritual of graduation is so important to students. In pursuing an efficient economic policy, however, or listening to Michael Jackson, or consuming a Lebanese dish, or attending a graduation, even under the divine gaze and presumably within the parameters of *sharīʿah*, the Islamic Secular sees no need to go beyond questions of efficiency, "soul," taste, or culture. Truth and meaning are simply not the Islamic Secular's only metrics of assessment.

This brings us back to the divide between the clear realism undergirding Ahmed's concept of "Islamic" and the nominalist bent of the Islamic Secular. The Islamic Secular neither represents nor attempts to apprehend a pre-existing universe of concrete ideas, actions, or artifacts. It is, rather, the product of an *orientation* toward the world that seeks to maximize worldly benefit and efficacy in full and conscious awareness of the adjudicative gaze and presence of the God of Islam. Ideas, actions, and artifacts become "Islamic," according to the Islamic Secular, not by apprehending, approximating, or reproducing some pre-existing Platonic archetype but by virtue of being a product of this orientation. Again, this does not mean that every thought or action of a Muslim is necessarily Islamic, even if this thought or action is Islamically permissible. It does mean, however, that, through an attachment to *taqwā*, *qurbah* obeisance, and oppugnancy, these things *can* become Islamic.

Of course, this perspective raises serious questions about the criterion by which one might distinguish, in concrete terms, what is Islamic from what is not (a criterion, incidentally, that I was also not able to glean from Professor

Ahmed's work). Are simply having a God-conscious orientation and seeking *qurbah* enough to secure a thought or action's status as Islamic? Are groups such as ISIS or the Nation of Islam to be considered Islamic, then, given that their God-consciousness, oppugnancy, and apparent desire to please the God of Islam (as so conceived) is beyond question? In short, is "Islamic" constituted by *any* good-faith attempt to earn divine pleasure, such that it might include ideas and practices that may be substantively wrong, *shar'an*?

In response to these questions, I would like to make two interrelated points. First, from the perspective of the Islamic Secular, ISIS and the NOI *would* be considered "Islamic," at least provisionally on descriptive grounds, in the same sense that the prayer of a person who unknowingly but in good faith prays with ritual impurities on his or her clothing or in the wrong direction is "Islamic." To say that such acts are not Islamic in this sense would be like saying that Nietzsche, Carl Schmitt, or even Hitler was not "rational." On the other hand, to the extent that we conclude that ISIS or the NOI fails to conform to agreed-upon meanings of scripture, acts in ways that damage Islam's plausibility structure, or frustrates values, truths, or interests that are widely recognized as normative in Islam, they may be deemed un-Islamic, in the same sense that we may deem Nietzsche, Schmitt, or Hitler to be unreasonable, because we reject the ends to which they seek to deploy their rationality. One might think here of the famous *ḥadīth* wherein the Prophet is reported to have said, "If a judge (*ḥākim*) rules on the basis of his independent effort to arrive at the truth and 'hits the mark,' he receives two rewards. And if he exerts such effort and rules but misses the mark, he receives one reward."[228] In earning reward, both of these actions must clearly be considered Islamic. In the case of the latter action, however, the *effort* is Islamic, while the *result* of this effort—the substance of the act itself—clearly is not.

This brings me to my second point. There is an important sense in which we must distinguish between what is *Islamic* and what is *Islam* (and who is a Muslim![229]) at any given point in time. As a quotidian orientation, the Islamic Secular may produce many candidates for inclusion in the composite "Islam" as a concrete, lived reality (distinct from the transcendent, universal ideal). Some of these candidates, through a process of communal sifting, debate, practical consideration, and collective mood, will not only prove to be consistent with religion-as-concrete-doctrine-and-practice but will gain admission into the panoply of communal norms. Others will either be rejected by the standards of religion-as-concrete-doctrine-and-practice, or—even if they meet this criterion—they may fail to evince an obvious, meaningful, or urgent enough contribution to Islam's efficacy or plausibility structure; or they may simply fail to capture a pressing interest or the collective mood to the point of rising to a communal norm. From the perspective of *process*, all of these candidates might be deemed Islamic, at least provisionally, even if they fail to gain communal acceptance as normative expressions of Islam. This is clearly what we see in the approach of the eponymous Abū al-Ḥasan al-Ashʿarī (d. 324/936?), when he titled his famous work on theological sects *Doctrines of the 'Islamics'* (*Maqālāt al-Islāmīyīn*), and included in it groups that never gained a major following or whose doctrines he himself considered to be outside of Islam.[230] While many of these views may have issued from motives and processes that might qualify as "Islamic," they never came to constitute "Islam," being either rejected as religion-as-concrete-doctrine-and-practice or failing to capture the collective mood of the community. In a similar vein, Ibn Taymīyah casts as "*islāmīyūn*" Muslim thinkers who took over from the Greek followers of Aristotle views he himself flatly condemned as contravening the *sharʿ*.[231]

Ideas and commitments that remain both within the parameters of the religiously permissible *and* garner sufficient communal support are eligible to become "Islam," again, not as the transcendent, universal ideal but as the concrete, normative, lived reality in any given time and place. I use "normative" here in the same way that Hodgson used "orthodox," to intimate a greater degree of play and fungibility, like the notes in a jazz piece as opposed to the strict, concerto-like adherence implied by orthodoxy.[232] Again, it is the community in any given time and place that is determinative. While certain economic, social, cultural, or political practices of a millennium ago or a hemisphere away may be or have been Islam as concrete praxis, they may be not be in another place today.[233] This is not to say that Islam, as a concrete, lived reality, is whatever Muslims do or whatever they say it is. It is to say that, as a normative, lived reality, Islam is *only* what Muslims, pursuing divine pleasure with due diligence and oppugnant vigilance in any given time and place, say it is. As a colleague of mine is fond of noting, "Islam has never been seen walking down the street."[234] At the same time, while the Islamic Secular respects the individual Muslim conscience, it does not vest the latter with absolute primacy, such that all heteronomous religious authority, including juristic articulations of religion-as-concrete-doctrine-and-practice, can be automatically indicted as authoritarian or oppressive, any more than the non-*sharʿī* articulations of non-jurists can be automatically dismissed as un-Islamic or as an encroachment upon the authority of the jurists.

To be sure, this situation is complicated by the fact that, unlike Christianity or the modern state, Islam never developed a mechanism for wiping the books clean, as a result of which many ideas, practices, and rules remain "on the books" long after their efficacy and even their recognized normativity have expired. Whether Muslims today or in the future will develop procedures for review and disposal that can be formally invoked and executed remains to be seen. I am speaking here simply of the principle, namely, the *sharʿī*/non-*sharʿī* distinction, by which Islam as a concrete, normative, lived reality in any given time and place, can be disaggregated and (re-)negotiated.

It should be clear from the foregoing that there are significant differences between Professor Ahmed's definition of "Islamic" and my own. It should also be clear, however, that there are important points of convergence: *inter alia*, we both object to the overly radical distinction between religion and culture; we both object to too radical a distinction between religion and non-religion and the zero-sum religious/secular divide; we both object to the Enlightenment monopoly on the definition of "religion," with all that it implies about religion's relationship with morality and the secular; and we both chafe at the notion that "Islam is . . . not interested in the richest possible unfolding of man's potentialities, in that it never conceived of the forming of men as civilization's principal and most noble task."[235] Most importantly, we are in full agreement on one fundamental and central goal: gaining more explicit recognition for the Islamic value of contributions from outside the sphere of authority represented by the *fuqahā'*-jurisprudents, that is, religion-as-concrete-doctrine-and-practice. We both recognize, in other words, the importance of a "space of knowledge, truth, thought and action [that] is conceived of as simultaneously *beside the law but within Islam*."[236]

Because Professor Ahmed saw no limits, however, to the jurisdictional boundaries of *sharīʿah* or its representatives and was not able to contemplate that possibility, he was forced to seek other means of producing a comparable effect, namely, by imposing strictures on the *fuqahā'*-jurisprudents from without, via the introduction of sources that fell outside their competence. The Islamic Secular, by contrast, insists not only that *sharīʿah* (and thus the authority of its representatives) is limited in its jurisdictional scope but that these limits are *self-imposed* and explicitly recognized *by* the *fuqahā'*-jurisprudents themselves. In fact, the whole theory of the Islamic Secular stands or falls on the validity of this claim. It is thus to it that I shall now turn.

2

Islam, *Fiqh*, the *Ḥukm Sharʿī*, and the Differentiated Realm

Between "Bad" and "Juristically Proscribed"

In his chronicle of pre-modern Egypt and Syria, the dean of Mamlūk historians, Taqī al-Dīn al-Maqrīzī (d. 845/1442), writes of the year 806/1403–04: "This was the first of the years of trials and tribulations during which Egypt was brought to ruin, most of its population perished, its conditions deteriorated, and its affairs were dislocated to a degree that announced the country's imminent demise."[1] Al-Maqrīzī is referring here to a period of extreme economic hardship.[2] Egypt had no silver mines, and the "silver famine" in Europe had contributed to a severe shortage of silver *dirhams*,[3] the most common denomination for everyday transactions. Meanwhile, plagues, regional shifts in trade patterns and the production of goods, alongside military threats and political instability all led to budgetary shortfalls.[4] In response, beginning in 803/1401 under Sultan Faraj Ibn Barqūq (regency: 801–08/1395–1405 and 809–15/1406–12), the Mamlūk government stepped up its production of copper coins known as *fulūs* (sg. *fals*). In 806/1403–04, it issued a decree making this specie, now traded in weight, the basic currency of commerce. Shortly thereafter, it moved to a non-metallic "money of account" to which all value was pegged and which became the basis of the Mamlūk monetary system.[5] Silver coins ceased to be minted, and the circulation of copper *fulūs* increased dramatically.[6] With this move, the government could consistently increase, or at least stabilize, its revenue relative to its expenses and debts, through the greater leverage it exercised over exchange rates and the ratio of value between gold, silver, and *fulūs*. But for everyday people, including farmers, the instability and inflation caused by this policy (aggravated by people's hoarding of what gold and silver did exist) decimated the purchasing value of *fulūs* and placed basic necessities beyond popular reach. This threatened Egypt with pauperization, a challenge with which it continued to struggle down to the end of the Mamlūk era.

Al-Maqrīzī not only decried this situation; he also expressed strong thoughts about its provenance and ultimate resolution. He traced it "solely to the malfeasance of the leaders and rulers and their negligence with regard to the public

The Islamic Secular. Sherman A. Jackson, Oxford University Press. © Oxford University Press 2024.
DOI: 10.1093/oso/9780197661789.003.0003

interest."[7] He recognized corruption and greed as contributing factors,[8] but he saw the ultimate culprit as bad economic policy.[9] In particular, the introduction of copper *fulūs* as the standard medium of exchange placed Egypt on shaky economic foundations. And the only way out of this situation would be to discontinue what al-Maqrīzī described as a juristically proscribed, vile, and unnatural innovation.

> Know—May God guide you to your own righteousness and inspire you to follow the straight path of your fellow humans— that the currencies that are legally, logically, and customarily acceptable are only those of gold and silver, and that any other [metal] is unsuitable as a currency. By the same token, the situation of the people cannot be sound unless they are obligated to follow the natural and legal course in this regard [i.e., the currency], namely, that they should deal exclusively with gold and silver for pricing goods and estimating labor costs.[10]

Al-Maqrīzī had actually served in the Mamlūk administration, occupying several positions, including that of *muḥtasib*, part of whose job it was to police the market.[11] He was also an accomplished Shāfiʿī jurist to whom Sultan Faraj once offered a chief judgeship.[12] His fame as a professional historian was well established, and he also wrote learned tracts on economics. This convergence of competencies made al-Maqrīzī particularly susceptible to blurring the boundary between law and non-law, the better to clothe his economic (and perhaps other) views with juristic authority. While the problem facing Mamlūk society was clearly economic, he cast the solution primarily in juristic (i.e., *sharʿī*) terms. As he put it, "juristically (*sharʿan*), logically, and customarily speaking," the only bona fide currencies are gold and silver.[13] This, he insisted, was "the natural, *legal* order" (*al-amr al-ṭabīʿī al-sharʿī*).[14] For, "silver is a *juristically* legal currency" (*fa inna al-fiḍḍah hiya naqdun sharʿīyun*) while "copper coins are the closest thing to nothing at all" (*al-fulūs innamā hiya ashbah shayʾin ilā lā shayʾ*).[15] Al-Maqrīzī's use of "*sharʿī*" here is overly prescriptive, implying that, because silver (and gold) is juristically sanctioned, everything else is not. And he tries to vindicate this disjunctive logic by insisting in broader religious terms that circulating copper coins "has no root among any community that believes in revealed religion, nor any legal (*sharʿī*) foundation for its implementation" (*lā aṣl lahā fī millah nabawīyah wa lā mustanad li fiʿlihā ʿan ṭarīqah sharʿīyah*).[16] Ultimately, al-Maqrīzī wants to condemn Mamlūk monetary policy not simply as an economist or a "concerned citizen" but as a jurist—that is, not simply as a bad or inefficient policy but as a juristically proscribed policy that violates the *sharʿ*.[17]

But did the policies in question really contravene the religious law? Did *sharīʿah* forbid the use of copper coins as a basic currency? Al-Maqrīzī's contemporary, the noted historian and Ḥanafī jurist Badr al-Dīn al-ʿAynī (d. 855/1451), who also served as *muḥtasib*, thought not. In fact, al-ʿAynī cites a unanimous consensus (*ijmāʿ*) to the effect that commercial exchange using copper coins was perfectly permissible.[18] Even al-Maqrīzī acknowledges that *fulūs* (and other "symbolic media of exchange" [e.g., sea shells]) had been used from time immemorial, though he insists that such media were only used for trifling purchases and were never taken as actual money (*naqd*), let alone the basis of an economy (pegged to a money of account or not).[19] Meanwhile, major Shāfiʿīs, such as al-Ṣuyūṭī (d. 915/1509), recognized the legality of using copper coins as money and traced this recognition all the way back to al-Shāfiʿī himself.[20] Other prominent Shāfiʿīs, including al-Ramlī (d. 957/1550) and al-Anṣārī (d. 976/1520), and even before them al-Nawawī (d. 676/1277), also identify the commercial use of *fulūs* as legitimate, pointing to no dissenting views on the matter within the school.[21] But, al-Maqrīzī's sense that Mamlūk monetary policy was so egregious seems to have blinded him to this well-established juristic view. For him, the economic effects of monetizing *fulūs* were so destructive that the practice itself *had* to be in violation of the religious law. In effect, he was equating "economically bad" with "juristically proscribed."

For the moment, let us indulge al-Maqrīzī in his righteous indignation. Would simply banning *fulūs* have produced the desired economic policy? From where, in other words, would the actual substance of such a policy come? Could *sharīʿah* be relied upon to provide all the details and adjustments needed to sustain its efficacy over time? Can any economic policy, Mamlūk or other, be entirely devoid of unintended or unavoidable side effects? What, then, would be the level of imperfection or entropy separating a "legitimate" from an "illegitimate" policy—or, as al-Maqrīzī might put it, a "*sharʿī*" from a "*ghayr sharʿī*" one?[22] Ultimately, what al-Maqrīzī seems to overlook—and this is the crux of the matter—is that the substantive efficiency of Mamlūk monetary policy is neither an exclusively moral nor an exclusively *sharʿī* affair. Rather, it is a prudential matter of economics whose substantive adjudication lies beyond the dictates and metrics of *sharīʿah*. This is not to deny or even question the moral dimensions of the problem, that is, whether it is right or wrong, *sharʿan*, to circulate *fulūs*. Nor is it to overlook the prudential element in *sharīʿah*-discourse itself (a matter to which I will return in Chapter 4). After all, such common and critical juristic categories as "*maṣlaḥah*" (attending benefit) and "*mafsadah*" (attending harm) are at least as prudentially as they are morally laden. And even where *sharīʿah* points to what is right or wrong in the abstract, the way to realizing or avoiding this in practical terms is almost always illuminated by non-*sharʿī* deliberations and insights. In sum, while *sharīʿah* may recognize or even extol the value of a healthy economy, *sharʿī* dictates alone cannot guarantee the practical efficiency of Mamlūk or any other economic policy. And to invoke *sharīʿah* and *sharʿī* arguments in this capacity is fundamentally to misapprehend the problem.

Beyond the *Ḥukm Sharʿī*

Meanwhile, it would be presumptuous to suppose that al-Ṣuyūṭī, al-Ramlī, al-ʿAynī, and other jurists who upheld the permissibility of using *fulūs* were any less concerned about the *ummah*'s welfare than was al-Maqrīzī. The fact that they held it to be juristically, that is, *sharʿan*, permissible to mint and circulate *fulūs* as money did not mean that they necessarily agreed with the specifics of Mamlūk financial or monetary policy. Nor did it necessarily imply any insensitivity on their part regarding the negative effects that might accrue to such policies. Nor, conversely, did their placing this action within the legal category of the permissible (*mubāḥ*) necessarily imply their belief that the resulting policies must therefore be efficient or practically good. These men were jurists, doctors of the law, whose stock-in-trade was the juristic ruling, the *ḥukm sharʿī*. And while the juristic ruling might imply the "efficiency" or "practical good" of some of what it dictates or sanctions,[23] it does not necessarily do so in all cases. The fact, for example, that it is juristically permissible for a woman to annul her marriage on grounds of her husband's insolvency does not guarantee the practical good or efficiency of this act in any specific instance.[24] In concrete terms, "good" or "efficient" and "juristically permissible" are often two distinct metrics of assessment that routinely rely upon mutually distinct modes and sources of inquiry.

Stated differently, to know the *ḥukm sharʿī* is not necessarily to know the practically good or efficient. Rather, to know the latter, one must routinely go beyond the *hukm sharʿī* to economics (in this case) or practical experience in business or finance. As al-Qarāfī succinctly put the matter: "Good, as a category, is broader than the legal ruling" (*al-ḥasan aʿamm min al-ḥukm al-sharʿī*).[25] On this understanding, given the everyday demands of prudence, practicality, and even ethics, "rule-following," that is, adherence to *aḥkām sharʿīyah*, does not and cannot encompass the entire normative practice of Islam. Failure to recognize this fact can only overburden (and over-authorize) the *ḥukm sharʿī* and its representatives, while also promoting misrecognition of the value and relevance of other modes and metrics of assessment, not to mention the role and authority of the sources, disciplines, and personnel behind these.

This is the key to understanding one of the fundamental arguments of this book: the *ḥukm sharʿī*, and therefore *sharīʿah*, is limited in the scope of its jurisdiction and what its sources can address authoritatively in concrete, substantive terms. Even on the understanding that *sharīʿah* confers a *ḥukm sharʿī* upon every human act, in the sense that every act falls into one of the "Five

Juristic Statuses,"[26] one must not assume that the *ḥukm sharʿī* thereby exhausts all Islamically relevant modes or metrics of assessment. To conclude, in other words, that it is juristically permissible (or impermissible) to circulate copper *fulūs* as the basic medium of commerce will not necessarily fulfill the Islamically mandated interest (*maṣlaḥah*) of devising a substantively efficient Mamlūk monetary policy. Rather, formulating such a policy requires other (i.e., non-*sharʿī*) metrics and repositories of knowledge.

The same applies to countless other aspects of Mamlūk life. For example, David Ayalon cites the view of al-Maqrīzī's contemporary and fellow Shāfiʿī jurist, historian, and *ḥadīth* expert Ibn Ḥajar al-ʿAsqalānī (d. 852/1449), that "The general condition declined any time a non-Mamlūk headed the Vizerate" (*inna al-wizāra in lam yataqalladhā turkī*^{un} *fasada al-ḥāl*).[27] Clearly, however, it remained juristically permissible, that is, *shar*^{ʿan}, for a non-Mamlūk to occupy this office. Ayalon also reports that the only gifts Mamlūk sultans appreciated receiving from the Maghrib were horses, and that they would be offended were the Maghrib's elites to send anything else.[28] Again, however, sending something other than horses surely remained juristically permissible, and the solution could not be sought in simply banning North Africans, *shar*^{ʿan}, from sending other gifts.

Something similar would apply in a modern context. Where Alasdair MacIntyre speaks, for example, of the moral/ethical incommensurability between various economic or social policies, it is often the case that no *ḥukm sharʿī* can be relied upon to resolve the dispute in question—for example, whether to support public or private schools—as both of these options are *prima facie* juristically permissible.[29] In all these cases, in other words, arriving at an appropriate decision entails considerations that go beyond the *ḥukm sharʿī*.

This understanding of the limits of what the *ḥukm sharʿī* can be reasonably called upon to do and how this relates to other regimes of knowing is more concretely laid out by al-Qarāfī. In *Sharḥ Tanqīḥ al-Fuṣūl*, he picks up on a discussion among his contemporaries regarding the principle that, whenever a person is given an equal choice between two acts, the two acts themselves must be assumed to be of the same legal status; otherwise, the person would be legally discouraged from performing one or legally encouraged to perform the other, and the two acts would not be of equal status. This logic is complicated, however, by a *ḥadīth* in which the angel Gabriel is reported to have come to the Prophet and offered him an equal choice between drinking from a chalice of wine and a chalice of milk. The Prophet chose the milk, to which Gabriel remarked, "Had you chosen the wine, your Community would have gone astray."[30] The question arises, then, of how these two choices could have been equal in terms of their legal status, while being so radically different in terms of the consequences attaching to them.

In his response, al-Qarāfī points to the difference between the *ḥukm sharʿī* that attaches to an act and the practical consequences of performing the act. He states explicitly, "Two actions may have the same *ḥukm sharʿī* while differing in terms of the consequences of engaging in them."[31] While it may be permissible for a man to engage in a particular act, such as building a house, buying a pack-animal, or marrying a woman, any *particular* house, pack-animal, or woman may be more or less beneficial or harmful to him. That their juristic status is equally permissible does not change this fact. The anticipated or possible consequences of an action do not necessarily change the basic *ḥukm sharʿī* that attaches to it. Nor does the *ḥukm sharʿī* automatically suspend the practical consequences attaching to an act.

Of course, as a Mālikī, al-Qarāfī recognized the principle of *sadd al-dharāʾiʿ* (blocking the means), on the basis of which a *prima facie* permissible act may be rendered impermissible whenever its commission is deemed a means to impermissible or otherwise undue consequences. The point, however, is that *sharīʿah* itself does not determine the presence or absence of these consequences. Those who can properly pronounce on such matters are qualified determiners of facts, as opposed to interpreters of texts (*qua* interpreters of texts). In other words, the act of selling guns *to those known to be intent on robbery* is "blocked" as impermissible, not the act of simply selling guns. Meanwhile, knowing who is intent on robbery is not a *sharʿī* determination. A jurist may (and ideally should) have knowledge of such matters as a function of his general knowledge of his environment and constituency; but this knowledge would come to him via his observation of social affairs, not as part and parcel of his training as a jurist. For this reason, his pronouncements regarding who is intent on robbery would not be authoritative simply because they came from him as an authorized jurist.[32] In sum, there is a difference between determining the legal status of an action and assessing the concrete consequences of carrying it out.

Moreover, an act's legal status cannot always be determined based on its practical implications. Divorce, for example, remains permissible, despite the catastrophic effects that might come in its train.[33] Al-Qarāfī applies this logic to the choice of drinking from either of the two chalices: "Its legal status is 'permissible.' Yet, Gabriel ultimately informed the Prophet that God had attached good consequences to one of these actions and bad consequences to the other. And these consequences are not in themselves the same as juristic rulings" (*wa dhālika ghayr al-aḥkām al-sharʿīyah*).[34] On the contrary, knowledge of the consequences of actions routinely lies beyond the *ḥukm sharʿī*.

It is this area "beyond the *ḥukm sharʿī*" that constitutes what I referred to and explained in Chapter 1 as the "differentiated realm": it falls outside the substantive reach of the *ḥukm sharʿī* and in this sense beyond Islam's *sharʿī* address proper. For this reason, when pursuing appropriate conclusions in this differentiated area, one cannot rely on the formal sources and methods of juristic law (*fiqh* and *uṣūl al-fiqh*) or even on the legal precepts or canons (*al-qawāʾid*) extrapolated from this law. For, in this differentiated realm, one is seeking not a *ḥukm sharʿī* per se but knowledge of the most efficient, beneficial, impressive, or profitable course of action, albeit within the bounds of permissibility drawn by *sharīʿah*. Stated differently, the question is routinely not whether a particular topic—politics or economics—falls within the parameters of Islam-cum-*sharīʿah* but whether and to what extent a particular political or economic question is *sharʿī* or non-*sharʿī*, even as a constituent of Islam as *dīn*.

It is important to bear in mind that this differentiated realm is not an independent, self-subsisting domain that can be concretely identified or pointed to as such. It is, rather, a residual realm, a contingent construct whose parameters emerge out of the asymmetrical relationship between the range of values, virtues, and interests identified with Islam as religion (healthy economy, good governance, harmonious marriages) and the nature of what the *ḥukm sharʿī* can be legitimately called upon to tell us as a *juristic* assessor of human acts. This differentiated realm emerges partly out of the fact that, contrary to the case of Christian authorities before the Reformation, Islam's jurists were more explicit and comfortable in recognizing the limits of their religion's concrete epistemological authority. We see this, for example, even in the likes of the "puritanical" "*sharīʿah*-maximalist" Ibn Taymīyah, when he asks rhetorically, having established that such pursuits as medicine, mathematics, and geometry are *ʿaqlī* as opposed to *sharʿī*, even as he recognizes their utility for Islam, "Can anyone be excommunicated for having embraced wrong views in the areas of mathematics, medicine, or the intricacies of logical reasoning?" (*hal yukaffar aḥad bi al-khaṭaʾ fī masāʾil al-ḥisāb wa al-ṭibb wa daqīq al-kalām*).[35]

By contrast, when Galileo (d. 1642) challenged the doctrine that the earth was the center of the universe, he ran afoul of the Christian Church's pretension to universal epistemological authority.[36] Essentially, he raised the question of whether the authority to decide cosmological truth resided unilaterally in science or in theology.[37] The Church responded by reaffirming its magisterium "on all matters of faith and morals," a category clearly expandable enough to draw in such questions as whether we live in a geocentric or a heliocentric universe.[38] This assertion implied not only the religious authority of the Bible but also the *interpretive* authority of the Church, as the sole determiner of scripture's meaning and scope.

Here is where Luther's doctrine of *sola scriptura*, that is, that "Scripture *alone* will be the rule of faith," became important.[39] Its basic point (and ultimate effect) was to curb the Church's epistemological authority and establish scripture as the sole basis of judgment-cum-excommunication. On the one hand, Luther's dictate might be seen as preserving religion by allowing it to sidestep various socio-political and intellectual challenges facing the Church, especially those connected with the emergence of modern science. Precisely in this capacity, however, it domesticated religion and subtly redefined it. For, as the exclusive preserve of scripture, religion could now be conceived of as relating to a particular kind of doctrinal statement, ultimate truth or quotidian activity. As modernity reached full tide, this shift rendered religion a relevant or appropriate consideration in some areas of life and an irrelevant or inappropriate consideration in others.[40] In turn, this development both informed and underscored the emergent meaning and importance of "differentiation," as that which separates the religious from the non-religious. Patricia Crone (d. 2015), a noted (if controversial) scholar of the pre-modern world, including Islam, summarizes the nascent understanding of "religion" as distinct from other categories of endeavor in the emerging industrialized societies of the modern West as follows:

> This is not to say that industrial society is hostile to religion; you may have as much of it as you like (communist countries were partial exceptions). But it will not allow you to embroil your religion in matters of public importance, be they political, social or cognitive. Religion is not allowed to impinge on such matters because it may not *underpin*: wherever an ultimate truth underpins a phenomenon, it creates a sacred cow, a holy institution, a dogma, something that cannot be changed. Dogmas would mean the end of modern science and scholarship.[41]

We might compare this attitude with the approach of al-Ghazālī to the general problem of a perceived conflict between religion and "science and scholarship" in Islam, wherein the latter is relegated to the realm of the non-*sharʿī* but not to a necessarily non-religious, secular domain. Al-Ghazālī addresses the views of those he identifies as "ignorant friends of Islam" (*ṣadīq*^{un} *li 'l-islām jāhil*^{un}) who condemn natural and other sciences developed by non-Muslims as contravening *dīn*. He insists that "God's concrete dictates (*al-sharʿ*) do not address these sciences in a manner that would either confirm or negate them" (*laysa fi 'sh-sharʿ taʿarruḍ*^{un} *li hādhihi 'l-ʿulūm bi 'n-nafy wa 'l-ithbāt*).[42] In fact, he makes it clear, in this same passage, that Islam is not served by condemning these non-*sharʿī* sciences. Elsewhere, meanwhile, he chides the Muslim community for their lack of attention to these very pursuits: "How many towns are there that are devoid of Muslim doctors, while it is not permissible to accept the expert testimony of non-Muslims in cases involving the religious law . . . . I wish I knew how the jurists could sanction the undertaking of communal obligations that are already being met to the neglect of communal obligations that are not being met."[43] Al-Ghazālī clearly recognizes here "communal obligations" (in this case medicine) that must be undertaken and fulfilled, despite the fact that they are *substantively* non-*sharʿī*, or outside the concrete dictates of God's *sharʿī* address. On this understanding, Muslim efforts to fulfill such non-*sharʿī* needs can be justifiably classed as "religious," given their direct (and intentional) contribution to the preservation of *dīn*, even as scripture itself is not the source of the substantive content of these pursuits.

We find a similar recognition of how epistemological boundaries can be negotiated without undermining the authority of religion or science[44]—and without the need for a separate, non-religious, secular realm in the modern Western sense—in the thought of al-Qarāfī and his Mālikī predecessor Abū al-Walīd al-Bājī (d. 474/1081). Responding to Mālik's earlier ban on astronomical calculation (*al-naẓar fi al-nujūm*), because it implies a claim to knowledge of the unseen, al-Qarāfī notes, following al-Bājī, that, being based on such mediating calculations as mathematics, astronomical knowledge is no different from predicting rain based on the appearance of rainclouds.[45] As such, it should not be judged inadmissible as a contravention of revelation or the religious law, even as it is not dictated by either. And yet, in contrast to what occurred in the Christian (and post-Christian) West, neither al-Qarāfī or al-Bājī or al-Ghazālī saw "outside the jurisdiction of the concrete dictates of scripture" or "the interpretive authority of the jurists" as necessarily falling "outside the parameters of *dīn*." In other words, unlike the differentiated realm in the West, the differentiated Islamic Secular is (or can be) a religious sphere.

To this I would add that the authority of Muslim jurists themselves as translators of the divine will into concrete *sharīʿah*-prescriptions was not co-extensive with that of scripture itself. Jurists routinely observed that not all verses of the Qurʾān are directly relevant to the production of *aḥkām sharʿīyah*,[46] some arguing that the number of "legal verses" was no more than five hundred (out of over six thousand).[47] Meanwhile, the Prophet openly acknowledged that there were worldly matters upon which he could not authoritatively pronounce.[48] This is important; for, once the notion of *sharīʿah* and its sources being coterminous with Islam is set aside, it becomes easier to see how a differentiated realm might co-exist outside *sharīʿah* yet inside Islam. Similarly, it becomes easier to see the Islamic Secular as taking—and seeking to take—nothing from *sharīʿah* or the jurists in order to redistribute it elsewhere, especially not outside Islam as religion.

Of course, if one does not recognize that *sharīʿah* has limits or boundaries, no such differentiated or secular realm within Islam can be assumed to exist. The religious law must be assumed to cover *all* human contingencies via an unbounded, undifferentiated, adjudicative authority, and everything that falls outside its scope must be assumed to fall outside Islam. These two interrelated tendencies—to see the scope of Islam's *sharʿī* address as all-encompassing, and to equate *sharīʿah* itself with Islam—have contributed much to the conclusions of scholars who specialize in Islamic law, as well as to the views of those who do not. What I am proposing is an alternate understanding, based on certain heretofore largely ignored features of the Islamic juristic tradition, a more critical engagement of certain modern truisms, and a less exclusivist attitude toward the idea of the "secular."

The Standard View

In his critique of what he termed "the totalizing 'legal supremacist' conceptualization of Islam as *law*,"[49] Shahab Ahmed observed that Western scholars of Islamic Studies, both those who specialize in Islamic law and those who do not, subscribe to the view that Islamic law is both the essence and the "final legitimate authoritative arbiter of what constitutes Islam/Islamic."[50] Beginning with Gotthelf Bergsträsser (d. 1933) and moving through legal scholars, anthropologists, historians, and 'generalists,' he traces an unbroken tendency in the West to equate Islam with Islamic law. This conflation implies that the scope of Islamic law is boundless, inasmuch as Islam itself is understood to cover "all and everything in the life of the individual."[51] The comprehensiveness of his coverage notwithstanding, Ahmed cites no scholars who dissent from this position and see *sharīʿah*'s jurisdiction as bounded.[52] Similarly, the idea that Muslim jurists themselves may have recognized *self-imposed* limits on *sharīʿah*'s authority is never contemplated. In the end, the impression one gets from Ahmed's survey is of a unanimous consensus among Western scholars on the unbounded nature of Islamic law.[53]

While we will see that no such consensus actually existed, it is true that leading scholars of Islamic law have long pointed to the all-encompassing and exclusivist nature of *sharīʿah*'s authority. In his seminal work, the celebrated (if controversial) Joseph Schacht wrote: "Islamic law is an all-embracing body of religious duties, the totality of God's commands that regulate the life of every Muslim in all its aspects; it encompasses on an equal footing ordinances regarding worship and ritual, as well as political and (in the narrow sense) legal rules."[54] In a spirit reminiscent of Hodgson, Schacht identifies *sharīʿah* as Islamic law proper, that is, as Islam's "religious law."[55] According to him, however, throughout its history, this law has coexisted alongside a "secular law" presided over and exercised by the political authorities.[56] Schacht casts this resort to "secular law" as part of Islamic law's natural entropy, an endemic dissonance between *sharīʿah* and quotidian reality, as part of the ongoing conflict between "theory and practice."[57] On the one hand, "The *sharīʿa* could not abandon its claim to exclusive theoretical validity"; on the other hand, "the scholars half sanctioned the regulations which the rulers in fact enacted, by insisting on the duty, already emphasized in the Koran . . . of obedience to the established authorities."[58] By modern times, this incongruity would be characterized as an outright contradiction. Thus, Schacht refers to modern "secular Islamic legislation" as a "contradiction in adjecto."[59] In other words, even more than in the pre-modern past, a piece of Muslim legislation is now *either* secular *or* Islamic. In sum, once we venture outside *sharīʿah* proper, we enter the realm of the "un-Islamic secular."

In a similar vein, Noel Coulson (d. 1986) insisted that "Sharīʿa is the sole criterion of behavior," and that "[T]he State [in Islam] exists for the sole purpose of maintaining and enforcing the law."[60] This implies, of course, that law—any law—can provide everything a successful state—any state—might practically need. Recognizing the challenge this posed for his original depiction, Coulson later wrote, "Islamic government has never meant, in theory or in practice, the exclusive jurisdiction of Sharīʿa tribunals."[61] Ideally speaking, however, *sharīʿah* remains, according to Coulson, "the sole criterion for behavior."

We should be clear about the basic assumption underlying the views of these two men: ideally, *sharīʿah*'s jurisdiction is total and exclusive; but in the real world, ideal theory breaks down, and Muslims are forced to resort to non-religious—what these authors understood to be "secular"—legislation. The secular for them is a complement neither to *sharīʿah* as law nor to Islam as religion; it is a non-religious (if not anti-religious) rival to both. On this understanding, any resort to secular norms, institutions, or modes of inquiry signals failure, in both pre-modern and modern Islam. Writing in the middle of the twentieth century, still within reach of powerful nineteenth-century European presuppositions, these scholars were clearly influenced by the Western secular and its antonymous relationship to religion as non-religious.

More recently, Wael Hallaq has written of *sharīʿah*: "As a representation of God's sovereign will, it regulates the entire range of the human order, either directly or through well-defined and limited delegation."[62] While this statement might appear to echo the totalizing views of Schacht and Coulson, Hallaq actually has a more nuanced understanding of the relationship between *sharīʿah* and the secular. As he puts it, "Sharīʿa rules over and regulates, directly or through delegation, any and all secular institutions. If these institutions are secular or deal with the secular, they do so under the supervising and overarching moral will that is the Sharīʿa."[63] Earlier, Hallaq had criticized Western scholarship's "repugnance toward religion," on the basis of which it set up a self-serving, false dichotomy between the rational/secular (us/West) and the irrational/religious (them/Islam).[64] He intimated that this was one of the ways that the West signaled its superiority over Islam. Having identified autonomous human reason as the true and proper ground of morality, the West could indict Islam as lacking true morality, based on its refusal to jettison heteronomy in the form of its commitment to *sharīʿah*. Hallaq categorically rejects this indictment and insists not only on Islam's/*sharīʿah*'s moral constitution but argues that it is ultimately through *sharīʿah*'s unbounded moral will that it is able to exercise authority over the entire expanse of human existence, including the secular realm. All political, social, and economic institutions are, as he puts it, "ultimately subordinate to Shariʿa."[65]

As a general proposition, most would agree with Hallaq's assertion of *sharīʿah*'s presumed normative superiority over the secular. There are ways, however, in which such an understanding can reach the point of diminishing returns. If, as Hallaq seems to imply, the divine sovereignty behind *sharīʿah* is decidedly moral and *sharīʿah*'s "moral will" is both superior and all-encompassing,[66] this superiority must ultimately obliterate the authority of all non-moral metrics of assessment. For, on this understanding, it becomes difficult to separate *sharīʿah*'s categorical superiority from morality's categorical superiority. But there are surely more things to know in life than what is morally right and wrong. This seems especially applicable to a religion such as Islam, which has long been viewed as inscrutably "worldly," even as it purports to be a religion. As we saw with al-Maqrīzī, there is often an incommensurability between the practical and the moral, not in the sense of the two being mutually exclusive but in the sense of their not always being subsumable under a single standard of judgment. The moral, in other words, does not always entail the practical, and the practical cannot always be meaningfully assessed morally. A mathematical statement may be mathematically correct or incorrect; but in neither case is it necessarily moral or immoral. Conversely, the most heroic act of sacrifice may be deeply moral; but it may not be practical in the least. Clearly, in such light, if practicality is enshrined as the absolute metric, morality must suffer; and if morality is enshrined as the categorically superior judge, it must (or may) trump all other metrics, including practicality, efficiency, order, and the like, with potentially catastrophic effects. On this understanding, the notion of morality's categorical superiority in the form of *sharīʿah*'s "overarching moral will" takes us to a point where "superior" can morph into "only," whereupon *sharīʿah* becomes an iteration of Kant's moral imperative[67] or perhaps Weber's "iron cage."

I concede that *sharīʿah* may rightfully sit in moral judgment over any act, idea or discipline or the ends to which these are put. In this sense it may be characterized as the morally superior metric. But I do not concede that *sharʿī* judgments encompass the full range of pertinent metrics in Islam. *Sharīʿah* cannot judge the substantive validity or practical value of such matters as whether gifting roses is an act of affection, whether water freezes at thirty-two degrees Fahrenheit, or whether a particular medicine will cure a theretofore unknown disease. By identifying *sharīʿah* with God's sovereign authority and then equating the latter with a moral authority to which everything is subordinated, Hallaq runs the risk of fashioning either a *sharīʿah* that can tell us everything (e.g., this economic policy is permissible because it includes no *ribā* or *gharar*, [i.e., nothing immoral]), on the assumption that all we need to know is the moral status of things, or a *sharīʿah* that can tell us nothing (i.e., this economic policy is permissible because it includes no *ribā* or *gharar*), whereas our real question is about economic efficiency. The former assumption, that *sharīʿah* tells us everything, or at least everything Islamically relevant, was what drove Schacht and Coulson to their conclusions about failure and secular legislation. In his critique of modern Islam, Hallaq also intimates that going outside traditional *sharʿī* assessments and institutions implies failure, as a departure from authentic Islam.[68] Ultimately, this intimates the same understanding of *sharīʿah*'s boundless and exclusive jurisdiction that we observed in Schacht and Coulson.[69]

Of course, Western scholarship is not alone in imputing boundless, exclusive authority to *sharīʿah* or in seeing Muslims resorting to anything beyond the *sharʿ* as a failure or violation, indeed, as a "secular" act in the modern Western sense. Many modern Muslims also subscribe to this understanding. The modern jurist ʿAbd al-Wahhāb Khallāf (d. 1375/1956), for example, sees the would-be existence or recognition of acts outside *sharīʿah*'s judgment as implying the latter's deficiency, a hapless descent into the (Western) secular. And his desire to preempt the encroachments of the latter prompts him to impute boundless, exclusive jurisdiction to *sharīʿah*.[70] In a similar vein, the late Mustafa al-Azami (d. 1439/2017) appears to leave no room for extra-*sharīʿah* assessments when he writes, "There was no aspect of behavior that was not intended to be covered by the revealed law."[71] The Malaysian intellectual Syed Muhammad Naquib al-Attas is even more emphatic: "Islām totally rejects any application to itself of the concepts secular, secularization, or secularism, as they do not belong and are alien to it in every respect."[72] Meanwhile, the Pakistani-American scholar Hina Azam clearly alludes to *sharīʿah*'s boundless jurisdiction when she writes, "All human interactions were to be governed, either directly or indirectly, by the divine will, rather than left to human negotiation, whether communal or individual."[73] And the Sudanese-American Abdullahi An-Naʿim sees *sharīʿah* as claiming an authority so universal and exclusive that it can only promote intolerance, which drives him to argue for a "secular state" in the modern Western sense.[74] Meanwhile, many who reject *sharīʿah* outright also do so on the assumption of its all-encompassing jurisdiction. We see this in Talal Asad's description of the view of the Syrian poet Adonis, according to him, a "self-professed atheist": "the religious law is monotheistic and totalitarian."[75]

All these proponents, whether their aim is to promote, domesticate, or reject *sharīʿah*, converge on the assumption of its unbounded jurisdiction. And for them, precisely because of this assumption, going beyond *sharīʿah* signals failure or violation (or success in the case of An-Naʿim and Adonis[76]), as a shift to the secular in the modern Western understanding of secular as non-religious.

The Bounded *Ḥukm Shar'ī*

My argument is that, in its depiction of *sharī'ah*'s scope, this standard view overlooks a critical and consistent feature of the classical juristic tradition. According to that tradition, *sharī'ah*'s unit of measurement is the *ḥukm shar'ī*, which subdivides into two types: (1) *ḥukm taklīfī*, or "injunctive ruling," (2) *ḥukm waḍ'ī*, or "declaratory ruling."[77] Injunctive rulings consist of commands—"Do!" or "Do not do!"—which confer upon the actions in question a legal status ranging from obligatory to forbidden, these constituting the aforementioned "Five Juristic Statuses" (*al-aḥkām al-khamsa/al-aḥkām al-taklīfīyah*).[78] Declaratory rulings, on the other hand, identify a given human act or natural occurrence as a cause (*sabab*), prerequisite (*sharṭ*), or impediment (*māni'*), indicating when or whether an injunctive rule actually applies or if a particular action is juristically valid. For example, the sun's passing its zenith is a legal *cause* activating the obligation to perform the noon prayer; reaching the age of majority is a legal *prerequisite* to this obligation; a woman's being on her menses is a legal *impediment* that blocks this obligation. Meanwhile, sibling-status between two people constitutes a legal impediment that renders their marriage to each other juristically invalid.[79]

Viewed from this side of certain developments that crystalized in post-formative jurisprudence,[80] the *ḥukm shar'ī* clearly emerges as a bounded entity, its jurisdictional boundaries assuming both horizontal and vertical dimensions. Its horizontal boundaries are coterminous with the Five Juristic Statuses and speak to the full panoply of matters upon which *sharī'ah* can pronounce authoritatively, either spontaneously (as with prayer or fasting) or in response to a human act or natural occurrence. These horizontal boundaries are expandable and not entirely exclusive of declaratory rulings, as future natural occurrences or human actions may engender additional, agreed-upon injunctive rulings, thereby expanding *sharī'ah*'s practical scope. But, unlike the case with injunctive rulings, humans are generally under no obligation to produce the referent of a declaratory ruling; nor do such basic requirements for legal responsibility (*taklīf*), as knowledge or capacity (*qudrah*), always attach to declaratory rulings. One acquires the right to inherit from a deceased relative, for example, even if one is a minor or does not know of that relative's existence; this relative's death is a legal cause that automatically obligates the distribution of his or her estate to legally defined heirs. Similarly, a husband's insolvency may constitute a legal cause for forcible divorce, even if he is unable, rather than unwilling, to support his wife.[81] Of course, where knowledge and capacity are inapplicable, so is morality. But morality is not always a relevant feature of declaratory rulings. This fact is nicely captured by the late Bernard Weiss (d. 2018) in his reference to declaratory rulings as "non-normative."[82] With injunctive rulings, by contrast, knowledge and capacity are always requisite, and acting (or not) in accordance with these rules generally carries moral significance.

Beyond questions of good and evil, Islam as religion recognizes any number of normative values, virtues, concerns, and interests whose instantiation must be pursued through means and metrics that may be prudential, practical, or even ethical but *not* necessarily strictly *shar'ī* or even strictly moral. Economics, public administration, fashion design, and modern physics are not *shar'ī* disciplines, even though they may be critical to the normative practice of Islam. While the action of a Muslim who produces a superior or inferior economic policy or theory of physics may be judged to be more or less valuable, it does not follow that this act is necessarily more or less *ḥalāl* or *ḥarām*. In and of itself, quantum physics is no more or less permissible than Einsteinian physics, even if one system proves more Islamically useful or scientifically correct than the other. In short, the horizontal scope of the values and interests that constitute Islam as *dīn* are broader than the moral (or prudential) reach of *sharī'ah* as juristic discourse. What we have, in other words, is a *shar'ī*/non-*shar'ī* divide *within* the circumference of Islam. And it is in this sense, not in the sense of some actions or occurrences falling within and some beyond the circumference of Islam, that I speak of *sharī'ah* as a horizontally bounded enterprise.

As for *sharī'ah*'s vertical boundaries, even when an act or event falls within *sharī'ah*'s horizontal boundaries, its appropriate or concrete instantiation may not be dictated or determined by *sharī'ah* itself. Instead, one may have to drill down beneath the surface of a *shari'ī* ruling and pursue the matter through other modes of assessment or expertise. For example, it is one thing to know, as an injunctive rule, that it is obligatory (*wājib*) for a man to support his family financially; it is quite another thing for him to know *how* to earn enough money to discharge this duty. *Sharī'ah* will not instruct him concretely regarding the latter. And it is the pursuit of this type of knowledge that takes one beneath the vertical boundary—beneath the "floor," if you will—of the injunctive ruling. Simply stated, knowing what to do in concrete terms is not as simple as knowing the *ḥukm shar'ī*. Rather, concrete decision-making routinely requires something additional, something that may lie within the *ḥukm shar'ī*'s horizontal boundaries but beyond (or beneath) its vertical boundaries.[83]

The notion of a vertical boundary is even more relevant to the declaratory ruling, or *ḥukm waḍ'ī*. The operative consideration here is not the status of an act or event as a matter of law but its actual occurrence or existence as a matter of fact. This introduces the all-important distinction between law and fact, as two distinct domains of inquiry in Islamic juristic discourse.[84] Ascertaining the existence of relevant causes, prerequisites, and impediments, such as the position of the sun or whether or not a woman is pregnant, relies almost entirely on non-*sharʿī* means of fact-determination—astronomy, shade-measuring instruments, sense perception, and, now, home-pregnancy tests and the like. In such light, the idea that *sharīʿah* possesses a totalizing, all-encompassing religio-legal jurisdiction that "covers *everything*" must be seen as an over-simplification of significant consequence.

Islamic Law: *Sharīʿah, Fiqh, Madhhab*

In what follows, I shall try to vindicate the notion that *sharīʿah*'s jurisdiction is bounded, based on testimony from the Islamic juristic tradition itself. Before doing so, however, I would like to explain my focus on the *ḥukm sharʿī* as the core and fulcrum of my thesis. This goes back to a point I made earlier, which is explicitly articulated by al-Qarāfī and generally recognized by what would emerge as the dominant trend in post-formative jurisprudence, following the so-called settling down of the schools of law (*istiqrār al-madhāhib*) and the crystallization of *uṣūl al-fiqh*. We should bear in mind that pre-modern jurists typically used the terms "*fiqh*" and "*sharīʿah*" interchangeably, in contradistinction to the modern reformist tendency to set them apart. Also, as we will see, pre-modern jurists had a similar understanding of "*madhhab.*"

According to al-Qarāfī, *sharīʿah* "from beginning to end is built on the discipline of *uṣūl al-fiqh*" (*al-sharīʿah min awwalihā ilā ākhirihā mabnīyah ʿalā uṣūl al-fiqh*).[85] The whole point of *uṣūl al-fiqh* is to identify the sources, methods, and indicants (*adillah*/sg. *dalīl*) for arriving at knowledge of what the Lawgiver has legislated (*sharaʿa*) as a *ḥukm sharʿī*. This understanding is explicitly confirmed by al-Qarāfī's Mālikī predecessor, Abū Bakr al-Bāqillānī (d. 403/1013), who notes, "[W]hat is sought by engaging juristic theory and its sources and indicants is simply the juristic ruling governing the acts of legally responsible persons."[86] We find a similar statement in the work of the Ḥanbalī turned Shāfiʿī jurist and legal theoretician, Sayf al-Dīn al-Āmidī (d. 631/1233): "The investigations of the legal theoreticians regarding the sources of juristic law do not go beyond determining the status of the indicants that lead to juristic rulings (*al-aḥkām al-sharʿīyah*) whose identity themselves is sought therefrom, along with the various types and rankings of these sources and the manner in which juristic rulings are derived from them."[87] In other words, the *ḥukm sharʿī* is the basic, fundamental unit of *sharīʿah*, and to speak of an individual *sharīʿah* rule is to speak of a *ḥukm sharʿī*. Cumulatively, it is the aggregate of individual *ḥukm sharʿī*s, deduced by the jurists from the sources of the law, that make up *sharīʿah*. This is eloquently captured by Bernard Weiss when he writes in his massive study of al-Āmidī: "Sharīʿa is, first and foremost, the totality of divine 'categorizations of human acts.'"[88]

In practical terms, "*ḥukm sharʿī*" can refer to either of two things: (1) "ruling" in the sense of the juristic status of an act or occurrence, according to one or more of the *madhhabs* or schools of law; or (2) "ruling" in the sense of the binding decree handed down by a judge or other government official. Of note is that a *ḥukm* in the second sense derives its validity and authority almost entirely from its validity as a *ḥukm* in the first sense. Indeed, according to al-Qarāfī, a "*ḥukm sharʿī*" in the first sense is distinguished from a "*ḥukm sharʿī*" in the second sense only by the fact that the latter is backed by the coercive power of the state, whereas the former is not.[89] In the post-formative period, all juristic interpretation took place under the auspices of one of the schools of law (*madhāhib*/sg. *madhhab*), and there were no independent, unaffiliated, authoritative interpreters of *sharīʿah*. For this reason, juristic law—*fiqh* or *sharīʿah*—was ultimately coterminous with "*madhhab*," itself the sum total of individual *ḥukm sharʿīs* (in the first sense just cited) produced by an interpretive community, or school of law. Neither *fiqh*, nor *sharīʿah* nor the *madhhab* could go any farther than the *ḥukm sharʿī* (again, in the first sense) could take it.[90] As such, any limits imputed to the *ḥukm sharʿī* were, ipso facto, limits that characterized *sharīʿah*.

Of Horizontal and Vertical Boundaries

Early Proponents of an Unbounded *Sharīʿah*

I noted earlier that Western scholars are not alone in imputing unbounded, undifferentiated jurisdiction to *sharīʿah*. This tendency is also not uniquely modern. We find it among Muslim jurists as far back to as the second/eighth century and the beginnings of Islamic jurisprudence. Yet, as explicit and straightforward as this formative perspective may have been, it did not endure as the predominant opinion on the matter. By the last third of the fourth/tenth century and the beginning of the fifth/eleventh, works on *uṣūl al-fiqh* began to characterize the *ḥukm sharʿī* as an explicitly bounded entity.

It was none other than al-Shafiʿī (d. 204/819), the reputed founder of *uṣūl al-fiqh* and eponym of the Shāfiʿī school, who first spoke of the unbounded nature of *sharīʿah*. In *al-Risālah*, he states unequivocally: "No situation befalls anyone who adheres to the religion of God but that there is in the Book of God an indication regarding the correct action therein" (*laysat tanzil bi aḥad min ahl dīn Allāh nāzilah illā wa fī kitāb Allāh al-dalīl ʿalā sabīl al-hudā fīhā*).[91] Al-Shāfiʿī's words are not only emphatic but unflinchingly broad. He makes no distinction between determining the meaning of scripture and determining the presence or absence of scripturally relevant facts, for example, the direction of the *qiblah* or the uprightness of a potential witness.[92] For him, all of this is included in an undifferentiated concept of *ijtihād*, or "determining the law."[93] According to the later Shāfiʿī jurist Badr al-Dīn al-Zarkashī (d. 794/1392), the early third-to-fourth-/ninth-to-tenth-century Shāfiʿī Ibn Surayj (d. 306/918) registered a similar opinion, insisting that everything on earth "must come under a legal ruling" (*lā yakhlū min ḥukm*).[94] Thus, at least on the surface, *sharīʿah* is depicted by these early scholars as unqualifiedly unbounded and as presumably covering everything in the most undifferentiated sense. Of course, it could be argued that what they were actually claiming was not that *sharīʿah* is categorically the sole metric of assessment but, rather, that it simply draws everything into the orb of its Five Juristic Statuses, as I suggested above. Still, there is no explicit acknowledgment, at least not in this early period, that the Five Juristic Statuses do not encompass all the metrics by which a human act or natural occurrence might be Islamically assessed.

Between Ibn Surayj and the next available writings on *uṣūl al-fiqh* there is a gap of more than half a century.[95] In the most fully developed of these later works, *al-Fuṣūl fī al-Uṣūl*, of the Ḥanafī Abū Bakr al-Jaṣṣāṣ (d. 370/980), we find an approach similar to that of al-Shāfiʿī, reflecting the unbounded nature of *sharīʿah*. Al-Jaṣṣāṣ makes no distinction between the Prophet's determinations of facts and his clarifications of the law or rules of conduct. In fact, he states explicitly that "there is no difference between *ijtihād* regarding matters of [how to conduct] wars and *ijtihād* regarding everyday rules of conduct" (*lā farq bayna al-ijtihād fī amr al-ḥurūb wa baynahu fī ḥawādith al-aḥkām*).[96] This statement is complicated, however, by his apparent recognition elsewhere of precisely this distinction between law and fact. In explaining, for example, the obligation to determine the "communal standards," or *al-maʿrūf*, by which to decide on the food and clothing due a nursing mother, he states that such decisions must be arrived at via "*itjihād*." He then breaks down *ijtihād* into various modes, some of which are clearly more geared to determining facts (e.g., determining the direction of the *qiblah*, the amount due for injuries or destroyed property) than to deducing rules from the sources. Yet, al-Jaṣṣāṣ refers to all this as simply "*ijtihād al-raʾy*."[97] In a similar context, however, he notes that the Prophet would consult his Companions regarding matters on which he himself had received no revelation, clearly implying a law/fact distinction.[98]

The basic tendency to cast the law as unbounded and undifferentiated is repeated by Ḥanafīs after al-Jaṣṣāṣ up to the end of the fifth/eleventh century. We find it in al-Dabūsī (d. 430/1030), al-Bazdawī (d. 482/1089), and al-Sarakhsī (d. 490/1097). In fact, unlike non-Ḥanafīs of the period, none of these jurists shows any interest in technical or substantive definitions of *fiqh*, *uṣūl al-fiqh*, or the *ḥukm sharʿī* that might implicate the issue of boundaries.[99] The Muʿtazilite Ḥanafī Abū al-Ḥusayn al-Baṣrī (d. 436/1044) breaks with this trend, briefly discussing the definition of "*fiqh*," "*uṣūl*," and "*uṣūl al-fiqh*," and even the meaning of "*sharʿī*." But, like the other Ḥanafīs cited, this is not theorized into an explicit concept of boundaries or a *sharʿī*/non-*sharʿī* (or *ʿaqlī*) divide.[100] In short, this inattention to definitions and boundaries appears to be a basic feature of early *uṣūl al-fiqh* works written in the "tradition-oriented" mode of the jurists (*ʿalā ṭarīqat al-fuqahāʾ*), that is, the Ḥanafīs,[101] as opposed to those written in the "theory-oriented" mode of the speculative theorists (*ʿalā ṭarīqat al-mutakallimīn*), which al-Baṣrī, even as a Ḥanafī, might be seen as representing. While the distinction between these two approaches is commonly recognized in standard Muslim accounts, it has not played much of a role in modern Western studies of Islamic law.[102]

A notable exception in this regard is my esteemed teacher, the late, most learned Professor George Makdisi, whose view on the jurisdictional scope of revelation-cum-*sharīʿah* in relation to the rise of the *ṭarīqat al-mutakallimīn* and the *ṭarīqat al-fuqahāʾ* challenges a core aspect of my thesis. Building on the nexus between law and theology and taking al-Shāfiʿī as his point of departure, Makdisi subscribes to the "standard view" that *sharīʿah* is normatively all-encompassing. According to him, al-Shāfiʿī's approach was as much a theological commitment as it was a method for deducing the law. In particular, his newly developed *uṣūl al-fiqh* was a Traditionalist attempt to preserve the primacy of revelation against the encroachments of theological Rationalism. Traditionalism affirmed the all-encompassing nature of revelation against Rationalist attempts to limit the latter's scope by invoking reason or other repositories of authority as alternative sources for theology *or* law. Accordingly:

> Shafiʿi's purpose in writing the *Risāla* was to counter any system of religious knowledge that pretends to go beyond the Koran and the Prophet's Sunna. In contrast to kalam [speculative theology], which went beyond the Scriptures to speculate about their author, God Himself, Shafiʿi's doctrine declared the Scriptures to be all that was needed for salvation. For Shafiʿi believed that the divine revelation, as expressed in the Koran and the Prophet's Sunna, *provides for every possible eventuality*.[103]

In this context, Makdisi sees the distinction later recognized between the *ṭarīqat al-mutakallimīn* and the *ṭarīqat al-fuqahāʾ* as "erroneous,"[104] a misrecognition of the true aims of *uṣūl al-fiqh* (which, again, al-Shāfiʿī had founded "as a vindication of Traditionalism").[105] Ultimately, this ostensibly benign distinction represented a *faux* normalization of Rationalism's success in "infiltrating" and "contaminating" the new discipline. The problem this poses for my thesis is simply this: If the conceptualization of *sharīʿah* as a bounded entity was merely the product of an *uṣūl al-fiqh* that had been "contaminated" by Rationalism (*ʿalā ṭarīqat al-mutakallimīn*), this conceptualization could be neither genuine nor settled, as I imply, but could only be contrived and, if history ever corrected itself, destined to be reversed. A thesis built on such precarious foundations must be equally precarious. Again, for Professor Makdisi, the presumption that the *ṭarīqat al-mutakallimīn* and the *tarīqat al-fuqahā'* arose as "innocently" co-equal approaches to *sharīʿah* is based on a (mis)reading of Islamic intellectual history that fails to appreciate the deep theological commitment undergirding al-Shāfiʿī's legal methodology and, ultimately, the normative aims of *uṣūl al-fiqh*.[106] Conversely, a proper understanding of that history rules out the notion of a bounded *sharīʿah* as the standard, normative view in Islamic jurisprudence, as I argue.

Professor Makdisi is certainly correct in seeing *kalām* as infiltrating *uṣūl al-fiqh*. But I am not sure that theology is the only or most productive angle from which to view the classifications *ṭariqat al-mutakallimīn* and *ṭarīqat al-fuqahā*.' As Aron Zysow suggests, "[T]he history of *uṣūl al-fiqh* is not a series of footnotes to al-Shāfiʿī's *Risāla*."[107] Indeed, away from al-Shāfiʿī's obsessions, it is not at all clear that it was necessarily theology—Traditionalism versus Rationalism—that separated the two approaches. When Bernard Weiss describes the *ṭarīqat al-fuqahā'* as the "tradition-oriented" approach of the Ḥanafīs, the tradition in question is not theological but legal, its primary commitment being "to provide a theoretical *justification* for a *tradition of law* that had been built up by their forebears in *fiqh*."[108] This *justificatory* approach might be contrasted with the *speculatively generative* approach of the *ṭarīqat al-mutakallimīn*, which went beyond the repository of Ḥanafī *fiqh*—as well as the Shāfiʿī, Mālikī, and Ḥanbalī *fiqh*-traditions—to speculate about law more generally, producing a legacy upon which all the schools could draw and to which they could all contribute.[109] The distinction, in other words, between the two approaches might be seen in legal and not necessarily theological terms, that is, between "speculative" and "justificatory" legal theories.

Meanwhile, to see scripture, as Traditionalism does, as the sole and all-encompassing source of knowledge about God—who transcends history—need not translate into the belief that scripture is the sole and all-encompassing source of how to instantiate Islam as quotidian practice *in* history. Limiting knowledge of God's *ḥukm sharʿī* to scripture, in other words, need not imply that speculating beyond scripture as a means of properly instantiating Islam on the ground takes on the same meaning as speculating beyond scripture for knowledge about God's nature or attributes. In *fiqh*, Traditionalist Shāfiʿīs could agree with Rationalist Shāfiʿīs on the role of *qiyās* (analogy), for example—including the hopelessly speculative enterprise of identifying the *ʿillah* or *ratio essendi*—while bitterly opposing any move by Rationalist Shāfiʿīs to admit *qiyās* into the sanctum of theology. In sum, their inevitable overlap notwithstanding, law and theology are simply not the same.

As approaches to law, Traditionalism and Rationalism did not line up against each other in the same way they lined up against each other in theology. Rationalist Ashʿarīs unanimously joined Traditionalist Ḥanbalīs and others in rejecting the Muʿtazilite notion that knowledge of what God rewards or punishes, that is, God's *ḥukm sharʿī*, can be known outside the data of scripture or rational extensions thereof. In other words, as approaches to law, the *ṭarīqat al-mutakallimīn* and the *ṭarīqat al-fuqahāʾ* need not be seen as zero-sum rivals paralleling Traditionalism and Rationalism as approaches to theology. Most important, the emergence of an understanding of *sharīʿah* as bounded and the parallel recognition of a *sharʿī*/non-*sharʿī* divide in law need not be seen as an exclusively Rationalist commitment or as a function of history gone wrong.

As we will see in my discussion of "*sharīʿah*-maximalism," below, the Traditionalists Ibn Taymīyah and Ibn al-Qayyim evince a clear affinity for the approach that Makdisi identifies with al-Shāfiʿī. But this applies far more to their theology than to their *fiqh*. Ibn al-Qayyim, for example, explicitly affirms that whatever serves the cause of justice is the law of God (*sharʿ Allāh*), even if its source is not scripture.[110] And Ibn Taymīyah openly recognizes scripture's practical limits, as we saw in what we quoted from him in Chapter 1.[111] In fact, a major feature of his campaign overall was that not every appeal to reason is necessarily an appeal to *kalām* or a challenge to scripture. While both these jurists remained guarded vis-à-vis the idea of a bounded *sharīʿah* and a *sharʿī*/non-*sharʿī* divide, neither opposed these ideas categorically. And, again, neither of these conceptual tropes was exclusive to Rationalism. Ultimately, the idea that *sharīʿah* is a bounded entity and not the exclusive repository of all Islamically relevant metrics of assessment was shared by *all* the *madhhab*s, including Traditionalist Ḥanbalīs. In fact, the big holdouts in this regard seem to be the Ḥanafīs, whose Rationalist tendencies are well known but whose *ṭarīqat al-fuqahāʾ* seems, as we will see, to be far less interested in the notion of a bounded *sharīʿah* or a *sharʿī*/non-*sharʿī* divide.[112]

The Emergence of the Theoretical Foundations of a Bounded *Sharīʿah*

In contrast to the approach of al-Shāfiʿī, Ibn Surayj, al-Jaṣṣāṣ, and the aforementioned Ḥanafīs, one detects during the latter part of the fourth/tenth century a countertrend toward greater recognition of jurisdictional boundaries. We get the first glimpses of this in the *Muqaddimah fī Uṣūl al-Fiqh* of the Mālikī jurist Ibn al-Qaṣṣār of Baghdad (d. 397/1007). Ibn al-Qaṣṣār has a palpably theoretical bent but is also tradition-oriented, grounding almost every position he takes in a view attributed to Mālik. Ibn al-Qaṣṣār speaks only indirectly to the issue of boundaries, but his intent is clear. He notes that the sun's decline from its zenith is a factual question whose determination does not fall within the jurisdiction of the jurist *qua* jurist. As such, according to him, it is improper to follow a jurist on such a matter by way of *taqlīd*.[113] The sun's position in the sky may be relevant to the obligation to pray, and in this capacity its status as a legal cause (*sabab*) is an actual *ḥukm shar'ī* on which a jurist *qua* jurist may speak with authority.[114] But the question of whether the sun has actually reached this or that position in the sky, as a matter of fact, is not within the exclusive competence of the jurist. Anyone—including those untrained in *sharī'ah*—can look upward and determine this fact for him or herself. According to Ibn al-Qaṣṣār, the jurist's pronouncement in this regard does not carry the authority of a pronouncement on law, clearly recognizing that his interpretive jurisdiction and authority are limited.

The idea that *sharī'ah* is bounded is expressed more straightforwardly by the Mālikī jurist and Ash'arī theologian, Abū Bakr al-Bāqillānī, who, like all the other non-Ḥanafīs we shall examine, wrote in the mode of the speculative legal theoreticians. Al-Bāqillānī appears to be the first theoretician to preface his discussion of *uṣūl al-fiqh* with a definition of *fiqh*: "Knowledge of the legal, as distinct from the rational, assessments governing the actions of legally responsible persons, which is arrived at through reasoned investigation" (*al-'ilm bi aḥkām af'āl al-mukallafīn al-shar'īyah allatī yutawaṣṣal ilayhā bi al-naẓar dūna al-'aqlīyah*).[115] As this definition includes the adjective "*shar'ī*," al-Bāqillānī goes on to highlight the distinction between the *shar'ī* and the non-*shar'ī*, explaining that those who know the assessments (*aḥkām*) of *sharī'ah* do not necessarily know the assessments dictated by reason (*'aql*), and those who know the assessments dictated by reason do not necessarily know the assessments of *sharī'ah*. Beyond his formal definition of "reason," we get a clearer sense of what he has in mind from the way he contrasts *aqlī* with *shar'ī*, the latter for him being synonymous with *fiqhī*. He notes that the designation "*fiqh*" in its technical sense does not apply to such things as grammar, medicine, or philosophy, all of which are "*'aqlī*." "*Fiqh*," rather, can only be applied to knowledge of the juristic, that is, *shar'ī*, assessments governing the actions of legally responsible persons, again, "*aḥkām al-mukallafīn al-shar'īyah*."[116]

Al-Baqillānī's allusions to a *shar'ī*/non-*shar'ī* distinction are clearer than those of Ibn al-Qaṣṣār. Moreover, he speaks directly to the question of the concrete basis upon which this distinction might be made. This is also the case with al-Ghazālī, who, like al-Bāqillānī, provides early in his *al-Mustaṣfā* a definition of *fiqh*: "knowledge of the established legal rules governing the conduct of legally responsible persons" (*al-'ilm bi al-aḥkām al-shar'īyah al-thābitah li af'āl al-mukallafīn*).[117] Al-Ghazālī notes in several places that this definition excludes such rational, or *'aqlī*, pursuits as mathematics, geometry, astronomy,[118] philosophy, grammar,[119] and medicine.[120] Echoing al-Bāqillānī, he states explicitly that knowledge of the *ḥukm sharʿī* is inextricably bound to the divine address, directly or by analogy. As he puts it, "The *ḥukm* in our view represents the Lawgiver's address whenever the latter attaches to the actions of legally responsible persons" (*al-ḥukm ʿindanā ʿibārah ʿan khiṭāb al-shāriʿ idhā taʿallaqa bi afʿāl al-mukallafīn*).[121] The idea that the *ḥukm sharʿī* is contingent upon revelation (in the broad sense, including Prophetic teaching) suggests that *sharīʿah*'s authority can extend only as far as revelation will take it. Al-Ghazālī does not back away from this implication but explicitly doubles down on it: "Where this address of the Lawgiver does not exist, there is no *ḥukm sharʿī*" (*idhā lam yūjad hādhā al-khiṭāb min al-shāriʿ fa lā ḥukm*).[122]

This degree of explicitness regarding *sharīʿah*'s circumscription appears to be al-Ghazālī's own contribution, as his teacher, Imām al-Ḥaramayn al-Juwaynī (d. 478/1085), seems less clear on the matter. Indeed, al-Juwaynī's legal theory is often so steeped in anti-Muʿtazilī polemics that it is often difficult to disentangle his jurisprudential from his theological commitments. But perhaps it was the depth and ferocity of this polemical posture, and the highly processed thought it produced, that allowed al-Ghazālī to glean the insights and perspectives that enabled him to see the matter as clearly as he did.

Al-Juwaynī's fundamental argument with the Muʿtazilites had been about the latter's insistence on turning rationally derived moral judgments into *aḥkām sharʿīyah* that bound God to reward or punish, independent of any self-disclosure from God. Against this position, al-Juwaynī (and Ashʿarites generally) insisted that it was God, not reason, that determined divine reward and punishment. And it was through God's concretely communicated *sharʿī* address that God disclosed this to humans. This clearly implies a distinction between the *sharʿī* and *ʿaqlī* and throws into relief the idea that, in the absence of God's *sharʿī* address, "there is no *ḥukm*." But al-Juwaynī seems less clear and direct on this matter of boundaries (on my reading of him) than his esteemed student.

In *al-Burhān*, al-Juwaynī cites the conventional description of *fiqh* as "knowledge of the rules that accrue to legal responsibility" (*al-ʿilm bi aḥkām al-taklīf*).[123] He follows this up with a slightly different wording, "knowledge of juristic rulings" (*al-ʿilm bi al-aḥkām al-sharʿīyah*), as if these two statements were synonymous and the wording were not important.[124] In his earlier (and less famous) work, *al-Talkhīṣ*, he adduced this latter wording as his preferred definition, holding it to be superior to that of al-Bāqillānī.[125] Unlike al-Bāqillānī, however, al-Juwaynī does not focus on or explain the word "*sharʿīyah*"/"*sharʿī*"; nor does he expound on the general definitions he puts forth. Overall, al-Juwaynī seems to have a latent awareness of a *sharʿī*/non-*sharʿī* divide, with all that it implies in the way of boundaries.[126] But he also insists, in a manner reminiscent of al-Shāfiʿī, that "there is no situation befalling God's servants but that there is a ruling from

God covering it" (*lā takhlū wāqiʿah ʿan ḥukm Allāh taʿālā ʿalā al-mutaʿabbidīn*).[127] Even this statement, of course, as we have seen, does not necessarily negate the idea of *sharīʿah* as a bounded entity. In al-Juwaynī's case, however, it appears to cloud more than it clarifies the issue.

Turning to Ḥanbalī theorists of the period, we can confirm that attentiveness to the question of scope and the *sharʿī*/non-*sharʿī* divide was not a purely Rationalist or Ashʿarī obsession. In his *al-ʿUddah fī Uṣūl al-Fiqh*, Abū Yaʿlā al-Farrāʾ (d. 458/1065), who played a pivotal role in the development of Ḥanbali jurisprudence, joins the tradition of laying out the meaning and contours of *fiqh* early on in his discussion. Echoing al-Bāqillānī, he states that the subject matter of *fiqh* is "knowledge of the legal, as distinct from the rational, assessments governing the actions of legally responsible persons" (*al-ʿilm bi aḥkām afʿāl al-mukallafīn al-sharʿīyah dūna al-ʿaqlīyah*).[128] He follows this immediately with the stipulation that "*fiqh*," as a technical term, does not apply to such things as "astronomy, medicine or philosophy."[129] Further on, he explains the distinction between "rational" (*ʿaqlī*) and "juristic" (*sharʿī*) as residing in the simple fact of the latter's reliance on revelatory indicants such as "the Qurʾān, Sunna, unanimous consensus (*ijmāʿ*), and analogy (*qiyās*)," whereas the former relies upon rational inquiry (*naẓar al-ʿāqil*).[130] While Abū Yaʿlā does not take up the *sharʿī*/non-*sharʿī* distinction directly, the theoretical line he draws between *sharʿī* and *ʿaqlī* clearly circumscribes and delimits both categories.

Abū Yaʿlā's student Ibn ʿAqīl (d. 513/1119) begins his *Al-Wāḍiḥ fī Uṣūl al-Fiqh* with a discussion of the meaning of "*uṣūl al-fiqh*" and its constituent parts, "*uṣūl*" and "*fiqh*," followed by suggestive allusions to the *hukm sharʿī* (to which he also refers as the "*ḥukm fiqhī*"). He cites what appears to be not simply his personal view but the going opinions in juristic circles at the time. "*Fiqh*," he notes, is "understanding of the juristic rules arrived at by way of rational investigation" (*fahm al-aḥkām al-sharʿīyah bi ṭarīq al-naẓar*) or "knowledge of the juristic rules arrived at by way of rational investigation of and extrapolation from the sources (*al-ʿilm bi al-aḥkām al-sharʿīyah bi ṭarīq al-naẓar wa al-istinbāṭ*).[131] Like his teacher, Ibn ʿAqīl notes that "*fiqh*" is a restrictive construct that applies only to the juristic rules governing the conduct of legally responsible persons. It does not apply to such pursuits as "grammar, medicine, lexicography, geometry or mathematics."[132] While Ibn ʿAqīl (like Abū Yaʿlā) does not actually define the *ḥukm sharʿī*, he makes it clear that "*sharʿī*" is a restrictive category, particularly in juxtaposition to what is " '*aqlī*," which apparently encompasses all other fields of knowledge and expertise.[133]

During roughly this same period (from the late fifth/eleventh century to the early decades of the sixth/twelfth century), Ḥanafī jurists appear to continue in the tradition of al-Jaṣṣāṣ, al-Bazdawī, and other early Hanafī predecessors, at least in their approach to the *ḥukm sharʿī*. This is evident in the works of the two great

Central Asian theorists, ʿAlāʾ al-Dīn al-Samarqandī (d. 539/1144) and Abū al-Thanāʾ Maḥmūd b. Zayd al-Lāmishī (d. later fifth/eleventh to early sixth/twelfth century). In neither al-Samarqandī's *Mīzān al-Uṣūl fī Natāʾij al-ʿUqūl*[134] nor al-Lāmishī's *Kitāb fī Uṣūl al-Fiqh*[135] is there any definitional treatment of *fiqh* or the *ḥukm sharʿī* that approaches the kind of coverage we find among theorists writing in the tradition of speculative jurisprudence. To the extent that there is any recognition of a *sharʿī*/non-*sharʿī* divide at all, it is far more implicit and transitory and even then remains inconclusive. This may be related to the Central Asians' engagement with their Ḥanafī counterparts in Iraq, who, coming out of Ḥanafism's early relationship with Muʿtazilism, assumed a more causal relationship between rationally deduced good and evil and juristic rulings. In other words, the elision of the rationally deduced judgments into the body of the *sharʿ* may have blurred for them the distinction between the *sharʿī* and the non-*sharʿī*, since, from a basic Muʿtazilī standpoint, non-*sharʿī*, *ʿaqlī* assessments not only bleed into but effectively constitute *sharʿī* rules.[136] Stated differently, if the *ʿaqlī* is understood not simply to cast light upon the *sharʿī* but to embody or constitute it, it may be difficult—if not moot—to make an explicit *sharʿī*/non-*sharʿī* distinction, certainly in contrast to what is *ʿaqlī*. This is the explicit understanding we glean from the Irāqī Muʿtazilī-Ḥanafī Abū al-Ḥusayn al-Baṣrī, according to whom the dictates of reason (*ʿaql*) can and should be assumed to constitute *sharʿī* rules *unless sharʿī* sources refute or turn one away from this conclusion.[137] For al-Baṣrī, in other words, the distinction between the *ʿaqlī* and the *sharʿī* is provisional, not inherent. This throws into relief the explicit distinction that Sunnī, that is, non-Muʿtazilī, theorists who wrote in the tradition of speculative jurisprudence consistently insisted upon between the *sharʿī* and the *ʿaqlī*, a view on which Ḥanafīs would not join them until well into the seventh/thirteenth century.

The Theoretical Consummation of a Bounded *Sharīʿah*

Turning to the latter part of the sixth/twelfth century and the early part of the seventh/thirteenth, we encounter a pivotal figure among those writing in the tradition of the speculative theoreticians. This is the famed Shāfiʿī jurist and Ashʿarī theologian Fakhr al-Dīn al-Rāzī (d. 606/1210), who, through a dramatic organizational innovation, solidified the conceptualization of *sharīʿah* as a bounded entity. In his highly informative tome on legal theory, *al-Baḥr al-Muḥīṭ*, the eighth-/fourteenth-century jurist al-Zarkashī singles out al-Rāzī as having started a new trend of sorts, referring to him as, "al-Imām Fakhr al-Dīn *and his followers*."[138] Even before al-Zarkashī, al-Qarāfī, in his works on *uṣūl al-fiqh*, had used the honorific *al-Imām* in reference to al-Rāzī with such veneration and frequency that it is not always clear that he is not speaking about Mālik! Ibn Khaldūn, by contrast, appears to play down the role and stature of al-Rāzī, claiming that al-Rāzī and al-Āmidī (d. 631/1233) merely summarized the *uṣūl al-fiqh* works of ʿAbd al-Jabbār (d. 415–16/1024–25), Abū al-Ḥusayn al-Baṣrī, al-Juwaynī, and al-Ghazālī. But none of these figures in pre-modern times came to enjoy the formal title "Imām" as a legal theorist.[139] In his entry on al-Rāzī, the noted biographer Ibn Khallikān (d. 681/1282) states that people became so preoccupied with his works that they "threw aside the works of his predecessors."[140] And in his description of al-Rāzī's *al-Maḥṣūl* (on *uṣūl al-fiqh*), the famed bibliographer Ḥajjī Khalīfah (d. 1067/1657 cites some twelve commentaries and abridgments of this work,[141] compared to four of al-Ghazālī's *al-Mustaṣfā*,[142] none of al-Juwaynī's *al-Burhān*,[143] and none on al-Baṣrī's *al-Muʿtamad*.[144] Of course, *Kashf al-Ẓunūn* is neither infallible nor exhaustive.[145] But this comparison does suggest something about the far-reaching impact of al-Rāzī.

It would presume too much, of course, to suggest that al-Rāzī's fame flowed entirely from his writings on *uṣūl al-fiqh*. In his study of al-Rāzī, Ayman Shihadeh shows how bold and innovative he was as a theologian and philosopher-ethicist.[146] Meanwhile, Sabine Schmidtke credits him with "thoroughly revis[ing] the Ashʿarite doctrine" and "serv[ing] as a model for later Ashʿarite theologians."[147] Yet, al-Rāzī's undeniable theological and even philosophical influence notwithstanding, *al-Maḥṣūl* includes a particular mode of systemization for *uṣūl al-fiqh* that distinguishes its author from all the major writers on legal theory before him. This, I would hazard, is probably what lay behind al-Zarkashī's intimation that al-Rāzī started a new trend in the discipline.

In his definition of *uṣūl al-fiqh*, al-Rāzī does not say anything fundamentally new, compared to al-Bāqillānī, al-Juwaynī, al-Ghazālī, Abū Yaʿlā, or Ibn ʿAqīl. He begins by identifying *fiqh* as "knowledge of the practical juristic rulings individually established via their textual indicants inasmuch as that they are not known by necessity to be a part of the religion" (*al-ʿilm bi al-aḥkām al-sharʿīyah al-ʿamalīyah al-mustadall ʿalā aʿyānihā bi ḥaythu lā yuʿlam kawnuhā min al-dīn bi al-ḍarūrah*).[148] He goes on to explain the word "juristic" (*sharʿīyah*), noting that it stands in contradistinction to "rational" (*ʿaqlīyah*) or, as he puts it, "*iḥtirāz*^{un} *ʿan al-ʿaqlīyah*."[149] "Rational," however, does not imply any particular system of reason, such as *ʿilm al-kalām*, Aristotelian logic, or 'Islamicized' Neoplatonism. It simply refers to the human faculty and what it can produce, unbound or uninformed by scripture. Al-Rāzī explains further that his use of the adverb "*shar*^{ʿan}" refers specifically to the fact that these assessments (*aḥkām*) can be made based only on the sources of *sharīʿah*.[150]

As for his formal definition of the *ḥukm sharʿī*, al-Rāzī is a bit more careful than his predecessors but, again, does not say anything fundamentally new: "the [divine] address that attaches to acts of legally responsible persons by imposing a duty or granting a choice" (*al-khiṭāb al-mutaʿalliq bi afʿāl al-mukallafīn bi al-iqtiḍā' aw al-takhyīr*).[151] The phrase "by imposing a duty or granting a choice" is a meaningful addition; but, since it was effectively implied in earlier definitions, I would not characterize it as new. It is at this point, however, that al-Rāzī offers his important organizational innovation, which sets the stage for a new chapter in the history of *uṣūl al-fiqh* and of the conceptualization of *sharī'ah* and its *ḥukm shar'ī* as bounded entities.

As far as I can tell, in none of the previous major works on *uṣūl al-fiqh* are injunctive (*taklīfī*) and declaratory (*waḍ'ī*) rulings, including the legal cause (*sabab*), legal prerequisite (*sharṭ*), and legal impediment (*māni'*), specifically recognized and gathered together as constituents of a composite *ḥukm shar'ī*. Where they are recognized as distinct entities, they tend to be scattered over various chapters in a manner that does not always obviate their connection one to the other. We already noted that Ḥanafīs writing in the tradition-oriented mode of the jurists showed little interest in the *ḥukm shar'ī* as a formal topic of discussion. But even jurists writing in the tradition of speculative jurisprudence—al-Bāqillānī, al-Juwaynī, al-Ghazālī, Abū Ya'lā, Ibn 'Aqīl, and, no doubt, others—did not gather these constituents in a single place and identify them as components of a composite *ḥukm shar'ī*. With al-Rāzī, however, this changed, and this shift proved seminal to later discussions of legal theory, especially, as we shall see, in the works of the Mālikī Shihāb al-Dīn al-Qarāfī.

Between al-Rāzī and al-Qarāfī stood the towering figure of Sayf al-Dīn al-Āmidī (d. 631/1234), a Shāfi'ī theoretician whose *al-Iḥkām fī Uṣūl al-Aḥkām* also gathers the *ḥukm taklīfī* and *ḥukm waḍ'ī* in a single place and defines them as constituents of a composite *ḥukm shar'ī*.[152] In fact, while al-Āmidī raises a number of technical quibbles with the "Imām" (al-Rāzī), his understanding of *fiqh*[153] and the *ḥukm shar'ī*[154] basically comports with that of al-Rāzī. Moreover, he explicitly recognizes the *shar'ī*/non-*shar'ī* divide.[155] This raises the question of why al-Rāzī should be preferred over al-Āmidī as the likely source of the development in question. The answer lies in chronology. In the introduction to his *al-Iḥkām*, al-Āmidī dedicates his effort to the Ayyūbid Sultan al-Malik al-Mu'aẓẓam,[156] who, according to Dominique Sourdel, summoned him to Damascus in 617/1220–21 and conferred upon him the chair at the 'Azīzīyah *madrasah*.[157] But al-Rāzī had reportedly already completed *al-Maḥṣūl* in 576/1180,[158] and Ḥājjī Khalīfah suggests 625/1228 as the year in which al-Āmidī completed his *al-Iḥkām*.[159] Thus, while al-Āmidī may have relied on al-Rāzī in writing *al-Iḥkām*, it was virtually impossible for al-Rāzī (who died in 606/1210) to have relied on al-Āmidī in writing *al-Maḥṣūl*. Of the two, in short, al-Rāzī is far more likely to have been the originator of this new approach.

I do not mean to imply by this brief survey that legal theorists writing in the tradition of speculative jurisprudence prior to al-Rāzī were entirely uninterested in the injunctive ruling (*ḥukm taklīfī*) and the declaratory ruling (*ḥukm waḍ'ī*), especially the former, and their respective constituents. But, again, none of their works included a formal section on these as constituents of a composite *ḥukm sharʿī*. Rather, the tendency was to discuss these entities discursively, as, for example, when al-Ghazālī, whose *al-Mustaṣfā* does not include a formal discussion of the legal impediment (*māniʿ*), notes that various contextual indicators (*qarāʾin*) remain probative as long as they "are not preempted by some legal impediment" (*idhā lam yamnaʿ māniʿ*).[160] Similarly, Ḥanafīs whose works do not appear to include formal discussions of the legal impediment often discuss legal competence (*ahlīyah*) in ways that are suggestive of it.[161] With al-Rāzī, however, for the first time, all these constituents were gathered in a single place and explicitly identified as elements of a composite *ḥukm sharʿī*.

The relevant section of the table of contents of Volume One of *al-Maḥṣūl* reads as follows: "(I) On the juristic ruling (*fī al-ḥukm al-sharʿī*); (II) Divisions of the juristic ruling (*fī taqsīm al-ḥukm al-sharʿī*); (a) On injunctive rulings (*fī al-aḥkām al-taklīfīyah*); (b) The division of actions into good and evil/bad (*inqisām al-fiʿl ilā ḥasan wa qabīḥ*); (c) On declaratory rulings (*fī khiṭāb al-waḍʿ*)."[162] To my knowledge, this kind of systematic, comprehensive organization of the *ḥukm sharʿī* is unprecedented in the history of *uṣūl al-fiqh*. The opening sentences of the subsection on declaratory rulings reads: "They say: Just as God's address comes bearing obligations or choices, it also comes to indicate that a thing has been rendered a legal cause, legal prerequisite or legal impediment."[163] "They say" here clearly indicates that al-Rāzī is not the origin of these itemized discussions; nor is that what I am claiming here. Rather, my claim is that al-Rāzī was an innovative *systematizer*. With him, the *ḥukm sharʿī* is definitively itemized as a complex, bounded construct in a manner that preempts any lingering thoughts about what it might include or exclude.

This is an extremely important development. For, if, as Bernard Weiss put it, "Sharīʿa is, first and foremost, the totality of divine 'categorizations of human acts,'" and if, as I laid out earlier, the *ḥukm sharʿī* is the fundamental unit of *sharīʿah*, this comprehensive definition of the *ḥukm sharʿī* empowers jurists to think about and theorize juristic law, that is, *fiqh*/*sharīʿah*, in a manner unprecedented in precision and concreteness, free of both over- and under-inclusiveness. This clarity in turn opens the way not only to a clearer understanding of juristic law but also to a clearer, more explicit and theoretically grounded recognition of the distinction between juristic law and juristic non-law, and between *sharʿī* and non-*sharʿī* law. This will clearly aid jurists in isolating the *non-sharʿī* dimensions of their own as well as others' assessments, and to recognize the value, status, and authority of modes and metrics of assessment beyond the dictates and instruments of *sharīʿah*.[164] *This* was the singular contribution of al-Rāzī.

Nowhere is the impact of this development more manifest than in the work of al-Rāzī's Mālikī commentator Shihāb al-Dīn al-Qarāfī, who wrote no less than three commentaries/abridgements of al-Rāzī's *al-Maḥṣūl*.[165] Al-Qarāfī's definitions of *fiqh* and the *ḥukm sharʿī* basically agree with those of "the Imām," but he does not follow the latter slavishly. While agreeing, for example, with the basic thrust of al-Rāzī's definition of *fiqh*, he sides with al-Āmidī in substituting "derivative" (*furūʿīyah*) for "practical" (*ʿamalīyah*) in order to include the actions of the heart, such as intention and sincerity, alongside those of the limbs.[166] On the other hand, he does not hesitate to defend al-Rāzī as, for example, against a piercing objection to the *sharʿī*/non-*sharʿī* distinction pressed by the Ḥanafī jurist, Najm al-Dīn al-Naqshuwānī (d. 651/1253). Al-Naqshuwānī had argued that "Everything in the world is created; and, as God is its Lawgiver (*shāriʿ*), everything is therefore *sharʿī*."[167] Included in al-Qarāfī's response is the insistence that "*sharʿī*" refers to those normative rules that issue from God concretely as Lawgiver, not to non-normative or descriptive "rules of nature" that are attributable to God as Creator. In other words, God's act of creating is different from God's acts of commanding, prohibiting, or communicating assessments. As nature has no will of its own, every thing and every occurrence in nature can be ultimately attributed to God's deliberate will. But nature cannot (or does not necessarily) speak for God. In this sense, not everything in the world is necessarily *sharʿī*, in the sense of communicating what God wants from humans.[168] As the carrier of what God concretely commands or sanctions, the *sharʿī* is distinguished from the *kawnī*, or God's simple act of creation. The *kawnī* may include things that God ultimately wills but does not concretely prefer (such as the disobedience that comes of the volition that God creates in humans). The former, however, is entirely a reflection of what God wills in the sense of concretely preferring and affirmatively sanctioning.[169] Clearly, on this understanding, not everything in creation is *sharʿī* in the normative sense.

But it is in his own treatment of the *ḥukm sharʿī* that al-Qarāfī makes his unique and seminal contribution. We may recall al-Rāzī's definition: "the [divine] address that attaches to acts of legally responsible persons by imposing a duty or granting a choice" (*al-khiṭāb al-mutaʿalliq bi afʿāl al-mukallafīn bi al-iqtiḍāʾ aw al-takhyīr*). Al-Qarāfī observes that this definition is incomplete and adds the following after "imposing a duty or granting a choice":

> . . . or what necessitates the application of a rule or its negation. That which necessitates the application of a rule are the legal causes, and that which necessitates its negation is the legal prerequisite by its absence and the legal impediment by its presence . . . and with this, the definition is straightened out and encompasses all the legal rulings. This is the view that I choose. And I have not seen anyone construct the definition (of the *ḥukm sharʿī*) in this way.[170]

In his *Muntahā al-Wuṣūl wa al-Amal ilā 'Ilmay al-Uṣūl wa al-Jadal*, Ibn al-Ḥājib, who died in 646/1259 and was one of al-Qarāfī's teachers, gives a definition of the *ḥukm shar'ī* that includes al-Qarāfī's addendum. On close examination, however, the two do not appear to attribute the same significance to this insight nor to want to do the same thing with it. Both reflect a palpable debt to al-Rāzī's systemization of the *ḥukm shar'ī*;[171] and both recognize the *shar'ī*/non-*shar'ī* divide.[172] In fact, based on the number of commentaries on Ibn al-Ḥājib's work, one could easily argue that he was the far more widely read.[173] But whereas Ibn al-Ḥājib's interest in the definition of the *ḥukm shar'ī* appears to be casual and almost perfunctory, al-Qarāfī sees it as the basis of a whole new theory for separating law from non-law. Thus, while al-Qarāfī's claim to precedence may be overstated, we are on stronger ground in viewing him as the first to see the broader implications of al-Rāzī's composite description of the *ḥukm shar'ī* for a formal theory of law.

Al-Qarāfī's neat and comprehensive definition proved critical to his unique construction of what I have termed elsewhere his "pure-law" conceptualization of *sharī'ah*, which restricts the authority associated with any juristic pronouncement strictly to what is formally "legal," that is, *juristic*, or *shar'ī*, therein.[174] In this respect, he clearly goes beyond Ibn al-Ḥājib, who, as far as I know, never produced anything of the sort. Indeed, it was al-Qarāfī who more clearly and forcefully than anyone before (and perhaps after) him put forth the argument that not everything a jurist says—even a *mujtahid* eponymous Imām, and even in the name of *sharī'ah*—should be clothed with *shar'ī* authority, a view that clearly implies limits to the jurists' authority *qua* jurists.[175]

In explicating the *shar'ī*/non-*shar'ī* distinction, al-Qarāfī notes that the *shar'ī* stands in contradistinction not only to what is known by formal reason but also to what is known by sense-perception (*ḥiss*), custom, common sense, and the like. As examples, he mentions mathematics, geometry, music, social customs, natural science, medicine, and commerce, while intimating that the list is open-ended.[176] He explicitly opposes the aforementioned view of the Ḥanafī al-Jaṣṣāṣ and his fellow Mālikī al-Qāḍī 'Abd al-Wahhāb (d. 422/1031), that there is no difference between a unanimous consensus reached on war-strategy and one reached on a juristic interpretation. He notes that the authority of the Community's (*ummah*'s) consensus is limited to what they assert based on revelation (*mā yaqūlūna 'an Allāh*), which does not include such things as war-strategy.[177] In other words, unanimous consensus is an interpretive instrument of the *shar'*, in that it lends authority to scriptural interpretations, while the substance of a war-strategy is neither deduced nor arrived at via the interpretation of texts. As such, in and of itself, no specific war-strategy can claim the juristic authority to bind the Community by way of unanimous consensus, any more than a unanimous consensus in the field of astronomy or music could exert such authority. One might be deemed wrong or even stupid for denying unanimously agreed-upon non-*shar'ī* findings, such and 3 x 4 = 12; but one could not be deemed sinful, disobedient, or in violation of the *shar'* for doing so.[178] Here again we see that, unlike many of his predecessors, al-Qarāfī imbues the *shar'ī*/non-*shar'ī* distinction with real power as part of a theory of law. Ultimately, while al-Rāzī pointed the way to a more systematic theorization of juristic law, al-Qarāfī brought this insight to its fullest expression via his "pure-law" conceptualization of *sharī'ah*. In his work, in a manner unprecedented in the history of Sunni jurisprudence, the categories of juristic law and non-law, that is, the *shar'ī* and non-*shar'ī*, as well as the distinction between these categories, reach their highest degree of clarity and explicitness.

Pursuant to this clarity, al-Qarāfī underscored, with a forcefulness also unique to him, the aforementioned vertical or subterranean boundary of the juristically "purely legal." He predicates this boundary on an important distinction between "*mashrū'īyat al-sabab*" or "*sababīyat al-sabab*," that is, the status of a thing or occurrence as a legal cause, prerequisite, or impediment, and its actual occurrence, that is, its "*wuqū'*," as a matter of fact.[179] He notes that the sources for determining status and occurrence are categorically distinct and that mastery over one does not necessarily entail mastery over the other. Thus, he speaks of "sources of juristic law," or *adillat mashrū'īyah*, and "sources of fact," or *adillat wuqū'*, noting that while the sources of juristic law (speaking in general terms across the schools) are approximately twenty in number, the sources for determining facts are countless and unending (*ghayr munhaṣirah*).[180] As an example, he cites the verse, "Establish the prayer at the sun's decline from its zenith" [Q. 17:83] as a *shar'ī* indicant that the sun's decline from its meridian is a juristic cause (*sabab*) obligating the performance of the noon prayer. By contrast, he cites fourteen different sources for establishing the sun's actual decline as a matter of fact. Neither the substance nor the status of any of these fourteen means and measures is dictated by the religious law. Nor does the religious law require one to rely on any particular one of these as opposed to any other.[181]

We should be clear about the ultimate meaning of all of this, relative to what I have been referring to as the "differentiated realm." The clear and distinct limits imputed to the *ḥukm shar'ī*, by al-Qarāfī and others, plainly imply that there are realms of knowledge, modes of inquiry and assessment, and spheres of authority and expertise whose substantive content and metrics of appraisal lie outside the moral or prudential calculus of *sharī'ah* proper. In other words, there are *aḥkām* (sg. *ḥukm*) other than the *aḥkām shar'īyah* (sg., *ḥukm shar'ī*) that are relevant to the instantiation of Islam as a lived reality. And there are authorities and disciplines other than the jurists and their *shar'ī* sciences that are equally critical. While al-Qarāfī is the most direct and comprehensive theorist making this point, the basic understanding of the bounded nature of the *ḥukm shar'ī* and the consequences thereof is not, as we have seen, unique to him; nor does it end with him. Al-Rāzī's *al-Maḥṣūl* continued to spawn discussions in *uṣūl al-fiqh* long after al-Qarāfī's time, discussions in which the composite, bounded *ḥukm shar'ī* became a standard feature, as did the *shar'ī*/non-*shar'ī* distinction that flows therefrom.

This distinction even influenced Ḥanafīs who engaged with "the Imām." We see this, for example, in the work of the Central Asian Ḥanafī-Māturīdī jurist, al-Qāḍī Ṣadr al-Sharī'ah 'Ubayd Allāh b. Mas'ūd al-Maḥbūbī al-Bukhārī (d. 747/1346). Ṣadr al-Sharī'ah wrote a commentary on his Ḥanafī predecessor al-Bazdawī's *Uṣūl* and entitled it *Tanqīḥ al-Uṣūl* (*The Refinement of* [al-Bazdawī's] *Legal Theory*). He explains that, in addition to what he drew from al-Bazdawī, *Tanqīḥ al-Uṣūl* included the cream of al-Rāzī's *al-Maḥṣūl*, alongside material from Ibn al-Ḥājib's *Muntahā al-Wuṣūl*.[182] Subsequently, however, Ṣadr al-Sharī'ah published a revised version, when he noticed that the copies in circulation had suffered certain corruptions, and he named this revised version *al-Tawḍīḥ fī Ḥall Ghawāmiḍ al-Tanqīḥ* (*The Clarifier in Removing the Ambiguities of the Refinement*).

Al-Tawḍīḥ became the object of at least twenty-five commentaries and super-commentaries, clearly bringing a multiplier effect to the views it contained. The most famous of these is the super-commentary by Sa'd al-Dīn al-Taftazānī (d. 792/1389), entitled *al-Talwīḥ ilā Kashf Ḥaqā'iq al-Tanqīḥ* (or more popularly *al-Talwīḥ 'alā al-Tawḍīḥ*).[183] Al-Taftazānī's *madhhab*-affiliation is a matter of dispute. Ḥājjī Khalīfah identifies him explicitly as a Shāfi'ī.[184] But there is language in *al-Talwīḥ* itself that strongly suggests that he was a Ḥanafī.[185] At any rate, while his connection to al-Rāzī is mediated through Ṣadr al-Sharī'ah, he joins the latter in recognizing the *shar'ī*/non-*shar'ī* distinction.[186]

In *al-Tawḍīḥ*, Ṣadr al-Sharī'ah parted with al-Bazdawī and joined al-Rāzī in putting forth a definition of *fiqh* that is followed by an explanatory discussion of the *hukm shar'ī*.[187] Al-Rāzī rather than Ibn al-Ḥājib provides the lead here.[188] Like Ibn al-Ḥājib, Ṣadr al-Sharī'ah endorses the view that the *shar'ī* is "that which could not be known in the absence of the divine address" (*mā lā tudrak law lā khiṭāb al-shāri'*).[189] But some of his language unmistakably echoes that of al-Rāzī (e.g., "*iḥtirāz*^{an} *'an*"); and, unlike the single sentence deployed by Ibn al-Ḥājib, Ṣadr al-Sharī'ah maps out some of the broader implications of the *shar'ī*/non-*shar'ī* divide, such as the fact that "*shar'ī*" excludes rational (*'aqlī*) and sentient (*ḥissī*)" assessments,[190] and that for Māturīdīs and Mu'tazilīs who recognize reason's ability to apprehend good and evil independent of revelation, ethics (*akhlāq*) is effectively a non-*shar'ī* discourse.[191] In the end, though a Ḥanafī, Ṣadr al-Sharī'ah's (and al-Taftazānī's) perception of the parameters of *sharī'ah* is consistent with the trend that began with al-Bāqillānī and culminated in al-Rāzī, al-Qarāfī, and others writing in the mode of the speculative theoreticians.

Not all Ḥanafīs from the seventh/thirteenth century onward who came to this perception necessarily drew on al-Rāzī. In his *Nihāyat al-Wuṣūl ilā 'Ilm al-Uṣūl*, Ibn al-Sa'ātī (Aḥmad b. 'Alī b. Taghlib: d. 694/1295) states that this work is based on his own summary of al-Āmidī's *al-Iḥkām fī Uṣūl al-Aḥkām* along with "adornments" added from al-Bazdawī's *Uṣūl*.[192] In taking this approach, Ibn al-Sa'ātī, according to Ibn Khaldūn, is the first theoretician to unite the "tradition-oriented mode of the jurists" with the "theory-oriented mode of the speculative theoreticians."[193] Ibn al-Sa'ātī defines *uṣūl al-fiqh* in a manner that clearly distinguishes the *shar'ī* from the non-*shar'ī*, contrasting "arriving at [knowledge of] juristic rulings" (*istinbāṭ al-aḥkām*) with "arriving at [knowledge of] the various professions (*istinbāṭ al-ṣanā'i'*).[194] Similarly, he itemizes the *ḥukm taklīfī* and the *ḥukm waḍ'ī* as constituents of a composite *ḥukm shar'ī*.[195] His doing so reopens the question of whether al-Āmidī or al-Rāzī was the more influential in post-seventh-/thirteenth-century *uṣūl al-fiqh*. Weiss seems to incline toward al-Āmidī.[196] I would tend to emphasize, as I explained previously, that al-Rāzī was certainly the *first* of the two to introduce the neat and comprehensive *systemization* of the *ḥukm shar'ī*. Meanwhile, while Ḥajjī Khạlīfah cites several commentaries/abridgments written on al-Rāzī's *al-Maḥṣūl*, he cites only one abridgment in his entry on al-Āmidī's *al-Iḥkām*.[197]

At any rate, what is indisputable is that, after the seventh/thirteenth century, *uṣūl al-fiqh* works, especially those written in the tradition of speculative jurisprudence, overwhelmingly tend to gather the *ḥukm taklīfī* and the *ḥukm waḍ'ī* together as components of a composite *ḥukm shar'ī*, routinely recognizing a *shar'ī*/non-*shar'ī* distinction.[198] This trend clearly opens the way to a more explicit theoretical recognition of the boundaries of *sharī'ah* and of juristic law and juristic non-law as two distinct areas of legitimate inquiry (in contrast to what is commonly pointed to as the totalizing, undifferentiated nature of Islamic law that recognizes no other legitimate, authoritative, "Islamic" modes of assessment or investigation). We see this recognition clearly in post-seventh-/thirteenth-century works written in the tradition of speculative jurisprudence. As for those written in the tradition-oriented mode of the Ḥanafīs, while there is less consistency, there is movement, albeit irregular, as in the works of Ibn al-Sa'ātī and Ṣadr al-Sharī'ah. This trend is interrupted by the seventh-to-eighth-/thirteenth-to-fourteenth-century Ḥanafī jurist Abū al-Barakāt al-Nasafī (d. 710/1310), whose *al-Manār* neither defines the *ḥukm shar'ī* nor gathers the *ḥukm taklīfī* and *ḥukm waḍ'ī* in a single place.[199] Meanwhile, the ninth-/fifteenth-century Ḥanafī Yūsuf b. Ḥusayn al-Karāmastī (d. 900/1494) does treat the *ḥukm shar'ī*, but his itemization and explication of its declaratory (*waḍ'ī*) side, especially the juristic impediment (*māni'*), remains rather opaque.[200] With the early-modern Ḥanafī master Ibn 'Ābidīn (d. 1252/1836) we come full circle to an open recognition of the *shar'ī*/non-*shar'ī* divide. Drawing directly from Ṣadr al-Sharī'ah, he writes,

"What is meant by *sharʿī* . . . is that which would remain unknowable absent an address from the Divine Lawgiver."[201] In sum, while recognition of the *sharʿī*/non-*sharʿī* distinction did not become a point of unanimous consensus, it clearly became the growing if not dominant trend all the way up to late-modernity.

Modern Continuities and Discontinuities

As for late-modern scholars, they routinely recognize the *ḥukm taklīfī* and *ḥukm waḍʿī* as constituents of a composite *ḥukm sharʿī*, but they often make no explicit reference to a *sharʿī*/non-*sharʿī* distinction. This is what we find in the two most popular late-modern works on *uṣūl al-fiqh*. Both Muḥammad Abū Zahra (d. 1394/1974) in his *Uṣūl al-Fiqh* and ʿAbd al-Wahhāb Khallāf (d. 1375/1956) in his *ʿIlm Uṣūl al-Fiqh* define "*fiqh*" as "knowledge of the practical juristic rulings acquired from their concrete sources" (*al-ʿilm bi al-aḥkām al-sharʿīyah al-ʿamalīyah min adillatihā al-tafṣīlīyah*).[202] Neither goes on, however, as was the tendency in pre-modern works, to define or even comment on the adjective "*sharʿīyah*." There is thus no contrast (*iḥtirāz*) between the *sharʿī* and anything else, *ʿaqlī* or otherwise, an approach that obviously lends itself to a more totalizing vision of juristic law.[203] I suggested earlier that Khallāf's tendency in this regard may have been connected to his fears about the encroachments of Western secularism. Perhaps Abū Zahrah nursed similar misgivings. Both men may have viewed expanding the boundaries of *sharīʿah* to the point of no limit as the most effective means of preempting the incursion of the Western secular into Islam as an alternative or substitute basis of adjudication. At any rate, with the effective disappearance of the *sharʿī*/non-*sharʿī* divide, the functional distinction between juristic law and non-law, so handsomely theorized by the likes of al-Rāzī, al-Qarāfī, and others after them, all but fades into the dust of the post-colonial stampede.

Yet, the tendency of these scholars to ignore the *sharʿī*/non-*sharʿī* distinction may have been less a matter of responding to the West than it was of their attachment to the Ḥanafī tradition. After all, other modern scholars, presumably just as concerned about Western influence, openly recognize and expound on the *sharʿī*/non-*sharʿī* divide. In his *Uṣūl al-Fiqh Alladhī lā Yasaʿu al-Faqīh Jahlah*, the Saudi Arabian jurist ʿIyāḍ al-Sulamī defines "*fiqh*" exactly as Abū Zahra and Khallāf do: "knowledge of the practical juristic rulings acquired from their concrete sources" (*al-ʿilm bi al-aḥkām al-sharʿīyah al-muktasabah min adillatihā al-tafṣīlīyah*).[204] He goes on, however, to explain "*sharʿīyah*" in a manner that clearly recognizes juristic and non-juristic assessments as distinct entities: "*sharʿīyah* excludes non-juristic (*ghayr sharʿī*) knowledge, such as assessing a particular linguistic expression to be sound or faulty, or knowledge of whether a particular medicine will benefit or harm a patient. The first of these is a linguistic assessment (*ḥukm lughawī*), the second a medical one ([*ḥukm*] *ṭibbī*)."[205] Of course, neither of the latter examples is presumed to be outside the notice of Islam as religion. In fact, language, as is well known, is key to the entire enterprise of *fiqh*. Thus, we see here, again, how an entity's removal from the sphere of the *fiqhī* or *shar'ī* does not necessarily place it outside the notice of Islam.

This same recognition of the *shar'ī*/non-*shar'ī* distinction appears in the work of the late Syrian Shāfi'ī jurist Wahbah al-Zuḥaylī (d. 1436/2015), who cites the exact words as al-Sulamī in his preferred definition of "*fiqh*"[206] and goes on to explain it in substantively identical terms:

> The qualifier "juristic" (*shar'īyah*) is derived from "law" (i.e., as derived from the sources by the jurists). This is to exclude judgments based on sense perception (*al-ḥissīyah*), such as "the sun is rising," as well as rational judgments (*al-aḥkām al-'aqlīyah*), such as "one is half of two" and "the whole is greater than the part," and other such matters, such as medical, geometrical, linguistic, and empirical judgments, such as our knowledge that Zayd is standing or not standing or that the subject of a verb is in the nominative case.[207]

In sum, while it would be wrong to claim a unanimous consensus among late-modern Muslim jurists on the *shar'ī*/non-*shar'ī* distinction, it is clear that such recognition is not a purely pre-modern phenomenon. In such light, assuming that this distinction is taken seriously and followed to its logical conclusion, there should be little difficulty in recognizing the authenticity of the claim that the Islamic juristic tradition, even in modern times, recognizes—as a function of its own self-imposed limits on *sharī'ah*'s *ḥukm shar'ī*—the existence of a differentiated, non-*shar'ī* realm within Islam, which I refer to as the "Islamic Secular."

Misrecognizing the Bounded Nature of *Sharī'ah*

From the time of al-Bāqillānī in the latter half of the fourth/tenth century, Muslim jurists writing in the tradition of speculative jurisprudence clearly recognized the *ḥukm shar'ī* and thus *fiqh*/*sharī'ah* as bounded entities. Even the Ḥanafī tradition, which initially did not recognize a *shar'ī*/non-*shar'ī* distinction, eventually included jurists who did. This feature of classical and post-formative juristic discourse has been lost on many influential, late-modern, post-colonial Muslim jurists; and most Western scholars, including Western Muslim scholars, seem to be no more mindful of it. *Fiqh* and *sharī'ah* have consistently been discussed in isolation from any consideration of the jurisdictional scope or boundaries of the *ḥukm sharʿī*, in which capacity the unbounded nature of *sharīʿah* is unquestionably assumed, as we saw in Schacht, Coulson, Hallaq, and others. Under the entry on "*aḥkām*" in the *Encyclopedia of Islam: New Edition*, for example, there is no discussion of boundaries or jurisdiction.[208] Similarly, in their otherwise thoughtful discussions on the *ḥukm sharʿī*, A. Kevin Reinhart and Ebrahim Moosa repeat this omission.[209] Even Mohammad Fadel, in the lengthy Introduction to his translation of al-Qarāfī's *Kitāb al-Iḥkām fī Tamyīz al-Fatāwā ʿan al-Aḥkām wa Taṣarrufāt al-Qāḍī wa al-Imām*, attaches no significance to jurisdictional boundaries, neither regarding Islamic juristic law nor the *ḥukm sharʿī*.[210] This is a particularly odd omission, given that this work by al-Qarāfī was explicitly dedicated to highlighting these very parameters. Meanwhile, Wael Hallaq and Adam Sabra display a similar lack of recognition in their reviews of my book on al-Qarāfī, neither of them committing a word to "pure law" or jurisdictional boundaries.[211] In fact, I myself was once blindsided by one of my graduate students who, after reading my book on al-Qarāfī, asked during class, "Dr. Jackson, didn't you see all of these connections to the Islamic Secular when you were writing this book?" My answer was a diffident, pensive "No."

If all these authors' assumptions (or perhaps the assumptions of the field at large) can so overwhelm their—indeed, *our*—interpretive faculties that we are prevented from recognizing a theme as clear and sustained as the *sharʿī*/non-*sharʿī* distinction in the thought of a jurist as relentless as al-Qarāfī and if other obsessions (e.g., *ijtihād* versus *taqlīd*, origins, ethics, certainty versus probability, etc.) can so thoroughly overshadow the same theme in the works of other major Muslim jurists, it is little wonder that the "totalizing 'legal supremacist' conceptualization of Islam as *law*" has so thoroughly influenced our thinking and has remained so thoroughly beyond critique for so long.

But there is another lesson in all of this (which Chapter 3 will draw out further): where the *ḥukm sharʿī* defines an action as merely "permissible" or obligates a man to support his family financially without telling him how to do so, a Muslim will routinely be forced to rely on non-*sharʿī* findings and deliberations, without which the *ḥukm sharʿī*'s injunctions or permissions will remain practically unfulfilled or meaningless. In this light, the *sharʿī* and non-*sharʿī* should not be seen as rival categories but rather as working in tandem. They should be recognized as equally relevant to the proper instantiation of Islam as concrete practice, as mutually dependent constituents in a relationship that is more complementary than hierarchical. Islamic law cannot be properly understood by focusing exclusively on its *sharʿī* side alone. Al-Qarāfī summarizes this lesson as follows, despite his orientation as the quintessential "jurists' jurist":

> Two great scholars once met, one of the rational and exact sciences (*maʿqūlāt wa handasīyāt*) the other of the transmitted and *sharʿī* sciences (*samʿīyāt wa*

> *shar'īyāt*). The former said to the latter, "Geometry is superior to *fiqh*, because it is certain, while *fiqh* is based on reasonable supposition (*ẓunūn*); and certainty is superior to reasonable supposition." The latter responded, "You are correct; from this perspective, it is superior. But *fiqh* is superior in that its fruits are one's happiness in the Hereafter, the bliss of Paradise and pleasing the All-Merciful, while geometry produces nothing of this." The former agreed. And both of these scholars, may God have mercy on them, approached this matter with fairness.[212]

This should temper the tendency to assume, in absolute, categorical terms, the primacy of the juristic (*shar'ī*) over the practical (non-*shar'ī*), or vice-versa. Both realms are integral to the proper instantiation of Islam as practice. Who, for example, could build a mosque, the quintessential *shar'ī* institution, without "*ma'qūlāt wa handasīyāt*"? The trick, of course, is to be able to determine which should be prioritized over which, when, and how. I would submit that these questions have always been part of what *fiqh*/*sharī'ah* in its best tradition has sought to negotiate.

Sharī'ah Minimalism and Maximalism

Ibn Ḥazm and the Ẓāhirī Project

Before ending this chapter, I must confront two (other) apparent challenges to my thesis that come from *within* the Islamic juristic tradition.

The first lies in the work of Ibn Ḥazm (d. 456/1064) and the overall Ẓāhirī approach. The challenge here is that the Ẓāhirīs argue in their own way for the bounded nature of *sharī'ah*, and this may prompt some to conflate my project with theirs. When Ibn Ḥazm insists, for example, that rulings based on analogical extrapolations (*qiyās*) are inadmissible and that everything for which the Qur'ān, Sunna, or the Unanimous Consensus (*ijmā'*) of the Companions provides no direct evidence must be assumed to be "licit" (*mubāḥ*), or unaddressed, the practical effect is a constriction of *sharī'ah*'s scope.[213] Of course, "licit" can be conceived of as either the result of what scripture directly designates as such or, in contrast to the mainstream position, as that which scripture effectively ignores, becoming permissible by default. As A. Kevin Reinhart summarizes the Ẓahirī program, however, according to them, "Revelation's writ ran to what it explicitly addressed and no more. . . . Revelation is applied strictly, but it applies to very little."[214] In sum, by first restricting the number of sources that can be counted as *shar'ī* and then designating everything outside their reach as unaddressed, Ẓāhirism potentially produces—in effect at least—a massive, non-*sharʿī*, differentiated realm, where normative action is not dictated by *sharīʿah* or its sources. And since the number of issues these limited sources can be assumed to address will be increasingly fewer over the course of post-Prophetic history relative to the number of issues they cannot address (especially in the absence of *qiyās*) the number of actions that are grounded in non-*sharʿī*, *ʿaqlī* deliberations will be far greater than those called forth by *sharīʿah* and its *sharʿī* authority.

Such progressive "juristic minimalism" may strike some as heading in the same direction as the Islamic Secular. But while the Islamic Secular also imputes boundaries to the reach of *sharīʿah*'s sources, the type of juristic minimalism represented by the Ẓāhirī approach is neither its aim nor its result. To say that *sharīʿah* is bounded does not—in the view of the Islamic Secular—connote any particular ratio of addressed to unaddressed issues, such that the latter must always be more than the former. Indeed, the Islamic Secular does its work even *within* the boundaries of what the law addresses, in the regions, for example, beneath the *ḥukm sharʿī*, however broadly or narrowly *sharīʿah*'s boundaries might be drawn. Similarly, unlike the Ẓāhirī approach, the Islamic Secular does not seek to restrict the number of *sharʿī* sources to anything less than what the *madhhabs* have traditionally recognized, including, *inter alia*, *qiyās* and juristic *ijmāʿ*.

Most important, the Ẓāhirī approach is basically silent when it comes to the prudential or practical concerns of the differentiated realm beyond the dictates of *sharīʿah*'s sources. While we may presume that the space engendered by the sources' silence will be filled with various modes of non-*sharʿī*, rational deliberation, there is nothing in Ẓāhirism approaching the Islamic Secular's explicit recognition of the appropriateness if not duty to pursue matters in this space in a spirit of obeisance and with an eye to fulfilling Islamically sanctioned needs and interests (*maṣāliḥ*/sg. *maṣlaḥah*). In contradistinction to the Islamic Secular, Ẓāhirism signals no recognition of activities outside *sharīʿah*'s exhortations as explicitly *religious* activity. While Ibn Ḥazm explicitly recognizes the religious value of medicine, genealogy, grammar and the like, this is only to the extent that these enterprises aid one in gaining knowledge of *sharīʿah*.[215] Outside this function, it remains an open question whether on a Ẓāhirī approach extra-*sharʿī* activity (such as setting the content of economic policy) can be considered "Islamic."

My point here is neither to repudiate nor cast aspersions on Ẓāhirī juristic minimalism, or juristic minimalism in general. It is simply to establish that Ẓāhirism and the Islamic Secular are two distinct projects that should not be confused or conflated with each other, their apparent (or even actual) overlap on various fronts notwithstanding.[216]

The *Sharīʿah*-Maximalism of Ibn al-Qayyim and Ibn Taymīyah

The second challenge is more substantive and comes from the direction of Ibn Qayyim al-Jawzīyah (d. 751/1350) and his teacher Ibn Taymīyah (d. 728/1328). These men significantly challenge—without, however, ultimately rejecting—the *sharʿī*/non-*sharʿī* divide upheld by theorists writing in the tradition of speculative jurisprudence.

Ibn al-Qayyim

While Ibn Taymīyah (as we will see) is more concerned about the theological implications of this distinction, Ibn al-Qayyim's concerns are more properly legal. In particular, he nurses misgivings about normalized encroachments upon *sharīʿah*, based on the notion that other reglementary regimes better serve the cause of justice and divine pleasure. The problem, in his view, begins with the rigid, superficial, and short-sighted interpretations of the jurists, which result in miscarriages of justice and the forfeiture of legitimate personal or communal interests, all in the name of *sharīʿah*. This in turn gives rise to calls for non-*sharʿī* alternatives, especially discretionary regulations proffered under the auspices of state-sponsored *siyāsah*.[217] Ibn al-Qayyim's response to this problem is to cast *sharīʿah* as totalizing, not only subsuming *siyāsah* but all reasonable inferences from the sources, through both formal analogy (*qiyās*) and the use of common sense, communal experience, rational induction, and the like. On this understanding, God's *sharʿī* address can cover every situation.[218] Part of the point of this "maximalist" construction is to weaken if not negate the *sharʿī*/non-*sharʿī* distinction in order to prevent the non-*sharʿī* from displacing or overwhelming the *sharʿī*. And, of course, to the extent that the *sharʿī*/non-*sharʿī* distinction is weakened or denied, so too is any recognition of an Islamic Secular.

We should be careful, however, about imposing too hasty or superficial a reading on Ibn al-Qayyim. As noted, even if we assume, as he clearly does, that *sharīʿah* confers a *ḥukm sharʿī* upon every human act in the sense that all acts fall into one of its Five Juristic Statuses, this does not necessarily imply that scripture or the *ḥukm sharʿī* encompasses all the Islamically relevant means or metrics of assessment that might be legitimately brought to bear on a given situation. For example, Ibn al-Qayyim insists that the Qurʾānic verse, "*Say, He made all good things lawful for you*" (*qul uḥilla lakum al-ṭayyibāt*) [5:4] informs us that all foods, drinks, clothing, and sexual arrangements that are "good" (*ṭayyib*) are permissible.[219] Of course, there is a difference between the Qurʾān's deeming good things permissible and its concretely telling us which things are good. Ibn al-Qayyim indirectly acknowledges this, as well as the fact that determining the "good" often calls upon metrics that fall outside scripture and the *ḥukm sharʿī*. He notes, for example, that, substantively speaking, much of the "good" the Qurʾān enjoins regarding spousal maintenance, fair treatment, and the rights and responsibilities of women "revert to what 'the people' recognize by convention to be good and not bad" (*mā yataʿārafahu al-nās baynahum wa yajʿalūnahu maʿrūf^an lā munkar^an*).[220] Of course, "the people" for Ibn al-Qayyim are not an independent source of *sharīʿah*, and their judgments must remain within the boundaries of what *sharīʿah* itself deems permissible. But in recognizing the people as a proximate source of "good," he acknowledges that neither scripture nor *sharīʿah* provides *all* the concrete judgments necessary to the production of proper *sharʿī* rulings, let alone the most proper or beneficial course of action to be taken in pursuit of legitimate human interests.

A similar analysis can be applied to Ibn al-Qayyim's treatment of "*al-siyāsah al-sharʿīyah*," with which he and Ibn Taymīyah are so closely associated. On the one hand, Ibn al-Qayyim acknowledges that *siyāsah* in the form of discretionary policies go beyond established juristic law, this being the whole point of the exercise. For him, however, this reach entails some clear liabilities, against which he seeks to expand the scope of *sharīʿah* to include things not normally recognized by the jurists' *fiqh*, in order to limit—if not dispense with—the need for *siyāsah* as a distinct and separate regime of rule-making. For example, he includes forms of courtroom evidence beyond those prescribed by *fiqh* and refers to all these as "*sharʿī*." On this understanding, a judge, according to him, should not release every thief for whose crime he lacks the testimony of two upright eyewitnesses, as prescribed in *fiqh*. Rather, "Whoever releases and absolves every such accused thief, despite the fact that this person's corruption is well known, saying, 'I will not hold him except on the basis of two upright witnesses,' violates '*sharīʿah*-based discretion' (*siyāsah sharʿīyah*)."[221] In other words, in the interest of protecting the integrity of *sharīʿah* as the sole guarantor of justice, extra-*fiqhī* forms of evidence are re-conceptualized and presented as *sharīʿah*. This is all grounded in Ibn al-Qayyim's argument that God's fundamental aim is justice and that, in the pursuit thereof, any means of establishing a fact more clearly than the jurists' "*sharʿī* (courtroom) evidence" must be accepted, *a fortiori*, as an expression of *sharīʿah*.[222] By casting all forms of evidence that serve justice as *sharīʿah*, including those that are not outlined in scripture or recognized by juristic *fiqh*, Ibn al-Qayyim undermines the role and legitimacy of extra-*sharʿī* rules, *qua* extra-*sharʿī* rules, since all rules are now essentially *sharʿī*. This is the point of his famous statement in *al-Ṭuruq al-Ḥukmīyah*: "Whenever the indicants of justice appear and uncover their face, by whatever means this occurs, there is the law and religion of God" (*sharʿ Allāh wa dīnuh*). The clear implication here is that there is no need to resort to anything outside *sharʿ Allāh wa dīnuh*.[223] In this way, Ibn al-Qayyim expands the frontiers of *sharīʿah* to the point of leaving no room, and no need, for extra- or non-*sharʿī* rules.

Yet, despite his clear misgivings about extra-*sharʿī* rules, Ibn al-Qayyim's juristic maximalism does not entirely negate the technical distinction between *siyāsah* and *sharīʿah*, between what is strictly *sharʿī* and what is not. Citing an earlier debate between his fellow Ḥanbalī Ibn ʿAqīl and an unnamed Shāfiʿī jurist who claimed, "There is no *siyāsah* that is not consistent with the *sharʿ*," Ibn al-Qayyim sides with Ibn ʿAqīl:

> Discretionary measures (*siyāsah*) are acts that render the people closer to wholesomeness and farther removed from vice, even if the Prophet, God's peace and salutations be upon him, did not institute this action and even if no revelation came down prescribing it. So, if you mean by "consistent with the *sharʿ*" that it does not violate the *sharʿ*, this is sound. But if you mean that there is no discretionary policy except in accordance with what the *sharʿ* actually prescribes (*mā naṭaqa bihi al-sharʿ*), this is wrong and amounts to an indictment of the Companions.[224]

Again, notwithstanding his clear preference for an expansive understanding of *sharīʿah*, the distinction between the actual *sharʿ* and what is simply consistent with it remains both clear and important for Ibn al-Qayyim. And, of course, non-*sharʿī*, differentiated deliberations will contribute handsomely to what constitutes "consistent with the *sharʿ*."

In fact, Ibn al-Qayyim's concern with maintaining the discretionary efficacy of *siyāsah* as a *sharʿī* enterprise, while also trying to preserve the primacy, autonomy, and integrity of *sharīʿah* as God's law, may have prompted him to express himself in ways that were not always consistent. This possibility seems to have informed the view of Khalid Masud, who concludes, on the one hand, that, despite his clear commitment to an expansive understanding of *sharīʿah*, "Ibn Qayyim was in favor of Ibn ʿAqīl's idea of *siyāsa* being independent of *sharīʿa*."[225] On the other hand, Masud writes, "Agreeing with Ibn Taymiyya, Ibn Qayyim maintained that just *siyāsa* completed the *sharīʿa*, rather, it was indeed *sharīʿa*. It was only a difference in terminology."[226] Again, the ambiguity (if not contradiction) here is easily traceable to Ibn al-Qayyim. In fact, elsewhere, he stresses the importance of grounding every ruling presented as "God's ruling," that is, *sharīʿah*, in an actual revelatory text (or its analogical extension), clearly implying, again, that *siyāsah* is merely consistent with *sharīʿah*, not substantively identical with it.[227] And yet, he wants to be able to hold and punish thieves in the absence of the required number of witnesses and for this to enjoy the full force of the *sharʿ*—for it to be taken as the application of *sharīʿah*. I suspect that Ibn al-Qayyim, unlike some modern proponents of including *siyāsah* as part of *sharīʿah*, probably recognized that his approach was a doubled-edged sword with significant boomerang potential. On the one hand, his ostensible inclusion of *siyāsah* in *sharīʿah* would neither eliminate discretionary measures altogether nor domesticate the state's or ruler's right to promulgate them. On the other hand, not only would including *siyāsah* in *sharīʿah* enhance the state's discretionary authority, but it would also confer an ominous degree of *sharʿī* insulation and legitimacy upon its discretionary acts. And yet, there could ultimately be no dispensing with *siyāsah* itself. Damned if you do, damned if you don't, which may explain Ibn al-Qayyim's attempt to both do *and* don't.

At any rate, notwithstanding his clear concern with preserving the primacy of *sharīʿah* relative to other modes of adjudication, there are discernible limits to Ibn al-Qayyim's *sharīʿah*-maximalism. Even where non-*sharʿī* modes of assessment are only tacitly acknowledged, or perhaps not acknowledged at all, they remain operative. Indeed, Ibn al-Qayyim himself acknowledges the need to rely on non-*sharʿī* modes of deliberation when he insists on the necessity of "*fahm al-wāqiʿ wa fiqhuh*"[228] or "*fiqh fī nafs al-wāqiʿ wa aḥwāl al-nās*,"[229] that is, a proper assessment of *factual* reality on the ground, as a prerequisite for reaching proper *sharʿī* conclusions. Clearly, such factual assessments rely by necessity on differentiated, non-*sharʿī*, *ʿaqlī* energies.

Ibn Taymīyah

As for Ibn Taymīyah, he considered the distinction between the *sharʿī* and the non-*sharʿī*, or *ʿaqlī*, as articulated by jurists writing in the tradition of speculative jurisprudence, to be dangerously overdrawn.[230] To begin with, *sharīʿah*, in his view, includes more than *fiqh*.[231] In addition to commands, prohibitions, and licenses, it comprises divine disclosures regarding socio-historical reality, nature, metaphysics, and, especially, theology and related doctrinal fundamentals.[232] Any field in which revelation imparts knowledge or in which it commands Muslims to acquire knowledge is, according to Ibn Taymīyah, *sharʿī*, at least to that extent.[233] On this understanding, he would count as *sharʿī* much of what the speculative theoreticians placed in the explicitly non-*sharʿī* realm of the "*ʿaqlī*." And in so doing he would draw the circumference of the latter—to the extent that he recognized it as separate from the former—much more narrowly than they would. This becomes easier to appreciate once we recognize that Ibn Taymīyah saw revelation itself as imparting, in addition to concrete practical-cum-moral guidance, "epistemic guidance" in the form of priming, prompting, tutoring, reinforcing, and directing primordial human reason to a proper appreciation of revelatory Truth.[234]

According to him, reason, as a primordial human faculty, carries what Jon Hoover insightfully refers to as the "foundational rules of thought":[235] like things are alike, things fall from up to down, a thing cannot simultaneously exist and not exist, the existence of a building implies the existence of a builder, etc. The encounter between revelation and primordial human reason, however, is ultimately dialectical: revelation prompts, directs, reinforces, and tutors reason; reason, thus primed and tutored, properly apprehends revelation and thereby increases its own appetite and appreciation for it. In this capacity, while the two remain ontologically distinct, the role of *ʿaql* in determining the substance of the *sharʿ* may be so inextricable that the two cannot always be meaningfully disaggregated.[236] By analogy, while the two elements obviously remain ontologically distinct, in their constitution as water, oxygen cannot be separated from hydrogen.

While insisting that reason does not independently establish *sharīʿah*, Ibn Taymīyah is critical of those who limit the latter's authority merely to the "acceptance of the reports of the truthful reporter" (*taṣdīq khabar al-ṣādiq*), that is, an acceptance on faith, with "faith" functioning as a faculty separate from reason.[237] For him, reason, that is, primordial *ʿaql*, is critical to processing and confirming revelation's Truth. And he considers reason's deployment in this capacity to be functionally *sharʿī*, that is, constitutive of *sharʿī* knowledge, a fact he captures in such phrases as "*ʿaqlī al-shāriʿ*" (Lawgiver's reasoning) or "*ʿaqlīyāt al-sharʿīyāt*" (legally/scripturally embedded reason).[238] In other words, all knowledge that results from this dialectic between scripturally tutored primordial reason and scripture is "*ʿilm sharʿī*," which is ultimately sublated into the *sharʿ*.[239] Clearly, if *sharīʿah* goes beyond *fiqh* to such topics as theology, exegesis, the lessons of morally wayward communities, and the like, *sharīʿah*'s jurisdictional boundaries must extend well beyond juristic law's *ḥukm sharʿī*. Just as clearly, "*sharʿī*" itself, as the adjectival extension of *sharīʿah*, cannot be as circumscribed or as differentiated from "*ʿaqlī*" as I and the pre-modern jurists catalogued above suggest.

There is, however, a tactical element to Ibn Taymīyah's approach, a full appreciation of which significantly tempers this conclusion. His basic aim in expanding the boundaries of "*sharīʿah*" and challenging the *sharʿī*/*ʿaqlī* divide is to bring *theology* more fully under the auspices of *sharʿī* deliberations, where it becomes the product of scripturally primed and tutored primordial reason engaging with scripture, rather than scripture being processed through the ostensibly autonomous, scripturally untethered reason of the speculative theologians.[240] Ibn Taymīyah makes a critical distinction in this regard between reason as the primordial human faculty (*gharīzat al-ʿaql*) and the various "systems of reason"—*ʿilm al-kalām*, *falsafah*, etc.—that might be erected based on the primordial faculty and then put forth as simply "reason," with the implication that such systems are as sound and authoritative as that upon which they are built.[241] This is the door that he fears being flung open to speculative theologians (*mutakallimīn*), philosophers, Sufis, and the like, empowering them to place other modes of knowing or systems of reason over scripturally tutored primordial reason as the primary instrument for discerning revelatory intent.[242] For Ibn Taymīyah, processing scripture through what he would describe as "non-*shar'ī*" systems of reason threatens to corrupt, subordinate, and undermine scripture by limiting its meanings to what these epistemologies might allow or dictate. He insists in this context that God's existence, for example, can be known through the human *fiṭrah*, or primordial reason's "foundational rules of thought," according to which rational creatures naturally discern from their own existence the existence of a Creator. The Rationalist proof, by contrast, built on the cosmological argument involving accidents and their contingency, renders any number of divine attributes mentioned in scripture "problematic."[243] This is what Ibn Taymīyah sees as being at stake in allowing for an entirely non-*shar'ī* regime of reason.

Again, Ibn Taymīyah is most insistent upon an expansive understanding of "*shar'ī*" (as the adjective for his expansive notion of *sharī'ah/shar'*) within a *theological* context. But even here there are concessions. For example, he notes that there are theologically relevant things that reason can know independent of revelation, such as the fact that every existing thing requires a producer.[244] And he famously distinguishes God's "*irādah kawnīyah*," or what God wills in the act of creation as a matter of fact, from God's "*irādah shar'īyah*," or what God wills or wants from humans as a matter of concrete preference. In this context, the idea that the *shar'ī*, as represented in God's *irādah shar'īyah*, is unbounded and coterminous with God's *irādah kawnīyah* would imply that what God wants to exist ontologically is indistinguishable from what God wants to exist *shar'an*. And this would lead to the kind of antinomianism that Ibn Taymīyah spent much of his career fighting against, especially among some Sufis, as it would imply that whatever we do and however we do it is what God wants, since both would be equally "God's will."[245] Clearly, on this understanding, God's *shar'ī* will, in the form of God's concrete *shar'ī* commands, must be limited relative to God's creative will in relation to everything that exists, including human acts.[246]

Thus, when Ibn Taymīyah turns to more strictly legal discussions, his recognition of *sharī'ah*'s boundaries becomes more manifest. Here "*shar'ī*" is the adjectival extension not of *sharī'ah* in his expanded sense but of the *ḥukm shar'ī* as the basic unit of *fiqh*. He acknowledges that some things are *'aqlī* (as distinct from *shar'ī*) and can be known only by reason (*tu'lam bi al-'aql faqaṭ*), such as medicine (*al-ṭibb*), arithmetic (*al-ḥisāb*), and the crafts and industries (*al-ṣinā'āt*).[247] In fact, he speaks of entire *'aqlī* disciplines and professions whose concrete substance falls outside the horizontal boundaries of God's *shar'ī* address:

> Those rational sciences that fall outside the construct of the *shar'ī* include those regarding which the Lawgiver issued no command or regarding whose substance the Lawgiver gave no indication (*lam yadulla 'alayh*), all of which follow

> the example of the crafts and industries (*al-ṣināʿāt*) such as farming (*filāḥah*), construction (*al-bināyah*) and textiles (*al-nisājah*).[248]

Elsewhere, he writes even more explicitly of *ʿaql* as a source of knowledge that is distinct from and independent of the *sharʿ*:

> As for those issues that are known by *ʿaql* independently, these include natural issues, such as the fact that a particular medicine will cure a particular disease. For such things are known by experience and analogy or by following doctors who know these things by experience or analogy. The same applies to such things as mathematics, geometry, etc. These are all among the things that are known by *ʿaql*.[249]

And yet, Ibn Taymīyah is explicit in his recognition that the functional integrity of *sharīʿah* as an applied system of socio-political ordering depends in part on the development of these and related non-*sharʿī*, differentiated disciplines. In fact, he insists, that where the Community is found lacking people to take up such disciplines and industries as farming, construction, textiles, and the like—precisely those endeavors he identified as falling "outside the construct of the *sharʿ*"—the Imām is to order persons to develop them.[250] Clearly, in a non-theological context, Ibn Taymīyah is more comfortable seeing the *sharʿī* as bounded, with the *ʿaqlī* as a differentiated, substantively autonomous realm. Here he differs more in degree than in kind from the speculative theoreticians surveyed above. In fact, in this more identifiably legal context, Ibn Taymīyah rejoins his Ḥanbalī predecessors Abū Yaʿlā and Ibn ʿAqīl, who recognized the *ʿaqlī* and the *sharʿī* (or *fiqhī*) as circumscribed and thus differentiated constructs. Later Ḥanbalīs, such as al-Ṭūfī (d. 716/1316) and Ibn al-Laḥḥām (d. 803/1401), continued to recognize this basic *sharʿī*/non-*sharʿī* divide.[251] In fact, Ibn al-Laḥḥām states with a casualness bespeaking general consensus within the school, "Juristic law has limits" (*al-fiqh lahu ḥudūd*).[252] None of this changes the fact that Ibn Taymīyah remains committed to a certain "*sharīʿah*-maximalism" in both theological and legal terms.[253] But as we have just seen, this commitment does not entirely negate, certainly not in a legal context, his recognition of a differentiated, non-*sharʿī* realm, in either the vertical or the horizontal sense.

As for the concept of the Islamic Secular per se, Ibn Taymīyah would clearly resent its application to the subject of theology. He would oppose the notion of an entirely differentiated, autonomous, non-*sharʿī ʿaql* as the basis of theological investigation. In *fiqh*, however—or perhaps, I should say, in the broader realm of Islamic law[254]—he clearly recognizes sciences, disciplines, and vocations that are not grounded in the revelatory sources but are integral to the proper instantiation of Islam in practice. Ultimately, Ibn Taymīyah's theological concerns and sensibilities do not pose a major problem for the Islamic Secular, as the latter's primary focus is not theology, and it is not called upon to do theological work. I would therefore simply cede to Ibn Taymīyah his *sharīʿah*-maximalism regarding theology, where he strives to shrink the arena of non-*sharʿī* reason—even if many jurists writing in the tradition of speculative jurisprudence would not accept such a concession.

Those jurists would also likely disagree with Ibn Taymīyah regarding the overall scope of what I have termed the Islamic Secular. Even though he ultimately acknowledges a differentiated, non-*sharʿī*, *ʿaqlī* realm, Ibn Taymīyah would want to draw its circumference as narrowly as possible, even in a non-theological context. This is evident in his bitter complaint (shared by Ibn al-Qayyim) against those who permit themselves "to go outside the *sharīʿah* of God and God's Messenger and disobey them, on the assumption that *sharīʿah* falls short of satisfying their best interests, an assumption based on ignorance, or ignorance joined by undisciplined passion, or just plain old undisciplined passion alone."[255] This statement, however, does not affect the basic integrity of the Islamic Secular. For, as we have seen, even Ibn Taymīyah recognizes that the religious law cannot dictate the full substance of the various "crafts and industries," including the most efficient way to farm, produce the most stylish belletristic work, or maximize the efficiency of an economic policy. Moreover, no matter where the boundaries of the Islamic Secular are ultimately set, they come at no cost to the integrity of the construct itself. In fact, negotiating the question of where these lines belong is precisely where the discourse on the Islamic Secular belongs. For, such discussion is likely to ensure that the construct does not grow static, overly authoritarian, or dogmatic, lessening the risk of its fossilizing and leading to the functional equivalent of Weber's "iron cage."

My final response to the challenge of Ibn Taymīyah (and Ibn al-Qayyim) is simply to offer the following: To the extent that their views are deemed incompatible with the concept of the Islamic Secular, they may simply be placed among the counterfactuals that fall between the two ends of the Kuhnian horseshoe (discussed in the Introduction) and threaten to implode my paradigm. The question then becomes whether the views of these two scholars (and those who agree with them) are damning enough to compel the search for a new theory that boasts fewer or less threatening counterfactuals than the Islamic Secular. The same applies to the challenges posed by those post-Rāzīan Ḥanafīs who continue to show little interest in formal definitions of *fiqh* or in a *sharʿī*/non-*sharʿī* divide. In the end, at any rate, we should remind ourselves that unanimous consensus (*ijmāʿ*) has never been a criterion for a juristic theory to be considered valid or authentically Islamic.

In closing and in preparation for the next chapter, I would like to reiterate and state more explicitly three points that have thus far been only casually stated or tacitly implied. First, to the extent that any of the jurists I have profiled recognize limits to the *sharʿī* as a category, these limits are *self-imposed* and emerge out of the jurists' own spontaneous, good-faith engagement with the sources and tradition of Islamic juristic law. As such, the differentiated realm does *not* emerge as a foreign construct imposed or even suggested from without. Second, given the self-imposed nature of these limits, Muslim jurists, with the possible qualified exception of Ibn al-Qayyim and Ibn Taymīyah, should not be seen as assuming any rivalry, let alone contradiction or hostility, between the *sharʿī* and the non-*sharʿī*, or differentiated, realms. On the contrary, the relationship between the two is assumed to be benign, if not complementary and synergistic. Finally, none of the jurists who recognize the differentiated, non-*sharʿī*, *ʿaqlī* realm see it as "secular" in the modern Western sense of falling outside the adjudicative gaze of the God of Islam and thus as constituting something "non-religious." Indeed, none of them go anywhere near the notion of proceeding "*as if* God did not exist."

3
The Islamic Secular

Between Divine Sovereignty and Divine Communication

In basic agreement with Durkheim, the contemporary West divides the world into two mutually distinct domains: secular and religious. The secular—macro and micro—is the realm where God's concrete address, divine presence, and adjudicative gaze are simply of no consequence. To do something secular, therefore, is to do something non-religious, or unrelated to God—"*as if* God did not exist." Shahab Ahmed eloquently lays out the implications this understanding has traditionally had for the study of Islam: "Is *x* religion and therefore Islam, or is *x* secular and therefore not-Islam? Is *x* sacred and therefore Islam, or is *x* profane and therefore not-Islam?"[1] We saw in Chapter 1, however, that religion, that is, *dīn*, can be thought of as a complex construct consisting of both religion-as-concrete-doctrine-and-practice and religion-as-orientation, these two facets corresponding, *mutatis mutandis*, to the *shar'ī* and non-*shar'ī* dimensions of Islam, respectively. This is the perspective of the Islamic Secular. At bottom, Islam's secular recognizes a distinction between the scope of God's activity as Sovereign-Creator and the scope of God's activity as Communicator of normative directives. On this distinction, *pace* Durkheim and the West, the whole of human life remains a single domain entirely blanketed by the adjudicative gaze and divine presence of the "Lord of the Worlds" (*rabb al-'ālamīn*). But this single reality is differentiated, in that God's *shar'ī* address, the repository of God's concrete, normative dictates, does not cover or determine it all.

On this understanding, there are areas of life in which Muslims cannot rely directly on revelation or its derivatives but must proceed on the basis of non-revelatory, secular knowledge. This knowledge is secular, however, only in the sense that it is non-*shar'ī*, that is, not deduced concretely from God's *shar'ī* address, as a result of which the latter does not, *ceteris paribus*, exercise any authority in determining its substance. But this secularity does not place this knowledge or its pursuit outside the notice of the divine gaze or the influence of the divine presence. Rather, it can be consciously pursued through the religious "orientation," or "obeisance," outlined in Chapter 1.[2] On this understanding, to do something 'secular' is not necessarily to do something non-religious or unrelated to God. Nor is religion relevant to some aspects of life but not to others. These are among the fundamental insights and assumptions of the Islamic Secular.

The Islamic Secular. Sherman A. Jackson, Oxford University Press. © Oxford University Press 2024.
DOI: 10.1093/oso/9780197661789.003.0004

But the contrast does not end with the Western secular. It extends to what Shahab Ahmed critically referred to as "the totalizing 'legal supremacist' conceptualization of Islam as *law*," both within and beyond the Western academy. By totalizing legal supremacy, Ahmed was referring to the categorical primacy and authority of the jurists and their juristic discourse. As we saw in Chapter 2, however, the Islamic juristic tradition exibits a clear recognition of the limits of *sharīʿah*, which even "*sharīʿah*-maximalists," such as Ibn al-Qayyim and Ibn Taymīyah, ultimately acknowledge, albeit often indirectly and with significant qualification. This is not to deny the existence of popular or even learned versions of the problem to which Ahmed referred. But if the general consensus of the Islamic juristic tradition is that there are Islamically useful, even necessary, forms of knowledge and human endeavor whose substance is not derived from God's direct communiqué, then clearly Muslim jurists, *qua* jurists, cannot rightfully exercise a monopoly over the substance of Islam or the Islamic. Even on the assumption that they may rightfully pronounce on the 'moral' status of all ideas and acts, in the sense that all of these come under one of the Five Juristic Statuses, this should not be understood to mean that these Statuses are the only Islamically relevant metric, or that jurists have the authority to determine or pronounce on the substance of non-*sharʿī* acts or ideas. Jurists cannot judge the mathematical validity of a mathematical equation, any more than their authority to pronounce on the permissibility of minting copper coins authorizes them, *qua* jurists, to decide whether or not this action is economically sound.

Following this lead, the Islamic Secular entails a more explicit recognition not only of the limits of the jurists' authority but also of the potentially religious-cum-Islamic value of the thoughts and actions of non-jurists. Even if *sharīʿah* is not the source of mathematics or economics and even if the jurists (qua-jurists) have no say in determining such subjects' concrete substance, this does not negate the religious value, utility, or positive status that Islam as a lived reality may attach to these non-*sharʿī* enterprises. On this understanding, not only is a 'secular' act not necessarily non-religious (let alone non-Islamic), but to do something religious or Islamic is also not necessarily to do something *sharʿī*, in pursuit of fulfilling some concrete dictate of *sharīʿah*.

My main objective in the present chapter will be to clarify the concept of the Islamic Secular by applying it to Islam in history, as both an analytical and a generative tool, with a particular focus on Islamic law. Analytically, this will entail a review of a highly influential and enduring theme that has informed the study of Islamic legal history virtually from its beginning: the cumulatively dystopian narrative of inexorable decline and rupture, culminating in Islamic law's displacement and the triumph of the modern Western secular. This narrative is partly held in place by interpretive presuppositions that shape the reading of Islamic legal and historical sources, key among these being the notion of a rigid, idealized *sharīʿah* vested with the authority to regulate "everything." My challenge to this dystopian narrative is not directed at its claim of *sharīʿah*'s decline or marginalization. It seeks, rather, to highlight the wages of failing to recognize the non-*sharʿī*, 'secular' dimensions of Islam-cum-*sharīʿah*, which breeds, on the one hand, a tendency to impute all decline and deviation to inadequacies in *sharīʿah* (or its interpreters) and, on the other hand, the notion that all purported invocations of something other than *sharīʿah* are necessarily manifestations of decline. The Islamic Secular points to a different set of interpretive possibilities. It uncovers, on the one hand, forms, dimensions, and complements of law that are Islamic but not *sharʿī*, and underscores, on the other hand, the fact that lapses in non-*sharʿī* production can exert no less an impact on Islam-cum-*sharīʿah* than do lapses in *sharʿī* production. In other words, not all decline (or success) with regard to Islam-cum-*sharīʿah* can be imputed to *sharīʿah* or its interpreters. And not every instance of going beyond *sharīʿah* is necessarily an indication of dereliction or decline.

As for the generative side of my thesis and its application, my goal is to examine what and how a conscious awareness of the Islamic Secular can contribute to the way modern Muslims negotiate reality—politically, culturally, interpersonally—with particular attention to the question of Islam's *nomos* or plausibility structure. The deeply internalized notion of an unbounded *sharīʿah* tends to generate a zero-sum understanding of the relationship between Islam-cum-*sharīʿah* and the secular. Both Islamists and secularists in the Muslim world tend to see Islam-cum-*sharīʿah* as contradicting and normatively marginalizing if not ideally preempting the secular. And both see the secular as a predatory, disjunctive force that is assumed to have a negative impact on Islam. Most Muslims, meanwhile, who formally identify neither as Islamists nor as secularists, are left bumbling about with a hodge-podge of attitudes and understandings, none of which enables them to assign the *sharʿī or* the non-*sharʿī* (*qua* non-*sharʿī*) its proper place. Part of my aim in the generative side of my analysis will be to look at what a conscious awareness of the Islamic Secular might contribute to a reassessment, renegotiation, and clearer understanding of issues now thought of as secular and thus as antagonistic toward, if not mutually exclusive of, religion.

As a preliminary to these topics, however, I must confront the challenge of nomenclature, specifically how the phrase "Islamic Secular" would read in Arabic. This is important for two reasons. First, for many readers, part of the criterion for measuring the authenticity of the Islamic Secular as an Islamic concept will be the relative ease with which it can be expressed in Arabic. Second, and related to the first point, all the standard, would-be Arabic candidates for translating the term are problematic, many producing what the average Arabic speaker would deem an oxymoron. This leaves a cloud of suspicion laced with confusion hovering about the Islamic Secular, potentially casting it as an alien concept that has been clumsily and unjustifiably grafted onto Islam.

Islām Mā Warā' al-Ḥukm al-Shar'ī

My choice for an Arabic translation of the "Islamic Secular" is *islām mā warā' al-ḥukm al-shar'ī* or, alternatively, *al-islām khārij al-ḥukm al-shar'ī*. These admittedly wordy renderings clearly diverge from what one would expect, as they do not include any of the most common words for "secular" in Arabic. But there is a reason for this omission, which I shall presently explain.

In the fall of 2018, I was invited to deliver the keynote lecture at a graduate student conference at the University of California, Santa Barbara, which was partly sponsored by some of my own students from the University of Southern California. I spoke on the Islamic Secular, and, following the conference, an Arab colleague published an article in an online Arabic journal in which he critically summarized my thesis. He expressed frustration with the term "Islamic Secular," particularly as he pondered how to translate it to an Arabic-speaking audience. He noted that to use "*islāmī* and *'almānī*'" in the same phrase would cause mass confusion.[3] For to a contemporary Arab, "People are either Islamic *or* secular, and an individual cannot be both at the same time." Indeed, "The Islamist (*al-islamī*) is a person affiliated with one of the Islamic movements, while the secularist (*al-'almānī*) detests nothing and no one more than s/he does the followers of the Islamic movements." For this reason, he argued, the phrase "secular Islamist" (*al-islāmī al-'almānī*), like "Islamic secularist" (*al-'almānī al-islāmī*), would be of a piece with "such fantasies as phoenixes and truly loyal friends."[4]

Of course, much of the problem he described stems from the fact that the pre-modern Arabo-Islamic lexicon never produced its own word for "secular," certainly not as commonly understood today. The Arabic word most commonly used today, *'almānī*, is a translation from Western languages, primarily English. By the time "secular" came to Muslim lands, it had already absorbed many of the ideological assumptions, aspirations, and polarities spawned by the European Enlightenment. To this we may add the colonial and post-colonial interpretive prism through which many modern Muslims, Islamist and secular alike, received the concept. Especially among those who saw Islam as the root of the contemporary Arab predicament, "secular," that is, *'almānī*, lost its neutral connotation as simply "non-religious" and tended toward something more aggressively "anti-religious." The same attitude would be found, ironically, among Islamists, who saw Islam as "the solution" in complete and uncompromising opposition to the secular.

Meanwhile, there was a Western contribution to the rise and spread of the adjective "Islamic" (*islāmī*), certainly as it functioned in the global discourse on Islam. As the formerly warring factions in Europe coalesced into "the West," "Islamic" became one of the West's reflexive counter-categories, forming a juxtaposition that carried not only religious but also geopolitical resonances, as captured by the ominously confrontational phrase, "Islam and the West." By comparison, "Judaism and the West," or even "Buddhism and the West," never got off the ground. Yet, as far-reaching as these geopolitical associations were, they could not obliterate the religious denotation of "Islamic." In the end, *islāmī*, as the Arabic translation of "Islamic," would come to be associated with a number of vaguely distinct yet overlapping meanings: an adversarial relationship with the West; the commitment to Islam as opposed to secularism; the promotion of Islam in its transcendent, pristine purity, away from all the dents and scratches inflicted by modernity.

Given this ambiguity, using either *al-islāmī* or *al-ʿalmānī* to translate "the Islamic Secular" has proved problematic. Regarding *al-islāmī*, as in my colleague's "*al-islāmī al-ʿalmānī*," if we take it to mean "Islamic as opposed to Western"—as an adjectival noun modified by the adjective "secular" (*al-ʿalmānī*)—we end up with some secularized version of Muslim opposition to the West. But this is neither the thrust nor ethos of the Islamic Secular. If we take *islāmī* to mean "Islamic as opposed to secularist," the addition of *al-ʿalmānī* as its adjective results in internal contradiction. The same would apply to using *al-islāmī* to refer to some form of pristine, purified Islam.

Of course, we could go with *al-ʿalmānī al-islāmī*, which would offer the advantage of more accurately positioning *al-islāmī* as the adjective. But *al-ʿalmānī*, even as an adjectival noun in the first position, also presents problems. First, on the assumption that scientific and technological progress require the marginalization of religion, some Arabs translate "secular" not as *ʿalmānī* (from *ʿālam*, relating to this world as opposed to the Afterlife) but as *ʿilmānī* (from *ʿilm*), meaning "knowledge-based," "science-based." The problem with this is that the "knowledge"/"science" in question is conceived of as both contrasting with and potentially marginalizing "religious" knowledge. This would obviously not capture the meaning of the Islamic Secular, as the latter assumes no such antipathy.[5] Second, the more common word for "secular," that is, *al-ʿalmānī*, has more than one meaning. Hans Wehr gives as its definition, "layman (in distinction of the clergy)."[6] This would be technically more promising, save for the presumption that pronouncements by laymen are normally secular and require qualification to render them religious or Islamic. Third, if, as my Arab colleague suggested, we take *al-ʿalmānī* to mean the opposite of *al-islāmī*, we confront two additional obstacles: first, the phrase becomes self-contradictory, that is, "the Islamic opposite of Islam"; second, if we take *al-ʿalmānī* as the opposite of religion, *al-ʿalmāni al-islāmī* simply implies Islam's would-be version of the Western secular, which, again, distorts the Islamic Secular's meaning. Of course, this phrase could also be taken to mean "the Islamic this-worldly." But this would leave no room for distinguishing the *shar'ī* from the non-*shar'ī* aspects of decidedly "this-worldly" activity. Finally, one might consider simply joining the two terms, in either order, by a hyphen, as in "African-American," implying a simple compound of co-equal parts. But for the average English speaker, the hyphen may not do away with the implicit noun–adjective relationship that has proved so problematic thus far. In other words, for most American English-speakers, African-Americans, like Irish-Americans or Arab-Americans, are still Americans.

There is another (though less common) translation of "secular," namely, *dunyawī*. This relative adjective (*nisbah*) was used in classical times to stress this-worldly as opposed to other-worldly interests *without* negating religion or the relevance of an Afterlife.[7] In this sense, it would constitute a rough equivalent of the secular in Islam. But here too there are problems. First, adding *al-islāmī* to *al-dunyawī* (i.e., *al-dunyawī al-islāmī*) would make no sense to a modern Arabic speaker. Second, adding *al-dunyawī* as the adjective to *al-islāmī* (i.e., *al-islāmī al-dunyawī*) would distort the Islamic Secular by rendering it an entirely worldly, non-religious enterprise. Of course, *al-islām al-dunyawī* might make some sense in Arabic, referring to an Islam that is concerned with worldly interests only. But this would be of no use in translating the Islamic Secular, since the latter entails *dīn*, which includes obeisance, *taqwā*, and *qurbah*. Also, *dunyawī*, as a relative adjective, was not really nominalized until modern times, the modern neologism *al-dunyawīyah* (as a noun) connoting the negation of religion and the Afterlife altogether. For this reason, *al-dunyawīyah al-islāmīyah* would convey the wholesale importation of the Western (macro-) secular. In sum, none of the "usual suspects" for conveying "Islamic Secular" in Arabic seem to work.

Despite these problems with modern Arabic words for "secular," however, the Islamic juristic tradition, classical and modern, clearly recognized the differentiated, non-*shar'ī* realm, as we saw in Chapter 2. As differentiation is the core and fulcrum of the micro-secular, this is the basis upon which I build my Arabic rendering for the Islamic Secular: *islām mā warā' al-ḥukm al-shar'ī* or, alternatively, *al-islām khārij al-ḥukm al-shar'ī*. Literally, *islām mā warā'a al-ḥukm al-shar'ī* translates into "Islam of the region beyond the juristic ruling."[8] In contrast to the spatial or ideational sense of *warā'*—"behind" as in "metaphysics," that is, "*mā warā' al-ṭabī'ah* (what lies behind nature)—I use *warā'* in the spatial sense of "beyond" as reflected in the classical reference to Transoxiana, that is, *mā warā' al-nahr* ("the region beyond the Oxus River"). I also use *warā'* in contradistinction to *ba'd*, in order to avoid the kind of temporal connotations that might suggest something along the lines of a post-*sharī'ah* reality, as contemplated by al-Juwayni and studied by Aḥmad Ahmad and Sohaira Siddiqui.[9] Similarly,

I omit the definite article from *islām* and use it in construct (*iḍāfah*) with the nominalizing *mā* and the rest of the phrase, in order to reinforce the notion of a space or region that is Islam but falls beyond the boundaries of the juristic ruling. In other words, *islām mā warā' al-ḥukm al-shar'ī* is an extra-*shar'ī* entity, not a post-*shar'ī* one and not one that is hostile toward *sharī'ah*.

Again, I admit that this rendering is prolix, and for this reason I also offer the more economical *al-islām khārij al-ḥukm al-shar'ī*, which essentially conveys the same meaning. My preference, however, remains with *islām mā warā' al-ḥukm al-shar'ī*, as it seems more effective in conveying the sense of a "realm" or "space" that is beyond the juristic ruling, even as both this realm and the juristic ruling remain equally within the circumference of Islam. In any case, both these more prolix options overcome the problems we saw with *islāmī*, *almānī* (or *'ilmānī*), and *dunyawī*, and both convey their meaning as easily recognizable constituents of the Arabo-Islamic linguistic heritage.

Islamic Law Beyond *Sharī'ah*

In the opening line of his article on *maẓālim*[10] tribunals, Jørgen Nielsen writes: "It hardly needs repeating that the Islamic law, the Sharī'a, virtually from the period of its formulation, had limited effect and application, especially in the commercial, criminal, and administrative fields."[11] This is one of the less charitable versions of what I referred to above as the dystopian narrative of Islamic law. One should not confuse this dystopian narrative with a similar sentiment expressed by pre-modern Muslims themselves, regarding the so-called *fasād al-zamān*, "the depravity of the times," or, more generally "decadence." The latter was more a social critique of a perceived falling away from religiosity, which resulted in moral decline and a failure to uphold Islamic standards, including Islamic law.[12] By contrast, the dystopian narrative of Islamic law relates to the substance of the law itself and implies its inherent deficiency and inability to live up to its own mandate and/or serve legitimate individual and communal interests. On this understanding, Islamic law is seen as requiring or giving way to supplemental and ultimately secular assistance, according to the common Western understanding of "secular" as the opposite of "religious."

The Dystopian Narrative of Islamic Law

This dystopian narrative, in various iterations, has a long pedigree in Western scholarship, going back as far as the nineteenth century and the beginnings of the Western study of Islamic law.[13] While it was never a point of full consensus,[14] we have seen how leading scholars of Islamic law, such as Schacht and Coulson, embraced it through the mid-to-late twentieth century. Other pioneers such as Hamilton Gibb (d. 1971) described a pattern of progressive juristic foundering that finally brought juristic law and theory "crashing to the ground."[15] In his 1997 study of the ninth-/fifteenth-to-tenth-/sixteenth-century Ottoman *sheikh 'l-islam* Ebu's-su'ud (d. 982/1574), Colin Imber echoes another version of the narrative: "Islamic jurisprudence in its traditional sense had a history of about 1000 years, from its obscure beginnings in the late eighth and early ninth centuries until its near-demise in the face of modernism in the late nineteenth."[16] According to Imber, the underlying causes of this dénouement were simple: "*sharīʿa* is in many respects impractical"[17] and its provisions are "unrealistic."[18] In still another version, Wael Hallaq is more specific. He sees the rise and imposition of modernity and the modern state as destroying the foundations of authority upon which Islamic law was built, distorting its epistemological outlook by radically separating the ontological "Is" from the normative and humanly pursued "Ought."[19] This is in addition to certain theological postulates woven into the fabric of classical Islamic jurisprudence, which allegedly marginalized reason and impeded Islamic law's ability to respond to the extra-scriptural or unprecedented.[20] According to Hallaq, prior to the rise of Western modernity, "To say that a rule of law [i.e., *sharīʿah*] prevailed in pre-modern Islamic societies, polities, and civilizations is merely to state the obvious."[21] This comes close to the view of many modern Islamists for whom the historical past stands as a blank canvas onto which to project *sharīʿah*'s full and ideal implementation, which was only disrupted by the incursions of the modern West.[22]

Sharīʿah and "Islamic Law"

In these and other iterations of the dystopian narrative, one notices a lazy ambiguity informing the terms "*sharīʿah*" and "Islamic law." At times they appear to be synonymous; at other times *sharīʿah* is identified with "religious law" while Islamic law implies or seems to function alongside an element commonly identified as "secular," that is, the law of the state or ruler. Occasionally, the religious and secular constitute a cooperative pair;[23] but more often they are depicted as rivals.[24] In fact, there is a nagging sense that the "secular" cannot be "religious," or vice versa, a notion whose Western provenance is obvious. This presumption isolates the putatively secular and religious elements of Islamic law in a manner that predetermines the meaning of Muslims' reliance on either at any given point in time: committed Muslims rely on religious law, while the less committed invoke the secular. In concrete terms, the secular generally implicated here is the broad category known as *siyāsah*, or discretionary powers of the Muslim state or ruler. Given *siyāsah*'s presumably secular character, alongside *sharīʿah*'s presumably religious character, any reliance upon the former raises questions about the integrity, applicability, and efficacy of the latter.[25] In the end, the lazy ambiguity informing common descriptions of *sharīʿah* and Islamic law injects a perduring ambiguity into our interpretations of Islamic legal history, as well as the meaning and validity of the dystopian narrative itself.

In his groundbreaking book, *Islamic Law and Legal System*, Frank Vogel, who was really the first scholar to focus on *siyāsah* as a central constituent of Islamic law, captures the problem surrounding the relationship between *sharīʿah* and *siyāsah* when he observes, "[T]he use of 'sharīʿa' imports constant confusion."[26] For, it is not clear, he writes, "whether (or when) siyāsa should . . . be understood as part of sharīʿa . . . or how 'ulamā' and qāḍīs may legitimately exercise some of the powers of siyāsa themselves, within a venture larger than the fiqh of their books."[27] This lack of clarity has obvious implications for any critical assessment of the dystopian narrative. For, how one measures the degree of Islamic law's decline or displacement will depend on both how secular or religious one understands *siyāsah* to be and how strictly limited to *sharīʿah* one understands Islamic law and the normative practice of Islam to be. If *sharīʿah* as "religious law" is inclusive of *siyāsah*, the mere invocation of the latter cannot be counted as a divergence from *sharīʿah*. Similarly, if "religion" is not limited to *sharīʿah* but may also include *siyāsah*, then going beyond *sharīʿah* to *siyāsah* need not imply a move toward secularization in the modern Western sense.

This is ultimately the argument of an important recent book by Khaled Fahmy, *In Quest of Justice: Islamic Law and Forensic Medicine in Modern Egypt*. Fahmy seeks to resolve the tension noted by Vogel in favor of an expansive understanding of *sharīʿah* that includes *siyāsah* as an integral constituent thereof. His primary focus is the role of forensic medicine in adjudicating legal cases, particularly those involving violent crimes. The basic question he poses is if and how forensic evidence, for example, autopsies, can be reconciled with Islamic law, given *sharīʿah*'s formalistic evidentiary rules, which require eyewitness testimony to substantiate such crimes as murder. Through detailed analysis of documents culled from the Egyptian National Archives, Fahmy shows that, rather than restricting themselves to juristic, that is, *sharʿī* evidence (*bayyinah*), Egyptian courts and authorities routinely availed themselves of forensic and related forms of extra-*sharʿī* proof, or at least extra-*sharʿī* means of producing *bayyinah*. In one case, a village strongman murdered an individual, forced the barber-surgeon to forge a death certificate, had the murdered man hastily buried, and intimidated his family into not going to the police. Given the lack of evidence, the *qāḍī* in the *sharīʿah*-court was forced to drop the case. But, after examining the forensic report and other corroborating testimony, the local administrative body, the Council of Gharbiyat Governorate, was able to convict the murderer.[28]

Fahmy cites numerous cases of this sort. And with each, his broader point is thrown into bolder relief, namely, that reliance upon non-*shar'ī* evidence is not, *pace* the dystopian narrative, a manifestation of decline, deviation, or secularization. While non-*shar'ī* forms of evidence may have no standing in *fiqh*, they are routinely recognized as constituents of *siyāsah*. And, against the view he attributes to scholars such as Hallaq and Asad, Fahmy insists that *siyāsah* is a constituent of *sharī'ah*.[29] Ultimately, in his view, it is only the reading of Islamic legal and historical sources that begins with the understanding that Islamic law is limited to *fiqh* that dooms the cases in question to being interpreted as unwarranted departures from the *sharī'ah* norm. Rather than decline-cum-secularization, Fahmy suggests, "bureaucratization" might be a better description of the resort to non-juristic norms,[30] a bureaucratization that was both accepted by the jurists and reflective of the seriousness with which Muslim states and rulers sought to uphold rather than circumvent, let alone cast aside, *sharī'ah*.[31]

Fahmy's interventions are important and insightful. I find myself at odds, however, with a critical aspect of his argument. At the most basic level, without redefining "secular" and "religious" such that they accommodate, if not entail, each other, arguing that the religious *sharī'ah* includes the secular *siyāsah* seems arbitrary.[32] It is like arguing that the modern religious church, while remaining entirely "religious"—*in the proper, the religious, sense*—can subsume the modern secular state, which remains entirely "secular"—in the sense of proceeding "*as if* God did not exist"—without fundamentally redefining "secular" or "religious." In my view, only by defining "secular" and "religious" along the lines of the Islamic Secular can one accommodate the idea of *siyāsah*, as a secular entity, being subsumed—not devoured, where its secularity dissolves—by Islamic law, as a religious entity. From the perspective of the Islamic Secular, it is not "Islamic law" as *sharī'ah* that subsumes *siyāsah* but "Islamic law" as a broader enterprise that is both religious and 'secular' and both includes and is partly differentiated from *sharī'ah*.[33] As for *sharī'ah* itself, I side with those who limit it to *fiqh*, a point whose implications I lay out further below and again in Chapter 4.[34] For now, let me try to clarify in a bit more detail how this perspective informs my disagreement with Fahmy.

The idea that Islamic law is broader than *fiqh* is profoundly welcome. But the claim that *siyāsah* is therefore part of *sharī'ah* does not necessarily follow. Fahmy is not alone, of course, in making this connection, as we saw with the *sharī'ah*-maximalism of Ibn al-Qayyim and Ibn Taymīyah.[35] In fact, their Ḥanbalī predecessor Ibn al-Jawzī (d. 597/1201) spells out explicitly the problem that many saw with *siyāsah*'s constituting a separate reglementary regime: "One who claims the need for *siyāsah* is claiming that there are deficiencies in *sharī'ah*."[36] This is not Fahmy's complaint, of course, and one need not be a *sharī'ah*-maximalist to question the idea of *siyāsah* falling outside *sharī'ah*. In his ground-breaking study of the formative period of Islamic law, Umar Wymann-Landgraf notes that Mālik's legal doctrine was routinely based on "considered opinion," or *ra'y*, rather than concrete scriptural indicants.[37] In his perceptive article on later Mālikī *fiqh*, Mohammad Fadel is even more explicit: "[A]t least in purely quantitative terms, rules derived from non-revelatory sources make up the vast majority of actual Islamic law."[38] By "legal doctrine" and "Islamic law," Wymann-Landgraf and Fadel could be referring to composite *sharīʿah* rules that break down into *sharʿī* and non-*sharʿī* elements, as discussed in Chapter 2. But the examples they adduce, taken at face value, rarely seem to suggest this. Rather, Wymann-Landgraf and Fadel seem to be pointing to the fact that non-*sharʿī* sources routinely gave rise to distinctly *sharʿī* rules.[39] This challenges the basic assumption of the Islamic Secular—that differentiated, non-*sharʿī* sources give rise *only* to non-*sharʿī* rules or to non-*sharʿī* aspects of *sharʿī* rules. More directly, their findings raise questions about the justification for placing *siyāsah* outside *sharīʿah*. For, if non-*sharʿī* sources can produce *sharʿī* rules, the mere fact that *siyāsah* is predominantly a product of non-*sharʿī* sources cannot be taken as proof that it falls outside *sharīʿah*.

Fadel is clear, however, that, in the post-formative period, "Mālikī works of *uṣūl* (*al-fiqh*) seem to share the fundamental premise of al-Shāfiʿī, namely, that Islamic law in the first instance means rules derived from revelation."[40] This reflects the widely diffused phenomenon we saw in Chapter 2, where jurists from across the schools point to the distinction between what is *sharʿī* and what is non-*sharʿī*, as part of the basic definition of *fiqh*. Meanwhile, the fact that a rule may appear to be impervious to *sharʿī*/non-*sharʿī* disaggregation does not necessarily mean that it is so.[41] Most important, even if we concede that non-*sharʿī* sources were often the basis of *sharīʿah*-rules in the early period described by Wymann-Landgraf, Fadel's depiction suggests that this approach atrophied progressively as *sharīʿah* passed into its post-formative stage and became the ward of *uṣūl al-fiqh*. The Islamic Secular simply assumes this post-formative backdrop, in the context of which non-*sharʿī* sources are presumed to produce or validate only non-*sharʿī* rules or non-*sharʿī* aspects of *sharʿī* rules. *Siyāsah*, I argue, by post-formative times, consists predominantly in non-*sharʿī* rules backed by non-*sharʿī* sources and in this sense falls outside the scope of *sharīʿah* proper. Again, however, "non-*sharʿī*" does not necessarily mean "non-religious" or "secular" in the modern Western sense. Nor does "outside *sharīʿah*" necessarily mean "non-Islamic" or "outside of Islam."

Returning to the perspective of Fahmy, if all law—*fiqh* and *siyāsah*—is *sharīʿah*, one might ask how the primacy of the state versus that of the jurists is negotiated when it comes to speaking authoritatively on *sharīʿah*-issues. What marks the boundary between their respective jurisdictions and competences as *sharīʿah*-authorities? Or is there no boundary? Can the dissent of a ruler or *maẓālim* magistrate on a matter of *sharīʿah* (i.e., *fiqh*) frustrate the consensus (*ijmāʿ*) that might otherwise be reached among the jurists?[42] Conversely, could a jurist discipline merchants, set food-safety standards, or establish zoning regulations, like a *muḥtasib*? And what are we to make of the jurists, as the self-appointed guardians of *sharīʿah*, in their perduring trans-generational suspicion toward the state, its discretionary powers, and the potential threat it poses to *sharīʿah*? Where the state's *siyāsah*-based economic, educational, or administrative policies fail, is *sharīʿah* also to be counted a failure? And would the state's presumably *siyāsah*-based abolishment of *sharīʿah*-courts, its nationalization of *awqāf*, its substantive reforms to penal, commercial, or family law, or its importation of foreign laws, all be considered *sharīʿah*?[43] Does not conflating *siyāsah* with *sharīʿah* confuse juristic authority with political authority, like comparing the executive orders of an American president with the jurisprudence of a US Supreme Court justice? Most important, has Fahmy adequately assessed the full price of including *siyāsah* as a part of *sharīʿah* and then handing this powerful composite over to the state?

Fahmy might respond that a regime of state-owned *siyāsah* that is separate from *sharīʿah* might pose equal dangers. In fact, placing *siyāsah* outside *sharīʿah* places it outside *uṣūl al-fiqh*'s criteria for assessing the substantive quality and legitimacy of views pretending to religious authority, leaving no formal grounds on which to evaluate the content of the state's discretionary rules or policies. We might recall, however, that part of Fahmy's argument is that *sharīʿah* itself, as the basis of state-authority, is not limited to "the parameters of *uṣūl al-fiqh* and the interpretive authority of the jurist." In fact, on his understanding, it is precisely the role of *siyāsah* to provide the state with a way around the constraints of *uṣūl al-fiqh* and *fiqh*, in the name of *sharīʿah* (as we saw in the case of the village strongman). From his perspective, in other words, *uṣūl al-fiqh* neither fully circumscribes *sharīʿah* or *siyāsah*. But if *uṣūl al-fiqh* does not exhaust the number and parameters of the sources of *sharīʿah*, this would seem to result in a *sharīʿah* that is both unbounded and undifferentiated—as unbounded and undifferentiated as are its sources. And here is where Fahmy and I part.

Whereas *uṣūl al-fiqh* sets concrete, objective parameters and metrics for assessing the validity of claims to *fiqh*/*sharīʿah*, perhaps *the* ultimate unresolved problem in Islamic legal history is the difficulty of developing comparable standards for rule-making outside the machinery of *sharīʿah*—building codes, speed limits, foreign policy, and the like. In this context, any attempt at a normative definition of Islamic law in the inclusive sense implied by Fahmy entails a necessary trade-off: if *siyāsah* is to be considered part of *sharīʿah*, the state must be credited not simply with political or discretionary authority but also with juristic, that is, *sharʿī*, authority; if *siyāsah* is not a part of *sharīʿah*, the substance of the state's policies can neither be assessed nor disciplined through the formal machinery of *sharīʿah*'s *uṣūl al-fiqh*. By contrast, the Islamic Secular confronts this trade-off head-on. It chooses to forfeit the advantages of including *siyāsah* in *sharīʿah* and accepts the cost of foregoing the full services of *sharīʿah*'s evaluative machinery in the form of *uṣūl al-fiqh*. It seeks to mitigate the consequences of this choice, however, by disaggregating state policy into *sharʿī* and non-*sharʿī* elements and then restricting binding, unassailable authority exclusively to what is *sharʿī* therein.[44] While this limits the contributions of *uṣūl al-fiqh* as an authoritative metric for assessing the substance-cum-legitimacy of state policy, it also frees the latter from the undue strictures of such a criterion. At the same time, it denies the state the ability to clothe its every discretionary policy with unassailable *sharʿī* authority.

Again, *pace* Fahmy (and others[45]) for whom "Islamic law" equals *sharīʿah*, and *sharīʿah* equals *fiqh* plus *siyāsah*, I include *siyāsah* in "Islamic law" but exclude it from *sharīʿah*. *Siyāsah* functions as a supplemental carrier of legal authority, in that it legitimizes the imposition of punitive and or corrective sanctions. In this capacity, it must be considered law. Meanwhile, to the degree that it is promulgated in a spirit of obeisance in pursuit of legitimate Islamic interests, it must (or can) be considered *Islamic*. These considerations are what prompted me to tax my reader's patience with the occasionally awkward use of "juristic" to refer to *sharʿī*—that is, that which is derived by the jurists from the sources of *sharīʿah*. This was in anticipation of having to accommodate other forms of Islamic rulemaking, namely *siyāsah* and its cognates, *maẓālim* and *ḥisbah*, large aspects of which are not derived by the jurists from the sources yet can be described only as both *law* and as *Islamic*, hence "Islamic law."

Many who object to my exclusion of *siyāsah* from *sharīʿah* and my reduction of *sharīʿah* to *fiqh* may do so on grounds similar to those articulated by Shahab Ahmed in his critique of the monopoly of the *fuqahāʾ*-jurisprudents. For these scholars, limiting *sharīʿah* to *fiqh* assures the primacy of juristic authority and risks placing it beyond critique. This in turn empowers the jurists to silence others based on an authority that only they as jurists are assumed to enjoy. I am alive to these concerns. But I would remind my reader of a point that I have made now several times, namely, that Islam and *sharīʿah* are not co-extensive: numerous issues that are clearly part of Islam (and even *sharīʿah*) lie outside the competence of the jurists. Those who oppose my limiting *sharīʿah* to *fiqh* may feel inclined do so because they, not I, effectively equate Islam with *sharīʿah*, which leaves no space for maneuver outside of *sharīʿah*-as-*fiqh*. Again, however, as I have argued, by now ad nauseam, the Islamic Secular recognizes an expansive realm beyond *fiqh*/*sharīʿah* that remains firmly within Islam. As such, limiting *sharīʿah* to *fiqh* does not translate into a monopoly of the jurists over Islam.

At the same time, the boundaries I impose on *fiqh*/*sharīʿah* should not be seen as an attempt to marginalize the role or importance of the *fuqahāʾ* and their discourse. In his effort to underscore the importance of the empirical side of Islamic law, Fahmy privileges what he refers to as "legal practice" over "legal thought,"[46] emphasizing the law as it is "practiced and applied, not only imagined and thought."[47] While it goes without saying (though not without caution[48]) that archival materials, which reflect the acts of executives rather than the thoughts of interpreters, better reflect the situation on the ground, the *meaning* of what happened in any particular instance can only be arrived at via comparison with some normative benchmark. Whether or not the state is abusing its power and encroaching upon the authority of *sharīʿah* or the jurists can only be determined once the theoretical boundaries of juristic and state authority have been established. And that can be done only on the basis of juristic theory (*uṣūl al-fiqh*) and its putative product, juristic law (*fiqh*), unless we assume these boundaries to be unilaterally imposed from without by the Muslim state, in which case the whole of Islamic legal history becomes an evolving *modus vivendi*. But this is precisely the dystopian narrative that Fahmy rejects. And it seems to me that it is not the archives but only the jurists' law and legal theory as "imagined and thought" that can substantiate his counterclaim that the normative baseline was not in all instances violated.

In what follows, I will try to vindicate, via direct reference to the classical and post-formative juristic tradition, the argument that *siyāsah*, like aspects of *maẓālim* and *ḥisbah*, participates in the Islamic Secular in that it relies on a legal authority other than, indeed beyond, *fiqh/sharīʿah*, that is, *warāʾ al-ḥukm al-sharʿī*. My claim is not that this is the position unanimously agreed upon by the jurists but that it is the predominant position among them. I will also lay out in greater detail why this perspective is preferable to, and has more explanatory and generative power than, the perspective that sees *siyāsah* as part of *sharīʿah*. These conclusions will force new questions about the past, present, and future of Islamic law. For, if Islamic law is not only broader than *fiqh/sharīʿah* but also includes non-*sharʿī*, 'secular,' *ʿaqlī* elements, we will need to look beyond the jurists and their *ijtihād* (or *taqlīd*) to explain important aspects of Islamic law's successes, failures, and silences, past, present, and future.

Siyāsah

It is not my aim in this section to present an exhaustive treatment of *siyāsah*. I have the more modest goal of substantiating the claim that *siyāsah*, like *maẓālim* and *ḥisbah* (which I discuss below), relies upon non-*sharʿī*, differentiated, Islamic Secular authority and energies in a manner that sets it apart from *fiqh/sharīʿah*. While I present each of these institutions (*siyāsah*, *maẓālim*, and *ḥisbah*) as separate entities, I do not mean to imply that they are hermetically sealed silos. In fact, later jurists are fond of citing the view, attributed to Ibn al-Qayyim, that a judge may or may not be authorized to resort to *siyāsah*, as *sharīʿah* itself imposes no normative rule in this regard: "*laysa fī dhālika ḥadd*^{un}

fī al-sharʿ."[49] Ultimately, the degree to which *siyāsah, maẓālim*, and *ḥisbah* are joined in a single authority or distributed over several is a matter of the terms of investiture, which are themselves informed by custom, the ruler's preferences, and conditions on the ground.

Given this background, the main point of this section is to show that *siyāsah*, as a largely non-*sharʿī* enterprise, is distinct from *sharīʿah* and that *maẓālim* and *ḥisbah* are essentially constituents of *siyāsah*, the super-category of legitimate discretionary rule-making authority. Especially regarding *siyāsah*, I will be forced to rely, as Kristen Stilt suggests, on general and passing descriptions of "what rulers [and other officials] actually did,"[50] since the institution itself is under-theorized in the Islamic tradition. Perhaps, however, this is as things should be. For, the fixed rules and parameters that a formal theory would produce would be the very antithesis of discretion itself, without which *siyāsah, maẓālim*, and *ḥisbah* lose much of their effectiveness.

One indication of the degree to which Muslim jurists conceived of *siyāsah* (and, to a lesser extent, *maẓālim* and *ḥisbah*) as an entity apart from *sharīʿah* is the fact that it is rarely discussed as a formal, substantive topic in manuals of jurisprudence or juristic law.[51] N. Hurvitz characterizes this lack of treatment as "[t]he omission of the rulers from the historical narrative of Islamic law."[52] As we will see, jurists did not entirely ignore rulers or state officials. But it is true that it is in works on government or judicature, not standard or even encyclopedic manuals of *fiqh* (*mutūn*/sg., *matn*), that one is likely to find substantive treatment of the non-*sharʿī*, legal institutions over which rulers and other government officials presided. In fact, were one to rely on *fiqh*-manuals alone, one might barely know of the existence of these institutions, let alone their status or function.

Some might argue that it is only on my limiting *sharīʿah* to *fiqh* that works on *sharīʿah* appear to exclude *siyāsah*. My response to this objection is that this is the understanding conveyed in the writings of the jurists themselves. While works on jurisprudence (*uṣūl al-fiqh*) lay out in great detail the qualifications required of those who produce the rules of *sharīʿah*, they never discuss the technical skills required for those who issue rules based on *siyāsah*. This, I argue, is because *siyāsah* is primarily the exercise of a non-*sharʿī*, discretionary authority (and skillset) to which the technical skills required to produce *sharʿī* rulings are largely irrelevant. Something similar, albeit to a lesser degree, can be said of *maẓālim* and *ḥisbah*.

Before turning to actual works on government and judicature, a word of interpretive caution is in order. One influential version of the dystopian narrative builds on a postulate whose mere assertion, if accepted as proof, can prejudice our reading of the sources and simultaneously foreclose the possibility of testing the postulate itself. Hamilton Gibb, for example, without providing evidence, presents this basic axiom as follows:

> Since God is Himself the sole Legislator, there can be no room in Islamic political theory for legislation or legislative powers, whether enjoyed by a temporal ruler or by any kind of assembly. There can be no "sovereign state," in the sense that the state has the right of enacting its own law. . . . The Law [*sharīʿah*] precedes the State, both logically and in terms of time. The State exists for the sole purpose of maintaining and enforcing the Law.[53]

On this basis, Gibb saw jurists such as al-Māwardī (d. 450/1058), a major writer on governance, as proffering theories that deviated from "the Law" and merely apologized for the illegitimate situation that had developed on the ground.[54] We will see, however, especially in light of the *sharʿī*/non-*sharʿī* distinction, that al-Māwardī, along with other major jurists from across the schools, contradicts Gibb's basic assertion and recognizes a legitimate rule-making authority beyond *sharīʿah*. To read al-Māwardī and these other jurists' works through the prism of Gibb's postulate not only jeopardizes our ability to hear what they are actually telling us, it also casts them as deviating from a norm whose authority itself is more assumed and asserted than actually proved. Even if we concede that the state has an absolute mandate to apply *sharīʿah*, the question is whether the state's legitimate rule-making powers are limited to *sharīʿah* exclusively. And here we must be willing to listen to what jurists have to say rather than subordinating their words to the dictates of an unproven postulate.

In their classic texts on government, *al-Aḥkām al-Sulṭānīyah*, both the Ḥanbalī Abū Yaʿlā and the Shāfiʿī al-Māwardī recognize the rule-making authority of *siyāsah* as separate from that of *fiqh/sharīʿah*. Both distinguish, for example, between *madhhab* and *siyāsah*,[55] *siyāsah* and *aḥkām al-sharʿ*,[56] *siyāsah* and *al-ḥukm wa al-qaḍāʾ*,[57] etc. In a similar vein, in his work on judicature, the later Mālikī jurist Ibn Farḥūn (d. 799/1397) contrasts the position of those who eschew *siyāsah* altogether, on the view that it violates the general canons of jurisprudence (*al-qawāʿid al-sharʿīyah*), with the position of those who exaggerate in invoking *siyāsah* and thus fling open the doors to abuse. He lauds, however, the position of those who take a "middle road," properly and successfully "joining *siyāsah* with *sharīʿah*" (*jamaʿū bayna al-siyāsah wa al-sharʿ*). In other words, Ibn Farḥūn clearly sees the two as distinct, if interdependent and occasionally interpenetrating, entities.[58] His references to the "middle road" and "joining *siyāsah* with *sharīʿah*" are repeated verbatim by the Ḥanafī ʿAlāʾ al-Dīn al-Ṭarābulisī (d. 844/1440) in his work on judicature.[59] Like Ibn Farḥūn, al-Ṭarābulisī sees *sharīʿah* and *siyāsah* as distinct, albeit mutually reinforcing, forces. In a demonstration of this relationship, he rehearses the standard Ḥanafī position that neither stoning plus flogging nor flogging plus banishment can be applied as punishment for a single act of sexual indiscretion, "except as a matter of *siyāsah*" (*illā an yakūna siyāsat^{an}*).[60] In other words, such compound punishments would be in technical violation of *sharīʿah*'s *fiqh* though perfectly consistent with Islamic law's *siyāsah*. In a similar vein, the seventh-/thirteenth-century Shāfiʿī jurist al-Fazārī insists that the prohibition against a judge from one school ruling based on another school's doctrine "is required by the administration of justice (*siyāsah*) . . . not by the Divine Law (*sharʿ*)."[61] Earlier, al-Māwardī had made the same point in even bolder terms:

> If he [a judge] is a Shāfiʿī, he is not bound to follow the views of al-Shāfiʿī in his rulings, unless his own independent interpretation (*ijtihād*) leads him to this. If his independent interpretation leads him to the view of Abū Ḥanīfa, he may adopt the latter. . . . Some jurists disallow this . . . to avoid suspicion of unfairness and bias. . . . But even if such disallowance might be dictated by *siyāsah*, the rules of *sharīʿah* do not bind him in this regard.[62]

Obviously, *siyāsah*, even as an expression of legitimate rule-making authority, cannot be a part of *sharīʿah* if the former's rules can be in violation of the latter's, or if the requirements of one can explicitly contradict those of the other.[63] Of course, over time, *siyāsah* may produce norms and policies that are absorbed into the body of *sharīʿah*—as we see, for example, with custom and, in this sense, the two may cohere as one.[64] Far more often, however, *siyāsah* operates on the basis of an authority and logic that produce rules whose substance lie *beyond fiqh/sharīʿah* and the *ḥukm sharʿī*.

The fact that al-Māwardī and Abū Yaʿlā both treat *siyāsah* as a formal topic of discussion shows how far back it has existed as a formally recognized institution, rather than being a later manifestation of state encroachment or juristic entropy. Both Abū Yaʿlā and al-Māwardī died in the middle of the fifth/eleventh century and had teachers who died in the latter half of the fourth/tenth. As their respective versions of *al-Aḥkām al-Sulṭānīyah* are palpably mature texts, it is almost certain that not all the ideas contained in these works originated with these men. At any rate, especially in their treatment of unrestricted and restricted *amīr*s (*wilāyat ʿāmmah, wilāyat khāṣṣah*) both assign a general duty to government officials to uphold the "rule of law," as well as the commonweal.[65] In fact, both Abū Yaʿlā and al-Māwardī recognize a *siyāsah*-based venue for the adjudication of *sharīʿah/fiqh* rules that is separate and distinct from the courts of the *qāḍī*s. *Siyāsah* here is not simply a convenient rule-making subterfuge pressed into service by rulers and government officials in pursuit of self-serving interests at the expense of *sharīʿah*. In fact, the jurists themselves viewed these fora as part of the overall apparatus necessary to uphold not only the rule of law, at the center of which lie the rules of *sharīʿah*, but also the extra-*sharʿī* dimensions of the common good. This perception comes through clearly in both al-Māwardī and Abū Yaʿlā. And their manner of presentation gives the distinct impression that Islamic law had long been recognized as a condominium of sorts between the jurists, state officials, and members of the community at large who might assist in ensuring the law's just and practical application, alongside the maintenance of the commonweal.[66]

Both al-Māwardī and Abū Yaʿlā, in their respective sections on "Installing Government Officials over Territories" (*Fī Taqlīd al-Imārah ʿalā al-Bilād*), portray the role of *amīr*s in the administration of justice as varying in accordance with circumstances, rank and the stipulations of appointment. This portrayal is separate from their treatment of the judicial process as such, which comes in a later, separate section in both texts. In the section under review, al-Māwardī and Abū Yaʿlā note that in a criminal case, a restricted *amīr* (*amīr wilāyah khāṣṣah*), who has no oversight powers over the administration of justice, cannot implement a prescribed punishment (*ḥudūd*/sg. *ḥadd*) where there is a conflict regarding litigants' retiring the evidentiary burden or there is a disagreement among the jurists regarding the applicable rule. For, such determinations fall outside his jurisdiction as a restricted *amīr*. But if there is no such conflict or disagreement, or there is disagreement but a judge settles it through his *ijtihād*, or the evidentiary dispute is resolved, then the following possibilities arise:

> The matter at hand will either involve a right of God or a right of humans. If it involves a right of humans, such as a case of false accusation (*qadhf*) or retaliation for loss of life or limb (*qiṣāṣ*), implementation will be determined by the manner in which the plaintiff chooses to proceed (*ḥāl al-ṭālib*). If s/he seeks the offices of a judge over those of an *amīr*, it becomes most appropriate (*aḥaqq*) for the judge to address his/her plea, as these are among the rights that judges are installed to ensure. But if s/he prefers to appeal to the *amīr* to exact punishment or retaliation, it becomes most appropriate for the *amīr* to do so. For, this does not entail the issuance of a legal ruling (*laysa bi ḥukm*); it is simply a matter of providing assistance in exacting a right. And the one most appropriate to offer such assistance is the *amīr* not the judge. If, on the other hand, the matter involves a pure right of God, such as a case of fornication or adultery—lashing or stoning—it becomes more appropriate for the *amīr* to exact punishment than for the judge to do so. For this is included among the dictates of *siyāsah* (*qawanīn al-siyāsah*) and the necessities of preserving and defending the Community, and because overseeing the commonweal is delegated to *amīr*s, who are installed to seek it out, not to judges, who sit back and wait to terminate individual disputes presented by litigants.[67]

This is an extremely important passage. It clearly establishes that the administration of justice was recognized *by the juristic tradition itself* as part of the state's or ruler's religious duty in confederation with the juristic establishment. It also shows that this recognition extends back at least as far as the fifth/eleventh century and almost certainly earlier, since, again, it is doubtful that these ideas originated with Abū Yaʿlā or al-Māwardī.[68] The passage also makes it clear that the state's or ruler's involvement in potentially shaping and certainly in upholding the law was not automatically perceived by the jurists as an encroachment upon or deviation from *fiqh/sharīʿah*—and certainly not Islamic law. Nor did this involvement necessarily imply impatience on the part of the state or ruler in the face of incompetence, corruption, or rigidity among the *fuqahāʾ*. What we see here, rather, is a recognition that the ideal relationship between the state and the jurists is one of cooperation, both being religiously responsible for upholding a normative Islamic order—including *sharīʿah* and Islamic law. In this context, it becomes clear that distinguishing *siyāsah* from *sharīʿah* should not be mistaken for a claim of zero-sum rivalry between the two.

Of course, history would repeatedly challenge this ideal, and such challenges would prompt jurists to retreat in protest and accuse the state of being an unreliable or insincere partner (with the latter occasionally reciprocating in kind). But this should not cause us to overlook or dismiss what the jurists recognized as the ideal, an ideal we see clearly here in al-Māwardī and Abū Yaʿlā, whose works are among the most authoritative in the history of this genre. Their words should serve as a check on the tendency to view *siyāsah*—even when deemed an institution external to *sharīʿah*—as an alien innovation that is secular in the modern Western sense, only coming into being in response to juristic corruption or incompetence, the increasingly formalistic nature of *sharīʿah*,[69] or the self-serving Machiavellian impulses nursed by Muslim rulers and governments.[70]

It is also clear from the statements by Abū Yaʿlā and al-Māwardī that *siyāsah* is distinct from *sharīʿah* and operates on a logic and authority that transcends it. Over time, this understanding would become so widely diffused that even the juristically minded al-Qarāfī, in a manual ostensibly devoted to *fiqh*, could openly acknowledge *siyāsah* as part of the state's rightful role in upholding the normative order, separate from the efforts of judges and jurists. He states explicitly, for example, that allowing *maẓālim* magistrates and police chiefs (*umarāʾ al-jarāʾim*) greater leeway in pursuing criminals is perfectly consistent with the principles of juristic law (*laysa mukhālif*^an^ *li al-sharʿ*), even if, as this juxtaposition clearly implies, the two jurisdictions remain distinct.[71] Elsewhere he clarifies this distinction by posing and responding to a hypothetical question regarding the legitimacy of what many today might term "man-made" law: "How can it be said that God has granted anyone the right to impose rules upon people? Does anyone have the right to impose rules except God?"[72] Of course, the ultimate question here is about the theoretical legitimacy of extra-*sharʿī* rules. Al-Qarāfī begins his response by pointing out that any layperson can impose a binding obligation upon himself or herself via a vow (*nadhr*), for example, "I vow to God that I will. . . ." or a "sworn commitment " (*taʿlīq*), for example, "By God, if such and such occurs, I will. . . ." He goes on to argue, *a fortiori*, that:

> If it is established that God has granted every legally responsible individual, even if s/he is an ignorant layperson, the right to originate obligations in this manner, while there is no necessity for such, it is all the more proper that God should grant this right to state officials (*hukkām*), given their knowledge and stature, due to the necessity of averting obstinacy, putting down corruption, extinguishing conflict and terminating disputes.[73]

Al-Qarāfī's response here reveals two things: first, he is not averse to extra-*sharʿī* rules and sees them, when properly devised and executed, as consistent with the overall aims of *sharīʿah*; second, the purpose of such rules is to uphold the rule of law and serve the commonweal. This was despite his deep and abiding concern about state encroachment on the integrity of *sharīʿah*, which underwrote his sustained effort both to clarify and fortify the latter's sacred boundaries.[74] Yet, the boundaries he seeks to impose are clearly directed toward the proper and efficient functioning of the condominium, by keeping the distribution of labor and jurisdictions clear and efficacious. To this end, he notes that the discretionary authority of rulers (*al-sulṭanah al-ʿāmmah*), as well as that of judges, is separate from and additional to (*zāʾid ʿalā*) the authority to issue juristic rulings proper, that is, *aḥkām sharʿīyah*.[75] And he clarifies the ways in which these jurisdictions relate to each other as follows:

> [J]udges rely on courtroom evidence (*al-ḥijāj*/sg. *ḥujjah*), *muftī*s rely on scriptural indicants (*al-adillah*/sg. *dalīl*), and the discretionary actions of the Imām that go beyond these rely upon (his assessment of) the pure or preponderant interests (*al-maṣāliḥ al-rājiḥah aw al-khāliṣah*) he identifies on behalf of the Community. And these latter are distinct from courtroom evidence and scriptural indicants.[76]

Again, far from expressing misgivings, let alone resentment, about the discretionary role of the state, al-Qarāfī idealizes a cooperative relationship between the jurists and the Imām, noting explicitly that, in contributing to the practical integrity of the rule of law and commonweal, governments are *not* in violation of the *sharʿ* but normatively serve the latter. In other words, *sharīʿah* and its practical administration are not sacred precincts from which the state is or should be categorically barred. Nor is the practical, non-*sharʿī*, Islamic Secular *ʿaql* upon which government officials rely in pursuing the rule of law and common good frowned upon or disguised as a would-be embarrassment or affront to *sharīʿah*. Clearly, on this understanding, as Fahmy suggests, the resort to *siyāsah* should not automatically be seen as a manifestation of deviation or decline. Yet, contrary to Fahmy's (and others') view, even as constituents of a cooperative condominium, *fiqh/sharīʿah* and *siyāsah* remain two distinct genera (as opposed to two species of a single genus [i.e., *sharīʿah*]).

In his study on Ḥanafī *fiqh*, Professor Baber Johansen also appears to contradict my understanding of a separation between *siyāsah* and *sharīʿah*. Speaking of *taʿzīr*, or extra-juristic, non-prescribed sanctions, he writes, "By the [second/] eighth century this category was already included into the *ŝarīʿa*."[77] He confirms that Muslim jurists also "accepted the siyāsa competence of the government" in this early period,[78] "[b]ut—contrary to *taʿzīr*—these *siyāsa* measures were not part of the *ŝariʿa*."[79] Later, however, he argues that *siyāsah* was admitted into the sanctum of *sharīʿah*, where it presumably remained.

> To the best of my knowledge, only postclassical authors—starting with Marĝīnānī at the end of the [sixth/] twelfth century, equate *taʿzīr* and *siyāsa*, thereby laying the foundations for a special form of *siyāsa* that included the *siyāsa* in the *ŝarʿīya*. The first monographs on the *siyāsa ŝarʿīya* within the Hanafite school seem to have been written in the [ninth/] fifteenth century.[80]

Johansen does not give a concrete reference in al-Marghīnānī (d. 593/1197); nor does he give the titles of the Ḥanafī books on *siyāsah sharʿīyah* to which he alludes. Standard Ḥanafī works on *fiqh*, however, all the way down to Ibn ʿĀbidīn, make an association between *taʿzīr* and *siyāsah* when discussing the aforementioned position that two punishments cannot be simultaneously applied for a single act of sexual indiscretion, unless the Imām sees fit to do so out of concern for the common good (*maṣlaḥah*). Al-Marghīnānī had cited this view in his *al-Hidāyah* in the chapter on prescribed punishments (*al-ḥudūd*), saying of the Imām's action, "And that would be a matter of *taʿzīr* and *siyāsah*" (*wa dhālika taʿzīr^{un} wa siyāsat^{un}*).[81] Assuming this to be the reference that Johansen had in mind, I see no indication in it that *siyāsah* has been included as part of *sharīʿah*. Of course, one could read the second "and" (*waw*) in al-Marghīnānī's wording as implying an appositional relationship between *taʿzīr* and *siyāsah*, and then, assuming that *taʿzīr* is part of *sharīʿah*, assume that *siyāsah* is too. But this reading, while plausible on its face, is neither conclusive nor particularly compelling. In fact, the great Ḥanafī jurist Ibn ʿĀbidīn states explicitly that *taʿzīr* and *siyāsah* are synonymous (*mutarādifān*),[82] while distinctly *not* giving the impression that *siyāsah* is a substantive part of *sharīʿah*.

Ibn ʿĀbidīn states that *taʿzīr* is a heightened regime of sanctions (*taghlīẓ*) for "offenses that are identified as such according to the general principles of the *sharʿ*, though the *sharʿ* itself does not address them specifically" (*jināyah . . . dākhilah taḥta qawāʾid al-sharʿ wa in lam yanuṣṣ ʿalayhā bi khuṣūṣihā*).[83] Drawing on the cumulative wisdom of the *madhhab*, he notes that "*siyāsah* refers to a ruler's undertaking an action based on some public good he sees in it, even if no specific textual indicant directing him to do so exists" (*al-siyāsah hiya fiʿl shayʾin min al-ḥākim li maṣlaḥah yarāhā wa in lam yarid bi dhālika al-fiʿl dalīlun juzʾīyun*).[84] What authorizes the ruler to undertake this action is that *sharīʿah* itself aims to curtail vice and promote the public good. In this sense, *siyāsah* derives its basic *mandate* from *sharīʿah*. The actual *substance* of what is applied in the name of *siyāsah*, however, is *not* derived from *sharīʿah* or its sources; rather, *sharīʿah* and *siyāsah* constitute two distinct regimes of rules.

This distinctness is clearly manifested in the example Ibn ʿĀbidīn adduces of the Caliph ʿUmar's banishing Naṣr b. al-Ḥajjāj from Medina because his good looks tempted the womenfolk. Ibn ʿĀbidīn notes that, while banishment may have been appropriate under the circumstances, according to the rules of *sharīʿah*, "a person's good looks do not give rise to any obligation to banish them."[85] We see a similar logic at work in Badr al-Dīn al-ʿAynī's commentary on al-Marghīnānī, where he states that the Imām *could* apply the two punishments for a single act of sexual indiscretion but "not as a prescribed punishment" (*lā ʿalā annahu ḥadd*).[86] In other words, the *substance* of what the Imām applied would not be prescribed by *sharīʿah*, even if *sharīʿah* could on its own terms sanction the *theoretical* application thereof.

From another perspective, following his teacher, the Shāfiʿī jurist ʿIzz al-Dīn Ibn ʿAbd al-Salām (d. 660/1262), al-Qarāfī notes that *taʿzīr* can be applied in response to deleterious acts even where they constitute no violation of *sharīʿah* at all. In fact, in an interesting display of the limits of juristic pluralism, he notes that , according to some, Ḥanafīs who publicly drink *nabīdh* (non-grape wine) can even be punished (*ḥaddan*), due to the harmful effects of drinking on the Community, even if, based on their interpretation of *sharīʿah*, these Ḥanafīs are technically guilty of no sin.[87] Again, even if *sharīʿah* mandates the resort to *siyāsah*, the actual rules of *siyāsah* do not necessarily revert to *sharīʿah* itself.[88] Thus, even where *taʿzīr* is identified with *siyāsah*, as in the example adduced by Professor Johansen, it does not necessarily follow that *siyāsah* must therefore be a substantive part of *sharīʿah*.[89]

As for the "*sharʿīyah*," in "*siyāsah sharʿīyah*," I am not sure why this must be taken to mean that *siyāsah* is an actual part of *sharīʿah*. Even *sharīʿah*-maximalists such as Ibn al-Qayyim recognize the difference between *sharīʿah*'s supplying the actual rules applied as *siyāsah* and these rules simply being consistent with the rules, broader aims, and objectives of *sharīʿah*. In fact, Ibn Taymīyah explicitly distinguishes between rules that are "a matter of consultation with the Imām and his issuing directives based on what serves the commonweal," and "*sharīʿah*-rules that bind everyone" (*min bāb mashūrat al-imām wa ḥukmih bi al-maṣlaḥah lā min bāb al-ḥukm al-sharʿī alladhi yalzam al-khalq kullahum*).[90] This distinction is also implied by al-Ṭarābulisī and Ibn Farḥūn in their use of "*siyāsah*," as we saw earlier.[91]

In sum, the view of the learned Professor Johansen notwithstanding, I still see *siyāsah* as operating on the basis of an authority largely distinct from that of *fiqh/sharīʿah*. *Siyāsah* carries the authority to interpret "facts on the ground" en route to fixing an ever-shifting, elusive, common good, as opposed to the authority to interpret scriptural texts and other sources of the "law" en route to fixing permanent rules that apply to an ostensibly fixed, formal reality, along with the mandate to negotiate these rules in light of actual reality. Still, as we have seen, jurists quite casually welcome this essentially non-*sharʿī* authority, duly exercised, as perfectly legitimate *sharʿan*.

There was, of course, palpable anxiety about this relationship between *siyāsah* and *sharīʿah*. On the one hand, to identify the two too closely would risk overempowering the state by enabling it to compete with *sharīʿah* by conflating every discretionary decree or policy with a presumably bona fide, unassailable *sharʿī* authority. We saw this fear earlier in Ibn al-Jawzī's protest and in Ibn al-Qayyim's vacillations[92] and again in Ibn Farḥūn's concern about those who exaggerate in invoking *siyāsah* and thus fling open the doors to abuse.[93] We also see it in al-Qarāfī's attempt to insulate *sharīʿah* from *siyāsah* by laying down a bright line between the two, delineating the boundary between "law" and "non-law"—a line so strict that Ibn Farḥūn and, after him, al-Ṭarābulisī claimed (wrongly in my view) that al-Qarāfī denied judges the right to resort to *siyāsah* in any way.[94] On the other hand, to separate *siyāsah* and *sharīʿah* too radically might not only impute deficiency to the latter but also lay the groundwork for the state to supersede it, via reliance on the more nimbly pragmatic policy-making powers of the ruler. This may be why Ibn Farḥūn and al-Ṭarābulisī took such umbrage at the position they impute to al-Qarāfī.[95] To their minds, al-Qarāfī's alleged restriction threatened to cripple judges, dooming them and the *sharīʿah* they represented to failure. And this, they feared, would open the field for any unscrupulous or overly pragmatic ruler or government official to claim that he had the unassailable right to intervene with a discretionary substitute of his choosing.[96]

In the end, at any rate, both sides evince a recognition of *siyāsah* and *sharīʿah* as distinct though interactive regimes of rulemaking. This is especially clear in the case of al-Qarāfī. Meanwhile, Ibn Farḥūn and al-Ṭarābulisī differentiate between "good" and "bad" *siyāsah*, the former qualifying as *sharʿī* and thus at times being equated with *sharīʿah*, the latter being cast as an explicit contravention of *sharīʿah* while still being considered *siyāsah*.[97] In each case, Islam-cum-*sharīʿah* and its principles are invoked as the immoveable standard by which the basic legitimacy of *siyāsah* is assessed, even though the rules or policies produced by the latter are not substantively traced to *sharīʿah* or its sources. In this context, the jurists' occasional rhetorical conflation of *siyāsah* with *sharīʿah*, as powerful as it may be, should not blind us to the fundamental distinction between the two.[98]

Maẓālim

In his general description of *maẓālim*, Jørgen Nielsen writes: "At the early stage in the development of Islamic institutions of government, *maẓālim* came to denote the structure through which temporal authorities took direct responsibility for dispensing justice."[99] While I agree with this general depiction, I disagree with the intimation that, in taking "direct responsibility for dispensing justice," "temporal authorities" were necessarily encroaching upon *sharīʿah* or Islamic law. Like *siyāsah*, *maẓālim*, in my view, while appreciably extra-*sharʿī* in substance, was not secular in the modern Western sense but remained a bona fide constituent of "Islamic law." Nielsen, on the other hand, argues that, "There are indications that the *maẓālim* jurisdiction was regarded by both [the early ʿAbbasid Caliphs al-Mahdī and al-Hādī] and by the *ḳādī*s [judges] and *ʿulamāʾ* [jurists] as a rival to the *sharīʿah* jurisdiction."[100] Part of what I suspect drives Nielsen to this conclusion is an interpretive point of departure that excludes any recognition of the distinction between the *sharʿī* and non-*sharʿī* dimensions of Islamic law. On this approach, anything outside the boundaries of *sharīʿah* and its strictly *sharʿī* entailments is perceived to be a rival to it.

As we shall see, however, alongside its *sharʿī* dimension, *maẓālim* (like *ḥisbah*) rests appreciably upon a palpably non-*sharʿī*, Islamic Secular authority and calculus. That the jurists recognized this authority is reflected in the fact that al-Maqrīzī (writing in 819/1416) subsumes *maẓālim* under the general designation of *siyāsah*.[101] Meanwhile, his Ḥanafī contemporary al-Ṭarābulisī (mistakenly) places the Mālikī al-Qarāfī's entire discussion of *maẓālim* (in which al-Qarāfī draws mainly on al-Māwardī) under the category of *siyāsah*, a mistake that he may have picked up from his Mālikī predecessor Ibn Farḥūn, which reflects the strong, almost unconscious, association between *maẓālim* and *siyāsah* in their minds.[102] Earlier, Abū Yaʿlā and al-Māwardī both included "looking into matters relating to the common good in which the *muḥtasib* is not quite able to set things right" as part of the job of the *maẓālim* magistrate,[103] both casting *ḥisbah* as falling halfway between *maẓālim* and the judicial process (*qaḍāʾ*).[104] Both of them also grant the *muḥtasib* the authority to apply *taʿzīr*,[105] which, as we have seen, jurists associated with *siyāsah*.[106] Again, however, while *maẓālim* and *ḥisbah* include aspects that are non-*sharʿī* and tend to fall more predominantly within the scope of *siyāsah*, they also include aspects that are *sharʿī* and fall legitimately within the province of *fiqh/sharīʿah*. For this reason, when jurists such as al-Maqrīzī or al-Ṭarābulisī equate *maẓālim* with *siyāsah*, or when other scholars such as al-Shayzarī (d. circa 579/1193) intimate that *ḥisbah* is a constituent of *sharīʿah*,[107] these authors must be understood as speaking in metonymical or synecdochic terms—*bi al-tajawwuz*—taking part of these institutions to represent the whole.

The clearly *sharʿī* dimension of *maẓālim* resides in the fact that, in theory, *maẓālim* proceedings cannot result in the application of any rule that is not recognized by *sharīʿah*. Both al-Māwardī and Abū Yaʿlā mention this stipulation explicitly: "*naẓar al-maẓālim lā yubīḥ min al-aḥkām mā ḥaẓarahu al-sharʿ*."[108] In actual practice, however, the examples they adduce suggest that *maẓālim* adjudication often goes beyond the substantive provisions of *fiqh*, even if it does not necessarily violate the latter. In fact, *mazālim* adjudication frequently appears to be a means of avoiding the burdens of formal, *sharʿī* judicial proceedings, albeit in the interest of the *sharʿ* and or common good.[109] Of course, the assumption that "Islamic law" equals *fiqh/sharīʿah* has prompted some to conclude that *maẓālim* proceedings are a remedial institution designed either to offset *sharīʿah*'s shortcomings or to ensure its application to powerful figures who might otherwise defy it. But in both al-Māwardī's and Abū Yaʿlā's depictions, not only is *maẓālim* not a remedial institution, but its application often *precedes* and may even preempt the judicial process as defined by *fiqh*. Yet there is no sense or suggestion that *maẓālim* and *sharīʿah* are inherent rivals or competitors.

Both al-Māwardī and Abū Yaʿlā cite several cases where adjudication runs not from the *qāḍī*'s court to the *maẓālim* tribunal but from the *maẓālim* tribunal to arbitration (*wisāṭah*) and then to the *qāḍī*'s court, the reverse of what one might expect on the traditional understanding of *maẓālim*.[110] The normative procedure governing these cases is described as follows: first they go to the *maẓālim* magistrate, who is authorized to launch an investigation (*kashf*), using fact-gathering tools not recognized in *fiqh*—for example, subpoenaing witnesses, relying on circumstantial evidence (*shawāhid al-aḥwāl*), applying pressure to litigants (*irhāb*, etc.). If this investigation uncovers the truth or brings the litigants to agreement, the case is closed. If not, it is handed over for arbitration (*wisāṭah*), which may involve not only government officials but also neighbors or business associates who know the litigants and/or the issue at hand. If this fails, the case then goes to court, where a judge will try it in accordance with the rules of *fiqh*.[111]

Al-Māwardī and Abū Yaʿlā cite several cases to explain the basic workings of this system. In one case involving several intertwining claims, the plaintiff wanted to frustrate the proceedings by forcing the defendant to give a sworn oath (*yamīn*) for every particular at issue, as would be allowed under the rules of *fiqh*. According to both al-Māwardī and Abū Yaʿlā, however, *maẓālim* magistrates are not bound by this rule and should not abide by it; rather, they should reduce the defendant's oaths to a single comprehensive oath in order to block the plaintiff's attempt at obstruction. Al-Māwardī continues:

> If the (*maẓālim*) investigation uncovers what enables us to know which of the litigants is right, this is accepted and acted upon. If it does not uncover that which can terminate the dispute, the litigants are handed over for arbitration, presided over by reputable neighbors or kinfolk. If this succeeds, the matter is terminated. If not, the case goes to court (*al-qaḍā'*), which is the end of the process (*wa huwa khātimat amrihimā*).[112]

Again, the *maẓālim* magistrate follows procedures that depart from those outlined in *fiqh*. The aim, however—at least in theory—is still the application of the rules (or at least the standards) of *sharīʿah*. We see this in al-Māwardī's and Abū Yaʿlā's descriptions of other cases involving, for example, unlawful confiscation of property (*ghaṣb*). They note that the *maẓālim* magistrate may simply rely on the official land registry (*dīwān al-ṣalṭanah*) and that the rightful owner does not have to present formal proof of ownership, that is, *bayyinah*, as defined in *fiqh*.[113]

By comparison, in his manual on *fiqh*, as part of his explanation of the rule governing land disputes, al-Māwardī cites as normative examples cases wherein the Prophet refused, in the absence of concrete evidence (*bayyinah*) or the claimant's sworn oath (*yamīn*), to grant property to one who claimed it, even where the claim seemed credible—a refusal clearly underscoring the centrality of formal evidence in settling disputes in accordance with *sharīʿah*'s judicial process.[114] Significantly, land registries are not a product of *fiqh*. The fact that al-Māwardī and Abū Yaʿlā recognize them as a basis for settling legal contests points to a conscious effort by the "condominium" between the state, the jurists, and the Community to develop and legitimate non-*sharʿī*, Islamic Secular instruments and institutions to assist them in the administration of justice.[115] Again, the aim in all of this is clearly to reconcile and serve the moral and practical vision of Islam-cum-*sharīʿah*, alongside the common good. As such, the invocation of these extra-*sharʿī* conventions need not be seen as flouting *sharīʿah* or Islamic law in favor of secular, "un-Islamic" alternatives.

In his book on *maẓālim*, Nielsen states that al-Māwardī's *al-Aḥkām al-Sulṭānīyah* was the definitive statement on this institution and that all writings on the subject after him followed his lead.[116] Both al-Māwardī and Abū Yaʿlā stress the *maẓālim* magistrate's reliance upon the ability to instill fear (*rahbah*), inspire awe (*haybah*), and wield coercive power (*saṭwah*), so as to drive litigants to abandon their obstinance.[117] Yet, both men see judges and jurists (among others) as indispensable features of the *maẓālim* tribunal, their function being to inform the magistrate of what will pass juristic muster in the sense of not violating the outer limits of *sharīʿah*.[118] Al-Māwardī and Abū Yaʿlā cite ten main functions of *maẓālim*, which can be reduced to five primary concerns: upholding the general *sharīʿah*-based order, putting down corruption among officials and non-officials, mediating public and private disputes, overseeing the payment of taxes and government salaries, and ensuring the prompt and proper application of judicial verdicts.[119] In all these instances, the *maẓālim* magistrate's primary role is one of discovery and enforcement, not deducing *sharʿī* rules. He deals, in other words, largely with the determination of facts on the ground and their legal or other implications, as well as how best to respond to these practically, not with the interpretation or derivation of *sharʿī* rules from the sources.

Having said this much, both Abū Yaʿlā and al-Māwardī impute to high officials such as the Caliph and the vizier the automatic right to preside as *maẓālim* magistrate.[120] Thus, a *maẓālim* magistrate *might* engage in actual legal interpretation; for these officials are both credited, in theory at least, with the ability to exercise *ijtihād*.[121] Outside circumstances where he happens to be a ruler or high official, however (or a *mujtahid* in his own right), issuing juristic rulings whose substance he has determined on his own, is *not* a function of a *maẓālim* magistrate. Even unrestricted *amīr*s (*amīr wilāyah ʿāmmah*) who are authorized to exercise oversight over the administration of justice (*al-naẓar fī al-aḥkām wa taqlīd al-qudāh wa al-ḥukkām*)[122] are not credited with the ability to engage in *ijtihād*. In fact, leaving aside the fiction that the Caliph and vizier are *mujtahid*s who can preside over *maẓālim* proceedings, *ijtihād*, or the ability to derive rules directly from the sources, is *not* included among the general qualifications for a *maẓālim* magistrate. Rather, the eligibility requirements (*shurūṭ*) cited for his office typically read: "That he be of lofty station, of heeded command, awe-inspiring, clearly abstemious and lacking in greed, and that he be devout, for his office requires the coercive power of security personnel alongside the judiciousness of judges."[123]

That *ijtihād* falls outside the competence of the everyday *maẓālim* magistrate need not be seen as a denigration of his stature. For, the coercive and discretionary powers he wields do not extend to judges. From this perspective, al-Māwardī and Abū Yaʿlā rank the *maẓālim* magistrate above the judge, noting that the former does what the latter is incapable of doing (*mā ʿajaza ʿanhu*).[124] Of course, the justice and rights upheld by the *maẓālim* magistrate are in theory defined by *fiqh/sharīʿah*. As for the non-*sharʿī* or *siyāsah* side of this office, it resides, again, in the alternate regime of discovery, evidence-gathering, and enforcement, including such tools as circumstantial evidence, subpoenas, pressure tactics, and the like.[125] Nowhere, perhaps, is the *sharʿī*/non-*sharʿī* contrast between what judges do and what *maẓālim* magistrates or government officials (*umarā'*/ sg. *amīr*) do, all in pursuit of the rule of law, more clearly manifested than in discussions on *jarā'im*, or criminal offenses, in books on government versus their treatment in books of *fiqh*.

I have long suspected that Abū Yaʿlā was first in writing his version of *al-Aḥkām al-Sulṭānīyah*.[126] Nevertheless, al-Māwardī's is a demonstrably richer text, containing significant segments not found in Abū Yaʿlā.[127] More importantly, al-Māwardī authored a major compendium of Shāfiʿī *fiqh* that has come down to us.[128] This enables us to compare directly what he says about *jarāʾim* as a matter of *fiqh* with what he says about them as a matter of government, that is, *siyāsah or maẓālim*. Therefore, I shall rely on al-Māwardī.

In the introduction to the section on *jarāʾim* in *al-Aḥkām al-Sulṭānīyah*, al-Māwardī notes that *jarāʾim* are offenses that God has legally prohibited and for which God has authorized the imposition of prescribed (*ḥadd*) or non-prescribed (*taʿzīr*) sanctions. Their practical adjudication includes two phases: (1) where charges or accusations are levied and guilt or innocence must be established in accordance with what he terms the dictates of "religious *siyāsah*" (*siyāsah dīnīyah*); and (2) where rights or guilt have already been established and must be recompensed in accordance with the dictates of *sharīʿah* (*al-aḥkām al-sharʿīyah*).[129]

It is primarily regarding the first phase that al-Māwardī indicates that offenses may be brought before either of two venues, one presided over by a judge, the other by an *amīr*. According to him, if a man is brought before a judge on charges of theft or adultery/fornication (*zinā*), the judge may not jail him in order to investigate these charges; nor is he permitted to try to pressure the man into confessing; nor is he even bound to hear the case, unless it is presented by a person from whom it is assumed the man is likely to have stolen (e.g., an employer). In a case of *zinā*, the judge may hear the case only if the man names the woman and describes what he did with her, such that the commission of the legally defined crime of *zinā* is established, as is the legally defined validity of his confession, as the relevant evidentiary burden in such cases.

By contrast, if either of these cases is presented before an *amīr* or law enforcement official (*amīr aw wulāt al-aḥdāth wa al-maʿāwin*), these officials may investigate the case and in so doing avail themselves of options that are not open to judges. Among other things, the *amīr* may consult his staff to see what they know about the man's character, even as a matter of hearsay, to determine if he is likely to engage in such behavior; and he may rely on circumstantial evidence, such as whether the accused is known to be a lady's man or was seen loitering around the scene of the crime or was caught with a tool typically used for theft in his possession. The *amīr* may even jail the accused to complete his investigation, some jurists limiting the period of detention to one month, others leaving it entirely to the *amīr*. Once in detention, assuming his preliminary investigations strengthen the case against the suspect, the *amīr* may physically strike (*ḍarb*) the accused to get him to answer questions (not to confess to the crime itself).[130] He may even force the accused to swear his innocence on pain of divorcing his wife, freeing his slaves, or donating his wealth to charity.[131] Al-Māwardī enumerates a total of nine options of which *amīr*s may avail themselves but to which judges have no legal access. Judges, for example, may not jail anyone except by due process of law as established in *fiqh* (*bi ḥaqq*^in^ *wajab*);[132] they have no right to resort to physical coercion, or to rely on circumstantial evidence, hearsay, or forced oaths; and they may not hand down life-sentences to petty criminals whose repeat-offenses threaten the commonweal.[133]

While al-Māwardī makes it is clear that the judge's "*sharī'ah*-court" is not the only venue before which such cases might be brought, it remains unclear (to me at least) why a case would come before an *amīr* or *maẓālim* magistrate rather than a judge. At any rate, al-Mawardī ends this introduction to *jarā'im* by reiterating that, in the fact-finding phase of a criminal case, the *amīr* relies on *siyāsah*-based principles, while the judge relies on *sharī'ah*-based procedural rules (*al-aḥkām*), clearly intimating that these are separate, if interactive, jurisdictions that rely on distinct regimes of authority, inevitable overlap between them notwithstanding.[134]

Regarding the second phase of adjudication, where rights and guilt are already established and must be recompensed, al-Māwardī restates the standard *fiqhī* rule that there are two means by which all rights or guilt may be legally established: juristically recognized courtroom evidence (*bayyinah*) and confession (*iqrār*). This rule applies whether the right or guilt in question is adjudicated before a judge or an *amīr*.[135] In other words, the alternate fact-finding procedures relied upon by *amīr*s or *maẓālim* magistrates do not necessarily entail alternate forms of proof per se but simply alternate ways of procuring or producing legally valid evidence or confession. Stated differently, juristic law does not dictate (even if it may circumscribe) the means or tactics to be used by non-judges, including *amīr*s and *maẓālim* magistrates, in procuring or producing legally valid proof or confession, though it does dictate the means or tactics that may be relied upon by judges. As for the implementation of punishment once guilt has been established, al-Māwardī states that judges and *amīr*s are equal in this regard (*yastawī fī iqamat al-ḥudūd 'alayhim aḥwāl al-umarā' wa al-qudah*).[136]

Following this introduction, al-Māwardī's substantive treatment of criminal offenses in *al-Aḥkām al-Sulṭānīyah* reads like any standard *fiqh* manual might, including such crimes as adultery/fornication (*zinā*), theft, wine-drinking, and the like.[137] In other words, his description of the bicameral system at work applies to the standard crimes identified in *fiqh* and not to some separate or irregular regime of offenses. When we turn, however, to al-Māwardī's eighteen-volume work on *fiqh*, *al-Ḥāwī al-Kabīr*, we get a different picture. While *al-Ḥāwī al-Kabīr* reflects a cooperative relationship between judges, the police, and government officials, there is no mention in it of a bicameral arrangement involving two distinct venues for settling cases. The closest we come to such an arrangement is in the section on judicature (*qaḍāʾ*) where there appears to be a division of labor between the judge and the police (*wulāt al-maʿāwin*) or *amīr*. Where there is a suspected crime involving a right of humans (*ḥaqq ādamī*), such as sexual calumny (*qadhf*) or a pure right of God (e.g., wine-drinking, abandoning prayer), a judge's knowledge of law and the legal process is required to establish legal guilt or innocence. Thus, the judge presides over the case and hands down the ruling. The *amir* or the police, in turn, implement the sentence as handed down. Where, however, there is an offense involving a right of God that it is committed in so public a fashion that a judge's legal acumen (*ijtihād*) is not required, the *amīr* is more entitled than the judge to hand down the sentence and implement the punishment, because this kind of public misconduct touches upon the state's ability to project its awe and preserve its overall efficacy. Even here, however, if there is any need to hear evidence, the judge presides over the case and the *amīr* simply implements the sentence.[138]

In none of al-Māwardī's treatment of criminal offenses in *al-Ḥāwī al-Kabīr* is there any mention of the *amīr*'s added powers of coercion or of additional means of uncovering evidence that *fiqh* does not accord to judges. Nor is there any sense, outside the political considerations just mentioned, that a case might be brought before one as opposed to another tribunal, judge versus *amīr*, in *al-Ḥāwī al-Kabīr*'s sections on *ḥudūd*,[139] murder (*qatl*),[140] judicature (*qaḍāʾ*), or courtroom testimony (*shahādah*).[141] What this suggests is that, while the manuals of juristic law, that is, *fiqh/sharīʿah*, define the rules to be relied upon by judges, including the evidentiary burden and procedural rules attached thereto, the concrete means by which *amīr*s or government officials, such as *maẓālim* magistrates, might produce such evidence fall largely *outside* the purview of *fiqh*-manuals as a genre.

In his brief look at *maẓālim* tribunals, N. Hurvitz insightfully speculates that *qāḍīs*' courts applied stringent rules of evidence to protect individual suspects from abuse but that this high-minded approach resulted in many criminals being left to roam the streets. The less stringent rules of the *maẓālim* tribunals, Hurvitz suggests, were designed to pick up the slack, in a spirit that was more cooperative than competitive.[142] This theory would explain and confirm Fahmy's interpretation of what happened in the murder case cited earlier: officials of the Gharbiyat Governorate did not abandon the basic standard of proof; they simply availed themselves, as the functional equivalents of *amīr*s or *maẓālim* magistrates, of non-juristically defined means of producing proof. Over the course of his treatment, al-Māwardī discusses the basic parameters and limits of such non-juristically-defined-evidence-gathering powers, even citing the views of other jurists in this regard. This occurs, however, in *al-Aḥkām al-Sulṭānīyah*, not in *al-Ḥāwī al-Kabīr*.[143] This suggests, again, that were one to rely on *fiqh*-books alone, one might well assume, based on the evidentiary requirements described therein, that much of Islamic law, including the rules enshrined in *sharīʿah*, was never applied. Or, whenever extra-juristic means of discovery or enforcement showed up in chronicles, biographical dictionaries, or archives, one might assume that this could only reflect an abuse of power, a disregard for Islamic law, decline, or secularization.

By contrast, al-Māwardī—who, like Abū Yaʿlā, was a prominent jurist and judge—recognized that, while these extra-juristic powers might go beyond *fiqh/sharīʿah*, they did not necessarily fall outside the bounds of Islamic law.[144] Thus, al-Māwardī ends his *al-Aḥkām al-Sulṭānīyah* by noting, "Most of this book of ours [on governance] covers what the *fuqahā'* ignored or fell short in clarifying. We simply included what they ignored and fully clarified what they fell short in clarifying."[145] In other words, there is a non-*sharʿī*, Islamic Secular reglementary regime that should be recognized, even by jurists, as a bona fide feature of governance and a constituent of "Islamic law," a reglementary regime that complements rather than rivals *sharīʿah*. This was an established perception almost a thousand years ago, long before it could have been the result of any half-hearted concession in the face of inexorable decline, government abuse, Westernization, or the rise of the modern state.

Ḥisbah

In her insightful book, *Islamic Law in Action*, Kristen Stilt confirms that *ḥisbah* relies simultaneously on the authority of *fiqh* and on that of *siyāsah*. According to her:

> In terms of constitutional structure, these two sets of influences correspond to two fundamental concepts of authority: the authority of doctrine, associated with the jurists who formulated it, and the authority of policy-based decisions (*siyāsa*), associated with the rulers. The *muḥtasib* was guided by and responsible to both sources of authority.[146]

Stilt's characterization shows that, alongside its *sharʿī* dimension, *ḥisbah* has an unmistakably non-*sharʿī* side. In her view, however, *ḥisbah* (like *siyāsah*) can be thought of as a constituent of *sharīʿah*. For, *sharīʿah*, as she sees it, equals Islamic law, and " 'Islamic law' . . . is intended to encompass *fiqh* and [she wants] to suggest that *siyāsa* might productively be considered *fiqh*'s necessary counterpart under the heading of Sharia."[147] This interpretation is neither unreasonable nor unprecedented. And Stilt is not overly doctrinaire in this regard. In her Conclusion to the book, she refers explicitly to the need to develop ways of assessing "when *siyāsa* has been considered a part of the broad notion of Sharia and when, and by whom, *siyāsa*-based actions were considered to fall outside the

Sharia."[148] I have sided, of course, with placing *siyāsah*—and, with it, aspects of *ḥisbah*—outside *sharīʿah*, partly in order to avoid misrecognizing, undervaluing, or occluding the explicitly non-*sharʿī* dimensions and commitments that inform these offices.

For his part, al-Māwardī—Stilt's main source for her theoretical discussion—raises *ḥisbah*'s non-*sharʿī* side to prominence, by highlighting a particular mode of *ijtihād* undertaken by the *muḥtasib* that stands in explicit contrast to that of the jurists. This is what al-Māwardī refers to as "*ijtihād ʿurfī*," or "independent practical discretion," as opposed to the "*ijtihād sharʿī*" or "*ijtihād ḥukmī*," that is, independent scriptural interpretation aimed at arriving at a *hukm sharʿī*, as practiced by jurists and judges.[149] Al-Māwardī cites *ijtihād ʿurfī* in several places over the course of his treatment of *ḥisbah*. Perhaps the clearest depiction appears in his discussion of zoning regulations. Here, he characterizes the *muḥtasib*'s job as protecting the common good and policing nuisances. If a person builds a structure that blocks a thoroughfare, the *muḥtasib* must order its demolition, even if the structure is a mosque. This standard applies as well to awnings, porticos, waterways, wells, and the like. In all such cases, the *muḥtasib* is to permit what is not harmful to the community and ban what is. And in determining which is which, he must rely on his *ijtihād*, that is, "*yajtahid ra'yah*." Here, however, al-Māwardī all but goes out of his way to clarify the distinction between these two modes of *ijtihād*:

> This is *ijtihād ʿurfī*, not *ijtihād sharʿī*. And the difference between the two is that *ijtihād sharʿī* seeks to ascertain a thing's status as a matter of *sharʿ* (*mā rūʿiya fīhi aṣl^{un} thabata ḥukmuhu bi al-sharʿ*), whereas *ijtihād ʿurfī* seeks to ascertain a thing's status as a matter of custom.[150]

In other words, the *muḥtasib*'s concrete, on-the-job execution is informed by a cumulative experience and practical knowledge that is largely unrelated to any ability on his part to extract rules from the sources of the *sharʿ*.

Of course, *sharīʿah* would cumulatively inform the *muḥtasib*'s perception of what is "beneficial" and what is "harmful," indeed, even, perhaps, what is normatively customary, that is, as a matter of recognized precedent. But much of this perception would come not through the study of texts but through transgenerational acculturation and socialization. As Stilt points out, after a certain point, most *muḥtasib*s had only "minimal education" in *sharīʿah*.[151] A *muḥtasib*'s practical sensibilities came to him, thus, much like Kantian sensibilities (e.g., transcendent reason, religion as morality) are assimilated by moderns who have never read Kant and know nothing about the Enlightenment. Like the *maẓālim* magistrate, the *muḥtasib* often enforced *sharīʿah* rules that were simply well known, generally agreed upon, or identified by the ruler as the *sharīʿah* rule *du* *jour*. In exceptional cases, he might, as a *mujtahid*, even derive such rules on his own.[152] But al-Māwardī is clear that *qua muḥtasib* he does not have the authority to derive and impose juristic rules (*aḥkām sharʿīyah*) based on his own *ijtihād sharʿī*.[153] In fact, in agreement with Abū Yaʿlā, he insists that if a slave complains about his master's failing to provide food or clothing, the *muḥtasib* can command the master to provide these. But if the complaint is about quantity or quality, the *muḥtasib* cannot impose anything specific. This is because, according to both Abū Yaʿlā and al-Māwardī, "Determining quantity or quality (*taqdīr*) requires *ijtihād sharʿī*, while insisting on the basic obligation to provide food or clothing does not."[154]

The jurisdictional boundary here is not entirely clear (or, shall we say, not entirely agreed upon). Jurists such as al-Qarāfī would consider the determination of quantity and quality to be matters of fact that fall beneath the "vertical boundary" of the *ḥukm sharʿī*.[155] As such, their determination would be *ʿurfī* rather than *sharʿī*, and this would expand the jurisdiction of the *muḥtasib* even *qua muḥtasib*. But we should be clear that such differences would be grounded ultimately in questions of what is factual versus what is legal, not in questions of what constitutes the parameters of the *muḥtasib*'s jurisdiction. While al-Qarāfī would differ with al-Māwardī and Abū Yaʿlā on whether quantity and quantity are factual or legal questions, they would all agree, as a matter principle, that the *muḥtasib* does not do *ijtihād sharʿī*.[156] In sum, however widely or narrowly one draws the line between the *sharʿī* and the *ʿurfī*, a sizeable amount of the *muḥtasib*'s work will fall outside the *sharʿī* and within the non-*sharʿī* realm of the Islamic Secular. This non-*sharʿī* activity can exert far-reaching if not determinative impact on the everyday normative order.

Stilt provides several insightful examples that demonstrate this point, one of which will serve here. In the year 776/1374, the Mālikī *muḥtasib* of Cairo, Shams al-Dīn al-Damīrī, set out to do the masses a favor by lowering bread prices, which everyone feared were about to spike in the face of impending low Nile levels. His decree was welcomed by the populace, but its deflationary impact soon caused bread supplies to dry up. People panicked, and in response the *muḥtasib* lifted all price restrictions. This quickly led to inflation, however, which decimated the poor. Six months later, after prices recovered, al-Damīrī decided on an even larger price reduction, which affected the bottom line of bakers and millers. In response, the former insisted that they would pay only so much for flour and the latter insisted that they would pay only so much for wheat. The grain importers who had arrived at the dock with fresh inventory refused to sell at these low prices and turned around to head for more lucrative ports, precipitating another round of hardship for the people.[157]

Clearly, as we saw with Mamlūk economic policy, these official actions greatly affected people's everyday lives. They were *not*, however—certainly not substantively speaking—dictated by *sharīʿah*.[158] On the contrary, they were non-*sharʿī*, practical, discretionary calculations aimed at serving the public good (however conceived).[159] Yet, they were also legitimate, *sharʿan*, having nothing (necessarily) to do with any abuse of power, corruption, or graft. They also clearly constituted law, as violators could be legally punished. And one can assume that they were Islamic, as they violated no *sharīʿah*-dictates and were clearly aimed at serving the Islamic interest of securing people's basic needs.

In the end, Stilt's informative review of *ḥisbah* makes it clear that Muslim society's legal (not to mention socio-political, economic, and cultural) order is not strictly a function of how assiduously *sharīʿah* in the form of juristic law is applied. Legitimately enacted, non-*sharʿī*, discretionary, Islamic Secular rules and policies have a far-reaching impact on the applied Islamic order. Recognizing this fact may bring us to a deeper appreciation of my alternative to Shahab Ahmed's understanding of the aforementioned statement of Ibn Qutaybah. Al-Damīrī's non-*sharʿī* miscalculations, like those al-Maqrīzī attributes to Mamlūk authorities in his time, had palpably negative consequences for Islam as a lived commitment. Yet, regarding those who would seek to halt these dislocations through "better" rules of *sharīʿah*, Ibn Qutaybah would likely ask: "What do they know of *dīn* who only *sharīʿah* know?"[160]

As *muḥtasib*, al-Damīrī's *ijtihād ʿurfī* was clearly aimed more at determining facts (i.e., what would be economically most advantageous for the populace) and how these could be brought about than it was at interpreting the sources of juristic law. On balance, the *muḥtasib* (like the *maẓālim* magistrate, *amīr*s and the ruler with his *siyāsah*) was far more vested with jurisdiction of *fact* than he was with jurisdiction of *law*, the latter being the primary preserve of the jurists. On this understanding, the actions of such officials fall more rather than less into the domain of the Islamic Secular. Keeping this in mind, we can see that the role of the Islamic Secular is more central than marginal to the rule of law and the maintenance of a normative Islamic order than may appear at first blush.

Historically speaking, certainly by post-formative times, Islamic law, that is, the composite of *fiqh/sharīʿah, siyāsah, maẓālim*, and *ḥisbah*, was not—and was never understood or intended to be, even by the jurists—the exclusive preserve and responsibility of the "*fuqahāʾ*-jurisprudents." On the contrary, it was a condominium, and maintaining the rule of law was the collective province and responsibility of the Community as a whole, including the state and its officials. Even Ibn al-Qayyim, who, as we saw, was a staunch *sharīʿah*-maximalist, enumerates several "vested authorities" (*wilāyāt*/sg. *wilāyah*), including the *muḥtasib* (everyone being technically responsible for commanding right and forbidding wrong), the *maẓālim* magistrate, the vizier, the governor, the exchequer, the secretary, and the judge—all of whom, in addition to the jurists, he holds responsible for upholding the normative Islamic order. "This," he insists, "is an obligation upon every Muslim who is capable of fulfilling it," and the only difference between Community members in this regard is their relative degrees of ability (*qudrah*).[161] Clearly, much of what the named authorities would rely upon in seeking to serve the rule of law and the commonweal would be non-*shar'ī*, Islamic Secular insights and deliberations.

One wonders, in such light, how much the modern Western presumption of a normative separation between the religious and the secular, between church and state, has informed the tendency among scholars to disaggregate Islam and Muslim society into jurists on one side and rulers on the other, with the rest of the Community now falling on one side, now on the other. The Western insistence on separating religion and state tends to cast the two as enemies. And this, along with certain facts of Muslim history, especially modern Muslim history, has dislocated in the minds of many Muslims (and non-Muslims) the idea of a cooperative relationship between the *shar'ī*, the non-*shar'ī*, and their respective personnel, particularly with regard to politics and governance. Against this mental habit, however, we might consider the view of the redoubtable Shāfi'ī jurist "*Sulṭān al-'Ulamā'*," 'Izz al-Dīn Ibn 'Abd al-Salām. He noted how difficult it is to arrive at an understanding, in concrete terms, of what will actually serve the interest (*maṣlaḥah*) of the Community and avert the harms (*mafsadah*) facing it, arguing that it is often impossible to arrive at anything but approximations (*taqrīb*) in this regard.[162] Precisely for this reason, however, he insisted, "Generally speaking, the reward that accrues to the just *imām*, official, and judge is greater than that of all other persons, by the unanimous consensus of the Muslims."[163] In fact, "The reward of the Caliph (*al-imām al-a'ẓam*) is greater than that of the *mufti* and the judge, because the benefits he brings and the harms he averts are more complete and far-reaching in scope.... Thus, Muslims are in unanimous agreement that undertaking political office is among the best forms of obedience to God" (*ajma'a al-muslimūn 'alā anna al-wilāyāt min afḍal al-ṭā'āt*).[164] Two points must be noted here. First, much of what al-'Izz alludes to entails Islamic Secular activity—the practical assessment of concrete interests and harms facing the Muslim Community on the ground. Second, this statement came from one of the most committed jurists and notoriously staunch, no-nonsense advocates and defenders of *sharī'ah* in the history of the Mamlūk period. Surely, in light of his claim, the notion that jurists ceded to the state only what the latter forced them to cede calls for reconsideration. So does the idea that blind hostility toward the state was the normative ideal for all jurists, or that jurists idealized the notion that "a society operating by the legal and cultural norms of the Shari'a was one that was largely self-governing ... [s]elf-rule [being] a marker of the state's absence."[165] To be sure, al-'Izz acknowledges that rulers and state officials throughout Muslim history have generally been corrupt.[166] But this takes nothing from what he sees as the normative status of the condominium, including the normative role of the state and other non-jurists in promoting the Islamic-cum-*shar'ī* norm and the common good.

The Islamic Secular: "Beyond the Law"

In a sense, the entire discussion thus far has been about the Islamic Secular as a domain and mode of engagement "beyond the law," that is, beyond the horizontal or vertical boundaries of *sharī'ah* and its *ḥukm shar'ī*. There are two other senses, however, in which I would like to invoke this trope relative to the Islamic Secular.

In the first sense, unlike the case above, "beyond the law" does not refer to non-*shar'ī* or *'aqlī* efforts to fulfill the law, for example, by figuring out how to earn enough money to satisfy the obligation to support one's family. Nor does it refer to the determination of the facts upon which the application of the law depends, for example, the sun's position in the sky or how a *maẓālim* magistrate might acquire pieces of evidence in a criminal case. Nor is "beyond the law" here a reference to the super-category of *siyāsah*, as a separate regime of supplemental, micro-secular rulemaking. In fact, it would be torturous to apply the word "*siyāsah*" to much of what will be discussed under the rubric, "beyond the law." "Beyond the law" in this first sense focuses on *how* and *by whom* the substance and authority of juristic law and its non-*shar'ī* complement is held in place. Building on the assumption that law is not self-sustaining, my investigation focuses on the role of the non-*shar'ī*, Islamic Secular in shaping and safeguarding *sharī'ah*'s (and, secondarily, Islamic law's) meanings and preserving their overall authority. My contention is that the non-*shar'ī*, Islamic Secular efforts of non-jurists are as critical (or nearly as critical) to maintaining the meanings and practical integrity of Islam-cum-*sharī'ah* as are the *shar'ī* efforts of the jurists.

But, before we get too far ahead of ourselves, let me spell out in more concrete terms the meaning and implications of "beyond the law" in this first sense.

Nomos and Plausibility Structure

In his book, *The Sacred Canopy*, Peter Berger introduced, in a sociological context, the concept of *nomos* or plausibility structure as the single most critical factor in collective meaning-making.[167] Berger described *nomos* as an "ordering of experience," the process of imposing meaning on the panoply of quotidian activity that makes up our socio-cultural existence.[168] While we are the authors of this "world-building enterprise," we are also partly its product. We externalize our inner thoughts and impulses by casting them out into the world. The cumulative result is "culture," which we confront as an object no less grounded in facticity than trees or cold weather. We then internalize this culture as part of the cognitive and affective apparatus through which we derive and produce meaning, self-understanding, and self-appraisal. As a society, consciously aware of this collective relationship to culture, we seek to stabilize our social order; for, according to Berger, the meaning-making *nomos* is a "shield against terror," allowing us to make sense of and impute value to everyday existence.[169] Socialization, in turn, is the process by which we collectively maintain this order, which is optimally achieved when we are able to keep the *nomos* "invisible." As Berger put it, "It is not enough that the individual look upon the key meanings of the social order as useful, desirable, or right. It is much better . . . if he looks upon them as inevitable, as part and parcel of the universal 'nature of things.' "[170] In the end, the interpretive schemas that we internalize through the *nomos* contribute significantly to the "meaning" we are able to impute to or extract from any external reality, be the latter social, cultural, political, interpersonal, or legal.

In a famous essay entitled, "Nomos and Narrative," published in 1983–84, Yale Law professor Robert Cover (d. 1986) converted the sociological concept of *nomos* into an instrument for examining law.[171] Cover suggested that the law student might identify the normative universe he inhabits with the rules, principles, material sources, and formal institutions of the law. But, while these are important, they are only a part of what should command his or her attention. According to Cover, "No set of legal institutions or prescriptions exists apart from the narratives that locate it and give it meaning."[172] These "narratives" are not solely (or even predominantly) a function of a community's dialectical interaction with the law or its sources. They come, rather, from "the trajectories plotted upon material reality by our imaginations."[173] "The varied and complex materials of that *nomos* establish paradigms for dedication, acquiescence, contradiction and resistance."[174] In other words, the *nomos*, according to Cover, is a "jurisgenerative" force that contributes critically to the creation and anchoring of legal meaning. And it does this largely through the sheer cultural power of the narrative it represents. As Cover put it, "The *nomos* that I have described requires no state. . . . [T]he creation of legal meaning—'jurisgenesis'—takes place always through an essentially cultural medium."[175]

Cover's point was that legal meaning is not the product of a naked, dialectical encounter between the interpreter and the interpreted text. It is, rather, the result of a triangular move in which the encounter with the text(s) is mediated by a *nomos*. As scholars of *sharīʿah*, many of us have encountered source texts that are adduced to justify particular rules, only to notice the surprisingly tenuous relationship between the text and the rule in question. Take, for example, the Qur'anic verse, "*And among the people are those who trade idle tales (*lahw al-ḥadīth*) in order, in ignorance, to steer people away from God's path and take the latter as sport.*" [31:6] This verse is routinely cited as a proof-text for banning singing, music, and musical instruments. Meanwhile, there are verses that clearly speak admonishingly (if not disparagingly) about poetry: "*And the poets, they are followed by those ever seduced. Do you not see them tumbling into every valley, lost to passion, saying that which they do not do—except those who believe and work righteous deeds, remembering God often*?" [26: 224–7] Yet, these are rarely taken to cast doubt on the permissibility of poetry, even the poetry of the pre-Islamic unbelievers. Clearly, something other than the words themselves are producing and holding certain meanings in place. According to Cover, this something is the *nomos*.[176]

Whence comes this *nomos*? Cover suggests that it is essentially a cultural product. I agree. But this conclusion raises interesting questions about the nature and viability of legal meaning itself. These questions are particularly applicable to a religious legal system, such as *sharīʿah*, where at least some of the meanings must be presumed to be transcendent and thus hostile, if not impervious, to change, especially by something as fickle as "culture" or "popular will." But even the authority of these "transcendent" meanings must ultimately be held in place by the religious Community itself. Speaking more specifically about meaning in a religious context, Berger referred to the *nomos* as a religion's "plausibility structure," that is, "those processes that ongoingly reconstruct and maintain [a] particular world[view]," against the backdrop of which a religion is able to sustain its normativeness and integrity.[177] According to him, "anyone who wants to maintain the reality of a particular religious system . . . must maintain (or, if necessary, fabricate) an appropriate plausibility structure."[178] Both Cover and Berger are clear that legal meaning (religious or other) is not self-constituting and that it cannot, at least not entirely, hold itself in place. But if *nomos* and plausibility structures actually work as these men suggest, it cannot be the jurists alone who determine the law and preserve the authority of its meanings. For, *nomos* and plausibility structures, or at least significant aspects thereof, are fashioned and maintained by acts and actors whose specialized theater of operation lies not only beyond the *sharʿ* but also beyond the expertise of the jurists.

Of course, we should not overstate matters. Part of the *nomos* in the case of Islam-cum-*sharīʿah* will result from Islam-cum-*sharīʿah*'s projecting its fundamental rules, values, and sensibilities so forcefully and consistently into Muslim socio-cultural and political space that they effectively become inextricable constituents thereof, often beyond notice. Similarly, the mimetic energies powered by the stature imputed to the Companions and Pious Ancestors (*salaf*)—real and imagined—will ongoingly anchor at least aspects of the prevailing narrative. But, for the vast majority of less central rules—and certainly unprecedented rules—that lie beyond the direct influence of these forces and projections, *sharīʿah* alone neither can nor will preserve the meanings of *sharīʿah*; neither can nor will the interpretive machinery of Islamic legal methodology (*uṣūl al-fiqh*). Indeed, even where this methodology can be credited with producing a particular meaning, we will need to go beyond that meaning and methodology themselves to find out what continues to hold them and their authority in place.

Let me try to give a brief example of what I am trying to get at here. In his famous book, *Ghiyāth al-Umam fī Iltiyāth al-Ẓulam* (*Rescuing Communities in the Midst of the Darknesses of Decline*), the celebrated Shāfiʿī jurist Imām al-Ḥaramayn al-Juwaynī takes his equally famous Shāfiʿī contemporary al-Māwardī (or perhaps it was Abū Yaʿlā[179]) to task for legally allowing protected religious Others, or *ahl al-dhimmah*, to serve as "executive viziers" (*wazīr al-tanfīdh*). An executive vizier, in contradistinction to a vizier (*wazīr al-tafwīḍ*), makes no decisions on his own but simply implements those of his superiors. In banning non-Muslims from holding this office, al-Juwaynī adduces four arguments grounded in Islamic legal methodology: (1) the Qurʾānic verse, "*Do not fill your entourage with people other than yourselves who spare no opportunity to cause you harm*" [3:118]; (2) the Qurʾānic verse "*Do not surrender the running of your affairs to Jews and Christians*" [5:51]; (3) a Prophetic *ḥadīth*: "I am absolved of responsibility for every Muslim who goes out of his way to keep company with polytheists; and (4) a precedent set by the second Caliph, Umar I, who rebuked one of his governors for employing a Christian secretary.[180]

Al-Juwaynī implies that the straightforward meanings of these sources lead unavoidably to the interpretation he wants to champion. None of the obvious ambiguity attaching to these sources give him pause, for example, what is an "entourage" (*biṭānah*); what is "the running of your affairs" (*wilāyah*), and how does it relate to the executive vizier with his limited, subordinate authority; did ʿUmar ban *all* Christian secretaries; what about ʿUthmān and ʿAlī? His rhetorical force also drowns out other *prima facie* relevant source material, for example, the Qurʾānic verses, "*Among the People of the Book are those who if entrusted with an entire treasure will promptly return it to you*" [3:75]; and "*They are not the same; among the People of the Book are a community who stand at night rehearsing God's verses and prostrating; they believe in God and the Last Day, they command what is good and forbid what is evil, and they compete with one another in righteousness. Indeed, they are among the righteous.*" [3:113–14]. On al-Juwaynī's rendering, the meaning of "Jews" and "Christians" is presumed to be general and unqualified, covering all Jews and all Christians at all times and places, under almost all circumstances and conditions.[181]

Clearly, however, it is neither the words alone nor al-Juwaynī's renderings alone that hold these meanings and the status of his argument in place. But perhaps a better way to get at the issue would be to ask what might alter their incumbency? Another overall vision or attitude toward Jews and Christians might dislodge it. But from where would that vision come? Maybe an individual experience by an extremely popular caliph or the Community at large; maybe just a widely circulated historical account validated by the Community's greatest historians; maybe a consistently maintained school curriculum or even a wildly popular heroic poem by a major poet—a contemporary Abū Tammām; or maybe an exposé about a Jew or Christian who developed and shared a cure for a deadly disease that had decimated the Muslim community. In the end, all these potential interventions—and this is the crux of the matter—would be essentially 'secular' and "beyond the law," as none of them would draw their concrete substance or authority from scripture or any other recognized juristic source. Nor would they be the preserve of the jurists *qua* jurists. Yet, all these activities would (or could) be pursued under the conscious awareness of the adjudicative gaze of the God of Islam, in an effort to normalize meanings deemed to be true(r) to God's will and of service to the concrete interests of the Muslim Community while not running afoul of the authority of *sharīʿah* itself. And to the extent that the right incentives backed these efforts, they would all be eligible for being considered "Islamic."

Of course, this perspective generates its share of liabilities. To begin with, if factors beyond the sources (*uṣūl*) of the law play a role in determining and preserving the substance and authority of the law, what is to ensure the primacy of the sources themselves in the interpretive processes that produce the law?[182] Similarly, what happens to the jurists' presumptive monopoly over the production of juristic meaning? Most importantly, what role does scripture play in informing the substance or directing the thrust of the non-*sharʿī* activities that produce, contribute to, and preserve Islam's *nomos* or plausibility structure, given the latter's critical contribution to the substance and authority of the *sharʿ*?

As a preliminary to my attempt to answer these questions, I call on the concept of what the Italian thinker Giambattista Vico (d. 1744) referred to as "*fantasia*," or "man's unique capacity for imaginative insight and reconstruction."[183] Imagination is the key element here, as it is the ground of what I referred to in Chapter 1 as obeisance, in contrast to obedience. Conscious obedience to a command requires that we first comprehend the command itself. This entails a type of reading that relies on what the scholar of Asian religion Alan Watts (d. 1973) refers to as "central vision," in contrast to "peripheral vision," which is used for such things as "seeing at night, and for taking 'subconscious' notice of objects and movements not in the direct line of central vision."[184] Peripheral vision is the instrument through which scripture and the tradition it spawns can be engaged with "imaginatively." This approach should be distinguished from engaging with these sources irrationally, irresponsibly, or self-servingly; for, on my approach, a conscious awareness of the divine gaze and presence of the God of

Islam normatively informs the process by which peripheral vision apprehends its object. Driven by this "orientation," various types of imagination—moral, practical, religious, aesthetic—may be deemed subjective and nonrational. But since they are fired by prejudgments that are themselves proper to a particular vision (in this case Islam), this subjective element is ideally reduced to a non-problem.

By engaging with the sources and tradition "imaginatively," then, I simply mean engaging with them in a manner that is not limited to "central vision." This is not the same as resorting to "figurative interpretation," or *ta'wīl*; in fact, it may not entail anything figurative at all. It is closer, rather, to what a teenager who has received no explicit curfew relies upon in discerning the right time to come home. What his parents tell him explicitly is neither ignored nor figuratively interpreted; on the contrary, he relies on the plain sense of what they say and do. And this reliance, together with his cumulative experience with their style, overall vision and expectations as parents, informs his *fantasia* and enables him, imaginatively, to fill in the gaps left by what they do *not* say or do. Applying this attitude to scripture, one can develop an interactive relationship between central vision, *fantasia*, and one's ultimate understanding of revelation, as well as the tradition this spawns, the four organically informing each other. MacIntyre captures much of this dynamic when he writes (in another context) of the relationship between the reader and scripture:

> The reader [i]s assigned the task of interpreting the text, but also ha[s] to discover, in and through his or her reading of those texts, that they in turn interpret the reader. What the reader, as thus interpreted by the texts, has to learn about him or herself is that it is only the self as transformed through and by the reading of the texts which will be capable of reading the texts aright.[185]

The process of constructing and preserving the appropriate *nomos* entails Muslims' moving through socio-cultural time and space, individually and collectively, imbued with visions, sensibilities, and aspirations that serve this interest. All of these come from an engagement with scripture and tradition through both central and peripheral vision, or *fantasia*, in tandem with the mimetic energies born of a connection with the Muslim past. On this understanding, the construction and preservation of *nomos* need not occur beyond the sources, in the sense of these sources playing no role in the process. Islam's foundational documents have already informed Muslim tradition and the Muslim past. Moreover, these sources are not semantically uniform: "revelatory" does not categorically equal "juristic." As such, the sources may be legitimately processed through modes of reading that go beyond the central vision of a strictly *sharʿī* gaze. Processed through central vision alone, a verse such as "*Is the reward for goodness anything other than goodness*" (*hal jazāʾu 'l-iḥsān illa 'l-iḥsān*) [55: 60] may command no specific, concrete action. But the peripheral vision powering *fantasia* might extract sensibilities from this verse that apply in every area of endeavor, including *fiqh*-cum scriptural interpretation. Jurists thus have no less use for *fantasia* and peripheral vision than non-jurists. In fact, without the benefit of the sensibilities, consciousness-raising, and insights that *fantasia* affords, the juristic enterprise is susceptible to compromise if not perversion.

The same applies to non-jurists. Most of the work of *nomos*-building consists of non-*shar'ī* activities that rely not on juristic interpretive acumen (language skills, knowledge of *ḥadīth*, etc.) but, more broadly speaking, on talent, genius, drive, taste, skill, and charisma, even common sense—all those non-*shar'ī* energies that back culture-production. Like jurists,' non-jurists' sensibilities are normatively primed by a scripturally imbued, tradition-informed *fantasia*, alongside a transgenerational mimetic energy, as part of a broader regime of what Ebrahim Moosa and, after him, Wael Hallaq (drawing on Foucault) nicely describe as Islam's "technologies of the self."[186] But there is no guarantee that every non-jurist (or jurist) will avail him- or herself of Islam's technologies of the self or engage with scripture and tradition in a manner that breeds proper prejudgments or "legitimate prejudices."[187] For this reason, depending on their orientation, the *nomos* they construct may end up weakening rather than strengthening Islam-cum-*sharī'ah*, constituting, in effect, a secularizing rather than an Islamicizing force. This possibility underscores the broader point that I am trying to make: the law *will* be affected by the prevailing *nomos*, whether those who construct it are pious or wicked, indeed, Muslims or non-Muslims—not only with regard to the law's specific meanings but also in terms of the degree of overall authority it enjoys.

The challenge, thus, unless one is willing to live a life of perpetual apology and adjustment, is how to confront the problem of *nomos* and plausibility structure head-on. As Richard Rorty reminds us, the task of anyone who wants to live according to a chosen norm is "to create the taste by which he will be judged."[188] Edward Bernays (d. 1995), the "father of modern propaganda," extends this insight a giant step further:

> The conscious and intelligent manipulation of the organized habits and opinions of the masses is an important element in democratic society. Those who manipulate this unseen mechanism of society constitute an invisible government which is the true ruling power of our country. We are governed, our minds molded, our taste formed, our ideas suggested, largely by men we have never heard of.[189]

Whether a society is democratic or not, poetry, architecture, education, city-planning, economics, technology, political philosophy, and now, journalism, film, advertising, and the like all have much more relevance to the substance and authority of the society's law than is commonly assumed.[190] All of these contribute directly or otherwise to the prevailing *nomos* and plausibility structure. How a people feels and thinks collectively about laws depends on more than just the laws' substance or jurisprudential basis. In America, for example, non-legal developments have certainly gone as far as legal ones (if not further) in explaining the legalization of same-sex marriage or how the Fourteenth Amendment could support "separate but equal" in 1896 (*Plessy v. Ferguson*) but the banning of racial segregation in 1954 (*Brown v. the Board of Education*).

Of course, we cannot assume that this modern understanding of the workings of *nomos* and plausibility structure extends seamlessly back into the pre-modern Islamic past. But the difference is more one of degree than of kind. In the introduction to his refutation of the *falāsifah*, for example, al-Ghazālī notes explicitly that he was moved to write this work upon seeing how strongly people were being influenced by such "highfalutin names as Socrates, Hippocrates, Plato, Aristotle, and the like" and the dangerous doctrines associated with these men.[191] Al-Ghazālī was not worried simply about the substance of Greek doctrine, which most people would not be able to understand; he was worried about these doctrines' association with these esteemed names and the authority and validation they and their legacy as a whole might draw from this. We find a similar logic, though expressed more aggressively, in Ibn Taymīyah's criticisms of such trends as Muslims dressing in a manner that defies the collective cultural authority of the Muslim Community, or celebrating non-Muslim holidays, or Arabic-speaking Muslims speaking other than Arabic. In fact, he explains the change in the direction of prayer (*qiblah*) from Jerusalem to Mecca as part of an attempt to keep Muslims from falling under Jewish cultural-cum-religious authority. For him, part of the whole point of Qur'ān 2:142–5 was "so that the Jews would not be able to argue against you on the basis of your following their practice, saying, 'They followed us in our direction of prayer, which comes close to their agreeing with us in our religion.' "[192] These examples (and I could cite more) reflect a clear recognition of the importance of what goes on "beyond the law" relative to the integrity and overall authority of the law.

In such light, the idea that the *fuqahā'* exercised a monopoly over *sharī'ah* and its meanings can be maintained only by ignoring or misrecognizing the impact of non-*shar'ī* elements on both the substance and the status of the law. Law follows at least as often as it leads, and a society whose economic, socio-cultural, and intellectual production is stagnant can hardly be expected to produce and sustain a legal system that commands widespread confidence and esteem, domestically or internationally. No one borrows from the legal systems of poor and undeveloped countries. And in this light one must understand that the *fuqahā'* have never exercised an actual monopoly over *sharī'ah*'s fortunes.[193] Nor, as an understanding of the Islamic Secular makes clear, was or is it uniquely their charge to do so. Today, jurists, *qua* jurists, can hardly be expected to produce alternatives to the prevailing global *nomos* that so threatens the authority and integrity of Islam-cum-*sharīʿah*—healthy economies, robust educational institutions, advanced technology, superior military might, competitive popular culture, political theory, a healthy political culture, and the like—any more than they were expected to do so in the past.[194]

As Jonathan Brown notes in his book on slavery, Muslim jurists had long recognized the abolishment of slavery as one of the ideals, or *maqāṣid*, of Islam.[195] While the modern West beat them to the punch, this was not the result of some unique moral insight that Euro-Americans suddenly happened upon. Instead, economic, social, and technological developments triggered changes in moral sensibilities and reasoning.[196] As Aristotle predicted, it was "when looms powered themselves" that a new *nomos* came into being, enabling humans to imagine the possibility and propriety of ending slave-labor.[197] Clearly, in this case, the non-juristic activity that changed the texture and valuation of manual labor would have been much more likely than juristic deliberation, or *ijtihād sharʿī*, to bring Muslims to the practical realization of what had long been recognized in theory as a bona fide Islamic ideal. Here, incidentally, one can see how the *maqāṣid al-sharīʿah* cease (or should cease) to be solely a tool for guiding the deliberations of jurists. Non-jurists can also be guided by the *maqāṣid* in contemplating how to deploy their non-*sharʿī* skills and talents in pursuit of divine pleasure and maintaining the integrity of Islam.

These issues bring new meaning to the question of the so-called crisis of authority in contemporary Islam. While the jurists may exercise an ostensible monopoly over juristic interpretation, the ability to inform and produce numerous aspects of Islam—including aspects of Islamic law—is diffused throughout the Community, far beyond the ranks of the *fuqahā'*. Precisely for this reason, the overall state of Islam-cum-*sharīʿah* in any given time or place never has rested and never will rest solely on the shoulders of the *fuqahā'*. The normative relationship between the producers and carriers of *sharʿī* and non-*sharʿī* knowledge and creativity is—or should be—far more complementary than categorically hierarchical. This, again, is clearly the point of Shaykh Yūsuf al-Qaraḍāwī's aforementioned insistence that Islamic culture is both religious and secular (*dīn wa dunyā*)."[198] His argument clearly reflects the importance of the interpretive and generative contributions of the Islamic Secular "beyond the law."

Efficient Decision-Making

The second sense of "beyond the law" concerns the challenge of individual and collective decision-making, not as part of the effort to uphold or fulfill the law but in pursuit of such quotidian interests as wealth, happiness, love, friendship, fun, civilization, and the like—interests that fall within the general notice of the *shar*ʿ but on which the *shar*ʿ provides no concrete instruction. Here, non-*sharʿī* Islamic Secular deliberations must be relied upon to lead the way. We are dealing, in other words, not with *sharīʿah*'s concrete dos and don'ts but with what *sharīʿah* simply allows, within the broad juristic category of the *mubāḥ*, or "permissible." As the *mubāh is* a juristic category, some might object that we are not really "beyond the law" here, or that we are so only in the sense I mentioned in Chapter 2. I want to suggest, however, that there is something far more subtle and consequential at stake.

Even as a juristic category, the *mubāḥ* admits countless choices that may be equally "permissible" from the standpoint of *sharīʿah*. While it may be necessary (as noted in Chapter 2) to go beneath its vertical boundary to arrive at a concrete decision, the actual act of settling upon a particular choice occurs neither in pursuit of fulfilling the *ḥukm sharʿī* itself nor simply because the act in question is permissible. Something beyond permissibility and *sharʿī* status determines this decision. For, the fact that an act is permissible, *sharʿan*, does not necessarily render it effective, socially appropriate, profitable, romantic, or chic. What is ultimately at stake in this second sense of "beyond the law" is whether the contributions of non-*sharʿī*, differentiated, 'secular' considerations are explicitly recognized and valued as "Islamic," as part of Muslims' decision-making apparatus, not simply on the level of the state (which is why the term "*siyāsah*" could not be aptly applied here) but also on the substate level of the individual and the Community. For, only on the basis of such recognition can individuals and communities often address the real issues behind many of their most pressing problems.

Take the matter of speed limits. Even if we determine the need to have them by acknowledging the broader interest of preserving life (*ḥifẓ al-nafs*), the question of what the actual speed limit should be remains outstanding. The mere fact that it would be permissible to choose 39 or 55 or 90 miles per hour would not determine the choice itself. For, the pertinent question would be not whether a particular choice is permissible but whether it is practically efficient—whether this or that permissible option serves the concrete interest at hand. But this determination cannot be concretely made based solely on the instruments of juristic law. "Efficient" is simply not a *sharʿī* category.[199] The choice would have to be made, therefore, based on such non-*sharʿī*, *ʿaqlī* skills and disciplines as engineering, actuarial science, practical experience, city-planning, public health, physics, and the like.

This same logic applies to countless issues in the public domain: FAA regulations, food-safety standards, building codes, education policy, zoning laws, tenure procedures, immigration policy, weapons development, term limits, and on and on. In all these cases, it is not the most pious or even the most juristically learned who will be most qualified to make the best choices but the most relevantly skilled. Even the staunch *sharīʿah*-maximalist Ibn Taymīyah acknowledges that those who are experts (*ahl al-khibrah*) in non-*sharʿī* fields are more knowledgeable and authoritative than the *fuqahāʾ* in those fields.[200] Meanwhile, to the extent that the religious-cum-Islamic value and relevance of applicable non-*sharʿī* disciplines are ignored, misrecognized, or religiously devalued, the quality of Muslim decision-making will suffer and potentially give way, out of frustration, to entirely Western secular deliberations, "*as if* God did not exist."

At stake in such decision-making challenges will often be the setting of communal *norms* as the most efficient means of avoiding the need to continually relitigate every detail of socio-political life. By norms, I am referring to a regime of permissible behaviors that are recognized as either appropriate or inappropriate in a given socio-political context, by virtue of which recognition communities are able to enjoy a modicum of convenience and predictability, gauge the practical utility of things, and assess community member's' character, competence, or reliability beyond questions of piety or presumed moral uprightness, *sharʿan*. Al-Qarāfī gives a clear example of the nature and challenge of norm-setting in a passing discussion on the probity (*ʿadālah*) of courtroom witnesses. He states that a person's probity may be impugned by his engagement in any number of otherwise perfectly licit (*mubāḥ*) acts, for example, "eating in the marketplace," *al-akl fī al-sūq*. By *sūq* here, al-Qarāfī has in mind those bustling, odiferous, bacterially rich meat and vegetable markets that still checker the old quarters of many cities in the Middle East (and no doubt elsewhere) today. The point of his statement is that if a person cares so little about his health and reputation that he is willing to be seen eating in such a place, he probably does not have the kind of personal dignity, or *murūwah*, that militates against lying under oath. For our purposes, what is important here is that, in and of itself, eating in the *sūq* is perfectly permissible, *sharʿan*. The person's probity is being impugned not because he has sinned or violated *sharīʿah* but because the plainly licit acts in which he is engaged tell us something negative about his character. Ultimately, however, it is culture-cum-custom not *sharīʿah* that establishes and preserves this norm. And, for al-Qarāfī, culture-cum-custom here is enough. He feels no need or pressure to make eating in the *sūq* forbidden, or *ḥarām*, *sharʿan*, to justify rejecting this person's *ʿadālah*. In fact, he explicitly groups such acts as eating in the *sūq* under a general category of "licit acts that compromise one's probity" (*al-mubāḥāt al-mukhillah bi al-ʿadālah*).[201] His discussion reminds one of some of the frustrations expressed by Muslim women when they are told that Muslim men's serial marriages and divorces, for example, are perfectly permissible, or *mubāḥ*, *sharʿan*. A full and explicit appreciation of the role of Islamic Secular norm-setting "beyond the law" might allow for more productive discussion and more effective collective decision-making in this regard.[202]

In many instances, the non-*sharʿī*, *ʿaqlī* skills and disciplines relied upon "beyond the law" will be generically indistinguishable, *mutatis mutandis*, from those developed and relied upon by non-Muslims; in fact, they may actually be developed by non-Muslims. This raises the question of what could render reliance upon such skills and disciplines "Islamic," as constituents of the "Islamic" Secular, and why (or if) it is important for them to be so. We may recall from Chapter 1 that "Islamic" ultimately expresses not simply a battery of concrete doctrines and practices but equally an orientation. It is reflective of the God-consciousness with which an activity is approached. On this understanding, even activities that comport with the law may not be fully "Islamic," in the sense that they may not be eligible for divine acceptance or reward. For, it is not merely the substance of the act that earns this eligibility; it is the God-consciousness (*taqwā*) and the intention to draw near to God (*qurbah*) behind the act. Al-Qarāfī is explicit on this point: "An act may not be accepted, even if it absolves its actor of religio-legal responsibility (*barāʾat al-dhimmah*) and is in itself legally sound."[203] Repaying a debt, for example, or providing financially for one's family, may fulfill one's legal obligation to do so; but, without the intention to please God, these acts earn no reward. This is different from the example of a prayer offered while unwittingly facing the wrong direction. What makes the latter act Islamic is the *intention* to please God in the manner that God has prescribed. Conversely, assuming that they fall within the parameters of the juristically permissible, a Muslim's *taqwā* and pursuit of *qurbah* can convert non-*sharʿī*, *ʿaqlī* skills and disciplines, even those developed by non-Muslims, into constituents of the Islamic Secular. Provenance alone is simply not the exclusively determinative factor.

This claim is confirmed by none other than "the obstreperous Ibn Taymīyah," as Shahab Ahmed uncharitably dubbed him.[204] According to Ibn Taymīyah, a skill, discipline, or even institution of non-Muslim origin may even qualify as *sunnah*, that is, as more than simply "Islamic" in the sense of being permissible. Responding to a hypothetical objection to entering bathhouses on the argument that the Prophet never did so (nor did Abū Bakr or ʿUmar) and that this action therefore violates the *sunnah*, Ibn Taymīyah insists that this argument would apply only if the Prophet (and his Companions) had had the occasion to enter bathhouses but refused to do so on principle. "But it is known," he continues, "that there were no bathhouses where they lived at the time."[205] This is similar, he insists, to the various foods, clothing, and dwellings that did not exist in the Hijaz during the time of the Prophet: "No one should think that it is *sunnah* to refuse to benefit from these things simply because the Prophet did not partake of them."[206] But Ibn Taymīyah does not stop here: he notes that the Prophet simply ate, wore, and rode what he found readily available in his land, among those things that

God identified as permissible. "Thus, whoever avails himself of the (permissible) things he finds in his land is following the *sunnah* (of the Prophet)" (*fa man ista'mala mā yajiduhu fī arḍihi fa huwa al-muttabi' li al-sunnah*).[207] Shortly thereafter, Ibn Taymīyah offers a broad, non-technical definition of *sunnah* that clearly captures the matter at hand: "The *Sunnah* is that which is established by *shar'ī* indicants to constitute obedience [or obeisance] to God and His Messenger, whether the Prophet partook of this thing or it was practiced during his lifetime or not" (*al-sunna hiya mā qāma al-dalīl al-shar'ī 'alayhi bi annahu ṭā'at*[un] *lillāhi wa rasūlih sawā'*[un] *fa'alahu al-rasūl aw fu'ila 'alā zamānihi aw lam yaf'alhu wa lam yuf'al 'alā zamānih*).[208] Ibn Taymīyah's reputation as a fierce opponent of unwarranted compromise and innovation (*bid'ah*), alongside his clear recognition of the wages of cultural and intellectual dependency, should prevent readers from taking his dictum to extremes that he would not countenance. The Islamic Secular adds to these fortifications via the vigilant spirit of "oppugnancy" at its core.[209]

As for why it is important that such acts be seen as "Islamic," here we return to the issue of cultural and intellectual authority. While seldom spoken of in these terms, this issue cannot be ignored or glossed over in any attempt to interpret Muslim life on the ground—as suggested by the nervous warnings wafting across the Muslim world about the West's cultural and intellectual imperialism (*al-ghazw al-thaqāfī, al-ghazw al-fikrī*), not to mention the concerns of Muslims in the West about assimilation, "selling out," and the like. Nor is this an entirely new issue; we saw how readily pre-modern Muslims recognized it in what I cited above from al-Ghazālī and Ibn Taymīyah regarding Greek philosophy, foreign languages, dress, and the *qiblah*. In a similar vein, in the introduction to his work on ophthalmology, *al-Istibṣār fīmā Tudrikuhu al-Abṣār*, al-Qarāfī notes that this treatise was written in response to questions put to the Ayyūbid Sultan al-Malik al-Kāmil (regency: 615/1218-635/1237) by the Norman king. He argues that it is important that Muslims be able to answer such questions "in order to avoid the stigma of being deemed inadequate (*waṣmat al-tanqīṣ*)," which will only increase the resolve and confidence of the opponents of Truth.[210]

All of this must be seen in the context of the fact that the world of culture and social interaction is much closer to the quotidian psyche than the reified world of law. And if, in the socio-cultural universe beyond what is *shar'ī*, everything estimable is not only "secular" in the modern Western sense but also the civilizational property of the West, then not only will the primacy of the Western secular be consummated, but so will the West's global hegemony, in which it leads and Muslims follow, in an "end-of-history" triumph of the secular over the religious. The Islamic Secular, by contrast, not only accommodates the skills and disciplines that power cultural and intellectual production without excluding or domesticating religion, but precisely because these are recognized as non-*sharʿī* (though still religious), it can facilitate exchanges between Islam and the West that are not necessarily confrontational, hierarchical, or mired in Nietzschean *ressentiment*. Of course, whether things from the West are successfully rebranded as indigenously Islamic (as happened with mosque architecture, Persian loan-words, or even bean pies) depends on the strength and quality of Muslim powers of appropriation. But, these too, in the final analysis, must be recognized as non-*sharʿī*, differentiated, Islamic Secular energies.

The Islamic Secular versus *Ijtihād*

Part of the value of recognizing the Islamic Secular "beyond the law" is that it preempts the tendency to subsume non-*sharʿī*, *ʿaqlī*, micro-secular issues into the realm of the *sharʿī*. Among the most common manifestations of this conflation, is the exaggerated focus on unmediated scriptural interpretation, or *ijtihād (sharʿī)*. *Ijtihād* is an important enterprise, and it would be foolish to deny its value in the modern world. But, strictly speaking, *ijtihād* (*sharʿī*) is relevant only to the production of *aḥkām sharʿīyah* (sg. *ḥukm sharʿī*). In cases where what is ultimately sought lies beyond the *ḥukm sharʿī*, *ijtihād* will not be able to reach it. Wael Hallaq perceptively reminds us that "colonialism was . . . a cultural project of control."[211] But as long as *ijtihād sharʿī*'s limited ability to address cultural and other non-legal challenges in a concrete, substantive fashion remains unrecognized, the result will be an over-investment in *ijtihād sharʿī*, which will send Muslims on false missions that ultimately lead to a loss of confidence in, and a misplaced frustration with, *sharīʿah*. Tariq Ramadan, a major proponent of *ijtihād*, comes close to acknowledging this problem when he writes:

> [A]fter constantly referring to *ijtihād*, *taqlīd*, and *iṣlāḥ* for over a century, Muslims—whether in Muslim majority societies or Western communities—still find it difficult to overcome the successive crises they go through and to provide something more than partial answers; and even the answers [they do put forth] remain constantly apologetic or [are] produced by mostly defensive postures."[212]

The panacean powers attributed to *ijtihād* are a direct function of the totalizing understanding of *fiqh/sharīʿah*, which recognizes no legitimate non-*sharʿī* realms of deliberation or production for anything connected with Islam. On this understanding, there is no legitimately Islamic space "beyond the law" and thus nothing besides *ijtihād* to consider in seeking knowledge and guidance for appropriate action. Again, however, where an interest (e.g., the most efficient, most profitable, or most romantic action) lies beyond the law, resorting to *ijtihād shar'ī* will amount to a fool's errand.

For example, in a scathing critique of marriage in early fourteenth-/twentieth-century Egypt, Muḥammad 'Abduh (d. 1322/1905) criticized the *fuqahā'* for their tragically transactional attitude toward matrimony, especially as it affected women. According to him, juristic discourses focused almost exclusively on sexual rights (mainly of husbands over wives) and were "entirely devoid of any reference to 'ethical/emotional obligations' (*wājibāt adabīyah*)."[213] This myopic perspective, according to 'Abduh, undermined the whole point of marriage, which was for two hearts and minds to come together in love and compassion (*mawaddah wa raḥmah*). Yet, it seems reasonable to assume that the jurists omitted "ethical/emotional obligations" because such amorphous preoccupations fell outside their *shar'ī* purview, as entities for which *sharī'ah* could prescribe no concrete instantiations in the form of specific acts. This does not mean, however, that they had no interest in or understanding of such issues themselves. The fact that they spoke as jurists in a specifically juristic context does not mean that they assumed that this is the only capacity in which *Islam* could speak.

In fact, in a recent article on al-Māwardī Marion Katz observes that this judge and jurist discusses marriage in almost purely transactional terms in his book on *fiqh* but uses more emotionally sensitive terms in his book on etiquette (*adab*). She writes, "Given that sexual enjoyment (*istimta'*) is the single most decisive factor in al-Mawardi's argumentation on the rights and duties of marriage in *al-Ḥāwī al-Kabīr* [on *fiqh*], it is striking to discover that he condemns it as the most morally blameworthy motivation for the contracting of a marriage in *Adab al-Dunyā wa al-Dīn.*"[214] In other words, the primacy of sex or love or compassion is not absolute in al-Māwardī's mind; it is contextual. In the context of discussing marriage as a transactional, *shar'ī* contract, "love and compassion" may be marginal, if not irrelevant. But where the topic is marriage as the ideal, normative relationship between men and women, these "*adabīyāt*" become central.

Even here, however, "love and compassion" can mean different things to different people in different times and places—from a husband's bringing home flowers to his wife in middle-class America to a man's bringing home a live goose to be plucked and cooked in poor parts of rural Egypt. The instantiation of love, in other words, is not a *shar'ī* determination but one arrived at via a culturally formed sense of propriety. Rather than recognizing this non-*shar'ī* dimension of the problem, however, 'Abduh doubles down on *ijtihād*, going back to the Qur'ān and Sunnah, and reiterating their provisions for marital bliss, especially for women: "All we have to do is hear the voice of our *sharī'ah* and follow the rulings of the Noble Qur'ān, the authentic Sunna of the Prophet and the ways of the Companions in order for women to find happiness in marriage."[215]

'Abduh's goodwill and eloquence notwithstanding, he seems to ignore the fact that, even if a man harbors the most intense love and compassion for his wife, those feelings alone do not guarantee that he will be able to express them in ways that are meaningful to her; nor will the fact that he is a devout Muslim who follows the Qur'ān and Sunna. A good Muslim can be a bad kisser, gift-buyer, dresser, or conversationalist or simply lack parenting skills. Thus, doubling down on scriptural exhortations to love and compassion would seem to be of little effect. Cultural literacy—indeed, a bit of *ijtihād 'urfī*—would more likely provide the solution. And, as I have argued repeatedly, cultural production is not, substantively speaking, a *shar'ī* enterprise. While the law may dictate the normative parameters within which cultural imagination must express itself, it cannot tell us in concrete terms what is pretty, fun, chic, or romantic in any given time or place.[216] The tendency, however, to 'over-*sharī'a*tize' matters, as Abduh appears to do here, blocks this insight from view.

A similar explanation might apply to the plight of Muslim women in the face of questionable behavior on the part of Muslim men (and vice versa). What is needed is not more *ijtihād* but a more sensitive, mutually empathetic culture, fashioned out of the energies of the Islamic Secular, which can establish and sustain salutary, recognizable, policeable norms that incentivize desired behaviors, such as expressing love in marriage, and disincentivize other behaviors, as we saw in the case of eating in the *sūq*. Such a paradigm requires, however, a recognition of the Islamic value and importance of non-*shar'ī*, differentiated skills and insights *beyond* the kind of knowledge provided by *sharī'ah*.

It is precisely when this recognition fails to materialize, however, that *sharī'ah* and the religious establishment end up shouldering responsibility for any dissonance between Islam and Muslims' legitimate aspirations in life. When Muslims rely entirely on *sharī'ah*-based commitments as the guarantor of financial well-being, healthy relationships, happiness, respect among nations, or even an effective health-care system, while ignoring the skills and disciplines that come under the sign of the Islamic Secular, the resulting failure can end up making religion feel like so much a waste of time. Indeed, as counter-intuitive as it may seem at first blush, one could argue that too much reliance on *sharī'ah*, to the point of overlooking the non-*shar'ī* Islamic Secular, can promote secularism and secularization in the modern Western sense almost as effectively as too little reliance.

But there is another side to all of this, that explains and partly vindicates the approach of 'Abduh (and others) and, to my mind, throws the point of the present project into relief. More than a century has passed since 'Abduh's death, and some of the enormous pressures under which he wrote may not be readily present in our minds today. 'Abduh faced assaults on *sharī'ah* from both British colonialists and an emergent Westernized Egyptian elite, *al-mutafarnijah*, which included

Muslims and Christians. At the hands of these forces, every manifestation of the non-*shar'ī* was likely to appear as a rival of rather than a complement to *sharī'ah*, with the expressed purpose of marginalizing if not proroguing the *shar'*. This fact comes through clearly in the recollections of 'Abduh's student Rashīd Riḍā regarding efforts to abolish *sharī'ah* courts and convert (or subsume) *sharī'ah* itself into a system of non-religious *qānūn*. By "*qānūn*," Riḍā was referring not to anything like Ottoman *siyāsah* but to a legal regime that was unabashedly secular, in the sense of being explicitly divorced from Islam as religion. As Riḍā put it:

> When the word '*qānūn*' is used in this context, it refers specifically to a system whose rulings fly in the face of the divine *shar'* and to what follows from that in the way of its implementation resting upon a decision of the parliament and a command from the ruler that it be applied, and to its being legislation that issues from this [colonial] government and falls under non-Islamic sovereignty (*siyādah ghayr islāmīyah*).[217]

Over the course of Riḍā's recollections, it becomes clear that he perceived the relationship between *sharī'ah* and *qānūn* (or *qānūn waḍ'ī* or *siyāsah madanīyah*) to be both mutually exclusive and zero-sum. The choice was thus between *sharī'ah* and its absolute, deliberate negation, in the name of a patently secularizing non-*shar'ī*—indeed, anti-*shar'ī*—*qānūn*. In such a context, it would be difficult, practically speaking, for him or 'Abduh to recognize (at least openly) any non-*shar'ī* modes of law without seeing himself (and perhaps being seen by others) as possibly providing the ink with which to sign *sharī'ah*'s death certificate.[218]

Faced with this challenge, 'Abduh and Riḍā responded with what they probably deemed to be the best if not the only means at their disposal: a *sharī'ah*-maximalism intended to function as a dike against the Western-secular deluge. For them, particularly on such issues as gender, where the hegemonic pretensions of Western modernity pressed hard and most incessantly, the distinction between the non-*shar'ī* and the anti-*shar'ī* became so blurred that it could be engaged with only agnostically, if at all. Because the secularizing attack on religion was directed first and foremost at *sharī'ah*, the main impediment to the privatization of *dīn*, the emergence of a strong resistance to anything non-*shar'ī* was almost inevitable. For to cede anything to the 'secular' non-*shar'ī*, or to a realm beyond *sharī'ah*, would be to risk playing into the hands of the enemy. As a result, their response was infused with a disquieting dubiousness regarding the entire region of *islām mā warā' al-ḥukm al-shar'ī*. This dubiousness, however, was less the result of a spontaneous reading of the sources and tradition of Islam-cum-*sharī'ah* than it was a reaction to the dichotomous secular/religious relationship that had developed in Western Europe and been delivered to the Muslim world through the barrels of guns.

Away from the battlefield, however, it is clear that both ʿAbduh and Riḍā recognized the legitimacy and necessity of non-*sharʿī* knowledge and pursuits. In binding the Imām to consult the learned (*mushāwarah*), for example, in his attempt to serve Community interests, they were cognizant of the need for doctors, engineers, military strategists, and the like.[219] And they recognized these as explicitly non-*sharʿī* pursuits that were neither concretely dictated nor governed by the sources of *sharīʿah*.[220] Nevertheless, the pressures of the day forced them, and no doubt many after them, into a corner, where open recognition of the non-*sharʿī* 'secular' could be seen only as serving the interests of those who opposed *sharīʿah*. *The Islamic Secular* seeks to break out of this corner, throw off this zero-sum religious/secular opposition, and place the non-*sharʿī* 'secular' back into the circumference of Islam as religion, where it properly belongs.

The "Islamic" in the Islamic Secular

The French political philosopher Charles-Louis Baron de Montesquieu (d. 1755) once observed, "A more certain way to attack religion is by favor, by the comforts of life, by the hope of fortune, by what makes one forget it; not by what makes one indignant, but by what leads one to indifference when other passions act on our souls and when those that religion inspires are silent."[221] My attempts at care and circumspection notwithstanding, many may suspect the Islamic Secular of nudging Muslims onto Montesquieu's slippery slope toward secularization in the modern, Western sense. Bit by bit, they might infer, and under pressure of the West's dominant cultural and intellectual authority, such a construct can only prompt Muslims to draw *sharīʿah*'s boundaries ever more narrowly, the better to maximize the area in which reason, science, custom, experience, cultural imagination, and the like can be freely invoked, ultimately, whether they intend so or not, at Islam-cum-*sharīʿah*'s expense.

This is a serious challenge, which I addressed in part in my earlier discussion of Ẓāhirī *sharīʿah*-minimalism. In addition to what I said there, however, I would like to offer two further points. The first, reiterated time and again throughout previous chapters, is that "*sharʿī*" and "religious" are neither coterminous nor synonymous. Whereas the *sharʿī* necessarily implies the religious, the religious does not necessarily entail the *sharʿī*, certainly not as a determinant of the concrete substance of religious acts.[222] For this reason, a diminution of the *sharʿī* does not necessarily imply a diminution of the religious. Conversely, even if the non-*sharʿī* area in which we deploy our secular skills and talents is extended maximally, this need not imply, *pace* Montesquieu, any decrease in the relevance of Islam as religion. For, again, the notion of proceeding "*as if* God does not exist" is alien both to Islam and to the Islamic Secular, even in the realm *mā warāʾ al-ḥukm al-sharʿī*. The whole point of the adjective "Islamic" in the Islamic Secular is to underscore the fact that the Islamic Secular remains a religious orientation to life. Thus, to be fair and accurate in our assessment of the Islamic Secular, we cannot minimize its Islamic side any more than we can detach it from its 'secular' side. Even when employing differentiated, non-*sharʿī*, secular skills and talents, the Islamic Secular's religious orientation—its *dīn*, *taqwā*, *qurbah*, and obeisance, not to mention its oppugnancy and conscious awareness of the presence and gaze of the God of Islam—must be recognized as continually informing their use.

Second, leaving aside the ends to which some may put it, Montesquieu's is a point worth considering. The greatest challenge to Islam (or any other religion) in the world today is not other religions, as Muslims generally believed to be the case in the pre-modern past; nor is it intolerance or persecution, as modern liberals would have us think today. It is, instead, the degradation of Islam's plausibility structure and the inability of Muslims to construct and preserve a viable alternative. This absence or weakness breeds Islam's (and every religion's) ultimate enemy: apathy born of irrelevance. Among the key ingredients of modernity's secularizing *nomos* is, of course, the culture that underwrites it. But, to borrow the insight of James Davison Hunter, "The only way to change culture is to create more of it."[223] As we have seen, culture-production is an overwhelmingly non-*sharʿī*, Islamic Secular enterprise. We might say the same regarding major aspects of the reigning intellectual paradigms that define the horizons of modern acceptability. In sum, to the degree that the non-*sharʿī* cultural and intellectual efforts of Muslims make or break Islam's *nomos* and plausibility structure, even the attempt to preserve *sharīʿah* for its own sake leads inexorably back to the Islamic Secular.

Still, the very idea of the non-*sharʿī*, Islamic Secular, and the parallel notion that *sharīʿah*'s jurisdiction is limited, will breed resistance among many Muslims and prompt them to try to expand the latter's scope, as a means, in their minds, of protecting Islam. This is what we saw in ʿAbduh and Riḍā (and before them Ibn al-Qayyim, Ibn Taymīyah, and Ibn al-Jawzī), and for precisely the same reason. But that was a hundred years ago (and much longer in the case of the latter). And it is to be hoped that the passing of time has rendered Muslims more capable of distinguishing the "extra-*sharʿī*" from the "anti-*sharʿī*," removing the cloud of suspicion from non-*sharʿī* activity and recognizing it (at least potentially) as Islamic. Moreover, it may be time to take stock of the cost of this defensive reflex, as well as what it might be concealing from us in the modern confrontation between the religious and the secular. Even were there no Islamic Secular and *sharīʿah* were accorded maximum authority, indeed totalitarian authority, this would not constitute any guarantee against the spread of secularization in the modern Western sense. For, ultimate secularization resides not in the simple act of moving away from religion-as-concrete-doctrine-and-practice (though that is certainly among its manifestations) but in the move away from a conscious awareness of the divine gaze and presence and, ultimately, the divine prerogative. Such a move can be brought about, however, almost as effectively by an over-emphasis on *sharīʿah*, whereby its assiduous application is assumed to guarantee success independent of God, as it can by rejecting or restricting the authority of *sharīʿah* outright.[224]

Even the Prophet, whose adherence to *sharīʿah* is beyond question, suffered unspeakable losses, disappointments, and setbacks: all of his children, for example, except one, perished before he did. And despite his undying, impeccable commitment to carrying out God's *sharʿ*, we read these words directed to him in the Qur'ān: "*Say, I do not control whether benefit or harm comes to me except by God's permission . . .* (*lā amliku li nafsī naf*ʿ*an* *wa lā ḍarr*an *illā mā shā' Allāh*) [7:188]. To look, then, to *sharīʿah* as a substitute for God, divine aid, and divine facilitation in the face of an earthly existence as fragile and precarious as our own may be no less secularizing in effect, indeed, no less *macro*-secularizing, than looking to reason, feelings, or modern science. Religiosity, certainly monotheistic religiosity, requires not merely adherence to rules but also open recognition of ultimate dependence on and indebtedness to God—in all areas of life. The Islamic Secular reinforces the centrality of this disposition. Equally important, even its 'secular' side, beyond *sharīʿah* and its *ḥukm sharʿī*, remains, normatively speaking, authentically religious and authentically Islam.

Coda: The Islamic Secular and the Challenge of Talal Asad

Having explicated the theoretical foundations of the Islamic Secular, I must now address a number of interpretive challenges emanating from the brilliant work of the foremost contemporary theorist of the secular in relation to Islam, Talal Asad. So large has been Asad's influence that, for many, the very phrase "Islamic Secular" will beg the question of how my thesis relates to his. Of course, there is asymmetry between his primarily anthropological approach and my more specifically juristic one, which complicates the prospects for a full comparison. But when Asad turns to secularization within Islam in particular, *fiqh* and *sharīʿah* assume a more central place in his analysis.[225] This increased focus on *fiqh/sharīʿah* suggests the appropriateness, if not necessity, of a comparison, especially since those who view the relationship between Islam and the secular through the prism of Asad's understanding may be led to read *The Islamic Secular* in that light.

Asad's work raises questions for the Islamic Secular on at least two fronts. First, secularization for Asad consists essentially in the privatization of Islam-cum-*sharīʿah*, whereby it ceases to be the basis of public law and morality. This process opens spaces to be filled by other reglementary regimes, including European codes, ultimately diminishing the practical authority of Islam as religion. Among the presuppositions informing this interpretation, however, is that "religion" and "*sharīʿah*" are coterminous, such that placing any limits or restrictions on *sharīʿah*'s jurisdiction moves in the same direction as Western secularization. Obviously, this view does not align with the Islamic Secular, which sees *sharīʿah* as bearing jurisdictional limits that are *self*-imposed. Taking their cue from Asad, however, those who view any limits on *sharīʿah* as necessarily implying secularization in the modern Western sense might be prone to misapprehending the Islamic Secular and casting it in a negative light.

Second, Asad compellingly catalogues and explains the dislocations that Western modernity has visited upon Islam-cum-*sharīʿah*, along with the general condition of religious decline that has accompanied this. By contrast, the Islamic Secular so thoroughly sublates the secular into the religious that it might be read as misrecognizing or pasting over the negative implications of the East/West encounter. In other words, if, as the Islamic Secular holds, there is no fundamental secular/religious antipathy in Islam, the spread of secular ideas, movements, and institutions cannot be counted as religious decline. Yet, the notion that there has been no religious decline runs counter to everything we know about Islam in the modern world. I should note that the Islamic Secular acknowledges religious decline. But it suggests that a major contributor to it has been not simply restrictions directly imposed on *sharīʿah* but insufficient investment in the 'secular' dimension of Islam, ultimately as a direct result of the inability to transcend the religious/secular binary. In other words, the Islamic Secular neither misrecognizes nor pastes over religious decline; it simply prioritizes a different set of causes, effects, and meanings in explaining it.

My aim in this final section is to lay out more fully and respond to the challenges posed by Asad (or those likely influenced by him) as part of my effort to secure a fairer hearing for the Islamic Secular.

The Asadian Frame

Asad's approach to the secular is not to define what it is but to catalogue what it does. As he puts it, "I think it [the secular] is best pursued through its shadows, as it were."[226] One is reminded here of the Muʿtazilite, ʿAbd al-Jabbār, who insisted that there was no point in definitions that cannot improve upon what we already know experientially: no definition of honey, for example, can make us more knowledgeable of what it is than our experience of tasting it.[227] Among the secular's "shadows," according to Asad, are the tendency of modern states to generate regimes of "self-discipline" by which populations are controlled or managed;[228] modern states' production of what purport to be equally owned national (or even global) identities and narratives, by which socio-religious difference is flattened or ostensibly transcended;[229] the creation of "public" and "private" as distinct spheres of endeavor with distinct modes of reasoning proper to each ("secular" reasoning belonging to the former, "religious" to the latter);[230] the invention of autonomous, self-owning, individual selves whose highest moral duty is to be true to their own dictates;[231] the parallel replacement of God by individual conscience;[232] the reduction of religion to morality;[233] and the denial of the right to inflict pain (or engage in violence) except in pursuit of the normalization of a liberal subjectivity.[234] All of these "shadows" point to secularism's program of establishing and maintaining the secular's hegemony over religion, expanding its authority at religion's expense, and ultimately reducing the sphere of religion (and thus religious freedom) to what the modern state is willing to let go.[235]

Asad's is a sophisticated, multifaceted, practical understanding of the secular as religion's superior Other. Ultimately, "secular" for him is a preeminently political construct, and secularism is the program by which modern states pursue the domestication of religion, denying religion its own story and ultimately assigning it a supporting role in the triumphalist, salutary, patronizing story of the modern state.

The Asadian Challenge

The essence of the Asadian challenge is articulated in the final chapter of his classic book, *Formations of the Secular*, entitled "Reconfigurations of Law and Ethics in Colonial Egypt." He contextualizes his discussion with two basic questions: (1) How did Muslims think about secularism prior to modernity? (2) What do Muslims today make of the idea of the secular? While Asad concedes the empirical plausibility of the claim made by some Muslim reformists that "secular life was always central in the past,"[236] he insists that, as an ideal, "secularism did not exist in Egypt [and by extension the Muslim world] prior to modernity."[237] He traces the rise of "Muslim secularism"[238] to a series of modern transmutations wherein Islamic meanings are not obliterated but sublimated into Western meanings, en route to becoming part of an arsenal of new conceptual tools with which the modern project of secularization can be carried out. *Sharīʿah*, for example, gets redefined as "religious law,"[239] a quaint deviation from "law" as it is commonly understood in the West, which is as "secular" and "administrative" law,[240] the instrument by which states "civilize" their populations.[241] "Civilization," in turn, is now aligned with the vision of liberalism.[242] Parallel to all of this is the emergence of such loaded terms as "progress," "agency," and "liberty," all of which give thrust and direction to Muslim aspirations to "become modern."[243]

Collectively, these transmutations contribute to and support the move to privatize religion by restricting *sharīʿah*, as "religious law," to the newly emergent domain of "family law." Asad questions the common assumption that colonial powers tolerated Islamic "family law" because it was so close to the hearts and minds of Muslims that any attempt to meddle in it would risk rebellion. He sees this view as superficial and misleading, part of a rhetoric of concealment. He writes, "I argue, on the contrary, that the *sharīʿa* thus defined is precisely a secular formula for privatizing 'religion' and preparing the ground for the self-governing subject."[244] In other words, renaming *sharīʿah* as "family law," or "the law of personal status" (*qānūn al-aḥwāl al-shakhṣīyah*) was "the expression of a secular formula, defining a place in which 'religion' is allowed to make its public appearance through state law."[245] By granting *sharīʿah* a "proper" place in the private domain, the public realm could be insulated from any claims of *sharīʿah*-jurisdiction beyond the private affairs of the family. Herein lay the secularization of Islam, a project that "delimits the sphere of religious rules,"[246] opens a space for the importation of Western codes and calls for "the installation of a particular conception of ethics and its formal separation from the authority of law, both of these being delinked from 'religion.'"[247]

To be sure, colonial power—brutal, directed, awful—played an obvious role in this process. But Muslims also contributed, routinely, in the name of reform. Asad cites in this context Muḥammad ʿAbduh's re-definition of the family as a "nuclear unit," en route to consummating the transmutation of individuals into "private beings" and recasting the family itself as a formal unit of society which the state has a justified interest in regulating.[248] He also discusses Qāsim Amīn's depiction of the family as a laboratory for the new civilizing mission, including, *inter alia*, the banning of polygyny.[249] But it is with the views of the British-trained lawyer Aḥmad Ṣafwat and his treatise *Baḥth fī Qāʿidat Iṣlāḥ Qānūn al-Aḥwāl al-Shakhṣīyah* that Asad is most substantive in his analysis. He focuses on Ṣafwat's complaint about the tendency to attribute "sacredness" (*qadāsah*) to *sharīʿah* and how this frustrates any prospects of adjusting its substance to the demands of modernity, including the changed status of women and the understanding of marriage as a partnership as opposed to a transactional arrangement of sexual usus and procreation.[250] In Asad's view, Ṣafwat's implied denial of this sacredness, presumably as a means of domesticating *sharīʿah*'s authority, constitutes the first step toward secularization. For, according to Asad, "It is when something is described as belonging to 'religion' and it can be claimed that it does not that the secular emerges most clearly."[251]

Ṣafwat consummates his move toward secularization with his attribution of uncharacteristically broad powers of discretion to the state. According to him, beyond what the Qur'ān absolutely obliges and forbids, the state has the power to regulate the expansive realm of permissible (*mubāḥ*) acts by temporarily suspending their permissibility or obliging their performance, as circumstances dictate.[252] It was widely recognized in pre-modern times that governments could regulate "rights" (or permissible acts) such as practicing medicine, setting up commercial businesses, and selling dangerous materials.[253] Following this precedent, modern states, according to Ṣafwat, should be able to regulate various aspects of marriage and divorce, including, for example, the means (having two witnesses) by which they are validated.[254] From Asad's perspective, this manner of distinguishing law (what a government can regulate) from morality/ethics (what religion authorizes individuals to do or leaves to their discretion) expands the authority of the state by "delimit[ing] the sphere of religious rules and open[ing] up the space for secular state law."[255] This expansion leads in turn to "the well-known story of the gradual narrowing of *sharīʿa* jurisdiction (that is, a restriction of the scope of 'religious law') and the simultaneous importation of European legal codes."[256]

Again, to the extent that secularization is identified with the "restriction of the scope of 'religious law'" and the power of the state to fill the breach, one can imagine how the Islamic Secular might be misread, built as it is on the notion of *sharīʿah*'s limited jurisdiction and the space this opens to non-*sharʿī* deliberations-cum-regulation by the state (in the form, e.g., of *siyāsah*, *maẓālim*, or *ḥisbah*). Taking Asad's thesis as their interpretive point of departure, secularists might view the Islamic Secular as the handmaiden of secularization and laud it on that basis. Islamists, on the other hand, or those opposed to secularization, might condemn it on the same misreading, believing that it artificially restricts *sharīʿah*'s jurisdiction and expands that of the (now secular) modern state at *sharīʿah*'s expense.

Again, there is no denying that modernity has subjected Islam-cum-*sharīʿah* to dislocation, including the restrictions it has placed on its application. On its face, Asad's explanation for all of this as "secularization" seems compelling. And if his explanation threatens the Islamic Secular with misreading, one might ask what the Islamic Secular has to offer in its stead.

The Islamic Secular's Response

We may begin with Asad's observation that prior to modernity, Muslims were "unmusical" (to use Weber's term) to the secular, certainly as an ideal in the form of secularism or secularization. His aim, as such, is to explore how modern Muslims received the construct as brought to them by the West. In an earlier segment of his book, he writes, "I draw my materials almost entirely from West

European history because that history has had profound consequences for the ways the doctrine of secularism has been conceived of and implemented in the rest of the modernizing world."[257]

I take issue here neither with Asad's approach nor with his basic assertion regarding the hegemonic expanse of the modern Western secular. I see a price, however, in taking the Western secular as the interpretive prism through which other articulations of the secular (and religious) are understood. "[T]he well-known story of the gradual narrowing of *sharīʿa* jurisdiction (that is, a restriction of the scope of 'religious law') and the simultaneous importation of European codes" might be a reasonable point of departure if we are speaking in general historical terms and largely from the vantage-point of the Western secular. But it can distort one's understanding of a concept of "secular" that *begins* with a recognition of *self*-imposed limits on what God dictates as law.

On Asad's approach, placing limits on *sharīʿah*'s jurisdiction is equated with privatization-cum-secularization. From the perspective of the Islamic Secular, however, limits are indigenous to the very concept and function of *sharīʿah* itself, part of its normative constitution. Similarly, the modern Western state began as a secular alternative to the existing religious order, injecting a zero-sum inflection into the relationship between religion and the state. By contrast, as we saw with such religious stalwarts as al-ʿIzz b. ʿAbd al-Salām,[258] Ibn Taymīyah,[259] al-Qarāfī,[260] and others—not to mention our discussion of *siyāsah*, *maẓālim*, and *ḥisbah*—while there was always tension between the state and the jurists in the Islamic world, there was never a presumption of zero-sum spoils between Islam-cum-*sharīʿah* and the state.[261] In sum, what Asad describes as "[T]he well-known story of the gradual narrowing of *sharīʿah* jurisdiction" reflects a late modern Western understanding of the normative relationship between religion and the state. From the non-Western perspective of the Islamic Secular, however, expanding state jurisdiction, especially into non-*sharʿī* areas, need not come at the expense of *sharīʿah* or religion nor amount to secularization. For, the non-*sharʿī* is not synonymous with the non-religious. And state expansion beyond the boundaries of *sharīʿah—warāʾ al-ḥukm al-sharʿī*—need not entail a loss of authority on the part of *sharīʿah* or religion.

Something similar might be said regarding the term "religion." While Asad does not subscribe to a universal definition of religion, he clearly sees the term as the antithesis of "secular." Moreover, for him, practically speaking, Islam as religion basically equals *sharīʿah*, which is why he sees a diminution in the scope of its authority as implying the same for religion. Again, this may be a reasonable point of departure in tracing the "shadows" of the Western secular, that is, religion shrinking as the secular expands. But it is not one from which the Islamic Secular can be fairly assessed or understood. Religion, according to the Islamic Secular, is broader than *sharīʿah* and includes both *sharʿī* and non-*sharʿī* elements, both within and beyond *sharīʿah*. On this understanding, even the restrictive redefinition of Islamic law as "family law" (a move with which I do not agree) would not necessarily result in a diminution of the scope of Islam as *dīn*.[262] Here, however, I should pause to clarify two points that may otherwise cloud the issue and lead to further misunderstanding.

First, Asad is correct in seeing the overall aim of the likes of Aḥmad Ṣafwat to be the domestication of *sharīʿah* and the emulation of European culture and civilization. Ṣafwat is clearly enamored of the latter, at one point stating explicitly that "the Western (system) is far superior to ours" (*wa al-gharbīyah arqā minnā kathīr*[an]).[263] But this fact alone should not be taken as the sole prism through which his treatise as a whole can be read and its implications assessed. *Pace* Asad, I read Ṣafwat's fundamental complaint as not being ultimately about the sacredness attributed to *sharīʿah* but about the sacredness attributed to what he identifies (sometimes rightly, sometimes wrongly) as the historically contingent aspects thereof, for example, the specific formulae used for divorce or the means by which marriages are validated. This kind of critique can be found, however, among pre-modern luminaries of the most orthodox bent, from Ibn al-Qayyim and Ibn Taymīyah to al-Qarāfī, Ibn Khaldūn, al-Ghazālī, and others, none of whom nursed any desire to domesticate *sharīʿah* or emulate foreigners.[264] We have seen how fervently al-Qarāfī disaggregated *sharīʿah* into juristic engagement with the transcendent sources of the law (*sababīyat al-sabab*) and the empirical assessment of ever-evolving facts on the ground (*wuqūʿ al-sabab*), clearly underscoring the historical contingency of various aspects of *sharīʿah* rules. In fact, his whole spirited campaign against what he dubbed "improper *taqlīd*" directly targeted jurists who failed to separate the factual (read: historically contingent) from the transcendent element of legal doctrines handed down from the past.[265]

Something similar can be said about the distinction Ṣafwat draws between law and ethics. We saw such a distinction in the line that Ibn Taymīyah drew between *sharīʿah* and *siyāsah*, and in the view al-Qarāfī cites on punishing Ḥanafīs who drink *nabīdh*-wine, despite their being guilty of no sin.[266] Al-Qarāfī also laid out the difference between the legal status of an act, that is, its *ḥukm sharʿī*, and the consequences of performing it, for example, marrying a particular woman or eating in the *sūq*. Of course, the consequences of acts, we might note, are the major focus of any ethics outside a Kantian frame.[267] In fact, classical Muslim orthodoxy as a whole might be characterized as lining up against Muʿtazilism precisely because of Muʿtazilism's failure to distinguish law from ethics (i.e., what we can know to be good or bad versus what we can know that God will reward or punish).[268]

My point here is that the Islamic Secular's sharing with Ṣafwat the critique of the blind sanctification of the past or recognizing the distinction between law and ethics should not be misunderstood or abused. For one thing, Ṣafwat may not be categorically wrong, as we have seen (Asad's interpretation of him notwithstanding). More important, even assuming that his view is wrong or exaggerated, the Islamic Secular takes its cue not from Aḥmad Ṣafwat or any other modern Muslim secularizing reformist but from al-Bāqillānī, al-Ghazālī, Abū Ya'lā, Ibn 'Aqīl, al-Qarāfī, Ṣadr al-Sharī'ah, and even Ibn al-Qayyim and Ibn Taymīyah, none of whom subscribed to secularism in any form. The Islamic Secular's de-sanctification of historically contingent features of Islam-cum-*sharī'ah*, its clear *shar'ī*/non-*shar'ī* distinction, and the discretionary powers it imputes to the state should no more be equated with modern reformist trends toward secularization than the views of these and countless other pre-modern authorities.

The second point has to do with the importation of European codes and how this relates to secularization. In some cases, for example, where such importation entails the unqualified allowance of *ribā* (interest, although this is not always an accurate translation) or the decriminalization of *zinā* for Muslims, *sharī'ah* and the divine authority behind it are clearly targeted and diminished. In this sense, such importation reflects an actual move toward secularization. But, barring such direct and flagrant contradictions and assuming what I have argued to be the self-imposed limits on *sharī'ah*, one might ask how the adoption of European codes in and of itself necessarily constitutes secularization, any more than what early Muslims adopted from pre-Islamic Arabians, Greeks or Persians. As Owen Chadwick asks rhetorically, "Could Christianity slowly turn into Islam without the world becoming in the least 'secularized' in the process?"[269] His point was that Islam is just as much a religion as Christianity; thus, for Islam to displace Christianity could hardly amount to secularization.

Let me be clear: the importation of European codes may constitute *kufr* (unbelief) or *fisq* (moral turpitude); or it may constitute "cultural apostasy" or a threat to the integrity of indigenous cultural or intellectual authority; or it may simply be a very bad idea. But how, assuming the binary relationship Asad posits between the "religious" and the "secular," does such importation in and of itself necessarily constitute secularization as the antithesis of religion? Is the meaning of "secular" now migrating away from an oppositional relationship to religion toward something closer to "foreign," "outside *sharī'ah*," or "anything that Muslims do not like or by which they feel threatened"? This question acquires added significance in cases where the imported foreign rules address identifiably non-*shar'ī* matters, such as speed limits, building codes, or medical licensing. When we describe the importation of such foreign rules as "secularization," are we suggesting that, normatively speaking, these rules *should* be "religious"? And by "religious," do we mean *shar'ī* or something else? I repeat, for the sake of clarity: the importation of European codes may constitute *kufr* or *fisq* or a treacherous bow to intellectual imperialism, in which case it would be appropriate, if not obligatory (*wājib*), for Muslims to oppose it. But to hold Christianity, Judaism, or the civilization of the West to be religiously unacceptable is not the same as deeming them "secular."

The Islamic Secular is alive to modernity's contribution to Islam-cum-*sharīʿah*'s declining fortunes, and even to the importation of Western codes as a manifestation of this. But because it does not view these developments through the prism of the Western secular, according to which the secular and the religious are mutually exclusive, it does not see the problem as one of secularization in the way that Asad does. On the contrary, from the perspective of the Islamic Secular, it is all too often not the contraction but the over-extension of *sharīʿah* that opens spaces to be filled by the Western secular. For, overextending *sharīʿah* denies the Islamic legitimacy of anything that cannot trace its provenance to hermeneutical engagement with scripture (or the *madhhab*s), frustrating the role of empirical assessment, *fantasia*, and all non-*sharʿī* production, ultimately consigning Muslims to sources and authorities outside Islam (now identified with anything "outside *sharīʿah*") to fill the breach. Stated differently, not only does the Islamic Secular identify a different set of causes for religious decline among Muslims; ultimately, it also embraces a different definition of religious decline itself, one that includes diminution in the value of (Islamic) 'secular' activity.

To give an example, as late as the fourteenth/twentieth century, failure to recognize that the amount of time pre-modern *fiqh* granted as a warranty period on real estate was the result of non-*sharʿī*, empirical determinations of fact, not the result of hermeneutical engagement with scriptural texts, prompted Egyptian jurists to reject anything beyond the maximum thirty-six-day period recorded in *sharīʿah* manuals, themselves presumed to reflect the pre-modern consensus. As a result, the Egyptian state ended up adopting the French *garantie décennale*, or ten-year warranty period, as thirty-six days would obviously not suffice in the case of modern office buildings or industrial plants.[270] The problem here stemmed not from a preference for secular over religious law, or for restrictions being placed on the scope of *sharīʿah*; it stemmed from the inability to see the category "religion" as including 'secular' elements (in this case the empirical, *ʿaqlī*, assessment of a reasonable warranty period) that are not the product of scripture or the *madhhab*s and are thus subject to legitimate change over space and time. Over-investment in *sharīʿah*, in other words, as both the sole metric of assessment and an enterprise limited strictly to hermeneutical engagement with scripture (or the *madhhab*s), led the state to conclude that *sharīʿah* in this instance was inadequate. And given the tendency to equate *sharīʿah* with Islam, this conclusion led to the view that assessing warranty periods should be placed outside the jurisdiction of Islam as *dīn*, rendering it a purely secular matter in the modern, Western sense.

One can imagine the cumulative effect of this kind secularization over time. And this brings us to the door of the second challenge posed by Asad: how the Islamic Secular explains religious decline.

Has Islam Become a Religion?

Western power clearly contributed to the Western secular's ability to reorient Muslim thought and sensibilities. Power alone, however, could not achieve this reorientation. In relative terms, the Mongols and Crusaders wielded equal, if not greater, power and inflicted perhaps far more physical devastation. Yet, neither was as successful in rearranging Muslim cognitive frames, including their perception of self and the world. I argue, in such light, that a major contributor to religious decline among modern Muslims has been their falling away from a functional recognition of the Islamic Secular, at the heart of which is the recognition that non-*shar'ī*, differentiated, secular activity is both practically valuable and Islamically necessary, as part of the apparatus for practicing and preserving Islam as *dīn*.

This falling away does not necessarily reflect a direct decline in religious commitment per se; in fact, it probably resulted, at least in part, from Muslim success at sublating the various non-*shar'ī* contributions to Islam's plausibility structure and concrete rules (*furū'*/sg. *far'*) into quotidian perceptions of Islam, whereby the *shar'ī*/non-*shar'ī* distinction effectively (and ideally) disappears on the level of everyday practice (as described in Chapter 1). In the end, at any rate, the combined effects of Western power, the Western secular (which positions religion as its binary Other), and Muslim misrecognition of the Islamic Secular effectively reduced Islam to undifferentiated "religion," along lines of what Leora Batnitzky describes in her book *How Judaism Became a Religion*. On this development, Islam could preserve itself only *as* religion, "*in the proper, the religious, sense*." And since the Western secular's "religion" is ultimately restricted to the dictates of scripture and its interpreters—*sola scriptura*—Islam was effectively reduced to formal religious doctrine, that is, theology and, especially, *sharī'ah*. From this position, its ability—and authority—to address pressing practical issues drastically declined, along with its ability to sustain a functional plausibility structure. This, and not simply the restrictions imposed upon *sharī'ah* from without, has contributed significantly to the opening up of spaces for Western secular regimes of socio-political ordering.

According to Batnitzky, prior to the rise of modernity, Judaism was not just a "religion"; it was a law, a practice, a culture, a language, a political arrangement, even a nationality.[271] But the modern (Protestant) redefinition of religion as private, internalized belief stripped all but the first of these aspects away, rendering the rest of them secular and migrating them out of what would become the common understanding of "religion" proper. In the case of Islam, the initial Muslim response to modernity's dislocating impact was to reject this disaggregation. But the process of reintegrating the now-secular features back into Islam required that their secular identity first be denied; for, the "secular" and the "religious" were now perceived as mutually exclusive domains. Accordingly, everything that was to be considered "Islamic" had to be rendered "religious," that is, concretely grounded in *sharīʿah*, as the sole repository of Muslim transgenerational hermeneutical engagement with scripture. Everything that was not "Islamic" (on this understanding) was subject to being either rejected or ignored. The late Ṭāriq al-Bishrī (d. 1442/2021), an astute observer of the nineteenth and twentieth centuries, notes that even some of the most ardent Muslim proponents and defenders of Islam limited their focus almost entirely to *sharʿīyāt*, or what was obligatory or forbidden (*al-furūḍ wa al-muḥarramāt*). This handed the practical aspects of economic, social, and political reform over to the proponents of secularist thought (*al-fikr al-ʿalmānī*), increasingly popularizing the notion that secular thought was the rightful home of these issues.[272] On this development, the entire realm of the non-*sharʿī* all but ceased to be recognized as Islam. Shahab Ahmed's aforementioned complaint is now not only apropos but thrown into relief: Muslims "would likely hesitate to think that a discourse on humour might somehow meaningfully be called 'Islamic' . . . by the same measure that [they] would likely *not* hesistate to classify . . . a treatise on the meaning of *jihād* as 'Islamic' "[273] Such mounting agnosia and practical irrelevance, now amplified by Western *and* Muslim proponents of secularism, cumulatively undermined the authority of and confidence in Islam-cum-*sharīʿah*.

Part of the explanatory power of Asad's analysis resides in how his mapping of Western polarities onto Islam facilitates an understanding of the phenomenon of religious decline among modern Muslims. It does so, however—to my mind at least—only according to those very polarities. Viewed from the vantage point of the Islamic Secular, decline is not simply a matter of Muslims becoming less religious (or more secular) in the modern Western sense or even of *sharīʿah*'s jurisdiction being restricted from without; it is equally (if not more) a matter of Muslims not being 'secular' enough in the Islamic Secular sense, which has led to *sharīʿah*'s jurisdiction ballooning to the point of misapplication and diminishing returns. By highlighting the *sharʿī*/non-*sharʿī* distinction and the wages of its misrecognition, the Islamic Secular offers an insight into religious decline among modern Muslims that is quite different from Asad's.

Asad recognizes that "the social and cultural changes taking place in the late nineteenth and early twentieth centuries—whether deliberately initiated or not—created some of the basic preconditions for secular modernity."[274] He cites in this regard the role of "the political authority of the nation-state," "the freedom of the market exchange," and "the moral authority of the family."[275] While these are all relevant, I would argue that there is also a place for considering "culture" in the common, everyday sense, a sense that places it, substantiely speaking, more explicitly "beyond the law" (*warāʾ al-ḥukm al-sharʿī*) and thus obviates *sharīʿah*'s limited impact on it. Al-Bishrī is clear and to the point in this regard:

> We may all recall what cinema and theater did to distort the image of the "average Aḥmad" (*ibn al-balad*) and the turbaned Azharī *shaykh* in the thirties and forties and to enhance the image of the *tarbush*-wearing "gentleman" (*afandī*) who had been educated in modern (read: Western) schools. They cast the former as usually crude, lustful and insolent, and the latter as usually understanding, kind and as one in whom the most praiseworthy traits were consummated.[276]

Al-Bishrī also cites, as a typical manifestation of the period's "West-toxification" (*maraḍ al-ifranjī*), the complaint of an upper-class father whose son traveled to Europe only to return "with contempt for his country and his people, having forgotten his native language."[277] So powerful were the cultural dislocations of the time that al-Bishrī characterizes cinema, theater, and the media in general as "weapons of mass destruction" (*asliḥat al-damār al-shāmil*), given their ability to instill, manipulate, or destroy perceptions of self and other.[278]

Even if we allow for an element of exaggeration or nostalgia in al-Bishrī's description, the actions and institutional developments he describes clearly reflect secularization, in that they point to the diminishing authority of native tastes and instincts, the sapping of native confidence, and the burnishing of the Western socio-political vision, with the cumulative effect of weakening the indigenous *nomos* and plausibility structure through which Islam-cum-*sharīʿah* sustains its status as normative. But these trends were not simply or even primarily a function of *sharīʿah*'s scope being limited to "family law"; nor would the mere (re-)expansion of *sharīʿah*'s jurisdiction beyond this restricted area necessarily reverse these trends. From the perspective of the Islamic Secular, the dislocations in question exerted their impact largely "beyond the law," in both the first and second senses outlined earlier.[279] For this reason, not *sharīʿah* or *sharʿī* activity but non-*sharʿī*, Islamic Secular efforts, operating similarly "beyond the law," would have been (and will be) far more likely to reverse these setbacks.

Stated differently, part of what drove Muslim efforts to align their perception of self and the world with that of the modern West was their infatuation with the latter as a culture and civilization.[280] The proximate path to reversing this phenomenon, however, would not be through more "religious" activity, that is, "*in the proper, the religious, sense*," nor through more fervent appeals to *sharīʿah* or *ijtihād*. It would be, rather, through more non-*sharʿī*, differentiated, 'secular' activity, through which Islam-cum-*sharīʿah*'s *nomos* and plausibility structure could be restored and, thus, Islam's prestige as a civilization reinstated. Not just more al-Ghazālīs and Ibn Taymīyahs, in other words, but, crucially, also more Sinans and Ulugh Begs!

This is not a new perspective in the history of Islam. We see it on display as far back as al-Qarāfī. While ophthalmology is clearly neither a dictate of *sharīʿah* nor a *sharʿī* pursuit, al-Qarāfī, even as the quintessential "jurists' jurist," recognized its importance for enhancing Islam's civilizational prestige, and from there the propriety of embracing its primacy and normativeness.[281] We saw a similar stance in al-Ghazālī's decision to address the *falāsifah*.[282] In both cases, secular activity—or at least partly secular activity, that is, Islamic Secular activity—not exclusively religious activity, "*in the proper, the religious, sense*," was recognized as the key to resisting the erosion of Islam-cum-*sharīʿah*'s stature and authority, such erosion being the functional equivalent of modern secularization. And yet—and this is the important point here—from the perspective of the Islamic Secular, unlike that of the Western secular reflected in Asad's analysis, this non-*sharʿī*, 'secular' activity was ultimately religious, equal in this regard to the architectural wonders of Sinan or Ulugh Beg cited in the Introduction. In sum, to see religious decline among modern Muslims solely through the prism of the Western secular/religious divide is to misapprehend both the problem and its solution.

As noted earlier, this perspective is indebted to a particular view of the concept of "differentiation." Here too, however, Asad and the Islamic Secular embrace different understandings. As we saw in Chapter 1, in applying the concept of differentiation to the Islamic Secular, I draw explicitly on the work of José Casanova and his influential book *Public Religions in the Modern World*. I argue that Islam as *dīn* can inform the substance of economics (recall al-Maqrīzī) or science (recall al-Ghazālī) without drawing concretely on the Qur'ān, Sunnah, or *sharīʿah*. In his engagement with Casanova, however, Asad questions the consistency of invoking differentiation and simultaneously arguing for a public role for religion. On the one hand, he argues, differentiation implies a walling off of religion from the secular spheres of politics, science, economics, and the like. On the other hand, any time religion takes itself seriously as it enters the public domain, it cannot remain "indifferent to debates about how the economy should run, or which scientific projects should be publicly funded or what the broader aims of national education should be."[283] In other words, religion cannot be both walled off from secular spheres and simultaneously directly involved in them.

Asad is proceeding, however, on the assumption of the Western secular and the binary opposition it posits between the secular and the religious. But, as I have noted, this is not an interpretive prism through which the Islamic Secular can be properly understood. According to the latter, "differentiation" is the separation not of the secular from the religious but of the *sharʿī*, as that which reclines upon revelation, from the non-*sharʿī*, as that which does not, within and not outside the circumference of Islam as *dīn*. On this understanding, there is no inherent contradiction between religion's embracing the secular as a differentiated realm, on the one hand, while simultaneously addressing political, economic, scientific, and other practical interests in the public domain as a non-*shar'ī* but religious activity, on the other.

I agree with Asad that secularism and secularization never existed in Islam prior to the Muslim world's encounter with Western modernity. But the reason for this was that there was no reason for secularism or secularization to exist. Muslims never developed or embraced as a dominant trend a mindset that pitted "religion" against the "secular" as binary opposites vying for a share of each other's real estate. Nor did the Muslim mainstream subscribe to a zero-sum competition between religion and the state. Nor was there ever an ideological commitment to proceeding "*as if* God did not exist." Instead, within the all-encompassing realm of the religious, some matters were identified as *shar'ī* and others as non-*shar'ī*. Jurists argued over how accurately this line was or could be drawn and how faithfully it was or could be observed. But these arguments did not mean that they could not recognize and call out "ignorant friends of Islam" or practitioners of "improper *taqlīd*" who tried to convert scripture or the *madhhab*s into a substantive source for everything. Over the course of their history, Muslims confronted some of the same challenges that appeared in the Christian West—the relationship between realism and nominalism, the relationship between law and ethics, the question of the meaning and scope of "divine law." And their answers often echoed insights and commitments landed upon in the West. One of the major arguments of this book, however, is that, even when Islam shares a doctrine or vocabulary with the West, its upshot need not necessarily follow the same dénouement that we witness in the West. Conversely, fleeing from a concept's or institution's associations with the West will not always deliver one to an accurate understanding of that concept or institution in Islam. For over a thousand years, Muslim jurists have recognized limitations on the scope of *sharī'ah*'s jurisdiction (again, as I define these). *Pace* Asad, however—or the understanding that many may draw from him—this did not mean that they attached any positive value, intentionally or otherwise, to secularism or secularization in the modern Western sense. This basic fact is fundamental to the vision of the Islamic Secular.

One can recognize the value of the secular—certainly as differentiation—without embracing secularism or secularization. If only by entailment, the Islamic juristic tradition's recognition of the *shar'ī*/non-*shar'ī* distinction was in effect a recognition of the (micro-)secular—Béteille's coveted "space." The fact, however, that this space constituted a "religious secular," that is, a secular *within* the boundaries of Islam, preempted—at least prior to the rise and influence of modern Europe—the emergence of any normative commitment to either secularism or secularization.

Today, the meaning of "secular" remains a topic of debate, even as the common Western understanding predominates and the category itself endures as an immoveable feature of the modern landscape. Nowhere, however, is its influence and relationship with its putative rival—religion—more topical than in discourses around the modern state, *the über*-framework that envelopes all contemporary life. In the West, the modern state emerged as a secular response to the "problem of religion." As Bernard Lewis summarizes the matter, "Christian struggles between Protestants and Catholics . . . devastated Europe in the sixteenth and seventeenth centuries and finally drove Christians in desperation to evolve a doctrine of separation of religion from the state."[284] Over time, this "solution" and the various assumptions that informed it, made their way into the Muslim world and, ultimately, the Muslim mind. As Asad (and others) makes clear, secularization, East and West, is a preeminently political commitment, aimed at facilitating the business of the modern state. Yet, it has been almost exclusively the common Western understanding of "secular" and "religious" that has governed discussions of the normative relationship between Islam and the modern state. The Islamic Secular—with its explicit recognition of self-imposed jurisdictional limits on *sharīʿah*, a *sharʿī*/non-*sharʿī* distinction within Islam, a clear commitment to maintaining the distinction between the historically contingent and the transcendent within religion, indeed, the very possibility of a "religious secular"—has not been part of the conversation.

One of my fundamental arguments is that Islam-cum-*sharīʿah* cannot be fully understood without duly considering the Islamic Secular. This includes Islam in the context of the most critical relationship that any religion must negotiate in the world today: its relationship with the modern state.[285] In fact, on a practical level, it might be argued that "religion" in the modern world *is* its relationship with the modern state. And here, perhaps more than anywhere else, the practical implications of the Islamic Secular come to the fore. The next three chapters, Part 2 of this book, will place the Islamic Secular in conversation with three important works that address the relationship between Islam and the modern state: Wael B. Hallaq's *The Impossible State*, Abdullahi A. An-Naʿim's *Islam and the Secular State*, and Andrew F. March's *Islam and Liberal Citizenship*. I begin with Professor Hallaq.

PART II

THE ISLAMIC SECULAR, MODERNITY, AND THE MODERN STATE

4
The Islamic Secular and The Impossible State

Basic Anatomy

In his response to Samuel P. Huntington's famous article "The Clash of Civilizations?" the late Fouad Ajami (d. 1435/2014) insisted that Huntington got things backward: "[L]et us be clear: civilizations do not control states, states control civilizations."[1] Over the course of his argument, Ajami depicts the "civilization of the West," including its "modernity and secularism," as imbuing modern, non-Western states with a new identity and vision that impel them to resist attempts by native civilizations—Hindu, Confucian, Islamic, Eastern Orthodox—to reassert themselves as the rightful definers of the prevailing order. This suggests that it is not a question of *whether* civilizations control states but of *which* civilizations control them. Be that as it may, Ajami is certainly correct in seeing this dance between 'pre-modern' civilizations and modern states as one of the defining features of the modern age. Even if we question his claim that states fully control civilizations, we can hardly deny that they try, any more than Ajami could deny that civilizations resist. Nowhere is this latter phenomenon more evident than in the case of Islam.

Like Ajami, most moderns grant the modern state a mandate to control or domesticate religion. Many Muslims, on the other hand, resist this presumption, either in direct reaction to it or based on a spontaneous reading of Islam in history. Much of what modern states assume the mandate to provide or regulate is commonly thought of as secular. In fact, modern states typically think of themselves as secular entities. We have seen, however, that "secular"—and, by entailment, "religious"—can be understood in ways that defy the commonly assumed secular/religious divide. As such, what a modern state sees as confirming or contradicting its secular identity and what a religion (in our case Islam) sees as affirming or compromising its religious integrity may differ, depending on the operative understanding of secular and religious in circulation. This is among the fundamental insights of the Islamic Secular.

It would seem appropriate, if not necessary, in such light, to factor this insight into any assessment of the normative relationship between Islam and the modern state. To date, however, such factoring has not obtained among scholars

The Islamic Secular. Sherman A. Jackson, Oxford University Press. © Oxford University Press 2024.
DOI: 10.1093/oso/9780197661789.003.0005

writing on the topic. Instead, far-reaching conclusions about the relationship between Islam-cum-*sharīʿah* and the modern state have been reached in the complete absence of any consideration of the Islamic Secular, despite the testimony of the Islamic juristic tradition regarding the Islamic Secular's centrality to the normative conception of Islam-cum-*sharīʿah*. This critical oversight is what this and the next two chapters will seek to address.

The Impossible State

In his provocative book, *The Impossible State*, Wael Hallaq, a leading scholar of Islamic law in the Western academy, insists that in attempting to negotiate its relationship with the modern state, Islam-cum-*sharīʿah* faces an impossible task. According to him, the modern state, by its very nature and definition, must seek to control or domesticate Islam-cum-*sharīʿah* in ways that the latter, by its very nature and definition, cannot countenance. The opening lines of his Introduction set the stage for this dilemma: "The argument of this book is fairly simple: 'The Islamic State,' judged by any standard definition of what the modern state represents, is both an impossibility and a contradiction in terms."[2] The modern state, according to Hallaq, entails an absolute, autonomous, transcendent sovereignty, which, within its territorial boundaries, implies universal political authority and coextensive legal jurisdiction. Meanwhile, *sharīʿah*, according to him, also claims unbounded jurisdiction, which is effectively coterminous with the all-encompassing authority of Islam itself. On this understanding, any attempt to conjoin Islam-cum-*sharīʿah* and the modern state results in a clash of unbounded jurisdictions. And, as the modern state will brook no challenge to its authority, it cannot possibly accord Islam-cum-*sharīʿah* the place assigned to it by any orthodox formulation of Sunni Islam.

Beyond the matter of jurisdictional boundaries, the modern state, according to Hallaq, recognizes no authority and no value higher than itself. In pursuit of its apex value of self-preservation, it operates solely on the basis of material interests—primarily the augmentation of power (especially economic and military)—not on the basis of morality. The modern state as such has no moral foundation. In and of itself, it cannot be good or sustain a common good or a commitment to producing morally good citizens.[3] This is why, for thinkers such as Alasdair MacIntyre, with whose project Hallaq identifies his own, the appropriate response for anyone attached to a tradition of virtues or morals is to reject the modern state.[4] Hallaq insists that Muslims must do the same, since Islam-cum-*sharīʿah* is ultimately a tradition of virtues, an all-encompassing moral vision, with which the modern state, lacking as it does any moral foundation, is simply incommensurable.

Hallaq places these arguments against the backdrop of the "modern condition" spawned by the Enlightenment. Modernity, he observes, not only dispenses with traditional faith-based morality; it replaces it with a "critical rationality" that is morally blind and attached to no prior principles, with the possible exception of "progress."[5] It is this modern condition that denies the state access to moral foundations and breeds a particularly modern set of dislocations: moral malaise, possessive individualism, degradation of the environment, militarism, cultural imperialism, and capitalist exploitation. These developments are as definitive of the age as they are inextricably woven into it. And because of this confluence of traits, Hallaq concludes, a functional political arrangement based on *sharīʿah* and Islamic principles of governance is simply impossible in the modern world.[6]

At bottom, there is a cumulative intimation in Hallaq's argument that raises the stakes significantly beyond what may appear on the surface. Hallaq implies that, as long as Muslims hold onto *sharīʿah* as a socio-political blueprint, they must either remain stateless or bear the cognitive dissonance of living under states that are un-Islamic. At the same time, he insists, "Islam . . . unless eviscerated, stands or falls on Sharīʿa."[7] If *sharīʿah* is the functional equivalent (or simply the essence) of Islam, on the one hand, and the modern state and condition are both immoveable and inherently antithetical to *sharīʿah*, on the other, it is difficult to see how the impossibility of which Hallaq speaks could be limited to the Islamic State. Rather, given the virtual identity he sees between *sharīʿah* and Islam, this impossibility would have to extend to Islam as religion. In such light, one wonders if what Professor Hallaq is really describing is not simply the "Impossible State" but the "Impossible Religion."

If we assume, however, the basic premise of the Islamic Secular as our point of departure, namely, that *sharīʿah* is a bounded entity, neither co-extensive nor identical with Islam, then a fully symmetrical clash of jurisdictions and thus the full impossibility of an Islamic State (or religion) must be reconsidered. If the state deems it necessary to control Islam *qua* religion, *in the proper, the religious, sense*, how much control will it deem necessary to exert over Islam-cum-*sharīʿah* in its non-*sharʿī*, 'secular' mode? In other words, one might ask not simply about the "possible" or "impossible" state but perhaps about the "half-possible" state, so to speak, that is, the Islamic State *warāʾ al-ḥukm al-sharʿī*.[8] In fact, given the ratio of non-*sharʿī* to *sharʿī* matters that typically define the quotidian role and mandate of modern states and given that the non-*sharʿī* can be thought of as no less religious—indeed, no less Islamic—than the *sharʿī*, one might argue, from the perspective of the Islamic Secular, that an Islamic State is more possible than Hallaq suggests.

Similarly, to the extent that degradation of the environment, militarism, cultural imperialism, and the like can be addressed as non-*sharʿī*, practical issues rather than as purely *shar'ī* matters, or what Hallaq describes as "moral" concerns, the idea of a categorical contradiction between Islam-cum-*sharī'ah* and the modern condition will also require reassessment. These two insights—the bounded nature of *sharī'ah* and the practical-cum-material dimensions of Islam-cum-*sharī'ah*'s overall vision, both of which are constituents of the Islamic Secular—will be the primary drivers of my critical engagement with Hallaq.

I should clarify that my overall aim is not to argue in favor of the Islamic State per se. It is, rather, to engage with Hallaq's understanding of the relationship between Islam-cum-*sharī'ah* and the modern state and to place that understanding in conversation with the Islamic Secular. This involves two main issues.

First, there is Hallaq's definition of "the state." Here my primary challenge will not be to the substance of his definition (which is not to say that I agree with it) but to the propriety and fidelity of its application. The paradigmatic "Islamic State" to which Hallaq applies his criterion is the modern descendent of the pre-modern Muslim political arrangement, whose Islamic nature and identity resided most fundamentally in its implementation of *sharī'ah*.[9] As a political arrangement, this Islamic State, on Hallaq's depiction, is essentially *shar'ī* through and through. Hallaq does not recognize the Islamic Secular or its commitment to Islam "beyond the law"; nor does he recognize differentiated, non-*shar'ī*, *'aql* as a legitimate source of things Islamic. On this understanding, the normative Islamic State lacks what he identifies as the essential features of a modern state. And this underwrites the categorical incompatibility he sees between the two. Yet, while Hallaq applies his definition of "the state" unqualifiedly to the Islamic State, I argue that it can only be applied qualifiedly to other modern political arrangements that nevertheless pass as states according to his criteria. This calls into question the implied uniqueness of the alleged impossibility of the Islamic State, according to Hallaq's theory.

The second issue relates to Hallaq's conceptualization of *sharī'ah*, particularly its relationship to reason. By "reason," I do not mean simply the linear faculty for refereeing claims to proper scriptural interpretation or the determination of empirical facts; I am referring additionally to modes of knowing that include such faculties as imagination, taste, talent, skill, *fantasia*, and the like, as suggested by the jurists' open-ended depictions of *'aqlī* in contradistinction to *shar'ī*, as discussed in Chapter 2. Engagement with this topic will bring us full circle to a discussion of the Islamic State in light of Hallaq's understanding of *sharī'ah*, compared to that of the Islamic Secular, touching upon various subsidiary issues along the way. For now, however, I would like to offer a few general observations that will hopefully diminish the likelihood of distorting or misapprehending Hallaq's thesis, or of disadvantaging, misrepresenting, or falsely privileging my own.

Avoiding Distortions and Straw Men

The Impossible State, umbilically tied to Hallaq's larger work, *Sharīʿa: Theory, Practice, Transformations*,[10] is a provocatively rich text, not every aspect of which is directly relevant to my analysis. As such, my critique of its main thesis should not be understood to extend to everything the learned Professor Hallaq has to say about Islam-cum-*sharīʿah* and its relationship to the modern world. Nor should it be read as an unqualified endorsement of the modern state or modern condition. Nor am I arguing that Islam views—or should view—the modern state as its normative mode of political organization. In fact, I have reservations about all these issues. I agree that the legal monism and "jurispathic"[11] tendencies of modern states pose significant challenges to Islam-cum-*sharīʿah*. And I am alive to the problem of contemporary Muslim regimes taking the modern state-structure as a convenient, autocracy-legitimizing leviathan.[12] Partly for these reasons, I do not believe that Muslims are necessarily bound to the modern state as some sort of would-be normative Islamic imperative. I also believe that various aspects of the modern condition, including many that come in for criticism by Professor Hallaq, are problematic for Islam.

But there is a difference, to my mind, between the modern state posing a challenge for Islam-cum-*sharīʿah* and the two constituting a categorical contradiction in terms. For, there is a difference between what political actors do with the modern state and the ostensibly inherent nature of that structure itself.[13] The modern state is neither a driverless vehicle nor in all its details an immutable given. Moreover, if Islam is to be held to a particular theory of the state, this theory should be extended across the board to include the Jewish State, the Hindu State, and the many other religiously informed or secular states across the globe. Otherwise, Hallaq's asserting the impossibility of the Islamic State in particular might be tantamount to asserting that cold water is wet, as if wetness were not a feature of hot or lukewarm water. Further, if we are to limit Muslims in their choices of political arrangements, this limitation should be clearly and identifiably dictated by their own tradition, not by preconceived interpretive presuppositions from without, for example, the presumed categorical conflict between divine and human will (discussed below). Finally, regarding the modern condition, there are two points to be considered.

First, while substantively unique in some ways, contemporary modernity is not the first "modern condition" that Islam has had to face. Muslims in second-/eighth- or third-/ninth-century Syria or Transoxiana had to make numerous adjustments unknown to the original Muslims of Arabia or even to the first Muslims of Syria or Central Asia. This is not to mention the situation during and after the Mongol invasions, the Crusades, or even (for some Muslims) Tīmūr Lenk (d. 807/1405). Why should Islam be able to face one "modernity"—indeed, even to appropriate aspects thereof as its own—but be so categorically unable to face another? Are we essentializing Islam in a manner that ultimately denies or misapprehends its traditional powers of appropriation?

Second, however problematic we may deem the present modernity to be, to assume that Islam's response can be mounted only on the basis of strictly *shar'ī* arguments and deliberations is to fall victim to the kind of over-inclusive understanding of *sharī'ah* that the Islamic Secular calls into question.

What Hallaq Is *Not* Saying

Given the force and detail of Hallaq's thesis, it is important to alert ourselves to a number of things that he is actually *not* saying, the better to recognize the importance of responding to what he *is* saying, directly or by implication. To begin with, while Hallaq does not formally define "Islamic State," he is not referring to the strident, utopian construct advocated and pursued by the likes of ISIS, *al-Qā'idah*, or Boko Haram. The Islamic State that Hallaq has in mind is closer to what I described some twenty-five years ago in my *Islamic Law and the State*: "[T]he Islamic State is a nation-state ruled by Islamic law."[14] While even then, I saw *sharī'ah* as a bounded entity that left room for reglementary activity beyond that of the *fuqahā'*, I now see much more clearly that "Islamic law" is a complex construct consisting more fundamentally of both *shar'ī and* non-*shar'ī* elements. Hallaq, on the other hand, sees *sharī'ah* as an unbounded, overwhelmingly *shar'ī* enterprise that only begrudgingly (if at all) recognizes non-*shar'ī* constituents, which themselves can never be legitimately pursued except as an extension or ward of *sharī'ah*.[15] On his understanding, the non-*shar'ī* is not only approached agnostically but is also subject to being dismissed as barely legitimate if not illegitimate. For, on his totalizing view of *sharī'ah*, it is difficult to distinguish "outside of *sharī'ah*" from "outside of Islam." Of course, this devaluation of the non-*shar'ī* necessarily promotes misrecognition of the Islamic Secular, occluding anything it might contribute to an assessment of the relationship between Islam-cum-*sharī'ah* and the modern state. My reassessment will hopefully reveal the impropriety and cost of this occlusion.

We should also note that Hallaq does not depict the contradiction between the Islamic State and the modern state in terms of the traditional religious/secular divide. In fact, unlike Andrew March and (especially) Abdullahi An-Na'im, Hallaq shows little interest in highlighting the secular nature of the modern state, certainly not as the most important contributor to its conflict with Islam.[16] This may raise questions about the propriety of placing his thesis in conversation with the Islamic Secular. But there are two points here. First, the fundamental conflict that Hallaq sees is between *sharī'ah* as the religious law of Islam and the materialist, power-driven, amoral modern state, which, invariably, if at times only indirectly, implies a secular/religious confrontation. Speaking of Islam in general, for example, he writes "By the rules of linguistic entailment . . . the 'religious' functioned in opposition to such concepts as 'rationalism' and, more starkly, 'secularism.'"[17] Second, Hallaq is unequivocal in tracing the provenance of the modern state to early-modern Europe. On this attribution, the state must be seen as the secular alternative to the religionized socio-political order it was designed to replace. Even scholars who reject the traditional "wars of religion" explanation for the rise of the modern state agree that secularization was part of its intended goal and that its basic character is "incomprehensible . . . apart from the notion that the Church is perhaps the primary thing from which the modern state is meant to save us."[18] On this provenance, the term "modern state" entails "secular" no less than "mother" entails "child," even if it remains possible (as Hallaq admits) for the state to evolve away from its present outlook, just as children eventually become adults.[19] Of course, the Islamic Secular implies a very different kind of secular. And part of my aim in placing it in conversation with *The Impossible State* is to investigate the relationship between Islam-cum-*sharī'ah* and the modern state when viewed through the lens of this alternate understanding of the secular—and the religious.

Meanwhile, though Hallaq remains pessimistic about the prospects of reconciling Islam-cum-*sharī'ah* with the modern state, he does not entirely foreclose the possibility. His basic argument is that the very nature of the modern state, as presently constituted, frustrates *sharī'ah* and its vision. Moreover, any reconciliation between the two will have to come from the side of *sharī'ah*, as the modern state is here to stay, at least for the foreseeable future. Still, assuming that Muslims are able to effect what he calls a "creative reformulation of Sharī'a and Islamic governance," Hallaq admits reconciliation as a theoretical possibility, albeit so remote as not to alter his basic thesis.[20] Crucially, however, the reason that this possibility is so remote is that *sharī'ah*, according to Hallaq, can be reconciled with the modern state only by betraying its own basic constitution, at the heart of which is its moral vision, which is held in place by a categorical refusal to separate the moral "Ought" from the ontological "Is."[21] Hallaq is not arguing here that the problem resides with the concrete substance of *sharī'ah*'s morality; rather, it is the fact that *sharī'ah* is morally constituted to begin with, which places it at odds with the materialist, amoral vision of the modern state.

Again, however, if, as I have argued, *sharī'ah* is committed to more than just morality and the range of its jurisdiction is not coterminous with that of Islam, then the conflict between Islam-cum-*sharī'ah* and the amoral modern state must diminish proportionally. I am not suggesting here that *sharī'ah* takes no interest in morality or even that morality is not in some sense its apex concern.

But *sharīʿah* also includes an abiding prudential imperative, which, alongside and even at times in competition with morality, has always informed Muslim jurists' negotiations with socio-political reality. They have always grappled openly with such questions as whether misappropriating another's property is always *ḥarām* (as, e.g., when a starving person eats from another's orchard without the owner's permission), whether a Muslim's inheriting (*mīrāth*, not *waṣīyah*[22]) from non-Muslim relatives is in every case forbidden, or whether accepting an interest-bearing (*ʔribā*) contract is always a sin (such as with home mortgages in the modern West). If, on its own accord—that is, not as a capitulation to the forces of modernity—*sharīʿah* has always included a prudential element that seeks to accommodate material interests, extenuating circumstances, practicality, and the like, then it is not entirely clear, *pace* Hallaq, why occasionally placing the prudential over the moral necessarily constitutes a violation of *sharīʿah* and its vision.

Hallaq is also not arguing that *sharīʿah* never achieved in pre-modern times the status of the applied "law of the land,"[23] such that its aspiring to such today would be an aberration—as some proponents of secularism or the dystopian narrative of Islamic law might claim. In fact, Hallaq maintains, "Until the early nineteenth century, and for twelve centuries before then, the moral law of Islam, the Sharīʿa, had successfully negotiated customary law and legal customary practices and had emerged as the supreme moral and legal force regulating both society and government."[24] Yet, whatever pre-modern Islam's political arrangement may have been, it was not, according to Hallaq, a state, as it lacked a state's essential form-properties.[25] Indeed, the introduction of the modern state ruptured this pre-modern arrangement and thoroughly dislocated *sharīʿah*. Again, while he does not claim that the problem begins with *sharīʿah*, Hallaq argues that it can be solved (to the extent that it can be solved) only by making adjustments to *sharīʿah*, adjustments that risk compromising its basic constitution and integrity. This claim is fundamental to Hallaq's thesis.

One final note before moving on to my concrete engagement with Hallaq. Hallaq's primary focus is the traditional Muslim world, most preeminently the Arab world. He outlines the problems confronting Muslims in Muslim-majority countries, as they grapple with their post-colonial reality of operating within the logic and confines of a modern political arrangement that has a decidedly foreign provenance and ethos. Muslims who live as minorities elsewhere (in the West, for example) are not included in his frame. This is neither a complaint nor a criticism: life is short, and we all have our specific interests. My point is, rather, that in engaging with Hallaq, I am assuming the same context he assumes, the Muslim-majority states of the Muslim world. I will have more to say about the Islamic Secular in a Muslim-minority context in my engagement with Andrew March in Chapter 6.

Hallaq and the Modern State

Hallaq acknowledges that there is a virtually endless list of definitions of the state.[26] He extracts from the aggregate of formulations by leading theorists what he presents as the *sine qua non* of any defensible definition of the state. As he puts it, "The Weberian bureaucratic, the Kelsenian legal, the Schmittian political, the Marxian economic, the Gramscian hegemonic, and the Foucauldian cultural can all be brought to bear upon a conception of the state."[27] The result is what he refers to as the "paradigmatic state," which possesses "properties that the state has in reality possessed for at least a century and without which it could never be conceived of as a state, being that essential."[28] These properties include: (1) the fact that the state is historically constituted by and embedded in a set of meanings and functions that are native to Europe; (2) its sovereignty, which negates the existence of any authority higher than its own; (3) its monopoly over law, legislation, and the use of legitimate violence; (4) its bureaucracy, characterized by an insatiable, mechanistic, regulatory appetite; and (5) its hegemonic engagement with the social order, which promotes the politicization of culture and the production of the modern "citizen," whose subjectivity is calibrated to the logic and sovereignty of the modern state.

Most of the thinkers upon whom Hallaq draws represent 'non-*shar'ī*,' or differentiated, modes of thinking (sociology, economics, culture). One wonders, therefore, about the propriety of placing them in conversation with Islam's *shar'ī* discourses. More substantively, what Hallaq appears to take from these thinkers' formulations are the various points on which they agree, their differences being either commensurable or inconsequential. But if Foucault essentially wants to do away with centralized, hierarchical sovereignty—indeed, with the very obsession with sovereignty itself—by "cutting off the king's head,"[29] while Schmitt wants a super-centralized *über*-sovereign who monopolizes the prerogative over the "exception," and if bureaucracy can be counted an essential form-property, while Weber (not to mention modern critics of the so-called administrative state) suggests ways in which bureaucracy undermines democracy (to which all Euro-American states subscribe),[30] then one would think that this diverse group of thinkers could be brought together only at the very highest level of abstraction. But, if this is the case, one wonders what Islam could possibly do at this altitude to disqualify itself from constituting a *bona fide* state. What would make *sharī'ah* (and its pluralistic ethos) functionally different from Foucault's challenge to centralized, hierarchical sovereignty? What would distinguish a Muslim ruler's *siyāsah* from the prerogatives of Schmitt's decider on the exception?[31] And why would bureaucracy be any less lethal to democracy than it is to the Islamic State? This question of why Islam should be disqualified absolutely on Hallaq's criterion, while

Euro-American (and other) states are accepted as states, even though they satisfy his criterion only qualifiedly, will reappear throughout my analysis.

In the meantime, there is an illocutionary subtlety attending Hallaq's description, which predisposes the reader to anticipate the coming conflict with Islam. Hallaq intimates that the form-properties he cites are not native to Islam-cum-*sharīʿah* and that the latter could accommodate them only by becoming something other than what it normatively is. This view is a function, however, of Hallaq's limiting Islam to *sharīʿah*, on the one hand, and his attributing totalizing jurisdiction to Islam's *sharʿ* on the other. On this understanding, the properties he lists would have to be dictates of *sharīʿah* for them to be considered native to Islam. But if, as the Islamic Secular maintains, *sharīʿah* is neither totalizing nor coterminous with Islam and both *sharīʿah* and Islam include non-*sharʿī* elements—indeed, non-*sharʿī* thinking—then there would appear to be a much greater possibility of congruence between Islam-cum-*sharīʿah* and Hallaq's form-properties. In other words, assuming the logic and calculus of the Islamic Secular, modern Muslim jurists and thinkers could subject all these properties to principled debate. And some of these jurists and thinkers might, in good faith and through due diligence, conclude that these properties, in full or in part, are reconcilable with and serviceable to Islam.

This assumes, of course, that modern jurists and thinkers enjoy the same interpretive and practical agency as their pre-modern forebears. At times, however, Hallaq gives the impression that authentic Islam-cum-*sharīʿah* is limited to what pre-modern jurists and theologians settled on and handed down as such.[32] Had the modern state's form-properties appeared on the "pre" side of modernity, pre-modern jurists might have legitimately processed them into *bona fide* Islamic institutions, as they did with numerous other entities that were known to be of non-Muslim, foreign origin. But the fact that the state emerged on this side of modernity seems to place this possibility, for Hallaq at least, beyond the reach of modern jurists. This is not what one would expect from a scholar who has been singular in his advocacy of the view that *ijtihād*, or independent, unmediated interpretation of the sources, was and remains a necessarily ongoing duty in Islam.[33] To argue as categorically as Hallaq does, however, that the modern state's sovereignty renders it irreconcilable with Islam-cum-*sharīʿah* is to argue that contemporary Muslims could never process the concept of state-sovereignty through the relevant *sharʿī* and non-*sharʿī* filters in a manner that renders it an acceptable feature of Islamic governance, even if they based this re-working on the same sources and interpretive methods of *ijtihād* enshrined by their pre-modern forebears.

We will return to this issue of pre-modern versus modern juristic authority more substantively below. For now, the point is methodological: by so severely limiting the interpretive authority of modern jurists, Hallaq can declare reconciliation between Islam-cum-*sharīʿah* and state-sovereignty to be impossible by effectively denying the legitimacy of any attempt by modern jurists to bring such reconciliation about.

Provenance

Of all the theorists Hallaq cites, the German thinker Carl Schmitt (1888–1985) clearly informs his thinking most.[34] This influence requires, however, a brief comment, lest Hallaq, a scholar of Palestinian descent, be unfairly interpreted if not abused. Schmitt was a controversial figure whose thought is often assessed through the prism of his association with the Nazis in Hitler's Germany and after. He sided with them after 1933 and, as the preeminent jurist of National Socialism, even defended Hitler's extra-judicial killings of political opponents. Yet, this dark background notwithstanding, Schmitt's work is recognized today as extremely rich, highly relevant, nuanced, and multifaceted. As such, one may invest in aspects of his theory without assuming or seeking to put them to Schmittian ends, as is obviously the case with Jewish scholars who invoke him. For his part, Hallaq does not simply borrow from Schmitt; in many instances he processes the latter's thought through a decidedly Hallaqian lens and adapts it to Hallaqian ends. In fact, in many instances, what he presents (and I respond to) as Schmittian is perhaps better understood as Hallaqian. At any rate, just as scholars routinely call upon Kant, Hume, or even the early Weber without being associated with the bitterly racist sentiments expressed by these authorities, that same scholarly courtesy should be extended to Professor Hallaq in the case of Schmitt and his infelicities.

Schmitt's influence on Hallaq begins with the first form-property: the modern state's European provenance. Hallaq cites Schmitt's view that the "state has been possible only in the West."[35] This Western provenance, in Hallaq's depiction, carries substantive implications that inform the remaining form-properties and reinforce the state's incompatibility with Islam-cum-*sharīʿah*.[36] In his view, the state was developed to address a European reality in a manner that resonated with European history, the European self, and the European imagination. To graft this system onto Islam, therefore, would be like forcing a man to wear shoes two sizes too small. But it is difficult to apply this logic to Islam, given what we know about Muslim intellectual and institutional history, in both the *sharʿī* and non-*sharʿī* realms. The "importation" and impact in the Muslim world of Hellenistic thought, which was explicitly pagan in origin and known to be so, is too well known to require more than a mention.[37] Meanwhile, George Hourani has convincingly argued that Zoroastrian dualists influenced the early Muʿtazilites (and the seminal, perduring influence of the Muʿtazilites on Muslim Rationalism is simply undeniable).[38] Nor was this kind of cross-fertilization limited to the world of ideas. Muslims appropriated numerous institutional structures, as any perusal of al-Māwardī's or Abū Ya'lā's sections in *al-Aḥkām al-Sulṭānīyah* on land surveyance, tax-collection, and the like readily reveals.[39] Earlier, we saw Ibn Taymīyah's attitude regarding the provenance of bathhouses[40] and al-Ghazālī's on sciences developed by non-Muslims.[41] We find a similarly revealing perspective in the redoubtable Shāfi'ī jurist 'Izz al-Dīn Ibn 'Abd al-Salām (d. 660/1261) with regard to general matters of *fiqh*:

> Question: "What do the jurists mean when they refer to "foreign dress"? Who are the "foreigners"? And what is the difference between "foreign" and "non-Arab"?
>
> Response: "Foreigners" refers to those we have been forbidden [by the Prophet] to imitate, such as the followers of the Persian kings during his time. This prohibition applies, however, only to what they do that is in violation of our religious law. What they do that falls under the legal categories of recommended, obligatory, or simply licit in our religious law is not to be abandoned simply because they practice it (*lā yutrak li ajli ṭa'āṭīhim iyyāh*). Indeed, our religious law does not forbid imitating those who do what God The Exalted has permitted.[42]

The modern state, as the basic structure of institutionalized political organization, may be a very bad idea; and there may be a thousand reasons why Muslims should or may reject it. But, given these testimonies and what is known more generally about pre-modern Islam, the mere fact that the state is a Western invention is not one of them, at least not if *sharī'ah*—not to mention the Islamic Secular—is the deliberative apparatus through which this decision is made. This is not to mention the long list of other modern Western products that would have to be rejected on a strict argument of provenance: democracy, Marxist critiques of capitalism, weapons systems, even tenure. In the end, again, assuming *sharī'ah* and/or the Islamic Secular to be the standard by which Muslims approach issues of provenance, we must admit the possibility that some modern Muslim jurists and thinkers may, in good faith, on *shar'ī* or non-*shar'ī* grounds, find reasons to accept the basic structure of the modern state as an Islamically legitimate institution. This is not to imply that the modern state structure is entirely problem-free, or that Muslims would find it so. But whatever problems it might present, provenance alone would not be enough to ban it categorically from consideration.

Sovereignty and Law

Hallaq's most definitive form-property is sovereignty, from which all subsequent properties essentially flow. Schmitt is clearly his point of departure here. Hallaq describes sovereignty as "the idea that the nation *embodying* the state is the sole author of its own will and destiny."[43] The modern state, in other words, is the repository of an autonomous, self-referencing authority that inheres entirely in the state *qua* state. This authority is original and authorizes the state both to legislate and to punish as it deems fit; it enables it to command loyalty, obedience, and sacrifice; and it recognizes no other authority outside or superior to itself to which it might be bound to pay homage. In its early modern European iteration, in the work of Thomas Hobbes (d. 1679), for example, sovereignty was identified with the prerogatives of the ruler, who essentially *was* the state, as reflected in Louis XIV's (d. 1715) famous statement "*L'état c'est moi*" (I am the state). But, with the help of John Locke (d. 1704) and others, sovereignty eventually migrated to "the people" (originally the bourgeoisie), and from there evolved into our contemporary concept of "popular sovereignty."[44] It is this popular sovereignty that is now most commonly imputed to the state, and Hallaq embraces it as an essential form-property, though he processes it through what he refers to as the "Hobbesian-Schmittian thesis."[45]

It was Hobbes who conflated the political authority of the state with God. Schmitt builds on this by essentially apotheosizing "the people" as the repository of popular sovereignty. But "the people," for Schmitt, are not simply the populace; they are *das Volk,* a more or less homogenous group bound by blood, history, affections, and, most importantly, a collective sense of destiny, something inscrutably "deeper than political ties." "*Das Volk* is a romantic ideal, a mythic body."[46] And, as the repository and protector of *das Volk*'s sacred will and destiny, the state is itself rendered sacred. Whereas popular sovereignty normally entails popular control over government, "the state," in Schmitt's thought, is a rarefied entity whose sacred mission hovers above the people and may transcend its will at any given moment. Indeed, as the actual holder of state power in the name of *das Volk,* the sovereign is authorized to rule *against* the people in the name *of* the people.[47] This sovereign, ideally (but not necessarily) an individual,[48] has the authority not only to make law but also to violate it, in the name and interest of the state as the repository of the sacred destiny of *das Volk.* This was the point of Schmitt's most famous statement: "Sovereign is he who decides on the exception."[49]

Hallaq imputes a version of Schmitt's view of sovereignty to the modern state, which both explains and underwrites his tendency to attribute God-like qualities to the state. He cites approvingly Schmitt's view that "[a]ll significant concepts of the modern theory of the state are secularized theological concepts."[50] Drawing as well on the work of Paul Kahn (who also cites Schmitt), Hallaq describes the state in language eerily connotative of divinity: omnipotent, omnipresent, known by its signs.[51] Through the influence of Schmitt, Hallaq recasts the modern state as "the new God" of modernity.[52] He writes, "The traditional God is replaced in modernity by the state,"[53] and he holds up this Schmittian sovereignty as normative for the state. Ultimately, it is the presumed normativity of the "Schmittian state" that renders the Islamic State so impossible. As Hallaq declares near the end of the book, "As long as the balance of power in the world remains in favor of a Schmittian state, Islamic governance as an existential entity will always be under fatal threat."[54]

Closely aligned with the notion of state sovereignty is Hallaq's third form-property: the state's monopoly over law and legislation. According to him, "sovereign will gives birth to the law," for, "The law constitutes the very expression of that will, it being sovereignty's most paradigmatic manifestation in the practice of governance."[55] Given, however, his Schmittian understanding of sovereignty, Hallaq goes on to characterize the state in its legislative capacity as "the god-like Law-giver par excellence,"[56] literally referring to it as "the God of gods."[57] While his focus here is the state's autonomy in its exercise of legislative sovereignty, Hallaq's aim is to emphasize this autonomy in the most absolute sense. The Caliph, as the political head of the Muslim *ummah*, could be perceived as a threat to the sovereignty of individual Muslim states, against which the latter would have to assert their autonomous right to rule and legislate. But this is not the argument Hallaq is making. Rather, he pits state sovereignty against divine sovereignty, noting explicitly that "it is the state that ratifies divine will, not the other way around."[58] In other words, in the modern state, state sovereignty is superior to divine sovereignty, in which context *sharīʿah* would be applied not because God said so but only if the state says so. And if the state decides that *sharīʿah* should not be applied, God could not second-guess or overrule the state. This perspective ultimately drives Hallaq to the rhetorical invocation of a new *shahādah*: "There is no god but the state."[59] And this consummates the categorical incompatibility he sees between Islam-cum-*sharīʿah* and the modern state.

There are several perspectives from which one might want to engage with Hallaq on all of this. To begin with, as previously mentioned, the quotidian business of modern states is on balance far more non-*sharʿī* than *sharʿī*. As such, the differentiated, non-*sharʿī*, Islamic Secular reasoning employed by Muslims in a presumably Schmittian Islamic State would be, *mutatis mutandis*, substantively indistinguishable from that employed in a non-Muslim Schmittian state (e.g., determining the minimum speed at which a plane must taxi for take-off or whether a particular chemical is dangerous enough to require regulation). It is thus difficult to see the problem with reconciling this kind of Islamic reasoning with the dictates of a Schmittian state. Indeed, one might ask what alternate modes of reasoning the latter would deem acceptable as a basis for developing such rules. Hallaq leaves us to assume that *sharʿī* reasoning is the only legitimate reasoning at a Muslim's disposal. And this assumption contributes significantly to the incompatibility he posits between Islam-cum-*sharīʿah* and his Schmittian state.

At the most basic level, Hallaq's argument is that *sharīʿah* and *sharʿī* reasoning, again, ultimately the only legitimately Islamic reasoning, can have no place in a modern state (which is for him a Schmittian state) because the latter is based on a transcendent authority that contradicts and does not recognize the divine authority upon which *sharīʿah* is founded. I would argue, however, that Schmittian sovereignty transcends the state more in theory than in actual practice; practically speaking, it inheres in "the people" and exceptionally "the sovereign." This is not a negation of transcendent sovereignty or authority per se but a recognition of its concrete meaning for human communities in real space and time. It is humans, in other words—not transcendent sovereignty itself—who, through whatever theological or other interpretive prisms drive them, concretize this sovereignty and execute it so concretized. On this understanding, one might ask what (in theory at least) prevents a modern Schmittian state, even as "the sole author of its own will and destiny,"[60] from adopting and implementing *sharīʿah*. Why would this be so "impossible"? Is not such voluntary surrender of human will to transcendent divine authority precisely what Muslims have done throughout history as part of the basic meaning and essence of "*islām*"? Here, however, we come to an unarticulated assumption that seems to drive much of Hallaq's thinking in this regard: a categorical conflict between divine and human authority, such that what humans do or devise on their own is presumed to contradict if not defy God's will and authority, and what God wills or dictates unilaterally is perceived as a categorical contradiction or denial of human authority.[61] From this perspective, the Schmittian state cannot accommodate the "Islamic State" because, for the latter, implementation of *sharīʿah* is a dictate of divine as opposed to human authority. Human authority, on the other hand, the basis of the Schmittian state, is presumed to be incapable of preserving its status and integrity as human authority while voluntarily choosing to apply *sharīʿah*, as God's law. Again, however, when we speak of "divine authority" (or any transcendent authority) we cannot ultimately mean much more than humans' recognition of that authority, which, in its actual playing out, admits a wider range of possibility than Hallaq seems to recognize. Of course, humans may choose, on the basis of human authority, to reject divine authority (and with it *sharīʿah*), and I suppose that highlighting this prerogative is often part of the whole point of invoking human authority to begin with. But there is nothing inherent in human authority per se that compels such rejection; it is only the preconceived assumption of a categorical, zero-sum conflict between the substantive dictates of divine and human authority that would necessitate such a result. Meanwhile, even the acceptance of divine authority does not necessarily guarantee the application of *sharīʿah*, given what humans bring to the practical meaning, concretion, and implications of divine authority. Even Muslims who in principle fully accept divine authority may choose not to apply *sharīʿah*, at least in part, for reasons both legitimate and not.

This brings me to a final and related point in this regard. Hallaq's assertion that it is the modern state—and nothing above or outside it—that decides what the law is and how to apply it implies that, normatively speaking, this is categorically not the case in Islam. But it has always been the *ummah* (including the state and the jurists) that decides what God's law is, the extent to which it is applied, and the modality of that application.[62] God has never been understood to come down and sit on any earthly throne to dictate the running of quotidian affairs. That Muslims presumed the exercise of human agency to be a normative feature of the administration of law is clear, for example, from the reception of 'Umar I's setting aside the punishment for theft during a famine, or his banning temporary marriage (*mut'ah*), or his doubling the punishment for drinking wine. Premodern Muslims never took such actions to mean that human authority (the jurists', the ruler's, the state's, the *ummah*'s) was somehow superior to or in competition with God's. While God was perceived as existing above the state, it was always humans, including those who ran the state, who concretized the meaning of divine sovereignty as expressed by the rules and application of *sharī'ah*.[63] The fact that modern Muslim autocrats may abuse the concept of state sovereignty neither negates this reality nor delegitimates the principle behind it, namely, that it is precisely the job of the *ummah*-cum-state to determine, *inter alia*, what *sharī'ah* is and how it should be applied, such juristic principles as *istiḥsān* (?equity), *maṣlaḥah* (legitimate interest) *sadd al-dharā'i'* (blocking the means), and the like assisting them in this regard. The *ummah*-cum-state was never categorically denied this role. Nor was the state's functioning in this executive capacity ever perceived, at least not by the mainstream, as turning the state into a "God of gods." In fact, failure on the state's (or *ummah*'s) part to exercise due diligence in determining *sharī'ah*'s proper content and application was deemed a dereliction of religious duty no less than was the open flouting of *sharī'ah*. This, as we have seen, is the clear and forceful message of such widely cited works as *al-Ṭuruq al-Ḥukmīyah* by the staunch *sharī'ah*-maximalist Ibn al-Qayyim, as well as al-Qarāfī's, Ibn Farḥūn's, and al-Ṭarābulisī's works on judicature and governance.[64] Clearly, in such context, the idea of state and divine authority-cum-interests being in categorical conflict with each other calls for reconsideration.

Meanwhile, closer to home, state sovereignty has almost always been qualified by history and socio-political reality. Expressions of sovereignty routinely amount to what Muslim jurists refer to as "general expressions that imply qualified meaning," *al-'āmm yurād bihi al-khuṣūs*. It is not that such expressions are meant to be understood absolutely but circumstances on the ground do not allow them to be applied as such; it is that circumstances on the ground are understood to inform their originally intended meaning. By analogy, "No vehicles in the park" is understood to have never intended to include baby strollers. Due in large part to the religious history out of which the modern state emerges, most modern states do not and cannot think of themselves as a "God of gods," their claims to autonomous, self-referencing, transcendent sovereignty notwithstanding. The American state, for example, explicitly declares itself to be a nation *under* God. And, despite its being supremely secure in its sovereignty and sovereign will, it could never contemplate reinstituting slavery, denying women the vote, or declaring that the God of Islam did or did not literally mount the Throne. Yet, one doubts that Hallaq would challenge the status of the United States as a *bona fide* state. Of course, Hallaq might insist that America does not subscribe to a Schmittian notion of sovereignty and that my comparison here is thus misplaced. But that would imply that not all states subscribe to what Hallaq claims is an essential form-property of all states. If, on the other hand, one argues that the US does wield Schmittian sovereignty (because, in theory, it must), then, if American psychological and socio-political history can qualify its sovereignty without violating Hallaq's criterion, why can't Islam, *sharīʿah*, or Muslim history do the same?

Even Schmitt's post-war Germany saw restrictions placed on its sovereignty, thanks to the country's historical experience with Hitler. The Basic Law of the German Constitution (*Grundgesetz*) states that some of its provisions cannot be amended, even by "popular sovereignty" or proper constitutional procedure. The German Federal Constitutional Court explained this in 1954 by affirming, "[T]he Basic Law has established an order of values that limits public authority. . . . Laws are not constitutional simply because they are formally lawful. They must also be materially in line with the highest fundamental values of the free democratic order as the constitutional order of values."[65] If this provision of the German constitution does not disqualify Germany as a *bona fide* modern state by violating its claim to absolute, unchallengeable, transcendent sovereignty, why should comparable appeals to *sharīʿah* as a counter to the modern state's transcendent sovereignty disqualify the Islamic State?

From another angle, liberal theorists routinely challenge the sovereignty of modern states based on such concepts as human rights.[66] They deny states the right to do all kinds of things, despite these states' status as legitimate sovereign states. We might say something similar about the way liberal and other theorists invoke "natural law." My point here is not that these appeals or interventions are always right or justified but that they reflect the existence of a transcendent authority outside or above the state that is routinely invoked against it. This, incidentally, is often the whole point and function of constitutions, whose authority is both prior to and superior to the state, state sovereignty, and even popular sovereignty. As one legal philosopher puts it, "The essential rationale of written constitutions is to remove certain important moral/political decisions from the ordinary business of lawmaking."[67] Of course, such limitations are precisely the kind of thing that Schmitt opposes.

But neither he nor Hallaq would deny liberal or constitutional states their status as states simply because they yield to appeals to human rights or the limitations imposed by constitutions.

I should clarify, as we conclude this discussion on sovereignty, that I agree with Hallaq that modern states routinely aspire to a tinge of supranatural mystique, an aura of ineffable majesty, as a means of drawing citizens into a sense of cosmic mission (and obedience/obeisance). William Cavanaugh has argued convincingly that modernity has promoted the "migration" of a sense of the holy from religion to the state.[68] To my mind, however, this remains far more aspirational than actual, especially in today's West and those areas under its influence, where state sovereignty must compete with a sovereignty that liberalism imputes to the individual, on the one hand, and neoliberalism imputes to the inscrutable "market," on the other. If the absolute sovereignty that Hallaq imputes to the modern state remains more aspirational than factual, then it seems unfair to deny state-status to political arrangements that do not recognize this absolute sovereignty absolutely. In sum, we need not judge an Islamic State that imputes a measure of transcendent sovereignty to *sharīʿah* as running afoul of Hallaq's criterion any more than we would pass such a judgment on non-Islamic, Western states that impute a similar transcendent authority to human rights, natural law, the liberal self, the market, or constitutions.

Violence, Sacrifice, Bureaucracy, Culture

As for the remainder of Hallaq's form-properties (violence, sacrifice, bureaucracy, and culture), all of them would yield a different conversation were the Islamic Secular and its *sharʿī*/non-*sharʿī* distinction duly considered, as all of them (some more than others) consist of non-*sharʿī* elements. To this extent, Muslims could produce and negotiate their substance without recourse to scriptural sources; nor would the reasoning that Muslims rely upon in these areas necessarily conflict with that deployed by modern secular states. Again, what would render these deliberations Islamic would be, *mutatis mutandis*, not their substance *per se* (assuming, of course, their basic status as *mubāḥ*) but the energies of *taqwā*, obeisance, and *qurbah* behind them and the Islamic ends to which they were put. In this sense, Hallaq's categorical claim that the modern state's monopoly over the legitimate use of violence, its demand of sacrifice, its bureaucracy, and state-sponsored culture-production are inconsistent with Islam seems overstated.

Take the issue of the modern state's monopoly over the use of "legitimate violence," as part of its exercise of sovereignty. This is not so unique to the modern state that it places it and Islam in a relationship of categorical mutual contradiction. Al-Qarāfī, for example, insists that the application of any rule whose implementation entails violence, such as the prescribed criminal punishments (*ḥudūd*), must be the preserve of the state. For, according to him:

> Were the implementation of these rules left to the public and the common people set out to lash fornicators and amputate the limbs of thieves, etc., tempers would fly, egos would be stirred up, and the people of character would be incensed. Chaos and strife would abound. Thus, the religious law (*al-sharʿ*) settled this matter by delegating (the implementation of) these rules to the state (*wulāt al-umūr*). The people surrender to this arrangement and accept it, willingly or unwillingly, as a result of which these grave liabilities are avoided.[69]

It goes without saying that other forms of "legitimate violence" such as jailing, imposing fines, and various types of non-prescribed punishment (*taʿzīr*) are also the exclusive prerogative of state authorities. The claim here is not that the reasons behind this monopoly are exactly the same as those motivating the monopoly claimed by the modern state, nor that these reasons issue from the same place psychologically. The argument is simply that there is enough overlap between Islam and the modern state in this regard to place these approaches in the same generic category—in Hallaq's terms, the "monopoly over so-called legitimate violence."[70]

As for sacrifice, here we return to the problem of unequal application, this time, however, within modern Western states. According to Hallaq, as part of their inherent nature, modern states intentionally breed in citizens a willingness to sacrifice for the state. This is achieved by the state's success at what Hallaq refers to as "epistemic-psychological assimilation,"[71] by which the state calibrates its citizens psychologically to identify state interests with their own. According to Hallaq, "The supremacy of the state as the highest value, which the citizen must always privilege, is not a value outside of, or external to, the citizen. There is nothing in the will of the paradigmatic citizen that is outside the will of the sovereign, since the latter will—as we have seen—subsumes not only individual will but also all other wills."[72] Thus, "for a citizen or a group of citizens to challenge the law of their own state is either a contradiction in logical terms (for that would amount to challenging their own will) or an act of extreme and radical violence representing an alternative popular will, an alternative sovereignty."[73] According to Hallaq, this is part of the very nature and metaphysic of the modern state. Yet, this is hardly the construction that most of us would put on the actions of a Claudette Colvin or Rosa Parks (d. 2005), both of whom, on Hallaq's theory, should have been willing to sacrifice themselves, their dignity, and everything else for the sake of the American state, as their state.[74]

Of course, these women were members of the broader Blackamerican community, whom political theorists have identified as a "counterpublic,"[75] imbued with what Charles Long referred to as "oppugnancy," a psychological "opacity"[76] that naturally resists attempts at penetration by the state or dominant culture.[77] But if America can qualify as a *bona fide* modern state, despite the continued presence in its midst of a transgenerational, opaque, and oppugnant counterpublic, why should the Islamic State's inability to achieve (or attempt) total "epistemic-psychological assimilation" disqualify it from constituting a state? The answer cannot be that the American state tried to assimilate Blackamericans but simply failed. For, over most of its history, America neither wanted to nor believed that it could successfully assimilate this "intellectually inferior" people.

Let me be clear. I agree that modern citizens are routinely called upon to make the ultimate sacrifice for "reasons of state." But I do not see this in the metaphysical terms that Hallaq does, according to which citizens are so transparent that there is virtually nothing in them to resist, complicate, or refract the state's attempts at virtual in-dwelling (*ḥulūl*). Moreover, Hallaq implies that if a state fails at least to *aspire* to this kind of in-dwelling, it cannot be a state. And since Islam could never legitimately countenance its state's aspiring to such ideological brainwashing, an "Islamic State" would be a contradiction in terms. My response to this perspective, however, is two-fold. First, non-Islamic modern states, as we have seen, routinely fail in this regard, while still retaining their status as states. Second, as we will see in our discussion of culture below, Muslim states have always been vested in promoting the kind of *nomos* and plausibility structure that normalize for its citizens (or subjects) certain behaviors or attitudes and marginalize others. In this regard, their difference from the modern state might, again, be better described as one of degree rather than kind.

But there is another perspective from which the state's form-property of "sacrifice" seems overstated. The idea that Muslims must be willing to make the ultimate sacrifice for the Muslim polity is as old as Islam itself. The Qur'ān is full of references in this regard: "*Fight in the path of God, but do not transgress; for God does not love those who transgress*" [2:190]; "*Those who migrate and are turned out of their homes and are assaulted in defense of My cause, who fight and who are killed, I will expiate their sins and grant them entrance into Gardens.*" [3:195]; "*Do not say of those who are killed in the path of God that they are dead; nay, they are alive, though you perceive not.*" [2:154]; "*The people of Medina and the Bedouin surrounding them have no right to abandon the Prophet nor to prefer their lives over his*" [9:120]. The whole institution of *jihād* stands or falls on this willingness to make the ultimate sacrifice. I agree that the commitment here is to the Community rather than the state as a rarefied entity. But the Community was always organized, even in pre-modern times, into something approaching a state; and the destruction of this "something" could not be meaningfully separated from the destruction of the Community itself. In such light, I do not know why Hallaq sees the idea of self-sacrifice in defense of the state as so categorically modern and alien to Islam. True, modern Muslim states routinely embark on irresponsible, immoral ventures of rank aggression in which they demand that their citizens (or those who make up their military) sacrifice their lives, a phenomenon also not unknown among pre-modern Muslim regimes. While such aggression obviously has no legitimacy in Islam, in cases where the call to sacrifice *is* considered Islamically legitimate, the difference between this and the call of the modern state is, again, one of degree rather than kind.

As for bureaucracy, Hallaq argues that the modern state carries out its business—"organization of control, governing, governmentality, and violence"[78]—through a sophisticated, multi-layered, administrative apparatus infused with a rationality that "precludes it from being determined by tradition or religious decree," while at the same time being so blindly instrumental that it routinely breeds "arbitrariness."[79] This bureaucracy is impersonal and omnivorous, invading every aspect of life, "from registration of birth to the certificate of death—and almost everything in between: schooling, higher education, health, environment, welfare, travel, labor, safety at work, public hygiene, parks and entertainment, etc."[80] By forcing citizens to jump through bureaucratic hoops in order to secure their basic needs and pursue their essential and non-essential aspirations, states are able to breed dependence and fear, producing subjectivities that reflect the state's logic and prioritization, culminating in not only the modern citizen but ultimately "the community of the state."[81] By contrast, Hallaq implies, Islam could never adopt such a bureaucracy and remain Islam.

Again, due consideration of the Islamic Secular and its *shar'ī*/non-*shar'ī* distinction might significantly alter the conversation here. According to Hallaq, bureaucracy is by definition an intrusion upon *sharī'ah*. But if one views bureaucracy as a non-*shar'ī* enterprise, it can be perceived of as both Islamic *and* as not necessarily encroaching upon *sharī'ah*. My argument is not that traditional Muslim polities deployed bureaucracy to the same degree or to the same ends as modern states. It is simply that pre-modern Muslim polities had bureaucracies and that these were predominantly non-*shar'ī* in origin, and even in substance. A quick perusal of a Mamlūk chronicle or a work such as Tāj al-Dīn al-Subkī's (d. 771/1370) *Mu'īd al-Ni'am* reveals a sprawling, intricate, constantly growing, and often burdensome bureaucracy, right down to the *amīr shikār*, or custodian of hunting birds and dogs, and the *bashmaqdār*, or royal carrier of the *sulṭān*'s shoes.[82] A good number of these institutions carry not Arabic but Turkish names, clearly underscoring their historical contingency and non-*shar'ī* origins. Hallaq could rightly point out that these bureaucracies tended to be patrimonial and thus lacked the impersonal character and reach of their modern descendants. But this was not categorically the case. When Ibn Bint al-Aʿazz (d. 665/1267), the Shāfiʿī Chief Justice under the Mamlūk *sulṭān* Rukn al-Dīn Baybars (regency: 658/1260-676/1277), refused to sign off on rulings handed down by "lower court" judges from other schools of law, Baybars was unable to dissuade his appointee from this obstructionism. But he also did not feel that he could fire or overrule the Chief Justice. Instead, he responded with more bureaucracy, installing four chief judges, one from each school, thus removing the matter from both his and Ibn Bint al-Aʿazz's personal discretion.[83] Again, my argument is not that this is the same as modern bureaucracy (1040 forms, 501c3-status, filibusters, filing deadlines, etc.). But Mamlūk bureaucracy was clearly historically contingent, rendering many of the differences between it and modern bureaucracy accidental rather than categorically inherent.

This raises the question of why a modern Islamic State that developed aspects of modern bureaucracy based on non-*sharʿī*, Islamic Secular energies and deliberations would be considered un-Islamic. Hallaq gives the impression that Islam frowns upon bureaucracy *tout court*, and he calls upon Ayatollah Khomeini (d. 1409/1989) as a witness in this regard.[84] But in the reference he cites, Khomeini's critique is actually of "superfluous bureaucracies," which he states, "have no place in Islam."[85] Even Hallaq would surely agree, upon reflection, that Khomeini's rhetorical depiction of a simple "folk-bureaucracy" can hardly be taken seriously as a general description of pre-modern Islam.[86]

Meanwhile, Hallaq seems to assume that there is nothing positive in modern bureaucracy that Islam might welcome and from which Islam and modern Muslims might practically benefit.[87] Certainly, however, the impersonal nature of modern bureaucracy is a double-edged sword. As noted earlier, it can promote secrecy, lack of transparency, insensitivity to unusual or extenuating circumstances, and a tendency to exclude "the people" from decision-making. At the same time, it is precisely these impersonal and what Weber called "rationalizing" aspects of bureaucracy that reduce corruption, cronyism, the inability to plan long term, and the discrimination routinely faced by the poor and minorities. On this understanding, I do not see how bureaucracy *in and of itself* is antithetical to Islam. What most modern Muslims probably want is the same as what everyone else wants: more and less bureaucracy—more to beat back cronyism, discrimination, graft, and the inability to plan; less to do the same, in addition to bringing "the people" more meaningfully into decision-making processes. Whether or not Muslims can strike this balance remains an open question. But to cast bureaucracy per se as intrinsically un-Islamic seems to me an overstatement. If Islam does not presently include a sufficiently impersonal, professionalizing, rationalizing bureaucracy, perhaps it should. And maybe it would behoove a modern Islamic State to acquire such a bureaucracy. Most importantly, determining the substance of most of this bureaucracy would fall outside the jurists' *shar'ī* jurisdiction and squarely within the non-*shar'ī* province of the Islamic Secular.

Regarding the state's involvement in culture for the purpose of producing the modern citizen, I have already remarked on aspects of this. I would simply add that, *pace* the impression Hallaq gives, pre-modern Muslim regimes also took an interest in shaping the sensibilities of its citizens—or, more properly, its subjects—on both *shar'ī* and non-*shar'ī* grounds. We saw earlier the example wherein Abū Ya'lā instructed *muḥtasib*s to order communities to hold the Friday Prayer in instances where it was debatable whether they were obligated to do so. This was for the explicit purpose of guarding against future generations' internalizing the idea that Friday Prayer could be ignored.[88] We saw it as well in al-Māwardī's view that it is more appropriate for state officials than it is for courts to punish offenses that constitute an affront to state power, a position clearly designed to normalize the state's awe, or *haybah*, in citizens' hearts and minds.[89] In fact, many have seen the (in)famous Inquisition or *miḥnah* as an attempt to shape the political culture of Islam.[90] Meanwhile, Kristen Stilt's study of the *muḥtasib* is replete with examples of the state trying to shape social psychology.[91] Even more explicit were the non-*shar'ī*, discretionary policies aimed at religious minorities, from how tall they could build their buildings to the size and color of the turbans they could wear, right down to the quality of the animals they could ride.[92] All of this was clearly part of an effort to normalize a way of life underwritten by a social hierarchy and psychology that signaled the superiority of Islam. Such facts might embarrass Muslims today, especially those who see such arrangements as religiously rather than practically mandated—that is, as *shar'ī* matters of law rather than non-*shar'ī*, Islamic Secular policies. And this embarrassment might even present problems for many of them in conceptualizing a modern Islamic State. But my point still stands: the difference between the interest that pre-modern Muslim regimes took in culture and the production of appropriate subjectivities and the interest that modern states take in such is one of degree, not kind.

Of course, Islam will always complicate such an enterprise through its insistence that ultimate allegiance is to God and not the state. But the state (be it a sulṭanate or *al-imāmah al-'uẓmā*) has always played an important role in preserving the integrity of Islam. While there will inevitably be disagreements over the status of state authority in relation to divine authority, it is doubtful that these can be successfully resolved by simply jettisoning the state. Like other states across the world that are informed by a particular ideological outlook, a state that is informed by Islam will retain an interest in calibrating the subjectivities of Muslims (and non-Muslims) "beyond the law" in ways that reinforce the normativeness and, indeed, the primacy of Islam's vision. In this capacity, once again, an Islamic State's difference with the modern state would be one of degree and not kind.

As I conclude this section, I must reiterate the basic point of this exercise. It is not my contention that the normative form of institutionalized political organization for Islam in the world today is the modern state. True, the modern state structure is a ubiquitous global fact. But as with the seminal, epoch-defining global facts of the past (agrarianism, tribalism, economies based on manual labor), Muslims may respond to this modern fact as they see fit—as a fact, however, and not necessarily as an ideal. They may reject the modern state in favor of either "cutting off the king's head" or some other arrangement. Or they may ask, as does Akeel Bilgrami, in a challenge to Foucault's "anti-statist neurosis,"[93] "Why can't we struggle to improve the state?"[94] Or they may adopt the modern state structure in its present form because they see it as accommodating their interests. Or they may seek to return to what I shall describe in Chapter 5 as the "empire state" of old.[95] My argument, at any rate, is that should Muslims choose the modern state, in whatever iteration they see fit, they would not be in violation of Hallaq's definition of the state any more than are any number of non-Islamic states today. Moreover, as we have seen, due consideration of the Islamic Secular and its differentiated, non-*shar'ī* modes of deliberation significantly alters the conversation around Hallaq's form-properties themselves, underscoring the weakness of his portrayal of the categorical impossibility of the Islamic State.

Beyond his ideal theory of the modern state, however, Hallaq's conceptualization of Islamic law is of critical importance. His understanding of *sharī'ah* as all-encompassing limits Muslims to *sharī'ah* as their point of departure in making any changes or adjustments to the relationship between Islam-cum-*sharī'ah* and the modern state-structure. Furthermore, if the state has amoral, material interests (and what state does not?), while *sharī'ah* is conceived of in entirely moral terms, the conflict between Islam-cum-*sharī'ah* and the state will appear to be all the more intractable. By contrast, the Islamic Secular introduces new possibilities and considerations, by joining a bounded *sharī'ah* with the ability to pursue practical and material interests in a manner that neither relies upon nor offends *sharī'ah*.

But if much of what Hallaq concludes about the relationship between Islam-cum-*sharī'ah* and the modern state is indebted to his particular understanding of *sharī'ah*, the same applies to me. It is thus to a discussion of our respective understandings of *sharī'ah* that I shall now turn.

Sharī'ah between Hallaq and the Islamic Secular

Several basic postulates inform Hallaq's understanding of Islamic law: "Islamic law" ideally equals *sharī'ah*; *sharī'ah* is unbounded; morality is the foundation and exclusive aim of *sharīʿah*; reason has no independent authority and no role outside interpretating the sources of *sharīʿah*. This last feature is critical, as it determines the extent to which non-*sharʿī*, Islamic Secular energies are recognized (or not) as playing a legitimate role in producing things Islamic. Again, "reason" here refers not simply to the linear faculty for assessing scriptural interpretation, empirical facts, or propositional truth-claims. Rather, as we saw with the legal theorists profiled in Chapter 2, the term "rational," that is, *ʿaqlī*, encompasses all modes of knowing that are not *sharʿī*, or contingent upon the sources of *sharīʿah*: imagination, talent, taste, *fantasia*, and the like. By universalizing the authority of *sharīʿah* and the *sharʿī*, however, Hallaq effectively obliterates the Islamic authority of all these forms of reason, leaving no basis other than *sharīʿah* and the *sharʿī* for negotiating reality in the name of Islam, either within or "beyond" the law. I argue that by so limiting Muslims' legitimate access to Islamic Secular reason, this expansion of *sharīʿah*'s jurisdiction to totalizing proportions promotes secularization in the modern Western sense. Moreover, it is a major source of the fundamental conflict that Hallaq assumes between Islam-cum-*sharīʿah* and the modern state.

Reason and Islamic Law

Hallaq's perspective on the role of reason in Islamic law goes back to a seminal issue in Islamic Studies regarding the conflict between "reason and revelation." The trope itself is not entirely indigenous to Islam[96] but seems to have been mapped onto Islam by Western scholarship. The Enlightenment's choice of Athens over Jerusalem clearly reflected the playing out of this conflict in Judaism and Christianity, signaling the emergence of reason as the ultimate basis of knowledge and highest marker of civilization.[97] Kant, for example, whose influence on modern Western thought is difficult to overstate, saw heteronomous, revealed religion as a danger to reason, because, as Jacqueline Mariña points out, he feared that "the individual comes to believe that the revelation and decrees of an all-powerful God absolves her of her need to exercise her capacity to gain insight into what is genuinely right."[98] Meanwhile, it is easy to imagine how Protestantism's *sola scriptura* could popularize the idea that, in a pre-modern civilization such as Islam, still given to a religious worldview, scripture would seek to assert its status as the highest, if not sole, epistemological authority against all comers, including reason.

These developments underwrote a tendency not only to look for a conflict between reason and revelation in Islam but also to superimpose this schema onto conflicts that might be meaningfully explained in other terms. For example, the early Ḥanafī jurist Bishr al-Marīsī (d. 218/833) accused al-Shāfiʿī of willfully distorting the meaning of scripture by drawing distinctions between injunctions of general (*ʿāmm*) and specific (*khāṣṣ*) import.[99] Rather than a conflict between reason and revelation, however, this disagreement could be understood as one between reason and reason, that is, between al-Marīsī's versus al-Shāfiʿī's reasoned approaches to scripture. Here both parties reject the other's system of reasoning without rejecting reason itself or the authority of the scriptural text upon which his counterpart has reasoned. But Western scholars seem not to have recognized such distinctions.[100] And the net effect has been the assumption that Muslim jurists placed a categorical premium on resisting or domesticating reason in favor of revelation, in order to preserve the integrity of *sharīʿah* as revealed law. Hallaq is emphatic in endorsing this sentiment.

The reason/revelation debate has long proceeded along zero-sum lines, virtually all the aforementioned non-*sharʿī* modes of knowing falling on the reason side of the ledger in presumed competition with revelation. For the formative period, reason as a category has been identified with *ra'y*.[101] "*Ra'y*" is a difficult term to translate but revolves around the notion of a broad, non-textual, reason-based, presumably good-faith approach to arriving at the law. Hallaq translates it as "discretionary reasoning,"[102] "considered opinion,"[103] or, more simply, "rationalism."[104] According to him, throughout the second/eighth century, *ra'y* was practiced across the board and had a generally positive meaning. During the second half of that century, however, a new phenomenon, the Traditionalist Movement, arose, insisting that legal views must be grounded in a more concrete and reliable source, namely the Sunna of the Prophet, which was transmitted through reports, or "traditions," known as *ḥadīth*. This "new" textual source of authority was identified as a constituent of revelation, and it challenged and gradually began to displace *ra'y* as a source of law. It was al-Shāfiʿī who championed this new juristic approach, turning against his erstwhile teacher Mālik b. Anas (d. 179/795) in Medina, as well as the followers of Abū Ḥanīfa (d. 150/767) in Iraq.[105] According to Hallaq, by the middle of the third/ninth century, the Traditionalists, *aṣḥāb al-ḥadīth* (Champions of *Ḥadīth*), had gained the upper hand, leaving "no room for reasoning not based on textual evidence, demanding that a choice be made between human authority, on the one hand, and Prophetic/Divine authority. Non-textual *ra'y* obviously was no match for the Sunna."[106] The Rationalists, *aṣḥāb al-ra'y* (Champions of Reason), pushed back, and things came to a head with the infamous Inquisition (*miḥnah*) at the beginning of the third/ninth century, in which Rationalist forces, backed by the state, persecuted the Traditionalists over the anomalous question of the created versus uncreated nature of the Qur'ān. The patron saint of Traditionalism, Aḥmad b. Ḥanbal, suffered during this ordeal, but he and his Traditionalist partisans ultimately triumphed. And in the aftermath—that is, the early decades of the fourth/tenth century—something momentous happened. As Hallaq describes it, "These intellectuals, locking their intellectual horns for over two centuries, finally settled on what I have elsewhere called the 'Great Synthesis,' namely the synthesis between reason and revelation."[107]

Not everyone, myself included, is convinced of the occurrence of a "Great Synthesis." For me, this is because I am not convinced of the zero-sum reason/revelation conflict that allegedly spawned the need for such, certainly not in a legal (as opposed to a theological) context. Certainly, there was tension over the role of reason and its proper interface with revelation in deriving the law; and reason was often invoked in instances where it should not have been, for example, in place of explicit revelatory dictates. But this is a problem concerning the improper *use* of reason, not an inherent, categorical conflict between reason and revelation.

In fact, at least two factors militate against the notion of such a conflict as typically described. First, the idea that either reason or revelation is wholly undifferentiated is suspect. Abū Dā'ūd al-Sijistānī (d. 275/889), a student of Ibn Ḥanbal and author of one of the canonical "Six Books" of *ḥadīth*, notes that jurists universally accepted *mursal ḥadīth* (e.g., where a Successor who never saw the Prophet narrates reports directly from him) until al-Shāfiʿī appeared and criticized the practice, after which some (but not all) jurists abandoned it.[108] Obviously, those who accepted such reports, both before and after al-Shāfiʿī, viewed them as a form of revelation, an embodiment of Prophetic teaching. They might thus invoke *mursal ḥadith* even in the face of *ḥadīth* with full chains, not to make room for a more rational over a more revelatory approach to law (from their perspective, both of these sources were revelation) but because one spoke to the issue at hand perhaps more directly or convincingly or practically than the other. We see this even in the way some jurists approach the Qur'ān, placing one verse over another with no hint of one being more authoritative or reason-friendly than its counterpart. Early Ḥanafīs, for example—the putative champions of *ra'y*—insist that the Qur'ānic verse, "*And do not prevent them [women] from marrying their husbands*" (*wa lā taʿḍilūhunna an yankiḥna azwājahunna*) [2:232] affirms women's agency in contracting their own marriages, more conclusively than verses that point to a need for a male spokesperson (*walī*) to represent the bride.[109] There is no sense of reason edging out revelation here or of a less than uniform attitude toward the authority of revelation as a whole. Nor would the introduction of *ḥadīth* material obligating the presence of a male guardian alter my point. For, that would simply entail, again, placing one form (or extension) of revelation in conversation with another, even if one of the concrete positions arrived at through this process might strike us today as more liberal (read: reason based) than the other.

As for reason, while it may be commonly thought of today as a single, undifferentiated entity, the same cannot be said of *ʿaql* in early Islam. *Qiyās* (analogy) differed from "common sense," which differed from Neoplatonism or the logic of legal dodges (*ḥiyal*/sg. *hīlah*), which differed from such interpretive principles as *naskh* (abrogation) or *takhṣīs* (specification of a general meaning)—not to mention what I said earlier about non-*shar'ī* reasoning overall. Given this variety and overlap of "reasons" and "revelations", the propriety of approaching the two camps as zero-sum rivalries in need of reconciliation is difficult to maintain. It is difficult, in other words, to justify gathering up everything associated with "reason" and categorically juxtaposing it to everything engaged as "revelation," such that one can neatly place the proponents of various approaches to *sharī'ah* in mutually distinct reason/revelation camps that might eventually come together through a "Great Synthesis."

As we have seen, the early debate between al-Shāfi'ī and Bishr al-Marīsī can be understood not as a conflict between reason and revelation but as one between different modes of reasoning.[110] Similarly, the conflict between al-Shāfi'ī and the Rationalist Ibn 'Ulayyah (d. 218/834) over the status of *aḥādī* ("solitary") *ḥadīth* that are not backed by unanimous consensus can be seen not as an attempt to make more room for reason and less for revelation but as a conflict over what should be functionally counted as revelation itself.[111] We know that many jurists looked to Medinese practice as reflections of Prophetic teaching, and, on this understanding, placing a Medinese practice over a sound Prophetic *ḥadīth* might be more a matter of revelation versus revelation than of reason versus revelation. Again, my point is not to deny the various tensions, conflicts, or preferences championed by and among early schools or jurists. I simply question whether they can be accurately summarized as a neatly bifurcated, categorical conflict between reason and revelation, especially in law.[112]

When the influential Mālikī jurist (and contemporary of al-Shāfi'ī) Asad b. al-Furāt (d. 213/828) returned to North Africa from the East, touting new, rationalized arguments, he was rebuked for doing so. He responded: "Do you not realize that, while the statements of the Ancestors may be *ra'y* to them, they are tradition for those after them?" (*amā 'alimtum anna qawl al-salaf huwa ra'y lahum wa athar li man ba'dahum*)."[113] Before that, Mālik is reported to have described his *ra'y* (or at least aspects of it) as his cumulative memory of what he had heard from "the people of knowledge and virtue and the Imāms who were emulated . . . whenever their views appeared to reflect what had been handed down from the Companions."[114] In a similar vein, Harald Motzki (d. 2019) notes that Ibn Jurayj (d. 150/767) would cite the exact same view of his fellow Meccan 'Aṭā' b. Abī Rabāḥ (d. 115/733), now in the form of the latter's *ra'y*, now in the form of a Prophetic *ḥadīth*.[115] Meanwhile, while al-Awzā'ī (d. 157/774), as we have seen, was numbered among the *aṣḥāb al-ḥadīth* and Abū Ḥanīfa was counted a champion of *ra'y*,[116] Ibn Qutaybah (himself associated with the Traditionalist movement) reports that al-Awzā'ī stated: "We do not hold it against Abū Ḥanīfa that he resorts to *ra'y*; for, all of us resort to *ra'y*. We simply hold it against him that Prophetic *ḥadīth* come to him and then he abandons these in favor of other things."[117]

Despite these considerations, Hallaq's "Great Synthesis" positions reason and revelation prior to this momentous event as bitter rivals. Speaking of the immediate aftermath of the Inquisition, he writes: "The final defeat of the rationalists implied (and in effect consisted of) an acknowledgment that human reason could not stand on its own as a central, much less exclusive, method of interpretation but had to operate solely, in the final analysis, in the service of revelation."[118] Not only does he homogenize both "reason" and "revelation" but his reference to "human reason" also masks the fact that what Rationalist theologians promoted and what Traditionalist theologians rejected—and the Inquisition was a *theological* not a *legal* contest—was not "human reason" per se but a particular system of reasoning, namely, the rationalist *kalām* tradition that had been built up primarily from the Hellenistic legacy. Despite Rationalism's sustained attempt to cast this reason as simply "reason" itself, Traditionalists never admitted it into the sanctum of theology, neither after the *miḥnah* nor after any would-be "Great Synthesis." Instead, in the face of Rationalist efforts to pass off *kalām* as transcendent reason itself, Traditionalist theologians remained fiercely vigilant, seeing all Rationalist claims made in the name of reason as potential Trojan horses designed to smuggle in *kalām*.[119]

The same cannot be said, however, of law.[120] Here Traditionalists allowed a role for speculative reason, even Greek-inspired speculative reason. In the Introduction to his book on *uṣūl al-fiqh* (which spawned important commentaries within the school), the staunchly Traditionalist Ḥanbalī jurist Ibn Qudāmah (d. 620/1223) rehearses the basics of Greek logic as one might find in any book on the subject written by a committed Rationalist.[121] His Ḥanbalī predecessor Abū Ya'lā is equally explicit in his commitment to reason, or *'aql*, in the introduction to his work on *uṣūl al-fiqh*.[122] By conflating theology with law, however, and equating reason with a particular system of reason, Hallaq gives the impression that a Traditionalist jurist *qua* jurist would be just as cautious about admitting reason into law as a Traditionalist theologian *qua* theologian would be about accepting its role in theology.

In reality, however, even Ibn Ḥanbal, the patron saint of Traditionalism, who would never admit speculative *kalām* into his theology, invokes common sense, discretionary preferences, and even speculative reasoning in his *fiqh*. For example, in response to his son 'Abd Allāh's question about a sound *ḥadīth* in which the Prophet forbade sleeping before the night prayer, Ibn Ḥanbal states, "Ibn 'Umar used to sleep before the night-prayer but made sure that there was someone around to wake him up."[123] The implication here is that it is permissible to sleep as long as one has someone around to wake one up in time, a clear common-sense deduction from the action of Ibn ʿUmar, despite the explicit prohibition expressed in the Prophetic *ḥadīth*. Meanwhile, in response to a man who asks about being commanded by his father to divorce his wife, Ibn Ḥanbal responds, "Don't divorce her." When the man reminds him that Ibn ʿUmar's father commanded him to divorce his wife, Imām Aḥmad retorts, "As if your father were ʿUmar's equal (*ḥattā yakūna abūka mithla ʿumar*)?"[124] Similarly, as we have seen, Mālik (also a collector of *ḥadīth*) relied on Medinese practice to direct his *raʾy* and assist him in determining the proper application of *ḥadīth*. In fact, in his massive study on Mālik, Umar Wymann-Landgraf writes, "Considered opinion [*raʾy*] stood at the heart of the Medinese tradition and was the crowning achievement of Mālik's legal reasoning, just as it was in the Kufan jurisprudence of Abū Ḥanīfa."[125] If Ibn Ḥanbal, Abū Ḥanīfa, and Mālik could all rely on various iterations of *raʾy*, I'm not sure I see how one can draw a categorical line between a commitment to reason versus a commitment to revelation in law, with the possible exception of Ẓāhirism in relation to the other schools.[126] Ultimately, I agree with Wymann-Landgraf when he concludes that there is a need for a "reassessment of the 'great synthesis' theory of Islamic legal origins, which has long held virtually unquestioned sway over the minds of most intellectual historians in the field."[127]

The importance of this discussion for our purposes is that Hallaq not only assumes a fundamental conflict between reason and revelation in Islamic law but he also maps this presumed conflict onto the modern period in a manner that inevitably casts a cloud over the Islamic Secular and its differentiated, non-*sharʿī*, *ʿaql*. By extending the conflict between reason and revelation to the realm of Islamic law, he implies that Muslim jurists *qua* jurists—Rationalist and Traditionalist alike—nurse (or should nurse) a natural suspicion toward "human reason." Against the backdrop of his critique of the "modern condition," this perspective ends up associating non-*sharʿī* reason with what he terms the "epistemic havoc wrought by modernity."[128] In such a context, modern jurists need to resist autonomous human reason as a contagion. Ultimately, this attitude toward "modern reason" (or, perhaps, "reason" in the modern world) drives Hallaq to an attempt to "*sharīʿatize*" reason, that is, to keep it domesticated, fettered, and subordinated to *sharīʿah*, in which capacity it can exercise no independent authority that might threaten or compromise *sharīʿah*'s sovereignty. The notion of a legitimately exercised non-*sharʿī*, differentiated reason is all but proscribed, and *sharīʿah*'s absolute, unrivaled supremacy and exclusive legal jurisdiction is confirmed,[129] "not only [as] the law of the land but also [as] the law of the heavens and everything lying in between, including politics and rule."[130] The price of this supremacy, however, as we suggested in Chapters 2 and 3 and will see further below, is that either *sharʿī* metrics are extended beyond their proper application, in which capacity they routinely frustrate proper assessment, or whatever issues *sharīʿah* metrics are deemed incapable of appropriately assessing remain beyond the legitimate reach of Muslims acting as Muslims.

The Curse of Modernity

Given Hallaq's well-known commitment to the view that Islam-cum-*sharīʿah* is firmly grounded in reason and not, *pace* the popular stereotype, crass fideism, the claim that he seeks to domesticate reason will strike many as a misguided interpretation of his oeuvre. His thesis that *ijtihād* never ceased is widely celebrated,[131] and his subsequent work even affirms the compatibility between reason and *taqlīd*, identifying the latter as "intelligent and creative,"[132] ultimately "a reenactment of *ijtihād*."[133] But, as mentioned earlier, Hallaq is forceful and consistent in his criticism of modern jurists who put forth views that are "entirely absent from the [pre-modern] *fiqh*,"[134] "hitherto unknown in the Malikite school,"[135] "unknown to Sharīʿa,"[136] "unknown . . . to pre-modern jurists of any strand,"[137] even if they arrive at these conclusions using the same sources and methods of *ijtihād* (or *taqlīd*) relied upon by their pre-modern forebears. He depicts reason in pre-modern Islam (albeit, presumably, as a ward of *sharīʿah*) as playing a decidedly positive role and as a manifestation of juristic ingenuity and acumen. But he looks upon modern jurists' use of reason with suspicion, viewing it as a sign of unwarranted capitulation to the forces of modernity. For modern Muslims, he implies, to venture outside the *sharʿī* is to risk landing outside Islam and falling prey to the corrosive effects of the modern condition.

This perspective comes through clearly in his analysis of the efforts of Muḥammad ʿAbduh, Rashīd Riḍā, ʿAbd al-Wahhāb Khallāf, and others. Of ʿAbduh's attempts to negotiate modern material interests, for example, he writes:

> [W]hile the determination of the value of an act is the province of reason, the penalty or reward that results from the commission or omission of the act is the jurisdiction of revelation. Thus, the use of reason is maximized, yet the religious tenor is not set aside. But the balance stands clearly in favor of an unprecedentedly favorable approach to materialism, whereby Muslims are called upon not to concern themselves overly with the hereafter to the detriment of their worldly life, since the best way to live as a Muslim is to pursue material progress. With this theology, ʿAbduh provided a break with pre-modern theological and juristic conceptions.[138]

It is difficult to see where ʿAbduh's view entails any shift to an "unprecedentedly favorable approach to materialism." As Hallaq himself acknowledges, ʿAbduh cedes adjudication of reward and punishment entirely to revelation; as such, determining what a Muslim may or may not do remains the province of scripture.

Nor is ʿAbduh's refusal to jettison the prudential in favor of the moral unprecedented, as we saw, for example, in the Ḥanafīs' re-processing of conditional sales (*bayʿ al-wafāʾ*) or the agonizings of Ibn al-Qayyim and Ibn Taymīyah over wealthy Coptic potential converts to Islam jeopardizing their inheritance based on the well-known *ḥadīth* barring interreligious inheritance.[139] In fact, the reasoning that Hallaq imputes to ʿAbduh reflects a straightforward application of the post-formative articulation of the doctrine of *al-ḥusn wa al-qubḥ al-ʿaqlīyān*, according to which reason—non-*sharʿī* reason—*can* make moral (and certainly practical) judgments, even if these do not reflect an extra-mental ontological reality or automatically translate into religious, that is, *sharʿī*, obligations.

Ultimately, ʿAbduh displays no artificial maximization of the use of reason beyond what pre-modern doctrine itself allows. And I do not see where his deployment of reason in pursuit of material interests (*maṣāliḥ*/sg. *maṣlaḥah*) can be equated with or dismissed as "materialism." In fact, his deliberations reflect precisely the logic and calculus of the Islamic Secular: differentiated, non-*sharʿī* reason deployed, within the bounds of the juristically permissible, in the service of procuring practical interests and benefits, as we saw in such pre-modern jurists as Abū Yaʿlā, al-Māwardī, al-Qarāfī, al-Ghazālī, Ibn Taymīyah, and others. Rather than breaking with "premodern theological and juristic conceptions," ʿAbduh's real indiscretion seems to be that he applied these in a modern context. Like his pre-modern forbears, he recognizes and imputes to non-*sharʿī*, Islamic Secular reason the authority to go beyond the moral metrics of *sharīʿah* as part and parcel of a process of negotiating and ideally reconciling, however imperfectly, Islam-cum-*sharīʿah*'s moral vision with the prudential-cum-material interests the Community has traditionally recognized.

Al-Ḥusn wa al-Qubḥ al-ʿAqlīyān

The pre-modern doctrine implicated in all of this, *al-ḥusn wa al-qubḥ al-ʿaqlīyān*, is pivotal. It speaks directly not only to ʿAbduh's approach but to Béteille's question about how much "space" religion/revelation leaves for the rational negotiation of quotidian reality.[140] According to Hallaq, Ashʿarite rationality, a major contributor to Islamic juristic thought, flatly denies that "sound human reason is, on its own, capable of distinguishing between right and wrong."[141] This conclusion is presumably what he sees ʿAbduh as flouting. But in the post-formative articulation of *al-ḥusn wa al-qubh al-ʿaqlīyān*, Ashʿarite jurist-theologians clearly acknowledge reason's ability to determine the moral, not to mention practical, value of acts.

This "new" articulation seems to have been popularized (though not originated) by al-Rāzī and spread from there.[142] In his commentary on his abridgment of al-Rāzī, al-Qarāfī lays it out as follows:

> What is meant by the "goodness" or "badness" of a thing is the degree to which it agrees or contradicts human nature (*al-ṭabʿ*), e.g., saving a drowning person or falsely accusing an innocent person; or (2) the degree to which it constitutes a virtue or a flaw, such as (when we say that) knowledge is good and ignorance is bad; or (3) the degree to which the act in question warrants praise or condemnation (read: reward or punishment) on religious grounds. The first two are rational (*ʿaqlī*) by unanimous consensus (*ijmāʿ*), while the third is juristic (*sharʿī*).[143]

Al-Qarāfī goes on to relate the well-known fact that the controversy in question goes back to early disputes with the Muʿtazilites. He adds, however, "We (Ashʿarites) and the Muʿtazilites agree that 'good' and 'bad' according to the first two definitions are known by reason independent of revelation" (*yastaqillu al-ʿaql bi idrākihimā min ghayr wurūd al-sharāʾiʿ*).[144] In other words, the dispute focused solely on the third point—whether our reason-based knowledge of an act's goodness or badness necessarily translates into knowledge of what God will or must reward or punish. Al-Qarāfī summarizes the matter as follows: "As for whether God will reward or punish an act, according to us, this is known only by the divine message (*al-rasāʾil al-rabbānīyah*), while, according to them, (i.e., the Muʿtazilites) it can be known by reason (*al-ʿaql*)" alone.[145] Reason for the Ashʿarites and the mainstream was not morally, let alone practically, blind or impotent. Rather, as al-Shāṭibī summarized the matter, "Reason is simply not a giver of divine law" (*al-ʿaql laysa bi shāriʿ*).[146] As for reason's ability to apprehend virtues and vices, material interests, harms and benefits, this was not a matter of dispute, a point explicitly confirmed by al-Qarāfī's Ashʿarite teacher, the redoubtable ʿIzz al-Dīn Ibn ʿAbd al-Salām: "Most worldly interests and liabilities are known by reason" (*muʿẓam maṣāliḥ al-dunyā wa mafāsidihā maʿrūf^{un} bi al-ʿaql*).[147]

In a possible effort to disguise change, the sixth/twelfth-century Ashʿarite heresiologist al-Shahrastānī (d. 548/1153) traced this understanding all the way back to al-Ashʿarī himself.[148] Al-Zarkashī, on the other hand (a Shāfiʿī, incidentally), traces it back to Abū Ḥanīfa.[149] Meanwhile, Ibn al-Qayyim and Ibn Taymīyah also endorse it, in some ways even more emphatically than the Ashʿarites, especially the idea that knowledge of what God will reward and punish is based strictly on scriptural indicants.[150] In short, *pace* Hallaq, there was a general Sunni consensus to the effect that reason *can* guide us to knowledge of what is good and bad, and certainly of what is practical and impractical.[151] What it *cannot* do—and this was also a point of Sunni agreement—is tell us independently of revelation what God will or must reward or punish. The issue, in other words, was whether reason had the ability to know and/or the authority to obligate (either us or God). The conclusion was that it had the former but not necessarily the latter.

Readers may notice that I have used "good" and "bad" for *ḥasan* and *qabīḥ*, instead of the more conventional "good" and "evil." I have done so to highlight an important nuance that these terms carry, particularly—though not exclusively—in a juristic as opposed to a theological context. The Muʿtazilites argued that good and evil inhere either in acts themselves (the Baghdādī school) or in the categories of mind through which reality is perceived (the Baṣran school).[152] On both views, good and evil can be apprehended by sound reason, unaided by revelation. And because what reason ultimately apprehends is assumed to be part of the natural order, inscribed upon creation by God, this finding can be assumed to be God's finding and thus to represent not only God's ontological will but God's deontological will as well. We can know, in other words, what God rewards or punishes by what reason discloses as good or evil, since what it discloses is effectively a reflection of God's (deontological) will.

In this theological context, the valence of *ḥasan* and *qabīh* is primarily moral—that is, "good" and "evil." To use Kantian terms, it carries a sense of duty, as distinct from interest or prudence. We see this moral inflection in the definition of *qabīḥ* related by the Zaydī Muʿtazilite, Mānkdīm (Aḥmad b. al-Ḥusayn b. Abī Hāshim al-Ḥusaynī) Shashdīw (d. 425/1034) from his teacher, the Sunnī Muʿtazilite chief, al-Qāḍī ʿAbd al-Jabbār (d. 415/1024): "a *qabīḥ* act is one that is committed by an able-bodied person for which he or she deserves censure" (*al-qabīḥ huwa mā idhā faʿalahu al-qādir ʿalayhi istaḥaqqa al-dhamm*).[153] In a legal, or *sharʿī*, context, however, not just considerations of conscience and duty but also of prudence and worldly interests, *maṣāliḥ*/sg. *maṣlaḥah* and *mafāsid*/sg. *mafsadah*, routinely factor into the assessment of acts. And here I must reiterate that what later Ashʿarites (and others) rejected was neither the notion that benefits and harms attach to acts themselves nor that God commands and prohibits acts in light of these.[154] It was the idea that these benefits and harms *compel* God to command or prohibit, reward or punish. Al-Qarāfī, for example, a staunch Ashʿarite, is explicit in this regard: "An inductive reading (of scriptural sources) points to the fact that harms and interests *precede* God's commands and prohibitions, while reward and punishment *follow* God's commands and prohibitions."[155] In other words, it is God, not harms and interests, that determine whether an act is rewarded or punished, even though God, in God's infinite wisdom and mercy, commands and prohibits acts based on what is beneficial and harmful in them, respectively.

Traditionally, *sharīʿah* rules are divided into two categories: *ʿibādāt*, or religious observances, such as prayer, fasting, and the like; and *muʿāmalāt*, or civil transactions, criminal sanctions, and the like. All of these are "moral," inasmuch as their commission or omission earn praise/reward or censure/punishment. But they are also tied to various interests. The primary interests of the *ʿibādāt* relate to the Hereafter, whereas the primary interests of the *muʿāmalāt* are connected to this world. These latter interests are especially (though not exclusively) the focus of discourses around the so-called *maṣāliḥ*/sg. *maṣlaḥah* (interests, benefits) and their opposite, *mafāsid*/sg. *mafsadah* (harms, corruptors). Felicitas Opwis notes in her study on the topic that, "*Maṣlaḥa*, which literally means a source of well-being and good, is sometimes translated as 'public interest' or 'social good.' "[156] It is often accompanied by a discussion of "appropriateness" (*munāsabah*), or the basis upon which the characteristics of a thing are deemed appropriate as a *ratio essendi* (*'illah*) in analogy, or *qiyās*. Here jurists, including Ash'arites, speak plainly of acts' benefits (*naf'*) and harms (*ḍarar*), as opposed (or in addition) to their exclusively moral implications or *shar'ī* status.[157] In other words, there is a palpable utilitarian bent to their juristic (*fiqhī*) deliberations.

In this context, al-'Izz Ibn 'Abd al-Salām describes *sharī'ah*-relevant benefits and harms as follows:

> Interests (*maṣāliḥ*) are of four types: physical pleasures (*al-ladhdhāt*) and the means thereto; and emotional pleasures (*al-afrāḥ*) and the means thereto. And harms (*mafāsid*) are of four types: physical pains (*al-ālām*) and the means thereto; and emotional pains (*al-ghumūm*) and the means thereto.[158]

Some of these interests and harms are explicitly identified by the *shar'*; but many are discovered by reason (again, broadly understood). Meanwhile, morally good or evil deeds are often accompanied by practically good or bad consequences that force one into a calculus of moral/practical balancing. Turning in a thief, for example, may be morally good; but the known corruption or ineptitude of the authorities may mean that this action is practically bad. Working at McDonald's, where one is compelled to sell pork, might be technically evil (*qabīḥ*); but the benefit of having a job may offset this evil, or at least the sin attached to it, *istiḥsān*[an]. In any event, the point of *sharī'ah* is to ensure that actions are pursued or avoided via means that are moral or, where this is not possible, in such a manner that the practical good outweighs any unavoidable moral evil.[159]

Clearly, morality is not the sole consideration of the law. There is nothing moral or immoral about eating fine food, striking Islamic coins, or using the latest or outdated technology; yet these are clearly interests and harms that the law would recognize as interests and harms, even as it seeks to ensure that they are addressed in a morally sound manner. In sum, *maṣāliḥ* and *mafāsid* refer to the practical-cum-material benefits and harms attaching to acts, with a view to the general welfare of the individual or community. In this legal (as opposed to theological) context, *ḥasan* and *qabīḥ* can connote both what is morally *and* what is practically/materially good or bad. It is this practical, material, prudential side that I am trying to capture by replacing the conventional "good and evil" with "good and bad."

Morality vs. *Shar'*

While a Muslim may—and should—pursue the *mu'āmalāt* with the intention of pleasing God, the obligation imposed by these rules is fulfilled by the commission of the commanded acts themselves even in the absence of such an intention. The *maṣlaḥah,* for example, behind obliging debtors to pay their debts is the benefit that creditors derive from receiving what they are owed; and this is realized upon payment, regardless of the payer's intention. The rule aims, in other words, not simply at making debtors moral or at upholding some public moral standard. The Community suffers practically from non-payment of debts, and avoiding this harm is the primary target of the rule. In fact, al-Qarāfī's explanation of the legal precept, "Discretionary punishments are sanctions that follow material harms even where there may be no sin" (*al-ta'āzīr ta'dīb yatba' al-mafāsid wa qad lā yaṣḥabuhā al-'isyān*) shows how practical/material interests may even trump morality.[160] This is the basis for disciplining Ḥanafīs (via *ta'zīr* or *ḥadd*) for drinking *nabīdh*-wine or minor children for inappropriate behavior, despite the fact that neither is technically guilty of any sin (the Ḥanafīs because their school approves of drinking *nabīdh,* and children because they are under no legal obligation [*taklīf*]).[161] Clearly, in such light, *sharī'ah* must be recognized as seeking to promote more than just morality. More important, Islam's extra-moral interests, within and beyond *sharī'ah,* clearly implicate the differentiated, non-*shar'ī* deliberations of the Islamic Secular.

From the opening paragraphs of *The Impossible State,* however, Hallaq explicitly identifies *sharī'ah* as "the moral law of Islam,"[162] a trope repeated *ad nauseum* throughout the book. "The law of the Muslim God is the Sharī'a, pure and simple. And Sharī'a is the moral code, *a representation of His moral will,* the first and final concern."[163] "Before being transcendental and theological, divine sovereignty was moral."[164] On this understanding, "Doing good is the heart and soul, the core and kernel, and the most pronounced message of the Qur'ān and therefore of Islam and Islamic governance."[165] That the "good" here is moral, not practical, is confirmed by what Hallaq contrasts it with, that is, the normative product of the modern state, "an exteriorized personality whose soul and spirit are of no concern but whose value resided in a political, materialistic, and efficiency-based conception of life."[166] Throughout the book, despite the distinction that the 'new' articulation of the doctrine of *al-ḥusn wa al-qubḥ al-'aqlīyān* draws between the *shar'ī* and the *'aqlī,* Hallaq insists that *sharī'ah* never recognized any distinction between "the legal" and "the moral," between law and morality.

We saw in Chapter 2, however, that the Five Juristic Statuses recognize a distinction between "must"—or even "may"—and "should." The fact that it is permissible for a man to marry or divorce a woman does not mean that he should do so, practically or even ethically speaking. Meanwhile, as we just saw, the doctrine of *al-ḥusn wa al-qubḥ al-ʿaqlīyān* recognizes reason's ability to arrive at moral and ethical conclusions that do not necessarily translate into law, or what God will or must reward or punish. Ultimately, Hallaq's denial of the distinction between law and morality effectively collapses the *ʿaqlī* into the *sharʿī* and implies that for a moral or ethical judgment to be Islamically valid, it must recline entirely upon the *sharʿ*. Practical, amoral judgments that neither derive from *sharīʿah* nor seek to promote its explicitly "moral vision" cannot be Islamically evaluated beyond their status as *mubāḥ*, or permissible. This is what he appears to have in mind in his critique of ʿAbduh and in his reference to "the rise of the legal" and "the rise of the political" as modern Western developments that separate the legal or political from the moral, which, he implies, is entirely alien to Islam.[167]

The problem, once again, is that the absence of a *sharʿī*/non-*sharʿī* distinction produces a zero-sum choice between the legal/political and the moral. From the perspective of the Islamic Secular, however, both the legal and the political can have *sharʿī* dimensions that recline upon *sharʿī* sources and speak more to the moral implications of legal or political acts while also having non-*sharʿī* dimensions that do not recline upon *sharʿī* sources and speak more to the practical or "political" side of such acts. This is thrown into relief by none other than the morally engaged *sharīʿah*-maximalist Ibn Taymīyah, who insists that, when it comes to administrative appointments that affect the material interests of the Community, considerations of competence must be measured with a non-*sharʿī*, practical calculus alongside but separate from the moral considerations pertinent to piety. He relates in this context the response of Aḥmad Ibn Ḥanbal to the question of whether a pious weakling (*ṣāliḥ ḍaʿīf*) or a strong miscreant (*qawī fājir*) should be appointed to head the army: "As for the strong miscreant, his power benefits the Muslims, while his corruptness affects only him; as for the pious weakling, his piety benefits him, while his weakness affects the Muslims."[168] Clearly, there is more at play here than a strictly moral calculus that is blind to the practical. And, once again, the importance of a differentiated, non-*sharʿī*, Islamic Secular calculus for negotiating the relationship between the two comes front and center.

Is vs. Ought

At bottom, Hallaq bases his argument that Islam never separated the legal from the moral on the claim that Muslims, unlike the modern West, never acknowledged a distinction between what he refers to as the "Is" and the "Ought," a position he traces all the way back to the Qur'ān itself: "In premodern Islamic tradition and its discourses, including its Qur'ān (obviously *the* founding text), the legal and the moral were not recognized as dichotomous categories, Is and Ought and fact and value being one and the same."[169]

The basic idea here seems to be that moral realism, or what Roberto Unger in modern times refers to as "the doctrine of intelligible essences" is the sole authentic position of Islam. According to this doctrine, the world is an objective reality that can be apprehended as such regardless of the perspective or predilections of the observer. A stone is distinguishable from a bird because it contains an objectively intelligible essence, "stoneness," that can be apprehended by the mind regardless of the pre-judgments or predisposition of the individual observer. Transferred to the world of morality, this objectivist ontology enables us to know that murder, theft, adultery, and the like are evil/bad because their moral essences are open to objective apprehension by our minds.[170] God's command, in turn, brings nothing to these acts that was not already there prior to the command itself, including the desert of reward or punishment.

In the West, Enlightenment thinkers rejected objectivist notions and insisted that morality was all a matter of perspective and convention (according to Unger, Hobbes was the beginning of this reaction). This "moral nominalism," as it came to be known, was built on the idea that an act—for example, adultery—is evil/bad, not because it is the repository of some evil/bad essence but simply because we, the constituents of society, *say* it is evil/bad. Coupled with such notions as "the individual" and "popular sovereignty," this position was used to challenge traditional religion-based morality as groundless. And in the minds of many, it set the modern world on a course toward moral malaise and confusion, a sentiment that we find in thinkers such as MacIntyre, who seems to see the stakes of the controversy in the same terms as Hallaq.[171] This critical perspective has led to the common assumption that realist, objectivist ontologies are the friends of religion, while nominalist perspectives challenge and undermine religion.[172]

This is ultimately what Hallaq assumes to be the position of Islam. To my mind, however, this is among the most unfortunate assumptions of *The Impossible State*, not because it misrepresents or overlooks later Sunnism's articulation of *al-ḥusn wa al-qubḥ al'-aqlīyān*—that nominalism *can* sustain a moral vision—but because it forfeits the opportunity to make an important point about the possibilities of religion in the modern world, possibilities that emerge out of an experience other than that of Western Europe. It is well known that the Ash'arites summarily rejected the realist ontology of the Mu'tazilites, and even Traditionalists, such as Ibn Taymīyah and Ibn al-Qayyim, insisted that, though some element (*ṣifah*) of good or evil must be assumed to inhere in scripturally commanded or prohibited acts, God was not *bound* to reward or punish on that basis. Al-Ghazālī powerfully summarizes the Sunni position when he asserts that *all* of God's actions (including those of commanding and forbidding) are voluntary (*jā'iz*) and none of them are independently incumbent (*wājib*) upon

God.[173] Yet, all of Sunnism was clearly and thoroughly committed to a religious worldview and a religion-based morality, clearly challenging the idea that religion requires a realist moral ontology.

Once again, however, Hallaq appears to take his cue from developments in the West. He writes:

> [I]f it is true—as many philosophers have already noted—that the distinction [made between Is and Ought] is modern, then the Sharīʿa could not have known it. But this is an argument by implication. More directly, there is absolutely nothing in the Sharīʿa and in premodern Islam as a whole to give rise to this distinction. And any argument that such a distinction existed in the Sharīʿa is one that ignores not only the thrust of the Sharīʿa as an ethical project but also both the quality and significance of the modern European political and legal divide between Is and Ought, thus navigating at the surface of this profoundly, and now universally, systemic distinction.[174]

It is beyond the scope of the present effort to unpack all the issues in this passage. It seems clear, however, that Hallaq's perception of how the Is/Ought argument (like the reason/revelation argument and the law/morality argument) developed and played out in the West informs his understanding of its applicability to Islam. Yet, whoever the "many philosophers" he refers to were, I doubt that they ever read al-Ashʿarī, al-Bāqillānī, al-Ghazālī, al-Juwaynī, al-Qarāfī, or even Ibn Taymīyah and Ibn al-Qayyim. As we have seen, the doctrine of *al-ḥusn wa al-qubḥ al-ʿaqlīyān*, to which they all subscribed in one form or another, clearly challenges the notion that "absolutely nothing in Sharīʿa and in pre-modern Islam as a whole" reflects a recognition of an Is/Ought distinction.

But even Hallaq's understanding of the Is/Ought controversy as it played out in the West appears to overindulge the narrative of the eventual winners, for whom nominalism was a means of breaking the back of traditional religion-based morality and denuding God (or the Church) of the authority to call the shots. In reality, however, this was not how the matter was always viewed. As Charles Taylor notes, "The fact/value split [wa]s first a theological thesis, and God [wa]s at first the sole beneficiary. . . . The thesis [wa]s propounded to defend God's freedom of choice."[175] In other words, by keeping the Is separated from the Ought, God could be *more* rather than *less* clearly recognized as being bound by nothing and thus empowered to make God's own moral decisions entirely and unilaterally as a function of God's autonomous will. As Taylor, notes, "For some thinkers the notion of a fixed and ordered cosmos, whose principles of justification could be found in itself, was incompatible with the sovereignty of God."[176]

For anyone who has sat with the writings of classical Sunni Muslim jurist-theologians, Traditionalists and Rationalists alike, this statement makes eminent sense and resonates strongly. For those jurist-theologians, like those in the West to whom Taylor refers, there is not and never was any necessary connection between the Is/Ought divide and the weakening of morality or religion. Pre-modern Islam certainly preserved both—the Is-Ought distinction and the efficacy of religion—even as its nominalism has remained mainstream for over a millennium. The real shift in the modern West was not from realism to nominalism per se but from God to humanity as the sole and unilateral *definer* of the Ought, that is, where the Ought as a moral category was not altogether denied.

In the end, it may be (though the forcefulness of Hallaq's assertions may drown this out) that Islamic nominalism (which recognizes both the authority of God *and*, especially as a constituent of the Islamic Secular, the authority, at least potentially, of differentiated, reasoned deliberations and principled social conventions, as part of a *religious* orientation) allows for flexibility and change in ways that realism does not. And in a world as enamored of the language of change, freedom and human agency as our own, it may be that Islamic nominalism, not realism or an Is/Ought unity, will best serve the interest of religion and alter the modern attitude toward it. This may be, at least in part, what even the late Patricia Crone had in mind when she suggested that "[I]f religion were to come back as a public force in western Europe, it would be more likely to be in the shape of Islam than in that of Christianity."[177]

Back to Reason

Again, Hallaq's argument is held together and policed by his conception of the role of reason in Islamic law. And here is where he is most at odds with the perspective of the Islamic Secular. I mentioned earlier that not every aspect of what must be regulated in everyday life—speed limits, building codes, FAA regulations, and the like—falls or can be placed under a *ḥukm sharʿī* (other than *mubāḥ*, which has no power to compel action and tells us nothing about substantive content). These are the areas in which the discretionary authority of governance most prominently assumes its relevance. Hallaq acknowledges this authority, under the rubric of *siyāsah sharʿīyah*. But he is palpably hesitant, if not unwilling, to recognize it as *differentiated* from the sources and authority of *sharīʿah*. In fact, he insists that *siyāsah* remains "subservient to Sharīʿa,"[178] insofar as "the much coveted prize of legitimacy . . . remain[s] defined by the Sharīʿa."[179]

Hallaq is certainly correct to see a connection between *sharīʿah* and legitimacy. But, as we saw in the example of the Mālikī *muḥtasib* who manipulated bread prices, mere conformity with the rules of *sharīʿah* is not enough to keep a government in a people's good graces. Legitimacy also requires that states effectively address a community's practical needs and aspirations. And, in their attempt to do so, states must often go beyond the machinery of *sharīʿah* proper and into the realm where differentiated, non-*sharʿī* reason exercises independent authority—where, *inter alia*, "a priori reasoning, experience, custom and common sense" (*al-ḍarūrāt wa al-tajārib wa al-ʿādāt wa al-ẓunūn al-muʿtabarāt*),[180] alongside imagination, taste, *fantasia*, and the like, are called upon to provide solutions. To the extent that he recognizes these at all, Hallaq wants to keep them as tightly tied to if not absorbed by *sharīʿah* as he can. Thus, he insists, "Unlike the modern state, in Islamic governance the Sharīʿa is unrivaled in this domain [of *siyāsah sharʿīyah*], and no power other than it can truly legislate. . . . The executive power was mandated by the Sharīʿa to legislate in limited and restricted spheres, but this right was *derivative, subsidiary*, and—compared to the modern state—*relatively marginal*."[181] Further, "[T]he powers conferred upon the ruler through *siyāsa Sharʿīyya* were not only consistent with the dictates of religious law; they were . . . an integral extension of this law."[182] "Therefore, ruling in accordance with *siyāsa Sharʿīyya* was in no way the unfettered power of political governance but in a fundamental way the Sharʿī exercise of wisdom, forbearance, and prudence by a prince in ruling the Sharīʿa's subjects."[183]

I agree with positioning *sharīʿah* as the ultimate anchor of any form of governance that purports to be Islamic. But Hallaq also expresses a deep distrust and ambivalence toward reason functioning outside its capacity as a ward of *sharīʿah*, almost as if "outside of *sharīʿah*" means "outside of Islam." This is what I referred to earlier as his attempt to "sharīʿatize" reason, which is reinforced by another aspect of his understanding of reason's role. According to Hallaq, "Ashʿarite legal theology, considerably dominating the Sunni scene, and sustaining therein most pre-modern legal theories of *uṣūl [al-fiqh]*, held human intellect to be largely incapable of any determination of the rationale behind God's revelation. God's ultimate wisdom was, in this theology, simply incomprehensible."[184] At best, according to Hallaq, "[T]he human mind is a tool that deciphers textual meanings within social contexts, but does not independently produce meanings of its own."[185]

Once again, law is conflated with theology. To say that God's actions are, *ghayr muʿallalah* in a theological (or philosophical) context simply means that they are "uncaused," that is, not the mechanical effect or product of any preexisting physical or ontological "cause," or *ʿillah*. In a legal context, however, it would mean that God's acts of commanding and forbidding are impervious to the powers of reason to discern any point, wisdom, or immediately practical purpose—that is, any *ʿillah* or *ratio essendi*—that any such command or prohibition might be understood to serve. As nominalist theologians, Ashʿarites were among the first to deny that God's actions were *muʿallal* in the first sense; but as Shāfiʿī, Mālikī, and, to a lesser extent, Ḥanafī jurists, they never denied that God's acts were *muʿallal* in the second sense.[186] Indeed, al-Qarāfī insists, quite matter-of-factly, that, whenever jurists come upon what they *think* may be reasonably taken as an appropriate *ratio essendi*, or *'illah*, they may attribute it to God's ruling, even as they acknowledge that they may be wrong.[187] On Hallaq's conflation of theology with law, however, reason becomes superfluous to the juristic enterprise beyond a certain juristic exegesis, in which it is not authorized to reach any normative conclusions on its own, including the discernment of the aims and purposes behind God's rules. But on this, understanding it is difficult to imagine how the reason-driven discretionary powers of the state, its "*siyāsah Shar'īyah*," could operate as "an integral extension of this law." For, if reason cannot penetrate the wisdom behind God's rules, how can it extend them? Similarly, if reason has no independent authority of its own, what role can it play in the non-scripture-based, discretionary, reason-driven dimensions of Islamic governance—the dimensions that address building codes, driver's licenses, regulating hazardous materials, and the like. To reiterate, al-Qarāfī's insightful assertion that "Good, as a category, is broader than the juristic ruling" (*al-ḥasan a'amm min al-ḥukm al-shar'ī*) clearly implies that knowledge of practical good—and bad—can and often must be reached outside the machinery of strictly *shar'ī* deliberation.[188]

In sum, on Hallaq's understanding of *sharī'ah* as unbounded, undifferentiated, entirely morally constituted, and impervious to reason, we are faced with a critical question: If reason is to remain "*sharī'a*tized" and limited to serving the meanings gleaned from scripture—presumably "moral meanings"—then on what basis are such issues as food-safety standards, traffic laws, administrative infrastructures, micro-biology, weapons development, and all the many amoral decisions confronting Muslim states to be deliberated? Stated differently, if reason is ideally subservient to *sharī'ah* and has little to no authority outside it, while *sharī'ah* itself is all-encompassing and all about morality, can there be any effective avenues to addressing amoral, practical, material issues, including those connected with good governance and the preservation of a healthy *nomos*, in the name of Islam? Ultimately, Hallaq's thesis leads inexorably to the conclusion that for all these issues Muslims must either adopt a modern Western secular approach (since amoral issues remain unreachable by an ostensibly totalizing *sharī'ah* and its *sharī'ah*-bound moral reason) or, precisely for this reason, they must simply leave these issues unaddressed (and perhaps content themselves with scientific, administrative, and other transplants from the West or elsewhere). On *this* understanding, Islam-cum-*sharī'ah* could not possibly fulfill the needs of a normatively operating modern state.

But it may be that only on Hallaq's particular understanding of Islam-cum-*sharī'ah* that an Islamic State would be "impossible." A different understanding of Islamic law might yield a different conclusion. Enter the Islamic Secular.

The Islamic Secular and the Islamic State

Shar'ī vs. Non-*Shar'ī*: Law vs. Fact

Part of the argument of this book is that Islam consists of both a *shar'ī* dimension, tied to *sharī'ah* and its sources, and a distinctly non-*shar'ī* dimension, loosely identified with *siyāsah* (broadly speaking and including its subsidiaries, *ḥisbah* and *maẓālim*) as well as a broad, private, and communal discretionary reasoning that extends to matters "beyond the law." Even within the law, as discussed in Chapter 3, *sharī'ah*'s optimal instantiation often includes non-*shar'ī*, *'aqlī*, considerations. Meanwhile, *sharī'ah*, *siyāsah*, and individual and communal discretion all draw upon a *nomos* that normalizes and privileges certain meanings and sensibilities, marginalizes others, and ideally bolsters the overall authority and efficacy of the law. At any given point in time, therefore, the overall state of Islamic law and governance depends on the combined efforts of Muslims (not just jurists) in all three areas: *shar'ī*, non-*shar'ī*, and *nomos*-building. The Islamic Secular cuts across all three of these areas, and its realm is where the bulk of the amoral, practical, and material interests of the Community, especially regarding governance, are pursued. Thus, any fair assessment of the relationship between Islam-cum-*sharī'ah* and the modern state must consider the contributions of the Islamic Secular.

Again, it goes without saying that *sharī'ah* is central to any system of Islamic governance. As such, *ijtihād* and/or *taqlīd* will play a critical role. On both approaches, however, there is a space/time differential between the indicants of revelation (the basis of *ijtihād*) or the conclusions of the *madhhab*s (the basis of *taqlīd*) and reality on the ground. For example, the Qur'ān speaks of husbands' obligation to supply "housing"; but what may have fulfilled this command in seventh-century Arabia will not do so in twenty-first-century America. Nor will what Mālik identified as pronouncements of divorce in second/eighth-century Medina necessarily constitute such today. In neither case, however, will changes in these rulings be a function of changes in the interpretation of the primary sources or the *madhhabs*. These will depend instead upon changes in the assessment of facts.

This law/fact distinction is one of the hidden elixirs of Islamic law and a major constituent of the Islamic Secular. We saw al-Qarāfī describe it earlier as the difference between the *status* of a thing as a legal cause, prerequisite or impediment—that is, *mashrū'īyat al-sabab* or *sababīyat al-sabab*—and the actual *occurrence* of a thing, i.e., *wuqū' al-sabab.*[189] In the case of the Qur'ānic mandate to provide housing, the question is not whether this obligation is an accurate deduction from scripture but whether this or that particular structure constitutes a "house" as a matter of fact.[190] And the relevance of this law/fact distinction stretches across virtually the entire *sharī'ah.*[191] Since I have discussed this in detail elsewhere, I will spare the reader all the intricacies of its mechanics here and try to limit myself to what is necessary.[192] But we should note the overall importance of this law/fact distinction not only to the proper application of the law but also to the overall issue of boundaries and jurisdiction. As al-Qarāfī summarizes the matter: "The jurisconsult does not give information about the *occurrence* of a legal *cause* that gives rise to a legal rule. He gives information only about the *status* of a legal rule [or cause] as a legal rule [or cause],[193] which applies to humanity until the coming of The Hour."[194] In other words, legal rules fall within the interpretive jurisdiction and authority of the jurists and their *fiqh*, while legal facts do not.

Of course, the application of all *sharīʿah* rules is contingent upon the presumed occurrence or absence of their respective legal causes, prerequisites, and impediments. Speaking from the perspective of quotidian reality, we may say that *sharīʿah* assesses every occurrence in terms of whether it constitutes a legal cause, prerequisite, or impediment and what—if any—legal rules it activates or affects. This means that, in attempting to determine the legal rule governing any particular event, there will be factual determinations that every *muftī*, judge, and government official will have to make. But it is the exception rather than the rule that these determinations can be made based on scriptural evidence or training in the law.[195] They typically require, rather, non-*sharʿī*, differentiated reason. Sometimes jurists will have easy access to this reason, for example, in the form of local custom or common sense. But sometimes factual determinations can be quite complex, as with determining the price or warranty period of a large piece of real estate. In such cases, jurists must either acquire knowledge of these facts through mastery of the relevant disciplines outside their juristic training or they must rely on other qualified determiners of fact. Failure or negligence in this regard will result in errors and miscarriages of justice. As al-Qarāfī laments, "How often the truth in a case escapes the *muftī* or judge because of their ignorance of mathematics, medicine, geometry (and the like). Thus, those of noble ambition should not neglect learning the various disciplines to the extent that they are able."[196] In sum, determining the relevant factual dimensions of a case may require that judges go beyond their training in *sharīʿah*, and their failure to do so may result in misapplications of the law. This requirement is even more applicable today, given the factual complexity brought to modern life by innovations in technology, financial instruments, social evolution, and the like.

Hallaq would probably place all of this under his description of reason "operat[ing] solely, in the final analysis, in the service of revelation," again, domesticating reason and subordinating it to scripture, the better to preserve the latter's primacy. But, if scripture in this context could be understood to address primarily one thing—law—while reason is understood to address primarily another—fact—then the interaction between the two could be more complementary than rigidly hierarchical, let alone competitive or antagonistic.

On this understanding, the conflict Hallaq wants to avoid need not be assumed to exist , at least not to the same degree. Similarly, it is one thing for mathematics or medicine to be used in ways that serve revelation once these disciplines have been developed; it is quite another to insist that revelation must be the actual source of these disciplines and/or the only legitimate incentive behind their development. Many disciplines (mathematics, medicine, architecture, metallurgy, among others) preceded the coming of revelation to Muḥammad, while others were developed by people who either did not believe in or had no reliable access to revelation.

More importantly, not only does Hallaq's depiction reduce Muslims to an entirely devotional mode of existence, taken seriously, it implies that jurists *qua*-jurists have the authority to pass judgement on the *substance* of all mathematical or medical issues. For, if all reason is necessarily *shar'ī* or subservient to *sharī'ah* and its sources, then all reason must fall under the jurisdiction of the jurists. And this leads precisely to the problem that al-Qarāfī—and the Islamic Secular—wants to avoid, namely, that of the views of jurists on issues outside their *shar'ī* competence being clothed with *shar'ī* authority. We saw an example of this in the recent controversy over the closing of mosques during the early stages of the COVID-19 pandemic. While the factual questions (the extent and infectious nature of the disease) clearly went beyond common knowledge, some jurists, while recognizing that scripture and/or the *madhhab*s recognized legal impediments (*māni'*) that might stay the communal obligation to perform prayers in mosques, refused or were hesitant to accept science (e.g., epidemiology) as the basis for confirming the factual presence of these impediments, preferring instead to rely on their own assessment of the relevant danger as the grounds for their *fatwā*s. While it was unfortunate that these jurists arrogated such technical knowledge to themselves, al-Qarāfī would have insisted that it was equally wrong for non-jurists to clothe the non-*shar'ī* dimension of these *fatwā*s with authority.

The overall point here is that even if reason is deployed in the service of *sharī'ah*, this does not mean, *pace* Hallaq, that it has no independent jurisdiction of its own. Nor must reason's service to revelation always be in a strictly *shar'ī* mode. There is an inextricably non-*shar'ī*, differentiated, Islamic Secular dimension to the application of *sharī'ah* that is just as critical to its maintenance and proper instantiation as the strictly *shar'ī* element. To conflate this non-*shar'ī*, Islamic Secular reasoning with *sharī'ah* itself defeats the whole function of the distinction.

Islamic Governance between Discretion and Juristic Law

Islam's non-*shar'ī*, differentiated, *'aqlī* element is even more integral, as we have seen, to the domain of *siyāsah*, or "discretionary rules and policies," which are foundational to Islamic governance. Yet, it is also in this area that such non-*shar'ī* rules and policies become a problem, one that sheds light on the impulse to force them back into the *shar'ī* domain. These rules and policies are backed by legal authority, namely, the state's right to back its discretionary rules with force, an authority that is recognized by the juristic tradition itself. Substantively speaking, however, they do not necessarily carry juristic or *shar'ī* authority, reflecting agreed-upon standards of derivation from *sharī'ah*'s sources. In other words, while these rules and policies can be enforced as law, their status as "discretionary" means that they are not subject to the kind of objective scrutiny that applies to the rules of *sharī'ah*—the concrete, formal rules of interpretation enshrined in *uṣūl al-fiqh* and *qawā'id* (legal precepts or canons). This becomes particularly problematic when such discretionary authority is placed in the hands of unscrupulous or incompetent rulers. Yet, to 'sharī'atize' this regime of authority would also defeat the purpose of its discretionary mandate, the whole point of which is to address the factually evolving and shifting interests of the Community, which cannot be achieved through fixed, unchanging, *shar'ī* rules.[197] Driverless cars may be judged *mubāḥ*, as a fixed *shar'ī* rule; but the discretionary rules and policies needed to regulate their use over time must continue to evolve and adjust with society and technology in order to remain effective in serving all the public interests involved.

My point here becomes clearer when we consider the fact that *siyāsah*'s mandate is not simply to determine the facts relative to the application of particular *sharī'ah* rules but also to lay down policies and regulations in areas where no *sharī'ah* rule—*qua* strictly *sharī'ah* rule—exists or (substantively speaking) *can* exist: speed limits, building codes, FAA regulations, immigration policy, tenure standards, medical licensing, food-safety standards and so on. Here, in contradistinction to the rules of *sharī'ah*, *siyāsah*-based rules are grounded in non-*shar'ī*, Islamic Secular deliberation. This distinction is clearly implied in the statement we saw earlier in al-Qarāfī: *muftī*s rely on scriptural indicants (*al-adillah*/sg. *dalīl*); judges rely on courtroom evidence (*ḥijāj*/sg. *ḥujjah*); and Imāms (i.e., governments) in their discretionary actions, rely on the pure or preponderant material interests (*al-maṣlaḥah al-khāliṣah aw al-rājiḥah*) of the Community.[198]

The legitimacy of a discretionary rule or policy is based not on its umbilical or genealogical ties to scripture but on the likelihood of its serving the Community's material interests, even as the latter are informed by the Community's transgenerational, *'aqlī* energies interacting with scripture, tradition and sociopolitical reality.[199] *Pace* Hallaq, however, these rules and policies could not be arrived at via a reason that "could not independently produce meanings of its own." In fact, *only* a reason that could stand on its own could produce such policies and regulations. As for *sharī'ah* or the strictly *shar'ī* alone, these simply cannot produce everything that is needed in the area of Islamic governance.[200] But once the Islamic Secular, with its differentiated, non-*shar'ī* reason—not to mention its broader definition of "Islamic"—is admitted into the conversation, it becomes far less obvious why Islamic governance or an Islamic State should be so "impossible."

In her study of *maṣlaḥah*, Felicitas Opwis describes classical scholars such as al-Juwaynī as insisting that, while the ruler has the right and responsibility to oversee both the religious and mundane interests of the Community, it is the religious scholars who are to direct him toward the substance of his decisions.[201] I have a different reading of al-Juwaynī, but I would prefer for the moment to take this opportunity to point out an important distinction between *maṣlaḥah* and *maṣlaḥah mursalah*. The former refers to the implicit, broader, or underlying aims of the law, which, through various modes of reading, are more concretely (albeit indirectly) extractable from the sources themselves. In this capacity, *maṣlaḥah* might be thought of as *shar'ī* and thus as falling within the scope of juristic authority. By contrast, *maṣlaḥah mursalah* is not concretely extractable from the sources but requires investment in the unarticulated spirit of the law. These are interests, as al-Qarāfī put it, that "the sources neither concretely validate nor invalidate" (*mā lam yashhad [al-shar'] lahu bi i'tibār wa lā ilghā'*).[202] The fact that the sources do not speak to these interests concretely renders them "untethered," whence their name: "interests untethered to texts," *maṣlaḥah mursalah*.[203] In pre-modern times, as members of the small elite of literate persons, jurists naturally assumed the right and responsibility to make determinations about what constituted a *maṣlaḥah mursalah*. And an inductive reading of scripture (*istiqrā'*), as suggested, for example, by al-Shāṭibī, could assist them in this regard. From another perspective, however, the question of which regulations or policies concretely serve these interests remains a question of fact. And over time, especially as we approach modernity and the proliferation of fact-determining disciplines—from actuarial sciences to modern astronomy—the presumption of juristic competence in this domain would naturally wane.

By contrast, the relationship between Islamic governance and the Islamic Secular acquires *added* significance in modern times. Every state today is faced with such challenges as developing immigration policies, national health-care plans, economic policies, new offices connected with the administration of justice, weapons systems, and so on. The answers to none of these challenges is substantively provided for by scripture or the *madhhabs*. And yet, because the Islamic Secular subsumes the relevant non-*shar'ī* forms of deliberation as part of Islam, pursuing these interests outside the instruments of *sharī'ah* and the *shar'ī* need not result in secularization in the form of going outside of Islam.

The Promise and Threat of Discretionary Authority

Given these realities, perhaps among the most important challenges for Islam today are: (1) how to bind the actions of Islamic government and limit its power in the realm *mā warā' al-ḥukm al-shar'ī*, where the strictures of *sharī'ah* proper and the interpretive constraints of *uṣūl al-fiqh* are of limited application; (2) how to bind or obligate the Community to act on the basis of rules and policies whose substantive content does not enjoy the authority of *sharī'ah*; and (3) how to secure a meaningful role for the Community in the decision-making processes of Islamic governance, including the expression of dissent, especially presuming the amorphous standard of "serving communal interests" that governs discretionary rules and policies, as opposed to the concrete and more objective criterion enshrined in *uṣūl al-fiqh* as the basis for assessing the substantive content of *shar'ī* rules. I will rely on al-Qarāfī for some preliminary responses to these challenges.

The challenge of state power is not new to Muslim jurisprudence. To understand al-Qarāfī's perspective on it, we must revisit his notion of "pure law." The point of this concept was to curb the potential "tyranny of the law," by limiting what was binding *and* unassailable, *shar'an*, in the pronouncements of *muftīs*, judges, and government officials to what was strictly legal—that is, *shar'ī*, or derived from *shar'ī* sources, either directly or as mediated through the *madhhabs*. This restriction raised problems, however, in actual practice. On the one hand, to grant the non-*shar'ī* factual assessments of judges, *muftīs*, and government officials full *shar'ī* authority would empower them beyond their presumed competence, especially regarding the assessment of legally relevant facts. Yet, as we have seen, all judicial rulings, *fatwā*s, and even government policies rely on such factual assessments. Thus, to deny the factual assessments of judges, *muftīs*, and government officials *all* authority would be to shut down the process of law and governance. Al-Qarāfī obviously does not want to do this. Instead, he develops and deploys the concept of what he refers to as the *taṣarruf*, which effectively cedes *provisional* authority to juristic and state determinations of fact but denies them *final* authority, thus creating a "para-legal" dimension of juristic pronouncements and state policies.[204]

As an institution, a *taṣarruf* is essentially a non-*shar'ī* discretionary act of finding. As a non-*shar'ī* pronouncement, it is not derived from scripture or the juristic aspect (i.e., *sababīyah* vs. *wuqū'*) of *madhhab* doctrine. For this reason, this finding may be provisionally *binding*, for the purpose of resolving the dispute at hand, but not *unassailable*, in that it may be legitimately challenged and, where appropriate, changed. Al-Qarāfī cites several examples and notes that discretionary actions are of many types. A particularly demonstrative example involves a judge buying or selling property on behalf of orphaned girls, absentees, or the mentally incapacitated. The *shar'ī* element of these transactions is the legal right to buy or sell; the non-*shar'ī*, discretionary element is the actual price at which the judge buys or sells the property. The default assumption is that the judge is acting responsibly and in good faith, buying or selling at a price that is not prejudicial to his wards. On this understanding, his action constitutes a valid, binding, ruling, a *ḥukm shar'ī*, which legally conveys the money to the orphans and the property to the buyer (or vice versa). Again, the right of an orphan to buy or sell property is confirmed in the *madhhabs* as a legal right, and, as the orphan's agent, the judge's act of buying or selling on her behalf is protected by the authority of the *madhhabs*. This right is "unassailable" in the sense that the cumulative *madhhab* tradition would not be willing, *ceteris paribus*, to relitigate it. But the price at which such property is bought or sold, however, is *not* a legal (read: *shar'ī*) question and thus *not* a constituent of the *madhhab*. Al-Qarāfī refers to the latter dimension of the judge's act of selling (i.e., setting the price) as a *taṣarruf*, a discretionary action that is "para-legal"—operating alongside or parallel to the law as a necessary though distinct element of its application.[205] Unlike its *shar'ī* dimension, this non-*shar'ī*, para-legal dimension may be provisionally binding, but it is *not* protected as unassailable by the authority of the *madhhab*. On this approach, al-Qarāfī is able to preserve the integrity of the legal process by confirming the provisionally binding authority of the discretionary dimension of judicial rulings without imputing over-inclusive authority to judges (or *muftīs* or government officials) by attaching unassailable, *shar'ī* authority to everything they say or do.

Outside the courts and the administration of justice, many—if not most—of the discretionary acts of governance, certainly in a modern context, will fall into the category of *taṣarruf*: FAA regulations, speed limits, education policy, building codes, zoning regulations, immigration policy, and the like. In terms of the concrete substance of their policies, government officials rely in these areas neither on scripture nor on the *madhhabs* but on their own (or their experts') good-faith assessment of what will serve the interests of the Community. Like that aspect of the judge's ruling represented by the price at which he sold the orphan's property, their assessments in these areas do not enjoy the unassailability of the *shar'ī* dimensions of judicial rulings, which, again, is derived from scripture or the *madhhabs*. The general presumption, assuming due diligence, is that these rules and policies are binding but not unassailable.[206] As such, their substance can be legitimately challenged whenever it is deemed to betray the pure or preponderant interests of the Community in any obvious or widespread way.

This leaves open the question of the concrete mechanism by which such challenges might be legitimately expressed, a question with which Muslims have struggled for over a millennium.[207] Indeed, one might say that this is perhaps among *the* foremost questions of Islamic governance in the Muslim world today: how to define and accommodate legitimate expressions of dissent. And failure to answer it will only bolster authoritarian tendencies, on the one hand, and strengthen Islamist and secularist reaction to these, on the other. But, whatever the answer might be—demonstrations, referenda, strikes, boycotts, recalls—it will *not* come out of an exclusively *sharʿī* mode of deliberation. Rather, the question of the most efficient way to institutionalize the accommodation of meaningful expressions of dissent will fall largely within the domain of the Islamic Secular.

To my mind, part of the problem with modern Islam's relationship to its heritage is not the latter's so-called rigidity or decline but the fact that modern Muslims' engagement with it remains almost exclusively *sharʿī* in focus. Their primary focus (in the interest of Islam) remains on reproducing the likes of Abū Ḥanīfa, al-Ghazālī, and Ibn Taymīyah, as if Islamic civilization were or even could have been built and sustained by these men alone. Little value or attention is attached to the critical role of the Sinans, Ibn al-Nafīses, Ulugh Begs and ʿUmar b. ʿAbd al-ʿAzīzes, or the mothers, wives, and sisters of numerous caliphs and scholars, or the countless unnamed administrators, agriculturalists, military geniuses, and wealthy businessmen and businesswomen who administered, fed, and defended the realm and financed its institutions. As critical as their contributions were, all these figures relied in the main on differentiated, non-*sharʿī*, Islamic Secular reasoning far more than they did on *sharʿīyāt*.

This misrecognition is partly why, even assuming a modern Muslim government's due diligence and the substantive probity of its policies, it may still face the problem of how to ensure or incentivize voluntary compliance. Even if a *siyāsah*-based policy clearly serves legitimate communal interests, in the absence of being associated with a *sharīʿah* rule that is identifiably based on scripture or the *madhhabs*, by which one can discern its concrete consequences for the Hereafter, the widespread notion that "Islamic" equals "*sharʿī*" leaves many Muslims insufficiently motivated to comply. In sum, the non-*sharʿī* is simply not Islamic enough and thus not sufficiently binding enough on the Muslim religious conscience to enlist voluntary assent in the name of Islam.[208]

One solution might be to connect the duty to comply with the authority traditionally conferred upon the ruler to issue discretionary policies.[209] But this would take us back to where we started and the question of how to domesticate that authority. Another approach might be what Rashīd Riḍā suggests, that is, that unanimous consensus (*ijmāʿ*), or even a majority consensus, among the Community's leadership (*ittifāq ahl al-ḥall wa al-ʿaqd kullihim aw aktharihim*) be considered dispositive as a *sharʿī* incentive and thus capable of compelling compliance on issues for which no textual evidence exists.[210] But this presents similar problems, in addition to those traditionally associated with *ijmāʿ* itself.[211]

A final (and cognate) approach might be to try to "sharīʿatize" the rational, non-*sharʿī* element of discretionary actions, rendering them extensions of *sharīʿah*, such that the rule or policy in question acquires *sharʿī* authority. This appears to be Hallaq's approach, part of the whole point of his "*sharīʿ*atization" of reason. But this method also carries liabilities. For, if *sharīʿah* is identified with every rational assessment a government makes, its authority as "God's law" is likely to atrophy over time, both because of the occasional failure of these rational assessments to deliver and because of the frequency with which discretionary rules and policies must change. This is in addition to the problem I cited earlier of how to protect the *sharīʿah* of the jurists from the *sharīʿah* of the state.[212]

By contrast, while the Islamic Secular does not directly solve the problem of compliance, it argues that by adjusting the relationship between Islam and *sharīʿah*, with the latter as a bounded rather than an unbounded entity and the former as the repository of not only *sharʿī* but also non-*sharʿī* but still religious authority, one can find resources within Islamic tradition (e.g., the *taṣarruf*) that point in the direction of meaningful bases of negotiation.

The Authority of the Islamic Secular

The Islamic Secular recognizes the realm *mā warāʾ al-ḥukm al-sharʿī* to be fully within the scope of Islam. On this understanding, just because *sharīʿah* does not obligate Muslims to do a thing does not mean that they have no reason to do it, in the name and interest of Islam. Even if an act is not binding on the 'moral' (or *sharʿī*) conscience, prudence or material interest can provide a sufficient motive to act in the name and interest of *dīn*, assuming, as the Islamic Secular does, that prudence itself is recognized as *dīnī* or "religious." Perhaps if we could get beyond the philosophical prejudice begun by Kant and the view that, when it comes to religion, morality is the only consideration that can legitimately compel action, the Islamic Secular's ability to motivate action in the name of religion might become more obvious.[213] We might be able to see that, if the rational assessment of the pure or preponderant interest of the Community is compelling enough, then, *dīn*—that is, obeisance, religion-as-psycho-dynamic-disposition, *taqwā*, and *qurbah*—can suffice as an incentive to act, even in the absence of a *ḥukm sharʿī* that legally or religiously—*in the proper, the religious, sense*—compels one to do so. In his discussion of the necessity of opening the means to desired or obligatory ends (*fatḥ al-dharīʿah*), just as we block the means to forbidden or undesirable ones (*ṣadd al-dharāʾiʿ*), al-Qarāfī insists that God may reward an act, even if it is not commanded, to the extent that it serves God's purposes.[214] Cumulatively, such actions could draw additional support from their sublation into the realm of the *maʿrūf*, or "communally recognized norms," or, conversely, the realm of the *munkar*, as incentives to avoid actions. As we find in the Qurʾān,[215] while the substance of such actions is clearly not dictated by scripture, scripture nonetheless underwrites the propriety of acting in accordance therewith, within the circumference of *islām mā warā' al-ḥukm al-shar'ī*.

On this recognition of the propriety of acting on the basis of differentiated, non–*shar'ī* Islamic Secular dictates, neither scripture nor *sharī'ah* need be challenged or threatened by the frequency of change or by the fact that discretionary policies occasionally fail. Rather, changes in policies and regulations could be indulged "safely," that is, within the non-*shar'ī* parameters of the Islamic Secular, without implying any deficiency in *sharī'ah* itself. Of course, the ultimate success of such policies and regulations—including their ability to command compliance—will depend as much on the strength and quality of the prevailing *nomos* and plausibility structure as it does on the substance of the policies themselves. This is another way in which the critical importance of the Islamic Secular is brought to the fore.

As for the question of communal involvement, this is a major concern of Ovamir Anjum in his insightful and thought-provoking book, *Politics, Law and Community in Islamic Thought: The Taymiyyan Moment*. Drawing on the *sharī'ah*-maximalism of Ibn Taymīyah, Anjum's point of departure shares much with that of Hallaq. He sees *sharī'ah* as essentially coterminous with Islam and, in that context, wants to show how the Community can be brought into the process of negotiating the politics that defines their lives. "Politics," according to Anjum, is *siyāsah*; but *siyāsah* is folded into *sharī'ah*, and he understands the latter in the broadest sense of encompassing virtually everything. He thus locates the key to Community enfranchisement in their ability to place limits on the authority of the jurists, such that the jurists cease to exercise a monopoly over determining the substance of *sharī'ah*. This, he proposes, can be achieved in two ways. First, by rejecting the "elitist" formal reasoning of the Ash'arites in favor of a natural reason (*fiṭrah*) shared by all, the views of the Community could gain just as much authority as those of the *fuqahā'*.[216] Second, by limiting the authority of the jurists as the exclusive definers of *sharī'ah* to those areas outside unanimous consensus, *sharī'ah* could become, in its most permanent features, the property of the Community as a whole.[217] Ultimately, on Anjum's Taymiyyan theory, the real importance of Community involvement in Islamic politics lies in its ability to preserve the integrity of the Faith through its collective infallibility, or *'iṣmah*, which the *Community*—and no one else (in Sunni Islam), including the jurists—inherited from the Prophet.[218]

Again, Anjum appears to embrace a Hallaqian understanding of Islamic law, including its reduction to a system of applied morality. Throughout his presentation, the key considerations are "good," "evil," "justice," "tyranny," "right," "wrong," and the like. Beyond a passing concern with the competence of certain government officials in their capacity as upholders of a *shar'ī* order, he directs little attention to such values as efficiency, prosperity, development, beauty, military power, or cultural influence. Here is where the perspective of the Islamic Secular is thrown into relief. According to the Islamic Secular, the Community, given its role in the concrete instantiation of Islam on the ground, is enfranchised via its right (if not duty) to participate in every aspect of governance in the domain *mā warā' al-ḥukm al-shar'ī*. This would include the pursuit of amoral, material, prudential interests, alongside or in conversation with the moral vision of Islam. And it would include the right to dissent and call for redress in the face of government *taṣarrufāt* that the Community deemed unjust, impractical, inefficient, or ill-informed.

Al-Qarāfī gives a striking example of this last point when he casts the Imām's declaration of *jihād*, along with other discretionary policies, as a *taṣarruf*, from which any reasonable Muslim could legitimately dissent: "If they command us to perform an act which they believe to be good, or forbid us to perform one which they believe to be evil/bad, it remains the right of anyone who disagrees with them not to follow them."[219] In other words, such commands do not constitute binding, unassailable *aḥkām shar'īyah*; they are only *taṣarrufāt*, in which capacity they can be legitimately challenged. Missing, of course, are the concrete mechanisms by which this back and forth might be held together. Here, however, as Anjum described his project, I see the value of my contribution, "not in elaborating robust political institutions, but in making such thinking possible by deconstructing the doctrines and developments that had foreclosed the very possibility of political thinking."[220]

To be sure, there is always more to "political thinking" than just "political thinking." As I mentioned, Islam's plausibility structure and *nomos*, which include the bulk of those issues Hallaq identifies with the modern condition, must also be addressed as part of any meaningful Islamic political thought. In his book *al-Ta'līm al-Dīnī Bayna al-Tajdīd wa al-Tajmīd* (*Religious Education between Renewal and Stagnation*), the late Shaykh Ṭaha Jābir al-'Alwānī (d. 1437/2016) pointed to the inadequacy of an exclusively *shar'ī* response to ideology—in his case, the waves of Western thought inundating Iraq in the mid-twentieth century. He noted that the *'ulamā'* tended to limit themselves to issuing *fatwās*, that is, *aḥkām shar'īyah*, that condemned communism, socialism, or what-have-you as Islamically unacceptable, or *ḥarām*. He notes the futility of such an approach and that he himself would "not try to fight ideologies with *fatwās*" (*lā uḥārib al-fikr bi al-fatāwā*).[221] Substantively speaking, ideologies—what one might call a major part of the modern condition itself—cannot be addressed by *fiqh* alone; they require the intervention of *fikr*, or reasoned discourse (not to mention material culture). When Hallaq asks, "How will this [Islamic] governance rebuff the forces of globalized culture, forces fully backed by the superior, positivism-grounded powers in the world?"[222] the answer must invariably be, "Primarily, through *fikr*, i.e., non-*shar'ī*, differentiated, *'aqlī* engagement, and not *fiqh*."

Stated differently, the challenge of confronting the modern condition is primarily not a *shar'ī* but a non-*shar'ī*, Islamic Secular challenge. And success in facing it will depend, in large measure, on non-jurist masters of various disciplines or areas of expertise—or, perhaps, on jurists who have gone beyond their juristic training to master other fields (as was often the case in pre-modern Islam). By restricting the Islamic to the *shar'ī*, however, Hallaq effectively places all of this beyond the quotidian gaze of 'common' Muslims, consigning them and their gifts to a spectatorial posture that renders them more rather than less susceptible to the hegemonic, Western forces of "epistemic-psychological assimilation" that Hallaq so dreads. From the perspective of the Islamic Secular, by contrast, non-jurist thinkers, administrators, inventors and financiers are looked to to play a major role in confronting the modern condition, relying primarily on energies that neither directly draw upon nor offend *sharī'ah*, in a manner that neither takes them outside Islam or the Islamic.

But perhaps the ubiquity of the modern condition itself should not be so casually assumed. Hallaq appears to join MacIntyre in the idea that, after the Enlightenment, a pervasive relativism, born of the lack of a common moral language and agreed-upon sources of moral reflection, denied the West a moral foundation upon which to erect its newly minted state. Hallaq knows of and acknowledges the existence of such moral language and resources in Islam, in the form of the lingering, albeit embattled, authority of "Qur'ān and Sunnah," the legacy of the *salaf*, or Pious Ancestors, the *madhhab*s, Islam's moral vision, and its "technologies of the self."[223] But he does not see this as providing an alternative to rejecting the Islamic State on the same grounds that MacIntyre rejected the Western state. His argument seems to be that the history of Europe, including the "modern condition," is effectively the history of the modern world, including the Muslim world, as a result of which Islam must be assumed to have undergone the same dislocation, relativism, and moral chaos witnessed in the West. But while some may argue that colonialism effectively rendered the history of Western Europe the history of the Muslim world, this argument, too forcefully put, risks overlooking any number of stubborn realities on the ground.

As late as the fifteenth/twentieth century, 'Abduh and Riḍā could still locate the aim behind the attempts of the British and Westernized Muslims (*al-mutafarnijah*) to destroy *sharī'ah* as residing in their desire to break the bonds of community, shared values, and identity among Muslims, thereby opening them to foreign influence and, ultimately, cultural and intellectual dependency.[224] Apparently, however, they did not succeed, at least not entirely, as it is still possible to walk down the streets of Cairo today and witness altercations in which total strangers intervene with the morally laden (and disarming) words, "*Ayb! Kidda 'ayb*!" (Wrong/shameful! This is wrong/shameful!), or the even more *sharī'ah*-laden "*Ḥarām; ḥarām 'alayk*!" (Forbidden; you should be ashamed!).

No one responds to such interventions with, "What do you mean?" Instead, the moral consensus is at least tacitly acknowledged and routinely runs its course. My point here is not to overstate this socio-cultural consensus but simply to question whether the Enlightenment should be unquestionably assumed to have had the same effect on *all* peoples—especially the un-Westernized masses who never experienced it directly.[225]

In this light, one might ask how justified we are in presuming that the moral malaise that befell Western Europe—and here I am speaking of the ability to recognize what is moral, not the commitment to practicing it—also befell the Muslim world. How do we explain, on this assumption, the fact that premarital sex, homosexuality, out-of-wedlock birth and possessive individualism are still nowhere near as acceptable in the Muslim world as they are in the West?[226] And how do we explain the rise and staying power of the likes of *al-Qāʿidah, ISIS, Boko Haram,* the *Ṭālibān*, and other groups, the substantive indecency of aspects of their programs notwithstanding? In sum, if the Islamic State is only impossible assuming the universality of the Western experience and the uniform spread of the modern condition across the globe, how impossible would it remain, assuming the absence of this universality and uniformity?

In closing, I would like to reiterate a few points that I have already made but which the cumulative weight and thrust of my arguments may have overshadowed along the way. While the Islamic Secular clearly implies that there are limits to the jurisdiction of *sharīʿah* and its *fuqahāʾ*, this should not be understood in the same light in which modern secularists, "progressives," and even some liberals may seek to construe these limits. As I hope to have established definitively, these are not limitations imposed on the Islamic jurisprudential tradition from without; nor are they invoked from within as a means of domesticating *sharīʿah*. Rather, they have been established, articulated, and defended by generations of Islam's finest juristic minds—men and women[227] whose entire lives had been devoted to piety and to upholding the sanctity and integrity of Islam-cum-*sharīʿah*, from Ibn al-Qaṣṣār in the fourth/tenth century to Wahbah al-Zuḥaylī in the fifteenth/twenty-first. As I have stated before, *islām mā warāʾ al-ḥukm al-sharʿī* remains authentic, *bona fide* Islam, and to operate within it is to operate within the circumference of Islam. The difficulties attending my use of the word "secular" notwithstanding, the Islamic Secular remains a part of Islam as religion, or *dīn*, which entails *taqwā*, *qurbah*, obeisance, "technologies of the self," the conscious awareness of the ubiquitous gaze of the God of Islam, and, lest we forget, *sharīʿah*, all as religiosity inflected commitments with a healthy strain of vigilance and oppugnancy.

Despite stereotypes about Muslims as "modern ancestors" who simply cannot separate the religious from the non-religious, the Islamic Secular's separation of the *sharʿī* from the non-*sharʿī* should *not* be seen as an attempt to placate or respond to this stereotype. Separating the *sharʿī* from the non-*sharʿī* is not the same—and is not intended to be the same—as separating the religious from the non-religious. Indeed, there is no inherently non-religious at all in the Islamic Secular. Nor has it been my intention to argue against the idea that Islam-cum-*sharīʿah* includes a moral vision. I have simply tried to show that Islam-cum-*sharīʿah*'s vision is not *exclusively* moral, that it also includes a prudential imperative, and that for over a thousand years Islamic juristic law has been engaged in a conversation about whether and how the moral and the prudential can be successfully negotiated. Finally, as I stated early on, the Islamic Secular has no interest whatever in secularization or secularism.

I should also reiterate that it has not been my aim to defend or promote the modern state as a normative form of political organization for Muslims. My argument is simply that, should Muslims decide to go this route, it would not entail an inherent, non-negotiable, self-contradiction, as argued by Professor Hallaq. Muslims may embrace the modern state and, in Akeel Bilgrami's words, "struggle to improve [it]";[228] or they may reject it for what they perceive to be its desire to domesticate religion; or they may see it as promoting nationalist navel-gazing and opt for a broader political arrangement and consciousness, such as the *ummah* or the caliphate; or they may move to a domestic version of the "empire-state" of old;[229] or they may simply seek to domesticate the modern state by, in Foucault's words, "cutting off the king's head." Personally, I suspect that greater utility might accrue to two other possibilities in this regard, both of which implicate the Islamic Secular.

First, whatever structural form a modern Islamic State might assume, to follow the West's lead in substituting laws and institutions for actual piety in leadership may be ultimately to mistake a religious menu for a secular meal, especially given the discretionary powers and deference that Islam-cum-*sharīʿah* has traditionally afforded Muslim rulers and states. As we are learning in the United States, even if we continue to call it one, a democracy cannot long endure if its political leaders are all autocrats, or its people are inclined to acquiesce to those who are. The Islamic State is no more a driverless vehicle than democracy is. Crucially, however, the inculcation of piety among Muslim leadership (including rulers, administrators, bureaucrats, security forces, and the like) occurs as much "beyond the law" and relies as much on Islamic Secular energies as it does on the substance and authority of *sharīʿah* itself. In such light, to ignore the Islamic Secular in the process of constructing an Islamic State may be to doom that process to failure from the outset.

Second, rather than "cutting off the king's head," it may be more germane and effective to "cut off the king's penis." One of the most pressing problems in the contemporary Muslim world is not simply the centralization of power, or even sovereignty per se (though these remain issues) but the abject determination on the part of those who come to power to ensure its continuation in their line, figuratively or literally—the military, the royal family, the sectarian or tribal junta, the Ba'th, or some other party This determination routinely compromises and corrupts the state's decision-making will, clouds its vision, and preempts its ability to recognize and pursue the real *maṣlaḥah rājiḥah aw khāliṣah* of the Community. Moreover, this "possessive statism" goes a long way toward sustaining a zero-sum, us-against-them attitude between the state and the people, in contradistinction to the condominium imagined by pre-modern jurists. In this context, the Community's interests all too often slam up against the overbearing interests of the incumbents to retain and pass on power, at all costs, which involves at times questionable relationships with imperial powers. Meanwhile, the signals generated by this determination to stay in power spawn and then feed upon an atmosphere of fear, if not paranoia. This stifles the Community's imaginative talents and creative energies and reduces their level of indulging these to what they perceive to be safe, whereas as immigrants to the West, for example, they are often among the most accomplished innovators. While it was far from a dictate of *sharī'ah*, eunuchs once played an important role in Islamic governance. Perhaps it is time to bring them back. That too, however, will ultimately require significant investment in the Islamic Secular.

5

The Islamic Secular and the Secular State

Basic Anatomy

Hallaq's *The Impossible State* argued that Islam-cum-*sharīʿah* cannot negotiate a legitimate relationship with the modern state. In *Islam and the Secular State*, Abdullahi An-Naʿim essentially argues the opposite. For An-Naʿim, the modern state is a decidedly secular entity, from which *sharīʿah* as the religious law of Islam must be separated. Moreover, he believes that the state must ultimately control or domesticate religion. This, however, does not render the modern state incompatible with Islam. For, An-Naʿim does not see separating religion from the state or the state's domesticating religion as subjugating or violating Islam or *sharīʿah*. On the contrary, according to him, this is the normative relationship, historically speaking, between Islam-cum-*sharīʿah* and the state. It is only the reactionary impulse of modern Muslims, especially Islamists, that has produced the idea of an "Islamic State" whose *raison d'être* is the implementation of *sharīʿah*. The aim of *Islam and the Secular State* is thus to disabuse Muslims of this mistaken notion and to explain the nature, merits, and Islamic legitimacy of the secular state as the normative political arrangement for modern Muslims.

Unlike Hallaq, An-Naʿim's theoretical point of departure is not the Schmittian state but the modern, liberal state. Like Hallaq's, however, his focus is on the relationship between Islam-cum-*sharīʿah* and the state in the traditional Muslim world. Also, like Hallaq, An-Naʿim does not factor the Islamic Secular into his deliberations. Instead, Islam is brought to negotiate its relationship with the secular liberal state on the understanding of *sharīʿah* as an unbounded and uniformly *sharʿī* entity. Ultimately, this conception of *sharīʿah* assumes greater significance for An-Naʿim than it did for Hallaq. For, An-Naʿim includes non-Muslims as a significant feature of his argument, which further problematizes state implementation of *sharīʿah*. It also exposes the extent to which the unarticulated assumption of legal monism (a one-size-fits-all approach to law) is grafted onto Islam-cum-*sharīʿah* by virtue of *sharīʿah*'s association with the modern state in the form of the Islamic State. An-Naʿim (like others) retrojects this assumption back into the pre-modern period, from where it is assumed to be Islam-cum-*sharīʿah*'s normative commitment throughout its history.

An-Naʿim's thesis is highly nuanced, eclectic, and rather discursive, laced at times with a stubborn ambiguity and a fluid use of key terms. This makes it

The Islamic Secular. Sherman A. Jackson, Oxford University Press. © Oxford University Press 2024.
DOI: 10.1093/oso/9780197661789.003.0006

difficult at times to describe his project without reproducing some of these ambiguities. My primary aim, nevertheless, will be to place An-Na'im's Secular State, undistorted, into conversation with the Islamic Secular, highlighting the extent to which his omission of the latter places important considerations, alternatives, and prospects beyond contemplation, thus misrecognizing the full range of possibility in the relationship between Islam-cum-*sharīʿah* and the modern, secular, liberal state.

My analysis will suggest that due consideration of the Islamic Secular calls into question the very need for a secular state as An-Na'im portrays it. I will also highlight ways in which his Secular State, by excluding the Islamic Secular, falls short of the neutrality it claims, ultimately restricting *sharīʿah*'s non-coercive role in society at large. I will also cover several subsidiary issues, including An-Na'im's concerns about the purity of religiosity, the question of human rights, and certain presumptions about Islam-cum-*sharīʿah* in history. In the end, my hope is that this chapter will demonstrate, once again, that neither Islam nor *sharīʿah* nor their relationship with the modern state or society (and therefore modernity) can be adequately understood without due consideration of the Islamic Secular.

The Islamic State, Secularism, and An-Na'im's Secular State

"In order to be a Muslim by conviction and free choice, which is the only way one can be a Muslim, I need a secular state. By a secular state, I mean one that is neutral regarding religious doctrine, one that does not claim or pretend to enforce Shari'a."[1] This is how An-Na'im opens his discussion of what he casts as the normative relationship between Islam-cum-*sharīʿah* and the modern state. He joins Hallaq in rejecting the idea of an Islamic State, in the form of a modern state ruled by and in the name of *sharīʿah*. For him, however, the chief inconsistency is not between Islam-cum-*sharīʿah* and the sovereignty of the modern state (although this, too, is an issue) but with the modern state's commitment to secularism, specifically, the separation between religion and state. Whereas for Hallaq, state implementation of *sharīʿah* remains paradigmatic, as it has been in mainstream Sunnism for over a millennium, An-Na'im argues that *sharīʿah* observance in Muslim society was always, and should remain, entirely "voluntary, a matter of personal choice and conviction."[2] Otherwise, he claims, such observance would be religiously counterfeit and corrosive.

The idea that state implementation and policing of religious rules and doctrines spoils religious sincerity is only part of the problem for An-Na'im. He also sees the Islamic State as exerting a deleterious effect on non-Muslims, who do not believe in Islam-cum-*sharīʿah* and for whom the question of sincerity (in relation to *sharīʿah* compliance) would not arise. The greater issue for him is thus that state-sponsored application of *sharīʿah* jeopardizes, if not frustrates, the values of constitutionalism, human rights, and citizenship. These, according to An-Naʿim, are the *sine qua non* of any acceptable, modern socio-political order. And his Secular State, in direct and explicit contrast to the Islamic State, is the only arrangement that can guarantee these values for everyone.

By "constitutionalism," An-Naʿim is referring to "the set of principles that limit and control the powers of government in accordance with the fundamental rights of citizens and communities,"[3] its ultimate aim being to uphold the rule of law, limit government, and protect human rights.[4] "Human rights" are the commonly referenced fundamental entitlements enshrined internationally "in the aftermath of the Second World War."[5] As for "citizenship," An-Naʿim describes it as "a particular form of membership in a political community of a territorial state,"[6] which implies "a shared understanding of equal human dignity for all and a fully inclusive and effective political participation to ensure the government accountability for respecting and protecting human rights for all."[7] As a value, citizenship also implies the prioritization of individual over collective or communal rights,[8] along with a positive valuation of pluralism, especially religious pluralism.[9] The individual is autonomous, self-sustaining, and possessed of an inherent right to pursue self-fulfillment unimpeded by any prior attachments, encumbrances, or commitments. An-Naʿim frames all this within a commitment to state neutrality, according to which "state institutions neither favor nor disfavor any religious doctrine or principle."[10] Of course, any official connection between *sharīʿah* and the state, as advocated by proponents of the Islamic State, would frustrate these values. Secularism and its concretization in a "secular state" is, again, therefore, the only option.

Regarding secularism itself, An-Naʿim rejects the notion that it is a modern, Western concept. In fact, he sees its association with the West as a major impediment to its acceptance among modern Muslims. His project seeks, thus, not only to dissociate secularism from the West but to rehabilitate and rescue it from the way it is commonly understood in the Muslim world.[11] This common understanding assumes that, under secularism, religion, in any explicit or organized form, must be separated not just from the state but also from society, the public sphere at large. The model is French *laïcité*, concretized in the Muslim world by the secularization project of Turkey's Mustafa Kemal Atatürk (d. 1357/1938) in the early twentieth century. Rejecting this form of secularism, An-Naʿim opts for a more American version, according to which the religious establishment is formally separated from the state, but religion itself is admitted into the public square, where it can freely participate in debates and negotiations over the form and substance of the general order, through what An-Naʿim refers to as "civic reason" (his version of Rawls's "public reason").[12] This process of negotiating the general order is what An-Naʿim refers to as "politics," and he sees the uniqueness of his definition of secularism as residing in its simultaneous insistence on keeping religion out of the hands of the state, while insisting that it be allowed to run its course in society at large, again, in the form of his "politics." His aim, in other words, is to secularize the state but not society. To this end, whatever constraints he seeks to impose on *sharīʿah*, he has no formal commitment to its abolishment. In fact, An-Naʿim sees his version of secularism as protecting *sharīʿah*, by allowing it to go as far in society as his "politics" may take it, while insulating both it and the populace at large, Muslim and non-Muslim alike, from the predations of a state bent on using *sharīʿah* to justify self-serving ends. For him, "[s]eparating Islam and the state while maintaining the connection between Islam and politics allows for the 'voluntary implementation' of Islamic principles in official policy and legislation."[13]

In the end, however, there is tension between An-Naʿim's commitment to secularism and the overall nature and value he imputes to religion. On the one hand, he insists that "[s]ecularism needs religion to provide a widely accepted source of moral guidance for the political community, as well as to help satisfy and discipline the needs of believers within that community."[14] On the other hand, he seeks to impose strictures on religion, especially, though not exclusively, "religion-as-*sharīʿah*," denuding it of all coercive authority, preventing it from spreading "disruptive" ideas (e.g., about women or non-Muslims), and requiring it to negotiate its status and authority through "civic reason." Ultimately, An-Naʿim wants to preserve the *moral* authority of religion, while denying it all *coercive* (read: political) authority, the latter being the exclusive preserve of his Secular State.

This concern with the authority to coerce in the name of religion is the core of An-Naʿim's project. It is not religion per se that he wants to separate from the state but religion that arrogates to itself the right to coerce, that is, religion plus political authority as a combined force, which is ultimately what makes the Islamists' Islamic State "Islamic" and is why An-Naʿim rejects it. Yet, his shifting uses of the terms "religious" and "Islamic" manifest an unresolved tension between his secular and religious commitments that bears significant consequences.

Normatively speaking, according to An-Naʿim, a state cannot be "Islamic"; it cannot rule in the name of *sharīʿah*. But there is another sense in which a state can and should be "Islamic," namely when, through the medium of his "politics," a Muslim community communicates its religious sensibilities to the state and the state, as part of the basic democratic process, incorporates these sensibilities into its laws and policies. Here, however, *sharīʿah* informs laws and policies not because God says so but because this is the will of the people. In yet a third sense, "Islamic" simply means "religious," "*in the proper, the religious, sense.*" On this understanding, individuals turn to Islam-cum-*sharīʿah* voluntarily, to regulate and enrich their personal and collective lives, independent of the state.

Ultimately, An-Na'im's Secular State remains attached to religion. But his failure to distinguish religion's *shar'ī* dimensions from its non-*shar'ī* dimensions blurs the distinction between "religion" and "religion-as-*sharī'ah*." On this ambiguity, the state ends up empowered to intervene and regulate religion any time it sees fit, as part of its commitment and mandate to keep *sharī'ah* (i.e., religion-as-*sharī'ah*, or *sharī'ah* plus coercive authority) at bay. By conceptualizing coercive religion-as-*sharī'ah* as unbounded and undifferentiated, in other words, An-Na'im is able to grant his purportedly neutral Secular State disproportionate power at religion's expense, not only in terms of regulating religion's attachment to the state but also in regulating its function in society. For, on his undifferentiated conceptualization of Islam-cum-*sharī'ah*, the distinction between religion and religion-as-*sharī'ah* effectively disappears, placing both equally under the regulatory power of the Secular State in relation to both the state and society.

The Basic Aim of the Present Analysis and Critique

My primary objective in engaging with An-Na'im is to highlight what I see as the cost of his not recognizing and thus excluding the Islamic Secular from his deliberations. While he speaks of the "differentiation of state and religious institutions in Islamic societies,"[15] this is limited to the distinction between the "religious establishment," that is, the *fuqahā'*, and the state, or "political establishment." It has nothing to do with any recognition of *sharī'ah* as a bounded entity or of a *shar'ī*/non-*shar'ī* divide. Meanwhile, An-Na'im's "politics," by which religious ideas can be voluntarily introduced into society, is a thoroughly secular enterprise that is patrolled by "civic reason," the whole point of which is to deny religion any coercive authority of its own at either the state *or* societal level. As long as *sharī'ah* remains undifferentiated, however, the process of separating it from the state cannot be easily distinguished from that of separating it from society. For, as we have seen, even non-coercive religious ideas (e.g., about women or religious minorities), can be deemed a threat. As such, the need for secular vigilance applies no less to the relationship between religion and society than it does to the relationship between religion and the state. Ultimately, in the name of domesticating *sharī'ah*, An-Na'im's secularism ends up replicating the Western secular by setting up a religious/secular divide that strongly privileges the secular over the religious, not only in relation to the state but also, again, in relation to society at large.

In place of An-Na'im's conception of *sharī'ah* as undifferentiated and all-encompassing, the Islamic Secular alters the basic problem by expanding the focus beyond *sharī'ah* to include *islām mā warā' al-ḥukm al-shar'ī*. This adjustment immediately diminishes the propriety, let alone necessity, of eliminating *sharīʿah* from state-sponsored law as the solution to many of the problems An-Naʿim raises. For, many of the constraints and limitations he seeks to impose on *sharīʿah* are already self-imposed by the Islamic juristic tradition itself. For example, viewed from the perspective of the Islamic Secular, the problem of distinguishing "transcendent" from "temporal" values, or "desacraliz[ing] [Muslim] perceptions of . . . worldly issues,"[16] fades appreciably, without having to remove *sharīʿah* from the state and without the need to over-regulate religion in society. Similarly, when An-Naʿim cites, as part of the rationale behind their secularizing programs, Sukarno's (d. 1390/1970) and Atatürk's appreciation of "the value of economic reasoning, as opposed to the conservative, fatalistic theology,"[17] one might recall that all of the jurists profiled in Chapter 2 (with the possible exception of al-Maqrīzī) would agree with this distinction and see it in terms of the difference between *sharīʿah* as a *sharʿī* enterprise and economics as a predominantly non-*sharʿī* enterprise, over whose substance the jurists *qua* jurists would exercise no monopoly, and regarding which non-jurists with economic knowledge would normatively carry the day. None of these jurists, pre-modern or modern, would see any need to separate *sharīʿah* from the state in order to be able to uphold or enact this kind of differentiation.

Throughout his thesis, An-Naʿim juxtaposes the categories "religious," "secular," and "political" according to general, popular understandings, except when he uses "secular" as a cognate of his formal definition of "secularism." While this usage is in some ways understandable, given the general diffusion of these "common sense" understandings, it becomes a liability when facing the need for a principled and consistent basis upon which to distinguish the secular/political from the religious. On An-Naʿim's more casual usage, "religious," "secular," and "political" end up meaning essentially whatever the state says they mean. And, given the explicit mandate he grants to the state to "regulate" religion, this can authorize ostensibly neutral states to disfavor religion without having to declare their true intention or take responsibility for doing so. For example, when describing the Turkish head-scarf controversy, in which the state banned women from wearing *ḥijāb*, An-Naʿim concludes, "The primary issue . . . has been how to distinguish between the 'public sphere,' from which the Constitutional Court says head-scarfs must be banned, and the 'private sphere' in which they are permitted."[18] In reality, however, the state gets to define not only what is public and what is private but also what is religious and what is not.

We see this in the example of the female cancer patient who wore a wig to cover her bald head, only to be summarily dismissed from her teaching post, as the state determined her action to be "religious."[19] Had the state reached the eminently reasonable conclusion that her act was "non-religious" (meaning, in the sense intended here by An-Naʿim, that it was not dictated by *sharīʿah*[20]), it would not have mattered whether it occurred in public or in private. And this is the point: this woman wore a wig not in fulfillment of any *sharīʿah* dictate but in pursuit of a non-*sharʿī*, practical, Islamic Secular interest, no different in effect from the color of shoes she chose to wear that day. But failure to recognize the Islamic Secular denied An-Naʿim (and the Turkish state) a formal basis upon which to make this *sharʿī*/non-*sharʿī* distinction, which left an overly broad and undifferentiated definition of "religion" in the hands of the state for it to react to as it saw fit.

In sum, An-Naʿim's non-recognition of the Islamic Secular denies him a principled, consistent basis upon which to distinguish what should be regulated as "religion"—that is, "coercive religion," or "religion-as-*sharīʿah*"—from what should not, in relation to both the state and society. Especially since the main problem for him is religion in the form of *sharīʿah* attaching to the state, it would seem crucial to identify *sharīʿah*'s jurisdictional boundaries, along with what is *sharʿī* and what is not *sharʿī* within these boundaries, in order to determine both what his Secular State *should* regulate and what the Islamists' Islamic State *could* justifiably (or not) implement as *sharīʿah*. From the perspective of the Islamic Secular, the issue is not simply the relationship between politics, economics, or law and religion in relation to the state or society but additionally which aspects of politics, economics, law, or religion are *sharʿī* and which are non-*sharʿī*. On An-Naʿim's undifferentiated approach, however, "religion," and the authority of the *fuqahāʾ* who represent it, balloons to omnivorous proportions that can then be domesticated only by overblown appeals to the "secular" or "political" as essentially "protected zones."

Even when religion in the broad, non-coercive sense enters An-Naʿim's "politics," the lack of clarity between the *sharʿī* and non-*sharʿī* can breed fear and suspicion about "*sharīʿah* creep," agitating the impulse on the part of the state to over-police. For, on the blurring of this distinction, Islamists' advocacy, for example, of a ban on gambling casinos (a *sharʿī* commitment) and their advocacy of certain regulations regarding immigration or health-care policy (non-*sharʿī* commitments) may prove indistinguishable from each other, both being treated—and rejected—as religion-as-*sharīʿah* attempting to shape the policies of the state. This is actually what brings such palpable urgency to An-Naʿim's project. And yet, in the absence of a clear "religion-as-*sharīʿah*" versus "religion-as-orientation" distinction (i.e., between the *sharʿī* and the non-*sharʿī*), it also leads to his version of "secular" acquiring the feel of the contemporary Western secular, in its oppositional, hierarchical, and effectively zero-sum relationship to "religion," despite his attempts to distance his project from the Western secular and his Secular State's claims to neutrality.

The Islamic Secular points to a different set of possibilities.

Two Necessary Digressions

An-Naʿim's conceptualization of *sharīʿah* as unbounded and undifferentiated will be the main driver of the conversation between his Secular State and the Islamic

Secular. There are two other issues, however, that appear on the surface to be tangential to that conversation but, in addition to their actual relevance, are so seminal and provocative in their own right that failure to address them would likely constitute a running distraction for the reader.

The Purity of Religiosity

The first is his claim that state implementation of *sharīʿah* spoils the religious piety of Muslims. Following his opening statement, An-Naʿim reiterates in several places the notion that, by the mere threat of coercion, state implementation of religious laws and doctrines undermines religion's authority and ultimately breeds hypocrisy.[21] If religious rules and doctrines are believed to issue from God, compliance with them must be voluntary and performed solely for the purpose of pleasing God; otherwise, An-Naʿim claims, it is not genuine. If the state inserts itself between the believer and God with the threat of sanctions designed to incentivize compliance, this can only contaminate the intention of the complier. Thus, An-Naʿim speaks of "free and honest compliance with Shariʿa" as "the only way to be a Muslim at all."[22] Given that I challenge An-Naʿim's logic and basic solution to what he sees as the threat posed by state implementation of *sharīʿah*, readers will want to know if the Islamic Secular is alive to this problem of contaminating religiosity and, if so, what it offers as a means of avoiding it.

There are three ideas that I would like to register in this regard. The first relates to the presumed logical entailment between the threat of coercion and the negation of religious sincerity. Simply stated, I do not see how an Islamic State's punishment of theft or murder detracts from the religious sincerity of Muslims who avoid these crimes as sins any more than the secular American state's punishment of theft or murder detracts from the religious sincerity of Jews and Christians (or Muslims) who avoid these crimes as sins. The fact that a state punishes murder—and that its citizens know and even fear this earthly punishment—does not prove that these communities avoid murder or theft only or even primarily for that reason; nor does it necessarily replace their religious motivations for avoiding these sins with secular, state-sponsored ones.[23] If, on the other hand, these sins are avoided *only* as crimes, that is, only out of fear of the state's punishment, then there was not likely much religious sincerity to be spoiled in the first place.

The second point has to do with the communitarian ethos that is clearly assumed by the Qurʾān and the Islamic juristic tradition but that An-Naʿim's individualist approach sidesteps entirely. If the Qurʾān speaks not only to individuals but to individual constituents of communities—*yā ayyuhā* ʾlladhīna *āmanū*—then the attempt to fulfill the *collective* duties imparted by scripture can be no less binding or religious and no less reflective of sincere religiosity than the attempts to fulfill *individual* obligations. Friday communal prayer (*ṣalāt al-jumʿah*), for instance, is no less obligatory for the community of individuals than are the five daily prayers for individuals *qua* individuals. The same goes for criminal sanctions or the remedies governing civil disputes, especially when these sanctions and remedies issue directly from God, that is, when the Community is simply imposing what they understand God to have commanded them to impose. An-Naʿim raises the question of how reliable our knowledge of God's commands and preferences can be (a topic I address below). But, assuming a satisfactory answer to this question, the basic point remains: communal commitment to coercing for the right reason, that is, out of a sense of a collective religious duty, should be considered no less a sincere religious act than voluntary, individual compliance. An-Naʿim might protest that communal coercion is still a threat to the religious sincerity of the individual (a point I also return to below). But this is to view the matter from a very particular, if unspoken, ideological perspective. Otherwise, the community of individuals has a duty to be religiously sincere *as a community*, which is what such implementation entails. Stated differently, there is a perspective from which one might ask whether *non-implementation* of *sharīʿah*'s coercive rules (e.g., collecting *zakāh*) or its criminal or civil sanctions reflects dereliction and insincerity and/or breeds religious hypocrisy, even on the level of the individual.

In theory, An-Naʿim acknowledges the importance of collective rights (less so, duties). But he renders these subservient to those of individuals. This is justified, according to him, because "respecting the freedom of opinion, belief, and association of individual persons is the only way in which the collective freedoms of ethnic or religious groups can be protected."[24] He does not tell us why this should be the case or how individuals *qua* individuals can be expected to resist state exercises or abuses of power. In fact, he does not tell us why the opposite should not be the case, that is, why respecting the rights and freedoms of collectives should not be the best way to protect the rights of their constituent members as individuals. Instead—his ceremonial nod to collective rights notwithstanding[25]—An-Naʿim essentially doubles down on the view articulated by another prominent liberal theorist, Martha Nussbaum, according to whom liberalism recognizes only the individual: "The central question of politics should not be, How is the organic whole doing? but, rather, How are X and Y and Z and Q doing?"[26] This view sets the stage for the third and perhaps most important point that I would like to consider in this regard.

In privileging non-coercion as the *sine qua non* of genuine religiosity, An-Naʿim's commitment to individualism, alongside certain presumptions about the nature of religiosity, overwhelms his recognition of Islam-cum-*sharīʿah* as a discipline and a system of law. As a discipline, I have in mind what Ebrahim Moosa and Wael Hallaq insightfully refer to as Islam's "technologies of the self," a tradition of supra-rational practices designed to produce and preserve a particular subjectivity—a set of proper instincts, pre-judgments, and disinclinations. These practices operate not through cognition but through the effects of practical training, a result witnessed with any committed practice, such as basketball practice, football practice, or violin practice. In the same way that such practices rely on what the French philosopher Henri Bergson (d. 1941) describes as mechanical memory, or "memory as habit,"[27] Islam's practices might be seen as relying on and seeking to cultivate "psychodynamic memory." George Clooney captures the logic here in a line from the movie *Three Kings*: "You *do* the thing that scares you shitless first, *then* you get the courage."

My point here is that certain practices are likely to produce certain enduring effects, regardless of their practitioners' sincerity or intentions. Even if one is forced to face a scary situation (as when one's older sibling forces one to stand up to a bully), surviving it is likely to render one a more courageous person.[28] Something similar can be said about Islamic law as practice: observing its dictates breeds or at least contributes to the instantiation of a particular subjectivity, a mode of being in the world, and even the instantiation of virtues, all independent of intention. Coercing people to pay *zakāt*, for example, can have the effect of making them more generous, empathetic, and God-conscious, which may in turn make them more likely to pay *zakāt* voluntarily. Even forced prayer can ignite a spiritual spark, or at least reinforce the normativity of prayer as a value. This is almost certainly what pre-modern jurist-theologians had in mind with their oft-repeated statement, "Faith increases through obedience and decreases through disobedience" (*al-īmān yazīd bi al-ṭā'ah wa yanquṣ bi al-ma'ṣiyah*).

On An-Na'im's approach, however, all possible benefits of compulsory implementation of any Islamic rule are viewed agnostically, if not rejected. In line with the liberal view of heteronomy as archenemy, he sees no positive role at all for coercion, at least not in religion.[29] The only tool that religion can rightfully exercise in his view is moral suasion. And, for him, religiosity, unlike secular civics, is not dialectical, in the sense of informing and being informed by principled regimes of forced compliance; it is a one-way street that runs from moral suasion to pure intention to obedience. On this understanding, the coercion implied by state implementation of *sharī'ah* can only spoil genuine religiosity.

In the real world, of course, as Paul Kahn reminds us, neither individual autonomy nor community is sustainable without order.[30] And in the face of violations of the normative order, we must acknowledge the role of coercion. Similarly, we must recognize *sharī'ah* for what it is beyond its status as a "technology of the self": *inter alia*, a system of applied law. In this capacity, its aim is to promote the practical and material interests (*maṣlaḥah*) behind its rules, regardless of the intentions, sincerity, or piety of the guilty parties or losing litigants, and beyond any positive impact its implementation may or may not have on an individual's religiosity. When a wife sues a husband for non-support (*nafaqah*) or seeks the termination of her marriage on those grounds, the law will determine her legal right to such, and then, if it decides in her favor, compel the husband to pay or divorce her. By paying or divorcing, the husband fulfills the proximate aims of the law, as applied law, regardless of his personal feelings or "religious sincerity."[31] The same applies, *mutatis mutandis*, to criminal sanctions (the issue of expiation notwithstanding): the point is to protect the community from harm and individuals from violations of their rights, above and beyond any impact this may have on making criminals or losers in civil lawsuits better Muslims.

In fairness, I should note that An-Na'im's logic is not entirely alien to the Islamic juristic tradition. Al-Qarāfī, for example, insists that, as a general principle, government intervention should be restricted to *mu'āmalāt*, or, civil transactions and criminal sanctions. He bars the state from intervening in "religious observances and the like," *'ibādāt wa naḥwuhā*, where, for example, it might seek to dictate where one places one's hands in the standing position of prayer. His argument is that the sole purpose of the *ibādāt* is to extol and worship God, which cannot be realized in the absence of the worshipper's proper intention (*nīyah*). And since the state is powerless to secure this intention, its intervention is superfluous.[32] Such a claim is not quite the same, however, as the claim An-Na'im is making, which is that government implementation spoils religion *tout court*. Where he and al-Qarāfī part ways is in the distinction noted earlier between the primary interests of the *mu'āmalāt* and those of the *'ibādāt*.[33] While intention is ultimately germane to both, *mu'āmalāt* also entail worldly interests that can be realized, even in the absence of a proper intention. Thus, even if we bar the government from intervening in the area of the *'ibādāt*, the same logic would *not* be consistent with the full aims of the *mu'āmalāt*. Separating *sharī'ah* from the state, in the sense of barring it from implementing the *mu'āmalāt*, would leave all the interests connected with the *mu'āmalāt* to be realized through voluntary compliance, leaving plaintiffs, victims, and society at large at the mercy of the piety of their legal adversaries, victimizers, and society's libertines. Meanwhile, *sharī'ah* itself as an applied order would atrophy significantly over time, as *mu'āmalāt* constitute the bulk of its rules.

An-Na'im views *sharī'ah*, however, entirely from the perspective of the (liberal) individual, whose inalienable freedom to choose underwrites An-Na'im's emphasis on moral suasion as the only legitimate card for religion to play. Again, however, beyond the world of interpersonal relationships, real and genuine threats to normative collective orders actually exist. And one need not be a radicalized Muslim 'Fundamentalist' to recognize that it is often necessary to raise power against such forces. As the celebrated Christian theologian Reinhold Niebuhr (d. 1971) reminds us, there are elements of our collective being "which belong to the order of nature and can never be brought completely under the dominion of reason or conscience."[34] People will not always cease to be dishonest or violent or predatory or lazy simply because their misdeeds are made known to them. It will often be necessary to *compel* them to right conduct.[35] The question, then—given both the right An-Naʿim grants to the Secular State to coerce and his appeal to a secularism that quarantines religion-as-*sharīʿah* from the state—is how a Muslim state's salutary power to compel citizens' behavior can be made ethical, moral, and righteous, indeed Islamic, if Islam and its practices are to be barred from attachment to the state. Who is to discipline the Muslim state, and on what basis? To whom should it answer, and by what mechanisms of accountability should it be guided? So far, the record suggests that secularism alone (i.e., separating *sharīʿah* from the state) offers few assurances as *sharīʿah*'s replacement.

But there is more to the problem of coercion than a strict focus on An-Naʿim's argument may allow us to see. By coercion, he is clearly referring to physical force. And by distancing his secularism from this form of coercion and aligning it with moral suasion, he gives the impression that the society he calls for is one that would be free of coercion, *tout court*. But, as Niebuhr reminds us, this kind of moralism merely conceals without eradicating the numerous forms of coercion enshrined by the status quo. It blinds and numbs us to the fact that "the coercive elements are covert, because the dominant groups are able to avail themselves of the use of economic power, propaganda, the traditional processes of government, and other types of non-violent power."[36] In the Muslim world, Islamist proponents of an Islamic State are far more likely to be on the receiving end of such coercive instruments (not to mention the more direct physical variety). But, as Niebuhr continues, "By failing to recognise the real character of these forms of coercion, the moralist places an unjustified onus upon advancing groups which use violent methods to disturb a peace maintained by subtler types of coercion."[37] My point here is not to take sides in these tragic contests but merely to suggest that, if Niebuhr is right about the ubiquity of non-violent modes of coercion (and readers might recall my discussion of Berger and Bernays from Chapter 3), then it may be a mistake to follow An-Naʿim in his insinuation that our choice is ultimately between an Islamic State that is coercive and a Secular State that is not.

This is not to deny the very real problem of Muslim states abusing and misapplying *sharīʿah*. Such abuse is especially problematic given the religious cynicism and hypocrisy that many of the men and women of power in the Muslim world display. Added to this is the post-colonial spirit of *ressentiment* that has gripped so many Muslims, especially radical proponents of the Islamic State, for whom gratuitous harshness, or *shiddah*, has morphed into an Islamic virtue.[38] But, while all of this may inform the actual experience of Muslims (and non-Muslims), it is also historically contingent and not a necessary feature of *sharīʿah* itself. Even when this *shiddah* extends beyond law to theology, providing political operatives, autocrats, and even well-meaning religious zealots with convenient means of shutting down dissent or bludgeoning adversaries into submission, it is still not an inherent dictate of state-sponsored implementation of *sharīʿah*. After all, none other than the "puritanical," "obstreperous" *sharīʿah*-maximalist Ibn Taymīyah (who knew a little about being targeted for his religious beliefs, having died in prison for them, but who would never advocate separating *sharīʿah* from the state) affirmed openly the distinction between a state's implementing rules in the name of *sharīʿah* and *sharīʿah* itself: "There are those who think that the *sharʿ* is simply an expression of whatever ruling a judge hands down. These people do not even distinguish between a learned, just judge and an ignorant, corrupt one. Instead, whatever a judge hands down they call '*sharīʿah*.'"[39]

Again, the problems that An-Naʿim raises are real for many Muslim (and non-Muslim) individuals and communities across the Muslim world, and these should be taken seriously. Ultimately, however, the question comes down to whether they result from the state's application of *sharīʿah* or from its *mis*application, including the conflation between *sharʿī* and non-*sharʿī* bases of authority, by which, for example, the substance of a particular economic, educational, foreign or health-care policy or a public ordinance can be proclaimed not only legally but also morally and religiously unassailable and binding on the Muslim conscience, as an expression of *sharīʿah*. To the extent that this kind of misapplication is the actual problem, An-Naʿim's proposed solution of the wholesale removal of *sharīʿah* from the state might be tantamount to wheeling in a canon to kill a fly. Even more important, if the preservation of religious sincerity is the primary concern, it is not at all clear, given all that has been said, how secularism—separating *sharīʿah* from the state—serves that interest.

Human Rights

The second ostensibly tangential issue relates to human rights (and, to a lesser extent, constitutionalism and citizenship, about which I will say more below). Human rights are part of the paraphernalia of late modernity, through which the West often signals its superiority over—and incompatibility with—Islam. As Michael Ignatieff notes in his book on the subject, "The challenge of Islam has been there from the beginning."[40] An-Naʿim, is careful to note, however, that in his view, "Shariʿa principles are basically consistent with most human rights norms, with the exception of some specific and very serious aspects of the rights of women and non-Muslims and the freedom of religion and belief."[41] In the face of these exceptions, he advocates that "we as Muslims consider transforming our understanding of Shariʿa."[42] He suggests that the final product of this transformed understanding be a negotiated construct somewhere between Islam-cum-*sharīʿah* as traditionally construed and universal human rights. In other words, he advocates a sincerely negotiated compromise and the avoidance of zero-sum retrenchment on either side.

There are two issues to be considered here. First, An-Naʿim's approach appears at times to reflect what Ignatieff calls "human-rights idolatry."[43] By "idolatry," Ignatieff means the tendency to worship certain features of an imagined human-rights scheme (formal equality or certain philosophical underpinnings, such as abstract universalism) while ignoring or excluding the potential contributions of those who refuse to bow to these features, rather than considering the ways in which native traditions might practically and meaningfully contribute to the lives and interests of the people whom human rights are supposed to serve. For example, al-Qarāfī's (and others') equating of the "rights of God" (*ḥuqūq Allāh*) with the sanctity and inviolability of the public space—including the right of Muslims *and* non-Muslims to be safe and secure from murder, dispossession, and the like—has clear human-rights implications, even if the substance, source, and philosophical underpinnings of these implications differ from those of the West.[44] Meanwhile, though Islam never committed to formal equality[45] between men and women (or Muslims and non-Muslims), it has spared Muslim women several indignities that American women suffered from the time of the country's founding, some of these well into the early decades of the twentieth century, for example, the denial of their right to sign contracts independent of their husbands or to claim their earnings or their children in cases of separation.[46]

The point here is not to make a zero-sum comparison between Islam and the West nor to deny the various challenges that Muslim women continue to face, including the pervasiveness of the male interpretive gaze and the seeming ubiquity of the male voice. But I see no justification for refusing to recognize the agency, equality, and even advantages Muslim women do enjoy, in the name of an absolute formal equality that is assumed but has never been proved to serve them better. If the human-rights interests of Muslim women are the real aim, how will these be served and how will their implementation prove any less coercive if they ultimately deny Muslim women their own story and insist on assigning them a supporting role in that of the modern West?

Second, in her influential article "What Are Human Rights? Four Schools of Thought," Marie-Bénédicte Dembour identifies four loosely constituted approaches to human rights: (1) the Natural School, (2) the Deliberative School, (3) the Protest School, and (4) the Discourse School.[47] While An-Naʿim clearly subscribes to the Natural School (with its claims and appeals to universality), I do not see why Islam should be limited to this school as its sole interlocutor. The Discourse School, for example, sees the Natural School's universalism as approaching belief in witches and unicorns. This is not to mention such articulations of human rights as those we find in the Eastern Orthodox Church, where such values as autonomy and individualism are conceived of not as absolutes but as values that must be negotiated, in status and substance, with both community (*Ekklisia*) and virtue.[48] In short, there is a case to be made that the conversation between Islam-cum-*sharīʿah* and human rights should be richer and broader than An-Naʿim seems to recognize.[49]

Third, and perhaps most important for our purposes, the juxtaposition of human rights to *sharīʿah* implies that it is an entirely *sharʿī* enterprise. This may be why so many Muslims reflexively balk at the notion. For them (and for An-Naʿim), human rights can only be Islamically authentic if they can be traced back to concrete indicants from Islamic scripture. Of course, on this logic, countless features of pre-modern Muslim civilization—from *madhhab*s to *madrasah*s to algebra—would be subject to dismissal. More directly, documents such as the Universal Islamic Declaration of Human Rights (1981), the Cairo Declaration on Human Rights in Islam (1990), or the more recent declaration of the Organization of Islamic Cooperation (OIC 2020) show that determining the substance and implications of human rights in Islam includes palpably non-*sharʿī*, Islamic Secular deliberations alongside *sharʿī* ones.[50] It is thus misleading to juxtapose human rights with *sharīʿah*, as if to suggest that only through *ijtihād sharʿī*, whose conclusions are drawn from scripture and juristic precedent, can Muslims arrive at an Islamically authentic commitment to human rights.

I do not mean to imply that by simply shifting the discussion from *sharīʿah* to the Islamic Secular one can efface all the problems that An-Naʿim sees in the relationship between Islam and human rights. But, as I argue below, many of the problems he raises regarding Islamic rules and policies associated with human rights, such as various forms of gender discrimination (e.g., unequal access to public forums or education), are (or may be) non-*sharʿī* and discretionary in nature. Moreover, if the Deliberative and Discourse Schools of human rights can challenge aspects of the Natural School's substantive commitments without being seen as turning away from human rights, a similar consideration should be extended to Islam. Something similar might be said regarding constitutionalism and citizenship. All in all, even beyond a fair consideration of what the Islamic Secular might contribute to these deliberations, the idea that the *only* effective means of accommodating human rights, constitutionalism, and citizenship is to separate *sharīʿah* from the state seems overstated if not misplaced.

The Naʿimian Secular State: Substantive Details

Having laid out my basic aims and addressed the likely distractions of religious sincerity and human rights, I now proceed to my detailed engagement with An-Naʿim's Secular State. I begin by noting that, as was the case with Hallaq, An-Naʿim is less categorical in his basic judgments than may appear at first blush. According to him, if properly understood or re-interpreted, *sharīʿah* could (with the exception of the *dhimmah* system, which must be abolished[51]) accommodate constitutionalism, human rights, and citizenship.[52] Because Muslims remain far from producing or accepting such re-articulations, however, this theoretical possibility does not diminish his preference for a Secular State. Or, perhaps, certain problematic rules of *sharīʿah* are seen as simply too firmly grounded in authoritative *sharīʿah* sources and precedents to be interpreted away.

An-Naʿim wants not only to propose his Secular State but to vindicate its adoption as the Islamic *norm*. He argues that Islamic law not only mandates the separation of *sharīʿah* from the state but that such separation is "*required by*—not merely tolerated or accepted by—Islam and Sharia."[53] Ultimately, An-Naʿim sees his proposal for a Secular State, as he defines it, as "more consistent with Islamic history than the so-called Islamic State model proposed by some Muslims."[54] He claims that "the states under which Muslims lived in the past were never religious."[55] Even when they aspired to be religious, their efforts inexorably resulted in a secular order. This is the reality that he calls on contemporary Muslims to recognize, resuscitate, and re-operationalize.

The Alchemy of the Secular

I will return to the question of the historical record below. For now, there is more to be said about the meaning of An-Naʿim's substantive claim that pre-modern Muslim states were "non-religious." As he puts it, "I am not claiming that the historical states of Islamic society were in fact secular states as defined in this book. Still, a clear understanding of at least the *non-religious* state should help to dispel the apprehensions among Muslims that the secular state is a Western imposition."[56] The difference he refers to between the modern "secular" state and the pre-modern "non-religious" state seems to be that, whereas the former mandates separation as a matter of principle, the latter entails separation by default, ultimately, because it must.

To explain why this is so, An-Naʿim introduces a rather sophistical argument grounded in the problem of epistemology. According to him, humans can never fully and objectively know the contents of the divine mind. For this reason, their interpretations of revelation can never claim definitively to represent divine truth or intent—a deficit, according to him, that not even unanimous consensus (*ijmāʿ*) is able to offset.[57] Accordingly, any move to invoke a particular interpretation as the basis of an applied *sharīʿah* order will be "political" rather than "religious."[58] For, it will entail an executive decision to choose among numerous legitimate possibilities, not a simple, direct transfer from the divine mind onto the socio-political plane. In other words, this choice will be made by humans (the state), not by God, and this renders the resulting order "political"—indeed, secular—rather than "religious."[59] This is partly what An-Na'im has in mind when he insists that "the state is a political entity that cannot be Islamic."[60]

An-Na'im appears to give little thought as to why this legal agnosticism should not connote an equally intractable religious agnosticism, if not atheism. How can we believe in God while not fully and objectively knowing God's essence, if we cannot believe that *X* is God's will unless we fully and objectively know God's mind?[61] Be that as it may, on An-Na'im's understanding, even if pre-modern Muslim states had applied *sharīʿah*, they would not have been religious. They could only have been "political" and "non-religious" because what they applied could not in any objectively knowable way be the law of God. Ultimately, this claim is designed to reinforce the argument that An-Na'im's Secular State, as an Islamic State that does not apply religious law, is *not* a modern Western invention but has precedence in Islam. As for the modern Islamic State, which purports both to be religious and to apply the law of God, An-Na'im argues that it has no such precedence and is in fact an aberration, a "contradiction in terms," albeit for reasons different from those adduced by Hallaq.

An-Na'im's epistemological argument is not new. Others have invoked it, principally for the same reason: to escape what is perceived to be the oppressive finality implied by state claims in the name of *sharīʿah*. We see it, for example, in Khaled Abou El Fadl's critique of the assumption that "human agents could possibly have perfect and unfettered access to the will of God and . . . that human beings could possibly become the mere executors of the Divine will, without inserting their own human subjectivities in the process."[62] Inattentiveness to this reality, he admonishes, can lead to and mask the exploitation of God's sovereignty and the marginalization of the majority of a population's right to regulate their own affairs.[63] In the hands of the state, "Shari'ah enables human beings to speak in God's name, and it effectively empowers human agency with the voice of God."[64] This, he claims, bolsters the argument that "secularism is necessary to avoid the hegemony and abuse of those who pretend to speak for God."[65] Ultimately, the learned Professor Abou El Fadl reaches a conclusion that is substantively indistinguishable from the one later articulated by An-Na'im:

> If a legal opinion is adopted and enforced by the State, it cannot be said to be God's law. By passing through the determinative and enforcement processes of the State, the legal opinion is no longer simply a potential: it has become an actual law, applied and enforced. However, the law applied and enforced is not God's law; instead, it is the State's law. Effectively, a religious State law is a contradiction in terms. Either the law belongs to the State or it belongs to God, and as long as the law relies on the subjective agency of the State for its articulation and enforcement, any law enforced by the State is necessarily not God's law. Otherwise, we must be willing to admit that the failure of the law of the State

is, in fact, the failure of God's law and, ultimately, God Himself. In Islamic theology, this possibility cannot be entertained.[66]

I shall ignore, in the interest of maintaining my primary focus, the full implications of the zero-sum conflict presumed here between God and humans. I will note, however, that if religiosity is contingent upon epistemological certainty and direct access to the divine mind, then not only the state but no one can be religious. For, the mandates to pray, fast, or eschew gossip cannot, on this understanding, be said with certainty to issue from God; they can only be the result of what humans impute to God. Closer to the matter at hand, both An-Na'im and Abou El Fadl depict *sharī'ah* as a simple, undifferentiated construct that is *shar'ī* through and through, with no distinction between the *shar'ī* and the non-*shar'ī*. This reinforces the ambiguity I referred to earlier between "*sharī'ah*" and "religion," effectively collapsing the two into synonyms. On this collapsing, "secular" assumes its meaning not only in contrast to *sharī'ah* (as that which must be removed from the state) but in contrast to *sharī'ah* and religion interchangeably. Because, in other words, *sharī'ah* is both substantively undifferentiated *and* coterminous with religion, any need to move away from *sharī'ah* entails a parallel move away from "religion," ultimately becoming an expression of the kind of secularism that An-Na'im theoretically disavows. By contrast, from the perspective of the Islamic Secular, one could move away from the *shar'ī* dimensions of Islam-cum-*sharī'ah*, while embracing its differentiated, non-*shar'ī*, 'secular' dimensions, without having to move away from religion per se nor necessarily removing *sharī'ah* from the state.

An-Na'im might object that such an understanding is based on a failure to appreciate the distinction he draws (or at least intimates) between religion-as-*sharī'ah* in the context of religion's relationship to the state, and religion-as-*sharī'ah* in the context of religion's relationship to society (i.e., via his "politics"). For, on this distinction, while moving away from *sharī'ah* in its attachment to the state may entail a move away from religion (as the state cannot be religious), there is no parallel need to move away from religion, even religion-as-*sharī'ah*, in relation to society; for both religion and *sharī'ah* function non-coercively in society, and society *can* be religious. This distinction, however, central as it may be to An-Na'im's argument, breaks down at critical junctures, often leaving religion-as-*sharī'ah* as vulnerable and circumscribed in its relationship to society as it is in its relationship with the state. For example, when An-Na'im speaks of the state's right and duty to "regulate" religion in the public space, with an eye to curbing the spread of problematic ideas enshrined by *sharī'ah*, such as *qiwāmah*, *jihād*, or *dhimmah*, given their possible influence on the general attitude toward women and non-Muslims, religion-as-*sharī'ah* ends up the target of restriction even in this plainly non-coercive relationship to society.[67]

This is further reflected in An-Na'im's disallowing the state to apply certain *sharī'ah*-rules even as the product of popular will. According to him, when religion-as-*sharī'ah* enters the public arena, even non-coercively, and its effects percolate up to the state, resulting in a voluntary collective will to apply *sharī'ah* rules as state law, "That cannot be accepted as sufficient reason for their enforcement by the state, because they would then apply to citizens who may not share that belief."[68] This poses an obvious challenge to the integrity of the democratic process. And in recognition of this, An-Na'im later equivocates, speaking of the possibility of "some" *sharī'ah* principles being democratically adopted as public policy or legislation, while others may not, clearly implying that "politics" may not always be allowed to run its course if it is too directly informed by *sharī'ah*.[69] In the end, the distinction between *sharī'ah* as a coercive instrument in the hands of the state and *sharī'ah* as a non-coercive instrument operating at the level of society simply does not hold up. Both may be targeted for restriction. And this raises questions about how much protection An-Na'im's secularism provides religion, even as a non-coercive participant in his "politics" at the level of society.

Part of my argument is that An-Na'im targets religion-as-*sharī'ah* more than is required by the interests he wishes to serve. The various non-*shar'ī* dimensions of *sharī'ah*—for example, what constitutes a "house" or "safe-keeping measures" (*ḥirz*) (in the legal definition of theft), or the meaning of "*qiwāmah*" in any given socio-cultural context—are more amenable to negotiation via his "civic reason" than he seems to recognize, whether these issues are contemplated in relation to the state or to society. By reducing *sharī'ah*, however—indeed Islamic law—to an undifferentiated, *shar'ī* "black box," An-Na'im forecloses possibilities for negotiating what would otherwise remain open to negotiation, as his Secular State, in contrast to the Islamic Secular, leaves no ground or medium for communicating across the religious/secular divide. This in turn opens avenues to his Secular State to step in and arbitrate, in a manner that purports (as it must) to be neutral, even as it displays a higher degree of vigilance toward views that are grounded in "religion," and certainly "religion-as-*sharī'ah*," than it does toward views that are purportedly "secular."

History

The epistemological argument is only half of An-Na'im's justification for his claim that the Secular State is the normative political arrangement in Islam. The other half, as I mentioned, is historical. Here, however, he goes against the established consensus of leading scholars of Islamic law and legal history. Hallaq, as we have seen, held not only that *sharī'ah* was the applied law in pre-modern Islam but also that it was unrivaled in its status as such. Before him, Schacht had written, "[T]he institutions concerning the *statut personnel* (i.e., marriage, divorce, and family relationships), inheritance and *wakf*, have always been, in the general conscience of the Muslims, more closely connected with religion than other legal matters, and therefore ruled by Islamic law."[70] Gibb, as we have seen, insisted that "The State exists for the sole purpose of maintaining and enforcing the Law."[71] And Intisar Rabb partly echoes this: "The foundational texts required the ruling authorities to enforce criminal laws. . . ."[72] Even proponents of the dystopian narrative (e.g., Colin Imber) acknowledge that Islamic law had a practical existence "of about 1000 years, from its obscure beginnings in the late eighth and early ninth centuries until its near demise in the face of modernism in the late nineteenth."[73] I am not aware of any specialist in Islamic law or legal history who agrees with An-Na'im that Islamic law was never applied by Muslim states and that compliance with *sharī'ah* was always strictly voluntary.

Nor does the concrete historical record appear to agree with An-Na'im. For example, the nucleus of my book *Islamic Law and the State* (which An-Na'im curiously ignores) was a controversy involving the application of *sharī'ah*.[74] As pre-modern Muslim historians tell it, the Chief Justice of Mamlūk Cairo was a stern individual who habitually refused to sign off on "lower court" rulings that did not reflect his stern views, leaving many judgements unenforced. This led to general complaints about the judiciary. On one occasion, the orphaned daughters of an *amīr* presented a case in which they claimed that they had purchased a mansion from the previous chief justice. When he died, his heirs claimed that their father had bequeathed the property to them as a charitable trust (*waqf*). At court on that particular day was a another senior *amīr* who, upon hearing the daughters' claim, launched into an attack on the judges. The Sultan, who was also present, proceeded to question the Chief Justice:

—*Qāḍī*, is this how the *qāḍīs* are?
Your highness, there are complications in everything.
—What is the situation here?
If the *waqf* is confirmed, the heirs reimburse the buyers.
—And if the heirs have nothing?
The *waqf* is confirmed, and the buyers receive nothing.[75]

At this, other parties came forth with complaints about the Chief Justice's sternness in handling their cases. Appalled at what he heard, the senior *amīr* exclaimed in disgust, "O *Qāḍī*, you may have your Shāfi'ī *madhhab*; we shall appoint a *qāḍī* from each of the schools of law!"[76] Sulṭān Baybars went on to appoint chief justices from each of the four Sunni schools to preside over the legal system of Cairo. Obviously, he would not have gone to such trouble for a legal system that was never applied.

An-Na'im might respond that, as interesting as all of this may be, it misses his fundamental point, namely, that, even if the law *was* applied, it was not "religious" and the state was not "Islamic" because, on his epistemological criterion, the law could not have been God's law and the state could not have been religious/Islamic. There are two responses here. First, An-Na'im anachronistically superimposes a modern argument onto pre-modern Muslim jurists that they would hardly have recognized. The Mamlūk state's application of the law could not have been religious for them because it is not religious for him; and it is not religious for him because its interpretation is not epistemologically certain. But this presupposes a necessary link between religiosity and rational certainty, as if the latter were a prerequisite for the former. While An-Na'im may not intend to make the connection, this is one of the ways in which modernity, particularly modern science, has signaled its superiority over religion, pressuring the latter to seek vindication in ever more sophisticated and desperate claims to rational certainty.

But this absolute requirement of certainty—and this is my second point—was simply not the posture assumed by pre-modern Muslim jurists. While they clearly upheld a valued and zealously guarded nucleus of certainties—*qaṭʿīyāt* (apodictic doctrines), *mujmaʿ ʿalayh* (doctrines backed by unanimous consensus), and *al-maʿlūm min al-dīn bi al-ḍarūrah* (doctrines that every Muslim knows as a simple matter of course)—and while certainty itself was valued in its own right, Muslim jurists were not epistemological Cartesians but were perfectly at home with the bulk of the religious law being grounded in simple reasonableness, as *ẓannīyāt*. To their minds, this did not detract from the status of the law as "religious law" or, indeed, as explicitly "God's law." If An-Na'im requires rational certainty as a prerequisite for considering rules deduced from scripture to be religious, he is free to do so. But I see no justification for superimposing that criterion onto pre-modern Muslim jurists and state officials who would not even have recognized, let alone agreed with, such an approach.[77]

The Wages of Rational Certainty: *Khilāf, Sui Juris*, and "Decreed by God"

It turns out, however, that rational certainty is a double-edged sword. On the one hand, according to An-Na'im's epistemological criterion, such certainty is essential to the law's constitution as "religious" and a true and reliable representation of divine intent. On the other hand, the very specter of certainty is what makes religious law so dangerous, since there can be no appeal from what has been certainly "decreed by God." This is among the reasons that An-Na'im prefers his Secular State to an Islamic State. The law of the Secular State is legitimated not by reference to its certainty or transcendence but by virtue of its being the product of non-discriminatory, democratic processes that are mediated through civic reason. On this nature and provenance, secular rules are more accommodating of dissent, and secular authority is far less onerous, final, and threatening to individuality and pluralism. To challenge secular rules is not to challenge the authority of God; nor are secular rules susceptible to the common assumption among followers of monotheistic religions that, just as God is one, so must be the correct understanding of God's will, all deviations from this single derivation being wrong and deserving of scorn, if not worse. For all these reasons, the psychological, emotional, and even physical cost of criticizing secular rules is far more bearable than that of criticizing religious rules, especially in public. In essence, An-Na'im sees the public invocation of religious law as a conversation-stopper. As he puts it, "[O]nce a principle or norm is officially identified as 'decreed by God,' it is extremely difficult for believers [not to mention unbelievers] to resist or change its application in practice."[78]

An-Na'im is right to point out the disturbingly harmful effects to which religious language and authority can be—and often is—put. This is especially the case given the modern Muslim tendency to overlook the law/fact and *shar'ī*/non-*shar'ī* distinctions, thereby sublating the presuppositions of the socio-political past into the realm of transcendent religion, where they take on an unwarranted authority, permanence, and unassailability that shackle modern Muslim/non-Muslim or gender relations, for example, to the fears, presumptions, and experiences of the pre-modern Muslim past.[79] The question, however, is whether this kind of conflation and the negative consequences it spawns is a necessary entailment of *sharī'ah*. If attaching *sharī'ah* and the religious phrase, "decreed by God," to the state necessarily reduces the possibilities of dissent and pluralism, such that these effects could be reversed only by detaching *sharī'ah* from the state, one would expect to find at least some indication of this problem among pre-modern Muslim jurists (and non-jurists), especially those affiliated with minority schools in various contexts. But this is generally not what we find. Rather, pre-modern jurists viewed the connection between *sharī'ah*, its language (including "God's law"), and the state as an unproblematic given, just as they viewed juristic disagreement and pluralism as natural and inevitable.

Citing Hallaq, An-Na'im acknowledges "the wide range of schools of jurisprudence and the strong disagreements among Islamic scholars on almost every conceivable subject."[80] But he ignores the fact that Muslim jurists explicitly theorized on questions of dissent and pluralism and on how to integrate all of this into a functioning legal order. Al-Qarāfī is a shining example of such theorizing. What is important in his thinking is that he is committed not simply to a broad, abstract ecumenicism but to the active protection of minority views that resist both forced induction into unanimous consensus (*ijmā'*) and being denied recognition as authoritative in real space and time. When all the schools agree on a doctrine, the latter is protected as an unassailable constituent of *ijmāʿ*. But al-Qarāfī wanted to emphasize in more concrete terms that disputed views that are not backed by unanimous consensus are *equally* protected, and neither the state nor the religious establishment can force a minority school or its members[81] to acquiesce to the majority.

In fact, in his effort to fortify this position, al-Qarāfī arrived at the counter-intuitive conclusion that disputed views (*mukhtalaf fīh*) are actually *more* inviolable than views backed by unanimous consensus (*mujmaʿ ʿalayh*). As he put it, "How strange it is that a judicial ruling involving a disputed (*mukhtalaf fīh*) question of law becomes stronger than one involving a legal question on which there is unanimous consensus."[82] His explanation was that, whereas a rule backed by unanimous consensus is protected only by unanimous consensus, a disputed rule is protected both by the unanimous consensus that holds all of the schools to be equally authoritative *and* the juristic principle that specific (*khāṣṣ*) indicants (in this case, those backing the view of the presiding judge and his school) take precedence over general (*ʿāmm*) indicants (the broader reservoir backing the views of the remaining schools). This is a standard feature of the basic concept and principle of *khilāf*, or principled disagreement. And even stalwarts such as Ibn Taymīyah insisted that the condemnation of opposing views should be generally reserved for those that are devoid of proof while violating unanimous consensus, not issues on which there is plausible, standing disagreement among the schools.[83] In fact, he writes, even if a view goes against those of the four Imāms, while grounding itself in a plausible interpretation of the Qur'ān, Sunna, and their spirit, it should be allowed to stand.[84] We need not delve into the intricacies of these doctrines or even assess their persuasiveness. What is important is the *value* clearly attached to dissent, minoritarian, or disputed views and their protection. We could easily cite other jurists who confirm this basic stance.[85]

In the case of al-Qarāfī, this position is reinforced by his formal recognition of what I refer to elsewhere as "*sui juris*," a Latin term that goes back to Roman times and means "of one's own right," which in Islam's case must be expanded to include "duties." The basic idea behind my use of *sui juris* is that the fundamental relationship between the individual Muslim and God is direct. For this reason, each individual is authorized or obligated to act upon the occurrence of the relevant legal causes (*asbāb*/sg. *sabab*) identified in the law.[86] While the relationship between the individual and God may be direct, the understanding of God's will is mediated through a corporate negotiation of the meaning of scripture, not dissimilar to Americans' reliance on the Supreme Court and its precedents for their understanding of their individually exercised Constitutional rights.

Al-Qarāfī does not hesitate, however, to qualify the relationship between the individual and God by removing some actions from the jurisdiction of individuals and placing them exclusively within the jurisdiction of the state (e.g., the punishment of criminals). On the other hand, while he believes in a strong state that is capable of overseeing the material interests and security of the Community, state intervention is for him the exception rather than the rule. As he put it, "There are three reasons that give rise to the need for judges or government officials (*wulāt al-umūr*). And whenever these reasons do not obtain, rules follow their respective legal causes, whether a judge [or government official] rules to this effect or not."[87] This is because, according to him, in his capacity as communicator on behalf of God, the Prophet spoke primarily neither *to* nor *as* the state but ultimately as Messenger to each individual member of the Muslim Community.[88] Thus, al-Qarāfī concludes:

> We are bound to follow every rule the Prophet conveyed to us from his Lord upon the occurrence of its legal cause, with no consideration of any ruling to be handed down by a judge and no authorization to be granted by any Imām. For, the Prophet simply conveyed to us the connection between these rules and their respective legal causes. Then he left the matter between humanity and their Lord.[89]

Again, we need not venture down a theoretical rabbit hole here. It is clear, however, that al-Qarāfī does not perceive *sharīʿah* as the all-encompassing, monopolized preserve of the Muslim state (and by extension the Islamic State), such that the only rights one enjoys are those that are generated unilaterally by the state. More importantly, even the application of *sharīʿah*'s rules is mediated, in al-Qarāfī's perception, through non-*sharʿī* deliberations. The reasons he contemplates for state intervention are not unilaterally dictated by *sharʿī* sources but are significantly informed by practical considerations. These include, according to al-Qarāfī: (1) the need that may arise for expert testimony to determine the actual occurrence of a legal cause (e.g., a husband's insolvency); (2) order and the containment of violence (e.g., in applying criminal sanctions); and (3) averting intractable legal disputes (e.g., whether an action falls under the rights of God or under the rights of humans).[90] The fundamental objective in all of this is clear, namely, to secure what the legal scholar Alan Watson identifies as the basic aim of *all* legal systems: order.[91] Ultimately, al-Qarāfī is thinking here practically, albeit in a spirit of obeisance, about how this basic objective might be best served. He is engaged, in other words, in primarily Islamic Secular deliberation, not strictly *sharʿī* deduction, the possibility that his conclusions may be ultimately sublimated into *sharʿī* doctrine (*fiqh*) notwithstanding.[92]

If al-Qarāfī and other pre-modern jurists could think practically about such issues without having to contemplate removing *sharīʿah* from the state apparatus, surely this possibility (if not duty) should extend to modern Muslims. It should also inform our perceptions of the normative relationship between the government and the governed in Islam. Neither the state nor the jurists can claim a monopoly on practical reasoning; nor does Islam as *dīn* categorically contradict such reasoning. In fact, among the starting points for a modern "Islamic Political Theory" might be a practical engagement with the principle of *sui juris*, by which the Community rationally contemplates how much individual (or sub-state group) autonomy must be forfeited to the state in order for the state to be able to function effectively and secure the Community's overall interests.[93] Meanwhile, al-Qarāfī's manner of proceeding clearly alters the conversation about whether the mere fact of *sharīʿah*'s attachment to the state undermines individual rights, pluralism, and the possibility of legitimate dissent. In fact, it directly calls into question the assumption that state implementation of *sharīʿah* summarily excludes non-*sharʿī*, differentiated, Islamic Secular deliberations from the process of determining the substance and parameters of such rights, pluralism, and dissent. One wonders how such an understanding might qualify An-Naʿim's declaration: "I need a secular state."

As for the phrase, "decreed by God," we might reconsider the oppressive finality that An-Naʿim imputes to it in light of what pre-modern jurists who used it actually meant by it. Al-Qarāfī uses "*ḥukm Allāh*," that is, "God's ruling," to refer to rulings handed down by judges, in which capacity other judges or jurists may not challenge them.[94] His purpose, however, is to preserve the integrity of the legal process *qua* legal process, not to confer infallibility upon a judge's view as "God's ruling." Nothing would prevent this same judge, upon further reflection, from issuing a different or opposite ruling in an identical subsequent case. And even his ruling in *this* case would not bar other jurists from debating and issuing *fatwā*s on the general topic—as opposed to the particular case under review. We find similarly explicit language regarding "God's ruling" in al-Ghazālī, as mentioned earlier.[95] Indeed, the sentiment is ubiquitous in Islamic legal literature. Yet, as a rule, Muslim jurists did not impute any substantive infallibility to views so described, such that other *mujtahid*s or even lay persons were barred from questioning or dissenting from them. In sum, attaching this kind of religious language to the state in the name of *sharīʿah* need not generate the liabilities feared by An-Naʿim. Meanwhile, An-Naʿim's sense that religion is a conversation-stopper assumes that religion is somehow unique in this regard—that reason, science, or political authority are not intended to play a similar role. In fact, however, the whole point of authority—any authority—resides in its ability, at least provisionally, to stop conversation! It seems to be uniquely religion, however, in An-Naʿim's view, that poses a *sui generis* danger in this regard.

An-Na'im might respond that the foregoing arguments are fine, as long as they are limited to the *fuqahā'* and the socio-political elite. In other words, even if the self-serving deployment of phrases like "decreed by God" does not paralyze this demographic, one cannot assume that they will not have a paralyzing effect on everyday Muslims. It is well known that Muslim "Fundamentalists," for example, routinely deploy this kind of language as a silencing mechanism against the masses and anyone who disagrees with them. But there are three brief points to make here. First, even within a single school, unanimous consensus is the exception rather than the rule. Assuming that the laity is not limited in its access to the *fuqahā'* as a whole, something of the indeterminacy of the law must reach them and inform the basic culture through which they process it. The issue, in other words, comes down not to *sharīʿah* but to the kind of civics developed and generally taught, a substantial element of which would necessarily draw on Islamic Secular considerations. Second, and relatedly, much of this language's power as a silencing mechanism reverts to a general lack of religious literacy, including a basic unfamiliarity with *khilāf*, *sui juris*, the *sharʿī*/non-*sharʿī* divide, the law/fact distinction, and the like. Muslim society today should be far more capable of disseminating such literacy than it was five hundred years ago. And if it does not, we might ask *why* it does not. The reasons behind such a failure could hardly be primarily *sharʿī* in nature. Finally, individual rights, pluralism, and dissent might actually be bolstered by an explicitly *sharʿī* claim that *sui juris*, for example, is "decreed by God." Given these considerations, it becomes far less obvious that the optimal solution to the problem of religious language is simply to remove *sharīʿah* from the state apparatus.

In the end, as suggested earlier, the root of the problem may be that An-Na'im has effectively reduced Islam to religion, "*in the proper, the religious sense*." To the extent that Islam-as-religion is no more than its *sharʿīyāt*, with no recognition of the process by which the latter are instantiated, including the distinction between *sharʿī* and non-*sharʿī* values, interests, and pursuits, questions of *mashrūʿīyah* (the legal status of things) will invariably overwhelm those of *wuqūʿ* (the actual occurrence or desired instantiation of things),[96] along with the entire calculus of how to negotiate benefits and interests. From here, all debates will be effectively reduced to competing parties' allegiance to scripture, since scripture is the sole source of the *sharʿī* status of things, and "*sharʿī*" and "Islamic" and "religious" are now all synonymous, and exclusively so. There will remain no other grounds, in other words, upon which to found legitimate Islamic argument. All dissent comes to be perceived as dissenting from the authority of scripture and what is understood to be "decreed by God."

The fact that An-Na'im does not recognize the Islamic Secular and its *sharʿī*/non-*sharʿī* distinction reinforces this tendency and predisposes him, no less than it does the 'Fundamentalists,' to reducing everything that is Islamically relevant to Islam's *shar'īyāt*, a move that inevitably marginalizes and ultimately frustrates Islamic debate beyond the circumference of *sharī'ah* and its sources.

Undifferentiated Religion and An-Na'im's Secular

Readers will recall from my discussion in Chapter 1 the Enlightenment project of micro-secularization, which aimed to "emancipate" such spheres as politics, economics, science, and the like from religion, so that the skills, metrics, and execution deemed proper to these domains would be free from the dictates of faith. This is also one of An-Na'im's aims. Because, however, he does not consciously recognize Islam's mode of differentiation, in which even religiously relevant non-*shar'ī* skills and metrics do *not* draw their substance or authority from *shar'ī* sources and can be engaged without relying on or offending *sharī'ah*, he is suspicious of religion's predatory propensities and wants to reinforce the boundary—indeed the wall—between the religious and the secular. He acknowledges, for example, that piety and practical skill may cohere in a single individual; but he is (rightly) leery of the over-inclusive claims of religious authorities, as well as the overly broad authority that the laity is prone to impute to them.[97] On this suspicion, he wants to keep those who exercise religious authority separate and distinct from those whose authority resides in their practical skills. As he puts it, "Allowing the same person to assert both types of authority is dangerous and counterproductive, because that makes it much harder to dislodge them without the risk of serious civil strife and violence."[98]

As we saw with al-Maqrīzī, religious knowledge can indeed be conflated with practical skill in a manner that produces bad policy that is then insulated in the name of religion. In this light, An-Na'im's point is well taken. To insist, however, that the practical can *only* be recognized and safely accorded its due if it is totally separated from religion is problematic. Because An-Na'im does not recognize a *shar'ī*/non-*shar'ī* distinction but only a religious/secular one, he can deploy only the bluntest instruments in attempting to isolate the practical from the religious, rendering the practical simply "secular" and implying inevitable conflict if not contradiction between it and the religious. To bolster this point, he invokes the names of classical jurists whom he sees as following this approach. He speaks, for example, of Ibn al-Qayyim and Ibn Taymīyah's insisting that appointment to political office be based on "secular," pragmatic skills and not piety, implying that they would see practical competence as "secular" and thus cordoned off from "religion" in the same way he does.[99] But one can hardly imagine Ibn Taymīyah, of all people, seeing the acquisition and application of practical skills as non-religious or secular in the modern Western sense. More importantly, one might ask about the plight of openly pious individuals who also happen to be competent in "secular," non-*shar'ī* endeavors. Without a criterion for distinguishing what is *shar'ī* from what is not, An-Na'im's Secular State might bar the secular skills of openly pious persons in the name of keeping the practical separate from the religious and the latter separate from the state. The would-be non-*shar'ī* contributions of *niqab*-wearing women or big-bearded, gown-clad, bead-thumbing men to economic policy, administrative law, or the independence of the judiciary, might be preemptively rejected as stealth attempts to "*sharī'*atize" the state.

Even if An-Na'im insists that his Secular State does not preclude such persons from bringing their "secular" skills to the challenges of the day, reservations will persist as long as he does not recognize the Islamic Secular. For, this lack of recognition can only enhance if not perpetuate the failure to distinguish piously developed skills that are religious and *shar'ī* from piously developed skills that are religious but non-*shar'ī*. As Ṭāriq al-Bishrī (hardly a 'Fundamentalist') has pointed out, while Coptic Christians often fear that an Islamic State can come only at the expense of their collective security and well-being, Islamic movements are no less fearful of being similarly marginalized under a secular state.[100] Indeed, here, one might ask how An-Na'im would respond to an openly committed Muslim who insists: "I need an Islamic State, one that will not deny me, as a religiously committed Muslim, as it does not deny secular or non-religious citizens, the right to direct the non-*shar'ī* skills and talents I develop in pursuit of God's pleasure to the cause of good governance or other challenges facing my country."[101]

The Nemesis of Neutrality

In theory, it is precisely this kind of discrimination that An-Na'im's principle of neutrality aims to address. According to that principle, "state institutions neither favor nor disfavor any religious doctrine or principle."[102] But if his Secular State is committed to keeping coercive religion (read: *sharī'ah*) separate from the state, the lack of an objective criterion for distinguishing what is "religious," that is, "*in the proper, the religious, sense*," (read: *shar'ī*) from what is not "religious" in this sense (read: non-*shar'ī*[103]) can render appeals to neutrality misleading and dangerous. For, it can empower the state to discriminate against religion in the name of neutrality, or "keeping the state free from coercive religion," by arbitrarily assigning the labels "religious" and "secular" as it sees fit. We saw this in the example of the Turkish cancer patient, when the state failed to recognize her action of covering her bald head as "secular."[104] An-Na'im himself recognizes a similar problem in the ban on *ḥijāb*, which he describes as "denying citizens who take Islam as a foundational force in their lives the right and opportunity to live by their own [religious] convictions," referring to this as an affront to human rights.[105] But rather than confront the need to draw the line between the religious and the secular more clearly and objectively, An-Na'im doubles down on the public-private argument cited earlier and suggests that the meaning of neutrality (which, again, necessitates distinguishing "religion" from "non-religion") be ongoingly negotiated over time through the medium of his civic reason.[106]

Even assuming such ongoing negotiations, the mandate An-Na'im extends to the state to "regulate and mediate the role of religion in public life" will impede its ability to remain neutral in actual practice.[107] Secularism is not an ontological given but an ideological commitment. As such, it requires conscious effort to legitimate and normalize its status.[108] Secularism's viability—like religion's—is contingent upon an appropriate *nomos* and plausibility structure, which must be ongoingly built and assiduously maintained. Ideas that threaten the integrity of this ideological ecosystem must be targeted for domestication, refraction, or destruction. An-Na'im gives as examples of such ideas the concepts "*qawamah* [*sic*], *dhimma* and *jihad*." According to him, "even if these principles are not enacted as state law or policy [i.e., even if they remain free of coercive force] . . . their moral and emotional impact on Muslims will severely undermine the ethos of constitutionalism, human rights and citizenship."[109] In other words, these principles, even if not coercively backed by the state, will breed intolerant and bigoted attitudes toward women and non-Muslims in a manner that frustrates these groups' ability to participate fully in public life. Of course, An-Na'im would prefer that such pollutants be neutralized through Muslim interpretive reform efforts. But society cannot always rely upon such efforts.[110] And the state must recognize the occasional need to step in and play its regulatory role.

Precisely in this context, An-Na'im concedes that neutrality may sometimes have to take a back seat. In his discussion of India, for example, he speaks of the state's need to "enhance and promote the legitimacy of secularism among different religious traditions rather than simply assuming that the value of secularism is self-evident or will be readily appreciated among all communities."[111] Again, his Secular State must actively promote and legitimize secularism. As for how this affects the state's commitment to neutrality, An-Na'im notes, on the one hand, that "complete neutrality" is impossible.[112] On the other hand, whether a particular departure from state neutrality is acceptable or not should remain the topic of ongoing debate and disagreement, mediated, again, through civic reason.[113]

There are several points I would like to make here. First, at the most basic level, the claim that the active promotion and legitimation of secularism can be reconciled with *any* notion of state-neutrality is mildly shocking in the degree of myopia it displays. The aim of such promotion and legitimation is clearly the domestication of religion, to the point that its ability to challenge the state or secularism is weakened if not undermined. How can a process with such clear and undeniable aims cast itself as neutral toward religion? Second, if the Secular State can indulge in what An-Naʿim accepts as necessary deviations from neutrality, will this be extended to the Islamic State as well? Third, state regulation of religion for the purpose of promoting secularism may encroach not only upon Muslims' *sharʿī* commitments but upon their non-*sharʿī* efforts as well, for example, their attempts to build and preserve the kind of *nomos* and plausibility structure that sustains if not enhances their commitment to religion, which, even as non-coercive actions, may include the expression of ideas that non-Muslims find offensive, disturbing, or threatening. Fourth, one wonders about the degree to which neutrality here is merely a stalking horse for state expressions of favoritism. As Yale law professor Stephen Carter points out, states are beholden to constituencies, and bigger constituencies are generally treated differently from smaller ones. The American state, for example, may put forth "neutral" reasons for building roads through sacred Native American land, but "nobody proposes to build a road through the Cathedral of St. John the Divine in Manhattan," not even for "neutral" reasons.[114] Similarly, *jihād*, *qiwāmah*, and *dhimmah* may be targeted for extirpation (for the reasons An-Naʿim gives); but no modern Western state (or even An-Naʿim's native Sudan) could get away with demanding the removal of images of a White, male Jesus, because of the psychological or emotional effects they might have on Blacks or women, or because of the attitudes of superiority they might engender in males or Whites.

Finally, state regulation of religion in the interest of preserving state neutrality is presumed unproblematically to serve the interests of religious minorities, who are presumed to see encroachments by the religious Other as the greatest threat to their own religion, which leaves them always preferring a secular order. But what if what religious minorities really fear *is* a secular order, which threatens to overwhelm them and erode if not destroy, by rendering irrelevant, their religious worldview? What if, on this understanding, a religious minority feels more threatened by a secular order than it does by an Islamic one? Of course, that would depend on what the constitution of such an Islamic order is in relation to non-Muslims. It is to this topic that I now turn.

Non-Muslims: Islam-cum-*Sharīʿah* between the Modern State and the Empire-State

For An-Naʿim, while state-sponsored application of *sharīʿah* threatens the religiosity, human rights, and citizenship of Muslims, its negative impact on non-Muslims is even greater. Even assuming the most humane and intelligent application of *sharīʿah*, non-Muslims will be left laboring under the oppressive authority of religious rules in which they do not believe. Of course, secular states bind us all to laws in which we may not believe, some of us even rejecting the rational, scientific, or cultural authority upon which such rules are based. But An-Na'im's argument is an extension of the Enlightenment vision, which looks upon religion as uniquely threatening in this regard.

As we shall see, much of what An-Na'im identifies in the way of problematic rules of *sharī'ah* falls outside the purview of my analysis proper. This is not an attempt to play down or evade the challenges posed by these rules. Substantively speaking, however, they constitute *aḥkām shar'īyah*, while my primary interest is in placing An-Na'im's Secular State in conversation with *islām mā warā' al-ḥukm al-shar'ī*. In other words, the *ijtihād shar'ī*, on the basis of which such rules might be modified, is not a constituent of the Islamic Secular per se. When An-Na'im speaks, for example, of certain Qur'ānic verses being taken as a justification for "denying women the right to hold any public office involving the exercise of authority over men" or for restricting their right "to appear in public or to associate with men," whether I agree with these interpretations or not, they implicate *ijtihād shar'ī*, as articulations of scriptural intent, and fall outside the purview of my primary focus on Islam's differentiated, non-*shar'ī* gaze. When, on the other hand, he speaks of "the regulation of women's dress"[115] or female access to education, the discussion might be reasonably construed as falling more directly within the purview of the Islamic Secular, as these rules can be seen as largely discretionary and thus non-*shar'ī* in nature.

Presently, however, my focus is on non-Muslims, and the issue is not (in the first instance at least) the substance of *sharī'ah*'s rules but whether and how they apply to non-Muslims. My attempt, in other words, will be to engage with An-Na'im on what appears to be his understanding not simply of the mission of the would-be Islamic State but of its basic structure and what that structure contributes to the question of whom *sharī'ah* is applied to and how. Ultimately, in my view, it is more the impact of certain assumptions about this basic structure than it is the substance of *sharī'ah* per se or its attaching to the state that breeds much of the problem that An-Na'im identifies.

In their book *Empires in World History*, Jane Burbank and Frederick Cooper describe an interesting difference between pre-modern empires and (modern) states. Whereas pre-modern empires maintain distinctions and hierarchy among the populations they incorporate, modern states (especially modern nation-states) tend to homogenize, at least in theory, divergent groups into an ostensible single "people," all equal and constitutive of a single political community.[116] In contrast to the modern state, the empire-state's basic point of departure is that "different people within the polity will be governed differently."[117] It is foremost a tax-taking not a legislating entity. In his study of late Ḥanafī jurisprudence, *Law, Empire, and the Sultan*, Samy Ayoub fleshes out some of the legal implications of this presumption. He notes, for example, that "Unlike [modern] state law, imperial law is negotiated, not imposed."[118]

Whatever degree of negotiability actually existed between imperial powers and their subjects, it is clear that the empire-state was not legally monistic; it did not insist on a single legal order applied uniformly across the board, as part of its intrinsic nature or as a sign of its sovereignty (let alone any commitment to equality). On the contrary, empire-states were quite comfortable with hierarchy and legal pluralism within their borders, a comfort usually expressed via a certain tolerance of minority groups via some form of subordinated communal autonomy. Nor was the empire-state, to return to Robert Cover's term, "jurispathic": it did not insist on a monopoly over law or legal interpretation, and it did not see the existence of alternate reglementary regimes within its borders as a threat to its overall integrity. Of course, there is nothing intrinsically inalterable about these features of empire-states or of modern states. As Burbank and Cooper point out, "both . . . could be transformed into something more like the other."[119] In the end, however, these distinctive tendencies are real, substantive, and operative.

I wish to argue three points: First, Islam-cum-*sharīʿah* in the pre-modern period functioned on the logic of empire, not that of the (modern) state, a logic that informed its basic structural impulses. Second, neither the form nor logic of Islam's empire-state was entirely dictated by *sharīʿah* per se. This form and logic were simply incorporated into Islam via a combination of *sharʿī* and non-*sharʿī* energies processing what was already in the soil of both Arabia and the conquered territories into which Islam spread. Third, and most important, many of the features of the so-called Islamic State that An-Naʿim finds most objectionable may be more attributable to the legal monism and jurispathic structural dictates of the modern state than they are to Islam-cum-*sharīʿah* per se. Because these features are not the exclusive product of fixed, transcendent *sharīʿah* sources or doctrines, an Islamic State need not necessarily be secularized in the modern Western sense of separating *sharīʿah* from the state in order to adjust or jettison various features that cause many of the problems that An-Naʿim describes regarding non-Muslims.

Ever since Hobbes, a basic presumption of the modern state has been some version of the social contract, according to which all citizens (and groups) forfeit a measure of autonomy in exchange for the state's guarantee of security. In the case of Islam, this basic point of departure is assumed to imply that religious others must forfeit *all* their autonomy and recognize *sharīʿah* as the exclusive law of the land. At the same time, Muslims are presumed to be religiously bound by *sharīʿah* to impose this one-size-fits-all order on non-Muslims. This is certainly the impression one gets from An-Naʿim. But I would hazard that this view is more indebted to a tendency to read *sharīʿah* through the prism of the basic presumptions of the modern state than it is to reading Islamic law on its own terms and in light of the logic of the empire-state on which it fed. Much of what defined the lives of pre-modern non-Muslims was the result of non-*shar'ī* rather than strictly *shar'ī* deliberations. As such, much of this could be modified or abandoned without relying upon or offending *sharīʿah*, let alone detaching *sharīʿah* from the state.

On this understanding, *pace* An-Naʿim, the Islamic State need not be rejected in order to accommodate alternatives to the one-size-fits-all arrangement that imposes *sharīʿah* indiscriminately upon non-Muslims, as a unified, religiously mandated law of the land. This becomes especially clear when one considers a number of relevant features in pre-modern Islamic juristic discourse.

Al-Shāfiʿī, Mālik, Ḥanafīs, and the Early Period

I begin with al-Shāfiʿī, the eponym of the Shāfiʿī school and purported founder of Islamic legal theory (*uṣūl al-fiqh*). In *Kitāb al-Umm*, he reflects an ancient *nomos* that sees non-Muslims, even when they are the numerical majority, as a subordinate, quasi-autonomous community within the Muslim empire-state. A Muslim ruler, under this arrangement, is not required to apply *sharīʿah* to non-Muslims but has a choice either to do so or not. Al-Shāfiʿī's interpretive point of departure is the Qur'ānic verse, "*So, if they come to you, either judge between them or turn away from them. But if you judge between them, do so on the basis of justice*" [5:42]. Of course, "justice" for al-Shāfiʿī is the law of Islam, and he cites the case of the Prophet's stoning a Jewish couple for adultery as an indication of the propriety of this view. But he insists here that the Prophet was not bound to apply *sharīʿah*, as an unsolicited religious duty; rather, his action was a voluntary response to a petition from the Jewish community that he preside over this particular case. Al-Shāfiʿī notes that the Jews in question were not protected religious others (*dhimmīs*) but simply parties to a mutual agreement of non-aggression (*muwādaʿah*).[120] From here, he insists that he knows of no reliable reports of the Prophet or any of the Rightly Guided Caliphs adjudicating among non-Muslims as an unsolicited religious duty.[121] The only reports he knows of that might even suggest this is one in which the second Caliph, ʿUmar b. al-Khaṭṭāb, forbade certain Zoroastrian practices that are forbidden in Islam,[122] and one in which the fourth caliph, ʿAlī b. Abī Ṭālib, is presented with a Muslim man who had illicit sex with a non-Muslim woman. ʿAlī's judgment was that the man was to receive the prescribed *sharīʿah* punishment (*ḥadd*), while the woman was to be "turned over to her religious community" (*tudfaʿ al-dhimmīyah ilā ahli dīnihā*).[123] Al-Shāfiʿī challenges the formal authenticity of both of these reports but sees the substance of ʿAlī's action as confirming his own position, that is, that the Imām is not automatically bound to apply *sharīʿah* to non-Muslims. In fact, at one point he asks rhetorically (in defense of his basic position) if leaving non-Muslims to their own devices regarding legal disputes could be more serious than leaving them to their *shirk*.[124]

It is clear that "justice" for al-Shāfiʿī is *sharīʿah*. But this should not be understood to apply to matters for which *sharīʿah* itself is not the mandated source of adjudication. It does not mean, in other words, that leaving others to apply something other than *sharīʿah* is *ipso facto* unjust. This is clear from al-Shāfiʿī's own position on applying *sharīʿah* to non-Muslims. On the one hand, he states that if non-Muslims approach the Imām and he agrees to adjudicate their case, he *must* rule according to the law of Islam. In fact, al-Shāfiʿī insists that were he himself to agree to adjudicate non-Muslim cases, he would overturn all of their marriages that had been contracted without witnesses or a male representative (*walī*) for the bride, as he would invalidate all the profits they had made from selling wine or pork.[125] But this is not before he makes it clear that his preference would be *not to rule*. And he lays down the specific conditions under which he would rule:

> I would not rule until I informed them that I will only allow them what is allowed to Muslims, and I will only deny them what is denied to Muslims. And I would inform them that I will only accept in their cases the testimony of free, upright Muslims. If they accept this and I see fit to rule, I will rule between them. If they do not agree to all of this, I will not rule.[126]

Clearly al-Shāfiʿī does not see his refusal to impose *sharīʿah* as unjust. Nor, more importantly, does he see the normatively functioning Muslim state as a legally monistic, jurispathic entity that is religiously bound to impose *sharīʿah* on all citizens (or subjects) as the exclusive and uniform law of the land. That al-Shāfiʿī in particular should cede this kind of autonomy to non-Muslims is significant, if not remarkable. For, of all the eponymous leaders of the Sunni *madhhab*s, he was alone in holding non-Muslims' unbelief (*kufr*), as opposed to their hostile aggression, to be the legal cause (*sabab*) obligating *jihād* against them.[127] Yet, he remains unperturbed by non-Muslim subjects of a Muslim empire-state applying rules that contradict *sharīʿah*. In fact, to the question of whether the Muslim community must rescue protected religious others (*ahl al-dhimmah*) if they are overrun by foreign powers that prohibit them from engaging in their polytheistic practices (*shirk*), drinking wine and eating pork, al-Shāfiʿī confirms that they must, despite his admission that this will facilitate these non-Muslims' return to drinking wine, eating pork, and worshipping other than Allāh.[128] We might note here that none of al-Shāfiʿī's views is argued on the basis of Prophetic *hadīth*. In fact, in setting up this particular argument, he all but forces his interlocutor to admit that there are no reliable Prophetic reports that require Muslims to rescue non-Muslims under such circumstances. The Muslim duty to come to their aid is simply the rational extension of the basic meaning and purpose of "protection."[129] In other words, this was essentially a conclusion to which the logic and calculus of the Islamic Secular contributed significantly.

Al-Shāfiʿī was not alone in his willingness to leave non-Muslims to their own devices, as long as their actions did not impinge on the rights of Muslims.[130] In the most authoritative early manual in the Mālikī school, *al-Mudawwanah al-Kubrā*, Saḥnūn (d. 240/854) poses the following question to Ibn al-Qāsim (d. 191/806), who had been Mālik's student for some twenty years: "According to Mālik, if four Muslims testify that a Muslim man had illicit sex with a non-Muslim woman (*dhimmīyah*), shall the man receive the prescribed punishment (*ḥadd*) and the woman be turned over to her religious community?" "Yes," replies Ibn al-Qāsim. "According to Mālik, she is turned over to her religious community, and the Muslim man receives the prescribed punishment for illicit sex."[131] The wording here suggests that Saḥnūn was not simply posing this question spontaneously but was trying to get confirmation on a view already in circulation. As mentioned, al-Shāfiʿī had cited an identical ruling in a report on the authority of the fourth Caliph ʿAlī Ibn Abī Ṭālib. His Yemeni contemporary ʿAbd al-Razzāq al-Ṣanʿānī (d. 211/827) cites a similar report in which the exact same ruling is attributed to ʿAlī, only through a different chain.[132]

Cumulatively, these reports suggest that the idea of non-Muslims policing their own communities in numerous areas of law was far from anathema to the early Muslim empire-state. And this "communitarian" perspective clearly placed non-Muslims beyond the reach of various aspects of *sharīʿah*. Meanwhile, the apparent absence of Prophetic *ḥadīth* on the topic suggests, again, that much of this policy was the result of non-*sharʿī*, Islamic Secular deliberation.[133]

The view of Mālik and al-Shāfiʿī was not universally shared, as few things are in *fiqh*. In *Kitāb al-Aṣl*, Abū Ḥanīfa's influential student Muḥammad b. al-Ḥasan al-Shaybānī (d. 189/805) insists that, outside the area of religious observances or *ʿibādāt*, non-Muslims are absolutely subject to Islam's substantive law, including the prescribed punishments for illicit sex. In fact, al-Shaybānī insists that non-Muslims can be punished for such indiscretions even based on non-Muslim testimony or confession.[134] Baber Johansen summarizes the basic Ḥanafī position as follows: "Within the territory of Islam, legal norms, with the exception of those for liturgical acts, are valid for all subjects of the Muslim government."[135] Yet, even here there are details that reflect the logic of the empire-state. For example, beyond the well-known exceptions to the rules on eating pork and drinking wine, al-Shaybānī notes that adultery is not a capital offense for non-Muslims as it is for Muslims. Rather, regardless of marital status, non-Muslims are subject only to the punishment for fornication (i.e., lashing—not stoning—even if their partner in crime is a married Muslim).[136] To be sure, this was less a gesture of tolerance than an expression and symbol of Muslim supremacy, the latter being reflected, interestingly, in the disqualification of non-Muslims from coming under the full application of *sharīʿah*—another counterintuitive feature of the logic of the Muslim empire-state.

The Post-Formative Scene

These early positions would soon be followed by a debate in the emergent field of *uṣūl al-fiqh* over whether non-Muslims in general were subject to the concrete rules of *sharīʿah* (*hal al-kuffār mukhāṭabūna bi furūʿ al-sharīʿah*). There was no unanimous agreement on the matter, some jurists arguing that they were, others that they were not. But the debate itself was far more theoretical than practical. Al-Rāzī summarizes the stakes and takeaways as follows: "The upshot of the disagreement [among the jurists] relates to the affair of the Hereafter. For there is no doubt that, if an Unbeliever dies in a state of Unbelief, he will be punished for his Unbelief. But will he be punished in addition for having not prayed, paid *zakāh*, or other such infractions?"[137] Again, we see that Muslim jurists were significantly "unmusical" to the jurispathic legal monism so foundational to the modern state. As applied to religious observances and certain other criminal sanctions (e.g., against wine-drinking), this is largely acknowledged in Western scholarship. But regarding the generality of laws governing civil transactions and criminal offenses, the dominant tendency is to assume that *sharīʿah* functioned in the pre-modern Muslim state as it presumably would in a modern state, that is, as the uniform law of the land.

In his book *Religious Pluralism and Islamic Law*, Anver Emon concludes that Muslim jurists were generally not willing to grant "legal authority to the *dhimmī*'s [non-Muslims'] legal tradition in the claim space of Sharīʿa" and instead "maintained that Sharīʿa provided the only doctrinal rules by which to govern an Islamic polity."[138] He explains this hegemonic tendency in terms of the notion that "legal systems do not contend with legal pluralism very well."[139] He also sees a universalizing impulse, born of the imperial ambition to reconcile the superiority of the Muslim state with the demands of governing a religiously diverse population. In other words, law, in his view, functions as the instrument through which minority communities are domesticated and their subordinate status confirmed.[140] In a similar vein, A. Kevin Reinhart explains the mandatory imposition of *sharīʿah* in terms of demographic changes that took Muslims from minority to majority status and replaced what he refers to as the "relativism" of the earlier period with a triumphalist universalism that was both kerygmatic and intellectual.[141] Meanwhile, according to Mohammad

Fadel, "[T]he political function of *dhimma*, or religious 'minority' status, was to generate some morally relevant basis upon which non-Muslims would be subject to the rules of Islamic law and thus establish peace between Muslims and non-Muslims."[142]

One wonders how much such views owe to the basic assumptions of the modern state, which holds the state to be the origin of all law (a presumption particularly strong among scholars trained in Western law). Emon, for example, acknowledges the imperial ethos of the Muslim empire-state but still sees in it a penchant for the legal monism characteristic of the modern state. As we saw in the views al-Shāfiʿī and Mālik, however, the universalist, homogenizing impulse Emon assumes was not necessarily the spontaneous impulse of jurists thinking in the context of the pre-modern Muslim empire-state. It was far more Muslim power and its accompanying sovereign-will that acquired a universalizing mission. And this power and will were neither expressed nor necessarily measured by the degree to which Muslims imposed *sharīʿah* (as explicitly reflected in the views of Mālik, al-Shāfiʿī, Ibn al-Qāsim, and others); it was by the degree to which the Muslim state could legitimately extract resources, services, and basic loyalty from religious minorities, as well as insulate itself from foreign and domestic aggression. While it may be paradigmatic of modern states to assert their sovereign-will by imposing monistic legal orders on constituent populations, there was no necessary connection between Muslim power-cum-sovereignty and the imposition of *sharīʿah* as the uniform law of the land, the basic Ḥanafī position notwithstanding. As for non-Muslim territories over which Muslim power extended, there was no categorical *sharʿī* mandate to impose a functional equivalent of colonial Britain's "Anglo-Muhammadan law," where *sharīʿah*-rules that offended British sensibilities were revised or eliminated.

Regarding Reinhart's view, one might ask why Mālik or al-Shāfiʿī would be any less triumphalist than later jurists, at least in terms of nursing a basic desire to impose *sharīʿah* uniformly across the board. Furthermore, why could not the majoritarian triumphalism of later centuries manifest itself in a move to bar non-Muslims from participating in *sharīʿah*, reflecting an explicit message of their inferiority, much like the *de facto* barring of Blackamerican soldiers from the "honor" of dying in combat during earlier periods of American history? As for Fadel's argument, one wonders if it does not overindulge the modern liberal obsession with eradicating specifically doctrinal conflict.[143] For, it seems to me that the only peace in which a pre-modern empire-state would be ultimately interested would be the one realized at the moment of conquest: surrender. Otherwise, I do not see how barring the building of churches, or the riding of certain animals, or the full and unqualified application of *ḥadd* penalties to non-Muslims would contribute to the cause of peace.

The Empire-State between *Sharīʿah* and the Islamic Secular

But the main argument I wish to make here is that the tendency among scholars in the Western academy and beyond to over-*sharīʿ*atize in their interpretations of Islamic legal history consistently misrecognizes the non-*sharʿī* Islamic Secular and in so doing distorts or misapprehends key relevant issues. My contention is not that Muslims had no desire to see *sharīʿah* applied broadly. It is that (1) this rarely approached the universalizing, homogenizing impulse of the modern state; and (2) it was infused with significant non-*sharʿī*, Islamic Secular energies, rules, and policies. In fact, the aspirations of the pre-modern Muslim state, and to a lesser extent of the jurists themselves, might be better understood as a commitment to applying "Islamic law" (as defined in Chapter 3) rather than simply "*sharīʿah.*" Emon seems to recognize something along these lines with his reference to "Rule of Law," which challenges restricting *sharīʿah* to the articulations of the jurists alone. As he puts it, "Sharīʿa as Rule of Law requires that we acknowledge the multiple sites of authority that animated and influenced juristic writings about Islamic legal doctrines, and which thereby constitute Sharīʿa as a whole, such as the governing and institutional setting that animated the jurists' legal culture (whether real or imagined)."[144] As we saw in Chapters 2 and 3, however, the jurists explicitly recognized the distinction in all of this between what was *sharʿī* and what was not. In such light, *pace* Emon (and others, including, at times, *sharīʿah*-maximalists such as Ibn al-Qayyim), it is my contention that jurists generally saw these extra-*sharʿī* elements *not* as *sharīʿah* but as non-*sharʿī* "Islamic law," a constituent of the Islamic Secular. This means that, in the case of non-Muslims, the mandate to apply the law, as well as the substance of what was applied, was often discretionary, differentiated, and 'secular,' not *sharʿī* or religious, "*in the proper, the religious, sense*"; and it was often practical, not strictly a dictate of Islam cum-*sharīʿah*'s "moral vision."

To be sure, the question of whether or not the Imām/state was obligated to impose *sharīʿah* on non-Muslims was complicated in pre-modern Islam and never a point of consensus, at least not unproblematically so.[145] Al-Māwardī, for example, under the heading, "On Applying Prescribed Punishments to Protected Religious Others" (*bāb mā jāʾa fī ḥadd al-dhimmīyīn*), cites a view, attributed to al-Shāfiʿī, that if protected non-Muslims seek his adjudication, the Imām has a choice to apply *sharīʿah* rules or not. He follows this, however, with another view (also attributed to al-Shāfiʿī) that leaves the Imām no choice but to apply the *sharʿ*.[146] This ambiguity ultimately evolves in the fully developed doctrine of the *madhhab* into three competing positions. In the first, the Imām has a choice to rule or not to rule, unless it was stipulated in the contract of *dhimmah* that *sharīʿah* will apply to the non-Muslims in question. In the second, the Imām is also given a choice, though the implication here is that he should rule and that, if he does, he must rule in accordance with Islam, except regarding such well-known exemptions as wine-drinking.[147] The third position is that the Imām is obligated to apply *sharīʿah* regarding the rights of humans (*ḥuquq al-ādamīyīn*) but not the rights of God (*ḥuquq Allāh*).[148] All of this is framed on the assumption that non-Muslims are actively seeking the Imām's judgment (*istaʿdaw ilaynā*), which suggests that the topic here is *dhimmah* contracts as constituents of a "negotiated *jizyah*," that is, *jizyah ṣulḥīyah*, offered to the vanquished prior to their actual defeat, as opposed to an ostensibly non-negotiable "*jizyah ʿanawīyah*," imposed pursuant to direct, physical conquest where the vanquished fight to the end.[149]

It is not always clear which of these assumptions—*ṣulḥ* or *ʿanwah*—is the focal point of discussion, but there seems to have been a broad trend among jurists to bring non-Muslims under the "rules of Islam" (*aḥkām al-islām*) as an automatic feature of a *dhimmah* contract.[150] Elsewhere, al-Māwardī himself subscribes to this view.[151] But here he cites, importantly, two mutually distinct interpretations of what "*aḥkām al-islām*" means. Some, he notes, held it to refer to *sharīʿah*; but others simply equated it with the legal sovereignty and power of Muslim rule more generally (*al-taḥakkum bi al-quwwah wa al-istiṭālah*).[152] The latter would invariably include not only *sharʿī* rules, such as the ten-percent tax *(ʿushr*) on *dhimmī* profits from "interstate commerce," but also numerous non-*sharʿī*, discretionary rules and policies, such as regulations on zoning or trafficking in hazardous materials or what currencies could be used in commerce.

Even with the strictly *sharʿī* rules, however, non-*sharʿī* considerations invariably bleed through. For example, al-Māwardī lists among the non-negotiable (*bi ghayr sharṭ*) stipulations of the *dhimmah* contract "that they do not engage any Muslim woman in illicit sex, not even in the name of marriage."[153] Targeting *zinā* is straightforwardly *sharʿī* enough; but tying this prohibition specifically to Muslim *women* speaks to something beyond the offense itself. This is not to mention the standard list of negotiable (*bi sharṭ*) stipulations, which include such things as dress codes for non-Muslims, the height of their buildings, the kinds of animals they can ride, and the requirement that they hold their burial services away from Muslim view.[154] Al-Māwardī also notes in this context that non-Muslims may adjudicate commercial and other civil disputes among themselves, a view we find with al-Qarāfī as well.[155] According to both, in disputes involving Muslims and non-Muslims, the law of Islam must be applied. But where the dispute is strictly between non-Muslims, the Imām has a choice to apply *sharīʿah* or not, assuming that no harm would come to Muslims.[156] Al-Māwardī confirms the pragmatic element informing these deliberations when he notes that the basic point of the *dhimmah* contract as a whole is "to strengthen Islam" (*taqwīyat al-islām*) and that the Imām should stipulate what best serves this interest, based on his assessment of the concrete circumstances on the ground.[157]

All of this challenges the notion of a categorical religious requirement that *sharīʿah* be automatically and uniformly applied to non-Muslims across the board, again, the standard Ḥanafī position notwithstanding. It is well known that non-Muslims were not bound by any of the rules of *ʿibādāt*. Outside the *ʿibādāt*, they could drink wine, eat pork, deal in *ribā* (?interest), marry—according to some, even incestuously—and divorce as they please, and, depending on circumstances, settle their own commercial disputes. As we have seen, some jurists also exempted non-Muslims from various aspects of the criminal law. Speaking, for example, of their exemption from *sharīʿah* rules governing *zinā*, al-Māwardī's contemporary, the Tunisian Mālikī jurist al-Lakhmī (d. 478/1085), insists that part of the whole point of the protection tax (*jizyah*) to begin with was to allow non-Muslims to maintain "their way of life" (*mā hum alayh*).[158] We also saw earlier that even Ḥanafīs, who hold non-Muslims to the rules of *zinā*, exempt them from capital punishment for this crime, a view we also find among Mālikīs.[159]

Considering all of this, one might ask what it even means to say that the Muslim state "applied" *sharīʿah* to non-Muslims. Would the aforementioned exemptions and adjustments be consistent with the meaning of "applying the law" to any group in any other context? Yet, while none of these exemptions was perceived as an affront to the sovereignty of the Muslim state, I suspect that the Muslim state would be far less tolerant of non-Muslims violating zoning regulations or the state's discretionary rules governing the sale of hazardous materials or pre-set wheat prices. Here, paradoxically, more rather than less than in the case of *sharīʿah*, the Muslim state would grant no "legal authority to the *dhimmī*'s legal tradition." Stated differently and perhaps more accurately (if counterintuitively), depending on the *madhhab* in question, non-Muslims' religion might formally exempt them from various aspects of *sharīʿah* but not from the "general Islamic order," or *aḥkām al-islām*. On this understanding, *pace* those who include discretionary rules of *siyāsah* as part of *sharīʿah*, it seems more accurate to speak of the Muslim state's interest in applying "Islamic law" (as described in Chapter 3[160]) rather than in simply applying "*sharīʿah*." Crucially, as I have already noted, "Islamic law" includes a significant non-*sharʿī*, Islamic Secular element. And to the degree that these Islamic Secular energies inform the normative Islamic order, Muslims can modify and adjust that order, as circumstances dictate, without relying on nor necessarily offending *sharīʿah*. The notion, therefore, that the only way to confer a meaningful degree of autonomy and protection upon non-Muslims or to take seriously their quotidian concerns and interests is to remove *sharīʿah* entirely from the state seems, again, overstated, if not misplaced.

But let us assume for the sake of argument that Muslims concluded that they were required, *sharʿan*, to apply *sharīʿah* to non-Muslims. Differences between the basic structure and presumptions of the modern state and those of the empire-state could give "applying *sharīʿah*" a meaning quite at odds with what An-Naʿim seems to assume. As we saw with al-Māwardī, al-Qarāfī, and al-Lakhmī, *sharīʿah* might, in fact, preserve rather than curtail various non-Muslim rights by insisting that they are exempted from this or that particular *sharīʿah* rule, as an actual dictate of *sharīʿah* itself. Such exemptions would apply not only to drinking wine, eating pork, or dealing in interest but also to marriage, divorce, fornication/adultery, and the like, in contrast to the dictates of the legal monism assumed by the modern state.

Some (including An-Naʿim) might dismiss this narrative as utopian, on the argument that, even if correct in theory, it cannot be accepted as a description of the applied order in actual practice. But that would be an argument against Muslim society and history, not Islam-cum-*sharīʿah* per se. My claim is not that this system was duly applied as a matter of fact but that it *could* have been applied as a matter of law, that is, in accordance with authoritative interpretations of Islam-cum-*sharīʿah*. Others might object, however, that, even if *sharīʿah* was applied in a manner that recognized non-Muslim rights and exemptions in the past, this can have no meaningful relevance today. For, the days of the empire-state—and empire-sensibilities—are gone, never to return (again, a sentiment perhaps stronger among scholars trained in Western law).[161] A recent episode involving Coptic Christians in Egypt, however, might temper some of this skepticism and add insight if not credence to the point I am trying to make.

In 2010, facing a rising tide of petitions from divorced Coptic Christians seeking to remarry, Egypt's High Administrative Court (*al-maḥkamah al-idārīyah al-ʿulyā*) issued orders to the Coptic Church to grant marriage licenses to Coptic divorcees. The Coptic Pope objected that this violated the religious freedom and sovereignty of the Coptic Church, according to which remarriage is an option only in cases of adultery or apostasy, and, even then, only for the aggrieved party. This doctrinal position clashed, however, with the secular principles of equality and state neutrality, according to which the Egyptian state would have to allow either everyone to remarry or no one to remarry. Given that divorce followed by marriage was permissible for the majority Muslim population, banning it across the board was not an option. Still, Pope Shenoudah III (d. 2012) insisted that the Coptic Church would not—indeed, could not—comply with the Egyptian state's order, as a matter of religious principle.

The matter grew serious and spawned large public demonstrations. (I was in Cairo at the time.) At the height of the controversy—and this is the crux of the matter for our purposes—Pope Shenoudah published a full-page editorial in the official daily newspaper *al-Ahrām*, in which he stated the following: "We simply ask the judges, if they wish to reconcile with the Church, to apply the Islamic *sharīʿah*" (*naḥnu naṭlub min al-quḍāh an yunaffidhū al-sharīʿah al-islāmīyah idhā arādū al-taṣāluḥ maʿa al-kanīsah*).[162] In other words, according to *sharīʿah*, in contrast to the laws of the secular Egyptian state, Christians have the right to follow their own rule in this regard, irrespective of what rule Muslims and others follow.

My claim here is not that Pope Shenoudah was advocating the application of *sharīʿah* after the fashion of the Islamists. In fact, the difference between the way these two groups relate to *sharīʿah* in the context of the modern state is precisely my point: *pace* An-Naʿim (and perhaps many Islamists), the legally monistic, jurispathic mode of a one-size-fits-all-uniform-law-of-the-land is *not* the only way that *sharīʿah* can be understood or applied. Pope Shenoudah was clearly not advocating any change in the Muslim right to no-fault divorce followed by remarriage; he simply objected to this right extending to Christians. And if we take his petition seriously, we might be forced to conclude that the empire-state sensibility is not as dead as An-Naʿim and others might assume.

At any rate, the takeaway here is that *sharīʿah* can function, *mutatis mutandis*, with one effect in a modernized version of an empire-state structure and with another in a legally monistic, jurispathic, modern state structure. Moreover, the decision to adopt one arrangement or the other, as well as the modality thereof, will owe as much to non-*sharʿī*, differentiated, Islamic Secular deliberations as it does to purely *sharʿī* deductions.[163]

All of this underscores the point I have made by now many times: given the *sharʿī*/non-*sharʿī* distinction implied by the Islamic Secular, the basic structure and governing principles of a Muslim state—or an Islamic State—are not entirely dictated by *sharīʿah*. We have just seen how relevant a fact this is for *sharīʿah*'s application to non-Muslims. It would be equally relevant to some of the issues An-Naʿim raises regarding women. When he speaks of women being denied the right to participate in public life, or of girls' being denied equal access to education, these challenges could be reasonably viewed as predominantly non-*sharʿī* matters of *siyāsah* or policy, not scripturally dictated *sharīʿah* rules.[164] As such, they could be debated, challenged, and changed without relying on or, *ceteris paribus*, offending *sharīʿah*. Meanwhile, precisely because these rules are non-*sharʿī*, or at least include significant non-*sharʿī* elements, Muslims and non-Muslims could negotiate them (or at least aspects of them) on a virtually level playing field. This assumes, of course, that circumstances on the ground make it reasonable to jettison the pre-modern assumption that all non-Muslims are hostiles lying in wait to undermine Islam, or the late modern fear-cum-suspicion that they are all in sympathy, if not cahoots, with post-colonial Western imperialists. Either way, few if any of these discretionary rules or the norms they spawn could be billed as "decreed by God," at least not fully.

In the end, as I suggested in my discussion of Hallaq, Muslims may opt for the modern state structure, with its one-size-fits-all presumption. And shorn of a recognition of the Islamic Secular, this choice will lend credence to An-Naʿim's call for a secular state. On the other hand, not only could Muslims recognize the importance of the Islamic Secular, instead of blindly adopting the modern state structure in its most common form, they could also opt for a different arrangement, perhaps a modern state in the form of a modified domestic empire-state—without the crass social hierarchy and religious chauvinism characteristic of the pre-modern age. Or they could opt for a centralized modern state committed to promoting an Islamic subjectivity while being neither legally monistic, nor jurispathic, nor oblivious to the spaces in which non-*sharʿī*, Islamic Secular deliberations reign supreme. As Burbank and Cooper note, the empire-state is amenable to permutations that make it akin to the modern state while avoiding some of the latter's most problematic features.

The Secular State and the Islamic Secular

Like Hallaq, An-Naʿim views the state as a modern, Western innovation. He does not seem to recognize, however, any parallel relationship between this Western provenance and the rise of the secular, including its oppositional relationship with the religious. Yet, from a historical perspective, one might view Western secularization not simply as a response to the problem of religion in Western Europe but also as an outgrowth of a pre-existing European political culture overall. Among the relevant features of that culture was a deep discomfort if not hostility toward the notion of religious pluralism and mutual co-existence, not simply among different religions but even among different denominations of the same religion. This is what England's Queen Elizabeth I (d. 1603) had in mind when she insisted: "There cannot be two religions in one State."[165] Her successor, King James (d. 1625), warned Protestant Puritans who rejected certain "Catholic-like" practices that they had better get with the program, "or else I will harrie them out of this land, or else do worse, only hang them, that's all."[166] As Owen Chadwick summarizes the European mindset, "Men believed that society could not cohere if it permitted difference in religion. Everyone saw how Catholic subjects were disloyal to Protestant sovereigns, Protestant subjects to Catholic sovereigns. Separate religions seemed to mean civil war or separate states."[167]

The famous Treaty of Westphalia of 1648 was supposed to address this threat of internecine violence. But the Westphalian order turned out neither to sanction nor to normalize religious pluralism. In fact, it catered to state confessionalism and ultimately strengthened the sentiments of such forces as France's powerful *politiques* in their commitment to "one king, one faith, one law."[168] As late as the eighteenth century, Rousseau (d. 1778) still had to change his denominational affiliation as he moved back and forth between France and Switzerland. And in nineteenth-century Germany, Karl Marx's Jewish parents (certainly his father) saw fit to be baptized as an investment in their general well-being.[169] In this context, secularization could be looked to as a remedy, inasmuch as the decoupling of religion from the state would leave the state with no reason to persecute, pressure, or discriminate against anyone on religious grounds.

By contrast, no such political culture of homogenizing, state-sponsored confessionalism generally characterized the pre-modern polities of Islam. The Shiite Safavid "purge" beginning in the tenth/sixteenth century was the exception that proved the rule, as neither the Shiite Fāṭimids nor the 'Shiite' Buyids engaged in such a policy. This is not to claim that these (or other) Muslim regimes were innocent of persecutions or discrimination (recall, for example, the Jews and Christians—and even Muslims—under the Fāṭimid Caliph al-Ḥākim bi Amr Allāh[170], or Jews under Almohad rule); nor is it to deny the long and painful record of Muslim political abuses more generally, or the outbreaks of bigoted religious zealotry, to which the ubiquitous invocation of "the depravity of the times" (*fasād al-zamān*) well attests. It is simply to point to a different political culture overall, one in which Muslim empire-states were neither morally nor existentially threatened by the mere presence of multiple religions in their midst, let alone multiple articulations of Islam.

Muslim chronicles and biographical dictionaries are replete with reports of scholars who move from one end of the Muslim empire to the other, never being forced or pressured by the state to change their theological or legal *madhhab*. Even in cases where Muslim states sought to police the boundaries of theology (as with the Rationalist-inspired *miḥnah* or the Traditionalist-inspired Qādirī Creed[171]), the most public form of religious identity, namely, affiliation with a school of law (*madhhab*) (or perhaps Sufism), rarely came within the province of what the state thought it could or should regulate. Again, there were episodes and tendencies, as reflected in the statement of the *al-Muwaḥḥid* (Almohad) ruler in Spain, Ya'qūb al-Ṭā'ir (d. 595/1199) in his attempt to displace the traditional *madhhab*s: "There is but this (pointing to the Qur'ān), this (pointing to books of Sunna) or the sword."[172] But such incursions rarely outlived a regime or dynasty to become part of the general political culture of Islam—until perhaps the rise of modernity. As we will recall from Chapter 3, even Bernard Lewis acknowledged that intramural religious conflict in pre-modern Islam never reached the level or scope of ferocity that became the norm in Western Europe.

Here, in fact, I must disagree with Professor An-Na'im regarding secularism's provenance as a political ideal. Not only is the modern state a Western invention, but, *pace* An-Na'im, secularism, that is, the commitment to separating religion from the state, is also a modern, Western innovation. Muslim states, unlike those of Europe, had little reason to secularize in this fashion—especially on An-Na'im's contention that these states were never religious. Beyond their divergent attitudes toward inter- and intra-religious pluralism, Samuel P. Huntington offers a summary of the difference between these two political cultures that is worth considering:

> In the Muslim world, the distribution of identities has tended to be U-shaped: the strongest identities and commitments have been to family, clan, and tribe, at the one extreme, and to Islam and the *ummah* or Islamic community, at the other. With a few exceptions, loyalties to nations and nation-states have been weak. In the Western world for over two centuries, in contrast, the identity curve has been more an upside-down U, with the nation at the apex commanding deeper loyalty and commitment than narrower or broader sources of identity.[173]

As the object of normatively "deeper loyalty and commitment," the Western state had incentives to homogenize that were much deeper and perhaps more urgent than those of Muslim states (until the rise of nationalism, which was obviously borrowed from the West). Even where the pre-modern Muslim state aspired to homogenization, to the extent that *sharīʿah* served as homogenizing agent, *khilāf* would cover Muslims, and non-Muslims would be exempt from numerous *sharʿī* rules, which would contribute meaningfully to the state's perception of which public actions violated its identity or sovereignty and which did not. In the main, there would be no blanket commitment to a religious monism along lines expressed by Queen Elizabeth I. Meanwhile, the non-*sharʿī* policies and regulations a Muslim state applied would already be differentiated from *sharīʿah* and thus require no additional separation. An-Naʿim's presumption that the Muslim state—presumably as a dictate of *sharīʿah*—is legally monistic and jurispathic and that Islamic law is itself *sharʿī* through and through occludes these facts and in turn recommends the wholesale separation of *sharīʿah* from the state as the singular solution.

But *sharīʿah* has never been a stranger to religious pluralism. And a modern state that reflected *sharīʿah*'s pluralistic, "empire-state" impulses (not to mention its openness to non-*sharʿī* differentiation) would be palpably less threatening to the interests that An-Naʿim prioritizes. I might note in this context, given the cynicism with which such a notion might be greeted at first blush, that there are even today modern states—India, Israel, Greece, Ghana—that function explicitly, to all intents and purposes as empire-states, applying different regimes of law to different segments of the population, at least in various areas of the law.[174] In such light, structurally speaking at least, the solution to the challenges An-Naʿim identifies might lie in the direction of removing not *sharīʿah* from the state but the state's legal monism and addiction to "jurispathy." By simply assuming *sharīʿah* to be the entire problem, however, one wonders how much An-Na'im's theorizing ultimately contributes to the problem it then sets out to resolve.

Of course, An-Na'im would insist that *sharīʿah*'s attachment to the state poses problems beyond the matter of structure. "Constitutionalism," "human rights," and "citizenship" imply complete equality for women and non-Muslims, while the *substance* of any number of *sharīʿah*'s rules (even beyond the question of *dhimmah*—inheritance, for example) directly violates this basic principle. Beyond the question of structure, in other words, either *ijtihād sharʿī* will sufficiently modify or interpret these 'problematic' rules away, or An-Na'im's criterion will not be met, leaving removal of *sharīʿah* from the state as the only option. As mentioned earlier, the Islamic Secular may contribute marginally to such efforts at conciliation, for example, by monitoring the factual changes that the legal tradition recognizes as a basis for modifying rules. And it may assist in the important process of distinguishing *sharʿī* rules from non-*sharʿī* policies. At the end of the day, however, such contributions can only go so far. The Islamic Secular alone, as the realm *warāʾ al-ḥukm al-sharʿī*, has no direct response to this aspect of the problem. It may contribute indirectly, through contributions "beyond the law" that modify the cultural sensibilities of Muslim men and women in a manner that produces a more balanced or female-sensitive regime of norms or interpretive prisms; or it may redefine "equality," or even displace it as the panacean standard for gender relations. Ultimately, however, this will be as far as the Islamic Secular can go in this regard.

Yet, the fact that aspects of the challenge of gender are more substantive than structural does not necessarily render the Islamic Secular, certainly as non-*sharʿī fikr*, entirely irrelevant to the topic of women. "Equality" as a construct is not self-authenticating, and its meaning, status, and proper application in concrete practical terms (one thinks of Affirmative Action) remain topics of reasoned debate. It is doubtful, for example, that an *ijtihād sharʿī* that rendered polyandry permissible (as opposed to simply banning polygyny) or that made it obligatory (*wājib*) for Muslim women to attend Friday Prayer, or that released husbands from the mandatory duty of financial maintenance (*nafaqah*) would amount to the equality that An-Na'im has in mind. In fairness, An-Na'im acknowledges that his secularism, like secularism everywhere, is "contextual, contested, and negotiated over time."[175] "Equality," in other words might be understood to mean equality regarding those issues on which men and women in any given society at any given time *should* be treated equally, not equality in the absolute. This is a perfectly reasonable approach. But it clearly implicates Islamic Secular deliberations that go beyond *sharīʿah* and its *ḥukm sharʿī* to contemplate and negotiate the socio-cultural and political *wāqiʿ* in pursuit of normative instantiations of "equality" that are calibrated to that *wāqiʿ* so understood, albeit in conversation with *sharīʿah*. An exclusive focus on *sharīʿah* alone, however, blocks from view the importance (if not possibility) of such religiously informed negotiations. Similarly, removing *sharīʿah* from the state would not change the fact that these are largely—and critically—non-*sharʿī*, Islamic Secular deliberations.

Something similar might be said regarding equality in the case of non-Muslims. Stephen Carter cuts to the heart of the matter when he describes how a leading evangelist once told him that Muslim inmates have all the rights that Christians have in American prisons. To this Carter responded, "No doubt they do. But they would prefer to have the rights they need as Muslims. The right to do everything that Christians are allowed to do is not the same as the right to follow God in their own way."[176] This raises questions about whether "equality," or at least "formal equality," as opposed to "accommodation," "equality of respect," or some related alternative is the best standard on which to negotiate a Muslim state's relationship with non-Muslims, in fact, whether holding an Islamic State to a standard of equality always serves non-Muslim interests.[177] Especially in a society where the overwhelming majority is presumed to be Muslim, one might ask whether and how removing *sharīʿah* from the state adds to the promotion of this particular interest. In fact, as we saw in the case of Pope Shenoudah, one might ask if it actually harms it. Ultimately, however, even this manner of presenting the problem partly distorts and misrepresents it. For, "applying *sharīʿah*" (as the opposite of removing it from the state) in a legally monistic, jurispathic Islamic State will produce one outcome, while applying it in an Islamic State in the form of a modernized empire-state will produce another. Whether Muslims choose one or the other of these arrangements will be as much an Islamic Secular as it is a *sharʿī* decision. In the meantime, to look to secularism—in the form of separating *sharīʿah* from the state—as the singular solution to the problem of equality would seem to entail a misdiagnosis of the problem.

Also beyond the matter of structure, part of the problem that state implementation of *sharīʿah* poses for An-Naʿim is that of jurisdiction, that is, by what authority *sharīʿah* should be adopted as state-law to begin with, particularly where this entails applying it to groups and individuals who do not believe in Islam? An-Naʿim would prefer that *sharīʿah* restrict its authority to his "politics", that is, non-binding public suasion and private indulgence. The very idea of grounding the public order in religio-political authority infuses the law with an authoritarian awe and heaviness that minimize the prospects for pluralism and discourages if not frustrates dissent, making it difficult to sustain open debate around critical issues affecting the commonweal. This is not to mention the deleterious impact that state implementation of religious law may have on the integrity of religiosity itself, what An-Naʿim might term, "the freedom to assent."

An-Naʿim's proposal to separate *sharīʿah* from the state as a means of avoiding these problems is intended to serve Muslims and non-Muslims alike. For Muslims (who are not of a single mind regarding *sharīʿah*) this would mitigate conflict by reducing negotiation to the ostensibly neutral instrument of "civic reason." To my mind, however, it is difficult to imagine why, after Islam has held acts such as adultery to be forbidden and punishable for over 1,400 years, a committed Muslim would suddenly be willing to present this rule before the bar of civic reason for review and possible recension. In fact, it may be both naive and dangerous to assume that a Muslim's acquiescence in the face of conclusions reached through such means can be unquestionably taken as actual agreement upon which a stable socio-political consensus can be built. Meanwhile, it might be useful to consider in this context the distinction between what might be proper for Muslims to debate through civic reason and what might not, based on the distinction between the *shar'ī* and non-*shar'ī* aspects of Islam-cum-*sharī'ah*.

For An-Na'im, of course, everything must be subjected to the process of negotiation through civic reason. This extends to non-Muslims as well, for whom separating *sharī'ah* from the state is also supposed to facilitate equal participation in the process of "debating . . . issues in relation to public policy and state law."[178] Again, An-Na'im draws no distinction between what is '*shar'ī*' and what is not, between, for example, what Christians might see as religious, "*in the proper, the religious sense*," such as no-fault remarriage, and what they might see as an important but more "secular" concern, such as whether to nationalize healthcare. It is doubtful, however, that Coptic Christians would be any more willing to accept Muslim views on the Coptic ban on no-fault remarriage than Muslims would be willing to accept Coptic views on the legality of pronouncing a triple Islamic divorce in a single sitting. This contrasts both groups' likely attitude toward negotiating such mutually shared, non-*shar'ī* issues as speed limits or national healthcare plans. Ultimately, on An-Na'im's approach, Muslims and non-Muslims might be more likely to *reject* each other's *unqualified* equal participation, whereas, on the approach of the Islamic Secular, they might be more likely to *accept* each other's *qualified* equal participation, the distinction between the *shar'ī* and non-*shar'ī* allowing them to recognize and accept the propriety of mutual negotiation on some matters even if not on all.

Were An-Na'im to recognize, as a structural fact, that *sharī'ah* is a bounded entity that leaves vast areas of public law and policy to differentiated, non-*shar'ī*, Islamic Secular deliberation, he might see less utility in banishing *sharī'ah* in the interest of non-Muslims. Al-Qarāfī, for example, while noting the general prohibition on admitting non-Muslim testimony where it impinges upon *sharī'ah* rules, states explicitly that their testimony *is* to be accepted on such matters as medicine or whether a product should be considered defective, even in cases involving Muslims.[179] Their relevance to the application of *sharī'ah* rules notwithstanding, these are identifiably non-*shar'ī* determinations, to which one's status as a non-Muslim is not a bar, at least not categorically. Centuries later, Shaykh Yūsuf al-Qaraḍāwī, a staunch contemporary proponent of the Islamic

State, displays a similar logic when he intimates that non-*shar'ī* rules and policies are open to universal debate. After observing that non-Muslims have the right to adjudicate family affairs and related matters according to their own rules, he states: "As for other areas, such as civil, commercial, and administrative regulations, non-Muslims relate to these as they relate to any other general legislation that may be borrowed from the West or the East and is approved by the majority."[180] In other words, it would be no less proper or acceptable for non-Muslims to debate these essentially non-*shar'ī*, 'secular' issues than it would be for Muslims to debate them.

Something similar could be said regarding the relationship between Islamists and lapsed or "secular" Muslims, an insight that may have contributed significantly to the efforts of Rached El Ghannouchi in Tunisia, for example, in his effort to negotiate and assuage fears about the relationship between *sharī'ah* and the pending constitution during the crisis of 2012–13.[181] Clearly, on the understanding I have laid out, for the state to "apply *sharī'ah*" does not preempt the adoption of any number of non-*shar'ī* rules, which the Islamic Secular clearly distinguishes from rules that are anti-*sharī'ah*. As *shar'ī* knowledge and commitment are irrelevant to numerous aspects of non-*shar'ī* rules, non-Muslims, as well as lapsed or "secular" Muslims, should be able to debate such aspects on an equal footing with religiously observant or Islamist Muslims. In fact, assuming the commonweal to be the actual concern, it is difficult to see why the views of a non-Muslim or a "secular" Muslim scientist or actuary should be categorically excluded from decisions about whether to authorize a vaccine against a deadly virus or how much traffic a proposed bridge or public building should be designed to bear.[182] Why should a non-Muslim's religion—*qua* non-Muslim—be a bar to his or her heading an Islamic State's Center for Disease Control? And why, generally speaking, in the case of lapsed Muslims, should we categorically overlook the distinction that Imām Aḥmad makes between the strong miscreant (*qawī fājir*) and the pious weakling (*ṣāliḥ ḍa'īf*)?[183] Why should the non-Muslim masses be deemed any less knowledgeable than Muslims when it comes to everyday problems of government bureaucracy or traffic jams?[184] Failure to recognize the Islamic Secular and the *shar'ī*/non-*shar'ī* distinction it implies leads to the misapprehension of these and countless other issues, again, directing An-Na'im (and others) to the singular solution of secularization or barring religion-as-*sharī'ah* from any attachment to the state.

The fact that An-Na'im does not recognize the non-*shar'ī* Islamic Secular also informs his view that *sharī'ah*'s attachment to the state precludes the possibility of a functional constitutionalism, human rights, and citizenship. I have already touched on aspects of this. I would add here only that I do not understand why An-Na'im overlooks the fact that Muslim states that attach themselves explicitly to *sharīʿah* routinely produce constitutions in which human rights and citizenship are explicitly mentioned. The 2005 Constitution of his native Sudan, for example, states under "Sources of Legislation" (5: 1), "Nationally enacted legislation having effect only in respect of the Northern states of the Sudan shall have as its sources of legislation Islamic Sharia and the consensus of the people." It goes on to state under "Citizenship and Nationality" (7: 1), "Citizenship shall be the basis of equal rights and duties for all Sudanese." Section 28 reads, "Every human being has the inherent right to life, dignity and the integrity of his person, which shall be protected by law; no one shall arbitrarily be deprived of his life." And section 142: 1 states, "The President of the Republic shall, after consultation within the Presidency, establish an independent Human Rights Commission."[185]

Many of the provisions of this Constitution, which include numerous points connected with human rights and citizenship, are the result of non-*sharʿī*, Islamic Secular deliberation. For example, citizenship is extended to "every person born to a Sudanese mother or father," and the President's Human Rights Commission consists of "fifteen independent, competent nonpartisan and impartial members." There is nothing in *sharīʿah* per se that would dictate such stipulations. My point here is that, as I suggested earlier, issues such as constitutionalism, human rights, and citizenship are (or can be) at least as reliant upon *fikr*, or Islamic Secular deliberation, as they are on *fiqh* or strict *ijtihād sharʿī*.

More importantly, this example reiterates two things: (1) there is (or can be) a significant degree of compatibility between *sharīʿah* and constitutionalism; and (2) *sharīʿah* does not necessarily provide everything a constitution needs (e.g., term limits, number of representatives, and the like). On both scores, the notion that the only way a state can accommodate constitutionalism or human rights or citizenship is to separate *sharīʿah* from its governing apparatus seems overstated. A more accurate conceptualization of *sharīʿah*—or more accurately, Islamic law—would include recognition of a vast non-*sharʿī*, Islamic Secular repository from which solutions to many constitutional matters (as well as matters concerning human rights or citizenship) might be drawn, all without relying upon or necessarily offending *sharīʿah*.

As I prepare to close, I would like to register two points. First, as in my engagement with Hallaq, it has not been my aim in engaging with An-Naʿim to defend the Islamic State per se in any particular iteration. My attempt has simply been to interrogate An-Naʿim's argument against the Islamic State in light of the Islamic Secular. By analogy, one might argue, as I would, that some of the arguments against same-sex marriage in the United States are simply bad arguments, for example, that the definition of "marriage" is a union between "one man and one woman." To point out such weaknesses, however, does not mean that one is necessarily in favor of same-sex marriage. It simply means that one does not believe that those particular arguments against it are sound or convincing, or that the issue itself is best served by continuing to debate it on the basis of such arguments.

Second, despite our disagreements, there are important points of agreement between An-Na'im's Secular State and my Islamic Secular. First, both recognize that "[t]here is . . . much more to Islam than Shari'a."[186] But, unlike the Islamic Secular, An-Na'im does not theorize this "much more," to the end of providing a reliable, formal criterion for distinguishing what is *sharīʿah* from what is not, within the circumference of Islam. Second, both recognize the difference between "the traditional 'minimal' imperial state of the past (what I call the empire-state) and the centralized, hierarchical, bureaucratic state of today."[187] But whereas An-Na'im apparently sees modernity as having birthed a political structure that is fixed and "irreversible,"[188] the Islamic Secular sees both the empire-state *and* the modern state as more malleable structures that are open to further possibility. Third, both An-Na'im and the Islamic Secular are adamantly opposed to the "over-*sharīʿ*atization" of the applied order. For An-Na'im, however, the optimal way of avoiding this is to remove *sharīʿah* from the state altogether, a move significantly indebted to the tendency to overlook the distinction between the *sharʿī* and non-*sharʿī* both within *sharīʿah* and beyond. For the Islamic Secular, the solution is not to remove *sharīʿah* but to ensure that what the state applies in the name of *sharīʿah* is in fact *sharʿī* and that the state not be allowed to impute to its discretionary, non-*sharʿī* rules and policies a binding, unassailable, *sharʿī* authority that it has no right to claim.

Here, in fact, we come to one of the more subtle yet far-reaching differences not simply between An-Na'im and the Islamic Secular but between the latter and the "over-*sharīʿ*atizing" impulse of Islamists who insist that the Islamic State must apply the *sharʿ*, the whole *sharʿ*, and nothing but the *sharʿ*. An-Na'im begins with the secular state and asks how religion can be successfully integrated into its mission. This point of departure raises the question of why *sharīʿah* should be applied as state law in the first place. The (secular) state's authority to coerce is assumed and unproblematically granted the authority to regulate religion. Religion, on the other hand, is not recognized as having any right to coerce or regulate the state. By contrast, Islamists begin with religion and view the state as a functionary thereof. In contradistinction to An-Na'im, they assume that it is religion's role to coerce behavior and to regulate the state. And any right the state might have to coerce behavior must be directly and concretely derived from religion (read: *sharīʿah*) and from religion alone (again, read *sharīʿah*).

Contrary to both perspectives, the Islamic Secular sees state and religious authority as distinct but not entirely separate or mutually exclusive; they are mutual participants in a complementary condominium rather than competitors in a zero-sum hierarchy. Ideally, each dialectically regulates and is regulated by the other in pursuit of the pure or preponderant interests of the Community. To be sure, this is a difficult balance to strike, let alone maintain. And An-Na'im seems to think that appeals to secular constitutionalism, human rights, and citizenship are simply the safest bet. Others, however, myself included, are less confident that appeals to such abstract constructs as "secularism" can suffice in the face of his Secular State's zealously guarded monopoly on power. If Islamists cannot be assumed to be angels who are immune to the temptations of power, I see no reason—in theory or in fact—to assume that secularists are.

Meanwhile, Islamists (or at least those An-Na'im has in mind) who also do not recognize the Islamic Secular tend to locate the solution to the problem of power in the abject domestication of the state, via the total *sharī'*atization of everything, in which capacity the state is portrayed as normatively exercising no power or authority beyond the discrete and identifiable dictates of *sharī'ah*. This applies especially, perhaps, though not exclusively, to certain articulations of Salafism, which perceives everything that purports to be religious but is not directly traceable to scripture as *bid'ah*, or "unsanctioned innovation," a betrayal of Islam. On this understanding, everything the state does (or should do or has a right to do) bears the presumption of being concretely dictated by *sharī'ah*. And on this presumption, autocracy—along with bad economic, educational, administrative, or other policies—can all be effectively *sharī'*atized, that is, camouflaged, insulated, and legitimated in the name of Islam-cum-*sharī'ah*, in a manner that effectively places all of this beyond critique.

This is among An-Na'im's greatest fears and underscores the urgency of his call for a Secular State.[189] Yet, such autocracy is precisely what the Islamic Secular seeks to preempt and delegitimize, not by separating *sharī'ah* from the state but by separating the *shar'ī* from the non-*shar'ī* in what the state has the right to impose and in what citizens have an even greater right to negotiate. To the extent that constitutionalism is, as An-Na'im puts it, "the set of principles that limit and control the powers of government," it would seem that the Islamic Secular's *shar'ī*/non-*shar'ī* distinction would be foundational to the demarcation of state power.

As should be clear by now, this *shar'ī*/non-*shar'ī* distinction is the Islamic Secular's primary obsession. In pre-modern times, the corporate authority of the *fuqahā'* went a long way toward institutionalizing it on a practical level, via the zealously guarded role the jurists played in defining the substance of *sharī'ah*. In many ways, their independence (sustained in part by the financial backing of the monied lay community), along with their ostensible monopoly on legal interpretation, enabled them to block the state from wrongful claims to specifically *shar'ī* authority. At the same time, their lack of martial power ensured that they would never take over the state, freeing the latter to promulgate its non-*shar'ī* discretionary policies and regulations. It is questionable whether such an arrangement could re-emerge under present conditions. But I hope I have shown that, however Muslims choose to proceed, their efforts to establish and maintain the desired balance will require significant investment in the Islamic Secular.

In the meantime, the idea of separating *sharīʿah* entirely from the state is likely to produce as much dislocation as the idea that the state could function on the basis of *sharīʿah* alone. Ultimately, Islam-cum-*sharīʿah* can never make permanent, unconditional peace with the state. For, to do so would be to forfeit its duty to moralize, humanize, communalize, judge, and enhance the efficiency of the state, not to mention criticizing and resisting it when appropriate. Yet, Islam-cum-*sharīʿah* can also not reject the state absolutely or declare itself to be at permanent, unconditional war with it. For, to do so would be to commit a similar dereliction. Not only is there a religious mandate for Muslims to organize politically, but the state serves any number of critical functions without which Islam-cum-*sharīʿah*, as a lived reality on the ground in the real world of global civilizational competition, would suffer mortally. This was the point of the redoubtable ʿIzz al-Dīn Ibn ʿAbd al-Salām when he emphasized the enormity of the reward awaiting just, competent state officials, based on the enormity of the harms they avoid and the benefits they bring to the Community.[190]

In Islam, the state (modern, empire, or other) is a means to promote and preserve the interests and integrity of the Islamic Community. Islam-cum-*sharīʿah* can neither consign nor abandon the Community to those who seize (or even legitimately come to) power. Nor—recalling from Chapter 3 the importance of the Islamic Secular "beyond the law" (and beyond the state)—can the state or *sharīʿah* alone be relied upon to construct and preserve the *nomos* and plausibility structure upon which their normativeness and efficacy so significantly rest. In the end, the Islamic Secular will always be integral to the preservation of the Muslim state, *sharīʿah*, and Muslim society. Not only does it consummate the process of separating the *sharʿī* from the non-*sharʿī*, thereby placing all the needed authorities and metrics of assessment in their proper place, but it also enables Muslims to recognize and ideally rise to the critical modern challenge of constructing Islam-cum-*sharīʿah*'s requisite *nomos* and plausibility structure, empowering them to do in the modern world what they so successfully did in the pre-modern world: "create the tastes by which one is judged."[191]

In closing, I must reiterate that An-Naʿim's focus is the majority-Muslim states of the contemporary Muslim world. As with Hallaq, my engagement with him assumes that same basic focal point. Discussing such matters as separating religion from the state in a non-Muslim context entails a very different set of considerations. As such, one should not mechanically extend my critical engagement with An-Naʿim (or Hallaq) to other contexts. Should White Evangelicals in the United States, for example, equate Christianity with Whiteness and see Whiteness itself as a "Christian race," the notion of religion's attachment to or separation from the state, especially given America's legal monism and jurispathic legacy, would take on a meaning, thrust, and set of problems entirely different from those we have been discussing.[192] Of course, the Islamic Secular would still play a role in navigating this terrain. But the relationship between Islam-cum-*sharīʿah* and a predominantly non-Muslim Western democracy is simply a different topic.

Yet, there *are* Muslims in the West. And the question of the normative relationship between Islam-cum-*sharīʿah* and the state is as urgent there as it is in the traditional Muslim world. It is thus to that topic that I shall now turn.

6
The Islamic Secular and Liberal Citizenship

Basic Anatomy

The primary focus of Hallaq and An-Na'im was the Muslim-majority states of the traditional Muslim world (An-Na'im including one non-Muslim-majority state where Muslims have constituted a significant, indigenous minority for centuries). While Western Europe's colonial and imperial legacy exerted far-reaching influence on these states, none of them were actual constituents of "the West." This is what distinguishes Andrew March's *Islam and Liberal Citizenship: The Search for an Overlapping Consensus.* Here the emphasis is on Muslim communities living as minorities in Europe and more focally the United States. And the fundamental question is how they as Muslims—or, more accurately, how Islam-cum-*sharī'ah*—can negotiate a normative relationship with a Western, liberal democracy as citizens thereof. Like An-Na'im, March takes the separation between religion and state for granted, as he does the notion that the state should control or domesticate religion. In contrast to An-Na'im, however, March's main focus is not on secularism per se but on liberal political theory and how Muslims can or cannot relate to it as the basis for negotiating Islam-cum-*sharī'ah*'s relationship with a modern, liberal, democratic order.

The central argument of *Islam and Liberal Citizenship* is that, contrary to what is commonly assumed in the West and even asserted by a minority of modern Muslim jurists and thinkers, the cumulative legacy of Islam's "*juridical and ethical tradition*"[1] is capable of accommodating liberal citizenship on the level of doctrine. By "liberal citizenship," March has in mind the general dictates of John Rawls's (d. 2002) "political liberalism," though he distills from the cumulative legacy of liberalism his own criteria for measuring compliance therewith. These Marchian criteria consist of four basic issues and their subsidiaries: (1) the permissibility, *shar'an*, that is, from the perspective of *sharī'ah*, of residing in non-Muslim polities; (2) the permissibility, *shar'an*, of being loyal to non-Muslim polities; (3) the permissibility, *shar'an*, of recognizing moral pluralism and non-Muslims as moral equals; and (4) the permissibility, *shar'an*, of solidarity with non-Muslim fellow citizens. By "Islam," March's main focus is the Islamic juristic tradition, that is, *fiqh* and *uṣūl al-fiqh*, diachronically read across Muslim history

The Islamic Secular. Sherman A. Jackson, Oxford University Press. © Oxford University Press 2024.
DOI: 10.1093/oso/9780197661789.003.0007

down to modern times, when some of its putative representatives, on March's depiction, are no longer trained in traditional Islamic law and jurisprudence. To this March adds exegesis of Qur'ān and *ḥadīth*, which he occasionally carries out himself. In the end, he concludes that there is a good-faith, plausible reading of Islam and its juristic tradition that accommodates his criteria and is consistent with the fundamental dictates of Rawlsian liberal citizenship. As he states in his concluding chapter, "[I]n all the areas in which this book set out to investigate the possibility of an overlapping consensus, Islamic views compatible with liberal conceptions of the demands of citizenship can be found."[2]

March is careful to note that his central focus is not Muslims as products of a particular culture or history; he is interested, rather, in the thoughts and attitudes that they bring to their engagement with liberal citizenship as a result and expression of their *doctrinal* commitment to Islam-cum-*sharīʿah*. He acknowledges that some may see this approach as infantilizing Muslims by reducing them to a mechanical impulse to surrender to religious doctrine, as if they were robotically driven by religion alone. He notes as well that some may see this particular focus as letting the West off the hook, by overlooking its misdeeds and their impact on Muslim perspectives on the West. March neither dismisses nor attempts to sidestep any of this. Instead, he insists that, for all that colonialism, Islamophobia, and American foreign policy may contribute to Muslim attitudes toward the reigning political order in (or of) the West, the issue itself remains no less about whether Islam-cum-*sharīʿah* can sanction full Muslim participation in a secular liberal democracy, as a matter of doctrine.[3] His project, therefore, is to distill from the aggregate of possible influences on Muslim thought and attitudes the doctrinal dictates of Islam-cum-*sharīʿah* as a distinct and legitimate topic of inquiry.

March's work is a welcome response to the tendency to over-invest in untutored stereotypes about Islam-cum-*sharīʿah* and its purportedly unqualified clash with the civilization of the modern liberal West. His intervention is particularly valuable at a time when attaching the label "illiberal" to Muslims invariably reinforces fears about the dangers they purportedly represent to and in the West. Instead of thoughtfully investigating the relationship between Islam-cum-*sharīʿah* and liberal democracy, many non-Muslim (and some Muslim) observers reflexively assume categorical, mutual exclusivity. And instead of comparing Muslim critiques of liberal theory with those of MacIntyre, Sandel, Walzer, Rorty, Fish, Dworkin, Kahn, Hauerwas, or Mills, these observers routinely equate anything short of complete conformity on the part of Muslims with religious bigotry, intolerance, an Islamic "will to power," or Muslims' plain old inability to get with the modern program. With the possible exception of Hauerwas, none of the aforementioned non-Muslim thinkers would be branded "conservative." Yet, this is the uncharitable fate awaiting any Muslim who is not unreservedly committed to liberalism's intellectual heritage.

March's work provides an opportunity to investigate the relationship between Islam and liberalism much more seriously. For that alone, his effort deserves commendation.

March's Framing and Its Implications

March's arguments are sophisticated, forceful, and often logically unassailable. Much of their strength, however, is sustained by the interpretive presuppositions that inform his framing of the conversation between Islam and liberal citizenship. Of course, we are all driven by presuppositions; the question is how transparent we are in presenting them and how convincing our arguments remain in the face of such transparency. March is effectively engaged in what I referred to in the Introduction as "Islamic Studies 2.0." As I also stated there, however, the credibility of a scholar's 2.0 depends largely on the reliability of the 1.0 on which it is built. I argue that March's presuppositions, which inform both his method and his conclusions, place important aspects of the American socio-political order and the nature and substance of Islam-cum-*sharī'a*h beyond consideration, which results in a view of the relationship between Islam and liberal citizenship that is mildly distorted and incomplete. As a preliminary, therefore, to my direct engagement with March's thesis, I would like to highlight five important aspects of his framing.

First, Rawlsian liberal theory is the medium through which March aims to investigate the relationship between Islam and liberal citizenship. To do this, he proposes bringing Islam-cum-*sharī'ah* and Rawlsian liberalism into conversation as "ideal theories." This presupposes, of course, that the Islamic juristic tradition can be safely and meaningfully processed as an ideal theory and that such processing sacrifices nothing on either side of the equation. By "ideal theory," March means a theory that is abstracted beyond the specificities of any particular society into a transcendent, normative ideal. The point is to theorize about society not as it is but as it ideally should be. In other words, society is never "post-colonial," "occupied," "racialized," or "militarily, economically, or intellectually dependent"; it is an abstracted, perfectly just society.[4] My point here is not to echo Marx's critique of philosophical idealism, which "thinks it has overcome the real world merely by transforming it into a 'thing of thought.' "[5] The problem, rather, is that March wants to place liberalism *as* an abstract, transcendent moral/political philosophy in conversation with *sharī'ah as* an abstract, transcendent juristic tradition. But this, I argue, defies *sharī'ah*'s inherent nature and weakens its ability to speak for itself as a juristic tradition.

This is not to argue that Islam-cum-*sharī'ah* cannot speak in the voice of philosophical idealism. As a discipline, *uṣūl fiqh* (and even moreso theology) routinely addresses profoundly abstract questions—for example, whether God can impose on humans a duty greater than they can bear—in a manner that is indubitably philosophical. But abstract, ideal moral/political philosophy as such was generally the province of the "humanistic" or *adab* tradition in Islam.[6] And this tradition was palpably distinct from the discourse of *fiqh/sharīʿah*, especially the *ḥukm sharʿī* and the permissible-impermissible metric at the heart of March's analysis.[7] Ultimately, neither in content nor in orientation was—or is—*fiqh/sharīʿah* abstract, transcendent political philosophy or "ideal moral theory."

Muslim jurists have long recognized this fact. Indeed, the tendency to approach *fiqh/sharīʿah* as ideal theory has been among the most pressing problems in Islamic legal history. We saw earlier how unidimensional abstract rule-following can preempt the ability to develop important remedial norms, such as the fact that perfectly licit acts may compromise one's probity (*al-mubāḥāt al-mukhillah bi al-ʿadālah*).[8] We see it as well in the occasionally stifling tenacity of such constructs as *dar al-ḥarb* (Abode of War), despite their clear historical contingency.[9] More directly, the central problem with *taqlīd* has been the tendency among *muqallid* jurists to treat *fiqh*-texts as compendia of transcendent rules that are impervious to the contingencies of quotidian flux. Al-Qarāfī, for example, is relentless in decrying this trend:

> Do not spend your life clinging slavishly to the contents of (*fiqh*) manuals. Rather, if a man comes to you from another locale seeking a *fatwā*, do not advise him on the basis of the custom of your country. Ask him about the custom of his country and advise and give him a *fatwā* according to that, not the custom of your country or what is preserved in your books. . . . Clinging slavishly to views that have been handed down from the past always constitutes error in religion and ignorance of the aims of the Muslim scholars and Pious Ancestors of old.[10]

Further, he writes, "Holding to rulings that have been deduced on the basis of custom, even after this custom has changed, is a violation of unanimous consensus and an open display of ignorance of the religion."[11] Of course, al-Qarāfī was not alone in this regard, as we saw with Ibn al-Qayyim and the critical role he attached to "*fahm al-wāqiʿ wa fiqhuh.*"[12] Similarly, speaking of the juristic duty to weigh harms and interests in crafting *fatwās*, Ibn Taymīyah invokes the ancient adage: "The rational man is not he who knows good from evil. He is, more simply, he who knows what is better and what is worse" (*laysa al-ʿāqil alladhī yaʿlam al-khayr min al-sharr wa innamā al-ʿāqil alladhī yaʿlam khayr al-khayrayn wa sharr al-sharrayn*), a calculus clearly more empirical than abstract.[13] In sum, *fiqh/sharīʿah* has long included, and consciously so, an inextricable role for differentiated, non-*sharʿī*, Islamic Secular deliberations, which are distinct from even if routinely in the service of the *ḥukm sharʿī* itself. Moreover, the normative role of the jurist's *fatwā* is often not to reflect the ideal but to instruct Muslims on how to pursue God's pleasure and divinely sanctioned human interests in this the real world, not in an ideal one.

March might respond that this argument misses his point. As he explains early on, were he to consider all the historical, political, economic, religious, racial, and other elements that contribute to the manifold encounters between Islam and the West, his project would be doomed, as he would not be able to isolate what Islam specifically contributes to its relationship with liberal citizenship. By contrast, he suggests:

> By studying the pattens of moral disagreement in their *specific points of contact*, by studying Islamic moral commitments in terms of a *juridical and ethical tradition*, and by abstracting ourselves from a political analysis of current events to something like an *ideal moral encounter*, it is possible to better understand whether a given political conflict actually has as its root a principled moral disagreement between competing ethical systems.[14]

In other words, as mentioned earlier, March wants to examine not how historically grounded grievances against the West define Muslims' relationship with liberal citizenship but how that relationship is defined by their principled doctrinal commitment to Islam-cum-*sharīʿah*. But if it is not modern Muslims' clinging to post-colonial grievances but the Islamic juristic tradition itself that insists that Islam's "*juridical and ethical*" judgments must be informed by assessments of concrete reality on the ground, we can only ignore the various ways that liberalism concretizes itself in America at the expense of distorting the approach of the Islamic juristic tradition that March purports to examine. Stated differently, even if Rawlsian liberalism can abstract itself out of quotidian reality, *sharīʿah* (including its Islamic Secular element) cannot. And to force it into an encounter with abstract rather than concrete reality—especially the latter's sustained as opposed to its episodic features—is simply to misunderstand and misrepresent it. In this light, even if March's conclusions about Islam and liberal citizenship turn out to be sound as far as they go, they cannot reflect the full picture.

The second feature of March's framing is indebted to the first. His proposal to place Islam and liberalism in conversation as "ideal theories" entails two prior moves. The first is to convert Islam as a whole into an expression of doctrine, that is, the *sharʿī* conclusions of the hermeneutic engagement with scripture. This follows Rawls's obsession with the problem of disagreements over doctrine as the fundamental cause of societal conflict. March casts Islam-cum-*sharīʿah* in a Rawlsian image by converting it into an articulation of scriptural and tradition-based answers to questions of religious, that is, *sharʿī*, permissibility.

Again, the impulse is understandable; but we have seen how the Islamic Secular routinely takes Islam's deliberations, including its juristic deliberations, *beyond* considerations of permissibility, permissibility alone not always determining the actual substance of decisions. This problem is further complicated by March's identification of doctrine with morality or ethics, which Islam-cum-*sharīʿah* also routinely transcends. Recall, for example, that the question of whether to promote commerce in copper coins could not be resolved solely on the basis of whether such commerce was moral or permissible, *sharʿan*. The same applies to such larger questions as Islam's relationship with liberal citizenship.

Reducing Islam to doctrine becomes an added liability in the post–September 11th era. As non-Muslim Americans struggle with their perceptions of Islam, restricting the conversation to questions of permissibility can promote the psychologically comforting jump from what Muslims *can* do to what they *should*, or perhaps *must*, do. In other words, because *sharīʿah* permits Muslims to be loyal, to live in solidarity with others, etc., many non-Muslim Americans may resent Muslims who find material, tactical, or strategic reasons not to be loyal or stand in solidarity with other Americans (as March defines these gestures), or to do so with significant qualifications. In fact, dissenting Muslims may end up more likely to be viewed as extremists, since their dissidence may be perceived as gratuitous rather than principled. Muslims who publicly demonstrate against a Salman Rushdie book or a Danish cartoon might be seen as less legitimate (and more threatening) than non-Muslim Blackamericans or Jews who demonstrate against KKK rallies. For, Muslims who engage in such activities are more likely to be seen as acting on religious doctrines that compel them to restrict free speech or impose *sharīʿah*, since religious doctrine is now understood to be their only basis of action as Muslims.

The second prior move is to treat Islam-cum-*sharīʿah* not just as doctrine but as a "comprehensive doctrine," an all-encompassing *sharʿī* outlook that speaks to every aspect of life.[15] As we will see, the problem of what to do with comprehensive doctrines is crucial to Rawls's (and March's) overall project. But we have also seen that the stereotypical notion of *sharīʿah* speaking to "everything" is misleadingly overstated. This raises questions about the propriety of treating *fiqh/sharīʿah* as a comprehensive doctrine. As a bounded entity, *fiqh/sharīʿah* simply cannot tell us all there is to know about Islam. Yet, March appears to proceed precisely on this presumption. In a general description of his project, he asks: "How would one begin to ask whether Islam can endorse 'the basic idea of society as a fair system of cooperation' and the idea of public reason? Where would one find this in the Qur'an or works of Islamic law?"[16]

The third feature of March's framing calls into question how abstract or transcendent his "liberal citizenship" or "society as a fair system of cooperation" actually is (or can be). March conceptualizes Muslims as almost exclusively those who have immigrated to the West from the traditional lands of Islam (or their progeny).[17] In and of itself, there is nothing wrong with this: every author has his or her interests, and every book is limited in what it can successfully cover. Moreover, in the aggregate, this demographic constitutes the majority of Muslims in the West. Yet, on this particular framing, neither Muslims, America, nor liberal citizenship can be seen as fully abstract, transcendent entities. For, all are embedded in socio-political, cultural, historical, and racial/ethnic specificity and flux. March might respond that I am distorting his thesis in order to avoid it, by bringing his ideal, transcendent liberal citizenship down to a level of concrete specificity where it can be more easily critiqued. But, based both on what he includes and excludes, I would argue that March's own depictions undermine his claim to transcendence.

Unlike the case in Europe, a significant segment of the Muslim population in America consists of trans-generationally native-born citizens—Blackamericans—whose legacy as Muslims began not with an act of immigration but with conscious acts of conversion—in America.[18] March indirectly alludes to this contingent when he speaks of those who enjoy "a certain cultural authenticity or demographic confidence,"[19] despite the fact that " 'American nationhood' has been constructed as 'white' or at least 'not black.' "[20] But, he largely ignores the implications of this variable for his thesis. In point of fact, negotiating one's relationship with American citizenship has *always* implicated race—for *everyone*.[21] In this capacity, liberal citizenship in America has always been mired in a concrete specificity that entails as many non-*shar'ī* questions of material interest, for example, how to negotiate race or confront racism, as it does ostensibly transcendent *shar'ī* questions of religious doctrine, for example, whether it is permissible, *shar'an*, to reside in America. By implying, however, that questions of doctrine are all that a Muslim—in fact, all that Islam-cum-*sharī'ah*—needs to confront in seeking to negotiate a normative relationship with America, March both subtly sanitizes liberal citizenship and distorts the nature and task of Islam-cum-*sharī'ah*.

Almost all the modern Muslim sources upon which March relies, especially the more rejectionist among them, intimate concerns about the loss of identity (*al-dhūbān*) as a consequence of living in the West, as if residence, solidarity, and the like necessarily imply assimilation, the uncritical quest for acceptance in exchange for adopting someone else's moral-cum-socio-cultural profile. This attitude is understandable, given the civilizing designs of the imperial powers and the post-colonial memory and response to these. But it hardly reflects a "transcendent" socio-political reality. For, it overlooks the fact that significant numbers of Muslims in America, namely, Blackamerican Muslims, are attached to a unique, proud, rich, "indigenous" Black *American* culture and identity—from jazz to Ebonics, from soul food and Hip-Hop to George Washington Carver. This attachment provides, at least partly and in theory, an alternative to the zero-sum options of rejectionism and assimilation. At the same time, it underscores the fact that March's inquiry does not begin from an ideal, Archimedean point of departure.

My point here is not to advocate focusing on one of these demographics over the other but to question the extent to which centering on either can be reconciled with a claim to transcendence. March might respond that his focus is not on Muslims (Blackamerican, 'immigrant', or other) but on Islam's doctrinal position(s) on the issues under review, abstracted out of any particular socio-political context.[22] But even leaving aside whether he actually achieves this aim of abstraction, returning to my earlier point, if the goal is to engage with Islam-cum-*sharīʿah*, we cannot overlook its insistence on a proper assessment of reality on the ground as part of the process of reaching a proper *sharʿī* ruling (read: doctrine) on any socio-political matter.[23] In other words, even if the question is how Islam, not Muslims, might respond to the challenge of liberal citizenship, the racial dimension of the American *wāqiʿ* must be considered. Otherwise, we end up misapprehending not only the reality of American liberal citizenship but also the functional nature of the Islamic juristic tradition with which we purport to place it in conversation.

The fourth feature of March's framing is the particular diachronic thrust he gives to *fiqh/sharīʿah*. He begins by conferring normativity upon what I would characterize as a 'Fundamentalist' imaginary. By Fundamentalist, I am not referring to radicalism or extremism or any particular Muslim political movement per se. Nor am I implying any commitment to literalism as a privileged hermeneutic.[24] By Fundamentalist, my reference is to three basic tendencies: (1) to ignore the distinction between apodictic (*qatʿī*) and probable (*ẓannī*) indicants, in which capacity solitary scriptural references are adduced to drown out other equally legitimate considerations and to cast damning aspersions on other views;[25] (2) to transcendentalize Muslim history through triumphalist readings of the past that are assumed to be binding on contemporary Muslims as their basis for processing *sharīʿah*, which is often accompanied by a paradoxical tendency to begrudge modern history and to view any attempt to adjust Islam to *it* as capitulatory, even as Fundamentalists themselves internalize aspects of this history as the prism through which they read the Muslim past;[26] and (3) to exclude, if not categorically reject, the category of "man-made law," which casts aspersions on most of what even the staunchest pre-modern defenders of *sharīʿah* (or "Islamic law") would recognize under such rubrics as *siyāsah*, *maẓālim*, and *ḥisbah*.

These tendencies significantly circumscribe traditionally recognized methods of juristic interpretive nuancing. Widely recognized instruments developed by classical and post-formative jurists for negotiating the gap between the ideal and the real, the moral and the practical, are effectively excluded from consideration.

Istiḥsān, maṣlaḥah mursalah, sadd al-dharāʾiʿ (and *fatḥ al-dharāʾiʿ*[27]), not to mention long-standing legal canons (*qawāʿid*), such as "difficulty justifies easing the ruling" (*al-mashaqqah tajlib al-taysīr*), are looked upon with suspicion. Thus, we encounter in March's argument such, seemingly apodictic statements as, "From the perspective of traditional Islamic legal, political, and ethical doctrines, the idea of Muslim citizenship in non-Muslim states is deeply problematic."[28] Even were we to concede such a claim on its face, that same literature includes equally urgent critiques of *Muslim* states—present and past—not to mention a set of juristic tools used to negotiate such catastrophes as the Mongol invasions, during which pre-modern Muslims—including jurists—lived under non-Muslim rule. Clearly, these jurists' *fatwās* did not reflect what they deemed to be the ideal. Yet, this did not detract from these *fatwās*' status as authentic "doctrine," bona fide *fiqh/sharīʿah*. Again, in real time and space, *fiqh/sharīʿah* is simply not always an expression of "the ideal." That Muslim jurists could accept living under the Mongols, *sharʿan*, does not mean that they would accept doing so as an expression of Islam's normative vision.

Similarly discounted in the Fundamentalist imaginary is the nature of *sharīʿah* as a discursive tradition wherein the dictates of scripture are transmitted and trans-generationally preserved by precedent, in which capacity scripture need not be directly quoted for its authority to be recognized or felt. One need not assume, in other words, that the view of those who quote scripture directly is necessarily more authentic than those of the *madhhabs*; nor should one assume that, because scripture is not directly affixed to a view in a *fiqh*-manual or *fatwā*, the view itself is not backed by scripture or an extension or inference therefrom.[29] On March's framing, however, the reader is prompted to identify "true Islam" with 'Fundamentalist' Islam, according to which scripture's authority can be represented only by its direct citation. Viewed through the prism of this imaginary, the Islamic juristic tradition is thrust into a position of apology, with obvious implications for the Islamic Secular. Not only does this approach cumulatively narrow the realm of the permissible, but it also implies a totalizing understanding of *sharīʿah*, which delegitimates everything that is non-*sharʿī* and misrecognizes the kind of factual, para-legal, discretionary, and *ʿaqlī* considerations "beyond the law" that are native to Islam-cum-*sharīʿah*'s differentiated realm.

Of course, it would be incorrect and misleading to exclude 'Fundamentalists' from the panoply of voices vying for primacy in modern Islam. But to position them as representative of the Islamic juristic tradition as a whole is simply to misrepresent the latter. By analogy, while it may be appropriate to study White Evangelicals in the US and to underscore the resonance of their message among segments of the population, it would be misleading to present White Evangelicals as the voice of global, trans-generational Christianity.

Fifth and finally, Paul Kahn makes an important distinction between liberalism as an ideology and liberalism as a general socio-political orientation underwritten by history—normalized, internalized, and then forgotten as history—what Rawls himself referred to as a society's "background culture."[30] In this latter sense, liberalism is a "political culture that has neither the sophistication of a theory nor the partisanship of a political party. This is the sense in which we speak of American political culture—or, more generally, of the West—as liberal."[31] There is an important distinction, in other words, between America as a liberal democracy, wherein political community is defined by the Constitution and a liberal background culture, and March's Rawlsian liberalism, where political community is defined in terms of liberal theory's specific understandings of "freedom," "equality," "reasonableness," a commitment to "public reason," and an "overlapping consensus" (all explained below), as well as March's aforementioned four-part criteria. The importance of this distinction is that the cumulative weight of March's argument promotes the identification of Rawls's liberal theory with American democracy.[32] And this can prompt readers to conflate the question of conciliation between Islam and Rawls with conciliation between Islam and American democracy. In such a context, any weaknesses detected in March's argument might be taken as signs of incompatibility between Islam and the US Constitution or America's liberal background culture.

I factor all of the foregoing into my reading of *Islam and Liberal Citizenship*. The main point of laying it out here is not to challenge March's conclusions but to empower the reader to understand and assess his (and my) arguments in light of his (and my) foundational presuppositions, as well as the logic and implications of the Islamic Secular.

Rawls, March, and the Basic Question

There are two formulations of the basic question that March sets for himself. In the first, he asks whether "Muslims, *qua* Muslims, can regard as religiously and morally legitimate the terms of citizenship in a non-Muslim liberal democracy."[33] In the second he asks, "Can there be an Islamic doctrine of citizenship in liberal democracies?"[34] There is obvious overlap between these two articulations, but they are not identical. In the first, the terms of liberal citizenship are presumably set, and the question is whether Islam can accommodate itself to these terms. In the second, the question is not whether Islam can reconcile itself with preexisting terms of liberal citizenship but, rather, what terms Islam itself would set for Muslims in constructing a polity defined as a liberal democracy. *Islam and Liberal Citizenship* seems to oscillate between these two articulations but to focus primarily on the first.

Rawls

As noted, Rawls is central to March's thesis. And March himself is clearly possessed of advanced knowledge of the Rawlsian tradition. To those unfamiliar (or only vaguely familiar) with Rawls, however, it may be difficult to grasp the full meaning or thrust of March's argument, or even to know in concrete terms what he means by "liberalism" beyond its everyday, non-academic use. As such, before moving to March's views proper, I shall offer a no-frills summary of the Rawlsian conceptual framework within which to situate *Islam and Liberal Citizenship*.

The literature on Rawls is staggering, and I doubt that it would yield a single, agreed upon view of his theory. In constructing my frame, I shall try to stay above the fray and limit my effort to the basics of Rawls's system. I rely on my own reading of Rawls, March, and a number of other scholarly presentations of Rawls's theory or aspects thereof. My hope is that the learned Professor March will recognize this as a sufficiently accurate and unbiased effort, designed neither to privilege nor to disadvantage his or my perspective.

Rawls's fundamental aim is to establish and sustain what is in his view is a well-ordered, just society characterized by fair and reasonable terms of socio-political cooperation. The unit of this society is not the group (religious, racial, etc.) but the individual. In fact, society itself, in Rawls's view, is not a "community" but the cumulative product of public negotiations between free and equal individuals.[35] "Free and equal" is a technical designation that goes back to the foundational myth upon which Rawls builds his theory. According to him, society should regard people as distinct from their accidental endowments and inherited advantages or disadvantages, neither privileging nor penalizing anyone on the basis of these. Thus, the well-ordered, just society cannot be fashioned by, or in the interest of, those who seek to preserve or advance their unearned advantages or to ensure that others continue to operate with unearned disadvantages. Thus, Rawls proposes that, in laying the theoretical foundation for society, we imagine ourselves in a pre-societal, "original position," wherein we have no concrete endowments (race, gender, age, intelligence), no ideological commitments (religion, political orientation), and no knowledge of what any of these factors will be upon entering society. In fact, "free" in this context refers to our being unencumbered by ideological or other prejudices (i.e., "comprehensive doctrines") that might bind us to a particular vision of ourselves or society as a whole. "Equal," meanwhile, refers to our equal ignorance of our own as well as others' eventual endowments, which forces us to theorize in the "original position" from behind a "veil of ignorance." This ensures that our deliberations will be objectively fair since we do not have enough knowledge to tip the balance in our favor.

The result of these deliberations will be a blueprint for a society that is fair and just. Moreover, the substance of this justice will not reflect any particular philosophical, religious, cultural, economic, or ideological theory or commitment. It will simply be "justice as fairness," that is, a freely and fairly negotiated socio-political arrangement that is the procedural equivalent of Kant's categorical imperative. As March puts it, "Political liberalism's claim to fairness is grounded . . . in its claim to be reasonable to all *citizens*, regardless of their comprehensive doctrines."[36]

Upon entering society, that is, beyond the "original position," there is another sense in which citizens remain free and equal. Individuals *qua* individuals are free to define for themselves what a "good life" is and to revise that definition over time. This freedom produces the immoveable fact of reasonable pluralism, born of the efforts of now socially embedded, free individuals (now in the sense of being unbeholden to others), who are attached to various comprehensive doctrines, to arrive at reasonable conceptions of the good. Because, however, everyone is equal in this regard, no one—including (in fact, especially) the state—has the right to coerce anyone else, except in ways that are mutually recognized as reasonable. This commitment to non-coercion, or neutrality, especially state neutrality, is fundamental to the Rawlsian vision, according to which it is wrong for anyone to use political power against their free and equal fellow citizens, except for reasons that *all* can accept.[37] And since no comprehensive doctrine or conception of the good is likely to enjoy universal consensus, an individual's *right* to engage in an act must be given precedence over the *good* of the act itself, since perceptions of the latter are open to dispute and daily revision. In this way, Rawls aims to grant individuals the maximum range of political rights (e.g., freedom of speech, freedom of conscience, etc.) that can be reconciled with all other citizens' right to the same. In short, his arrangement is underwritten by a spirit of reciprocity.

The result of this social blueprint is not chaos; for, individual claims to rights *can* be denied. But they can be denied only on the basis of what Rawls refers to as "public reason," the public exercise of the rational faculty in a manner that others can recognize as reasonable, meaning that they could see themselves reaching the same rational conclusion. There are actually two approaches to this appeal to public reason, the first favored by March, the second by Rawls. In the first, one transcends, sets aside, or brackets one's own comprehensive doctrine and puts forth reasons that can be recognized as reasonable by *any* reasonable person, including those who do not share one's ideological commitment. For example, Jews, Christians, and Muslims may all have scriptural justifications for banning heroin. Being religion-specific, however, these justifications are not likely to appeal to atheist or agnostic citizens. But Jews, Christians, and Muslims could bracket their ideological commitments and simply put forth justifications that *all* "reasonable persons," regardless of ideology, could recognize as reasonable grounds for prohibiting the sale or use of heroin (e.g., its association with crime, or its impact on the economy).

On the second approach, favored by Rawls, all parties hold onto their respective comprehensive doctrines, but *within* them search for reasons that others who do not have the same ideological commitment may still recognize as reasonable (e.g., heroin's health implications or its impact on the family). In both cases, the resulting consensus is assumed to enjoy stability because it has been reached voluntarily. One might argue, however, that the second approach yields a more stable consensus, since each party has arrived at it on its own terms, and from its own point of view. In other words, their agreement is more than just a practical compromise.

At any rate, whenever, on either of these two approaches, society reaches a mutually voluntary agreement, it achieves what Rawls refers to as an "overlapping consensus." And comprehensive doctrines that are willing and able to participate in this kind of negotiation are recognized as "reasonable." For Rawls, this overlapping consensus is the ultimate key to the depth and long-term stability of a well-ordered, just society's fair and reasonable terms of socio-political cooperation. While everything else is effectively a means, achieving this overlapping consensus is the ultimate end.

One final feature of Rawls's liberalism merits mention. Rawls states explicitly that his is a "*political* liberalism," in contrast to what he refers to as "Enlightenment liberalism."[38] The latter is grounded in and constitutes a comprehensive doctrine that governs every aspect of life. Jeremy Bentham's (d. 1832) Classical Utilitarianism would be an example of Enlightenment liberalism, as it reduces every action to a concrete calculus of pain and pleasure, whether the context is interpersonal, political, a church, a club, a hospital, etc. By contrast, Rawls restricts his liberalism to society's "basic structure," that is, the basic political, economic, and social institutions that define public life.[39] His liberalism is "political" both in the sense of being "free standing," or independent of any comprehensive doctrine, and in the sense of being expressly limited to fair and reasonable cooperation *regarding the basic structure*. The importance of this qualification is thrown into relief by Rawls's insistence that his political liberalism is *not* political in the commonly understood sense of seeking to advance or defend one's power advantage vis-à-vis others (often in the service of some comprehensive doctrine). In fact, according to him, that is being "political in the wrong way." The aim of his political liberalism is fair and reasonable *cooperation*, not the pursuit of personal or group advantage.

In sum, Rawls's political liberalism aims at reconciling free and equal citizens into an arrangement of fair and reasonable socio-political cooperation regarding society's basic structure, in a manner that is stable over time, observes state neutrality, and privileges individual rights derived from free-standing perceptions of the good over conceptions of the good derived from comprehensive doctrines that are collectivist, abstract, and tend toward universalization.[40]

The Rawlsian March and the Marchian Rawls

As previously stated, virtually every aspect of Rawls's theory remains the object of debate. March recognizes this fact and offers responses to the most common controversies.[41] While the basic Rawlsian frame that I have laid out remains the conceptual backdrop against which March places Islam in conversation with liberal citizenship, he makes adjustments along the way, revealing his own independence as a liberal thinker. For example, while Rawls restricts political liberalism to society's "basic structure," or the basic political concerns and dictates of "constitutional democracy,"[42] March extends it to churches, mosques, families, and substate entities in general. As he puts it, "liberalism establishes a certain range of civil rights and liberties for all citizens and does not recognize the right of any cultural or religious authority to deprive its members of these rights any more than it does the state."[43] Similarly, Rawls notes that part of what makes political liberalism "political," as opposed to the universalizing aspirations of "Enlightenment liberalism," is its embeddedness in a concrete background culture, or "certain fundamental ideas seen as implicit in the public political culture of a democratic society."[44] March tends, on the other hand, to emphasize political liberalism's transcendence and to play down its embeddedness in *any* inherited political culture. In fact, he occasionally juxtaposes "tradition" and "authority" with "reason" and implies that, reason, in contradistinction to tradition, is neutral, its point of departure being nowhere and thus everywhere—Kant writ large.[45]

As we will see, beyond their relevance to the conversation between Islam and liberal citizenship, these and related adjustments alert us to a distinctly "Marchian" element in the liberalism at the heart of March's comparison.

The Marchian Challenge

Turning to March's perception of the basic challenge that liberal citizenship poses for Islam, I begin by noting the different priorities he sees liberalism assigning to the secular and the religious. According to March, the demands of liberal citizenship do not simply run parallel to the various commitments or comprehensive doctrines that citizens may have. Liberalism assumes primacy. And here is where the challenge begins. According to March, while political liberalism does not seek directly to deny any religious truth or value, "it does not allow religious doctrine or law to triumph in coercive state institutions," or "religious truth to be brought to bear on society at large." Rather, "When the two conflict, public reason trumps religious reason."[46] It is this liberal commitment to what March describes as a "form of secularism" that, according to him, many believers find objectionable and see, in his words, as "tantamount to denying religion."[47]

> For them, there is no neutral space where religion is neither affirmed nor denied. By not affirming it, it is denied. And yet, we are asking for a religious justification of this state of affairs. How could this possibly be? How could there be religious reasons for religion being superseded by secular authority, even secular authority that does not seek to transform all believers into unbelievers?[48]

It is perhaps beyond the scope of March's project to define "religion." He does appear to echo, however, Bruce Lincoln's notion of that which "speak[s] of things eternal and transcendent with an authority equally transcendent and eternal."[49] It is clear, moreover, that "secular" and "religious" are binary opposites for March. Meanwhile, "religious reason," in March's view, is undifferentiated and all-encompassing, qualities reflected in the fact that (according to him) there is no neutral space in which religion is "neither affirmed nor denied." But this zero-sum presumption is not entirely consistent with the distinction that Muslim jurists draw between the *sharʿī* and non-*sharʿī* dimensions of religious reasoning, the latter admitting precisely of the possibility of religion, "*in the proper, the religious, sense*," being neither affirmed nor denied, "*lā nafyan wa lā ithbātan*."[50] In such instances, the propriety of a thing is determined not by the fact that religious doctrine directly dictates, affirms, or permits it but by the practical implications of partaking of it, as we saw in al-Ghazālī's assessment of non-Muslim natural sciences or Ibn Taymīyah's attitude towards bathhouses, Greek ideas, or vocabulary. On March's approach, however, only that which Islam confirms as "doctrine," the product of the combined authorities of "religious reason" and scripture, can legitimately determine the relationship between Islam and liberalism. His aim is thus to find *within* the scope of Islamic doctrine, thus defined, the means to reconcile Islam with liberal citizenship.

March explicitly rejects various pseudo- alternatives to his basic commitment, including: (1) seeking to replace Islam's religious doctrines with new ones from outside that avert conflict with liberal citizenship; and 2) augmenting Islam's beliefs with new ones from outside that do the same work. In other words, a Muslim could replace his or her religious beliefs with alien ones that teach that such acts as blasphemy, apostasy, or adultery carry no sanctions or are mild or uncertain enough to be ignored; or he or she could add new beliefs from outside the Faith that qualify the original beliefs to the point of effectively neutralizing them, in both cases "not thinking about (or . . . forgetting) what God might have said about the matter."[51] March dismisses these alternatives because he wants to address the challenge of liberal citizenship on the basis of plausible interpretations *from within* Islam. And he wants to pursue this seriously, not settling for superficial congruences that hide, distort, or misrepresent the true nature either of Islam or political liberalism or the apparent conflict between them. He seeks an "overlapping consensus," in other words, that is authentic and genuine, not simply pragmatic or apparent.

While Muslims may thus passively accept the fact of their existence in America, agreeing to pay taxes and generally obeying the law, March is looking for something more; he is looking for Muslims' positive affirmation on doctrinal grounds of America's legitimacy.[52] While, *da'wah*, for example, or inviting others to Islam, might be offered as a justification for Muslim residence in the US, as long as non-Muslims remain little more than potential converts, as opposed to free and equal citizens who deserve respect as such, this Islamic justification will fall short of the liberal (or Marchian) criterion for an overlapping consensus.[53] In other words, even if they come from within Islam, facile and potentially insincere justifications that merely *appear* to accept the terms of liberal citizenship will not do for March. Nor, conversely, will watered-down versions of the demands of liberal citizenship that lower the bar for Islam.

Islam and Comprehensive Doctrines: Between March and Rawls

I have already registered my view on Islam-cum-*sharīʿah*'s constituting a "comprehensive doctrine." But just as comprehensive doctrines are critical for Rawls, this understanding of Islam-cum-*sharīʿah* informs March's argument throughout. Whereas Rawls was dealing, however, primarily with Western comprehensive doctrines already rooted in the background culture of the West, March is dealing with Islam as represented primarily by Muslims in and from the traditional lands of Islam. Whereas Rawls could assume a certain affinity between Western comprehensive doctrines and the background culture of Western liberal democracies, March enjoys no such advantage.[54] In fact, as comprehensive doctrines go, Islam is generally perceived to be both *sui generis* and recalcitrant. As the late Ali Mazrui (d. 1435/2014) once put it, "Islam in the twentieth century has posed the greatest cultural resistance to western imperialism."[55] This naturally breeds a certain dubiousness about the prospects of reconciliation between Islam and liberal democracy, as well as the degree to which Muslims can be trusted to play by liberalism's rules.

Ultimately, the question comes down to whether Muslims will be asked to live as *full* liberal citizens or as *fully* liberal citizens. In other words, will reinterpretations of *sharīʿah* that bring it into conformity with liberal positions be enough to sustain a genuine overlapping consensus? Or must *sharīʿah* as a "comprehensive doctrine" be set aside in favor of liberal positions that are explicitly the product of liberalism's "public reason"? Stated differently, will Muslims be willing, in cases of conflict, to abandon their supposed "comprehensive doctrine" in favor of liberal positions and liberal modes of justification? Or will Islam-cum-*sharīʿah*'s tenacious hold on Muslims keep them from becoming more than "resident aliens," who outwardly adjust their behavior, pay taxes and obey the law but live in sustained, disquieting, internal conflict with liberalism and its primordial instincts, internally refusing to allow these to trump their "religious reason" in cases of conflict?[56]

For his part, Rawls was clear that "no one is expected to put his or her religious or non-religious doctrine in danger" (even if they must give up the notion of imposing it or using the state to guarantee its success).[57] March, however, is more transparent in acknowledging liberalism's quiet interest in a certain "ordering of the soul," as a potentially necessary antidote to the intransigence of Islam as a comprehensive doctrine. After all, if not only the state but also society at large, including religious communities, are to be barred from denying individuals certain rights, at some point these communities, being steeped as they are in their respective comprehensive doctrines, must be "calibrated," "programmed," or "disciplined," either by the state or by some other instrument of Gramscian hegemony, into voluntarily recognizing these rights as inviolable.[58] Otherwise, states will be constantly forced to intervene in communal affairs, which can only jeopardize over time the image of state neutrality and/or the stability of the overlapping consensus itself.

That liberalism is not above this kind of non-violent coercion is explicitly acknowledged by one of its most enthusiastic supporters, Brian Barry, whose view March cites in cataloguing some of the critiques of liberalism:

> We have to abandon as illusory the hope that people might be left undisturbed in the dogmatic slumbers while somehow being cajoled into accepting liberal policy prescriptions. Dogmatism must give way to scepticism before the appropriately attenuated concept of wrongness can become attractive. . . . There is no way that non-liberals can be sold the principle of neutrality without first injecting a large dose of liberalism into their outlook.[59]

March does not see in this stance the dangers that liberalism's critics see. In fact, a similar sentiment appears to lurk behind the distinction he himself draws between behavior and belief, between what he describes as Muslims' willingness to uphold the requirements of "justice" in liberal society and their actual affirmation of the validity of liberal "citizenship." "One meets the requirements of justice merely by not breaking just laws; one affirms a doctrine of citizenship only by giving certain types of reasons for not breaking them."[60] The difference is between action and affect, between simply obeying the law and believing-cum-feeling that the law *should* be obeyed. Ideally, the "right kinds" of reasons for obeying the law are those that are not simply believed in but on some level actually *felt* to be right and thus worthy of more than simple rational assent—something closer to a somatic resonance. Part of liberalism's mission is thus to ensure that these feelings find their place in citizens' hearts.

And yet, there must remain a safe distance between these carefully instilled "affective reasons" and any particular comprehensive doctrine (including liberalism itself), lest the latter spill over into public debate and jeopardize the integrity of liberalism's purportedly free-standing consensus. Despite the more tolerant attitude we saw in Rawls, March seems to suspect that Islam-cum-*sharīʿah* as a comprehensive doctrine must be properly domesticated in order to open up spaces for alternate bases of belief and feeling.[61] And he is not alone. Even Muslim liberals in the West have insisted that *sharīʿah* be checked at the door of public negotiation, in favor of public reason as the exclusively authorized means of producing the "right kinds" of reasons for complying with liberal views and policies.

The Primacy of Public Reason

We saw earlier An-Naʿim's invocation of what he terms "civic reason." In a similar vein, Mohammad Fadel, a leading Muslim-American proponent of Rawlsian liberalism, has argued that Tunisia's move to ban the practice of polygyny based on reinterpretations of *sharīʿah* would not pass liberal muster. According to him, in approaching the matter the way they did, Tunisian Muslims remained committed to their comprehensive doctrine, only a different interpretation of it. Fadel notes that "from a Rawlsian perspective, at least some rules of Islamic law will have to be revised to meet the requirements of public reason,"[62] which he defines as "limit[ing] citizens to advance only such positions as they may justify on grounds that they reasonably believe others as free and equal could reasonably accept."[63] In this case, he insists, "Tunisian legislation prohibiting polygamy . . . is an example of Islamic modernist legislation that violates public reason because the justification given is theological, namely, that the Qur'an, properly read, prohibits polygamy, rather than being rooted in public reason, for example, that it is harmful to women and children."[64] In other words, it is not enough to adopt the position of liberalism (in this case, no polygyny); one must also adopt and internalize its logic, which will in turn inform the way one thinks, feels, and negotiates societal issues moving forward. Of course, the cumulative effect of this kind of normalized avoidance can only be a reordering of the Muslim soul, as the status of the Qur'ān, Sunna, and the like as bases of doctrine can hardly evade alteration (if not demotion) over time.[65]

Fadel's approach answers definitively the question of whether, in cases of conflict, various provisions of *sharīʿah* must be reinterpreted or abandoned to the dictates of public reason. Again, however, Rawls himself does not appear to require so drastic a move. In a lengthy footnote in *Political Liberalism* (a reprint of his essay, "The Idea of Public Reason Revisited"), Rawls engages with Abdullahi An-Naʿim's *Towards an Islamic Reformation*, praising An-Naʿim precisely for his commitment to reinterpreting *sharīʿah* for the purpose of accommodating constitutionalism. He writes, "Now that historical conditions have changed, An-Naʿim believes that Muslims should follow the earlier Mecca period in interpreting Shari'a. So interpreted, he says that Shari'a supports constitutional democracy."[66] Now, An-Na'im made it clear that the reasons undergirding his position might differ from those put forth or deemed acceptable by non-Muslims. As he put it, "Non-Muslims may have their own secular or other justifications. As long as all are agreed on the principle and specific rules of constitutionalism, including complete equality and non-discrimination on grounds of gender or religion, each may have his or her own reasons for coming to that agreement."[67] Rawls responds with unqualified enthusiasm: "This is a perfect example of overlapping consensus."[68] In sum, Rawls (like An-Naʿim) accepts as sufficiently liberal what Fadel rejects as "theological."

March does not go as far as Fadel, at least not explicitly.[69] But it is difficult to miss the tension coursing through *Islam and Liberal Citizenship* about what to do about Islam-cum-*sharīʿah* as a comprehensive doctrine. On the one hand, the optimal manifestation of Muslims' full embrace of liberal citizenship seems to be for them to declare, openly and unequivocally, that in cases of conflict they are willing doctrinally to abandon (i.e., not simply to ignore or agree not to pursue) 'problematic' *sharīʿah* provisions in favor of positions that are not only sanctioned but also produced by liberalism's public reason.[70] On the other hand, too explicit or uncompromising an insistence on this point might jeopardize the entire project, given the fact of Islam-cum-*sharīʿah*'s tenacious hold over Muslims as a comprehensive doctrine.

March might respond that, instead of tension, what is really on display here are two equally acceptable approaches to Islam-cum-*sharīʿah* as a comprehensive doctrine: one in which it speaks in its own voice in ways that are reconcilable with liberal citizenship; the other in which it abandons its voice and adopts that of liberalism, or public reason. The fact, however, that this equal choice is neither clear nor consistently articulated suggests a certain diffidence, itself designed (perhaps) to preserve the option of demanding, when deemed necessary or likely to succeed, that Muslims abandon their comprehensive doctrine in favor of liberal justificatory arguments.

Part of my argument, by contrast, is that, on the Islamic Secular's *shar'ī*/non-*shar'ī* distinction, there are significant areas wherein Muslims need not speak directly in the voice of *sharī'ah* or Islamic scripture yet can participate fully in public negotiations without offending *sharī'ah* or scripture. In other words, because Islam-cum-*sharī'ah* is *not* a comprehensive doctrine, we need not assume that every disagreement with liberalism will require Muslims to decide whether or not to abandon or interpret away some or another Islamic "doctrine."

The Rawlsian/Marchian theories described above form the backdrop against which March constructs and responds Islamically to his criteria for liberal citizenship. These criteria are not directly dictated by liberalism but reflect March's own understanding of what would constitute a reasonable standard, according to liberal theory, for measuring Muslim commitment to liberal citizenship. As he puts it, "The point is to identify authoritative Islamic reasons for endorsing what *this author* regards as the most reasonable moral principles for regulating social cooperation."[71] For each of his four questions (and their subsidiaries), he presents the would-be objections of those whose readings of Islam's juristic tradition bring them to a rejectionist conclusion. This is followed (much later) by the views of those whose readings align more positively with his four-part criteria, the ultimate intimation being that these should be accepted as dispositive.

March's ordering here is not inconsequential. His overall aim is apparently to highlight the magnitude of the challenge facing the attempt to reconcile Islam-cum-*sharī'ah* with liberal citizenship, from which vantage point the significance of his achievement will be thrown into relief. But by beginning with an exclusive focus on jurists and thinkers who flatly go against his criteria for liberal citizenship, March gives the impression that this is not only the older view but also the more authoritative or "going" (*mashhūr*) opinion in Islam, against which all other views must be seen not only as coming later but as also having to overcome a presumption that is not native to the Islamic juristic tradition itself but is ultimately installed by him. As we will see, this manner of proceeding, while perhaps useful for March's purposes, comes at the price of distorting the Islamic juristic tradition that he purports to represent.

March's Response to the Challenge of Islam and Liberal Citizenship

March does not assume that the Islamic juristic tradition, beginning in its premodern past, speaks directly to the issue of liberal citizenship. His task, as such, is what Rawls referred to as "conjecture"—arguing, in good faith, "from what we believe, or conjecture, are other people's basic doctrines, religious or secular, and try[ing] to show them that, despite what they may think, they can still endorse a reasonable political conception that can provide a basis for public reasons."[72] In other words, March's task is to extract from the Islamic juristic tradition a doctrinal position that vindicates the Muslim embrace of liberal citizenship along Rawlsian lines. His extractions may not reflect with full fidelity the sources from which he draws; for, liberal citizenship is a new phenomenon that Islamic tradition can be assumed to have addressed only partially, if at all. Meanwhile, for any number of reasons (e.g., lack of interest, simple bias, an incomplete understanding of liberalism or *fiqh*) modern Muslims may not see all the possibilities for reconciliation that exist. March will thus seek to undertake this task on their behalf in a manner that flies above these impediments. On the one hand, he writes, "The conjecturer's job is not to create Islamic arguments but to find them and analyze them in terms of their nature as reasons for action."[73] At the same time, there is clearly a subjective element informing this process. As he puts it: "[T]he conjecturer looking to present Islamic arguments endorsing the liberal terms of social cooperation might neglect incompatible positions or treat the tradition in an eclectic, á la carte context-free way."[74]

Conjecture and Islam's Ostensible Default Position

March's conjecture begins with what he presents as the Islamic juristic tradition's default position: a patently rejectionist attitude toward Muslims residing in non-Muslim polities. This sets the stage for a negative response to his remaining criteria on *a fortiori* grounds: if Islam-cum-*sharīʿah* will not permit Muslims to reside in a country, one can not expect it to permit them to be loyal to that country or to stand in solidarity with its citizens.

In crafting this depiction of Islamic tradition, March relies on four main authorities: (1) Sayyid Quṭb (d. 1386/1966); (2) a certain ʿAbd al-ʿAzīz b. Ṣāliḥ al-Jarbūʿ (b. 1387/1967), whom he describes as a "Saudi Arabian dissident" who "justif[ied] the September 11th attacks";[75] 3) the modern Lebanese jurist, Khālid ʿAbd al-Qādir; and 4) the celebrated pre-modern Algerian born and later Moroccan Mālikī jurist, Aḥmad b. Yaḥyā al-Wansharīsī (d. 914/1508). Others—for example, the modern Bosnian Salafī jurist Sulaymān Topolyak and pre-modern jurists such as al-Juwaynī and al-Sarakhsī—are brought in more tangentially to support, qualify, or fill out the view fashioned out of the works of these four. March himself adds a number of his own interpretations of Qurʾān, Sunna, and Muslim history as reinforcement. This is the portal through which he invites his reader to indulge his survey of the Islamic juristic tradition.

Quṭb, a non-cleric, is the leading contributor to the interpretive prism through which March reads the Islamic juristic tradition.[76] Al-Jarbūʿ, on the other hand, is a cleric who is in sympathy with the 'Fundamentalist' imaginary described above. ʿAbd al-Qādir is a modern *faqīh*, writing in the traditional mode of juristic discourse; and al-Wansharīsī is a traditional, pre-modern *faqīh/ʿālim*. Not only does March begin his inquiry with the question of Muslim residence, he begins his conjecture with these four scholars. Quṭb and al-Jarbūʿ are flatly rejectionist, and ʿAbd al-Qādir is presented as going along with this stance. Al-Wansharīsī, meanwhile, plays the pivotal role of justifying March's attribution of this rejectionist stance to the pre-modern or classical tradition as a whole. The importance of al-Wansharīsī's role emerges against the backdrop of what March describes as his basic methodological commitment: " 'Canon First' Or: Theorize from More Orthodox Sources to Less."[77] In other words, the views he presents first should be assumed to be more authoritative and orthodox. Only when these are found lacking, inconclusive, or ill suited to the task at hand will he move to less orthodox views. The reasonable inference to be drawn from this is that Quṭb and al-Jarbūʿ represent the more orthodox position and that any relaxation of this position on the part of others is a move to a less orthodox stance. Subtly implied by this filiation is that the more relaxed position constitutes a chronological and doctrinal evolution *away* from the more Islamically authentic view and is informed by a willingness to make certain concessions to the forces of modernity.

March is on solid ground in depicting al-Wansharīsī as standing against Muslims residing in non-Muslims lands, particularly Spain following the fall of Granada in 1492 CE. Crucially, however, this is not simply Spain or "non-Muslim lands" in the abstract; this is post-Muslim Spain in actual fact, where Christian authorities eventually went so far as to ban "Arabic dress" and even speaking the Arabic language[78]. In such light, the move from al-Wansharīsī's position on post-Muslim Spain to a conjecture about America would seem to require an inquiry into the relevant differences between the two. This would include the reasons behind al-Wansharīsī's view as well as a critical analysis that separates the legal (*sharʿī*) aspects thereof from those aspects that are factual, historically contingent, or discretionary, that is, non-*sharʿī*. March does cite the various reasons al-Wansharīsī gives in support of his position, for example, that such residence "causes the loss and abandonment of prayer" or that it subjects God and God's word to the "scorn of infidels."[79] But he does not disaggregate any of these.[80] Instead, he presents both al-Wansharīsī's position and the reasons behind it as undifferentiated, *sharʿī* statements of law, imputing a finality and unassailability to al-Wansharīsī's view (and with it the alleged view of the Islamic juristic tradition) with which it would otherwise not be vested.

For his part, in accordance with the best tradition of *fiqh* as it had developed by his time, al-Wansharīsī displays a palpable recognition of the impact of facts on the law. The section of his work from which March draws is a *fatwā* that al-Wansharīsī wrote in response to a question that included details reaching far beyond the simple matter of residence in a non-Muslim land. Specifically, it inquired about Muslims expatriated to North Africa from Spain following the fall of Granada who, in their romantic recollections of the "good ole days" in Iberia, disparaged the lands of Islam, extolled the economic and other advantages of living in non-Muslim Spain, and suggested that *hijrah* should be *from* the lands of Islam *to* the lands of Unbelief, clearly revealing the extent to which they had fallen under the cultural and intellectual authority of the Unbelievers.[81] Even at the height of his indignation, however, al-Wansharīsī prefaces his response with a gesture toward the law/fact distinction. He notes, for example, that one might be forced to choose between living in a place where there is public justice and private sin (*ʿadl wa ḥarām*) and living in one where there is public injustice but the ability to maintain proper behavior in private (*jawr wa ḥalāl*). In fact, he notes that a country in which God's rights are violated (*balad fīhi maʿāṣ*^{in} *fī ḥuqūq Allāh*) might be preferable to a country in which the rights of humans are violated (*balad fīhi maʿāṣ*^{in} *fī maẓālim al-ʿibād*).[82]

Obviously, a full assessment of the permissibility, *sharʿ*^{an}, of residing in non-Muslim Spain requires a clear-eyed assessment of the facts on the ground viewed through the prism of such considerations. True to this standard, the remainder of al-Wansharīsī's response reflects the fact that, *on his assessment of these factual considerations*, his opinion was that Muslims were not permitted to live in conquered Spain. His Islamic Secular interpretation of the facts, in other words, played an integral role in his *fatwā*. Elsewhere in the same work, al-Wansharīsī cites approvingly the view of the North African Mālikī jurist al-Māzarī (d. 536/1141) that there may be valid reasons for Muslims to reside in non-Muslim lands, such as "necessity" (*iḍṭirār*) or a factual interpretation of circumstances on the ground that points to a benefit in doing so, "such as the hope that they will guide non-Muslims and turn them away from their misguidance."[83]

My point here is not that March's presentation of al-Wansharīsī is invalid on its face. But if al-Wansharīsī is this responsive to the facts on the ground in the very source upon which March relied in presenting his view, then conjecturing on his behalf about America as a site of liberal citizenship would seem to require consideration of any number of well-known facts about America, such as the fact that Islam is among the fastest-growing religions in this "non-Muslim" polity, that Muslims often find themselves freer to practice aspects of Islam there than in some Muslim-majority countries, that the US Constitution explicitly protects religion (however understood), and that a major contingent of the Muslim community in America consists of trans-generationally native-born converts who hail from a "counterpublic" notorious for its resistance to assimilation. With these facts in mind, it would be reasonable to conjecture that al-Wansharīsī might have adopted a more accommodating position, or perhaps multiple positions, on Muslim residence in a non-Muslim land such as America.

I want to emphasize that al-Wansharīsī is the *mainstay* of March's attribution of the rejectionist position to the classical tradition. While he also adduces testimony from the also traditional 'Abd al-Qādir, who makes some statements that could be taken to support March's claim, in the closing summation of his work from which March draws, 'Abd al-Qādir states explicitly: "Residing in non-Muslim lands is permissible on the condition of ample access to religious freedom" (*taṣiḥḥ al-iqāmah fī dār al-kufr bi sharṭ tawāfur al-ḥurrīyah al-dīnīyah*).[84]

This leaves Quṭb and al-Jarbū' to consolidate March's argument. And there are two points to be made in their regard. First, March is correct in noting that I do not believe that the views of 'Fundamentalists' can or should be summarily dismissed. Rightly or wrongly, they resonate among significant segments of the Muslim Community, and their proponents often enjoy significant standing among certain demographics.[85] Even this, however, cannot gainsay my second point, namely, that even if 'Fundamentalist' views are popular and in certain circles even preferred over those of the *fuqahā'*, that does not mean that they represent the legacy of the Islamic juristic tradition as a whole. And it is the latter that March purports to represent first and foremost throughout *Islam and Liberal Citizenship*: "Canon First."

In several places, March describes how daunting the challenge posed by Islam's "*juridical and ethical tradition*" is, noting, for example, that the "Canon First" principle binds him to "traditional and authoritative voices" and that "it is precisely these voices (particularly in the Islamic tradition, where they are likely to be medieval or earlier) that are least likely to offer anything promising in the way of an overlapping consensus with modern liberal concerns."[86] Yet, when he finally gets around to introducing authorities who do allow Muslim residence in non-Muslim lands, his sources go all the way back to the second/eighth century and the famed disciple of Abū Hanīfa, Muḥammad b. al-Ḥasan al-Shaybānī (d. 189/805), and from there extend all the way up to modern times.[87] In other words, these authorities are not newly discovered; nor do their views appear later in the history of the Islamic juristic tradition. March simply delays citing them until well after the views of their rejectionist counterparts have been carefully installed as the going opinion. The effect of this is to imply that the perspective of Quṭb and al-Jarbū' is normative and can be taken as the predominant view of the Islamic juristic tradition, to which others' views must then respond and vindicate themselves if they are to be recognized as authentic.

Cumulatively, this positions jurists who support residence in non-Muslim polities as apologists who have deviated from the ostensible Islamic norm. A clear manifestation of this is March's response to Shaykh 'Abd Allāh b. Bayyah's positive assessment of "neutralist secularism" (*ʿalmānīyah muḥāyidah*): "[I]t is appropriate to ask what is Islamic about these arguments."[88] My point here is not that Bin Bayyah is right (I obviously do not agree with his use of *ʿalmānīyah*, and I think he overindulges the idea that majorities and minorities are or can be equidistant from "neutral" states.[89]) Nevertheless, it is odd that Bin Bayyah should be called to some standard beyond his religious commitment and extensive training as a jurist, and that an alien (read: 'Fundamentalist') standard should determine the "Islamicity" of his tradition-bound view. Equally curious is that this question (about how Islamic a view is) is never directed at the views of rejectionist thinkers.

Meanwhile, baked into March's critique is the notion that "Islamic" equals *sharʿī* and that any position not entirely dictated by *sharīʿah* cannot pretend to "Islamicity." To be both non-*sharʿī* and Islamic, in other words, is part of March's unimaginable, a direct result of his perception of *sharīʿah* as unbounded and consubstantial with Islam. Bin Bayyah's position, in turn, cannot be Islamic because March cannot see it as *sharʿī*. The views of Quṭb and al-Jarbūʿ, on the other hand, never run afoul of this standard because they are never seen as venturing outside of what March deems to be *sharīʿah* or its sources. Clearly, the 'Fundamentalist' imaginary has become March's touchstone, by which fidelity to the Islamic juristic tradition as a whole is ultimately measured.

Eventually, however, the impression that the rejectionist position is standard is overturned, in the last third of March's book, where we begin to hear more from the likes of Yūsuf al-Qaraḍāwī, Bin Bayyah, Fayṣal al-Mawlawī (d. 1432/2011), Rashīd Riḍā, and others. By that time, however, it has become difficult *not* to see these views as a digression from what March has carefully positioned as the established rule—a *ḥukm sharʿī* that, incidentally, holds no normative place for the Islamic Secular.[90] In fact, March's privileging of thinkers who reflect a 'Fundamentalist' imaginary contributes directly to his non-recognition of the Islamic Secular. As we will see, this enables him to tell us perhaps both too much and too little about the relationship between Islam-cum-*sharīʿah* and liberal citizenship.

Liberal Citizenship between March and the Islamic Secular

As mentioned, each of March's four basic questions entails a series of subsidiary queries. "Residence in a non-Muslim state" implicates being subjected to non-Muslim laws, accepting the predominance of non-Muslims over Muslims, strengthening the unbelievers, "friendship" (*walāʾ*) with non-Muslims, and living in sinful environments.[91] "Loyalty to a non-Muslim state" implicates questions such as whether one can join a *jihād* against the state or fight in its defense (against Muslims or non-Muslims), and whether one considers the state to be legitimate and inviolable.[92] "Solidarity with non-Muslims" entails issues of intimacy, mutual reliance, and a willingness to contribute to common socio-political goals, as well as the question of whether and how this is all consistent with the dictates of Islamic brotherhood/sisterhood.[93] "Recognition of non-Muslims and pluralism" implicates questions of equality, justice across community lines, and respecting non-Muslims' rights, as well as their prerogative to choose and revise their conceptions of the good.[94] I will ignore for the moment, for the sake of staying on task, the unidirectional nature of March's inquiry. It seems clear, however, that Rawlsian liberalism, like the paradigmatic state for Hallaq and the Secular State for An-Naʿim, is the standard by which March is judging Islam, the latter being authorized to make no counter-judgments or demands of its own. On this approach, one wonders if March's overlapping consensus might not ultimately lend itself more to consuming than it does to including Islam.

March on Islam's Response to His Four-Part Criterion

At any rate, now drawing primarily on the pre-modern and modern clerical class, as distinct from thinkers such as Quṭb, March responds to all of his questions and their subsidiaries by arguing that, through proper conjecture, one can fashion conciliation between Islam-cum-*sharīʿah* and liberal citizenship out of authoritative views within the Islamic juristic tradition. Again, for us, the central concern is not so much whether March succeeds in demonstrating this claimed compatibility as it is the meaning, terms, and hidden costs of that compatibility so argued. By limiting his focus to moral doctrine and questions of permissibility, March effectively marginalizes if not excludes matters of prudence and material interest. Moreover, his understanding and particular sequencing of the jurists and thinkers he cites places non-*sharʿī*, Islamic Secular considerations much farther away from the quotidian gaze and sensibilities of Muslims, including jurists, than an approach from *within* the Islamic juristic tradition would warrant or reflect. In fact, by failing to recognize the Islamic Secular's *sharʿī*/non-*sharʿī* distinction, March's thesis threatens to transform the pursuit of societal peace into a mechanism for domesticating Muslims, as it reduces them to "doctrine" and then on that basis calls on them to adjust to and negotiate with the non-negotiable dictates of the liberal state. At the same time, it fails to recognize the non-*sharʿī*, non-doctrinal, material interests that doctrinally committed Muslims might pursue and regarding which they might potentially reach (or not) a genuine overlapping consensus with non-Muslims, without relying on or giving offense to religious "doctrine," or *sharīʿah*.

In his critical engagement with Rawls, Sheldon Wolin argues that the former's ultimate obsession was stability and that he viewed religion, in the form of a comprehensive, totalizing doctrine, as the greatest threat thereto. According to Wolin, the domestication of religion was for Rawls the *sine qua non* of any stable political order. Rawls's point of departure was the Reformation and the death and destruction attending Western Europe's so-called wars of religion. His basic question was, "[H]ow is a just and free society possible under conditions of deep doctrinal conflict with no prospect of resolution?"[95] Whereas thinkers before him, such as Locke (d. 1704), had located the solution in the principle of toleration and ending state sponsorship of religion, such that the state no longer did religion's bidding, "Rawls contends that toleration is insufficient and that religions must importantly conform to what the state needs."[96] We have seen liberalism's quiet interest in the reordering of the soul and how that interest is perhaps stronger in March than in Rawls. But that is not quite the focus here. Wolin's critique is not so much of Rawls targeting religion as it is of his singular obsession with the political consequences of strongly held *beliefs*, an obsession that promotes the notion that resolving conflicts over *doctrine* is the key to everything. For Rawls, it seems, "religion" *is* "doctrine," or "strongly held *beliefs*," and it is precisely for this reason that he targets these as mortal threats.

But this ignores, according to Wolin, and raises beyond our analytical reach, the more immediate problem of competing *interests*. As Wolin sees it, Rawls's focus on managing doctrine/belief went against the basic insight of America's "Madisonian liberalism," which relied on the "fragmenting effect of the pluralism of interests and beliefs" to domesticate majority rule and direct citizens toward social cooperation, as part of the pursuit of self-interest.[97] Socio-political cooperation is underwritten, in this framework, not by "public reason" but by the recognition that the successful pursuit of one's own interests is most likely enhanced by compromises with the interests of others, including others with whom one might morally or doctrinally disagree.[98] For Wolin, liberal democracy is about the messy business of accommodating disagreement over competing interests, not about forging agreement over doctrines and beliefs by casting them into a public melting pot heated by the flame of public reason. On this understanding, he argues that "*Liberalism* [the title of Rawls's book] does less for democracy than it does for liberalism."[99]

For our purposes, the most relevant take-away from Wolin is the understanding that the Rawlsian focus on doctrine marginalizes, if not obliterates, material and other interests that may be equal or even further-reaching in their socio-political implications. As applied to Islam-cum-*sharīʿah*, Rawls's focus promotes the tendency to look upon material interests as almost an afterthought, if not a perversion of Islam's normative religious commitment to doctrine. Yet, it is precisely the realization and avoidance of material and other interests and harms, *maṣāliḥ* and *mafāsid*, that Muslim jurists have always contemplated, processed, and sought to reconcile with doctrine, in the very name of Islam-cum-*sharīʿah*. And given that so much of this negotiation falls into the non-*sharʿī* realm of the Islamic Secular, to omit the latter from Islam's "*juridical and ethical tradition*" is simply to misunderstand and misrepresent it. Even if March's Islamic responses to his four-part criterion and their subsidiaries prove plausible, his singular focus on doctrine would render them incomplete, if not misleading, as they would occlude a major and inextricable component of Islam-cum-*sharīʿah*'s native calculus.

Let me try to give an example from each of his four questions to demonstrate the point I am trying to make.

Residence

In his response to the question of Muslim residence in non-Muslim polities, March introduces several pre-modern and modern scholars (e.g., al-Nawawī, Ibn Taymīyah, Rashīd Riḍā, Tariq Ramadan) from whom we did not hear when he catalogued the ostensibly default, rejectionist position, along with other scholars, such as al-Qaraḍāwī, who seem to have qualified or changed their rejectionist sentiments over the course of March's presentation. Based on these "new" sources, March identifies six arguments in support of Muslims' residing in non-Muslim states: (1) the inconclusiveness of the scriptural texts that prohibit such residence; (2) the existence of other texts of scripture that contradict the prohibiting texts; (3) the fact that Muslims may be able to "manifest their religion" even in the absence of sovereign authority; (4) the fact that *hijrah*, even if obligatory, is not feasible for most Muslims; (5) the fact that such residence entails potential benefits to Islam, for example, spreading the faith; and (6) the fact that *hijrah* may be understood as spiritual migration from sin rather than physical relocation.[100]

Reasons (3), (4), and (5) clearly implicate interests and show the extent to which they can modify doctrine, while (1), (2), and (6) might arguably be adduced in support of these interests. Cumulatively, at any rate, the list raises a number of questions.

First, if the issue can be adjudicated based on interests that may or may not obtain (or may obtain to this or that degree) as a matter of *fact*, what is the point of treating Islam-cum-*sharīʿah* as a comprehensive doctrine that delivers fixed, inalterable yes/no answers to questions of permissibility? March implies that we cannot always know whether it is permissible for Muslims to reside in non-Muslim lands as a matter of transcendent doctrine, since this permissibility is partly determined by circumstances on the ground, as the wording of (3), (4), and (5) clearly suggests. Such contingency is what March's commitment to an "ideal moral encounter" would seem to preclude. Yet his arguments here suggest that conciliation can be reached only in contemplation of a real rather than an abstracted society.

Second, why were these considerations of material interests (and alternative texts) not factored into the presentation of the "rejectionist" jurists and thinkers cited earlier? Were these interests (and texts) not part of their hermeneutic?

Third, even if we conclude that it is permissible, *shar'an*, for Muslims to reside in America as a matter of law or doctrine, what does that tell us about how Muslims *will* or *should* act as a matter of material interest or fact? At one point, with a clear emphasis on doctrine, March depicts Shaykh Yūsuf al-Qaraḍāwī as singling out the question of the permissibility of residing in non-Muslim lands as "the first of 'juridical' questions facing Muslim minorities," implying that impermissibility is a formidable presumption to overcome.[101] In the work from which March draws this view, however, al-Qaraḍāwī points to certain *interests* that are served by Muslim residence in the West, which clearly inform his view regarding its permissibility. He writes, "Considering that Western nations have come to lead and direct the world, politically, economically, and culturally, there must be an influential Muslim presence in the West, given their status as a Community that has a global message. This is a reality we cannot afford to deny." Thus, he concludes, "In this light, there is no room for even asking about the permissibility of Muslims residing in non-Muslim lands."[102] Al-Qaraḍāwī's position reflects, *pace* the impression one gets from March, the fact that there is an inextricable, non-*shar'ī*, differentiated, Islamic Secular calculus *beyond* (or perhaps alongside) the dictates of doctrine and abstract questions of *ḥarām* versus *ḥalāl*, which is part and parcel of the concrete instantiation of Islam-cum-*sharī'ah* in any given place and time and on any given issue.

Given this fact, looking to doctrine alone, in the form of decontextualized texts of scripture or the entries in *fiqh* manuals, cannot be a reliable basis upon which to approach the question at hand. Meanwhile, as a matter of methodology, it hardly seems accurate to think of al-Qaraḍāwī and others who follow his approach as having capitulated to the times, unless we are willing to pass a similar judgment on al-Qarāfī, Ibn Taymīyah, al-Ghazālī, al-Māzarī, al-Juwaynī, al-Wansharīsī, and others, based on the way they engaged with the socio-political realities of their times in the pre-modern Muslim past.

Loyalty

March's criterion for measuring Muslim loyalty to non-Muslim states is quite different from what one would normally understand by "loyalty." According to him, "Islamic doctrine"[103] or "Islamic juristic discourses" make it clear that (1) Muslims may never fight against Muslims on behalf of non-Muslims regardless of the cause; (2) war for the sole purpose of expanding Muslim rule is just and a legitimate form of *jihād*; (3) all Muslims, regardless of domicile, may be obligated to participate in a *jihād* if called upon to do so by a legitimate Imām; (4) Muslims may not advance the cause of unbelievers or uphold non-Islamic rulings and truth-claims; and (5) Muslims may not sacrifice their lives in defense of a non-Muslim polity.[104] In the aggregate, according to March, all of these points make it impossible, at least *prima facie*, for Muslims to embrace "even minimal bonds of loyalty" in accordance with the demands of liberal citizenship.[105] Moreover, exemptions based on conscientious objection or professed pacifism do not apply to Muslims; for, according to March, the Muslim objection is likely to be tied to doctrinal dictates, such as "the principle of *walā' wa barā*'" (affirming one's loyalty to Islam alone and disavowing all other loyalties), the duty to be in solidarity with fellow believers across citizenship boundaries, or a simple "unwillingness to form deep bonds of solidarity with non-Muslims."[106] In short, according to March, "The Islamic case is special . . . because objections to fighting come . . . from a doctrine of loyalty to the global political community of fellow Muslims (the *umma*)."[107]

It is difficult to miss the 'Fundamentalist' imaginary coursing through March's perspective. We saw it, for example, in the casting of man-made law as a categorical contradiction of Islam, a perspective that culminates in such overly broad and vague notions as "non-Islamic rulings."[108] We see it here again in such extrapolations as "a Muslim may not recognize his non-Muslim state's unqualified right to exist . . . he may not regard himself as under any personal duty of restraint toward his state of citizenship, and . . . he may not feel he can defend his state of residence, even against a non-Muslim aggressor, solely because of the non-Islamic character of that society's political system."[109] We see it in the unqualified claim that Muslims may never fight or die on behalf of non-Muslims.[110] We see it in the manner in which Qur'ān and Sunnah are invoked not as *dalīl*, or indicants, but as decontextualized, apodictic proof, often presented as representing Islamic tradition as a whole.[111] And we see it in the way that modern history has apparently transformed "non-Muslim" into "colonialist/imperialist, hostile enemy" whose status as an ally[112] or protected religious other (*dhimmi*) with whom Muslims might cooperate and/or be bound to protect is no longer imaginable. Again, March gives the impression that the ultimate source of all of this is the pre-modern Islamic juristic tradition. But it seems that something quite extraneous to that tradition is at work here.

Ultimately, March's aim is to extricate Islam from this rejectionist posture by showing that adjustments can be made, either to his liberal criteria or to Islamic doctrine, that will salvage the permissibility of Muslim loyalty to a non-Muslim state while contradicting neither Islam-cum-*sharī'ah* nor liberalism. To this end, he renegotiates his criteria down to the following three postulates:

(1) Hostilities on the part of Muslim forces against a non-Muslim state are justified only in self-defense or to counter aggression and not to facilitate the spread of Islam or to change the government of a state in which Muslims are not oppressed.[113]
(2) In conflicts between a non-Muslim state in which Muslims live and a Muslim force, a Muslim may forswear on grounds of principle any active aid to the Muslim force and promise to engage in no violent activities against their non-Muslim state.[114]
(3) In conflicts when the non-Muslim state in which Muslims live is under attack by another non-Muslim force, and thus no conflict of loyalty or theological imperative is at stake, it is permissible to contribute in some substantive way to the self-defense of the non-Muslim state.[115]

This set of adjustments, March concludes, "represents an equilibrium between the concerns of political liberalism and those of Islamic doctrine."[116] He explains that a Muslim may justifiably refuse to engage in combat against his fellow Muslims, if his reasons are "grounded in some theological imperative to not commit an act."[117] What is *not* justified, is for a Muslim to refuse to engage in such combat out of indifference or contempt for the legitimate interests of his non-Muslim state of residence. In other words, the "right reasons" for refusing to fight in defense of non-Muslims, even if theological, must be accompanied by an *affective* attachment to his state of residence that precludes any indifference toward it or any hostile action against it. To be sure, there is a lingering tension here (think back to the invocation of the principle of *walā' wa barā'*). But most of this is ostensibly offset via appeals to the Islamic principle requiring Muslims to uphold their pacts with non-Muslims[118] and to the views of certain outlying scholars who allow serving in non-Muslim armies.[119]

Difficulties remain, however, on the question of legitimacy. According to March, to recognize the legitimacy of non-Muslim states goes against the basic logic of *jihād*. For, were these states actually recognized as legitimate, there would be no point or justification in waging *jihād* against them. Therefore, according to March, "Muslims will have to depart from classical jurisprudence and endorse the efforts of Modernists to revise the classical *jihād* doctrine."[120]

In reality, according to the actual dictates of classical *fiqh*, non-Muslim states were subdued either by force (*'anwat^{an}*) or by treaty (*ṣulḥ^{an}*), and it is difficult to imagine how a treaty of non-aggression (*hudnah, muhādanah*) could be entered into with a state that was not considered legitimate, at least enough to be expected to uphold its end of the bargain, including such acts as granting "temporary citizenship" or safe passage (*amān*) to Muslims. Moreover, where the Imām entered into a peace treaty with a non-Muslim entity, there was no consensus in classical *fiqh* that required him to hold the latter to *sharīʿah* (presumably the *sine qua non* of legitimacy, according to March). Ibn Qayyim, for example, states unequivocally that, while the contract of *dhimmah* (where non-Muslims reside in Muslim lands) binds non-Muslims to the rules of Islam (*aḥkām al-islām*), peace treaties (*hudnah*) may explicitly exempt them from the rules of Islam in their own lands.[121] Similarly, as the Ḥanafī al-Sarakhsī notes, Muslim courts in Muslim lands were not bound to hear cases involving offenses against non-Muslims living in non-Muslim lands subdued by treaty, even if the non-Muslims in question traveled to *dār al-islām* for adjudication, a policy clearly implying at least the partial legitimacy, even if by default, of the non-Muslim order.[122] On a more mundane level, marriages of non-Muslims in non-Muslim polities who convert to Islam are recognized by Muslim jurists as valid marriages, including those that were not contracted according to the rules of Islam.[123]

Clearly, Muslim jurists' understanding of *jihād* was driven by something other than the presumed legitimacy or illegitimacy of non-Muslim polities. And clearly, to the extent that legitimacy was an issue, it was not categorically measured by the level of non-Muslim compliance with or implementation of *sharīʿah*. In contrast to the legally monistic, jurispathic logic of modern states—and more in conformity with the imperial logic of the pre-modern empire-state—Muslims sought first and foremost to spread Islam's *power*, not its legal system.[124] In modern times, the colonial experience that saw the West use its power to dislocate *sharīʿah* has significantly distorted this distinction and bred the notion that power always is and has been used to gut the law of the vanquished. But this distinction, between spreading power and spreading law, was clearly evident among Islam's pre-modern jurists. And it is difficult to see how March's reading on this point reflects the criterion he invokes as "Canon First."

March begins with Sayyid Quṭb's rebuke of modern Muslims who, buckling under "the pressure of modern values" apologize for the fact that Islam's permanent approach to foreign policy is to offer all of humanity three choices: (1) conversion to Islam; (2) payment of the *jizyah* (poll tax) in exchange for non-conversion; or (3) war. Those Muslims who apologize for this approach, according to Quṭb, have adopted a "defeatist" position, in which *jihād* is turned into a defensive enterprise.[125] In March's view, if *jihād* is purely for defensive purposes, there can be no free-standing obligation to wage war against non-Muslim states that are not hostile, and these states must be viewed, therefore, as legitimate. March is of two minds, however, about fully extending this logic. On the one hand, he sees it as contributing to the possibility of reconciling Islam with liberal citizenship (inasmuch as it implies the legitimacy of non-Muslim polities). On the other hand, he joins Quṭb in criticizing it as ultimately *faux* and defeatist. As he puts it, "Affirming the 'defeatist,' 'defensive' interpretation of the Islamic doctrine of *jihād*, according to which non-Muslim states have the right to equal recognition with Muslim states, is precisely what is required for a Muslim citizen of democracy."[126] And, "Whereas the classical doctrine articulates no absolute right to recognition for non-Muslim polities, 'modernist' authors underline the defensive aspect of *jihād*."[127]

Once again, Quṭb is the touchstone for March. And he casts those whose views contradict Quṭb's as "defeatist," "defensive," and "Modernist," clearly signaling capitulation on their part to the forces of modernity, a capitulation that drives their attempts at apologetic reinterpretations of *sharīʿah*. Interestingly, by "Modernists," March is not referring to such thinkers as Fazlur Rahman, Abd al-Karim Soroush, or the late Muḥammad Shaḥrūr (d. 1441/2019). Rather, his list includes the likes of Maḥmūd Shaltūt (d. 1383/1963), Muḥammad Abū Zahrah, Wahbah al-Zuḥaylī, Muḥammad Ramaḍān al-Būṭī (d. 1434/2013), Khalīd ʿAbd al-Qādir, and, ultimately myself, all writers whose point of departure is the classical juristic tradition.[128] Few would think of these scholars as "Modernists"; in fact, March later characterizes al-Qaraḍāwī and al-Mawlawī (whose scholarly profile is indistinguishable from that of the aforementioned scholars (with the exception of myself)) as "conservative."[129] By casting them here as Modernist, the aim and effect is to reinforce the logic and normativity of the Quṭbian perspective—that *jihād* can be understood as a defensive enterprise only by those who have capitulated to the forces of modernity.[130] When, in the course of this argument, he cites my article "Jihad and the Modern World," March acknowledges that I grounded my arguments in classical *uṣūl al-fiqh*.[131] Specifically, I argued—relying on the law/fact distinction so powerfully articulated by al-Qarāfī—that, as the world has evolved *as a matter of fact* out of the ancient "state of war," where war was the default presumption and the distinction between defense and offense was blurred, into an overall state of peace, where peace has become the presumption and war the exception, the obligation to wage aggressive *jihād* has lapsed. But March challenges the legitimacy of relying on such empirical assessments in adjudicating the law, despite what we have seen even in pre-modern *sharīʿah*-maximalists such as Ibn al-Qayyim and his teacher Ibn Taymīyah.

More directly, March draws on Quṭb to challenge the idea that non-Muslim hostility could have been the only reason for aggressive *jihād* in the first place, such that its disappearance as a legal cause (*sabab*) could justify retiring the obligation to wage *jihād*. Referring to Quṭb's commentary on Qurʾān 8:61, March writes, "Equally important seems to be the belief that in Islam there is a *categorical* Divine command to not passively tolerate systems of unbelief when capacities permit."[132] Now, Quṭb may be right or wrong in his interpretation of Qurʾān 8:61 and related verses, on the basis of which he sees the point of *jihād* as toppling "systems of unbelief." But that was (and is) simply *not* the prevailing understanding of the Islamic juristic tradition which March purports to represent;

and it is difficult, again, to reconcile the prominence he gives to Quṭb with his own principle of "Canon First."[133]

To be clear, by definition, *all* hostile "others" presided over "systems of unbelief." But we saw earlier with al-Shāfiʿī, Mālik, Ibn al-Qāsim, al-Lakhmī, and others not only a tolerance of non-Muslim reglementary regimes but also a near-refusal to 'honor' non-Muslims with the imposition of *sharīʿah*. Meanwhile, al-Shāfiʿī was explicit in recognizing that the protection under which *dhimmah* brought non-Muslims allowed them to eat pork, drink wine, and even worship other than Allah.[134] And in response to the question of whether he assumes any responsibility for the groundless (*bāṭil*) rulings of non-Muslim judges in cases where he himself refuses to adjudicate their disputes, he answers plainly in the negative. In fact, he insists that *dhimmīs* *must* accept *either* the rule of *sharīʿah* *or* that of their own traditional courts, morally retrograde (*ʿalā ghayr al-ḥaqq*) though the latter may be, clearly identifying the maintenance of order, not the extended application of *sharīah*, as the governing interest.[135] Similarly, we saw with al-Māwardī, Ibn al-Qayyim, al-Qarāfī, and others an explicit permission for peace treaties to extend to non-Muslims the right to live according to their own norms in their own lands.[136] In sum, as important as it may be for March's overall argument, classical jurists were simply *not* preoccupied with questions about the legitimacy of non-Muslim regimes. In fact, far more than the substance of non-Muslim reglementary régimes, fiscal concerns routinely appear as the major driver of juristic discussions on non-Muslims.[137]

Beyond this, Muslim jurists' most fundamental concern was with non-Muslim *power* and, more specifically, with what that power might do to them, as it could not be assumed that power-wielding non-Muslim states would recognize the "legitimacy" of Muslim states. As al-Qarāfī summarized the general Muslim sentiment: "It is their nature to hate us" (*jubbilū ʿalā bughḍinā*), and, "If they gain the upper hand over us, they will annihilate us and seize control over our bodies and our property."[138] In this context, the aim of *jihād* was *not* the installation of substantively "legitimate" (presumably *sharīʿah*-based) regimes but, rather, the neutralization of the threat of non-Muslim power. After all, even in Muslim polities, once non-Muslims agreed to pay the *jizyah*, they were generally free to continue with significant aspects of their non-Muslim reglementary order, depending on circumstances and on the Muslim ruler's practical assessment of how best to promote the interests of Islam.

All in all, March is free to rely on Quṭb as the basis of his understanding of Islamic doctrine, an understanding that he (and others) may deem superior to that of the Islamic juristic tradition. But he should not pretend that Quṭb speaks for that tradition. Nor should he try to recast the latter through a Quṭbian prism or force it to speak in a Quṭbian voice.

Again, the real point of my critical engagement with March is to reiterate the inextricable intertwinement between the *shar'ī* and the non-*shar'ī* in the instantiation of Islam-cum-*sharī'ah* as a lived reality, and thus as an interlocutor with liberal citizenship or any other form of life. On this understanding, the question of loyalty, like March's other criteria, cannot be adjudicated solely as a matter of transcendent, ideal doctrine. To put it more directly, to treat these issues purely as matters of transcendent doctrine is to distort the way Islam-cum-*sharī'ah* has always processed socio-political reality and would do so today in negotiating a relationship with liberal citizenship. Beyond questions of doctrine and permissibility, or perhaps alongside them, the question of the relevant Muslim interests to be served or threatened must also be considered. And this makes for a target that is constantly moving rather than fixed.

Of course, in this post–September 11th moment, when Islam and Muslims are suspect entities in the West and many non-Muslims are clamoring for reliable, definitive answers to allay their fears about Islam (or to indict it), some may see this kind of nuancing as dangerous if not irresponsible. They may fear that, if it cannot be shown definitively, based on fixed and stable doctrines, that Islam requires Muslims to be loyal to the nation in which they live, there can be no guarantee that Muslims will not be disloyal—or worse. I will have more to say about such concerns in the closing segment of this chapter. For now, let me simply offer the following.

First, March's thesis does not bind Muslims to be loyal; it simply authorizes them, by making it permissible, *shar'an*, for them to be loyal. Second, just because Islamic doctrine does not compel Muslims to be loyal (again, in the Marchian sense), it does not follow that Muslims' interests will automatically push them away from, rather than toward, greater loyalty. Taking Wolin's understanding of democracy as the messy business of managing competing interests, there could be long-term, Islamically legitimate *maṣāliḥ* that are served by Muslim loyalty to a liberal state or at least by the avoidance of disloyalty (again, as March defines these concepts). As mentioned in Chapter 4, Muslims do all kinds of things for non-doctrinal reasons, simply because they see it in their Islamic (or personal) interest to do so. Third, the affective element in March's "loyalty" seems to be a one-way street that flows from Muslims to non-Muslims. There is no comparable value or emphasis placed on the need for non-Muslims to be affectively attached to Muslims and their interests, preferences, or understandings of the good (another point explored at the end of this chapter). At least as much as "doctrine," this is likely to inform Muslim attitudes toward "loyalty."

Finally, to reduce "loyalty" to a matter of fixed, transcendent doctrine may ultimately reduce Muslims to a blind loyalty, loyalty no matter what. And here the question becomes not only whether this is good for Muslims but also whether it is good for America. Surely it would be more in America's interest for the American state to be held to living up to basic expectations of justice, fairness, decency, and responsiveness to the legitimate interests of all its citizens as a means of earning, en route to ensuring, their loyalty.[139] As Edmund Burke once reportedly put the matter, [T]o make us love our country, our country ought to be lovely."[140] Indeed, recent years have shone a bright light on the cost of government being able to take blind loyalty for granted. In such light, might not Muslims play a positive role in reinforcing what is to be generally expected from the American state as part of the price of loyalty?

In a reference to the abolitionist John Brown (d. 1859), March notes that "the United States prior to the Civil War was not a just society."[141] This injustice ostensibly justified (or at least made understandable) Brown's actions. But, presumably, only Brown and his fellow abolitionists believed that they were justified at the time. What if Muslims should similarly see fit to act as the scorned carriers of the nation's conscience on issues regarding which the rest of society has lost its way? Might not March's binding them to a transcendent, unchanging doctrine of blind loyalty undermine this important socio-political role and prerogative? In fact, might not Muslims' unwillingness to bear the cost of speaking truth to power (and occasionally to the powerless)—even where they are not bound *shar'an* to do so—ultimately constitute an act of *dis*loyalty?

Pluralism and Solidarity

Beyond the relationship between Islamic doctrine and the liberal state, the third and fourth elements of March's criterion speak primarily to how Muslims relate to non-Muslims in a predominantly non-Muslim *society*. This includes: (1) recognizing the right of non-Muslims not to be Muslim and therefore to hold beliefs and values that are incommensurate with those of Islam; (2) affirming equal justice as "the regulatory principle of relations between communities divided by metaphysical beliefs";[142] and (3) affirming "an Islamic foundation for the belief that contributing to the welfare of non-Muslim societies and participating in their political life are permissible and not in conflict with any core Islamic conception of the good or of justice."[143]

At bottom, March's point of departure echoes the assumption that has weighed on the Western political imaginary since at least the time of Rousseau (d. 1778): "It is impossible to live in peace with people one believes to be damned; to love them is to hate the God who punishes them; it is an absolute duty either to redeem or torture them."[144] As March puts it (rhetorically), "Why should we restrain ourselves in the realm of public justification to include people whom we may think are wrong?"[145] Of course, "wrong" in this context could mean either subscribing to views or *doctrines* that one finds morally objectionable from one's perspective as a Muslim; or it could mean pursuing *interests* that run counter to one's own, even if one does not deem these to be immoral or even practically misguided. We have seen that even staunch *sharī'ah*-maximalists such as Ibn Taymīyah recognized the distinction between judging non-*shar'ī* and *shar'ī* views.[146] And even regarding the latter, Muslims of the deepest doctrinal commitments have long defied the logic of Rousseau (and March), openly countenancing the views of co-religionists whom they believed to be wrong, Ḥanafīs, Mālikīs, Shāfi'īs, and Ḥanbalīs all accepting each other as orthodox and authoritative, despite their substantive mutual disagreements.

As for the relationship with non-Muslims, Muslim jurists and state officials have routinely, and as a matter of principle, recognized their right to do all kinds of things that Muslims find morally objectionable. It would seem, thus, to be a stretch to assume that Muslims cannot find common ground with non-Muslims on issues of common *interest* simply because the latter are non-Muslims, as if issues of public safety or clean air or water in and of themselves could divide the two groups. In fact, this takes us back to my earlier comment about the assumed makeup of the Muslim community. One need only recall what some of America's top Blackamerican non-Muslim athletes were willing to risk in order to come to the defense of Muhammad Ali in 1967 or Malcolm X's commitment to the broader non-Muslim Blackamerican community, even after his return from pilgrimage to Mecca in 1964. Beyond the basic question of their status as *mubāḥ*, these were all primarily matters of interests, not doctrine. And the priority, urgency, and optimal mode of contemplating and pursuing them would be through Islamic Secular deliberations. Given the extent to which March ignores or misrecognizes these non-*shar'ī* modes of thinking as legitimately Islamic, one wonders how accurately he can predict how Muslims might legitimately proceed in their relations with non-Muslims (or liberal citizenship).[147]

Regarding justice, March invokes the issue of non-Muslim "rights," based on his understanding of the place of rights in Islam-cum-*sharī'ah* as a whole. He writes, "[A]ccording to the ('orthodox') doctrine of Ash'arism . . . all rights and obligations obtain because God has chosen them and informed us of them. . . . That is, all rights and claims are 'statutory' in the sense of being created by God in the act of revelation."[148] Moreover, he notes, even where Islam guarantees justice, the rights it accords non-Muslims are not equal rights.[149] Once again, his mission is to find within the Islamic "*juridical and ethical tradition*" articulations of Islamic doctrine that can overcome or offset these obstacles, thus allowing for a full, or at least reasonably meaningful embrace, of equal rights as a constituent of liberal citizenship.

I discussed the matter of formal equality in my engagement with An-Na'im, noting how the pervasive logic of legal monism adopted by the modern state forces the presumption that everyone will be equally served and satisfied with the same regime of rights. March too assumes (apparently) that non-Muslims would be pleased if they enjoyed all the rights that Muslims enjoy (and, conversely, that Muslims are equally served by all the rights that non-Muslims seek).

But this is often far from the reality on the ground. As for whether Muslims can contribute to the welfare of non-Muslims, in addition to what I just mentioned about Blackamericans, we can dispense with this question via the classical tradition's well-known recognition of the right of a Muslim to bequeath up to one-third of his estate to a non-Muslim, even a non-relative. Again, my primary concern is not with whether March is correct in his conclusions, as far as these go (e.g., regarding equal rights), but on how his framing forecloses possibilities that the Islamic Secular would otherwise allow us to see, and how its omission affects our understanding of the relationship between Islam-cum-*sharīʿah* and rights as a constituent of liberal citizenship.

March's notion that *all* rights in Islam are "statutory" reflects the common misunderstanding of Ashʿarite doctrine I discussed in Chapter 4. To reiterate, while post-formative Ashʿarites limited divine reward and punishment to actions addressed by scripture (directly, analogously, or inductively), they did not limit all rights to revelation. In affirming, for example, the evil of falsely accusing an innocent person, which they acknowledged as being knowable independent of revelation, they were obviously attributing to all persons the right not to be wrongly accused. This does not mean that all such rights were recognized as justiciable in court; but neither is every right that *sharīʿah* confers upon Muslims, for example, a parent's right to be honored by his or her children. In sum, even on doctrinal grounds (taking Ashʿarism, as March does, as Islamic orthodoxy), there is no reason why the source of numerous rights could not be extra-revelatory.

Pace March, it is not necessarily the case that the only obligation of justice that Muslims have toward non-Muslims is a "statutory" one.[150] Islam-cum-*sharīʿah* has traditionally recognized numerous non-revelatory, conventional rights under the rubric of *maʿrūf*, or that which society has conventionally recognized as good.[151] In other words, much of the discourse around rights falls (or could fall) into the *ʿaqlī*, non-*sharʿī* realm of the Islamic Secular.[152] This becomes even clearer when we consider the kinds of extra-statutory, non-*sharʿī* rights included in the *siyāsah* rules and policies promulgated by the pre-modern Muslim state, which are not grounded in Islamic doctrine, or *aḥkām sharʿīyah*, but in assessments of public utility and interest.

We saw in earlier chapters that numerous aspects of the basic operation of any modern state falls into the non-*sharʿī* realm of the Islamic Secular: traffic laws, medical licensing, building codes, the concrete details of government bureaucracy, term limits, tenure procedures, and the like. These rules and policies tend to impinge upon people's everyday lives far more immediately than many of the concrete prescriptions of *sharīʿah*, especially in the case of non-Muslims, who are exempt from numerous aspects of the *sharʿ*— the entire realm of *ʿibādāt*, marriage, divorce, and even some aspects of criminal law.

Precisely, however, because these discretion-based rules and policies do not derive from *sharīʿah*, it is difficult to imagine reasons to exclude non-Muslims from the "rights" (and responsibilities) they confer, to say, for example, that non-Muslims do not have the equal right to obtain a driver's license or establish a commercial business.

More importantly, as I mentioned in my discussion of An-Naʿim, inasmuch as these rules and policies are non-*sharʿī*, it is difficult to imagine reasons to exclude non-Muslims from the process of negotiating their substance—at least reasons that would not also justify excluding Muslims. In fact, it is precisely in this vast area of non-*sharʿī*, Islamic Secular concerns that a genuine overlapping consensus between Muslims and non-Muslims would appear to be least problematic and most likely to occur. For, *sharīʿah* contributes little if anything to the concrete substance of most of these rules (e.g., speed limits, four-year terms of office, one book, a second book project, and four or five peer-reviewed articles for tenure). And, unless we assume that Muslims *qua* Muslims know more about building codes, medical licensing, or public administration than do non-Muslims *qua* non-Muslims, there is no reason why the two groups could not participate in setting the rules and policies governing these matters on an equal footing. We might remind ourselves here of the view of the "conservative" Shaykh Yūsuf al-Qaraḍāwī, when he hints at basic equality between Muslims and non-Muslims in terms of how they relate to non-*sharʿī* rules.[153] Of course, these considerations do not resolve all the tensions between Islam and liberal citizenship, and that is not my claim. It does demonstrate, however, that a full and accurate assessment of the relationship between Islam and liberal citizenship—or Muslims and non-Muslims—must include the Islamic Secular dimension of Islam-cum-*sharīʿah*, which an exclusive focus on Islamic "doctrine" occludes.

Regarding Muslim solidarity with non-Muslims, we must remind ourselves that March's focus is not on the relationship between Muslims and non-Muslims per se, but, as I intimated earlier, on the relationship between a concretely imagined group of Muslims and non-Muslims. Otherwise, the relationship between Blackamerican Muslims and Blackamerican non-Muslims would seem to render this question all but moot. But even beyond this consideration, if we admit interests and harms (*maṣāliḥ* and *mafāsid*) into the equation—as opposed to limiting ourselves to doctrine—the very question of solidarity becomes more complex. By solidarity, March's primary concern is with whether "it is permissible for a Muslim to form common social, economic, and civic goals with non-Muslims" and whether "[i]t is permissible for a Muslim to participate in a political system not based on Islamic justice or Islamic public justification."[154] We have seen the fallacy of the presumption that Muslims will (or should) proceed in the public domain strictly on the basis of "Islamic" [read, according to

March: *shar'ī*] "public justifications." It is also unclear in this context exactly what March means by "Islamic justice." How does issuing tickets to traffic-code violators relate in his scheme to "Islamic justice"?

Equally important, solidarity is not always expressed via agreement. Purely on the basis of interests (not doctrine), Muslims may perceive the common good differently from the way their compatriots see it, seeing as good or harmful what the latter see in opposite terms. This underscores the problematic nature of what appears to be March's (and Rawls's) blanket assumption that the whole point of joining in on public discourse is to promote cooperation. To extend the lesson of the famous *ḥadīth*, "Help your brother whether he is an oppressor or is oppressed" (*unṣur akhāka ẓālim*^{an} *aw maẓlūm*^{an}), it may be necessary to help one's society by *refusing* cooperation and seeking to disrupt its operations.[155] As full members of American society, Muslims may see fit to enter the public square precisely for the purpose of thwarting rather than promoting collaboration, despite the fact that it might be doctrinally permissible for them simply to go along with the status quo. This insight is precisely what a singular focus on doctrine blocks from view. And this underscores the clear and critical role of the Islamic Secular in arriving at a fair and accurate assessment of the relationship between Islam and liberal citizenship.

It bears repeating, however, that, despite the substantive disagreements I have with various aspects of March's thesis, my argument is not that he fails to demonstrate Islam's compatibility with liberal citizenship as he defines and argues this. In fact, I join him in his basic conclusion: there are authoritative Islamic arguments that make it permissible, as a matter of doctrine, for Muslims to live in non-Muslim polities, maintain a meaningful degree of loyalty to these states and societies, recognize non-Muslims' rights as non-Muslims, and join in solidarity with their non-Muslim compatriots. But as March himself acknowledges through the testimony of the rejectionists he cites, doctrine could also be invoked to support the opposite view. Doctrine alone, however, that is, *shar'ī* hermeneutics devoid of non-*shar'ī* considerations, has never been the sole medium through which Islam-cum-*sharī'ah* moves through time and space. The identification and pursuit of interests and the avoidance of harms, including many that lie "beyond the law," have always been part of Islam's concretion as a lived reality. The Islamic Secular, in sum, has always been a key constituent of Islam-cum-*sharī'ah* on the ground—any ground. My argument, therefore, is that, because March's reading of the Islamic juristic tradition fails to recognize the bounded nature of *sharī'ah* and the resulting reality and significance of *islām mā warā' al-ḥukm al-shar'ī*, his conclusions do not and cannot fully reflect the normative relationship between Islam and liberal citizenship.

In fact, given the nature of "public reason" and its centrality to liberalism's process of negotiation, even were March to include the Islamic Secular as part of his calculus, questions would remain about how the practical and material interests of Muslims would fare under the diluting, homogenizing (if not hegemonic) effects of liberalism. Yet, he (and no doubt others) would surely ask, if the appeal is not to be to liberalism-cum-public reason as referee, via what media should Muslims seek to negotiate their relationship with American liberal democracy, as doctrinally committed Muslims? To this and related questions I shall now turn in the final segment of this chapter.

Islam, Liberalism, and American Democracy: An Alternate Approach

Standing Where I Sit

I begin with the perspective from which I approach this topic. As a Blackamerican Muslim, I sit at the intersection of American Blackness, Islam, and the American project. From my perspective, all three—race, religion, and politics—are inextricable features of the American *wāqiʿ*, or socio-political reality, all three informing the liberal democratic order with which March calls upon Islam-cum-*sharīʿah* to negotiate its relationship. As we have seen, from the perspective of the Islamic Secular, the tools and metrics for apprehending any concrete socio-political *wāqiʿ* are predominantly non-*sharʿī*. March, however, aligns the American socio-political order with the ideal theory of Rawlsian liberalism, on the one hand, and Islam with *sharīʿah* as a comprehensive doctrine, on the other, both of which, according to him, if I understand him correctly, theoretically transcend socio-political specificity. I propose a different negotiating platform, one that includes: (1) a fuller fleshing out of the skeletal image of America's socio-political reality; (2) a fuller appreciation of *islām mā warāʾ al-ḥukm al-sharʿī*; and (3) a fuller appreciation of the distinction between America's liberal background culture—including its constitutional basis—and liberalism as a formal political theory.

There are three main reasons for suggesting this alternate approach (in addition to the fact that American democracy long preceded Rawls). First, race, religion, and politics all implicate concrete Muslim interests whose practical pursuit neither *sharīʿah*'s *ḥukm sharʿī* alone nor Rawlsian/Marchian liberalism adequately recognizes or addresses. Second, and relatedly, unlike the situation in Western Europe where liberalism was born, the primary fault line in America has been neither doctrinal nor rational but pre-rational and affective—more bluntly, racial. For this reason, requiring that public commitments be rationally justified and vindicated through a public reason that assumes no socio-political, economic, or cultural hierarchy fosters a false homogenization that doubly penalizes Muslims as minorities (especially since most of them are or are seen as racial minorities), once by denying their pre-rational commitments a fair hearing and again by rendering them the target of falsely homogenized, alienated Whites (especially working class) who see Blacks and Muslims (and others) as disproportionately benefiting from the liberal order. In other words, given public reason's commitment to exclusively rational justification, it cannot be relied upon to mend the pre-rational divisions that divide Americans. Third, liberalism tends to break down communities into autonomous individuals, even as being recognized as "individuals" is not equally open to all Americans. As a simple everyday fact, Blackamericans are more likely to be judged and pre-judged as members of a broader collective than by their individual talents or crimes. For them (and other racial minorities) "individualism" is a luxury that is largely limited to the possessors of the lone "invisible" American race: Whiteness. Meanwhile, privileging individualism ignores the communitarian dimension of who we *all* are (or aspire to be) as humans, and in so doing risks the perversion of this fact by more nefarious forces in society and politics, even as individualism makes it difficult if not impossible for religious communities to preserve the authority and integrity of their Faith as a way of life.

On all these fronts, my argument is simple: if Islam-cum-*sharīʿah*, as nothing but doctrine, is left to negotiate its relationship with American citizenship, with nothing but liberalism and its public reason as mediator, Muslims will be shortchanged and unable to address some of their (and in some cases America's) most pressing issues. Therefore, I suggest that Islam-cum-*sharīʿah*, beyond doctrine and including the Islamic Secular, on one side, and the US Constitution, beyond liberalism but including America's liberal background culture, on the other, are more fitting interlocutors. As we shall see, this engagement draws more on non-*sharʿī*, differentiated *fikr* than it does on undifferentiated *sharʿī fiqh*, underscoring, again, the critical role of the Islamic Secular.

Race

By "race," my proximate focus is the public identity-marker of Blackamericans, the descendants of America's slaves. Blackamericans are not immigrants who voluntarily determined how much of their original culture and history they would dump into the Atlantic en route to a newly chosen home. American Blackness was largely fashioned *in* America rather than being brought *to* it fully developed from without. This is undoubtedly what James Baldwin had in mind when he insisted, "Negroes do not . . . exist anywhere other than in America."[156] In fact, according to Baldwin, Blackamericans are "the world's first genuine black Westerner[s]."[157] Baldwin was not touting Blackamericans' Western-ness as some long-sought, celebrated achievement; he was simply recognizing the result of four-hundred years of hard-lived history-cum-cultural and socio-political ingenuity. I would qualify his insight, however, with the equally important insight of the late Charles Long:

> It would be difficult, if not impossible, to make the case for the non-Western identity of the black community in America, though several make this claim. The element of truth in this claim is that though we are Westerners, we are not Westerners in the same way as our compatriots, and thus we afford within America an entrée to the *otherness* of humankind.[158]

Among the major challenges confronting Islam-cum-*sharīʿah* in the modern world is how to respond to issues that are unprecedented or "new," not necessarily in the sense of having no prior existence in Muslim lands but often in the sense of not being entirely analogous to cognate realities in the modern West, realities that typically shape the interpretive prisms through which we moderns study and evaluate non-Western phenomena. Institutionalized, structural racism, is one such challenge. To be sure, distinct peoples (*aqwām*/sg. *qawm*) always existed in Muslim societies, and there were group rivalries, attitudes, and, for a time, even a social hierarchy between Arabs and non-Arab "clients" (*mawālī*/sg. *mawlā*) that many today would identify as racist (though language here tended to trump skin-color).[159] In fact, works such al-Jāḥiẓ's (d. 255/868) *Fakhr al-Sūdān ʿalā al-Bīḍān* (*Blacks' Boasts Against Whites*) confirm the existence of specifically anti-black (and anti-white) prejudice. When the great Persian (Sunnī) poet Saʿdī(d. 690/1291) states, "You can't wash the black off an African,"[160] one can assume that he and his anticipated audience perceived blackness to be a stain. Meanwhile, the custom in some contemporary Arab communities of referring to blacks in general as "slaves" (*ʿabīd*/sg. *ʿabd*) is unmistakable in its suggestion of an inherited racial hierarchy, at least socially speaking. Speaking of slaves, scholars have argued that in some times and places (e.g., Mamlūk Cairo) even black slaves were socially inferior to white slaves.[161]

Of course, the very notion of "white slaves" contradicts the foundational logic of modern racism. Meanwhile, across the Muslim world, not all "blacks" were associated with Africa, there was no "One-Drop" rule, and dark skin did not automatically trump all other endowments, such as learning or genealogy. Prominent Arab scholars, for example, recognized the black African Aḥmad Bābā al-Timbuktī (d. 1036/1627) as the *mujaddid*, or "Renewer of the Faith," of the tenth/sixteenth century.[162] Centuries earlier, in 659/1261, a black man escaped the Mongol destruction of Baghdad the previous year and made his way to Mamlūk Cairo, claiming to be a member of the ʿAbbāsid house. Amid great fanfare, his genealogy was publicly confirmed and he was recognized as al-Mustanṣir,

"Commander of the Faithful" (*amīr al-mu'minīn*), "the black Caliph" (*al-khalīfah al-aswad*).[163] This was the opposite of what we find half a millennium later in America, where a darker-skinned mulatto's "blue blood" would not prevent him or her from being disowned (or sold), and neither Washington's nor Jefferson's non-white offspring would have been eligible to be president. In sum, structurally speaking, the presence of racial prejudice notwithstanding, no functional equivalent of "Whites only" signs was ever institutionalized in the lands of Islam.[164]

Still, given the cumulative record, one could hardly deny the fact of racial prejudice—including anti-black prejudice—in Muslim history, even if it differed from what we now recognize as institutionalized racism.[165] Precisely on this difference, however, one might be hard-pressed to find in Islam's juristic tradition legal precedents, *aḥkām shar'īyah*, that address racism as a consciously sustained ideology and mode of societal (or global) ordering backed by official power. Both within the academy and beyond, this juristic silence might bring those who see *sharī'ah* as the unbounded equivalent of Islam to conclude that, in practical terms, Islam is indifferent to institutionalized racism and that the latter is irrelevant to any assessment of Islam's normative function in the modern world.[166] To this we might add that the field of Islamic Studies in general has tended to be racially agnostic, "the West," for example, rarely being discussed as "White" but almost always as a racially non-descript entity (though "the Greeks" seem to be unspokenly racialized as White). Ultimately, however—and this is the thesis of the Islamic Secular—even were Muslims to bring modern racism in its institutionalized form under a specific *ḥukm shar'ī*, that is, as *harām* (forbidden), to condemn a thing, *shar'an*, is not the same as prescribing a concrete, practical program for eradicating it. As the aforementioned Shaykh al-'Alwānī might put it, racism cannot not be fought with *fatwās* alone.[167] In the end, if Islam is limited to *sharī'ah* and its *ḥukm shar'ī*, it may not be entirely clear that Muslims are religiously obligated (or even encouraged) to fight against racism or, if they are, how they are to do so, beyond simply condemning racism on strictly moral grounds.

We see something along the lines of this logic expressed by South Africa's Muslim Judicial Council (MJC) during the period of apartheid in the 1960s. Against the efforts and criticisms of their more activist anti-apartheid brethren, they protested:

> Has the [apartheid] government forbidden the worship of Allah? Has the government closed down or ordered the demolition of any mosque in a declared white area? If our government has ordered our Muslims to desert the faith of our forefathers, then our *ulema* [religious scholars] would have been the first to urge us to resist, even to the death.[168]

As morally repugnant as institutionalized anti-Black and (more directly) anti-Colored racism might have been, in other words, it did not violate any *ḥukm sharʿī* in the sense of denying Muslims the right to do (or not do) anything that Islamic "doctrine" required them to do (or not do). It has been observed that the MJC approached apartheid from the perspective of the Islamic juristic principle of *hifẓ al-dīn*, "preservation of religion."[169] On this approach, in their view, religion, *in the proper, the religious sense*, could simply be successfully preserved and practiced under apartheid. In such light, one might oppose apartheid, even as a Muslim; but such opposition would be seen as "secular," as seeking to promote "non-religious" rather than properly religious or Islamic ideals and interests, which the MJC did not see as being mortally threatened by apartheid.

This tendency to equate Islam as a whole with *fiqh/sharīʿah* subtly throws out of focus the fact that not everything that threatens Islam necessarily does so because it is a direct threat to the application of *fiqh/sharīʿah*. Nor, conversely, can *fiqh/sharīʿah* provide all the concrete analyses and solutions needed to combat every such threat. Even if institutionalized racism does not force Muslims to violate any specific *ḥukm sharʿī*, in that they can still pray, fast, wear *ḥijāb*, marry, inherit, build mosques, avoid alcohol, and eschew *ribā*, it may still undermine Islam and Muslims. Yet, *how* racial subjugation saps Muslims' self-confidence and resolve, how it breeds complexes that predispose them to self-doubt and self-hatred or to preferring the ways of the "superior" group over Islam, how it facilitates the voluntary forfeiture of economic rights and resources, how it impedes the acquisition of the cultural and intellectual authority necessary to the health and longevity of Islam's requisite *nomos* and plausibility structure, how it demoralizes Muslims and in turn potentially renders truth— about themselves as well as the Other—subservient to "victory," in fact, how it inhibits the dominant group's ability to give Islam a fair hearing, as Islam is invariably viewed as the Faith of "inferiors"—all of this, as well as what to do about it, is apprehended primarily not through the hermeneutics of *fiqh/sharīʿah* contemplating scripture but by Islamic Secular *ʿaqlī* energies contemplating and interacting with socio-political reality. Even if *fiqh/sharīʿah* should address these issues so understood, the most it could provide would be a *ḥukm sharʿī* that condemns racism as *ḥarām*, or "impermissible," which is different from telling Muslims what, if anything, to do about it. Again, as Shaykh al-ʿAlwānī might put it, institutionalized racism cannot be fought with *fatwā*s alone.

This strictly doctrinal approach and the massive oversights it breeds are essentially what we see in the view of South Africa's MJC: because apartheid is not perceived as impeding the application of any *ḥukm sharʿī*, it falls outside the purview of what a Muslim can legitimately contemplate as an Islamic concern. In a similar fashion, March's restricting Islam to doctrine—*aḥkām sharʿīyah*—places all of the aforementioned challenges and interests outside the purview of what

Muslims in America can (or should) consider and pursue as explicitly Islamic interests. Yet, if Muslims *qua* Muslims cannot negotiate the challenge of racial hierarchy in America, how can they successfully negotiate a dignified existence with liberal citizenship as American citizens?

In contradistinction to March's restricted focus on *sharʿī* doctrine, the Islamic Secular admits all of the aforementioned concerns into the purview of what Muslims can and should address, both as religious/Islamic activity and as part of their negotiation with liberal citizenship in America—as Americans. This alone is a strong argument for the necessity of including the Islamic Secular in any discussion of the relationship between Islam and American liberal citizenship.

As for liberalism (as the co-medium of negotiation between Islam and liberal citizenship), it too faces problems in confronting race and racism. Liberalism emerged out of Western Europe's efforts to reconcile doctrinal conflicts over religion into a political arrangement that could avert internecine violence and sustain the public peace. In other societies—traditional African societies, for example, or even ancient Rome, as we saw with Cicero—one might no more ponder converting the public order to one's religious outlook than one would ponder converting it to one's tribe or kinship group.[170] In fact, even in societies where conversion was the desired result, the process did not necessarily mean force and internecine violence. In his book *Conversion to Islam in the Medieval Period*, Richard Bulliet argues that the central lands of Islam (Iran, Iraq, Syria, Egypt, North Africa) did not become simple-majority Muslim for some two hundred and fifty years after the initial conquests, much longer than any sustained campaign of forced conversion would have taken.[171] In any case, not only is Western Europe's story not the story of Islam, it is not the story of America, where racial rather than doctrinal conflict has been the primary driver of history. In contrast to the "Wars of Religion" that defined modern Europe, it was race that colored the bloodiest war in American history. In fact, according to Matthew Frey Jacobson, it is America that produced the distinctly racial understanding of "difference,"[172] effectively operationalizing the principle of *E pluribus duo*—"from the many two," White and non-White, a distinction that hardly captures the fundamental division in seventeenth and eighteenth century Europe.[173] Meanwhile, the historian Henry Adams (d. 1918), grandson of President John Quincy Adams (d. 1848), insisted that American history without the clue of race is "a nursery tale."[174] Given that the problem that liberalism was designed to address was not America's signature problem, one wonders about the propriety of appealing to it as the ultimate medium and referee in negotiating an American reality in which race plays such a central role.[175]

No one has been more forceful in underscoring liberalism's problematic relationship with race than the late Charles W. Mills (d. 2021).[176] Mills pointed out that by ignoring "*the* distinctive injustice of the modern world," that is, racial injustice, Rawls's liberalism effectively raised the problem of race beyond critique, folding this blind spot into his overall theory.[177] He viewed Rawls's theory in its present form as incapable of—indeed, as disinterested in—addressing the problem of racial hierarchy. It is important to understand in relation to this point that Islam in America has always had a racial connotation, socially if not legally, as a non-White religion—a reality that immigrant, Blackamerican, Latino, Native-American and even White American Muslims confront, albeit in different ways. If Mills is right and Rawlsian liberalism is insufficiently attuned to the problem of race, while I am right in seeing Islam in America as inescapably racially inflected, then liberalism as a political theory is fatally "unmusical" to a basic feature of American life that informs the lived reality of both Islam and liberal citizenship for Muslims in this country.

While Mills is critical of what he terms Rawls's "Racial Liberalism,"[178] he believes that Rawls's racial agnosia can be edited out of his theory and that the liberal project itself, including parts of the Rawlsian apparatus, can and should be salvaged.[179] I am not so sure. But I want to go beyond Mills and argue that liberalism is inadequate to the problem of race in America on yet another level, one that also has an impact on the lives of Muslims. As its etymology suggests, liberalism is grounded in a commitment to freedom. But this is a very particular understanding of freedom. Liberalism's freedom extols as an intrinsic good our individual autonomy and our right to choose, unilaterally, our life plans, with the expectation that we will be able to vindicate these choices and plans through public reason. As the communitarian thinker Daniel Bell suggests, however, this perspective implies that *un*chosen attachments are somehow wrong or inferior, since they do not accept the burden of rational vindication as the price of public recognition, participation, or respect.

The problem here is that reason can only mediate the appropriateness of attachments whose source itself is reason. Yet, all of us maintain and are partly constituted by unchosen, pre-rational attachments. As Bell puts it, "I didn't [rationally] choose to love my mother and father, to care about the neighborhood in which I grew up, to have special feelings for the people of my country, and it is difficult to understand why anyone would think I have chosen these attachments, or that I ought to have done so."[180] In other words, such attachments are not reasoned choices but unreasoned facts of human existence. Yet, this does not render them any less legitimate or operative in informing one's sense of self or the world, including one's relationship with others. From this communitarian perspective, freedom might be thought of not simply as the right to exert one's individual autonomy but equally importantly as the right to maintain and extol the broader, unchosen aspects of who one is, unmolested by demands to vindicate these rationally, especially through the third language of public reason.

This may be ultimately why thinkers such as Carl Schmitt, with his *das Volk*, continue (however problematically) to command our attention. There is simply something intuitively compelling about the idea of natural (or imagined) bonds tying us to our group and enabling, if not compelling, us to sacrifice some of our individual interests for the sake of the group. Paul Kahn characterized this kind of attachment as simply "love," which "works through a kind of double-movement that is simultaneously a realization and a sacrifice of the self."[181] Much earlier, Ibn Khaldūn had famously referred to it as *ʿaṣabīyah*, which he saw as foundational to the procurement and exercise of all socio-political power.[182]

Duly considered, such perspectives might enable us to see more clearly that at the heart of our problem in America is not merely the substance of our respective doctrinal commitments but also what I would term "the tragic consequences of love." This dialectical, involuntary force both binds us to our respective groups and brings us face to face with the fact that we do not and cannot love everyone equally. Rawls's denial of community was based in part precisely on this fact, his fear of communally defined love prompting him to try to individuate us and place reason over love and *ʿaṣabīyah* as a means of enhancing the possibilities of mutual co-existence. But the affective, pre-rational, unchosen communal attachments of Americans, even as individuals, doggedly persist; and denying them only exacerbates and promotes further misdiagnosis of the problem. When people feel that the legitimacy of their unchosen bonds of communal love and attachment is being questioned or denied, they will often experience this as a mortal threat, with hatred of perceived Others welling forth as a defensive reflex. At bottom, the challenge for America is that its racial, ethnic, and religious groups are essentially "aggregates of love," "regimes of *aṣabīyah.*" And the question is how a multiplicity of such aggregates and regimes, bound not by reason but by largely unchosen, pre-rational, affective forces, can be honestly and effectively reconciled into a functional political arrangement.

Liberalism seems to think that this conciliation can be achieved by the power of public reason to domesticate love or *ʿaṣabīyah* in the same way it domesticates doctrine. But this assumes a particular understanding of the relationship between reason and the self, namely, that the former always drives the latter rather than the other way around. This, however, is by no means a settled matter. In the West, Hobbes famously suggested that reason was ultimately dependent upon affect: "Thoughts are to the Desires, as Scouts and Spies, to range abroad, and find the way to the things desired. . . . [T]he mind is moved by desire, the active element of the self."[183] Much earlier, al-Ghazali had essentially made the same point. Responding to his Muʿtazilite interlocutors' moral objectivism, he protested, "You have erred in stating that reason (*al-ʿaql*) is a motivator (*dāʿin*); nay, reason is merely a guide (*hādin*), while impulses and motives (*al-bawāʿith wa al-dawāʿī*) issue from the self (*al-nafs*), based on information provided by reason."[184]

If liberalism, in its commitment to exclusively rational negotiation, cannot penetrate the true source of our competing affective commitments, because these are ultimately pre-rational, then the liberal peace that purports to resolve our conflicts must leave many of us either out in the cold or seething in white-hot anger beneath the surface. This includes, however, not only Blacks and Muslims but also working-class "ethnic Whites," who, "inexpert in Reason," as Shahab Ahmed might put it, cannot accommodate themselves to the would-be consensus fashioned by liberal (and other) elites but who also can neither avoid nor neutralize the effects of this consensus. These Whites, whom Matthew Frey Jacobson refers to as "Ellis Island" Whites, live under the patronizing gaze of a "Whiteness" whose normative image and expression is presided over by their "Plymouth Rock" betters, whom Ellis Island Whites see as looking down on them. To give an example, Joan Williams, a self-defined "silver-spoon girl" from an elite WASP background and now a distinguished professor of law, recalls her experience with a working-class Italian boy with whom she fell in love at age sixteen. Upon meeting his family, she recalls being later told how his father had grumbled, "She looked at us like a fucking anthropologist."[185]

Far more than empathy, however, let alone exogenous solidarity, what these disgruntled masses want is power, the kind that could insulate them from such judgments and ideally confer upon them a degree of validation and unaccountability regarding their attitudes towards others, especially non-Whites, whom it is simply easier (and often safer) to look down upon and blame for their woes than it is to confront their Plymouth Rock betters.[186] Ultimately, their desire for this kind of power renders them ripe for conscription by more nefarious forces in this country. Speaking of how liberal condescension drove working-class Whites into the arms of the far right, the aforementioned Joan Williams recounts the testimony of an anthropologist describing her fieldwork with this group:

> A [White] gospel singer told Hochschild how much she loved Rush Limbaugh. Hochschild was mystified until she realized that [this woman's] attraction to Limbaugh stemmed from her sense that Limbaugh was defending her against insults she felt liberals were lobbing at her—that "Bible-believing Southerners are ignorant, backward, redneck losers. They think we're racist, sexist, homophobic, and maybe fat." Limbaugh protected their pride.[187]

Let me be clear: it is not my contention that liberalism is somehow more responsible than conservatism for America's racial caste system.[188] After all, racial hierarchy, which long preceded Rawls, is what many (White) conservatives (and White liberals) want to maintain first and foremost. Nor do I subscribe to the insinuation that "Plymouth Rock" Whiteness is an exclusively liberal preserve. Nor do I believe that conservatives are innocent of deliberately stoking the resentments of working-class Whites—often identified as their base—and weaponizing these against Blacks, Muslims, and others. As the White Evangelical scholar Randall Balmer argues, white supremacy and racial segregation have informed the political platform of the "religious right" longer and more centrally than even such matters as abortion.[189] But if March is suggesting that Muslims should negotiate their relationship with American citizenship specifically through the machinery of Rawlsian/Marchian liberalism, one must take full account of the wages of such a proposal, both hidden and apparent.

It is difficult to imagine liberalism's public reason mending the divide between Plymouth Rock and Ellis Island Whites. In fact, if identity as an attachment to a broader unchosen collective has any value at all, it is difficult to see how *any* subaltern group survives liberalism's liquifying effects, especially given the inevitable if unacknowledged hierarchy built into public reason itself. In the absence of such mending, it is difficult to imagine Ellis Island Whites—steeped in a sense of being falsely homogenized and betrayed by the counterfeit promise of a Whiteness that is supposed to insulate them from Plymouth Rock's contemptuous gaze and empower them to judge others and not be judged—nursing feelings of loyalty, solidarity, or equality with Blacks or Muslims (or others), whose interests they see the liberal consensus placing over theirs, and whose identity they do not see the liberal consensus eroding as it does theirs.[190] This resentment may be (mis)directed even more forcefully toward 'immigrant' Muslims, who are often perceived as foreign yet tend (or are assumed) to be college-educated and solidly middle class, who "talk White," own businesses, and live in the suburbs.

If non-college-educated Whites (the majority) are made to question their place in the putative consensus forged by liberalism's public reason, surely, so the sentiment goes, Blackamericans, Muslims, and others—"*Jews will not replace us!*"—should not be allowed to assume a place of uncontested American belonging.[191] Viewed from this perspective, if not only Muslims' endorsement of loyalty, solidarity, and equality *vis á vis* non-Muslims but also non-Muslims' endorsement of these values *vis á vis* Muslims is among the fundamental dictates of liberal citizenship, then Rawlsian/Marchian liberalism may ultimately end up complicating rather than facilitating the way there.

In fairness, there is more to this impasse than the ideological strictures of liberalism. There is also a structural misdiagnosis. At slight risk of overstatement, America might be described as an empire-state that sees itself as a nation-state. By "empire-state," I do not mean to focus on America's exploits abroad (as objectionable as these may be) but to suggest that, as Americans, we are not—and probably never will be, except through unacceptable levels of physical and psychological violence—a single people. We are a single political community, made up of several peoples, indeed a "community of communities." By analogy to an earlier chapter in the history of Islam, as Americans, we might be described as a single *sha'b*, or geographically defined group, but not as a single *qabīlah* (tribe)[192] or *qawm* (people)[193] bound by a single biological, cultural, historical, or socio-psychological heritage. The whole notion of the existence in our midst of "discrete and insular minorities" confirms this fact.[194]

This fragmented nature may be why Europeans who visited America in earlier centuries doubted its very viability. Sigmund Freud, for example, described America as "a mistake, a giant mistake."[195] Alexis de Tocqueville (d. 1859) explicitly expressed his belief that the differences between Blacks and Whites were simply irreconcilable.[196] Even allowing for exaggeration in these articulations, the undeniable structural feature of America as a motley collection of different "peoples," some already present, some coming voluntarily, others involuntarily, some coming early, others late, some coming as members of or joining the "dominant group," others persisting as perpetual "minorities," all trying to forge a single political community—this unwieldly convergence inexorably pits the interest of assimilation against "the tragic consequences of love": White love of Whites, Jewish love of Jews, Black love of Blacks, Asian love of Asians, Latino love of Latinos, Muslim love of Muslims.

In this context, those who extol the lofty aims of "public reason" should also acknowledge its limits. In addition to its limited ability to reach the pre-rational and affective, a society as steeped in racial hierarchy as America necessarily consists of dominant and non-dominant groups. To imagine in this context that one group's centuries-long dominance will not tip the scales of "public reason" (i.e., what society deems "reasonable" or not) in its favor only reinforces that group's privilege by thickening the clouds of pretension that conceal its unacknowledged advantages and raise these beyond critique. Once again, given that the majority of Muslims in America are racial minorities (socially, where not legally[197]), liberalism stands as a precarious interlocutor for Islam-cum-*sharīʿah* to use in negotiating its relationship with American citizenship, given the centrality of racial hierarchy to the American *wāqiʿ*. Meanwhile, restricting Muslims to *sharʿī* "doctrine," to the exclusion of the Islamic Secular, only lowers the prospects of their effectively negotiating this basic American challenge.

Religion

Richard Rorty once described liberal society as "one which is content to call 'true' (or 'right' or 'just') whatever the outcome of undistorted communication happens to be, whatever view wins the free and open encounter."[198] Even Rorty's status as a non-Rawlsian cannot gainsay the fundamental role of public reason as the ultimate authority and arbiter in negotiating liberal theory's public order.

The broader implication of Rorty's insight is that "truth" cannot precede or transcend society but can only be a product of it and can claim in society only the authority brought to it by its proponents' prevailing in public debate through public reason. In other words, a Rawlisan/Marchian society can proceed—despite the presence of dominant and non-dominant groups—*as if* what prevails as "reasonable" equals what is substantively "true." Liberalism as such, functions as the default morality—and for some, no doubt, the default piety. March leaves little doubt about this when he insists, as noted earlier, that "When the two conflict, public reason trumps religious reason" and in his disallowing "religious truth to be brought to bear on society at large." This alone is enough to raise suspicions about the dangers that liberalism poses to religion, including Islam. Part of my argument, however, and the whole point of the Islamic Secular, is that Islam, while obviously committed to a transcendent Truth, is ultimately about *more* than just truth. For this reason, I shall focus on the wages of Rawlisan/Marchian liberalism for the more pragmatic, prudential side of Islam as *dīn*.

In arguing his case, March begins with his definition of "liberal citizenship" and asks how Islam might be successfully fitted into it as so defined. He does not ask what Muslims, as full-fledged co-owners of the American project, might recognize as necessary to sustain the integrity of Islam, beyond its ultimate truth and the ability to remain within the boundaries of the juristically permissible, as if Islam (or any religion) could be practically sustained on that basis alone. My proposal is to shift the terms of inquiry from truth and permissibility to Muslim practical needs and interests, within the parameters of Islam and the American constitutional arrangement. This also shifts the emphasis from a presumed desire or obligation to implement or impose *sharīʿah* to the question of how to sustain the universe of values, meanings, virtues, and priorities that preserve the status of Islam-cum-*sharīʿah* as an ideal *within* the Muslim community, the question of actual application being secondary. By "secondary," I do not mean "unimportant," or that Muslims can or should simply ignore this interest. Ultimately, however, a person is as good as he or she *wants* to be, and the enduring communal commitment, the top *farḍ kifāyah*, for Muslims in America must be to preserve the primacy and integrity of that want.[199]

Even if Muslims are not able to sanction co-religionists who drink alcohol or fornicate, the crucial question is whether and how they can practically sustain, as a communal value, the belief and sensibility that alcohol consumption and fornication are Islamically forbidden and wrong. Similarly, while the pursuit of perfect justice and a "politics of personal destruction" may become so normalized in society that they become difficult (if not impossible) to avoid, the question is whether and how Muslims as a community will be able to preserve the practical status of such core Islamic values as mercy (*raḥmah*), forbearance/resilience (*ṣabr*), reliance upon God (*tawakkul*), forgiveness (*ʿafw*), fault-covering (*satr*), and the consigning of absolute justice to the Ultimate Forum. If, finally, the dominant culture comes to see the universalization of rules and values as a function of the these rules' and values' truth, the question becomes whether Muslims, especially given the widely diffused presumption of legal monism, will be able to maintain collectively their practical recognition of the distinction between rules and values that Islam intends to be practically universalized and rules and values that it does not.

Ludwig Wittgenstein (d. 1951) argued that the preservation of meaning requires not a theory of language, signs, or symbols but a form of life, a culture, a semantic frequency on which meanings, values, and sensibilities can safely travel, arrive, and be decoded with fidelity.[200] Stanley Hauerwas registers a similar view when discussing the challenge of preserving Christianity's basic integrity. According to him, foundational Christian values and concepts cannot be understood by individuals approaching them from the perspective of nowhere and everywhere. Proper understanding requires, rather, explicit reliance upon Christian tradition and community as the semantic point of departure and referee. Otherwise, one cannot arrive at and sustain a proper understanding or valuation of such Christian concepts as "sanctification," justification," "sin," "salvation," or even beliefs about God and Jesus.[201] Ever since Kant's invocation of *Sapere aude* ("Dare to think for yourself"), tradition and, albeit less directly, community, have been stigmatized as impediments to progress and self-realization. But Hauerwas makes it clear that tradition for him is "not a 'deposit' of unchanging moral 'truth', but is made up of the lives of men and women who are constantly testing and developing that tradition through their own struggle to live it."[202] Tradition is sustained, moreover, not by individuals acting as detached free agents but as individuals acting as members of a community, not just contemporaneously but trans-generationally across space and time, participants in an ongoing conversation between the living, the dead, the unborn.

I wish to argue something similar for Islam, especially in a minoritarian context such as America, where an Islamic form of life cannot be assumed but must be somehow simulated. What Muslims in America need first and foremost is a *nomos*, a plausibility structure or communicative field that can sustain the habits of heart and mind that dialogically feed upon and nurture the truth, authority, and efficacy of Islam-cum-*sharī'ah* as a way of life. This commitment to *nomos* and a plausibility structure must be American Muslims' *primary collective commitment*. This implicates tradition, not as a mere repository of iron-handed authority but as the collective memory of the Community's mistakes, successes, genius, failures, wisdom, villains, and heroes, all of which inspire humility and resolve no less than they spawn cautionary, death-defying and life-affirming reflexes that, promote pride and and perspicacity and provide Muslims with a way out of their status as "orphans of modernity." Yet, these are ultimately the very bonds of community that liberalism is inclined, if not committed, to loosening if not undoing.[203]

We get a sense of what is at stake in all of this when we consider the negative connotations that have accrued to such staples of Islam as *Allāh*, *sharīʿah*, *jihād*, prayer, or even ablution anywhere outside the home or mosque. We see it as well in how such words as *tawḥīd*, *ribā*, *zinā*, or *shirk* (which even non-Arabic-speaking Muslims know and use) have lost their awe, gravity, priority, and urgency. While no monotheistic religion can dispense with a functional category of exclusion, for American Muslims, even the mere public utterance of the word *kāfir* (one who does not believe in Islam) is effectively proscribed as a threat to social peace, the functional equivalent of the "N" word.[204] Meanwhile, the internalization of *ʿibādah* as simply "worship," to the exclusion of "obeisance," nudges Muslims toward the voluntary privatization of Islam, "religious freedom" being openly acknowledged as the freedom to believe, pray, fast, and build mosques but far less so as the freedom to "take Islam to the streets" or to the halls of power or to those places where beauty, morals and prevailing ideologies are made. Such developments can only put distance between future generations and Islam's normative ethos and meanings.

In such light, it becomes clear that, just as the sustainability of liberalism relies on a broader culture of tolerance, debate, and "a certain form of secularism,"[205] Islam has background requirements as well. And in the interest of sustaining Islam's integrity, it is not enough for Muslims to have the theoretical right to remain within the boundaries of the "permissible" or even to do what *sharīʿah* merely requires them to do—especially if the psychological, emotional, and spiritual price of doing so remain so high as to render this right almost meaningless. Elsewhere, March notes that "the state's mere tolerance of homosexual acts and lifestyles while denying public recognition through extending the right of forming legal unions is a form of stigmatization that marks homosexuals as less than equal."[206] In a similar vein, Islam-cum-*sharīʿah* cannot negotiate its relationship with American citizenship purely on the basis of state recognition of what is obligatory or forbidden, *sharʿan*.

Let me share a personal experience that might add some flesh to these skeletal allusions. Several years ago, about to board an early flight out of Detroit, I stopped at the airport's Burger King to get an egg-and-cheese croissant. Standing in front of me was a well-dressed, middle-aged Blackamerican gentleman sporting an elegant gold crucifix that rested proudly about his chest. When the attendant came out and slid a bunch of wrapped sandwiches into the bin, he said to her: "Excuse me, miss, what's in these sandwiches? Please don't tell me swine, 'cause I ain't eatin' no swine." Of course, this obviously Christian gentleman may have had a personal aversion to pork. A more likely explanation, however, is that his reaction went beyond him as an individual and reflected the success of the Nation of Islam in redefining aspects of Blackamerican cultural orthodoxy. Prior to the rise of Islamic movements in Blackamerica, I am unaware of any aversion to eating pork among Blackamerican Christians. While the Nation's influence may not have spread across the entire Blackamerican community, it was apparently broad enough to ensure that, despite its status as a traditional constituent of soul food, Blackamerican Muslims would generally not be judged negatively for refusing to eat pork.

This reshaping of Blackamerican culture went beyond the question of permissibility. It did not simply allow or permit Muslims to eschew pork, as they had not been forced to eat it prior to this development. Nor would Muslims be in violation of any *ḥukm sharʿī* had they simply refrained from eating pork while pursuing no efforts to normalize this posture in the broader culture of Blackamericans. This change made it possible, however, for Muslims to uphold their religious obligation without stigma, fear, psychological dislocation, or turmoil. As Rorty suggested, the Nation of Islam had succeeded in creating the tastes in the broader Blackamerican community by which Blackamerican Muslims would be judged.[207] Clearly, their efforts went beyond the dictates of the *ḥukm sharʿī*, beyond considerations of individual choice, and beyond any vindication by public reason. Moreover, this was a communal effort that included, before and after the fact, the policing of cultural boundaries.

According to March, however, if I understand him correctly, liberalism does not permit communities to wield this kind of authority. Indeed, it protects individuals not only from the state but from any such authority that communities as sub-state entities might wield.[208] In effect, liberalism needs us to think, feel, and argue in liberal terms, not only in public but at home, in the mosque, at work, and with friends.[209] This is how it sustains its status as the default morality (if not the default piety). Meanwhile, by limiting our gaze to the theatre of doctrine—the permissible versus the impermissible—Marchian liberalism diverts attention away from the fact that Muslims will not be able to achieve the kind of cultural change they need—to shape the tastes by which they are judged, as a legitimate *maṣlaḥah*—via strict reliance on *sharīʿah* and its *ḥukm sharʿī* alone. On the contrary, such change is the domain of the Islamic Secular writ large.

Politics

In a 1973 interview, the German-Jewish immigrant to America Hannah Arendt (d. 1975) made the point I alluded to earlier, that America is not a nation-state united by a common biological, historical, linguistic, or socio-psychological heritage. This fact, she noted, baffled Europeans, who have had a hard time understanding that one becomes an American simply by assenting to an idea: the US Constitution. While this curious feature of Americanness stood out to Arendt, it has been lost on many among the dominant group of Americans today. The Blackamerican public intellectual Albert Murray once observed that, while Blackamericans are constantly judged, *qua* Americans, in terms of their degree of conformity to White standards, no one judges the Americanness of White Americans based on the extent to which they live up to the standards of the Constitution. For Murray, because Blackamericans, even in their critique of the American state and dominant culture, were historically truer to the Constitution, they are more authentically American.[210] White Americans, by comparison, and seemingly only White Americans, are able to erect all kinds of requirements for full Americanness other than adherence to the Constitution, as if America were a seamless extension of Europe, where the state represents an ostensible "single people" and sits atop a single cultural orthodoxy, amorphous as it may be, which the state and all patriotic citizens are called upon to police in the name of the republic.

Against this backdrop, I would like to note that, while American constitutionalism may be grounded in a broad and imprecise liberal background culture, neither Rawls's nor March's liberal theory is part of the US Constitution. As such, in posing the question of the relationship between Islam and "liberal democracy," one must distinguish between "liberal" in the sense of a liberal background culture and "liberal" in the sense of a commitment to Rawls or March. I propose that Islam-cum-*sharīʿah*, including the Islamic Secular, negotiate its relationship with American citizenship through the US Constitution and America's liberal background culture instead of through Rawlsian-Marchian liberalism. By "liberal background culture," I am referring (beyond the problem of race) to the status and role of appeals to such staples as freedom, justice, equality, and pluralism (however vaguely understood) as legitimizing agents in American public discourse. My argument is that, while Islam did not install this background culture, it can accommodate it, partly as an echo of its own ethos and historical memory, and partly in recognition of what the Qur'ān and Islamic juristic tradition recognize as a society's *maʿrūf*—conventionally recognized socio-political norms that do not contravene *sharīʿah*.[211] Or perhaps it would be useful to add what the Moroccan jurist Aḥmad al-Raysūnī refers to as *taʿāruf*, or "reasoned convention," which he distinguishes from *maʿrūf*/*ʿurf* by the fact that *taʿāruf* is the result of reasoned debate, whereas *maʿrūf*/*ʿurf* is more an expression of trans-generational spontaneity.[212] Either way, impulses and principles already present in Islam's historical memory, ethos, and juristic tradition, rather than crass pragmatism, back my appeal to America's liberal background culture. Equally important, beyond whatever legitimacy Muslims might extend to this background culture, *sharʿan*, their actual engagement with it, including their possible challenges and contributions to it, will rely on Islamic Secular energies as much as it does on *shar'ī* ones, if not more.

The US Constitution between *Sharī'ah* and the Islamic Secular

Before proceeding further, however, I must clarify my endorsement of the US Constitution, lest I be suspected of trying to hide the ball (*taqīyah*) by turning a blind eye to the actual dictates of Islam-cum-*sharī'ah*. In fact, a number of common assumptions about the Constitution and Islam have already led to similar charges against me. Perhaps the most direct and strident of these was put forth by Vincent Cornell in his critique of an earlier articulation of mine on the matter. He writes:

> The ideological universalism of US democratic constitutionalism confronts Sherman Jackson with a dilemma far greater than he acknowledges in his book. If, as he seems to believe, the secular and non-Muslim origin of the Constitution means that it is not founded on the same principles as the Shari'a, then the Constitution can only be seen as an ideological rival to the Shari'a, and US democracy must be seen as a counterideology to Islam.[213]

Cornell's point of departure appears to be the 'Fundamentalist' imaginary of Usāmah b. Lādin (d. 1432/2011), whose view he quotes at the beginning of his essay: "You [Americans] are the nation who, rather than ruling by the *sharia* of God in the Constitution and Laws, choose to invent your own laws as you will and desire." As we can see, there is no distinction in this conceptualization of "the Constitution and Laws" between '*shar'ī*' and 'non-*shar'ī*' contributions, the only legitimate law presumably drawing its substance directly and entirely from *sharī'ah*. This is the basis of the rejectionist stance of those whom Cornell refers to as "Shari'a fundamentalists." And this is the view he apparently assumes in anyone (myself included) who assigns *sharī'ah* a place of primacy in the lives of Muslim-Americans.

In a brief (equally strident) online response to Cornell,[214] I clarified that neither the non-Muslim nor the secular origins of the Constitution necessarily render it Islamically invalid for Muslim-Americans as the basis of political community in the US. More concretely, the fundamental clash that Cornell sees between *sharī'ah* and the Constitution would obtain only on the assumption that both pretend to totalizing, universal claims to ultimate truth. *Pace* Cornell, however, I argue that the US Constitution makes no such pretension (indeed, such would violate its Establishment Clause), and *sharī'ah*, as we have seen, is also a bounded entity that does not speak to everything. Rather than a transcendent, totalizing statement of truth, the Constitution is a negotiated compromise, a split-the-difference agreement, over how political rights and protections for

Americans are to be distributed and adjudicated. That there may be provisions thereof with which Muslims disagree, or even see as violating this or that detail of *sharīʿah*, need not necessarily alter its status as an actionable agreement.

When the Prophet sat to negotiate the famous Treaty of Ḥudaybīyah with the pagan Meccans, the latter refused to acknowledge his prophethood, denied God's attribute as "The All-Merciful, The Mercy-Giving" (*al-raḥmān al-raḥīm*), and would not allow Muslims to make the pilgrimage to Mecca that year—all offenses against, if not violations of, Islam. In fact, the Meccans included other stipulations that could easily be seen as unjustly tilting the Treaty to their advantage.[215] Despite these infelicities, however, the Prophet agreed to and held himself bound by this Treaty, clearly recognizing the practical, long-term benefit to be derived therefrom.[216]

By embracing the Constitution, I am not endorsing any of the pretensions to transcendent, ultimate truth that some (e.g., Cornell) may impute to it. I am simply recognizing its practical authority as the basis of America's political arrangement, itself a 'non-*sharʿī*,' practical arrangement that was not the direct product of scriptural sources. On this distinction, I do not hold Muslims *qua* Muslims to be religiously bound (i.e., *sharʿan*), to believe in the US Constitution as an articulation of ultimate truth. Rather, Islam, in my view, simply *permits* Muslims to accept the Constitution as a political pact, and the real incentive to embrace it comes largely from the Islamic Secular side of deliberation and the material benefits it confers upon Muslims, including an ability to pursue their "primary communal commitment," as articulated above. As I have written elsewhere (in the same book criticized by Cornell, incidentally), according to the US Constitution,

> the US government cannot force a Muslim to renounce his or her faith; it cannot deny him or her the right to pray, fast, or perform the pilgrimage; it cannot force him or her to eat pork, shave his beard, or remove her scarf (*ḥijāb*); it cannot deny Muslims the right to build mosques or schools or to vote or to hold public office; it cannot deny them the right to criticize and seek to change government officials and policies, including the person and policies of the president. . . . Surely it must be worth asking if Muslims in America should conduct themselves as "nouveau free" who squander these and countless other rights and freedoms in the name of dogmatic minutiae, activist rhetoric and uncritical readings of Islamic law and history, rather than turning these to the practical benefit of Islam and Muslim-Americans.[217]

It is on this basis that I argue(d) that Muslims in America should embrace and defend the Constitution. For, without it, there simply is no viable form of politics for them, no way, especially in this charged, post–September 11th atmosphere, for them to confront their political adversaries, assert their political rights, promote their own vision, and negotiate the terms by which they will live their lives. In the face of prejudice, abuse, and threats from various quarters, the Constitution, duly upheld, may be the only political trump card that Muslims hold. And, as Hobbes (I believe) once observed, when a community finds itself bereft of political trump cards, clubs become its adversaries' trumps!

As for *sharīʿah*, Cornell's notion that it and the Constitution clash at the level of universal truth is tied to the notion that Islam-cum-*sharīʿah* is all about truth, and that as truth it must pretend to a Kantian universalism modeled on the categorical imperative. This understanding is reminiscent of March in his construction of Islam-cum-*sharīʿah* as a "comprehensive doctrine." We have seen, however, that while Islam obviously entails a claim to ultimate truth, Islam-cum-*sharīʿah* is not *only* about truth;[218] nor does it seek necessarily to universalize all of the truths it espouses in the manner implied by Cornell, as we saw, for example, with al-Shāfiʿī and his attitude toward protecting non-Muslims' right to worship other than God.[219] There is a practical, prudential, material side to Islam, in other words, that, while inseparable from its constitution as religion, does not seek to promote or defend any truth per se; nor do the *sharʿī* categories of *sharīʿah* as a would-be "comprehensive doctrine" encompass all of the metrics of assessment that may be relevant to this non-*sharʿī*, practical domain. When the Qurʾān commands Muslims, "*Prepare in facing them in battle what you can in the way of power and tethered horses*" [8:60], there is no ultimate truth in the resulting technology or strategy developed or deployed; nor is their status as "permissible" (*mubāḥ*)—or even "obligatory" (*wājib*)—the only Islamically relevant metric of assessment upon which Muslims will rely in developing and evaluating their efforts. Rather, non-*sharʿī*, Islamic Secular, metrics, such as effectiveness, are also germane.

Given this practical side of Islam-cum-*sharīʿah*, what Muslims and non-Muslims develop in the domain of the Islamic Secular need not be assumed to draw the two groups into 'religious' conflict, since the bulk of what is developed here will draw on non-*sharʿī* as opposed to *sharʿī* sources and energies. This applies to constitutions as well. Constitutions are not about universal, ultimate truth (at least not primarily); they are about practical, political arrangements. In the US, the practical, prudential challenges of competing interests and "aggregates of love" are at least as relevant to the maintenance of the constitutional order as are doctrinal differences or competing claims to universal truth. Herein lie the relevance and utility of the Islamic Secular as an alternative to Marchian liberalism and purely *sharʿī* metrics as media through which Muslims might negotiate Islam's relationship with American citizenship and constitutionalism.

Protecting the Protection

In more concrete terms, my alternate approach builds on the communitarian ethos of the Qur'ān coupled with a model of political community inspired by my reading of an essay by Michael Walzer, "What Does It Mean to be an 'American?'"[220] The key notion I draw from this essay is that of "protecting one's protection." Walzer describes America as essentially the land of hyphenated citizenship—Asian-American, Arab-American, Irish-American—a concept that would make little sense in Europe, where there is no such thing as "Asian-Europeans" or "Italian-Frenchmen."

There are two sides, however, to the American hyphen. The left side is the place of *parochial* community, the location of many-ness, where ethnic, cultural, racial, and religious difference and diversity live and thrive. Here is where citizens embrace and celebrate their concrete distinctiveness and unchosen commitments and draw the most meaning and happiness in their private, communal, and even broader socio-cultural lives. For, it is here that the specificities of parochial regimes of love and belonging resonate with value, meaning, beauty, confirmation, and reciprocity, and where the deepest sense of moral and cultural community is experienced. In short, the left side of the hyphen is the home of *'aṣabīyah* and all its tragic and joyful consequences. Those who prioritize this side, however, do not necessarily see their Americanness as a challenge to or contradiction of their racial, cultural, or religious consciousness. They see it, rather, more as a qualifier thereof, the hyphen working essentially "like a plus sign."[221]

By contrast, the right side of the hyphen is the home of *political* community, the singular hub that holds the various ethnic, cultural, racial, and religious spokes together in a workable balance. This is the place of oneness, the *unum*, where the democratic framework sets the rules and seeks to ensure fair and sufficient terms of socio-political cooperation. It is also here that many Americans identify the "greater good" and where they see the ultimate aim of the American project residing. They envision the right side of the hyphen as ideally subsuming the left and collapsing all difference into a single, homogenized community, a melting pot. *Pace* liberalism, however, it is not the force of reason—and certainly not public reason—that these citizens believe can domesticate "love" and offset its tragic consequences; it is the simple recognition of political community as the highest possible value and commitment, which is usually what they mean by "patriotism." In theory, they want not so much to eliminate ethnic, racial, cultural, and religious difference as to disempower them. In practice, however, in their quest to transcend or blend together competing parochial perspectives, they often fail to recognize their own perspective, including their perspective on America, as itself parochial—not to mention the fact that, in many instances, their real commitment is to raising their own parochial perspective beyond recognition and critique *as* parochial.[222]

In deploying the concept of "protecting one's protection," I view the American project from the left side of the hyphen. I also make a conscious commitment to uphold, if not strengthen, the unitary democratic framework within which Americans can indulge their ethnic, religious, and cultural differences and pursue the activities and practices that preserve their integrity. This commitment is grounded in my recognition that the left side of the hyphen is only as secure as the right side is solid, operative, and mutually recognized. In other words, Muslims in America can pursue their "primary communal commitment" only if the American constitutional order is secure and functional. On this understanding, especially given what I said earlier about the Constitution and its not being a competing claim to ultimate truth, it would be imprudent for Muslims not to be loyal to this constitutional arrangement as members of the American political community, even as they retain various parochial interests and commitments that set them apart from other Americans. In short, it is clearly in their interest to "protect their protection." As for solidarity, moral pluralism, and the like, these are as much the product of Muslim "politics," which this political arrangement supports, as they are of Islamic "doctrine."

There are two modes of Muslim politics under this arrangement. The first is Rawls's "politics in the wrong way," where, in pursuit of their "primary communal commitment," Muslim values or interests may clash or simply not relate positively to those of other citizens. Here their aim is not to promote the common good per se but to maximize or protect the good that serves Islam's concrete interests, including its requisite *nomos* and plausibility structure. Even this good, however, must be pursued in a manner that does not lose sight of the interest of "protecting the protection." Either because they lack the relevant resources in the way of alliances, money, social and political capital, or adequate organization, or because "the protection" allows others to deploy their superior resources to opposite ends, Muslims may lose some battles. But this need not result in their abandonment or rejection of the overall political arrangement. Rather, Muslims can accept such non-lethal losses, yet to fight another day.

What they cannot accept (at least not on principle) is unequal protection or a formal political arrangement that guarantees that they cannot win. It is here that my commitment to America's liberal background culture and constitutional arrangement, as distinct from Marchian liberalism as a political theory, is most thrown into relief. Independent of the justificatory burden of public reason, with its liquifying effects, the commitment to "protecting the protection" entails the explicit right of Muslims to pursue their own vision of the good, both morally and practically, while being assured basic protections and without having to subject the unchosen aspects of their identity as Muslims to a justificatory process that is stacked against the very idea of unchosen-ness. The theoretical attraction of liberalism, especially for minorities, begins with its promise of neutrality and the equal empowerment of everyone to negotiate their choices, against the threat of false homogenization or domination. In practice, however, liberalism has difficulty accommodating the encumbered individual for whom the very idea of *choice* may occasionally contradict what conscience dictates as *duty*. For the encumbered (as opposed to the autonomous) self, as Michael Sandel, explains, "Where freedom of conscience is at stake, the relevant right is [often] to perform a duty not to make a choice."[223] Of course, not all duties are necessarily *shar'ī*. In fact, non-*shar'ī* deliberations will routinely drive this side of Muslim politics.

Muslims may oppose this or that non-Muslim value, doctrine, or interest not out of a sense of being compelled to do so, *shar'an*, but because they feel duty-bound on practical grounds to protect and promote their interests (*maṣāliḥ*/sg. *maṣlaḥah*) as Muslims, which, in addition to scripture (or the *madhhab*s) are ongoingly informed by circumstances on the ground. Take, for example, the issue of same-sex marriage. As I have noted elsewhere, pre-modern Muslim jurists acquiesced to the Zoroastrian custom of men marrying their mothers, sisters, or daughters, despite their seeing this as morally repugnant and blatantly in violation of the moral vision of *sharī'ah*.[224] Even Ḥanafīs, who tended to go further than the other schools in extending *sharī'ah*'s application to non-Muslims, allowed such marriages. The great Ḥanafī jurist al-Sarakhsī, for example, wrote: "If a protected non-Muslim male (*dhimmī*) marries a female relative, i.e., a mother, daughter or sister, we do not intervene, even if a judge knows this to be the case, unless they seek our intervention."[225] By analogy, certainly as applied to non-Muslims in America (the overwhelming majority in the country), a good-faith engagement with the Islamic juristic tradition *could* bring some Muslims to the conclusion that it is permissible, *shar'an*, for them to acquiesce to same-sex marriage, in the same way they acquiesce to non-Muslims' right to drink wine, eat pork, or worship Jesus, even as they hold all of these things, substantively speaking, to be religiously unacceptable (i.e., *ḥarām*) from their perspective as Muslims.

In the present context, however, the question is whether Muslims *should* acquiesce to same-sex marriage. Here, taking the aforementioned "primary communal commitment" as their point of departure, other Muslims might conclude that such an allowance could only strengthen and ultimately normalize a sexual ethic that threatens or degrades the *nomos* and plausibility structure upon which the survival of Islam's own moral ethic relies. On this essentially non-*shar'ī*, Islamic Secular calculation, they will likely conclude that their interest lies in opposing same-sex marriage. While this clearly contradicts the interests of another group of Americans, this should be seen as an expression of Muslim politics in pursuit of Muslim interests, not necessarily as an expression of ultimate truth nor as an attempt to impose *sharī'ah* on American society. Indeed, while *sharī'ah* is obviously a contributing factor in these deliberations, the Islamic Secular is far more determinative. Stated differently, beyond their commitment to Islam as religion, *in the proper, the religious, sense*, Muslims, like everyone else, have material and other *interests*. In such light, once again, *sharʿī* doctrine—permissible versus impermissible—is neither always a reliable basis upon which to predict what Muslims will do nor to understand their political decisions after the fact.

The second mode of "politics" entails contests wherein the basic point of departure is not Muslims' "primary communal commitment" or the specific interests of Islam or Muslims per se but the American (or local) commonweal and its practical, material interests, which are grounded in such differentiated, Islamic Secular metrics as efficiency, safety, the most economical, and the like: medical licensing, zoning laws, FAA regulations, gun control, or whether there should be a single-payer healthcare system. Even if *sharīʿah* contributes to these deliberations by lending a general directionality to Muslim thinking, the concrete details of their reasoning will be primarily determined by Islamic Secular deliberation, much of which will be substantively indistinguishable from the deliberations of many non-Muslims. For example, the presumed permissibility, *sharʿan*, of owning a gun may yield to factual assessments of the level of gun violence in the local or national community, bringing Muslims to favor or not effective restrictions on gun ownership. Or it may prompt them to consider, rather than dismiss out of hand, proposals to require every household to have a gun on hand, as a means of discouraging home invasions. This, incidentally, is the mode of Muslim politics where the possibility of a genuine overlapping consensus is, theoretically, most likely, given the level of reliance on Islamic Secular as opposed to strictly *sharʿī* energies.

In the end, among the advantages of this alternative to Marchian liberalism is its ability to avoid the large though often masked liabilities of false homogenization. It allows Americans, Muslim and non-Muslim alike, to remain consciously a single *shaʿb* while also belonging to different *qabāʾil* (sg. *qabīlah*) or *aqwām* (sg. *qawm*), accommodating multiple racial, ethnic, cultural, or religious American authenticities, limiting the singularity of American authenticity to the commitment to American political community, the mutual commitment to "protecting the protection." This domesticates "public reason's" push toward singularity-cum-conformity[226] and has the potential to tame the so-called culture wars over whose culture shall become "the" or "our" American culture; for not only will everyone be able to recognize and celebrate his or her parochial commitment, all ethnic, racial, cultural, and religious commitments will be recognized *as* parochial.

This arrangement, I hasten to add, does not condemn communities to isolation in hermetically sealed silos. They can and almost certainly will expand, contract, gain converts, and atrophy over time, as we have seen in the diachronic swelling of the ranks of "Whites," the fluctuating fortunes of ethnic identities, and the now expanding ranks of those collectively referred to as "people of color."[227] More importantly, communities will feel less of a need to assimilate to alien norms and standards in order to feel authentic *as* Americans. And this will reduce the tendency to see parochial communities as threats to the republic. It will also afford more "discrete and insular" communities, including, for example, Blackamericans, Native-Americans, Latinos, and even "plebeian" Whites, greater facility in addressing issues that may be unique to them and only properly appreciated or understood by them, instead of their having to sit by and watch numerous matters go unaddressed (or inadequately addressed) simply because they fall outside the socio-political gaze and understanding of the dominant group and its "public reason."

To be sure, the "tragic consequences of love" will remain a challenge. For, part of what is implied by the very notion of love is involuntary discrimination. Marchian liberalism avoids this problem, not by solving it but by essentially denying it, by denying the legitimacy of the unchosen and assuming reason's ability to neutralize love's discriminating propensity. By contrast, there are two ways in which my alternative to March's approach speaks to and ideally mitigates this challenge. First, in discussing the problem of love (in another context), Stanley Hauerwas points to the need for an "overriding obligation" other than liberalism (which he rejects) that can offset the ravages of what he refers to as "discriminating" love. He sees the "non-discriminating" love of the Church as just such an obligation.[228] Like Hauerwas, I also see the need for an "overriding obligation," and I see Islam as *dīn* fulfilling this role. Unlike Hauerwas, however, I see *all* love as ultimately discriminatory. As such, I would not characterize Islam's utility as *dīn*, even as an "overriding obligation," as "non-discriminating love," as he characterizes that of the Church. Yet, by placing God-consciousness, that is, *taqwā*—the same force behind the Islamic Secular's obeisance—between Muslims and those who are not the objects of their love, Islam as *dīn can* domesticate the tragic consequences of love. Muslims can be fair, cooperative, empathetic, and even in solidarity with those who fall outside the reach of their love or *ʿaṣabīyah*, simply because God tells them to be.

This obviously applies to Muslims' relationships with fellow Muslims who hail from different ethnic, racial, or cultural backgrounds. But my argument is that it extends to non-Muslims as well: "*So, if they [non-Muslims] come to you, either judge between them or turn away from them. But if you judge between them, do so on the basis of justice*" [5: 42]; "*Do not allow the enmity of a people to cause you to transgress. Be just. That is closer to piety*" [5: 8]; "*And do not allow the enmity of a people, reflected in the fact that they prevented you from entering the Sacred Mosque, to cause you to transgress. Rather, cooperate [with them] in goodness and piety, but do not cooperate in sin and transgression*" [5: 2]; "*We simply feed you in pursuit of God's pleasure. We desire neither remuneration nor thanks from you in return*" [79: 9]. In sum, while love may clearly be *a* source of fairness, cooperation, and solidarity, at least among those it binds, it is not the only possible source. And its "tragic consequences" can be offset or overridden by commitments other than liberalism's liquifying public reason, including Islam as *dīn*.

Second, while the "tragic consequences of love" may negate our ability to love everyone equally, they do not negate our ability to love outside our group. Loving someone and loving everyone (within or beyond our group) are two different things, as are loving and loving equally. Moreover, not loving a group or person is not the same as hating them, and it should feel neither normal nor justified to hate those we simply happen not to love. Loving and hating are not our only options. Meanwhile, our racial, cultural, and religious commitments are both concentric and overlapping. Blackamericans, White Americans, and Asian-Americans, for example, are not of a single religion; nor are Muslims or Christians of a single race, ethnicity, class, or culture. It is far more the cumulative historical fact of living together than it is any political theory of cooperation that enhances our civic energies, sensibilities, and resilience as Americans. Organic, supra-group empathy, solidarity, and cooperation are cultivated neither by "public reason" (certainly not *only* by public reason) nor by a *ḥukm sharʿī* (or *only* by a *ḥukm sharʿī*). Rather, this is achieved by something closer to Vico's *sensus communis* (communal sense) or what I would call "public sensibility," an experientially acquired and shared sense of empathy and propriety in dealing with one's fellow citizens.[229] Ultimately, the living together that sustains this "public sensibility" is secured not by naive and inflated altruistic expectations from the left side of the hyphen but by the left side's proper appreciation of and full commitment to the right. Even in the absence of love, in other words, one can recognize the propriety of—and if not the propriety of, then his or her own interest in—honoring the basic rights and humanity of others.

Here, in fact, is where "protecting the protection" takes on its fullest meaning. To "protect my protection" means protecting the democratic framework within which I can pursue, *inter alia*, my "primary communal commitment" as a Muslim and operate as the distinct entity I am. This means that I am guaranteed certain basic rights and considerations, which largely revert to America's socio-political *maʿrūf*, or "liberal background culture." These entitlements are not a function of love but of the constitutional framework as a political arrangement. Yet, in order for that framework to work effectively for me, it must work for all the other constituents of the American project, upon whom the overall strength of the framework itself depends. Stated differently, for me to be able to "protect my protection," I must commit to "protecting the protection" of all Americans, including those whom I do not love (certainly not as I love my own) and those whose substantive, left-side commitments I fundamentally oppose. They, in turn, must also commit to protecting mine.

It is important to remember, however, that this commitment is to protecting *basic* rights and considerations, not to protecting everything that everyone might want to do or for which they might be able to put forth "reasonable" vindications. Defending someone's rights is not the same as defending their values. I must support the right of LGBTQ-citizens to such basic rights and considerations as fair housing, fair employment, equal voting rights, healthcare, public safety, courtesy, and the like; but that does not mean that I must morally sanction homosexual acts, support same-sex marriage, or endorse gay pride parades. In turn, LGBTQ citizens must support my right to build mosques, be free of discrimination at work, and remain safe from discriminatory surveillance and intimidation by the government; but that does not mean that they must support polygyny or other features of *sharīʿah* or endorse Muslim candidates for public office. Similarly, this commitment means that I must oppose anti-Semitic attempts to deny Jews their basic right to respect and security; it does not mean that I must join Jews in their support for Israel or turn a blind eye to Israel's abuse and mistreatment of Palestinians. In each of these scenarios, the latter issues fall into the realm of politics "in the wrong way," while the former are removed from politics in this sense and cordoned off as part of everyone's guaranteed protection.

This arrangement goes further, I think, than Marchian liberalism in recognizing and negotiating both "false homogenization" and "the tragic consequences of love"—Jewish love of Jews, White love of Whites, Muslim love of Muslims. By not denying the affective element of collective (and, ultimately, individual) identity, it avoids the problem of forcing certain communities underground or into socio-cultural pressure-cookers where their forced acquiescence to the dictates of "reason" is taken for actual agreement and where the easiest outlet for their frustration and resentment becomes hatred of others whom they perceive as unfairly benefitting from a *faux* consensus. Similarly, it reduces the incentive and ability of *ʿaṣabīyah* and love commitments to hide behind sophisticated, rationalized justifications, in which skill at finessing the third language of "public reason" masks the true loves and hatreds still resident in our hearts, allowing us to pretend that they are not operative. Ultimately, accepting the reality of inevitable clashes of commitments and interests may make for a more honest politics and thus far fewer surprise uprisings, psychological dropouts, and socio-political inexplicables.

Admittedly, none of this does away with conflict altogether. But however contentious our politics may become, to the extent that the left side of the hyphen remains steadfast and serious in its commitment to the right, we should be able to recognize and maintain the distinction between those whom the political theorist Chantal Mouffe characterizes as "enemies" and those whom she describes as simply "adversaries."

> [W]ithin the context of the political community, the opponent should be considered not as an enemy to be destroyed, but as an adversary whose existence is legitimate and must be tolerated. We will fight his ideas but we will not question his right to defend them. The category of "enemy" does not disappear but is displaced; it remains pertinent with respect to those who do not accept the democratic "rules of the game" and who thereby exclude themselves from the political community.[230]

Muslim-Americans, including those with the deepest commitments to Islam-cum-*sharīʿah*, can have many adversaries in America without having enemies. And they will have adversaries, precisely because they have values and interests whose liquification through liberalism's "public reason" they cannot accept. Still, they can embrace, in a meaningful way, as members of a single political community, loyalty, solidarity, and "equality" with non-Muslim Americans, without having to embrace Marchian liberalism, on the one hand, and without having to reject their own story as Muslim-Americans, on the other—not to mention America's constitutional arrangement and liberal background culture. This arrangement, to my mind, represents a fuller understanding of the possible relationship between Islam and liberal citizenship. And, in all of this, crucially, failure to recognize the status and role of the Islamic Secular will hamper not only the Muslim ability to rise to this and related challenges but also the ability of non-Muslim observers to analyze and assess this relationship properly.

In closing, I would like to reiterate three brief points, in the interest of preempting misunderstanding. First, as I indicated earlier, while the context of my engagement with Hallaq and An-Naʿim was the traditional Muslim world, the assumed context here is Muslim-minoritarian America. It is neither my understanding nor my intent that what I propose here should be applied to the Muslim world in general. Second, the bulk of my analysis, as well as my Islamic alternative, is largely the product of Islamic Secular deliberation, not of *ijtihād sharʿī* in pursuit of binding, permanent, ostensibly universal "doctrines," or *aḥkām sharʿīyah*. There is, in other words, a decidedly provisional dimension to the applied substance of my thesis, being grounded as it is not simply in the immoveable sources of Islam-cum-*sharīʿah* but also in the unpredictable vicissitudes of American life. In such light, my proposal should be taken as the beginning rather than the end of a conversation. Finally, it should go without saying (though I suspect it will not) that the Islamic alternative I am proposing will not solve or anticipate all the problems connected with the relationship between Islam and liberal citizenship. But, as I also hope to have shown, neither does Marchian liberalism. The question, therefore, should not be which approach is right and which is wrong; the question should be how the advantages and shortcomings of one compare with those of the other. Horseshoes, not circles.

Conclusion

As part of his critique of Kant (among others), the German anti-Enlightenment thinker J. G. Hamann (d. 1788) insisted, "God is a poet, not a geometer. . . . The greatest error in the world is 'to confuse *words* with *concepts* and *concepts* with *real things*.'"[1] Kant's categorical imperative insisted that, once we arrive at knowledge of right/moral action, there is nothing else to consider. For, "an action done from duty derives its moral worth, not from the purpose which is to be attained by it, but from the maxim by which it is determined."[2] The only possible exception in this regard revolved, for Kant, around the question of scope: "Canst thou also will that thy maxim should be universal law?"[3] Hamann viewed Kant's approach as an elegant but ultimately misguided attempt to hide behind abstract concepts and categories as shields against the terror of life's vagaries. For Hamann, "Universalism is an idle craving, an attempt to reduce the rich variety of the universe to a bleak uniformity, which is itself a form of not facing reality, attempting to imprison it in some prefabricated favorite logical envelope."[4]

Speaking more directly to the subject of this book, Hamann also insisted, "A religion is true not because it is rational but because it is face to face with what is real."[5] Beyond any attempt to explain, understand, or provide pre-set prescriptions for every detailed occurrence in life, religion fails most fundamentally if it does not inspire humans to face and, in a spirit of due-diligence and obeisance, move beyond the limitations of these very prescriptions, morally, ethically, and materially. Between quotidian reality and *any* system of abstract prescriptions lies the stuff of everyday human existence, which will crush to powder any attempt at circumscription. Ultimately, no battery of abstract rules, no exclusively *ḥukmī* approach to life, can concretely address every quotidian contingency nor amount, in its attempt to do so, to more than a Kantian chimera. In the real world, as much as religion relies on revelation, it relies on reason, or *ʿaql*—not simply in its narrow capacity as a scriptural decoder or referee of claims to propositional truth but also in the broader sense of imagination, taste, talent, *fantasia*, experience, phronesis, and the like. These are the media through which any meanings or visions of religion as might emerge from the hermeneutical engagement with scripture will be successfully concretized, transferred onto the quotidian plain, and sustained trans-generationally in real time and space, for the individual as well as the collective. To refer to such energies and efforts as "non-religious" because they or their manner of deployment are not concretely

The Islamic Secular. Sherman A. Jackson, Oxford University Press. © Oxford University Press 2024.
DOI: 10.1093/oso/9780197661789.003.0008

grounded in or dictated by scripture is to view them through the prism of a very specific, overly narrow, and historically contingent understanding of "religion."

This is ultimately the critique this book directs at the tendency, within the Western academy and beyond, to impute exclusive, totalizing jurisdiction to Islam's *sharīʿah*. On such an imputation, "Islam" and "*sharīʿah*" become coterminous, as do the terms "*sharʿī*" and "religious." The scriptural sources of *sharīʿah*'s *ḥukm sharʿī* are assumed to exhaust religion and thus provide the Muslim with his or her only legitimate response to everything in life. Reminiscent of Kant's universalist position on morality, such a view presumes that God's transcendent *sharʿī* dictates tell Muslims everything they need to know Islamically and that once they come to know these, there is no Islamic justification (or need) to go beyond them and nothing more to consider in pursuing the proper instantiation of Islam as a lived commitment to God. On this understanding, Islam-cum-*sharīʿah* is effectively reduced to an all-encompassing constellation of perfectly-fitting "geometric forms," "favorite logical envelope[s]." And God, as *shāriʿ*, becomes the functional equivalent of a Totalizing Geometer, Author of a comprehensive set of *sharʿī* categories that perfectly and without exception envelop and provide specific instructions for every human contingency. *Sharīʿah* and the *sharʿī* alone constitute the "religious"; and the "religious" alone, *in the proper, the religious, sense*, constitutes the Islamic. Beyond these *sharʿī* dictates, Muslims have nothing of their own to contribute. And wherever the dictates and metrics of *sharīʿah* do not determine the substantive content of their endeavors, that content, *qua* content, falls outside the circumference of Islam as *dīn*, outside "religion," and outside the "Islamic."

This book has demonstrated that such a totalizing understanding of *sharīʿah* was not the prevailing perception of pre-modern Islam's juristic tradition, especially among those writing in the dominant mode of the speculative legal theoreticians, *ʿalā ṭarīqat al-mutakallimīn*. As far back as the fourth/tenth century and extending all the way up to the fifteenth/twenty-first, Muslim jurists have explicitly recognized *sharīʿah* and its derivative category, "*sharʿī*," as bounded entities that do not cover everything needed to concretize the vision of Islam-cum-*sharīʿah* in real space and time. Medicine, grammar, farming, weapons systems, educational institutions, and countless other practical disciplines have all been recognized as integral to the health and perpetuation of Islam, in which capacity they all constitute (or can constitute) Islamic pursuits and without which Islam as a lived reality cannot be sustained. At the same time, jurists have been explicit in recognizing such disciplines as identifiably non-*sharʿī* pursuits, whose substance is *not* directly derived from nor dictated by the sources of *sharīʿah*. In this context, "Islamic" is not synonymous with "*sharʿī*" or "religious," *in the proper, the religious, sense;* nor is "non-*sharʿī*" necessarily synonymous with "non-religious" or "non-Islamic." Rather, like "religion," "Islamic" includes both *sharʿī and* non-*sharʿī* concerns and artifacts.

I have identified the distinction between the *shar'ī* and the non-*shar'ī* with what came to be known in the West as "differentiation," the basis of one of two distinct modes—macro and micro—of the secular as a category. In the West, however, differentiation referred to the separation of religion from those domains that had been "liberated" from it and declared non-religious—economics, science, politics, and the like—such that these could operate free of any constraints or interference that religion might impose. The non-religious was thus identified as the secular, and the secular and the religious were conceived of as binary opposites. By contrast, based on the understanding of *sharī'ah* as a bounded subset of Islam and of Islam itself as an unbounded mother-discourse, one can discern a clear distinction between the *shar'ī* and the non-*shar'ī* *within* Islam. As the non-*shar'ī* does not derive its substance or authority from the sources of *sharī'ah*, it is identified with the "secular" in the simple sense of being "differentiated" from *sharī'ah* and its sources. Farmers, mathematicians, and poets cannot be taught their crafts by jurists nor by the sources of juristic law; nor can jurists sit in judgment over the substantive quality of their work. As we have seen, even such staunch *sharī'ah*-maximalists as Ibn Taymīyah acknowledge this fact.[6] Yet, this does not render such non-*shar'ī* pursuits secular in the sense of non-religious. For, neither the religious nor the Islamic in Islam is limited to the "*shar'ī.*" Nor, for that reason, are the religious and the secular mutually exclusive. Ultimately, what we end up with in Islam is a "religious secular," a secular that is (or can be) Islamic in the sense of falling *within* the circumference of Islam and the psychodynamic energies that define the normative relationship between humans and God, even as the determination and assessment of its concrete substance falls outside the dictates and jurisdiction of *sharī'ah*, as a bounded regime of concrete divine directives. This realm, within Islam but outside *sharī'ah*, is the "Islamic Secular" or, alternatively, "Islam's secular."

This manner of conceptualizing the relationship between *sharī'ah* and Islam underscores one of the most important conclusions of this book: Islam as *dīn* consists of not one but *two* distinct yet mutually reinforcing registers of religiosity, one *shar'ī*, or religious, *in the proper, the religious, sense*, the other non-*shar'ī*, in effect, ultimately a religious secular. Earlier Western scholars were onto something when they insisted that Islam is an unbounded discourse that recognizes no distinction between the sacred and the profane. What they apparently did not recognize, at least not fully, was that Islam maps *two* distinct registers of religiosity onto the panoply of life. By limiting themselves to religion *in the proper, the religious, sense*, Western scholars tended to view that mode of religiosity, at the heart of which is *sharī'ah*, as Islam's singular mode of religiosity, which was charged, as such, with encompassing everything in life. Such a view, I have argued, distorts our understanding of Islam-cum-*sharī'ah* in history, by limiting what we can identify as legitimately driving that history, as well as the fortunes of *fiqh* and the *fuqahāʾ* over the course thereof. Meanwhile, among the corollaries of this distortion is the singular focus, virtually from the beginning of Islamic legal studies in the West, on *ijtihād sharʿī*, as that upon which Islam rises or falls. This book has argued that neither *fiqh* nor the *fuqahāʾ* nor *ijtihād sharʿī* can be credited or shouldered with producing the educational institutions, weapon systems, textiles, medical treatments, or farming innovations upon which the collective welfare, self-sufficiency, and success of the Community depends. As al-Qarāfī so memorably summarized the matter, "Good, as a category, is broader than the juristic ruling" (*al-ḥasan aʿamm min al-ḥukm al-sharʿī*).[7] For this reason, the state of Islam at any given time and in any place can be understood and properly assessed only with an eye to *both* registers of Islam's two-pronged religiosity.

While these two registers are mutually distinct, they are also mutually dependent, the quality of each informing the other. As the guardian of Islam's "technologies of the self," the *sharʿī* dimension helps to sustain the health and clarity of a Muslim's linear and non-linear faculties, including his or her skill, *fantasia*, and the "integrity of the want" behind his or her endeavors. Meanwhile, as the guardian of Islam's *nomos* and plausibility structure, the non-*sharʿī* Islamic Secular preserves the integrity of the meanings and overall authority of Islam-cum-*sharīʿah* within society. On this understanding, neither the achievements of Islam's "Golden Age" nor its failures in its "Age of Decline" can be chalked up exclusively to the *sharʿī* side of the ledger.

This is the second major argument of this book: the Islamic Secular must be recognized as part and parcel of Islam-cum-*sharīʿah*, without which the relationship between the latter and quotidian reality cannot be adequately understood. Nowhere is this clearer than in attempts to assess the relationship between Islam and the modern state, with which all religions in the modern world must negotiate their standing and functional relevance. Such was the focus of the last three chapters of this book. In each I demonstrated how due consideration of the Islamic Secular alters the conclusions that might otherwise be reached. The Impossible State proves less impossible than Hallaq assumes; the Secular State proves less necessary than An-Naʿim assumes; and the mere fact that Islam-cum-*sharīʿah* can accommodate liberal citizenship on the level of "doctrine" proves less meaningful than March assumes. In each case, my main point was not to refute these scholars' theses but to cross-examine them in light of the Islamic Secular.

Beyond the theater of Western scholarship, this book also suggests that it may be time for modern Muslims to acknowledge that their project of seeking to preserve the integrity of Islam by restricting its normative discourses and metrics of assessment entirely to *sharīʿah* and the *sharʿī* has failed and may have played into the hands of the perceived enemy. By this I do not mean that the Muslim juristic establishment as a whole has failed, any more than I mean to absolve it of any particular instance of dereliction. Nor is this a veiled indictment of non-jurist activists who, in often enviable displays of courage, sacrifice, and dedication, have spearheaded Muslim revivalist movements and "the return of Islam." In the real world, however, life often leaves us with no other option but experimentation. And, as I believe Karl Popper once observed, successful civilizations are not those whose experiments never miss the mark but those that develop the means and will to detect and eliminate error. This book argues that failure to recognize the Islamic Secular is a serious error that calls for detection and elimination.

But not only must Muslims recognize the Islamic Secular as an integral part of Islam, they must also understand that the domain of *islam mā warā' al-ḥukm al-shar'ī* is not an epiphenomenal dead-zone that can be either benignly ignored or expected to take care of itself. The Islamic Secular is a domain filled with issues that require serious and sustained intellectual, creative, and imaginative attention, along with the development of metrics of assessment that empower Muslims to confirm the modern good and weed out the modern bad, as a matter of principle rather than fear, sycophancy, or *ressentiment* vis-à-vis the West. The fact that this activity is "secular," that is, non-*shar'ī* as opposed to *shar'ī*, must not prevent Muslims from recognizing it not only as important but also as "religious" and, *in potentia*, "Islamic."

Today, far too much Muslim talent, genius, and money is lost to the idea that only those whose activity is strictly *shar'ī*, that is, religious *in the proper, the religious, sense* (issuing *fatwā*s, providing religious education, building mosques, fighting *jihād*, etc.) are involved in Islamic activity. In fact, far too many talented and wealthy Muslims fail to see themselves as religious or Islamically important at all, simply because their callings and resources are not clerical. Viewed from the perspective of the Islamic Secular, however, the religious-cum-Islamic value of their non-*shar'ī* contributions is thrown into relief. In fact, I am reminded here of Egypt's notorious *al-Gamā'ah al-Islāmīyah* (no strangers to armed *jihād*) and their description of "the real enemy (*al-'adūw al-ḥaqīqī*) from which all of our Muslim peoples suffer and regarding the identity of which none of us disagrees: poverty and lack of development" (*al-faqr wa al-takhalluf*).[8] How can those who, in a conscious spirit of *taqwā*, *qurbah*, and obeisance, contribute directly and significantly to the reversal of this deficit be seen as engaging in non-religious, non-Islamic, "secular" activity? This brings us to the third major insight of this book: Preserving the integrity of *sharī'ah* alone is not sufficient to preserve the integrity of Islam; indeed, decadence in the area of the Islamic Secular will prove no less deleterious to Islam-cum-*sharī'ah* than feeble, impoverished, or overly pragmatic approaches to *sharī'ah* itself. No matter how important *ijtihād shar'ī* and its personnel may be, where the need is for products of Islamic Secular energies and deliberations, no amount of *ijtihād shar'ī* will put things right.

Modern Muslim states are unprecedented in their degree of centralization and the expanse of issues over which they are expected and/or authorized to govern. Viewing this vast area as exclusively *shar'ī*, such that *sharī'ah* becomes the sole medium through which these matters can be legitimately negotiated, generates a self-fulfilling cycle of failure and disappointment. For, much of what modern states are called upon to provide or regulate—from building codes to immigration policies to national health-care plans—falls squarely within the domain of the differentiated, non-*shar'ī*, Islamic Secular. Not only are many of these issues not successfully adjudicated on the basis of *shar'ī* sources alone, but the modes of reasoning by which they are negotiated are also routinely shared among Muslims and non-Muslims alike, boldly underscoring the extent to which *sharī'ah* and its personnel are often not the issue. Indeed, these modes of reasoning are shared not only by Muslims and non-Muslims but also by clerics and non-clerics within the Muslim community, including rulers and other state-officials.

This takes us to the fourth major insight of this book. The common assumption of a hopelessly zero-sum relationship between Islam-cum-*sharī'ah* and the authority and jurisdictional profile of the modern state is overdrawn. In the West, the modern state began explicitly and consciously as a secular, non-religious alternative to a putatively religious order, with the understanding that the conflict between religion and the state was inherent if not absolute. There is no reason, however, given their own history, including the juristic recognition of the *shar'ī*/non-*shar'ī* distinction, for Muslims to assume that Islam must also take (or took) such a view as its point of departure. If the modern state can be entrusted with powers of coercion that are categorically denied to religion, based on little more than the political culture and experience of Western Europe, then the historical experience of Islam should be granted comparable consideration, and along with this, the authority to adjust this formula as Muslims see fit. In short, it may be time for Muslims, secularist and Islamist alike, to abandon as their theoretical point of departure the assumption of full, zero-sum conflict or even antagonism as the default relationship between Islam-cum-*sharī'ah* and the state, especially given the expanse of the differentiated, non-*shar'ī*, Islamic Secular realm, where the state and religion, *in the proper, the religious sense*, do not necessarily come into mutual conflict.

Of course, against the backdrop of the contemporary Muslim predicament, this suggestion will strike some as naively optimistic—if not callous or collaborationist—given the tragic problem of power and the question of the Community's fate at the hands of dictatorial governments and unscrupulous rulers who use Islam as either a cover or a foil. This is not a new problem in Islamic history. And we have seen the attitude and proposals of such pre-modern stalwarts as Ibn Taymīyah, al-Qarāfī, Ibn al-Qayyim, and al-'Izz b. 'Abd al-Salām, who advocated a condominium between the state and the Community, including the jurists. Yet, whatever the answer to the problem of power in a modern context might ultimately be, if what is proposed is limited entirely to laws and procedures, on the assumption that power cannot be made moral, that the powerful are by nature impervious to the influence of religion, and that Muslims must thus abandon the idea of Islam's transformative capacities exerting any positive effect on Muslim political leaders, then it seems that the nature of the state for modern Muslims, whatever it is called, has already been determined. In fact, when all is said and done, this particular capitulation may constitute the ultimate secularization, at least of the state, and, over time, perhaps Muslim society as well. If, on the other hand, Islam is not deemed impotent in this regard, then developing the appropriate delivery system for Islam's transformative powers will necessarily implicate the Islamic Secular and the mass of energies "beyond the law" at least as much as it implicates the *shar'ī* machinery of *sharī'ah*, if not more.

For Muslims in the West, the Islamic Secular plays a different but no less critical role. While modern history has clearly weakened Islam's plausibility structure in the traditional Muslim world, it has not entirely degraded it. Embattled though it may be, Islam's trans-generational legacy continues to bequeath to majority-Muslim societies a universe of presumptions, sensibilities, and tastes, along with a collective memory, that dialogically feeds upon and nurtures Islam's foundational meanings and authority. In the West, by contrast, Muslims are challenged by the absence of communal forms of life that can anchor, reinforce, and lend resonance to the values and meanings of Islam. In this context, the very status of Islam in the hearts and minds of Muslims depends on their ability to build a *nomos* and to create, or at least contribute to, the tastes by which they will be judged and judge others within society. (This is in addition to the challenges inherent in navigating, and ideally neutralizing, American society's racial hierarchy.) Much if not most of this activity, however, falls under the sign of the Islamic Secular. And recognizing it as *Islamic* activity (or at least as activity that can and should be Islamic) is as important for Muslims in the West as is their recognition of the normative status of Islam's *shar'ī* dictates. No part of this argument should be viewed as playing down or marginalizing *sharī'ah*. But, to rephrase the pivotal insight of al-Qarāfī: Good—especially practical as opposed to merely moral good—is broader than the juristic ruling. The same can be said of the practical and morally bad. In sum, the domain of the Islamic Secular, in both the East and the West, is exceedingly vast and exceedingly important.

As noted several times over the course of this book, the Islamic Secular participates in the same generic category as the modern Western secular, which is why it remains an Islamic *Secular*. But it has a palpably different thrust and ethos. Unlike the competitive relationship between the religious and the secular in the West, Islam's secular does not exist at the expense of its religion. There is no categorical hostility or hierarchy between the two; nor is there any recognition of the propriety of proceeding "*as if* God did not exist." The Islamic Secular has no interest in privatizing or compartmentalizing religion. It does not even recognize a normatively "non-religious" realm. In fact, the Islamic Secular would agree in the main with the general sentiment of Hamann: "Better to deny religion altogether, like an atheist, than to reduce it to a tame and harmless exercise within an artificially demarcated zone that it must not transgress."[9] In other words, unlike the Western secular, the Islamic Secular implies a commitment neither to secularism nor secularization. Both are alien to its constitution and its thrust. This is the fifth major insight of this book.

While it remains religious, however, the Islamic Secular proceeds on the recognition that Islam-cum-*sharīʿah* is not an exclusively moral or ethical discourse. This is the sixth major insight of this book. Unlike the reasoning behind *fiqh*, the Islamic Secular's reason is not exclusively linear; and the good it seeks is not exclusively moral. While the Islamic Secular remains committed to the proper instantiation of *sharīʿah*'s moral vision, it routinely goes beyond it to the practical, the prudential, and even the simply enjoyable, forcing such categories into negotiation with the moral. As indicated earlier, the Islamic Secular assumes that there is more to know about life lived Islamically than simply what is morally good and what is morally bad.[10]

Of course, there are those who would reduce all good and bad to the moral/ethical realm. To my mind, however, it is difficult to see how such a move could avoid a commitment to a totalizing vision of *sharīʿah*. For, if Islam-cum-*sharīʿah* is all about morality/ethics and ethics is presumed to encompass everything, then Islam-cum-*sharīʿah* must be the concrete source of everything and every judgment. Such a position is incompatible with the Islamic Secular because it is incompatible with the practical exigencies of everyday life that lie beyond considerations of what is moral or ethical, permissible or impermissible. Two mutually contradictory economic policies may both be moral or ethical, *sharʿan*, in the sense of falling within the parameters of the juristically permissible; in the final analysis, however, something other than morality or ethics will determine our choice of one over the other—as good or bad *policy*. Meanwhile, the resolution of this disagreement over whether all good can be reduced to what is moral/ethical will likely recline more on Islamic Secular *fikr* than on Islamic *sharʿī fiqh*.

Viewed from the perspective of Hamman's critique of Kant, the Islamic Secular might be thought of, at least in part, as the "Poetics of Islam-cum-*sharīʿah*"—a *poiesis*, or imaginative-cum-creative activity, that is concretely dictated neither by Islam nor by *sharīʿah* but without which neither Islam nor *sharīʿah* can fully realize itself in the world.[11] As poetics is distinct from hermeneutics, the Islamic Secular's primary focus is not so much on meaning as it is on effect, that is, on how and in what ways Muslims might properly respond to Islam-cum-*sharīʿah*'s push to go beyond its direct dictates in pursuit of the religion's optimal instantiation.

Its differentiated *'aql* is not synonymous with the abstracting, universalizing episteme of Kant but often resembles the culturally-cum-historically grounded phronesis of Aristotle.[12] It is embedded, in other words, in a trans-generational, communal narrative mimetically laced with historical memories that are themselves normatively informed by Islam's "technologies of the self." It routinely invokes not simply the "grammar of *fiqh*" but a broader, creative syntax by which one can tap into and build upon Islam's "rhythmic meter," its *qāfiyah*, as it were, in the form of Islam's overall normative vision.[13] Here, what may appear (viewed through a strictly linear gaze) to violate that vision may actually be consistent with it, just as the sound plural ending "*ūn*," according to the conventional norms of Arabic poetry, can be counted as rhyming with the sound plural ending "*īn*." Imām Aḥmad's position on the pious weakling versus the strong miscreant might also be seen as an example of this "poetic" synthesis. Meanwhile, Talal Asad's insistence that "It is precisely an achievement of secularism that makes 'religion' an autonomous domain and 'religious discourse' a[n exclusively] technical language" may be more insightful than appears at first blush.[14]

This brings us to the seventh and final major insight of this book. The Islamic Secular joins heaven to earth and in so doing upsets many of the assumptions of binary opposition embedded in our modern universe of first-order meanings: religious/secular, reason/revelation, man-made/divine, historically contingent/transcendent, and moral/practical. While the Islamic Secular recognizes that each side of this set of binary pairs is different from its counterpart, difference is not the same as opposition. The *shar'ī*, for example, differs from the non-*shar'ī*; but both can be reconciled as religious. The same applies to the moral and the practical, reason and revelation, the historically contingent and the transcendent, the man-made and the divine. Such reconciliations suggest the need for caution when using Western[15] definitions, presuppositions, and bifurcations beyond the circumstances and ideological commitments that produced them. Of course, *qua* experience, the Western experience is eminently valid, as are all experiences *qua* experiences. But that is no reason to grant the Western experience unqualified, universal authority as everyone's presumed point of departure.

If the "Islamic Secular" comes off initially as an oxymoron, it may be because the incumbency and cognitive mass of the Western definitions and presuppositions that drive our modern thinking and sensibilities will not allow us to see it otherwise. The way past this agnosia, however, is not simply to discard the Islamic Secular. It is to interrogate—fairly, honestly, and courageously—the substance and universality of the definitions and presuppositions that inform our modern thinking, shape our modern sensibilities, and drive our modern perspective on the world.

Notes

Introduction

1. Available at https://www.c-span.org/video/?170651-1/james-baldwin-speech I use "Blackamerican" to signal the uniqueness of Blacks' relationship to the American hyphen compared to other ethnic Americans, Blacks being the only group whom upon their arrival could not write a letter home.
2. I capitalize "Black" (and "White") when speaking in the context of America, where these are intentionally fashioned socio-political categories that go beyond skin-color. Outside the US (and South Africa) I leave black and white in lower case, as falling outside the processes that make Blackness and Whiteness in the US.
3. See Ṭ. 'Abd al-Raḥmān, *Rūḥ al-ḥadāthah: al-madkhal ilā ta'sīs al-ḥadāthah al-islāmīyah*, 4th ed. (Casablanca: al-Markaz al-Thaqāfī al-'Arabī, 2016), 11.
4. See his "The Muslim *Fiqh* as a Sacred Law. Law and Ethics in a Normative System," in Baber Johansen, *Contingency in a Sacred Law: Legal and Ethical Norms in the Muslim* Fiqh (Leiden: E. J. Brill, 1999), 1–76, esp. 42–72.
5. These quotes were part of an argument presented by one of OUP's readers of the original manuscript for this book.
6. This is not to mention the number of "*mā shā' Allāhs*" one might hear bellowing from bars, nightclubs, casinos, and other such places in the Muslim world.
7. J. Stout, *The Flight from Authority: Religion, Morality, and the Quest for Autonomy* (Notre Dame: University of Notre Dame Press, 1981), 17. See also Talal Asad's discussion of meaning in his *Genealogies of Religion: Discipline and Reasons of Power in Christianity and Islam* (Baltimore: The Johns Hopkins University Press, 1993), 43–8, esp. 43–4.
8. Stout, *Flight*, 17–21. See also B. Nongbri, *Before Religion: A History of a Modern Concept* (New Haven: Yale University Press, 2013), 18, for a similar if not more blunt perspective.
9. See T. Asad, *Formations of the Secular: Christianity, Islam, Modernity* (Stanford: Stanford University Press, 2003), 192.
10. See Charles Taylor, *A Secular Age* (Cambridge, MA: The Belknap Press of Harvard University Press, 2007), 54.
11. C. Calhoun, "Rethinking Secularism," *Hedgehog Review*, *19*:3 (2010): 1–7 at 2.
12. T. Fitzgerald, "Critical Religion and Critical Research on Religion: Religion and Politics As Modern Fictions," *Critical Research on Religion*, 3:3 (2015): 303–19 at 311. Fitzgerald continues: "The Peace of Westphalia of 1648, taken by theorists in international relations to be a watershed event in the emergence of the modern world order of secular states, is always concerned with the Christian Prince and his religion, either

Catholic or Lutheran, and its references to the secular does not yet demarcate a *non-religious* government. It distinguishes between the temporal and the ecclesiastical and the term secularization refers to the transference of properties from one kind of Christian institution to another." Emphasis original.

13. N. Keddie, "Secularism and Its Discontents," *Daedalus* (Summer, 2003): 14–30 at 4.
14. See O. Chadwick, *The Secularization of the European Mind in the 19th Century* (Cambridge: Cambridge University Press, 1975), 78. In fact, according to Chadwick, nineteenth-century French Communists explicitly appealed to the idea of the early Christian community's sharing of common property, and German Communists went so far as to claim that "*Christianity is Communism*." See Chadwick, *Secularization*, 75. Emphasis original.
15. See Johansen, "Muslim *Fiqh*," 43.
16. Johansen, "Muslim *Fiqh*," 43; see also 44–5.
17. Johansen, "Muslim *Fiqh*," 46–7.
18. J. Schacht, *The Origins of Muhammadan Jurisprudence* (Oxford: The Clarendon Press, 1950), v.
19. Johansen, "Muslim *Fiqh*," 65.
20. C. Hayes, *What's Divine About Divine Law? Early Perspectives* (Princeton: Princeton University Press, 2015), 1.
21. Hayes, *What's Divine?* 2.
22. Hayes, *What's Divine?* 2. Emphasis original.
23. This is clear in the case of Ash'arites and Traditionalists. The Ḥanafī-Māturīdī Ibn al-Humām asserts, however, that "All Ḥanafīs (read: Māturīdīs) believe that good and evil can be known in the manner affirmed by the Mu'tazilites." See Kamāl al-Dīn Ibn Abī Sharīf al-Maqdisī, *al-Musāmarah fī sharḥ al-musāyarah*, 2 vols. (Cairo: al-Maktabah al-Azharīyah li al-Turāth, 2006), 2: 38. (The quote is from Ibn al-Humām's *al-Musāyarah*, included in the body of the text.) Ibn al-Humām goes on to state, however, that, whereas the Mu'tazilites hold that what reason uncovers as good or evil compels (*yūjib*) God to issue rulings in accordance therewith, the Māturīdīs reject this notion and hold God to be entirely autonomous in the rules God imposes. His Ash'arite commentator, Kamāl al-Dīn al-Makdisī, adds that all Sunnīs agreed on this. See *al-Masāmarah*, 2: 42.
24. On this realism/nominalism divide, see Hayes, *What's Divine?* 195–9. Speaking of Islam, we should note that the idea that the divine law is simply what God identifies as law does not mean that God is oblivious to the effects or consequences of what God commands or prohibits, or that reason is incapable of apprehending good and evil in the world or in what God commands or forbids. The question in Islamic intellectual history was whether God was *bound* to reward or punish *because* of what reason determined to be the inherent goodness or badness of an act, essentially whether God could be compelled by some authority outside God's self. Even the Mu'tazilites' opponents, including Traditionalists, acknowledged that reason could make moral judgments. And (later) Ash'arites insisted that God's commands and prohibitions routinely follow human interests, i.e., that God commands and forbids what is beneficial and harmful, respectively, *because* it is beneficial or harmful. This, however—and this was their point—was a function of God's inherent wisdom, mercy, goodness, and

"character," not of God's being *compelled* to do so by the inherent qualities of the acts in question.

25. Hayes, *What's Divine?* 198. Emphasis original.
26. See, e.g., A. Emon, *Islamic Natural Law Theories* (New York: Oxford University Press, 2010). We will encounter echoes of this as well in the discussion of Shahab Ahmed in Chapter 1.
27. As A. Emon explains (and this is not his position), "To claim that Sharīʿa and *fiqh* are different and distinct is in large part to emphasize the limited authority of the *fiqh* based on human epistemic limitations, and thereby create space for others to contribute legitimately to the ongoing development of *fiqh* norms in a changing world." See his *Religious Pluralism and Islamic Law:* Dhimmīs *and Others in the Empire of Law* (New York: Oxford University Press, 2012), 9. I should add that recognizing the limits of human interpretation is not a uniquely Muslim perspective. Speaking of the classical tradition, Baber Johansen notes that, "while all scholars and schools of *fiqh* equally derive their norms from the revelation no scholar's and no school's normative interpretation of the revelation can claim a privileged access to truth. All scholars and schools of *fiqh* share the same activity: probable, but fallible interpretation of infallible texts." See his "Muslim *Fiqh*," 37 and 65–6. I would add, however, that it is one thing to say that no scholar or school's normative interpretation can claim universality; it is quite another to negate the truth or divine authority that this view carries for the jurist and his or her school here and now.
28. See Abou El Fadl, "Islam and the Challenge of Democratic Commitment," *Fordham International Law Journal, 27*:4 (2003): 4–71 at 64.
29. See Abou El -Fadl, "What Type of Law Is Islamic Law," in *Routledge Handbook of Islamic Law*, eds. K. Abou El Fadl, A. A. Ahmad, and S. F. Hassan (London and New York: Routledge, 2019), 11–39 at 20–1. See also his *Reasoning with God: Reclaiming Shariʿah in the Modern Age* (Lanham, MD: Rowman and Littlefield, 2014), xl–xlvii.
30. See al-Ghazālī, *al-Mustaṣfā min ʿilm al-uṣūl*, 2 vols. (Būlāq: al-Maṭbaʿah al-Amīrīyah, 1324 AH), 2: 376. The distinction is cited by jurists and theologians across the schools of law and theology. But see Badr al-Dīn al-Zarkashī, *al-Baḥr al-muḥīṭ*, 6 vols., eds. ʿA. ʿA. al-ʿĀnī, S. al-Ashqar, and ʿA. Abū Ghuddah (Kuwait: Wizārat al-Awqāf wa al-Shuʾūn al-Islāmīyah, 1413/1992), 1:35, where he notes, on the authority of al-Ghazālī's teacher al-Juwaynī, that most other jurists, in fact, "the masters" (*al-muḥaqqiqūn*) ignored this distinction and referred to both types of indicant as simply *dalīl*. See also Abū Isḥāq al-Shirāzī, *al-Lumaʿ fī uṣūl al-fiqh*, ed. ʿA. al-Khaṭīb al-Ḥasanī (Bahrain: Maktabat al-Niẓām al-Yaʿqūbī al-Khāssah, 1434/2013), 81, for an identical view, al-Shirāzī noting, however, that *dalīl* can point to a conclusion that is either certain or probable.
31. Al-Ghazālī, *al-Mustaṣfā*, 2: 364. In fact, according to al-Ghazālī, even apodictic indicants do not necessarily point to an ontologically verifiable rule "out there," though he acknowledges that some groups hold that they do.
32. Abou El-Fadl, "What Kind of Law," 21. See my discussions in Chapter 2 and Chapter 4, however, on *sharīʿah* as a strictly "moral" vision.

33. See, e.g., al-Zarkashī, *al-Baḥr*, 6: 235–68, esp., 6: 241, where he cites the view of al-Māwardī and al-Rūyānī: "Most jurists are of the view that all of the competing views are true, that every *mujtahid* is correct both in the sight of God (*fīmā 'inda Allāh*) and in terms of (the applicable) ruling." This is not, however, the only view that al-Zarkashī cites.
34. In fact, even al-Māturīdī's more rigid expression of the fallibilist (*mukhaṭṭi'*) position held that jurists who missed the mark incurred no sin and could even be rewarded for their good intentions though not for their *ijtihād* per se. See A. Zysow's insightful discussion of fallibilists and infallibilists in his *The Economy of Certainty: An Introduction to the Typology of Islamic Legal Theory* (Atlanta, GA: Lockwood Press, 2013), 259–77, esp. 271 on al-Māturīdī. See also Shihāb al-Dīn al-Qarāfi, *Sharḥ tanqīḥ al-fuṣūl fi ikhtiṣār al-maḥṣūl fi al-uṣūl*, ed. A. F. al-Mazīdī (Beirut: Dār al-Kutub al-'Ilmīyah, 1428/2007), 426–8, where, though a *mukhaṭṭi'*, he insists that, even if the correct view is solitary, the individual *mujtahid* must follow what appears to *his* mind to be God's ruling (*ḥukm Allāh*) *as* God's ruling.
35. See Chapter 3, in the section "*Sharī'ah*' and 'Islamic Law.'" I ignore, incidentally, as irrelevant in this context, that *fiqh*, according to some jurists, is technically a product of *ijtihād*, rules that do not require such interpretive effort (e.g., that adultery is forbidden) technically not qualifying as *fiqh*, though they obviously remain a part of *sharī'ah*. This distinction, however, is not what those who point to the difference between *fiqh* and *sharī'ah* generally have in mind. See, e.g., Jalāl a-Dīn Muḥammad b. Aḥmad al-Maḥallī, *Sharḥ al-waraqāt fī uṣūl al-fiqh* (Beirut: al-Maktabah al-'Aṣrīyah, 1434/2013), 15–16.
36. See the important work by G. Makdisi, *The Rise of Humanism in Islam and the Christian West* (Edinburgh: Edinburgh University Press, 1990).
37. A. El-Shamsy, *Discovering the Islamic Classics: How Editors and Print Culture Transformed an Intellectual Tradition* (Princeton: Princeton University Press, 2020) esp. Ch. 8.
38. Asad, *Formations*, 1. Emphasis mine.
39. A. Hughes, *Islam and the Tyranny of Authenticity: An Inquiry into Disciplinary Apologetics and Self-Deception* (Sheffield, UK: Equinox Press, 2015).
40. Hughes, *Tyranny*, xvi–xvii, 57–74 and passim.
41. Hughes, *Tyranny*, xiv.
42. Hughes, *Tyranny*, xii. Elsewhere he adds "democracy" (*Tyranny*, xiii) and "love" (*Tyranny*, 40). At *Tyranny*, 54, he writes: "Perceived to exist outside of time, modern-day Muslim activist scholars seek to make the Qur'an, and by extension Islam, compatible with the West. This is not scholarship, but theological advocacy." Of course, non-Muslim scholars compare aspects of Islam with the intellectual heritage of "the West" (Aristotle, Kant, Marx, Foucault, Rawls, capitalism) and may even pursue reconciliation between the two, without jeopardizing the status of their efforts as legitimate "scholarship."
43. Hughes, *Tyranny*, xv. Emphasis original.
44. Hughes, *Tyranny*, xvi.

45. Hughes, *Tyranny*, xii: "One would think, indeed hope, that scholars who spend their time studying Islam within the secular discipline of religious studies would not be so quick to make pronouncements about what is or what is not authentic Islam." But the historical record to which Hughes would bind scholars in pursuit of "objective" scholarship is replete with the efforts of pre-modern Muslims to articulate normative understandings of Islam, from Rābiʿah al-ʿAdawīyah to Ibn Taymīyah. One might ask, therefore, if the study of Islam, even by *non-Muslim* scholars, can fully avoid engaging with and assessing "pronouncements about what is or what is not authentic Islam."
46. Teaching *of* versus teaching *about* religion strikes me as a vague criterion that is also potentially mutually contradictory. If students/readers accept a teacher's/scholar's presentation of a religion's truth-claims as true, the teacher/scholar is suspected of the teaching *of* religion; if students/readers reject the truth-claims as false or process them agnostically, the teacher/scholar is seen as simply teaching *about* religion. And yet, equating the latter outcome with "objectivity" entails precisely the kind of ideological pre-commitment that "teaching *about* religion" is supposed to avoid.
47. Hughes, *Tyranny*, 2.
48. See his "Thesis on Method," *Method and Theory in the Study of Religion*, *17*:1 (2005): 8–10 at 9.
49. See T. Fitzgerald, "Bruce Lincoln's 'Theses on Method': Antithesis," *Method and Theory in the Study of Religion*, *18*:1 (2006): 392–423 at 410.
50. In one of numerous examples, in *Tyranny*, 80, Hughes presents my depiction of the hesitancy that some Muslims feel about the US Constitution as if this were my position, and then he goes on to ignore or distort virtually everything I say on the matter: "For Jackson, Muslims must question the Constitution not only because it separates church and state (something that his version of Islam opposes) but even more significantly, it is a document that is inferior to God-given Muslim law (*sharia*), something that is grounded in authoritative Muslim sources." Compare this with what I actually wrote in *Islam and the Blackamerican: Looking Towards the Third Resurrection* (New York: Oxford University Press, 2005), 145–9, esp. 148, and my discussion on the US Constitution in Chapter 6 below.
51. In his magisterial work on the rise and spread of secularism, Charles Taylor states openly that his view of secularization "has been shaped by my own perspective as a believer." See his *Secular Age*, 437. Meanwhile, Hughes's attempt to police the boundaries of what is permissible in the "secular academy" explicitly asserts the primacy of the secular over the religious, while assuming that this entails no ideological bias or commitment.
52. One might also consider as examples Fred Donner's *Muhammad and the Believers: At the Origins of Islam*, Patricia Crone's *God's Rule: Government and Islam*, Wael Hallaq's *The Impossible State*, and Andrew March's *Islam and Liberal Citizenship*.
53. Sherman A.Jackson, *Islam and the Problem of Black Suffering* (New York: Oxford University Press, 2009), 100. *Mea culpa*. Al-Maqdisī was offering a commentary on a Māturīdī text, in which capacity his explications might be considered valid insights into Māturīdī doctrine. But they cannot be considered a Māturīdī confirmation thereof, as I implied.

54. Jackson, *Islam and the Problem of Black Suffering*, 112, 113, 114, 196, 201. *Mea culpa.* I am not aware of anyone else having pointed out these mistakes.
55. Today, "Black," as in "Black Lives Matter," is taken to be an unproblematically positive term. But this was not always the case, even among Blackamericans. The situation began to change in the 1960s, James Brown's 1968 hit, *Say It Loud, I'm Black and I'm Proud*, being among the cultural artifacts both signaling and contributing to this transformation.
56. R. Rorty, *Contingency, Irony and Solidarity* (Cambridge: Cambridge University Press, 1989), 7. Bracketed segment mine. While Rorty saw the Romantics as positioning imagination over reason as the central human faculty, I am not sure—which speaks to the profundity of his argument, not its weakness—that I am prepared to go that far.
57. See, e.g., Humaira Iqtidar's critical comment on my article, "The Islamic Secular," in *American Journal of Islamic Social Sciences, 34*: 2 (2017): 35–8.
58. See S. Mahmood, "Can Secularism Be Other-wise?" in *Varieties of Secularism in a Secular Age*, eds. M. Warner, J. Vanantwerpen, and C. Calhoun (Cambridge, MA: Harvard University Press, 2010), 282–99 at 293.
59. N. Ghobadzadeh takes up the question of the secular in modern Shiism in his *Religious Secularity: A Theological Challenge to the Islamic State* (New York: Oxford University Press, 2017). His project, however, which builds on that of Abdullahi An-Na'im, "challenges the legitimacy of the Islamic state" and seeks "the emancipation of religion from the state" (p. 4). This is patently different from my project. Meanwhile, while there is *prima facie* overlap, e.g., in our mutual challenge to the religion/secular dichotomy in Islam, Ghobadzadeh neither fully theorizes nor consistently sustains this. He notes, for example, "to be religious is to be secular and to be secular is to be religious" (p. 7). But on this identity, I am not sure how religion can then be separated from the state without also separating the secular, in which case the overall aim of his project becomes difficult to grasp. At any rate, Ghobadzadeh's "religious secularity" is distinct from and in some instances contradicts my concept of a "religious secular."
60. See T. S. Kuhn, *The Structure of Scientific Revolution*, 2nd ed. (Chicago: The University of Chicago Press, 1970).
61. See I. R. al-Fārūqī, "Islamization of Knowledge: Problems, Principles and Prospective," 15–63, available at https://www.academia.edu/5737422/Islamisation_of_Knowledge_Problems_Principles_and_Prospective_Ismail_al_Faruqi
62. Al-Fārūqī, "Islamization of Knowledge," 48
63. Al-Fārūqī, "Islamization of Knowledge," 25–6.
64. Al-Fārūqī, "Islamization of Knowledge," 16–17.

Chapter 1

1. Indeed, according to Talal Asad, "The terms 'secularism' and 'secularist' were introduced into English by freethinkers in the middle of the nineteenth century in

order to avoid the charge of their being 'atheists' and 'infidels,' terms that carried suggestions of immorality in a still Christian society." See his *Formations*, 23.

2. See Asad, *Formations*, 25.
3. See J. Casanova, "Secularization Revisited: A Reply to Talal Asad," in *Powers of the Secular Modern: Talal Asad and His Interlocutors*, eds. D. Scott and C. Hirschkind (Stanford, CA: Stanford University Press, 2006), 12–30 at 23.
4. Charles Taylor notes, for example, that while the pervasiveness of the closed "immanent frame" in which we now live, where science, technology, and social ontology bind us to a "natural" or "this-worldly" mindset that dispenses with any reference to the "supernatural" or "transcendent," it remains an open question "whether for purposes of ultimate explanation, or spiritual transformation, or final sense-making, we might need to invoke something transcendent." See his *A Secular Age*, 594. This latter point essentially captures the theme of A. T. Kronman in his *Confessions of a Born-Again Pagan* (New Haven: Yale University Press, 2016).
5. J. Casanova appears on the surface to contradict this when he writes, "[T]he majority of Americans are humanists, who are simultaneously religious and secular." See his *Public Religions in the Modern World* (Chicago: University of Chicago Press, 1994), 38. Similarly, he notes that priests in medieval Christendom could be both "religious" and "secular." See *Public Religions*, 13. I understand this to mean that the particular activity in which they are engaged determines whether priests or Americans are in a religious or secular mode of being and that the activity in question remains either secular *or* religious, not secular *and* religious simultaneously.
6. E. Durkheim, *The Elementary Forms of Religious Life*, trans. C. Cosman (New York: Oxford University Press, 2001), 38. Durkheim asserted further that this conceptualization was "the hallmark of religious thought." (p. 36)
7. Asad, *Formations*, 22.
8. There is push-back against the idea of the secular's global expansion. See, e.g., M. Marty, "Our Religio-Secular World," *Daedalus*, 132:3 (2003): 42–8; J. Miller, "What Secular Age?" *International Journal of Politics, Culture and Society*, 21:1/4 (2008): 5–10.
9. Calhoun, "Rethinking Secularism," 1. We saw a cognate of this earlier in Hughes, where he chides Muslim scholars for their normative statements about Islam but mentions "the secular discipline of religious studies" as if "secular" were the equivalent of "neutral" and "unbiased." See note 45 of the Introduction to this text.
10. Asad, *Formations*, 21–66.
11. T. Fitzgerald, *The Ideology of Religious Studies* (New York: Oxford University Press, 2000), 8.
12. Fitzgerald, *Ideology*, 9.
13. J. K. A. Smith, *How (Not) to Be Secular: Reading Charles Taylor* (Grand Rapids: William B. Eerdmans Publishing Company, 2014), 26.
14. See his *Public Religions*, 234. Of course, as we shall see, "secularization" is not quite the word I would use for any institutionalization of the Islamic Secular.
15. Keddie, "Secularism and Its Discontents," 30.

16. Ashis Nandy, e.g., seems to think of secularism and secularization as primarily political constructs. See his "An Anti-secularist Manifesto," *India International Centre Quarterly*, 22:1 (1995): 35–64. Talal Asad also refers to secularism as a "political doctrine." See *Formations*, 1. And Saba Mahmood speaks plainly of "political secularism." See her "Can Secularism Be Other-wise?" Meanwhile, Olivier Roy writes: "Secularization is a social phenomenon that requires no political implementation," a view one would assume extended naturally to secularism. See his *Secularism Confronts Islam* (New York: Columbia University Press, 2009), 8. Peter Berger, on the other hand, highlighting the link between secularism, secularization, and the Enlightenment, seems to be more sensitive to their epistemological role and impact. See his *The Desecularization of the World: Resurgent Religion and World Politics*, ed. P. Berger (Grand Rapids: Eerdmanns Publishing Company, 1999), 2–4. José Casanova points to a dual meaning of secularization, one socio-political (or institutional), the other more epistemological, focusing on "beliefs and practices." See his "Secularization Revisited," 16. See also N. Hashemi, *Islam, Secularism, and Liberal Democracy: Toward a Democratic Theory for Muslim Societies* (New York: Oxford University Press, 2012), 106, where he speaks of philosophical, sociological, and political secularisms.
17. Cited in C. Taylor, "Modes of Secularism," in *Secularism and Its Critics*, ed. R. Bharghava, 6th ed. (New Delhi: Oxford University Press, 2007), 31–53 at 33–4. Emphasis mine. See also Taylor, *A Secular Age*, 126, where the Latin is rendered "even if God did not exist."
18. See Chapter 4.
19. Asad, *Formations*, 1.
20. J. Casanova, *Public Religions*, 12–15.
21. In fact, the ongoing conflict between the dual authority of the Church and the State has been summarized as follows: "What was required to transcend this impasse, of course, was some concept of sovereignty that would eliminate the dual claims to superior authority on the part of the pope and emperor." See B. Nelsen, *The Making of the Modern State: A Theoretical Evolution* (New York: Palgrave Macmillan, 2006), 34–5.
22. See Casanova, *Public Religions*, 13–15.
23. One gets a sense of what was claimed and lost in the aims of the modern movement known as Radical Orthodoxy. In their edited volume on the topic, John Milbank, Catherine Pickstock, and Graham Ward speak of recovering a "Christian ontology" and returning to "patristic and medieval roots, and especially to the Augustinian vision of all knowledge as divine illumination, a notion which transcends the modern bastard dualisms of faith and reason, grace and nature." See their *Radical Orthodoxy: A New Theology* (London: Routledge, 1999), 2.
24. Taylor, *A Secular Age*, 2.
25. Taylor, *A Secular Age*, 2.
26. See B. Nongbri, *Before Religion: A History of a Modern Concept* (New Haven: Yale University Press, 2013), 4.
27. Casanova, *Public Religions*, 15.
28. See, e.g., Taylor, *A Secular Age*, 44–5, 146.

29. Casanova, *Public Religions*, 36.
30. R. Tarnas, *The Passion of the Western Mind: Understanding the Ideas That Have Shaped Our World View* (New York: Ballantine Books, 1991), 285–6.
31. One gets a glimpse into the awkwardness of a non-religious identity in traditional Muslim society from a story told by the litterateur Aḥmad Amīn about a modern Egyptian fellow who traveled to Europe only to return to his village and declare that he was an atheist. When they dismissed his claim as nonsense, he retorted in protest, "I swear by God Almighty, I am an atheist!" (*uqsim bi 'llāh al-'aẓīm ana mulḥid!*) Cited in Y. al-Qaraḍāwī, *al-Ḥurrīyah al-dīnīyah wa al-ta'addudīyah fī naẓar al-islām* (Beirut: al-Maktab al-Islāmī, 1428/2007), 13.
32. Ibn al-Rāwandī rejected revelation as superfluous but did not categorically reject the existence of God, which he saw reason as a sufficient basis for establishing. Al-Rāzī also ridiculed the notion of prophecy and rejected Islam outright. But this hardly made him an atheist or a macro-secularist (See the discussion below in the section, "The Secular: Macro- and Micro-Modes"). The Neoplatonic scheme of emanation and the ultimate struggle to reunite with The One can hardly be described as non-religious. See, e.g., M. Fakhry, *A History of Islamic Philosophy*, 3rd ed. (New York: Columbia University Press, 2004), 97–106. See also, however, M. M. Sharif, ed., *A History of Muslim Philosophy*, 2 vols. (Karachi: Royal Book Company, 2018 [reprint]), 1:434–49, esp., 448, where he concludes that al-Rāzī "believed in man, in progress, and in God the Wise, but in no religion whatever."
33. See Ṭ. Husayn, *Ḥadīth al-arbi'ā'*, 3 vols., 15th ed. (Cairo: Dār al-Ma'ārif, n.d.), 2:23. Abū Nuwās's debauchery was the stuff of legend. About to be introduced to the Abbasid Caliph al-Amīn (d. 198/813) by his friend, al-Kasā'ī (d. 189/805), the renowned grammarian and narrator of one of the seven canonical recitations of the Qur'ān, Abū Nuwās nearly sent his friend into coronary arrest when he confided in him, "I want to kiss him!" (*al-Arbi'ā'*, 1:31–32). Yet, early jurists often lauded the poetry of Abū Nuwās, and al-Shāfi'ī (d. 204/819), eponym of one of the four Sunni schools of law, is even reported to have narrated *ḥadīth* from him (*al-Arbi'ā'*, 1:23). On the other hand, Ṭaha Ḥusayn reports that "our modern morals and customs" will not allow the publication of a poem recited by the Companion Ibn 'Abbās at the Sacred Mosque upon being asked if reciting poetry invalidates ablution; nor will they allow the publication of what the Successor 'Abd Allāh Ibn al-Zubayr recited upon meeting the poet al-Farazdaq, whose wife had complained about him; nor could we publish the Companion Ḥassān b. Thābit's satire of Hind, the wife of Abū Sufyān. See *al-Arbi'ā'*, 2: 42–3.
34. See, e.g., O. Hamdan, "The Second *Maṣāhif* Project: A Step Towards the Canonization of the Qur'anic Text," in *The Qur'ān in Context*, eds. A. Neuwirth, N. Sinai, and M. Marx (Leiden: E. J. Brill, 2011), 795–835.
35. See Muḥammad b. Ismā'īl al-Bukhārī, *Ṣaḥīḥ al-bukhārī*, 9 vols., ed. Q. al-Shamā'ī al-Rifā'ī (Beirut: Dār al-Arqam b. Abī al-Arqam, n.d.), 8:570.
36. See Ibn Taymīyah, *al-Tuḥfah al-'irāqīyah fī al-a'māl al-qalbīyah* (Cairo: al-Maktabah al-Salafīyah, 1386/1967), 39.
37. See, e.g., Ṭ. Al-Bishrī, *al-Ḥiwār al-islāmī al-'almānī* (Cairo: Dār al-Shurūq, 1417/ 1996), 39.

38. I have in mind here James Davison Hunter's notion of "life-boat theology," i.e., "seeing the world as a sinking ship on its way to judgment and hell," wherein the goal becomes to turn away from it and "rescue as many as possible on the lifeboat of salvation." See his *To Change the World: The Irony, Tragedy and Possibility of Christianity in the Late Modern World* (New York: Oxford University Press, 2010), 4.
39. I should be clear that ascetic movements and inclinations were well represented in Islam long before modernity. But it is one thing to see specific and concrete forms of ascetic practices as part of the practice of Islam and quite another to see Islam itself as an exclusively ascetic commitment. In other words, it is one thing to see sex, money, and power as things that can be pursued licitly within the boundaries of the law, even as one *personally* eschews them for spiritual reasons (i.e., as a matter of voluntary spiritual discipline); it is quite another to see Islam-as-religion as categorically frowning upon such pursuits.
40. See Casanova, "Secularization Revisited," 17.
41. Cited in Asad, *Genealogies*, 22, note 21. On differentiation, see below.
42. In fact, as we will see in Chapter 3, some modern Arabs translate "secular" as "*ʿilmānī*," i.e., related to knowledge/science, as opposed to "*ʿalmānī*," or "this-worldly."
43. See B. Turner, *Weber and Islam: A Critical Study* (London: Routledge and Kegan Paul, 1974), 163, 164, 168.
44. Keddie, "Secularism and Its Discontents," 22.
45. Asad summarizes a typical defense of the secularization thesis as follows: "[I]n order for society to be modern it has to be secular and for it to be secular it has to relegate religion to nonpolitical spaces because that arrangement is critical to modern society." See *Formations*, 182. One wonders, incidentally, how much this description owes to the European as opposed to the American experience. As Casanova points out, "[T]he standard explanations of the phenomenon in terms of general processes of modernization are not persuasive, since similar processes of modernization elsewhere (in the United States or in the cultural areas of other world religions) are not accompanied by the same secularization results." See "Secularization Revisited," 17.
46. See his "An Anti-secularist Manifesto," 64.
47. DuBois spoke of double consciousness as "this sense of always looking at oneself through the eyes of others, of measuring one's soul by the tape of a world that looks on in amused contempt and pity." See W. E. B. DuBois, "Strivings of the Negro People," *The Atlantic*, 80 (Aug., 1897): 1–10 at 4, available at https://www.theatlantic.com/magazine/archive/1897/08/strivings-of-the-negro-people/305446/. This is repeated in DuBois's more famous 1903 classic *The Souls of Black Folk* (reprint) (Greenwich, CN: Fawcett Publications, Inc., 1961), 16–17. He went on to explain this double consciousness in terms of a contradiction of double aims: "The double-aimed struggle of the black artisan, on the one hand to escape white contempt for a nation of mere hewers of wood and drawers of water, and on the other hand to plough and nail and dig for a poverty-stricken horde, could only result in making him a poor craftsman, for he had but half a heart in either cause." "Strivings," 5; *Souls*, 17.
48. I will return to this point in Chapter 3.
49. See Chadwick, *The Secularization of the European Mind*, 66.

50. See, e.g., Taylor, *A Secular Age*, 25–7, 30–41, 98–9, and passim; P. L. Berger, *The Sacred Canopy: Elements of a Sociological Theory of Religion* (New York: Anchor Books, 1990), 111–13, 118, and passim; M. Gauchet, *The Disenchantment of the World: A Political History of Religion*, trans. O. Barge (Princeton: Princeton University Press, 1997).
51. The basic principle of logical positivism was famously articulated by the British mathematician William K. Clifford (d. 1879): "[I]t is wrong always, everywhere, and for anyone, to believe anything upon insufficient evidence." Cited in A. McGrath, *The Twilight of Atheism* (New York: Galilee Doubleday, 2006), 90.
52. Taylor adds as a complement to this "emptying" the parallel development of what he terms the "buffered self," which seeks to insulate itself from the horrors or influences of the world's charged presence by essentially blocking them out. This buffering of the self protects us from the dangers of the charged order *and* assuages our fears about having abandoned our search for the Originator thereof. See *Secular Age*, 37–41, esp. 41. One wonders how Taylor's buffered self might map onto what Charles Long refers to as Black Religion's "oppugnancy," which also entailed an attempt to buffer the self, not against the "charged" cosmos but against the predations of the White man and the critical categories of the Enlightenment used to subjugate Blacks. See C. Long, "The Oppressive Elements in Religion and the Religions of the Oppressed," in C. Long, *Significations: Signs, Symbols, and Images in the Interpretation of Religion* (Aurora, CO: The Davies Group, 1995), 171–86 at 180. Long's essay originally appeared in the *Harvard Theological Review* in 1976.
53. By contrast, as Taylor put it, "[D]isbelief is hard in the enchanted world . . . God figures in this world as the dominant spirit, and moreover, as the only thing that guarantees that in this awe-inspiring and frightening field of forces, good will triumph. . . . In general, going against God is not an option in the enchanted world." See *A Secular Age*, 41.
54. The *falāsifah* (sg. *faylasūf*), e.g., al-Farābī and Ibn Sīnā, were the Muslim champions of "Islamicized" Hellenistic thought, most prominently Neoplatonism.
55. See F. Rahman, *Major Themes of the Qur'ān* (Chicago: University of Chicago Press, 2009), 69. But also see his whole discussion of Nature, 65–79.
56. See Abū Ḥāmid al-Ghazālī, *Iḥyā 'ulūm al-dīn*, 4 vols. (Cairo: Dār Iḥyā' al-Kutub al-'Arabīyah, n.d.), 3:214.
57. *Iḥyā'*, 3: 215.
58. In fact, al-Ghazālī's main goal is to highlight how the *dunyā* can be misused and mismanaged by rendering it subservient to base and immediate passions that block out and take one away from God. This is what he refers to as "blameworthy *dunyā*" (*al-dunyā al-madhmūmah*). While he habitually speaks negatively of *al-dunyā*, he makes it clear that his reference in doing so is to "blameworthy *dunyā*," not "*al-dunyā*" in general. As he put it, "We will only treat blameworthy *dunyā* in this book." See *Iḥyā'*, 3: 214. For an insightful view that runs counter to mine, however, i.e., that *dunyā* was secular and thus non-religious and distinct from religion as *dīn*, see R. Abbasi, "Did Premodern Muslims Distinguish the Religious and the Secular? The *Dīn-Dunyā* Binary in Medieval Islamic Thought," *Journal of Islamic Studies*, 3:2 (2020): 185–225.

See also his *Beyond the Realm of Religion: The Idea of the Secular in Premodern Islam*, PhD dissertation, Harvard University, 2021, where he expresses the same view. See also, A. Mustafa, "Innovation in Premodern Islam: Between Non-Religion, Irreligion and the Secular," *Journal of Islamic Studies* 34:1 (2023): 1–41 at https://doi.org/10.1093/jis/rtac029

59. Al-Ghazālī, *Iḥyā'*, 3: 214.
60. Al-Ghazālī, *Iḥyā'*, 3: 215. See also Abū Ḥāmid al-Ghazālī, *al-Iqtiṣād fī al-i'tiqād* (Cairo: Muṣṭafā al-Bābī al-Ḥalabī wa Awlāduh, n.d.), 114, where he notes that *al-dunyā*, "is homonymous (*mushtarak*), applying, on the one hand, to extravagance in enjoyment, pleasure, and going beyond what is necessary or vital, while also applying, on the other hand, to everything one needs before death. The former is the opposite of religion, the latter a prerequisite for religion."
61. Cited in T. N. Madan, "Secularism in Its Place," in *Secularism and Its Critics*, 6th ed., ed. R. Bhargava (New Delhi: Oxford University Press, 2007), 297–320 at 318.
62. See, e.g., al-Ghazālī, *al-Iqtiṣād*, 87, where he states that *taklīf* is communicated through the medium of God's speech (*kalām*) (which includes, by extension, the teachings of God's Messenger), implying, as we will see in Chapter 2, that *taklīf* can go only as far as God's speech (on this expanded understanding) will take it.
63. W. M. Watt, *Muhammad at Mecca* (Oxford: Clarendon Press, 1953), 24–5.
64. *Public Religions*, 19. See also Taylor, *A Secular Age*, 425 and, especially, 816, note 5 where a slightly different and multifaceted understanding of differentiation is cited.
65. See his essay, "Religious Rejections of the World and Their Directions," in *From Max Weber: Essays in Sociology*, eds. H. H. Gerth and C. Wright Mills (New York: Oxford University Press, 1946), 328. Emphasis original.
66. I have long questioned the interpretation of Weber's reference to himself as religiously "unmusical" to mean that he was not religious. On my reading, Weber simply sought to establish his distance from those more frenetic, charismatic forms of religiosity. See, e.g., his "The Social Psychology of the World Religions," *From Max Weber*, 287: "The sacred values that have been most cherished, the ecstatic and visionary capacities of shamans, sorcerers, ascetics, and pneumatics of all sorts, could not be attained by everyone . . . . 'Heroic' or 'virtuoso' religiosity is opposed to mass religiosity. By 'mass' we understand those who are religiously 'unmusical.'" This is all he says. Meanwhile, in a letter to the German sociologist Ferdinand Tönnies in February of 1909, Weber wrote: "It is true that I am absolutely unmusical in matters religious and that I have neither the need nor the ability to erect any religious edifices within me—that is simply impossible for me, and I reject it. But after examining myself carefully I must say that I am neither anti-religious nor irreligious. In this regard too I consider myself a cripple, a stunted man whose fate it is to admit honestly that he must put up with this state of affairs (so as not to fall for some romantic swindle). . . . For you a theologian of liberal persuasion (whether Catholic or Protestant) is necessarily most abhorrent as the typical representative of a half way position; for me he is in human terms infinitely more valuable and interesting . . . than the intellectual (and basically cheap) pharisaism of naturalism, which is intolerably fashionable and in which there is much less life than in the religious position (again depending

on the case, of course)." See J. T. Kloppenberg, *Uncertain Victory: Social Democracy and Progressivism in European and American Thought, 1870–1920* (New York: Oxford University Press, 1988), 498, note 104. Cf., meanwhile, A. T. Kronman, *Confessions*, 3: "The great German social historian Max Weber, who was also deeply interested in religious phenomena, was once asked if he was a religious man himself. He replied that he was not—that he was 'unmusical' when it came to religion."

67. Stout, *Flight*, 245.
68. In his introductory essay, "The Ethical Significance of Kant's Religion," J. R. Sibler writes: "That Kant was a religious man there can be little doubt." See Kant's *Religion within the Limits of Reason Alone*, trans. T. M. Greene and H. H. Hudson (New York: Harper One, 1960), lxxix.
69. See Kant, *Religion within the Limits*, 5–7: "But if, now, the strictest obedience to moral laws is to be considered the cause of the ushering in of the highest good (as end), then, since human capacity does not suffice for bringing about happiness in the world proportionate to worthiness to be happy an omnipotent moral Being must be postulated as ruler of the world, under whose care this [balance] occurs. That is, morality leads inevitably to religion." See also N. Smart et al., eds., *Nineteenth Century Religious Thought in the West*, vol. 1 (Cambridge: Cambridge University Press, 1985), 8; also E. Fackenheim, "Immanuel Kant," *Nineteenth Century Religious Thought*, 17–34, where it is noted that Kant argues that morality is the highest sphere of rationally accessible truth.
70. According to Stout, these were his two main concerns. See *Flight*, 130–1.
71. Greene and Hudson, "Introduction," *Religion within the Limits*, lxxvi. See also Asad, *Genealogy*, 255: "The essence of religion—as Kant put it, and other moderns agreed—was its ethics." Of course, as Elizabeth Shakman Hurd points out, the ultimate ground of Kant's morality was not scripture or church authority but transcendent reason. "Kant anchors rational religion in the law of morality rather than anchoring morality in ecclesiastical faith. This allows Kant to retain the command model of morality from Augustinian Christianity while shifting the proximate point of command from the Christian God to the individual moral subject." See E. S. Hurd, *The Politics of Secularism in International Relations* (Princeton: Princeton University Press, 2008), 25.
72. See Kant, *Religion within the Limits*, 7–8.
73. See N. Stolzenberg, "The Profanity of the Law," in *Law and the Sacred*, eds. A. Sarat, L. Douglas and M. M. Umphrey (Stanford: Stanford University Press, 2007), 34. See also J. M. O'Sulllivan, "Church and State According to Luther," *Studies: An Irish Quarterly Review*, 3:10 (1914): 6.
74. See S. Wolin, *Politics and Vision: Politics and Change in Western Political Thought* (Princeton: Princeton University Press, 2006), 147
75. O'Sullivan, "Church and State," 6.
76. See, e.g., M. Zarqā, *Fatāwā muṣṭafā al-zarqā* (Damascus: Dār al-Qalam, 1420/1990), 405. Of course, this was not limited to the Ḥanafī school. For example, Ibn Rushd cites a unanimous consensus (*ijmā'*) on the ban on Muslims inheriting (*mīrāth* not *waṣīyah*) from non-Muslim relatives. Nevertheless, faced with a spate of wealthy

Christians who wanted to convert to Islam but balked at losing their inheritance, Ibn al-Qayyim and Ibn Taymīyah inclined toward allowing them to inherit from their non-Muslim relatives, effectively implying that this rule was not intended to function as a bar to conversion. See Ibn Rushd, *Bidāyat al-mujtahid wa nihāyat al-muqtaṣid*, 2 vols., eds. 'A. M. Mu'awwaḍ and 'A. A. 'Abd al-Mawjūd (Beirut: Dār al-Kutub al-'Ilmīyah, 1418/1997), 2: 523, where, despite the eventual consensus he cites, he also cites some early dissenters who allowed Muslims to inherit from non-Muslims but not the other way around. On Ibn Qayyim and Ibn Taymīyah, see Ibn Qayyim al-Jawzīyah, *Aḥkām ahl al-dhimmah*, 3 vols., eds. A. al-Bakrī and A. al-'Arūrī (Dammām: al-Ramadī li al-Nashr, 1418/1998), 2: 853–72, esp. 2: 253–8.

77. J. Casanova, "The Secular and Secularisms," *Social Research*, 76:4 (2009): 1049–66 at 1049.
78. *A Secular Age*, 437. Meanwhile, Peter Berger characterized secularization as "a globalized *elite* culture." See his edited volume, *The Desecularization of the World*," 10. Emphasis original.
79. See my *Islam and the Problem of Black Suffering*, 139–40.
80. For more on this point, see the section "Beyond the *Ḥukm Shar'ī*" in Chapter 2.
81. See, e.g., Nongbri, *Before Religion*, 12, 16; L. Batnitzky, *How Judaism Became a Religion: An Introduction to Modern Jewish Thought* (Princeton: Princeton University Press, 2011), 1; W. T. Cavanaugh, *The Myth of Religious Violence: Secular Ideology and the Roots of Modern Conflict* (New York: Oxford University Press, 2009), 60, 61, 69ff; and W. C. Smith, *The Meaning and End of Religion* (Minneapolis: Fortress Press, 1991), 18–19, though Smith is clear on the difference between the term itself and how it came to be used by moderns.
82. See J. Z. Smith, "'Religion' and 'Religious Studies': No Difference at All," in *On Teaching Religion: Essays by Jonathan Z. Smith*, ed. C. I. Lehrich (New York: Oxford University Press, 2013), 80. This article was originally published in 1988.
83. See, e.g., A. K. Molnár, "The Construction of the Notion of Religion in Early Modern Europe," *Method and Theory in the Study of Religion*, 14:1 (2002): 47–60 at," 47, though he later claims (p. 51), "The experts of divinity started using the word religion only around the middle of the seventeenth century." See also S. Engler, "'Religion,' 'the Secular' and the Critical Study of Religion," *Studies in Religion*, 43:1 (2014): 419–42 at 423–4.
84. See D. L. Pals, *Eight Theories of Religion* (New York: Oxford University Press, 2006), 4. Von Harnack affirmed this in a speech he gave in Berlin in 1901. See C. H. Long, "The Study of Religion: Its Nature and Discourse," *Significations*, 23. Incidentally, early proponents of the History of Religion did not entirely abandon the notion of Christianity's superiority. See, e.g., R. Otto, *The Idea of the Holy*, trans. J. W. Harvey (Mansfield, CT: Martino Publishing, 2010), 1: "Christianity not only possesses such conceptions [about God] but possesses them in unique clarity and abundance, and this is, though not the sole or even the chief, yet very real sign of its superiority over religions of other forms and at other levels." Otto's work was first published in 1912. Nor has the attitude completely receded: we see manifestations of it, even if deployed to different ends, in Marcel Gauchet's *The Disenchantment of the World: A Political History of Relligion*, transl. O. Barge (Princeton: Princeton University Press, 1997). On p. 9, e.g.,

we read "The so-called 'major religions' or 'universal religions,' far from being the quintessential embodiment of religion, are in fact just so many stages of its abatement and disintegration. The greatest and most universal of them, our own, the rational religion of the one god, is precisely the one that allows a departure from religion."

85. See J. Wach, "Introduction: The Meaning and Task of the History of Religions (Religionswissenschaft)," *The History of Religions: Essays on the Problem of Understanding*, 2nd impression, eds. J. M. Kitagawa, M. Eliade, and C. H. Long (Chicago: University of Chicago Press, 1969), 1–19 at 7.
86. C. H. Long, "African American Religion in the United States of America: An Interpretive Essay," in C. H. Long, *Ellipsis: The Collected Writings of Charles H. Long* (London: Bloomsbury, 2018), 199–211 at 203. See also J. Z. Smith, "Religion, Religions, Religious," in *Critical Terms for Religious Studies*, ed. M. C. Taylor (Chicago: University of Chicago Press, 1998), 269–84 at 269, where he notes that the early study of religion in the West depicted it as "a category imposed from the outside on some aspects of native culture."
87. Smith, *How (Not) to Be Secular*, 70.
88. M. Eliade, *The Sacred and the Profane: The Nature of Religion* (Orlando: Harcourt, Inc., 1987), esp. 202–04. The book originally appeared in 1957.
89. See Pals, *Eight Theories*, 70–71.
90. Cited in R. T. McCutcheon, "The Category 'Religion' in Recent Publications: A Critical Survey," *Numen* 42:3 (1995): 284–309 at 299. Perhaps Smart had in mind such characterizations of Eliade's as the following: "[N]on-religious man in *the pure state* is a comparatively rare phenomenon. . . . [T]he modern man who feels and claims he is nonreligious still retains a large stock of camouflaged myths and degenerated rituals." See Eliade, *Sacred and Profane*, 204–05. Emphasis original.
91. J. Z. Smith, "Religions," 273.
92. Scholars have described this division in terms of substantivist versus functionalist approaches to the study of religion. See, e.g., R. Cipriani, *Sociology of Religion: An Historical Introduction*, trans. L. Ferrarotti (New Brunswick: Transaction Publishers, 2000), 2–10; W.T. Cavanaugh, *Myth*, 57–58, 102–18. Others, however, e.g., Russell McCutcheon, characterize this shift as a move from normative to descriptive concerns. See R. McCutcheon, "What Is the Academic Study of Religion?" at http://religion.ua.edu/wp-content/uploads/2017/07/mccutchintrohandout.pdf
93. C. H. Long, "Human Centers: An Essay on Method in the History of Religions," *Significations*, 77.
94. Indeed, the encounter with Islam prompted W. C. Smith to suggest that we might abandon the term "religion" altogether. See his *Meaning and End*, 15, 17, 50, 119–53.
95. Fred Donner gives a list of major nineteenth- and twentieth-century scholars of Islam who argue that the Prophet's movement was social, economic, or nationalistic, as opposed to "religious," clearly reflecting the bifurcation that had developed in the West between "religion" and other pursuits. For these scholars, Islam had to be *either* a social *or* a religious *or* an economic *or* a nationalistic movement and could not have been simultaneously all of these as an expression of "religion." See his *Muhammad and the Believers: At the Origins of Islam* (Cambridge, MA: The Belknap Press of Harvard University Press, 2010), xi–xii.

96. See C. Adams, "The History of Religions and the Study of Islam," in J. M. Kitagawa, M. Eliade and C. Long, eds., *The History of Religions*, 177–93 at 178. He adds, "As time has gone by, it has proven increasingly difficult to see a direct and fructifying relationship between the activities of Islamicists and those of historians of religion."
97. C. Adams, "History," 187.
98. J. Z. Smith, "Religious Studies: Whither (wither) and why?" 66.
99. J. Schacht, *Introduction*, 1.
100. Both Schacht's *An Introduction to Islamic Law* and Coulson's *A History of Islamic Law* (Edinburgh: Edinburgh University Press, 1964), appeared in 1964.
101. J. Z. Smith, "Religions," 281. Elsewhere, Smith describes as "pathetic" the notion that this high number of definitions is "proof that religion is beyond definition." See Smith, "'Religion and 'Religious Studies,'" 80.
102. See S. F. Hoyt, "The Etymology of Religion," *Journal of the American Oriental Society*, 32:2 (1912): 126–9. The terms in question were: (1) *religare*; (2) *ligare*; (3) *religio*; (4) *relegere*; (5) *diligo*.
103. See Hoyt, "Etymology," 127. See also R. Gothóni, "Religio and Superstitio Reconsidered," *Archiv Für Religionspsychologie/Archive for the Psychology of Religion*, 21:1 (1994): 37–46 at 37–8, where he renders it "to re-trace or re-read." Another alternative is to re-gather together, re-arrange, based on its origin in *legere*, "to gather together, to arrange." See B. Saler, "Religio and the Definition of Religion," *Cultural Anthropology* 2:3 (1987): 395–9 at 396. See also, however, Nongbri, *Before Religion*, 26–9 for other "meanings" and intimations before and after Cicero.
104. See Hoyt, "Etymology," 126; Gothóni, "Religio and Superstitio," 40–1; Saler, "Religio," 396.
105. Gothóni, "Religio and Superstitio," 39.
106. See Shakman Hurd, *Politics*, 33–4. She notes that, "At the time, early Christians were referred to as atheists because they did not belong to a recognizable *traditio* and did not acknowledge the gods of others." *Politics*, 34.
107. See Gothóni, "Religio and Superstitio," 37–40.
108. See Gothóni, "Religio and Superstitio," 40.
109. See Gothóni, "Religio and Superstitio," 41.
110. W. C. Smith, *Meaning and End*, 38.
111. Cavanaugh notes how this essentially sets the stage for the "invention," domestication, and compartmentalization of religion in the modern world, where it is distinctly separated from politics and the political. See *Myth*, 57–101.
112. L. Gardet, *Encyclopedia of Islam*, 2nd ed., 12 vols., eds. P. J. Bearman et al. (Leiden: E. J. Brill, 1960–2005), II: 293–96 at 293.
113. The late Samuel P. Huntington (d. 2008) famously insisted that Islam had failed or refused to recognize the principle of rendering unto God what is God's and unto Caesar what is Caesar's. Instead, according to him, "In Islam, God is Caesar." He also wrote, "The separation and recurring clashes between church and state that typify Western civilization have existed in no other civilization. This division of authority contributed immeasurably to the development of freedom in the West." See his *The*

Clash of Civilizations and the Remaking of the World Order (New York: Simon and Schuster, 2011), 70. See also B. Lewis, "The Roots of Muslim Rage," *The Atlantic* 266:3 (1990): 47–60.

114. Al-Ghazālī, e.g., spoke of "the religious order" (*niẓām al-dīn*) at the center of which is the Imām (read: state) and the religious law. See his *al-Iqtiṣād*, 113–14. Meanwhile, the famed lexicographer Ibn Manẓūr (d. 711/1311) lists Islam-as-concrete-doctrine-and-practice as one of the meanings of "*dīn*." See his *Lisān al-'arab*, 6 vols., eds. 'A. 'A. al-Kabīr, M. A. Ḥasab Allāh, and H. M. al-Shādhilī (Cairo: Dār al-Ma'ārif, n.d), 2: 1469.
115. This triumph was clearly ideological. As far back as 1889, Max Müller refuted the *religare*-thesis and argued that *religio* could only have derived from *religere*, meaning, "respect, care, reverence," i.e., a psychodynamic disposition. See Gothóni, "Religio and Superstitio," 41. Yet, Gothóni notes, "Despite the conclusion of philologists that Cicero's etymological derivation is preferable, Lactantius' fabrication is curiously enough still the one presented under the entry on the concept of religion in nearly all encyclopedias and handbooks." See "Religio and Superstitio," 43. Cavanaugh, on the other hand, upholds the derivation of *religio* from *religare* but sees it as "a virtue which directs a person to God by means of bodily ritual practices." See W. Cavanaugh, "The City: Beyond Secular Parodies," in *Radical Orthodoxy: A New Theology*, eds. J. Milbank, C. Pickstock, and G. Ward (London and New York: 1999), 182–200 at 191.
116. See his *God and Man in the Koran: Semantics of the Koranic Weltanschauung* (Tokyo: The Keio Institute of Cultural and Linguistic Studies, 1964), 219–29. C.f., W. C. Smith, who suggested that *dīn* as religion came to the Arabs from the Persian *dēn* as a phonemically transmitted, "fully international term." See his *Meaning of Religion*, 100, 101.
117. Interestingly, one of the arguments put forth in favor of *religare* or *religere* was that a single word could not have simultaneously contradictory meanings, in *any* language. See Saler, "Religio," 397.
118. Izutsu, *God and Man*, 224.
119. Ibn Taymīyah, *al-Īmān* (Damascus: al-Maktab al-Islāmī, n.d.), 221.
120. See al-Ghazālī, *Iḥyā'*. See also above in the section, "Of Definitions and Usages," on the West's binary separation between religious "faith" and religious "doctrines and practices."
121. Al-Shāṭibī, *al-Muwāfaqāt fī uṣūl al- sharī'ah*, 4 vols., ed. M. 'A. Drāz (Cairo: al-Maktabah al- Tijārīyah al- Kubrā, n.d.), 1:66.
122. Speaking of all religion in the pre-modern world, Stanley Tambiah writes: "[T]he reification of religion as a great objective phenomenon or an entity of speculative interest did not exist. Religion was something one felt and did, so to say. . . . It is essentially in the modern period, since the Enlightenment, that a particular conception of religion that emphasizes its cognitive, intellectual, doctrinal, and dogmatic aspects, gained prominence." See S. Tambiah, *Magic, Science, Religion, and the Scope of Rationality* (Cambridge: Cambridge University Press, 1990), 4.
123. Al-Qarāfī, *al-Furūq*, 4 vols. (Beirut: 'Ālam al-Kitāb, n.d.), 2:161.

124. See the section "The Secular in Historical Perspective" earlier in this chapter.
125. Al-Qarāfī, *al-Furūq*, 2:161. But see the entire discussion from 2:157–63. It is not uncommon for books of theological creed, i.e., *uṣūl al-dīn*, to include segments on the Imāmate. See, e.g., Abū Manṣūr 'Abd al-Qāhir al-Tamīmī al-Baghdādī, *Kitāb uṣūl al-dīn* (Beirut: Dār al-Kutub al-'Ilmīyah, n.d.), 270–94; Abū Ḥāmid al-Ghazālī, *al-Iqtiṣād*, 113–18 ; Abū al-Thanā' Maḥmūd b. Zayd al-Lāmishī, *Kitāb al-tamhīd fī qawā'id al-tawḥīd* (Beirut: Dār al-Gharb al-Islāmī, 1995), 148–61.
126. Gothóni, "Religio and Superstitio," 44.
127. See C. H. Long, "Study," 7.
128. Long, "Study," 24.
129. See Immanuel Kant, *Religion within the Boundaries of Mere Reason and Other Writings*, 17th printing, trans. and ed. A. Wood and G. Di Giovanni (Cambridge: Cambridge University Press, 2016), 4.
130. N. Smart et al., *Nineteenth Century Religious Thought*, 9; see also B. A. Gerrish, "Fredrich Schleiermacher," *Nineteenth Century Religious Thought*, 123–56 for a summary of his thought.
131. See, e.g., N. Adams, "Shapers of Protestantism: F. D. E. Schleiermacher," *The Blackwell Companion to Protestantism*, eds. A. McGrath and D. C. Marks (London: Blackwell Publishers, 2004), 66–82 at 71–2, where they summarize Kant's view as follows: "[T]he only thing humans can know are the presentations of their minds. The only things of which we have such presentations are objects in the world. We have understanding when sense experience (provided by objects) and concepts (provided by the mind) are combined. God, however, is not the kind of object which provides us with sense experience. For that reason, we cannot have knowledge of God. Rather, God is the product of [practical] reason and is an idea by which we measure our actions in the world." Or, as Jacqueline Mariña puts it, "*Genuine* religion can exist only in the context of the prior moral commitment of the good individual who hopes that the world is ultimately ordered towards the good—and that it thereby has a meaning—and that there exists a Being that can guarantee this." See her "Kant, Schleiermacher, and the Study of Theology," in *Theology, History and the Modern German University*, eds. K. M. Vander Schel and M. P. DeJonge. (Tübingen: Mohr Siebeck, 2021), available in pdf with pagination 1–24 at https://www.academia.edu/38954292/Kant_Schleiermacher_and_the_Study_of_Theology Emphasis original.
132. See Chapter 2, on Ibn Taymīya, *fiṭrah*, and the "foundational rules of thought."
133. See, e.g., Schleiermacher, *On Religion: Speeches to its Cultured Despisers*, trans. and ed. R. Crouter (Cambridge: Cambridge University Press, 1996), 3–54.
134. Schleiermacher, *On Religion*, 22.
135. Schleiermacher, *On Religion*, 16.
136. Schleiermacher, *On Religion*, 22. He adds, "Thus, religion maintains its own sphere and its own character only by completely removing itself from the sphere and character of speculation as well as from that of praxis." *On Religion*, 23.
137. C. H. Long, "The Oppressive Element in Religion and the Religions of the Oppressed," *Significations*, 180. Again, Long's "oppugnancy" might be thought of

as the Blackamerican response to the ravages of a White-dominated socio-political world, in the same way that Charles Taylor's "buffered self" is the European response to the vulnerabilities induced by the "charged presence" of the "physical" world. See note 52, in the section "The Secular: Macro- and Micro-Modes" of this chapter.

138. On these features of *mysterium tremendum*, see Otto, *Idea of the Holy*, 10, 18, 20, 21.

139. Berger had argued that early modern Protestantism's success in stripping the world of mystical or supernatural elements destroyed religion's "sacred canopy," thereby sapping its ability to sustain its relevance in the modern world and spawning the rise and diffusion of a secular (i.e., non-religious) worldview. See P. L. Berger, *The Sacred Canopy: Elements of a Sociological Theory of Religion* (New York: Anchor Books, 1990), 110–13. The book first appeared in 1967. Berger later reversed his position on the pervasiveness and inevitability of secularization. See his *The Desecularization of the World*, 1–18.

140. See W. C. Smith, *Meaning and End*, 112.

141. For the view that religion-free zones have always existed in Islam, see Thomas Bauer, *A Culture of Ambiguity: An Alternative History of Islam*, transl. H. Biesterfeldt and T. Tunstall (New York: Columbia University Press, 2021), 130.

142. See, e.g., al-Bukhārī, *Ṣaḥīḥ al-bukhārī*, 1: 58. Incidentally, this is the first *ḥadīth* in al-Bukhārī.

143. See al-Bukhārī, *Ṣaḥīḥ al-bukhārī*, 1: 89; Muslim b. Ḥajjāj, *Ṣaḥīḥ muslim*, 5 vols. (Beirut: Dār Ibn Ḥazm, 1416/1995), 1: 47.

144. See, e.g., T. Izutsu, *God and Man*, 220: "[T]he meaning of the word *dīn* contains among others a remarkable semantic element of 'obedience' (*ṭā'ah*) and 'servantness' (*'ubūdiyyah*)." See also Ismā'īl b. Ḥammād al-Jawharī, *al-Ṣiḥāḥ tāj al-lughah wa ṣiḥāḥ al-'arabīyah*, 6 vols., ed. A.'A. 'Aṭṭār (Beirut: Dār al-'Ilm li al-Malāyīn, 1376/1965), 5: 2118–19; Ibn Manẓūr, *Lisān al-'arab*, 2: 1469; Muḥibb al-Dīn Abū Fayḍ al-Sayyid Muḥammad Murtaḍā al-Ḥusaynī al-Wāsiṭī al-Zubaydī al-Ḥanafī, *Tāj al-'arūs min jawāhir al-qāmūs*, 10 vols. (Cairo: Dār al-Fikr, n.d.), 9: 208, where *ṭā'ah* is identified as the "basic meaning" (*aṣl al-ma'nā*).

145. See Ibn Taymīyah, *Amrāḍ al-qulūb wa shifā'uhā* (Cairo: al-Maṭba'ah al-Salafīyah wa Maktabatuhā, 1386/1966), 12–13.

146. This is what Leora Batnitzky sees Schleiermacher doing. See her *How Judaism Became a Religion*, 25: "No single thinker did more to define the modern concept of religion than Schleiermacher, the founder of liberal Protestant theology. . . . Schleiermacher agrees with the cultured despisers of religion that it is wrong to mix religion and politics, but he also argues that religion in that sense is not true religion. Instead, Schleiermacher alleges that the essence of religion constitutes a unique and separate dimension of experience—by definition, separate from all other spheres of life, such as politics, philosophy, morality, and science—and is characterized by what Schleiermacher calls intuition and feeling: 'religion's essence is neither thinking nor acting, but intuition and feeling.'" It could be argued, however, that Schleiermacher is less extreme than Batnitzky suggests in separating religion from the other spheres. For he insists that religion, i.e., "intuition of the universe," is the necessary ground for all other ruminations (*On Religion*, 24). As he put it, "To want to have speculation and

praxis without religion is rash arrogance" (*On Religion*, 23). He simply insisted that these other ruminations *in and of themselves* are not religion, and that religion should not be held accountable for them. In other words, "thought," including "religious thought," is distinct, in the final analysis, from the "intuition" that prompts it. In a similar manner, the Islamic Secular would insist, as we will see, that not every thought that emerges as a result of its religious "psychodynamic orientation" is necessarily Islam.

147. Variants of this point were raised by one of the manuscript's anonymous reviewers.
148. On plausibility structure, see below.
149. Thus, Talal Asad refers to "Muslim secularism" as a response to the impositions of Western power, describing it as being "preoccupied less with theology than with separating religion from politics in national life." See his *Genealogies of Religion*, 229.
150. See my *Islamic Law and the State*, 140 and 140–1, where *Islāmī* is described as, "serving as a powerful and virtually unassailable authenticator of the cultural and other predilections of various Muslim communities."
151. See my *Islam and the Blackamerican*, 84, 154–6, 159, 164.
152. See K. GhaneaBassiri, *A History of Islam in America* (Cambridge: Cambridge University Press, 2010), 318.
153. *Islam and the Blackamerican*,160–1. The "Five Juristic Statuses," or "*al-ahkām al-khamsah*," include: (1) obligatory (*wājib* or *farḍ*); (2) recommended (*mandūb*); (3) neutral (*mubāḥ*); (4) discouraged (*makrūh*); and (5) forbidden (*ḥarām*). For a more detailed treatment, see my *Islamic Law and the State*, 116–23. Jurists also speak of *ʿafw* (non-accountability) but this relates more to the state of mind or degree of capacity of the actor than to the actual act itself. See, e.g., al-Shāṭibī, *al-Muwāfaqāt*, 1:166–8.
154. See, e.g., B. Lawrence, "Afterword: Competing Genealogies of Muslim Cosmopolitanism" in C. Ernst and R. C. Martin, eds., *Rethinking Islamic Studies: From Orientalism to Cosmopolitanism* (Columbia, SC: University of South Carolina Press, 2010), 3-2-23 at 311. This was simply a misreading of my thesis.
155. M. G. S. Hodgson, *The Venture of Islam: Conscience and History in World Civilization*, 3 vols. (Chicago: University of Chicago Press, 1974), 1: 59. Emphasis original. Perhaps Bruce Lincoln, who also taught at the University of Chicago, provides a thicker description of what Hodgson may have had in mind here: "Religion, I submit, is that discourse whose defining characteristic is its desire to speak of things eternal and transcendent with an authority equally transcendent and eternal." See his "Theses on Method," 8.
156. See J. Abu Lughod, "The Islamic City—Historic Myth, Islamic Essence, and Contemporary Relevance," *International Journal of Middle East Studies* 19:2 (1987): 15–76 at 162.
157. Abu Lughod, "Islamic City," 162.
158. On al-Faruqi's attitude toward the problem of Islam and culture, see Z. Grewal, *Islam Is a Foreign Country: American Muslims and the Crisis of Global Authority* (New York: New York University Press, 2014), 140–1.
159. Berger, *Sacred Canopy*, 46.
160. Berger, *Sacred Canopy*, 47.

161. Berger, *Sacred Canopy*, 46.
162. See H. R. Niebuhr, *Christ and Culture* (New York: HarperSanFrancisco, 2001), 30. The book originally appeared in 1951.
163. Cited in H. R. Niebuhr, *Christ and Culture*, 102.
164. This might be seen as bolstering the argument of those who reject religion on the charge that it is "man-made," which is taken to mean "untrue," an argument never made about man-made science, democracy, or human rights. Beyond this double standard, moreover, lies an unexamined assumption of an absolute conflict between God and humans, such that if an entity is "man-made" it cannot be consistent with what God wants. If, however, the argument is not that "man-made" equals not "untrue" but simply "not transcendent" (c.f. Kant), can *any* religion that is concretized in real space and time be exclusively transcendent? Have we not seen what has become of Kant's claims of transcendent reason?
165. Cited in H. R. Niebuhr, *Christ and Culture*, 30. Meanwhile, Kathryn Tanner notes: "The intrinsic character of Christianity is also put at risk by the recognition that Christian social practices are pulled in novel directions by their transplantation beyond a Western orbit." See her *Theories of Culture: A New Agenda for Theology* (Minneapolis: Fortress Press, 1997), 95.
166. See Y. al-Qaraḍāwī, *Thaqāfatunā bayna al-infitāḥ wa al-inghilāq* (Cairo: Dār al-Shurūq, 2005), 21. Of course, al-Qaraḍāwī's point could be restated by saying that the Islamic culture we need is not an exclusively *shar'ī* culture and that what is "Islamic" encompasses both *shar'ī* and non-*shar'ī* ideas, actions, and artifacts.
167. Hodgson, *Venture*, 1: 29.
168. Hodgson, *Venture*, 1: 57.
169. Hodgson, *Venture*, 1: 75.
170. Hodgson, *Venture*, 1: 315.
171. Hodgson, *Venture*, 1: 57.
172. Hodgson, *Venture*, 1: 58.
173. Hodgson, *Venture*, 1: 58. Emphasis original.
174. Hodgson, *Venture*, 1: 67.
175. On the Ṣābi'ī families, see *EI2*, 8: 672–5, some of whose members, including the famed Hilāl al-Ṣābi'ī (d. 448/1055), ultimately converted to Islam.
176. In fairness to Hodgson, I should note that he was not the beneficiary of the kind of critical investigation into the category "secular" that became commonplace in the decades following his untimely death. Had he witnessed this development, he might have revised his thesis, or at least his vocabulary.
177. Hodgson, *Venture*, 1: 75.
178. Hodgson, *Venture*, 1: 75.
179. Hodgson, *Venture*, 1: 320.
180. Hodgson, *Venture*, 1: 57. "One can speak of 'Islamic literature,' of 'Islamic art,' of 'Islamic philosophy,' even of 'Islamic despotism,' but in such a sequence one is speaking less and less of something that expresses Islam as a faith."
181. See my *On the Boundaries of Theological Tolerance in Islam: Abū Ḥāmid al-Ghazālī's Fayṣal al-Tafriqa* (Karachi: Oxford University Press, 2002), 123.

182. Jackson, *Boundaries*, 123.
183. Hodgson, *Venture*, 1: 34. See also 1: 79–80.
184. Hodgson, *Venture*, 1: 88.
185. Hodgson, *Venture*, 1: 88. Emphasis original.
186. Hodgson, *Venture*, 1: 75.
187. Hodgson, *Venture*, 1: 75.
188. Hodgson, *Venture*, 1: 75.
189. Hodgson, *Venture*, 1: 57. At *Venture*, 1: 72, Hodgson notes: "From the most essential religious avowals through the realms of uniform cult and law to the most localized and incidental custom, all can be derived in this perspective from islâm, and all can be included in Islamic beliefs and ways."
190. Hodgson, *Venture*, 1: 89.
191. Hodgson, *Venture*, 1: 74. Emphasis mine.
192. S. Ahmed, *What Is Islam? The Importance of Being Islamic* (Princeton: Princeton University Press, 2016), 431.
193. Ahmed, *What Is Islam?* 477. Emphasis original.
194. Ahmed, *What Is Islam?* 120. Emphasis original.
195. Ahmed, *What is Islam?* 488.
196. See Abū Muḥammad ʿAbd Allāh b. Muslim Ibn Qutaybah, *ʿUyūn al-akhbār*, 4 vols. (Beirut: Dār al-Kutub al-ʿIlmīyah, 1418/1998), 1:42. Emphasis mine. Ahmed provides a full transliteration of the relevant passage along with his own translation on p. 487.
197. See Ibn Qutaybah, *ʿUyūn al-akhbār*, 1:42. My translation differs slightly from Ahmed's. Also, I would note that, in Ibn Qutaybah's time and place, many of the non-*sharʿī* disciplines—the arts, engineering, medicine, and the like—would depend on direct support from those in authority, which would explain, in part at least, the relevance of his reference to "the quality of those in authority."
198. Ahmed, *What Is Islam?* 318. Emphasis original.
199. Abū Bakr Aḥmad b. ʿAlī b. Thābit al-Khaṭīb al-Baghdādī, *al-Taṭfīl wa ḥikāyāt al-ṭufaylīyīn wa akhbāruhim wa nawādir kalāmihim wa ashʿārihim*, ed. B.ʿA. al-Jābī (Beirut: Dār Ibn Ḥazm, n.d.), 44.
200. At one point, for example, Ibn al-Jawzī (the Ḥanbalī!) relates the story of a family planning to ask Abū Ḥanīfa about the financial status of one of his disciples who wants to marry their daughter. The lad is worried that he will not measure up and seeks Abū Ḥanīfa's aid. The latter advises him as follows: "When you enter my presence, reach down and grab your crotch." When the family finally asks Abū Ḥanīfa about the young man's financial suitability for marriage, he is reported to have responded, "I saw him with the equivalent of ten thousand *dirhams* in his hand!" See Jamāl al-Dīn Abū al-Faraj ʿAbd al-Raḥmān b. ʿAlī Ibn al-Jawzī, *Akhbār al-adhkiyāʾ*, ed. B. ʿA. al-Jābī (Beirut: Dār Ibn Ḥazm, 1424/2003), 110.
201. Ibn al-Jawzī, *Akhbār al-adhkiyāʾ*, 21.
202. See Ṭ. Ḥusayn, *Ḥadīth al-arbiʿāʾ*, 3, 2: 43. Obviously, Sufyān al-Thawrī's judgment was based on a significantly broader reading of the poetry of Abū Nuwās. Still, one could ask, on Ahmed's bifurcation, "What was al-Thawrī doing reading Abū Nuwās?"

203. Ahmed, *What Is Islam?* 405. Emphasis original.
204. Ahmed, *What Is Islam?* 435. Emphasis original.
205. Ahmed, *What Is Islam?* 435. Emphasis original.
206. Ahmed, *What Is Islam?* 540.
207. Ahmed, *What Is Islam?* 435.
208. W. Montgomery Watt, *Islamic Fundamentalism and Modernity* (London and New York: Routledge, 1988), 13–14.
209. Ahmed, *What is Islam?* 437. Emphasis original.
210. See Muḥammad b. ʿAbd al-Karīm al-Shahrastānī, *al-Milal wa al-niḥal*, 2 vols., eds. A. A. Mahnā and A. H. Fāʿūr (Beirut: Dār al-Maʿrifah, 1417/1997), 2: 487–90. These men would clearly come under Hodgson's "Islamicate," though one would not think of them as "secular" thinkers.
211. Clearly, in other words, not everything from the Muslim past is *prescriptively* Islamic today, even if it was in the past and may be deemed *descriptively* so today.
212. Ahmed, *What is Islam?* 540. One is reminded of a similar sensibility expressed by the late Ali Mazrui (d. 1436/2014): "Prophet Muhammad was the last prophet (*nabī*), but was he the last messenger (*rasūl*)? Let's accept that he was the last *rasūl* in the form of a human person. But could *time* be a continuing cosmic *rasūl*, or at least a *risālah*? Is history a continuing revelation of God? Is expanding science a non-carnate *rasūl*? If God reveals Himself incrementally, and if history is a continuing revelation of God, should we not re-examine Muhammad's message in the light of new installments of Divine Revelation?" See his "Liberal Islam versus Moderate Islam: Elusive Moderates and the Siege Mentality," *American Journal of Islamic Social Sciences*, 22:3 (2005): 83–9 at 86–7.
213. Ahmed, *What Is Islam?* 470–1.
214. Ahmed, *What Is Islam?* 350. Emphasis original.
215. Ahmed, *What Is Islam?* 424.
216. Ahmed, *What Is Islam?* 513.
217. Tambiah, *Magic*, 7.
218. Tambiah, *Magic*, 7.
219. See, al-Bukhārī, *Ṣaḥīḥ al-bukhārī*, 4: 541–2; 9: 792 (where the wording is "before Him" (*qablah*). See also Ibn Taymīyah's discussion in *Majmūʿat al-rasāʾil wa al-masāʾil*, 5 vols. (Beirut: Dār al-Kutub al-ʿIlmīyah, 1421/2001), 5: 349–61.
220. See, e.g., Ahmed, *What Is Islam?* 486.
221. Tambiah, *Magic*, 6. One is reminded, incidentally, of Nietzsche: "You desire to LIVE 'according to nature'? Oh, you noble Stoics, what fraud of words! Imagine to yourselves a being like nature, boundlessly extravagant, boundlessly indifferent, without purpose or consideration, without pity or justice at once fruitful and barren and uncertain: imagine yourselves INDIFFERENT as a power—how COULD you live in accordance with such indifference? To live—is not that just endeavoring to be otherwise than Nature? Is not living, valuing, preferring, being unjust, being limited, endeavoring to be different?" See F. Nietzsche, *Beyond Good and Evil* (San Bernardino, CA: Millennium Publications, 2014), 6.
222. In fact, according to Fazlur Rahman, "From the Greeks through Hegel it has often been said that 'nothing' is an empty word without any real meaning, since

'there can be no nothing and we cannot imagine it.'" See his *Major Themes of the Qur'an*, 3.

223. Some may see this as implicating a position on the question of whether reason can know good and evil independent of Revelation. I will have more to say about this in Chapter 4. For now, let me just note that the question of whether reason can know good and evil is separate from the question of whether good and evil are ontologically inscribed upon creation. Good and evil based on convention, such as the pre-Islamic Arabian *ma'rūf*, are equally discoverable by reason, independent of a realist presumption.
224. Muslim jurists may grant certain principles or considerations precedence over the plain sense of Revelation, as with *istiḥsān, sadd al-dharā'i', takhṣīṣ al-'āmm*, and the like. In these instances, however, Revelation remains primary, the ultimate goal being to serve its message as understood. In a similar vein, the Qur'ān may place a principle, such as order, over its explicit commitment to morality, as when it allows pagan men who married their widowed stepmothers to remain married to them after their conversion to Islam, despite the Qur'ān's describing this practice as an abomination. [4:22] But this does not render the principle of order a "higher" truth than Revelation. Incidentally, the issue of whether it was permissible for pre-Islamic men who converted to remain married to their stepmothers was controversial. For the view I cite here, see Muḥammad al-Ṭāhir Ibn 'Āshūr, *Tafsīr al-taḥrīr wa al-tanwīr*, 30 vols. (Beirut: Mu'assasat al-Tārīkh, 1420/2000), 4: 75–6, where he states that he knows of no instances where the Prophet imposed separation after Revelation prohibited the practice. On the other hand, the early Ḥanafī jurist al-Jaṣṣāṣ contradicts Ibn 'Āshūr, noting that he knows of no instances in which the Prophet allowed a man to remain married to his father's wife, even if the latter marriage had been contracted prior to Islam. He acknowledges, however, that there was disagreement on the matter. See his *Aḥkām al-qur'ān*, 3 vols., ed. 'A. M. 'A. Shāhīn (Beirut: Dār al-Kutub al-'Ilmīyah, 1415/1994), 2: 153–4, and 2:167.
225. Ahmed, *What Is Islam?* 325.
226. C. Shannon, *Conspicuous Criticism: Tradition, The Individual, and Culture in Modern American Social Thought* (Scranton, PA: University of Scranton Press, 2006), 202–03.
227. One thinks here of the 1.5 to 2 hours it takes to make seven ambits around the *ka'ba* during *ḥajj* and why Muslims continue to return to this taxing ritual again and again, with sweet dread.
228. See al-Bukhārī, *Saḥīḥ al-bukhārī*, 9:767–8. Incidentally, to say that the views of the NOI, for example, violate Sunni orthodoxy and therefore do not constitute Islam is not to impugn their religious sincerity, as one writer seems to claim I do. See Z. Grewal, *Islam Is a Foreign Country*, 95 and 369, note 31.
229. Again, as we saw, for example, in Hodgson's "Islamicate," non-Muslims have long been recognized as contributing to the constitution of the "Islamic" without being seen as contributing to the constitution of "Islam" as an ideal. Sabian and Coptic contributions to Islamicate society did not render them Muslims. Nor were their actions themselves, as distinct from the results thereof, necessarily deemed "Islamic." One might note in this regard the *ḥadīth* in Muslim and al-Bukhārī wherein the Prophet states: "Verily, God will aid this religion even through the deeds

of shameless men" (*inna Allāh la-yu'ayyid hādhā al-dīn bi al-rajul al-fājir*), clearly speaking to the results as opposed to the psychodynamic drivers of their acts. See Muslim, *Ṣaḥīḥ muslim*, 1: 99; al-Bukhārī, *Ṣaḥīḥ al-bukhārī*, 4: 494.

230. See Abū al-Ḥasan ʿAlī b. Ismāʿīl al-Ashʿarī, *Maqālāt al-islāmīyīn wa ikhtilāf al-muṣallīn*, 2 vols., ed. M. M. ʿAbd al-Ḥamīd (Cairo: Maktabat al-Nahḍah al-Miṣrīyah, 1389/1969). Incidentally, I beg to differ with Ahmed on his reading of al-Ashʿarī's statement in the introduction to this work. He reads "*ḍallala baʿḍuhum baʿḍan*," as "some of them led others astray." I translate this phrase as "some of them *deemed* others to *be* astray," which al-Ashʿarī then qualifies with, "except that Islam gathers them together and encompasses them all." In other words, they may all be equally "Islamic" in the sense I have laid out here, but they do *not* all equally represent Islam, as Ahmed seems to suggest. There is a presumption, in other words, of normativity informing al-Ashʿarī's statement that Ahmed seems to miss. See Ahmed, *What Is Islam?* 5.
231. See Jalāl al-Dīn al-Suyūṭī, *Juhd al-qarīḥah fī tajrīd al-naṣīḥa* (Beirut: al-Maktabah al-ʿAṣrīyah, 1430/2009), 31. This is an abridgment of Ibn Taymīyah's *Naṣīḥat ahl al-īmān fī al-radd ʿalā manṭiq al-yūnān*. Wael Hallaq has translated al-Suyūṭī's abridgment with a masterful introduction. See his *Ibn Taymiyya Against the Greek Logicians* (New York: Oxford University Press, 1993).
232. Hodgson, *Venture*, 1: 351.
233. Thus, "Islamic Science" or "Islamic Economics," e.g., can change or even prove to be "wrong" without undermining the integrity of Islam. In a similar vein, slavery or certain gender restrictions can be authentically Islamic in one time and place but not in another.
234. I picked up this pithy insight from Ebrahim Moosa.
235. Ahmed, *What Is Islam?* 342 (citing Gustave von Grunebaum).
236. Ahmed, *What Is Islam?* 454. Emphasis original. We might note in this context, and given what has been said thus far, the Islamic Secular's (and Ahmed's) departure from the view of Thomas Bauer who sees such designations as "Islamic medicine" as oxymorons. He writes: "[S]ome speak unthinkingly of 'Islamic medicine', ignoring that medicine in the cultures of the Near East constituted a separate subsystem of society. It had its own experts, whose knowledge was committed exclusively to the standards of its own discipline. Theologians or other religious experts had no say in it." See his *Ambiguity*, 130. For Bauer, the "Islamic," like the "religious," is basically limited to the views of "[t]heologians and other religious experts." Overall, he seems to recognize no *sharʿī*/non-*sharʿī* distinction, only a "religious"/"non-religious" or "Islamic"/non-"Islamic" one. Otherwise, however, I am in sympathy with much in this insightful book.

Chapter 2

1. Taqī al-Dīn al-Maqrīzī, *Kitāb al-sulūk li maʿrifat duwal al-mulūk*, 12 vols. in four parts (Cairo: Maṭbaʿat Dār al-Kutub wa al-Wathāʾiq al-Qawmīyah, 1435/2014), 3:3, 1127.

2. A. Allouche treats this in his study of al-Maqrīzī's *Ighāthat al-ummah bi kashf al-ghummah*, which was a direct response to this situation. See A. Allouche, *Mamluk Economics: A Study and Translation of al-Maqrīzī's* Ighāthah (Salt Lake City, 1994). According to Allouche, al-Maqrīzī's final version of *Ighāthah* was probably completed in 809/1406. See *Mamluk Economics*, 5–7.
3. See Allouche, *Mamluk Economics*, 18. See also W. C. Schultz, "'It Has No Root among any Community That Believes in Revealed Religion, Nor Legal Foundation for Its Implementation': Placing al-Maqrīzī's Comments on Money in a Wider Context," *Mamlūk Studies Review*, 7:2 (2003): 169–81 at 180, where he notes, "There were no active gold, silver or copper mines in Egypt in the Mamluk period."
4. For a sense of the scope and magnitude of routine financial outlays, see D. Ayalon, "The System of Payment in Mamluk Military Society I," *Journal of the Economic and Social History of the Orient*, 1:1 (1957): 37–65; "The System of Payment in Mamluk Military Society II," *Journal of the Economic and Social History of the Orient*, 1:3 (1958): 257–96.
5. On money of account, see H. Kato, "Reconsidering al-Maqrīzī's View on Money in Medieval Egypt," *Mediterranean World*, *21* (2012): 33–44, at 37–43. See also F. C. Lane and R. C. Mueller, *Money and Banking in Medieval and Renaissance Venice* (Baltimore and London: The Johns Hopkins University Press, 1985), 7: "Present day coins have inscriptions stating their value: one cent, five cents. . . . Medieval coins generally had no inscription stating their value. Their names were derived from the title of the ruler who issued them. . . . When counted out in payment, the coins were evaluated in denominations that did not appear on the coins: they were valued in pounds, shillings and pence, or other terms, just as we evaluate nickels and dimes in dollars and cents. They were evaluated in monies of account whose names differed from those of most of the coins used as the means of payment."
6. Allouche, *Mamluk Economics*, 16–19, esp. 17.
7. Allouche, *Economics*, 24. Allouche translation.
8. See, e.g., Allouche, *Mamluk Economics*, 15, 52.
9. See, e.g., Allouche, *Mamluk Economics*, 83, 85.
10. Allouche, *Mamluk Economics*, 80. Allouche translation.
11. Allouche, *Mamluk Economics*, 3–4. See also K. Stilt, *Islamic Law in Action: Authority Discretion, and Everyday Experiences in Mamluk Egypt* (New York: Oxford University Press, 2011).
12. See N. Rabbat, "Who Was al-Maqrīzī? A Biographical Sketch," *Mamlūk Studies Review*, 7:2 (2003): 1–19 at 15–16. According to Rabbat, this occurred around 813/1415. Al-Maqrīzī declined.
13. See *Igāthat al-ummah bi kashf al-gummah*, ed. K. H. Farhāt (Giza: 'Ayn li al-Dirāsāt wa al-Buḥūth al-Insānīyah wa al-Ijtimā'īyah, 2007/1427), 155. I reference the Arabic original here simply to highlight al-Maqrīzī's specific use of the term "*shar'*"/"*shar'ī*."
14. Al-Maqrīzī, *Ighāthah*, 155.
15. Al-Maqrīzī, *al-Nuqūd al-islāmīyah* (aka, *Shudhūr al-uqūd fī dhikr al-nuqūd*), in *Thalath Rasā'il* (Constantine, Algeria: Maṭba'at al-Jawā'ib, 1298/1881), 17. Emphasis added. Incidentally, in this work al-Maqrīzī excoriates Sultan Faraj by name and

refers to him as "the ruler with the most detestable manner of proceeding and the basest soul." See *al-Nuqūd*, 16.

16. Allouche, *Mamluk Economics*, 77.
17. Allouche, *Mamluk Economics*, 18. Here Allouche points to al-Maqrīzī's tendency to moralize on the matter, overplaying the role of mismanagement. Meanwhile, Schultz in "It Has No Root," p. 180, points to the practical calculus, above and beyond any attending moral considerations, that drove Mamlūk policy.
18. See Badr al-Dīn Maḥmūd b. Aḥmad b. Mūsā b. Aḥmad b. al-Ḥusayn al-ʿAynī, *al-Bināyah sharḥ al-hidāyah*, 13 vols., ed. A. Ṣ. Shaʿbān (Beirut: Dār al-Kutub al-ʿIlmīyah, 1433/2012), 8: 414.
19. See al-Maqrīzī, *al-Nuqūd*, 18.
20. See Jalāl al-Dīn al-Ṣuyūṭī, *al-Ḥāwī li al-fatāwī*, 2 vols. (Beirut: Dār al-Kutub al-ʿIlmīyah, 1408/1988), 1: 95–105, esp. 96, 100, 104. It has been suggested that al-Maqrīzī was merely relying on a basic prohibition in the Shāfiʿī school against the use of *fulūs* as currency. See, e.g., A. Allouche, *Mamluk Economics*, 20; W. Schultz, "It Has No Root," 178. Both appear to rely on R. Brunschvig, "Conceptions monétaires chez les jurists musulmans (VIIe-XIIIe siècles)," *Arabica*, *14* (1967) 113–43. On p. 139 Brunschvig writes: "il [al-Shāfiʿī] nie sans ambages le caractere monétaire des *fulūs*," and he references *al-Umm*, 3:86 [old Būlāq edition]. It is true that al-Shāfiʿī states there that *fulūs* "is not a medium of exchange" (*laysa bi thaman li al-ashyā'*). But it is not entirely clear whether he means that it is not a medium of exchange as a matter of *fact* (i.e., custom) or that it *cannot be* a medium of exchange as a matter of *law*. For at *al-Umm*, 3:28 [old Būlāq edition], he states: "If someone contracts a loan or sale with someone via *fulūs* or *dirhams*, then the Sultan invalidates the use of either, such a person is only entitled to the equivalent of the *fulūs* or *dirhams* through which they contracted the loan or sale" (*man sallafa fulūs[an] aw dirāhim aw bāʿa bihā thumma abṭalahā al-sulṭān fa laysa lahu illā mithlu fulūsih aw dirāhimih allatī aslafa aw bāʿa bihā*). Similarly, we read in al-Nawawī, *Kitāb al-majmūʿ*, 23 vols., ed. M. N. al-Muṭīʿī (Cairo: Dār Iḥyā' al-Turāth al-ʿArabī, 1415/1995), 9: 493: "If *fulūs* comes to circulate in the same way that [standard] money does, the rules of *ribā* do not apply to it. This is the sound position and the one explicitly referenced (in the school)." Thus, while the status of *fulūs* in terms of whether the rules of *ribā* (or *zakāt*) apply to it or whether it is customarily used as money may be an issue, I see no evidence of its use as currency being flatly banned in the Shāfiʿī school, beginning with al-Shāfiʿī himself. One might note in this context the argument among early-modern jurists as to whether paper money was subject to the rules of *zakāt* or *ribā*, even as they did not question its status as valid tender. See, e.g., Abū Bakr Ḥasan al-Kishnāwī, *Ashal al-madārik sharḥ irshād al-sālik fī fiqh imām al-a'immah mālik*, 3 vols. (Beirut: Dār al-Fikr, 1420/2000), 1: 370–1, 2: 223.
21. See Abū Yaḥyā Zakarīyah al-Anṣārī, *Asnā al-maṭālib sharḥ rawḍ al-ṭālib*, 9 vols., ed. M. M. Tāmir (Beirut: Dār al-Kutub al-ʿIlmīyah, 1434/2013), 4:37; 4: 51. See also Abū Ḥāmid al-Ghazālī, *Iḥyā'*, 3: 222, where copper is cited as a currency without objection. For additional views on both sides of the issue, see M. A. Haneef and E. R. Barakat, "Must Money Be Limited to Only Gold and Silver? A Survey of *Fiqhi* Opinions and

Some Implications," *Journal of King Abdulaziz University: Islamic Economics, 19*:1 (2006): 21–34, though there seems to be some conflation between the question of money as an object of *ribā* (?interest) and money as a medium of exchange.

22. Again, al-Maqrīzī uses these designations in an overly prescriptive sense, in contrast to the descriptive sense in which I use them. See the section "Differentiation" in Chapter 1.
23. A verse such as "*likay lā takūna dūlat*^{an} *bayna al-aghniyā' minkum*" (so that wealth is not simply recycled among the rich) [59:7], e.g., clearly points to the practical benefits of the command in question.
24. The reference here is to the Shāfi'ī ruling on insolvent husbands. See Shams al-Dīn Muḥammad b. Aḥmad al-Shirbīnī (d. 977/1570), *al-Iqnā' fī ḥall alfāẓ abī shujā'*, 2 vols. (Cairo: Muṣṭafā Bābī al-Ḥalabī, 1359/1940), 2: 146–7.
25. Al-Qarāfī, *Nafā'is al-uṣūl fī sharḥ al-maḥṣūl*, 4 vols., ed. M.'A. 'Aṭā (Beirut: Dār al-Kutub al-'Ilmīyah, 1421/2000), 1: 179.
26. See note 152 in Chapter 1.
27. Ayalon, "System of Payment II," 280. He adds: "This statement of the famous scholar is of great significance, for al-'Aṣqalānī was neither a mamluk like Baybars al-Manṣūrī nor a son of a mamluk like Ibn Taghribirdī and Ibn Iyās, who might be suspected of being favorably disposed toward the ruling class."
28. Ayalon, "System of Payment II," 264. He attributes this assessment to Ibn Khaldūn.
29. See A. MacIntyre, *After Virtue*, 2nd ed. (Notre Dame: University of Notre Dame Press, 2003), 7.
30. Al-Qarāfī, *Sharḥ tanqīḥ*, 280.
31. Al-Qarāfī, *Sharḥ tanqīḥ*, 280: "*anna al-shay'ayn qad yastawiyān fī al-ḥukm al-shar'ī fa yakūn ikhtilāfuhumā bi ḥasab al-'āqibah lā bi ḥasab al-ḥukm al-shar'ī.*" The text actually reads "*bi ḥasab al-'āfiyah*," which is clearly a mistake. See also al-Qarāfī's discussion at *al-Furūq*, 2: 12–13.
32. Indeed, there may be facts that are relevant to determining the consequences of an act that are so intricate that they lie beyond a jurist's ability to know (e.g., scientific, economic, or social facts). In such cases, deferring to his pronouncements regarding these issues would risk distorting the law. Thus, a jurist may have to rely on other expert finders of facts, including facts that are relevant to applying the principle of *sadd al-dharā'i'*. On *sadd al-dharā'i'* as a juristic principle, see al-Qarāfī, *al-Furūq*, 2: 32–4. I will have more to say about the law/fact distinction in Chapter 4.
33. One is reminded here of a *hadīth* that appears in al-Nasā'ī, wherein a man complains to the Prophet that his wife does not rebuff the advances of other men. When the Prophet advises him to divorce her, he replies that he fears that he might not be able to live without her (*innī akhāfu an tatba'ahā nafsī*). The Prophet retorts, "Then, keep her" (*fa amsikhā*). Clearly, this man's problem could not be resolved by a *ḥukm shar'ī* that simply rendered it permissible for him to divorce or remain married to his wife. On the various narrations of this *hadīth* and the controversy surrounding its authenticity, see M. N. al-Albānī, *Ṣaḥīḥ sunan al-nasā'ī bi ikhtiṣār al-sanad*, 3 vols. (Riyādh: Maktab al-Tarbīyah al-'Arabī li Duwal al-Khalīj, 1408/1988), 1: 680–1, 1: 731–2.

Al-Albānī appears to consider it sound. See also Ibn Taymīyah, *Majmūʿat al-fatāwā*, 32: 92–3 for a discussion of the *ḥadīth*'s authenticity and meaning.

34. Al-Qarāfī, *Sharḥ tanqīh*, 280–1.
35. Ibn Taymīyah, *Minhāj al-sunnah al-nabawīyah fī naqḍ kalām al-shīʿah al-qadarīyah*, 9 vols., ed. M. R. Sālim (n.p., 1406/1986), 5: 93. By "*daqīq al-kalām*," Ibn Taymīyah could also be referring to language and linguistics.
36. See D. L. Lindberg, "Galileo, the Church and the Cosmos," in *When Science and Christianity Meet*, eds. D. L. Lindberg and R. L. Numbers (Chicago: University of Chicago Press, 2003), 33–60 at 45.
37. His place in modernity's science/religion mythology notwithstanding, Galileo was neither a freethinker nor opposed to religion. As Lindberg notes, "Every one of the combatants, whether church official or disciple of Galileo, called himself a Christian; and all, without exception, acknowledged the authority of the Bible." See Lindberg, "Galileo," 58.
38. "The Council decrees that, in matters of faith and morals . . . no one, relying on his own judgment and distorting the Sacred Scriptures according to his own conceptions, shall dare to interpret them contrary to that sense which Holy Mother Church, to whom it belongs to judge their true sense and meaning, has held and does hold, or even contrary to the unanimous agreement of the Fathers." See Lindberg, "Galileo," 45. While the conflict over interpretive authority was real, I am inclined to accept Lindberg's advice and avoid the conclusion that the matter was all about religion versus science/reason. Many other issues (e.g., personal ambitions, personality clashes, careers, politics, etc.) also imposed themselves. Even on the merits, Lindberg notes further: "In support of heliocentric cosmology were no scientific proofs, but scientific opinions and arguments. . . . Thus, it was not (as members of the Inquisition saw it) divinely inspired biblical certainties against convincing scientific demonstrations, but biblical certainties against improbable scientific conjectures. From the church's perspective, no choice could have been easier." "Galileo," 48–9.
39. Stout, *Flight*, 43.
40. See, e.g., E. R. Gane, "Luther's Views of Church and State," *Andrews University Seminary Studies (AUSS)*, *8*:2 (1970): 127: "Bishops' courts, he [Luther] argued should deal only with 'matters of faith and morals, and leave matters of money and property, life and honor, to the temporal judges.' "
41. See P. Crone, *Pre-Industrial Societies: Anatomy of the Pre-Modern World* (London: Oneworld, 2020), 221. Emphasis original. This was a reprint of the 2015 edition.
42. Abū Ḥāmid al-Ghazālī, *al-Munqidh min al-ḍalāl wa al-muwaṣṣil ilā dhi al-ʿizzah wa al-jalāl*, eds. J. Ṣalība and K. Iyāḍ (Beirut: Dār Maktabat al-Hilāl li al-Ṭibāʿah wal al-Nashr, 1986), 102. Earlier he had noted, speaking of mathematics, that this discipline "is connected to arithmetic, geometry (*handasah*), and astronomy (*ʿilm hayʾat al-ʿālam*)" and that "none of this implicates religion (*al-umūr al-dīnīyah*), positively or negatively." *Al-Munqidh*, 101. For a similar view on the relationship between Islam and science, see Ibn Khaldūn, *al-Muqaddimah*, ed. Ḥ. ʿĀṣī (Beirut: Dār Maktabat al-Hilāl li al-Ṭibāʿah wa al-Nashr, 1986), 309, where he speaks of the Prophet's mission

being to teach "concrete religious doctrine and practice (*al-sharāʾiʿ*), not medicine (*ṭibb*) and other such everyday pursuits." Ibn Khaldūn goes on to cite numerous sciences that became part of Muslim civilization, essentially casting all of them as constituents of what I describe herein as the Islamic Secular.

43. See his *Iḥyāʾ*, 1: 22. Again, recognizing medicine as a communal obligation, *sharʿan*, is not the same as *sharīʿah* providing the substantive content of medicine.
44. My argument is not that there can be no conflicts or contradictions between science and religion (though I believe we should be careful about overindulging our modern bias that holds that, in any such perceived conflict, science must be right, and religion is wrong; after all, science changes). My argument is simply that Muslim jurists deliberated the matter in a spirit that did not see science and religion as *categorically* antithetical.
45. See Shihāb al-Dīn al-Qarāfī, *al-Dhakhīrah*, 14 vols. (Beirut: Dār al-Gharb al-Islāmī, 1994), 10: 55–7.
46. See, e.g., Abū Yaʿlā, *al-Uddah*, 2: 445.
47. See, e.g., al-Ghazālī, *al-Mustaṣfā*, 2: 350; Aḥmad b. Saʿīd b. ʿUbayd Allāh b. ʿAbd al-Razzāq al-Hindī (aka Mullā Jīwan), *Nūr al-anwār fī sharḥ al-manār*, 2 vols., ed. M. A. ʿAbd al-ʿAzīz (Beirut: Dār al-Kutub al-ʿIlmīyah, 2018), 1: 21. C.f., however, al-Qarāfī, *Sharḥ tanqīḥ*, 424–5, where he notes that al-Rāzī also placed the number of "legal verses" at five hundred, with which al-Qarāfī disagrees, noting that verses that speak, e.g., of God's attributes or the fate of past communities are often instructive in assessing the legal status of acts.
48. See, e.g., Muslim b. Ḥajjāj, *Ṣaḥīḥ muslim*, 4:1464, where, in response to the complaint of a group of farmers who acted on his view that he saw no point in their pollinating their date trees, only to have the trees' produce diminish, the Prophet responded: "If you found benefit in that (pollination), you should have continued to do it. I simply expressed a (non-revelational) point of view. Do not hold me accountable for personal (non-revelational) views. But when I inform you of something on the authority of God, take it; for, I will never invent lies against God."
49. Ahmed, *What Is Islam?* 120.
50. Ahmed, *What Is Islam?* 117.
51. Ahmed, *What Is Islam?* 119. See also Hodgson, *Venture*, 1: 74: "Sharīʿah in principle . . . covers every human contingency, social and individual, from birth to death."
52. Curiously, he overlooks my book *Islamic Law and the State*, in which *sharīʿah*'s boundaries are discussed in detail. In fact, Chapter 4 of that book is entitled, "The Limits of Law: Against the Tyranny of the *Madhhab*."
53. Ahmed, *What Is Islam?* 117–29.
54. Schacht, *An Introduction to Islamic Law*, 1. As Ahmed points out, Schacht was one of Bergsträsser's students who published the latter's book on Islamic law in 1935 after Bergsträsser's death in 1933. In this work, Bergsträsser registers a view almost identical to that of Schacht. See Ahmed, *What Is Islam?* 118. Earlier, in his *Origins of Muhammadan Jurisprudence*, v, Schacht wrote: "[L]aw lay to a great extent outside the sphere of religion, was only incompletely assimilated to the body of religious duties, and retained part of its own distinctive quality." Some may read this as recognizing a

distinction between *sharī'ah* in its mature form and Islam as religion. What Schacht is actually articulating, however, is his view that much of the concrete material that came to constitute the religious law originated outside the religion, in early Arabia or elsewhere, but that once the religious law absorbed this material it was no longer recognized as having a foreign provenance.

55. Schacht, *Introduction*, 54.
56. Schacht, *Introduction*, 54–5.
57. See, e.g., Schacht, *Introduction*, 76–85. See also N. J. Coulson, *A History of Islamic Law* (Edinburgh: Edinburgh University Press, 1964), 120–34. Referring to the pre-modern period, Coulson writes: "Sharī'a law had come into being as a doctrinal system independent of and essentially opposed to current legal practice." See *History*, 120. Practice diverging from theory is apparently understood to be a *sui generis* trait of Islam.
58. Schacht, *Introduction*, 84. See Chapter 3, where I offer an alternate thesis.
59. J. Schacht, "Problems in Modern Islamic Legislation," *Studia Islamica*, *12* (1960): 99–129, at 120.
60. N. J. Coulson, "The State and the Individual in Islamic Law," *International and Comparative Law Quarterly*, 6:1 (1957): 49.
61. Coulson, *History*, 134.
62. W. B. Hallaq, *The Impossible State: Islam, Politics, and Modernity's Moral Predicament* (New York: Columbia University Press, 2013), 51.
63. Hallaq, *Impossible State*, 51.
64. W. B. Hallaq, *Sharī'a: Theory, Practice, Transformations* (Cambridge: Cambridge University Press, 2009), 5. See also Hallaq, *Impossible State*, 113.
65. Hallaq, *Impossible State*, 51.
66. Hallaq, *Impossible State*, 49.
67. Kant was clear: "The moral worth of an action does not lie in the effect expected from it, nor in any principle of action which requires to borrow its motive from this expected effect." See Immanuel Kant, *Groundwork of the Metaphysic of Morals*, trans. T. K. Abbott (San Bernardino: Digireads.com Publishing, 2017), 16. Alasdair MacIntyre sums up this stance as follows: "Kant argues that my duty is my duty irrespective of the consequences, whether in this world or the next." See his *A Short History of Ethics: A History of Moral Philosophy from the Homeric Age to the Twentieth Century*, 2nd ed. (Notre Dame, IN: University of Notre Dame Press, 2009), 196.
68. See, e.g., Hallaq, *Sharī'a, Theory, Practice*, 495, 488 and passim; "Juristic Authority vs. State Power: The Legal Crisis of Modern Islam," *Journal of Law and Religion*, *19*:2 (2003–2004): 243–58.
69. I will return to this theme in Hallaq in Chapter 4.
70. See A. Khallāf, *al-Siyāsah al-shar'īyah aw niẓām al-dawlah al-islāmīyah fī al-shu'ūn al-dustūrīyah wa al-khārijīyah wa al-mālīyah* (Cairo: Maṭ ba'at al-Taqaddum, 1397/1977), 11.
71. M. M. al-Azami, *On Schacht's Origins of Muhammadan Jurisprudence* (Oxford: The Oxford Centre for Islamic Studies and The Islamic Texts Society, 1996), 13.

72. *Islām and Secularism* (Kuala Lumpur: International Institute of Islamic Thought and Civilization, 1993), 25. The modern movement *al-Qā'idah* does al-Attas one better: "We believe that secularism (*'ilmāniyya*)—in all its forms, appellations, and political parties—constitutes flagrant unbelief leading one to fall outside the community of believers. He who believes in secularism, calls to it, supports it or rules by it is an infidel associationist regardless of whether he claims adhesion to Islam or pretends to be a Muslim." See B. Haykal, "On the Nature of Salafi Thought and Action," in *Global Salafism: Islam's New Religious Movement*, ed. R. Meijer (New York: Columbia University Press, 2009), 53. While the Islamic Secular also has no interest in secular*ism*, this articulation appears to proscribe any recognition of the "secular" on *any* definition.
73. See Azam's groundbreaking study, *Sexual Violation in Islamic Law: Substance, Evidence, and Procedure* (Cambridge: Cambridge University Press, 2017), 67.
74. See A. An-Na'im, *Islam and the Secular State: Negotiating the Future of Sharī'a* (Cambridge, Mass: Harvard University Press, 2008). I engage with An-Na'im more fully in Chapter 5.
75. Asad, *Formations*, 54, 56.
76. My point here is simply that An-Na'im ultimately joins Adonis in the latter's secularism, in terms of separating *sharī'ah* from the state. It is *not* my insinuation that An-Na'im joins Adonis in his atheism or that he aims, like the latter, to separate *sharī'ah* from society. On An-Na'im's secularism, see Chapter 5.
77. Scholars have put forth various translations of these terms. R. Mottahadeh, e.g., in *Lessons in Islamic Jurisprudence* (Oxford: Oneworld, 2003), 55ff., uses "injunctive" and "declaratory" for the *ḥukm taklīfī* and the *ḥukm waḍ'ī* respectively, while B. Weiss uses "normative" and "non-normative." See B. Weiss, *The Search for God's Law: Islamic Jurisprudence in the Writings of Sayf al-Dīn al-Āmidī* (Salt Lake City: University of Utah Press, 1992), 2.
78. See Chapter 1, note 133.
79. Again, for a more detailed treatment, see my *Islamic Law and the State*, 116–23.
80. The division between "formative" and "post-formative" is a contested boundary, both in terms of when it occurred and in terms of its meaning and implications. Recently, Intisar Rabb has offered three distinct phases of development: (1) the founding period (seventh to ninth centuries CE); (2) the period of textualization (tenth and eleventh centuries CE) including the so-called "closing of the gates of *ijtihād*"; and (3) the period of synthesizing textual and interpretive authority that followed. It is roughly this third period and after that I am referring to here. See I. Rabb, *Doubt in Islamic Law: A History of Legal Maxims, Interpretation, and Islamic Criminal Law* (Cambridge: Cambridge University Press, 2015), 8–9. Meanwhile, L. Salaymeh has criticized such notions as "formative," "post-formative," and the like as part of the Orientalist obsession with "origins" and, from there, "maturity" and "decline." My use of "post-formative" has nothing to do with these concepts but simply recognizes that *sharī'ah* eventually became the ward of *uṣūl al-fiqh*, whereupon all legal arguments assumed the authority of and drew their own authority from the latter.

See Salaymeh, *The Beginnings of Islamic Law: Late Antique Islamicate Legal Traditions* (Cambridge: Cambridge University Press, 2016) 84–104, 136–42.

81. See al-Qarāfī, *al-Furūq*, 1: 161–2.
82. Weiss, *The Search for God's Law*, 2. He refers to the *ḥukm taklīfī* as "normative."
83. I will return to this point in more detail in Chapters 3 and 4.
84. I will discuss this in more detail in Chapter 4.
85. Al-Qarāfī, *al-Furūq*, 2: 223.
86. Al-Bāqillānī, *al-Taqrīb wa al-irshād (al-ṣaghīr)*, 3 vols., ed. ʿA. Abū Zayd (Beirut: Mu'assasat al-Risālah, 1418/1998), 1: 274: "*iʿlamū anna al-maṭlūb min al-naẓar fī uṣūl al-fiqh wa adillatih innamā huwa ḥukm fiʿl al-mukallaf al-sharʿī.*" I shall generally use the somewhat cumbersome "juristic law" for *sharīʿah* to make room for what I shall present in Chapter 3 as non-juristic or non-*sharʿī* law, namely *siyāsah*, which I also count as "Islamic law."
87. See al-Āmidī, *al-Iḥkām fī uṣūl al-aḥkām*, 4 vols. (Riyadh: Dār al-Ṣumayʿī li al-Nashr wa al-Tawzīʿ, 1424/2003), 1: 21: "*mabāḥith al-uṣūlīyīn fī ʿilm al-uṣūl lā takhruj ʿan aḥwāl al-adillah al-muwaṣṣilah ilā al-aḥkām al-sharʿīyah al-mabḥūth ʿanhā fihi wa aqsāmihā wa ikhtilāf marātibihā wa kayfīyat istithmār al-aḥkām al-sharʿīyah ʿanhā.*"
88. See Weiss, *The Search for God's Law*, 1. "Divine categorization" was Weiss's translation of "*ḥukm sharʿī*." He continues: "The medieval Muslims were in fact more concerned with the explication of the concept of a divine categorization of an act than with the explication of the concept of Sharīʿa as such." See *The Search for God's Law*, 1–2. In a technical sense, I agree with Weiss. I shall argue, however, that this does not mean they were necessarily unaware of the broader implications of the nature of the *ḥukm sharʿī* for Islamic law as a whole.
89. See Chapter 1, however, where this is modified to accommodate rules based on *siyāsah* or "discretion."
90. For more on this point, see my *Islamic Law and the State*, 113–41. I will treat the details and nuances of this matter in Chapter 3.
91. Muḥammad b. Idrīs al-Shāfiʿī, *al-Risālah*, ed. A. M. Shākir (Cairo: al-Maktabah al-Ilmīyah, n.d.), 20. See also 477.
92. As A. El Shamsy notes in his depiction of early Shāfiʿī scholars following the lead of their eponym: "Although the determination of the *qiblah* represents an empirical matter while legal theory involves interpretive judgments, at least in the early centuries Shāfiʿī jurists do not seem to have drawn any distinction between the two." See El Shamsy, "Rethinking *Taqlīd* in the Early Shāfiʿī School," *Journal of the American Oriental Society*, *128*:1 (2008): 1–24 at 14–15.
93. See, e.g., al-Shāfiʿī, *al-Risālah*, 487–503.
94. Al-Zarkarshī, *al-Baḥr al-muḥīṭ*, 1: 165.
95. See A. El Shamsy "Bridging the Gap: Two Early Texts of Islamic Legal Theory," *Journal of the American Oriental Society*, *137*:3 (2017): 505–36. By introducing the works of Ibn Surayj (d. 306/918) and al-Khaffāf (fl. first half of the fourth/tenth century), El Shamsy has basically cut in half the gap traditionally presumed to exist between al-Shāfiʿī and the next works on *uṣūl al-fiqh*.

96. *Uṣūl al-jaṣṣāṣ* (a.k.a. *al-Fuṣūl fī al-uṣūl*), 2 vols., ed. M. M. Tāmir (Beirut: Dār al-Kutub al-'Ilmīyah1420/2000), 2: 97. But see the whole discussion at 2: 93–8. See also, however, D. Stewart, "Muḥammad b. Dā'ūd al-Ẓāhirī's Manual of Jurisprudence, *Al-Wuṣūl Ilā Ma'rifat al-Uṣūl*," in B. Weiss, ed., *Studies in Islamic Legal Theory* (Leiden: E.J. Brill, 2002), 99–158 at 106–07, where he discusses the early effort of al-Jāḥiẓ who died in 255/869.
97. Al-Jaṣṣāṣ, *Uṣūl*, 2: 249.
98. Al-Jaṣṣāṣ, *Uṣūl*, 2: 208.
99. See, e.g., Abū Zayd al-Dabūsī, *Taqwīm al-adillah*, ed. K. M. al-Mays (Beirut:Dār al-Kutub al-'Ilmīyah, 1421/2001); Fakhr al-Islām 'Alī b. Muḥammad al-Bazdawī, *Uṣūl al-bazdawī*, ed. S. Bakdāsh (Beirut: Sharikat Dār al-Bashā'ir al-Islāmīyah, 1436/2014); Abū Bakr Muḥammad b. Aḥmad b. Abī Sahl al-Sarakhsī, *Uṣūl al-sarakhsī*, 2 vols., ed. R. al-'Ajam (Beirut:Dār al-Ma'rifah,1418/1997). There is, I should note, at least one place in al-Sarakhsī's work that appears to reflect a distinction between the *shar'ī* and non-*shar'ī*, where he discusses the Companions' reactions to the Prophet's proposed war strategy and to his advice on pollinating trees. See *Uṣūl al-sarakhsī*, 2: 92–3. Still, this does not appear to be a central concern of his or one grounded in any interest in a theoretical definition of law. See also 2:267–303.
100. See Abū al-Ḥusayn al-Baṣrī, *al-Mu'tamad fī uṣūl al-fiqh*, 2 vols., ed. K. al-Mays (Beirut: Dār al-Kutub al-'Ilmīyah, 1403/1983), 1: 4–5. See also the discussion below in the section, "The Emergence of the Theoretical Foundations of a Bounded *Sharī'ah*," where I note that the *shar'ī* and non-*shar'ī*/*'aqlī* are not as distinct for al-Baṣrī as they are for Sunnī theorists writing according to the *ṭarīqat al-mutakallimīn*.
101. "Tradition-oriented" is a phrase I take from B. Weiss. See his *The Search for God's Law*, 19, 20.
102. See, e.g., 'Abd al-Wahhāb Khallāf, *'Ilm uṣul al-fiqh*, 14th ed. (Beirut: Dār al-Qalam, 1361/1942), 18; Muḥammad Abū Zahra, *Uṣūl al-fiqh* (Cairo:Dār al-Fikr al-'Arabī, n.d.), 15–20. See also my discussion of Professor Baber Johansen's view on the law/fact divide in Chapter 4, note 191.
103. Makdisi, *Rise of Humanism*, 15. Emphasis original.
104. Makdisi, *Rise of Humanism*, 13.
105. Makdisi, *Rise of Humanism*, 11.
106. Makdisi, *The Rise of Humanism*, 13–14.
107. Zysow, *Economy of Certainty*, 2. See also Weiss, *The Search for God's Law*, 19 for a similar perspective.
108. Weiss, *The Search for God's Law*, 19. Emphasis mine.
109. This would explain the phenomenon of Mālikīs or Ḥanafīs writing commentaries on works on *uṣūl al-fiqh* written by Shāfi'īs and vice-versa. Meanwhile, according to Weiss, and as we saw with al-Baṣrī, even some Ḥanafīs wrote in the speculative tradition, *'alā ṭarīqat mutakallimīn*. See Weiss, *The Search for God's Law*, 19.
110. See below, in the section "Ibn al-Qayyim" in this chapter.
111. See the section "The Islamic Secular's Religion" in Chapter 1.
112. Again, however, as mentioned in the Introduction, I will defer on this point to those more learned in the Ḥanafī tradition.

113. Abū al-Ḥasan ʻAlī b. ʻUmar b. al-Qaṣṣār, *al-Muqaddimah fī uṣūl al-fiqh*, ed. M. al-Sulaymānī (Beirut: Dār al-Gharb al-Islāmī, 1417/1996), 20–31.
114. On the *ḥukm waḍʻī* as a species of the *ḥukm sharʻī*, see my *Islamic Law and the State*, 119–21.
115. Al-Bāqillānī, *al-Taqrīb*, 1: 171–2. The book is preceded by a lengthy introduction of some 170 pages. Al-Bāqillānī's work proper begins on p. 171.
116. Al-Bāqillānī, *al-Taqrīb*, 1: 172; see also 1:221–24.
117. Al-Ghazālī, *al-Mustaṣfā*, 1: 4.
118. Al-Ghazālī, *al-Mustaṣfā*, 1: 3.
119. Al-Ghazālī, *al-Mustaṣfā*, 1: 4.
120. Al-Ghazālī, *al-Mustaṣfā*, 1: 5.
121. Al-Ghazālī, *al-Mustaṣfā*, 1: 55. Al-Ghazālī uses only the word "*ḥukm*" as opposed to "*ḥukm sharʻī*." It is always clear, however, that the latter is his meaning. For this reason, I add "*sharʻī*" to some of my translations of his quotations for the sake of clarity.
122. Al-Ghazālī, *al-Mustaṣfā*, 1: 55.
123. Imām al-Ḥaramayn Abū al-Maʻālī˜ Abd al-Malik b. Abd Allāh b. Yūsuf al-Juwaynī, *al-Burhān fī uṣūl al-fiqh*, 2 vols., ed. ʻA. M al-Dīb (al-Manṣūrah: Dār al-Wafā', 1418/ 1997), 1: 78.
124. Al-Juwaynī, *al-Burhān*, 1: 79. Emphasis mine.
125. Al-Juwaynī, *al-Talkhīs fī uṣūl al-fiqh*, 3 vols., ed. ʻA. J. al-Niyābī and S. A. al-ʻAmrī (Beirut: Dār al-Bashā'ir al-Islāmīyah, 1417/1996), 1: 105–06. In *al-Burhān*, al-Juwaynī is assumed to have backed away from views he expressed in *al-Talkhīṣ*, *al-Burhān* reflecting his more mature thought. In this case, however, *al-Burhān* gives no more clarity on the matter.
126. See, e.g., al-Juwaynī's discussion in *al-Burhān*, 1: 82, where he distinguishes the judgments of reason from those of revelation when it comes to good and bad. See also his discussion under the caption, "On the meaning of juristic rulings (*fī al-aḥkām al-sharʻīyah*)," *al-Burhān*, 1: 213–14.
127. See al-Juwaynī, *al-Ghiyāthī, ghiyāth al-umam fī iltiyāth al-ẓulam*, 2nd ed., ed. ʻA. al-Dīb (Cairo: Maṭbaʻat Nahḍat Miṣr, 1401/1981), 430. At p. 431 al-Juwaynī notes that some Shāfiʻīs disagreed with this and allowed that there might be situations regarding which there is no ruling. Al-Juwaynī flatly rejects this claim. Again, however, this could simply mean that for him everything falls under one of the Five Juristic Statuses, not that the latter exhaust all legitimate metrics of judgment. Felicitas Opwis suggests that al-Juwaynī expressed the view that the law was all-encompassing in *al-Burhan*, 2: 805 and 116, but I have not been able to confirm this view based on this reference. See her Maṣlaḥa *and the Purpose of the Law: Islamic Discourse on Legal Change from the 4th/10th to 8th/14th Century* (Leiden: E. J. Brill, 2010), 43 and note 122.
128. Abū Yaʻlā Muḥammad b. al-Ḥusayn al-Farrā', *al-ʻUddah fī uṣūl al-fiqh*, 2 vols., ed. M.ʻA. A. ʻAṭā (Beirut: Dār al-Kutub al-ʻIlmīyah, 1423/2002), 1: 17–18.
129. Abū Yaʻlā, *al-ʻUddah*, 1: 18.

130. Abū Ya'lā, *al-'Uddah*, 1: 26–32. This should not be understood as preempting the possibility of revelation and reason operating side by side. Indeed, Abū Ya'lā's student Ibn 'Aqīl notes explicitly that it is not possible to know legal rulings without engaging in rational contemplation of the sources. See Abū al-Wafā' 'Alī Ibn 'Aqīl, *al-Wāḍiḥ fī uṣūl al-fiqh*, 5 vols., ed. G. Makdisi (Beirut: al-Sharikah al-Muttaḥidah li al-Tawzī', in a commission by Franz Steiner, Stuttgart, 1417/1996), 1: 46. In a similar vein, the Central Asian Ḥanafī 'Alā' al-Dīn al-Samarqandī observed: "Everything that reason and revelation calls us to, such as faith in God and the basics of worship, is good, according to reason and the *shar'*, unlike what our natural inclinations (*ṭab'*) may call us to" (*kullu mā yad'ū ilayhi al-'aql wa al-shar' dūna al-ṭab' fa huwa ḥasan^{un} 'aql^{an} wa shar'^{an} ka al-īmān bi 'llāh ta'ālā wa aṣl al-'ibādāt*). See 'Alā' al-Dīn Shams al-Naẓar Abū Bakr Muḥammad b. Aḥmad al-Samarqandī, *Mizān al-uṣūl fī natā'ij al-'uqūl*, 2nd ed., ed. M. Z. 'Abd al-Barr (Cairo: Maktabat al-Turāth, 1418/1997), 46. The problem, in other words, is with automatically conflating "natural inclinations" (*ṭab'*) with reason (*'aql*) and/or the *shar'*.
131. Ibn 'Aqīl, *al-Wāḍiḥ*, 1: 1–2; 1: 47.
132. Ibn 'Aqīl, *al-Wāḍiḥ*, 1: 2.
133. Ibn 'Aqīl, *al-Wāḍiḥ*, 1: 44–6.
134. Al-Samarqandī, *Mīzān al-uṣūl*, 24–66.
135. Abū al-Thanā' Maḥmūd b. Zayd al-Lāmishī, *Kitāb fī Uṣūl al-Fiqh*, ed. 'A. Turkī (Beirut: Dār al-Gharb al-Islāmī, 1995), 53–66.
136. On this relationship, see A. Zysow, "Mu'tazilism and Māturīdism in Ḥanafī Legal Theory," in B. Weiss, ed. *Studies in Islamic Legal Theory* (Leiden: E. J. Brill, 2002), 235–65.
137. Abụ al-Ḥusayn al-Baṣrī, *al-Mu'tamad*, 2: 403–04.
138. Al-Zarkashī, *al-Baḥr al-muḥīṭ*, 1: 142. Emphasis mine.
139. Ibn Khaldūn, *al-Muqaddimah*, p. 288.
140. Ibn Khalikān, *Wafāyāt al-a'yān wa anbā' abnā' al-zamān*, 8 vols., ed. I. 'Abbās (Beirut: Dār al-Ma'rifah, n.d.), 4: 249.
141. Ḥājjī Khalīfah, *Kashf al-ẓunūn 'an asāmī al-kutub wa al-funūn*, 3 vols. (Beirut: Dār al-Kutub al-'Ilmīyah, 1413/1992), 2: 1615–16.
142. Khalīfah, *Kashf*, 2: 1673.
143. Khalīfah, *Kashf*, 1: 242.
144. Khalīfah, *Kashf*, 2: 1732. Hajjī Khalīfah also mentions that al-Rāzī took from al-Baṣrī's work.
145. We know, e.g., that the Sicilian Mālikī, al-Māzarī (d. 536/1142), wrote a commentary on al-Juwaynī's *al-Burhān*, entitled *Īḍāḥ al-maḥṣūl min burhān al-uṣūl*, as did the Egyptian al-Muẓaffar b. 'Abd Allāh al-Muqtaraf (d. 612/1215). And there is no entry in *Kashf al-ẓunūn* on 'Abd al-Jabbār's *al-'Umad*. Similarly, we know that al-Qarāfī wrote commentaries on *al-Maḥṣūl*, none of which appear on Ḥajjī Khalīfah's list; nor does the abridgment of Amīn al-Dīn al-Tabrīzī (d. 621/1224) cited by the modern jurist Ibn 'Āshūr. See his *al-Tawḍīḥ wa al-taṣḥīḥ li mushkilāt kitāb al-tanqīḥ*, 2 vols. (Tunis: Maṭba'at Nahḍah Nahj al-Jazīrah, 1341/1923), 1: 63.

146. A. Shihadeh, *The Teleological Ethics of Fakhr al-Dīn al-Rāzī* (Leiden: E. J. Brill, 2006).
147. S. Schmidtke, "The Muʿtazilite Movement (III)," *The Oxford Handbook of Islamic Theology*, ed. S. Schmidtke (New York: Oxford University Press, 2016), 174.
148. Al-Rāzī, *al-Maḥṣūl fī ʿilm uṣūl al-fiqh*, 6 vols., ed. Ṭ. J. al-ʿAlwānī (Beirut: Muʾassasat al-Risālah, 1418/1997), 1: 78.
149. Al-Rāzī, *al-Maḥṣūl*, 1: 79.
150. Al-Rāzī, *al-Maḥṣūl*, 1: 96: *wa qawlunā sharʿ*[an] *ishārah ilā mā nadhhab ilayhi min anna hādhihi al-aḥkām lā tathbut illā bi al-sharʿ*.
151. Al-Rāzī, *al-Maḥṣūl*, 1: 89.
152. Al-Āmidī, *al-Iḥkām*, 1: 131–75.
153. Al-Āmidī, *al-Iḥkām*, 1: 19–20.
154. Al-Āmidī, *al-Iḥkām*, 1: 131–2. Having raised certain technical objections early on, al-Āmidī later states his preferred definition of the *ḥukm sharʿī*: "the divine address that affords some legal benefit" (*khiṭāb al-shāriʿ al-mufīd fāʾidat*[an] *sharʿīyah*). *Al-Iḥkām*, 1: 132. In explaining this, however, he ends up agreeing with al-Rāzī in substance. *Al-Iḥkām*, 1: 131–75.
155. Al-Āmidī, *al-Iḥkām*, 1: 20: "Our statement *'sharʿīyah'* stands in contradistinction to that which is not *sharʿī*, such as matters that are known by reason or by the senses" (*wa qawlunā al-sharʿīyah iḥtirāz ʿammā laysa bi sharʿī ka al-umūr al-ʿaqlīyah wa al-ḥissīyah*).
156. Al-Āmidī, *al-Iḥkām*, 1: 16.
157. D. Sourdel, *EI2*, 1:4: 34. Sourdel gives the title of al-Āmidī's work as *Iḥkām al-ḥukkām fī uṣūl al-aḥkām*.
158. See ʿAlwānī's Introduction to his edition of *al-Maḥṣūl*, 1: 48.
159. Khalīfah, *Kashf*, 1:17.
160. Al-Ghazālī, *al-Mustaṣfā*, 1: 223. Nor does al-Ghazālī draw these constituents into a unified composite in his earlier work on *uṣūl al-fiqh*, *al-Mankhūl*.
161. See, e.g., al-Sarakhsī, *Uṣūl*, 2: 305–10; al-Bazdawī, *Uṣūl*, 706–91.
162. See al-Rāzī, *al-Maḥṣūl*, 1: 420. Of course, this corresponds with al-Rāzī's order of treatment in the text.
163. Al-Rāzī, *al-Maḥṣūl*, 1: 109.
164. This includes non-juristic law, as we will see in Chapter 3.
165. These include *Tanqīḥ al-fuṣūl*, *Sharḥ tanqīḥ al-fuṣūl*, and *Nafāʾis al-uṣūl fī sharḥ al-maḥṣūl*. In *al-Dhakhīrah*, which is an earlier work on Mālikī *fiqh* to which he attached *Tanqīḥ al-fuṣūl* as an introduction, al-Qarāfī notes that he based the latter on four sources: al-Qāḍī ʿAbd al-Wahhāb's *al-Ifādah* on *uṣūl al-fiqh*; Abū al-Walīd al-Bājī's "*Jumlat al-ishārah*" (which presumably refers either to *al-Ishārah fī maʿrifat al-uṣūl wa al-wijāzah fī maʿnā al-dalīl* or *al-Ishārah fī uṣūl al-fiqh*); Ibn al-Qaṣṣār's *al-Muqaddimah fī uṣūl al-fiqh*; and al-Rāzī's *al-Maḥṣūl*. See al-Qarāfī, *al-Dhakhīrah*, 1: 55. In *Sharḥ tanqīḥ al-fuṣūl*, p. 32, however, al-Qarāfī gives the title of his introduction to *al-Dhakhīrah* as "*Kitāb tanqīḥ al-fuṣūl fī ikhtiṣār al-maḥṣūl.*" He also cites "*Sharḥ al-Maḥṣūl*," (i.e., *Nafāʾis al-uṣūl*), in *Sharḥ tanqīḥ al-fuṣūl*, p. 44. This would suggest that al-Qarāfī wrote *Tanqīḥ al-fuṣūl*, and then *Nafāʾis al-uṣūl fī sharḥ al-maḥṣūl*, followed by *Sharḥ tanqīḥ al-uṣūl*. Incidentally, al-Bājī (at least in his *Iḥkām*

al-fuṣūl fī aḥkām al-uṣūl) may be added to the list of pre-Rāzian works that do not itemize and gather the constituents of the *ḥukm sharʿī* into a single composite.

166. Al-Qarāfī, *Sharḥ tanqīḥ*, 46; Al-Qarāfī, *Nafāʾis*, 1: 28–9. Here again we see the simultaneous recognition of *dīn* as religion-as-concrete-doctrine-and-practice and religion-as-psychodynamic-orientation.
167. Al-Qarāfī, *Nafāʾis*, 1: 33.
168. Al-Qarāfī, *Nafāʾis*, 1: 33. This is reminiscent of the oft-stated position of Ibn Taymīyah on the distinction between God's creative will (*irādah kawnīyah*) and God's normative will (*irādah sharʿīyah*).
169. For more on all of this, see my *Islam and the Problem of Black Suffering*, 86–7.
170. Al-Qarāfī, *Sharḥ tanqīḥ*, 93. Emphasis mine.
171. See, e.g., Ibn al-Ḥajib, *Muntahā al-wuṣūl wa al-amal ilā ʾilmay al-uṣūl wa al-jadal* (Beirut: Dār al-Kutub al-ʿIlmīyah, 1405/1985), 32.
172. See Ibn al-Ḥājib, *Muntahā al-wuṣūl*, 45.
173. Aron Zysow notes that some seventy commentaries were written on Ibn al-Ḥājib's work. See Zysow, *The Economy of Certainty*, 200–01.
174. See my *Islamic Law and the State*, 114–23, for a detailed treatment of this doctrine.
175. For more on this point, see my *Islamic Law and the State*, 124–9. See also the section "Islamic Governance Between Discretion and Juristic Law" in Chapter 4.
176. See, e.g., al-Qarāfī, *Sharḥ tanqīḥ*, 45, 373; *Nafāʾis al-uṣūl fī sharḥ al-maḥṣūl*, 1: 177; *Tamyīz*, 196.
177. Al-Qarāfī, *Sharḥ tanqīḥ*, 332 and 422, for a similar view. I will use "Community" with a capital "C" to refer to the *ummah* and "community" with a lower case "c" to refer to smaller or more local collectives of Muslims.
178. This is separate, of course, from the question of whether one might be bound to follow the Imām's instruction to implement such a policy as a matter of *siyāsah*. For more on this point, see the section "*Siyāsah*" in Chapter 3.
179. For his most detailed statement in this regard, see al-Qarāfī, *al-Furūq*, 4 vols. (Beirut: ʿĀlam al-Kitāb, n.d.), 1: 28–9. See also my *Islamic Law and the State*, 124–7.
180. Al-Qarāfī, *al-Furūq*, 1: 128; al-Qarāfī, *Sharḥ tanqīḥ*, 434. Meanwhile, in *al-Dhakhīrah*, 10: 86, which I take to be an earlier work, he cites only seventeen such sources.
181. Al-Qarāfī, *al-Furūq*, 1: 128.
182. Ṣadr al-Sharīʿah al-Bukhārī, *al-Tawḍīḥ fī ḥall ghawāmiḍ al-tanqīḥ*, in Saʿd al-Dīn al-Taftazānī, *Sharḥ al-talwīḥ ʿalā al-tawḍīḥ*, 2 vols. (Cairo: Muḥammad ʿAlī Ṣubayḥ wa Awlāduh, n.d.), 1: 11 (bottom segment).
183. See, Khalīfah, *Kashf*, 1: 496–9. The *Talwīḥ* and the *Tawḍīḥ* are commonly published together as commentary and super-commentary, under the title *Sharḥ al-talwīḥ ʿalā al-tawḍīḥ*.
184. Khalīfah, *Kashf*, 1: 496.
185. In discussing the relation between general (*ʿāmm*) and specific (*khāṣṣ*) expressions, e.g., al-Taftazānī states that general statements are definitive in what they indicate, "according to '*us*,' in contradistinction to al-Shāfiʿī." See al-Taftazānī, *al-Talwīḥ*, 1: 74–5. Emphasis mine.

186. See al-Taftazānī, *al-Talwīḥ*, 1: 19–22.
187. Ṣadr al-Sharīʿah, *al-Tawḍīḥ*, 1: 16–26.
188. Ṣadr al-Sharīʿah also refers to Ibn al-Ḥājib as "*al-imām al-mudaqqiq*." But this is a more general use of the honorific. When he uses it to refer to al-Rāzī, he clearly uses the definite article as "*alif-lam al-ʿahd*," as in the common reference to the Qur'ān simply as "*al-Kitāb*." In other words, when applied to al-Rāzī, the definite article is effectively italicized to make him "*the* Imām." See Ṣadr al-Sharīʿah, *al-Tawḍīḥ*, 1: 11.
189. Ṣadr al-Sharīʿah, *al-Tawḍīḥ*, 1: 26; Ibn al-Ḥājib, *Muntahā al-wusūl*, 45: "the meaning of [a proof] being *sharʿī* is that it is known on the basis of the *sharʿ*" (*maʿnā kawnihi sharʿīy*^{an} *anna ṭarīqat maʿrifatihi al-sharʿ*).
190. Ṣadr al-Sharīʿah, *al-Tawḍīḥ*, 1: 19.
191. Ṣadr al-Sharīʿah, *al-Tawḍīḥ*, 1: 26–7. Ṣadr al-Sharīʿah builds on a mild mischaracterization of the Ashʿarī position here, for which al-Taftazānī kindly takes him to task. See al-Taftazānī, *al-Talwīḥ*, 1: 27.
192. Aḥmad b. ʿAlī b. Taghlib Ibn al-Saʿātī, *Nihāyat al-wuṣūl ilā ʿilm al-uṣūl*, ed. S. al-Sulamī (Mecca: Maʿhad al-Buḥūth al-ʿIlmīyah wa Iḥyāʾ al-Turāth al-Islāmī, 1418/1998), 3–5.
193. Ibn Khaldūn, *al-Muqaddimah*, 288.
194. Ibn al-Ḥājib, *Muntahā al-wuṣūl*, 9.
195. Ibn al-Saʿātī, *Nihāyat*, 141–202.
196. Weiss, *The Search for God's Law*, 22.
197. Khalīfah, *Kashf*, 1:17.
198. See, e.g., Najm al-Dīn al-Ṭūfī, *Sharḥ mukhtaṣar al-rawḍah*, 3 vols., ed. A. al-Turkī (Damascus: Muʾassasat al-Risālah, 1435/2014), 1: 247, 1:433ff.; al-Zarkashī, *Baḥr*, 1: 175ff., 1: 305ff.; al-Shāṭibī, *al-Muwāfaqāt*, 1:109ff.
199. Abū al-Barakāt ʿAbd Allāh b. Aḥmad al-Nasafī, *al-Manār*, ed. I. Qabalāt (Beirut: Dār al-Kutub al-ʿIlmīyah, 1437/2016).
200. See al-Karāmastī, *Zubdat al-wuṣūl ilā ʿumdat al-uṣūl*, ed. ʿA. Ḥajqalī (Beirut: Dār Ṣādir, 1428/2008), 76–87. In fact, only the legal cause (*sabab*) and prerequisite (*sharṭ*) are mentioned by name here, though his treatment of legal competence (*ahlīyah*) at times echoes the definition of the legal impediment (*mānīʿ*).
201. Muḥammad Amīn Ibn ʿĀbidīn, *Radd al-muḥtār ʿalā al-durr al-mukhtār sharḥ tanwīr al-abṣār*, 12 vols., ed. A. ʿAbd al-Mawjūd and A. Muʿawwaḍ (Beirut: Dār al-Kutub al-ʿIlmīyah, 1415/1994), 1: 118.
202. Abū Zahra, *Uṣul al-fiqh*, 4; Khallāf, *ʿIlm uṣūl al-fiqh*, 11. In place of "from," Khallāf has "acquired from their concrete sources" (*al-muktasabah min adillatihā al-tafṣīlīyah*).
203. See Abū Zahrah, *Uṣūl al-fiqh*, 23: "The divine address that attaches to acts of legally responsible persons by imposing a duty or by granting a choice or by positing (a relationship between an act or occurrence and an obligation or prohibition)" (*al-khiṭāb al-mutaʿalliq bi afʿāl al-mukallafīn bi al-iqtiḍāʾ aw al-takhyīr aw al-waḍʿ*). See also Khallāf, *ʿIlm uṣūl al-fiqh*, 100, where he gives essentially the same definition, with no mention of *sharʿī* in it.
204. See ʿI. al-Sulamī, *Uṣūl a-fiqh alladhī lā yasaʿu al-faqīh jahlah* (Riyadh: Dār al-Tadmurīyah, 1429/2008), 11. Al-Sulamī does not restrict himself to the mode of the

speculative theoreticians but includes the perspective of the "*fuqahā*," i.e., Ḥanafīs, as part of the general discussion in this work.

205. Al-Sulamī, *Uṣul al-fiqh alladhī*, 12.
206. W. al-Zuḥaylī, *Uṣūl al-fiqh al-islāmī*, 2 vols. (Damascus: Dār al-Fikr, 1406/1986), 1: 19.
207. al-Zuḥaylī, *Uṣūl al-fiqh al-islāmī*, 1: 21. See also 'Abd al-Karīm Zaydān, *al-Wajīz fī uṣūl al-fiqh* (Beirut: Mu'assasat al-Risālah, 1980), 9, for a substantively identical view.
208. D. Sourdel, *EI2*, I: 257. Interestingly, in the entry on *sharīʿah*, published in 1997, N. Calder notes: "Western studies on *fiḳh* [*fiqh*] are still dominated by the work of Joseph Schacht, who produced the articles *fiḳh* and *sharīʿah* for *EI1*, the former slightly edited for *EI2*." See *EI2*, IX: 323. In the entry on *fiḳh* in *EI2*, Schacht echoes a familiar theme: "All aspects of public and private life and business should be regulated by laws based on religion: the science of these laws is *fiḳh*." See D. Sourdel, *EI2*, II: 886.
209. See A. K. Reinhart, "Islamic Law as Islamic Ethics," *The Journal of Religious Ethics*, *11*:2 (1983): 186–203, esp., 192–6; E. Moosa, "Allegory of the Rule (*Ḥukm*): Law as Simulacrum in Islam?" *History of Religions*, *38*:1 (1998): 1–24, esp., 5–7; 21–4. On p. 5, Moosa does say of the *ḥukm*: "It represents the most powerful rhetorical and practical criterion that differentiates a religious existence from a nonreligious existence." But this does not engender any discussion of jurisdictional boundaries or the distinction between law and non-law *within* the domain of religion. Moreover, it clearly implies that non-*sharʿī* is by definition non-religious. Similarly, Reinhart, drawing partly on Hodgson, notes a distinction between "Islam as a religious system," which he identifies with *fiqh*, *sharʿ* and *sharīʿah*, and "Islam as the whole" (p.186), but this distinction is not further theorized.
210. Fadel does speak of the jurisdictional boundaries separating government officials, e.g., judges and official translators from property assessors and so on, but none of this is based on any law/non-law distinction, i.e., the idea that certain matters lie *outside* the jurisdiction of judges and jurists because they are *non-legal*. See M. Fadel, trans., *The Criterion for Distinguishing Legal Opinions from Judicial Rulings and the Administrative Acts of Judges and Rulers: al-Ihkam fi Tamyiz al-Fatawa 'An al-Ahkam wa Tasarrufat al-Qadi wa'l-Imam* (New Haven: Yale University Press, 2017), 44–6.
211. See W. B. Hallaq, "Review of Islamic Law and the State: The Constitutional Jurisprudence of Shihāb al-Dīn al-Qarāfī," *Islamic Law and Society*, *5*:1 (1998): 127–30; A. Sabra, "Review of Islamic Law and the State: The Constitutional Jurisprudence of Shihāb al-Dīn al-Qarāfī," *Journal of Law and Religion*, *15*:1/2 (2000): 413–16.
212. Al-Qarāfī, *al-Furūq*, 2: 221. We see a related understanding of this complementarity in the work of the Mālikī jurist and social commentator Ibn al-Ḥājj (d. 737/1336) who notes that, assuming that one intends to please God, there is no difference between prayer and the various crafts and professions (*ṣanāʾi*) in terms of their constituting acts of worship (*ʿibādah*). In fact, according to Ibn al-Ḥājj, after fulfilling the basic religious observances (*al-mafrūḍāt*), such 'secular worship' may even be superior, "because its benefit passes to others, and that is weightier in the scales

and greater in the sight of God." See Ibn al-Ḥājj, *al-Madkhal*, 4 vols. (Cairo: Dār al-Fikr, n.d.), 4: 2–3.

213. See, e.g., Abū Muḥammad ʿAlī b. Aḥmad b. Saʿīd Ibn Ḥazm, *al-Iḥkām fī uṣūl al-aḥkām*, 8 vols. (Beirut: Manshūrāt Dār al-Āfāq al-Jadīdah, 1403/1983), 4: 2–16, esp. 15–16.
214. A. K. Reinhart, *Before Revelation: The Boundaries of Muslim Moral Thought* (New York: State University of New York Press, 1995), 16.
215. See, e.g., Ibn Ḥazm, *Marātib al-ʿulūm* in *Rasāʾil ibn ḥazm al-andalūsī*, 4 vols., ed. I. ʿAbbās (Beirut: al-Muʾassasah al-ʿArabīyah li al-Dirāsah wa al-Nashr, 1983), 4:61-90, esp. 75-6, 82-3, 87, 90.
216. I should also distinguish the Islamic Secular from what Sohaira Siddiqui describes as the "legal minimalism" of al-Juwaynī. See Siddiqui, *Law and Politics under the Abbasids: An Intellectual Portrait of al-Juwayni* (Cambridge: Cambridge University Press, 2019), 264–70.
217. For a more detailed discussion of *siyāsah*, see Chapter 3.
218. See, e.g., Shams al-Dīn Abū ʿAbd Allāh Muḥammad b. Abī Bakr, Ibn Qayyim al-Jawzīyah, *Iʿlām al-muwaqqiʿīn ʿan rabb al-ʿālamīn*, 4 vols., ed. M. M. ʿAbd al-Ḥamīd (Mecca: Dār al-Bāz, n.d.), 1: 332.
219. Ibn al-Qayyim, *Iʿlām*, 1: 324.
220. Ibn al-Qayyim, *Iʿlām*, 1: 324–5.
221. Ibn al-Qayyim, *al-Ṭuruq al-ḥukmīyah fī al-siyāsah al-sharʿīyah*, ed. M. J. Ghāzī (Cairo: Maṭbaʿat al-Madanī, n.d.), 20. As we will see in Chapter 3, this is different from the *siyāsah* described by Abū Yaʿlā and al-Māwardī in their respective *al-Aḥkām al-sulṭānīyah* works.
222. Ibn al-Qayyim, *al-Ṭuruq al-ḥukmīyah*, 16–19; *Iʿlām*, 4:373.
223. Ibn al-Qayyim, *al-Ṭuruq al-ḥukmīyah*, 19.
224. Ibn al-Qayyim, *al-Ṭuruq al-ḥukmīyah*, 17–18.
225. K. Masud, "The Doctrine of *Siyāsa* in Islamic Law," *Recht van de Islam, 18* (2001): 1–29 at 12.
226. Masud, "The Doctrine of Siyāsa," 13.
227. See, e.g., Ibn al-Qayyim, *Iʿlām*, 1: 39, 1: 44.
228. Ibn al-Qayyim, *Iʿlām*, 1: 87–8.
229. See Ibn al-Qayyim, *al-Ṭuruq al-ḥukmīyah*, 5, where he notes, "There are two types of *fiqh*, both indispensable to the judge: (1) *fiqh* regarding the general rulings governing cases; (2) *fiqh* regarding quotidian reality and the circumstances of the people" (*fiqh fī nafs al-wāqiʿ wa aḥwāl al-nās*).
230. See, e.g., Ibn Taymīyah, *Majmūʿat al-fatāwā*, 4th ed., 37 vols. (in 20 books), ed. ʿA. al-Jazzār and A. al-Bāz (Al-Manṣūrah: Dār al-Wafāʾ li al-Ṭibāʿah wa al-Nashr wa al-Tawzīʿ, 1432/2011), 19: 165–8. All my references are to volume number, not book number. See also his *Darʾ taʿāruḍ al-ʿaql wa al-naql*, 11 vols., ed. M. R. Sālim (Cairo: Dār al-Kutub, 1391/1971), 1: 198.
231. Ibn Taymīyah, *Majmūʿat al-fatāwā*, 19: 167.
232. Ibn Taymīyah, *Majmūʿat al-fatāwā*, 19: 165–6. At 19: 165, he notes that early scholars explicitly included theology under the designation of *sharīʿah*, as in the theological

work by the Ḥanbalī theologian Ibn Baṭtah (d. 387/997), *al-Ibānah 'an sharī'at al-firqat al-nājiyah wa mujānabat al-firaq al-madhmūmah*, 4 vols., ed. S. 'Imrān (Cairo: Dār al-Ḥadīth, 1427/2006).

233. Ibn Taymīyah, *Majmū'at al-fatāwā*, 19: 125.
234. See Ibn Taymīyah, *Majmū'at al-fatāwā*, 19: 123–6. See also the important study by Jon Hoover, *Ibn Taymiyya's Theodicy of Perpetual Optimism* (Leiden: E. J. Brill, 2007), 29–32. I see now that Ibn Taymīyah would have rejected or at least significantly qualified what I have written elsewhere: "While scripture may be the object of the theologian's thinking, scripture does not prescribe any particular method or modality for that thinking. The Qur'ān is not a book of logic, nor a manual on formal reasoning or systematic thinking. To be sure, the Qur'ān points to several prerequisites for receiving and benefitting from its guidance, e.g., humility, God-consciousness, and a willingness to use one's mind. In several places it even models rational arguments against the rejecters of truth. But while the Qur'ān urges its audience to 'think' (*tafakkur*), 'ponder' (*tadabbur*), and 'reason' ('*aql*), it never tells them *how* to do any of this." See my *On the Boundaries of Theological Tolerance in Islam*, 13.
235. Hoover, *Ibn Taymiyya's Theodicy*, 32. See also pp. 39–44 on the relationship between *'aql* and *fiṭrah*, i.e., primordial disposition, or what Hoover renders "the natural constitution."
236. Hoover (if I understand him correctly) registers a different perspective. According to him, "To put the matter another way, revelation embodies true rationality." See Hoover, *Ibn Taymiyya's Theodicy*, 31. Without challenging this basic claim, I see Ibn Taymīyah as laying more emphasis on the primordial human faculty and its congruence, properly groomed, with revelation than on revelation as the actual source or embodiment of this primordial faculty. We do not learn that things fall from up to down or that water consists of hydrogen and oxygen from scripture. Moreover, reason might include or guide us to many things that are not embodied in or confirmed by revelation, "*lā nafy*^{an} *wa lā ithbāt*^{an}," such as medicine, astronomy, or the social sciences.
237. See, e.g., Ibn Taymīyah, *Dar'*, 1: 198–200; and *Majmū at al-fatāwā*, 19: 230, 19: 232.
238. Ibn Taymīyah, *Majmū'at al-fatāwā*, 19: 123, 124–6. See also Ibn Taymīyah, *Dar'*, 1: 198, where he insists again that the opposite of the *shar'ī* is not the *'aqlī* but the *bid'ī*, or that which is related to "unsanctioned innovation." I should note that the use of "legally" here should not be taken in its restricted sense, as Ibn Taymīyah explicitly states that *sharī'ah* is broader than *fiqh*. Perhaps "scripturally embedded" or "religiously embedded" would be closer to the mark. But given that "*shar'ī*" does imply law, which tends to be thought of in the West as distinct from scripture and religion, these terms would also fall short.
239. Ibn Taymīyah, *Majmū'at al-fatāwā*, 19: 123.
240. This is clear from several of Ibn Taymīyah's discussions in this regard. See, e.g., *Majmū'at al-fatāwā*, 19: 123–6; and 19: 165–8. See also C. S. El-Tobgui, "Ibn Taymiyyya on the Incoherence of the Theologians' Universal Law: Reframing the Debate Between Reason and Revelation in Medieval Islam," *Journal of Arabic and Islamic Studies, 18* (2018): 63–85. Though El-Tobgui does not make much of it, I see

a critical distinction in Ibn Taymīyah's thought between "reason" as the primordial human faculty and "systems of reason" built up from this faculty.

241. See, e.g., *Dar'*, 1: 89–91, esp. 89: "Do you mean by 'reason' here the primordial faculty within us or those forms of knowledge that we innovate through this faculty?" (*a ta'nī bi al-'aql hunā al-gharīzah allatī fīnā am al-'ulūm allatī istafadnāhā min tilka al-gharīzah*). See also Hoover, *Theodicy*, 32.

242. Ibn Taymīyah, *Majmū'at al-fatāwā*, 19: 166. Interestingly, among Ibn Taymīyah's main targets in this regard is al-Rāzī—the theologian, not the legal theorist!

243. Simply stated: All existents are possessed of accidents. All accidents require a producer. To avoid infinite regression, there must be at some remove an unproduced Producer, i.e., God. Thus, we read in the popular mnemonic poem still used in traditional circles today: "Regarding His existence, there is apodictic proof: the fact that all temporal existents require a producer" (*wujūduhu lahu dalīl*[un] *qāṭi' ḥājatu kulli muḥdath*[in] *li al-ṣāni'*). See Abū Muḥammad 'Abd al-Wāḥid Ibn 'Āshir, *al-Murshid al-mu'īn 'alā al-ḍarūrī min 'ulūm al-dīn* (Beirut: Dār al-Fikr, 1416/1996), 5. Obviously, by this argument, God, as the accident-free, Unproduced Producer, cannot mount the Throne, have a face, or indulge affective traits such as wrath or pleasure—all mentioned in scripture—since all of these imply accidents.

244. See, e.g., Ibn Taymīyah, "*al-Kalām 'alā al-fiṭrah*," in *Majmū'at al-rasā'il al-kubrā*, 2 vols. (Cairo: Muḥammad 'Alī Ṣubayḥ wa Awlāduh, n.d.), 2: 337.

245. See, e.g., my *Islam and the Problem of Black Suffering*, 138–9.

246. We should also recall from Chapter 1 his rejection of the notion that God wants nothing from us beyond what is concretely expressed in revelation, clearly imputing boundaries to the latter.

247. Ibn Taymīyah, *Majmū'at al-fatāwā*, 19: 124.

248. Ibn Taymīyah, *Majmū'at al-fatāwā*, 19: 125: "*mā kharaja min al-ulūm al-'aqlīyah 'an musammā al-shar'īyah wa huwa mā lam ya'mur bihi al-shāri' wa lam yadulla 'alayhi fa huwa yajrī majrā al-ṣinā'āt ka al-filāḥah wa al-bināyah wa al-nisājah*." See the discussion in this chapter, in the section "Beyond the *Ḥukm Shar'ī*," for the earlier reference in this regard.

249. Ibn Taymīyah, *Minhāj al-sunnah*, 5: 93. He adds, incidentally, "This being the case, a man being considered a believer or an unbeliever or as upright (*'adl*) or corrupt (*fāsiq*) is a *shar'ī*, not an *'aqlī*, matter."

250. See Ibn Taymīyah, *al-Ḥisbah fī al-islām* (Beirut: Dāral-Fikr al-'Ilmīyah, n.d.), 26.

251. See Najm al-Dīn al-Ṭūfī, *Sharḥ mukhtaṣar al-rawḍah*, 1: 212, 133–4, 135, 138–9; Abū al-Ḥasan 'Alā' al-Dīn Muḥammad b. 'Abbās al-Ba'lī, known as Ibn al-Laḥḥām, *al-Qawā'id wa al-fawā'id al-uṣūlīyah wa mā yata'allaq bihā min al-aḥkām al-far'īyah*, ed. A. Faḍīlī (Beirut: al-Maktabah al-'Aṣrīyah, 1418/1998), 17. Al-Ṭūfī's work is a commentary on his abridgement of a work on *uṣūl al-fiqh* by the staunchly traditionalist Ḥanbalī Ibn Qudāmah (d. 620/1223), in which the latter also sees *fiqh* as a bounded construct that is distinct from exegesis or grammar but does not isolate and discuss "*shar'ī*" as extensively as do the others. See Ibn Qudāmah, *Rawḍat al-nāẓir wa junnat al-munāẓir* (Beirut: Dār al-Kutub al-'Ilmīyah, 1401/1981), 4.

252. Ibn al-Laḥḥām, *Qawāʿid*, 17.
253. See, e.g., Ibn Taymīyah's statement in *al-Ṭuruq al-ḥukmīyah*, 145.
254. See Chapter 3 on the distinction I draw between *fiqh/sharīʿah* and Islamic law.
255. Ibn Taymīyah, *Majmūʿat al-fatāwā*, 19: 167.

Chapter 3

1. Ahmed continues: "Is *x* prescriptive/proscriptive discourse, such as creed and law, and therefore Islam, or is it non-prescriptive/proscriptive discourse such as love-poetry or wine-poetry and thus not-Islam? Is *x* devotional and therefore Islam, or is *x* not devotional and therefore not-Islam?" See Ahmed, *What Is Islam*? 196.
2. See the section "The Conceptual Landscape: Secular, Religious, Islamic" in Chapter 1.
3. I shall focus primarily on "*al-islāmī al-ʿalmānī*" because this was the choice of my Arab colleague, which I suspect related to his sense that *al-ʿalmānī al-islāmī* would be a bridge too far for most Arabic speakers. At any rate, I also discuss the latter option below.
4. https://nohoudh-center.com/articles/-الأس تاذ-صديقي-بَدَأَهُ-حوار-معًا-علم اني-إسل امي
زمَن-عبد-الحكيم-جاكسن%D9%90ش
5. I might note, incidentally, that Edward Lane's painstaking lexicon has no entry on *ʿalmānī* or *ʿilmānī*. As Lane died in 1876, this would suggest a surprisingly late entry of these words into common Arabic usage.
6. H. Wehr, *A Dictionary of Modern Written Arabic*, 3rd ed., ed. J. M. Cowan (Ithaca, NY: Spoken Language Services, Inc., 1976), 636.
7. Again, see the views of Rushain Abbasi and A. Mustafa in Chapter 1, note 58 where it is argued that *dunyā* was indeed the secular opposite of the religious.
8. The phrase "*al-islām khārij al-ḥukm al-sharʿī*" translates into "Islam outside the juristic ruling."
9. See A. Ahmad, *The Fatigue of the Shariʿa* (New York: Palgrave Macmillan, 2012); S. Siddiqui, *Law and Politics under the Abbasids*.
10. For a general description of *maẓālim*, see the discussion below.
11. J. Nielsen, "*Maẓālim* and *Dār al-ʿAdl* under the Early Mamluks," *The Muslim World* 66:2 (1976): 114–32 at 114.
12. Some will recognize here echoes of Charles Taylor's "secular 1." But I would argue that there was never an ideology or movement committed to this mode of the secular in pre-modern Islam. Even those erroneously dubbed atheists, e.g., Muḥammad b. Zakarīyah al-Rāzī, opposed revealed religion and its God, not religion per se, not belief in God, and not necessarily belief in a Hereafter per se.
13. See, e.g., D. S. Powers, *Law, Society and Culture in the Maghrib, 1300–1500* (Cambridge: Cambridge University Press, 2002), 1.
14. See, e.g., R. Peters, "Murder on the Nile: Homicide Trials in 19th Century Egyptian Sharīʿa Courts," *Die Welt des Islams, 30* (1990): 98–116 at 115, where he partially

challenges this view: "[I]t is clear that until the introduction of French law codes in 1883, the Sharīʿa was fully applied in homicide cases side by side with secular criminal justice." See also K. Stilt, *Islamic Law in Action: Authority, Discretion, and Everyday Experiences in Mamluk Egypt* (New York: Oxford University Press, 2011), 1–2, note 3, where she cites post-Schachtian efforts to challenge the dystopian narrative. In a separate vein, Frank Vogel largely averts the dystopian narrative, or at least one side of it, by dividing Islamic law into microcosmic (*fiqh*) and macrocosmic (*siyāsah*) dimensions. While the microcosmic dimension may have atrophied over the centuries, the same cannot be said, certainly not with the same meaning, about the macrocosmic dimension. See his *Islamic Law and Legal System: Studies of Saudi Arabia* (Leiden: E. J. Brill, 2000).

15. See H. A. R. Gibb, "Al-Mawardi's Theory of the Caliphate," in *Studies on the Civilization of Islam*, eds. S. J. Shaw and W. Polk (Boston: Beacon Press, 1962), 151–65 at 164 (Reprinted from *Islamic Culture*, IX [1937]: 291–302).
16. Imber, *Ebu's-suʿud: The Islamic Legal Tradition* (Stanford: Stanford University Press, 1997), 24.
17. Imber, *Ebu's-suʿud*, x.
18. Imber, *Ebu's-suʿud*, 37. Norman Calder echoes the same sentiment when he writes, "*Sharīʿa* . . . represents an ideal (unreal) governmental system." See Calder, "*Sharīʿa*," in EI2, IX: 323–26 at 325.
19. Hallaq, *Sharīʿa*, 500; Hallaq, *Impossible State*, 10, 74–5, 89–90, and passim. I will discuss Hallaq in detail in Chapter 4.
20. Hallaq, *Sharīʿa*, 502–04 ff.
21. Hallaq, "Juristic Authority," 254.
22. See, e.g., Stilt, *Islamic Law in Action*, 4.
23. See, e.g., Stilt, *Islamic Law in Action*, 25–6, though the "political" is still depicted as "secular." See also the view of R. Peters in note 14 of this chapter.
24. See, e.g., I. Lapidus, "The Separation of State and Religion in the Development of Early Islamic Society," *International Journal of Middle East Studies*, 6 (1965): 363–85 at 364. "Governments in Islamic lands were . . . secular regimes . . . fully differentiated political bodies without any intrinsic religious character." Jørgen Nielsen contrasts *sharīʿah* with secular law, as in the title of his book, *Secular Justice in an Islamic State: Maẓālim under the Baḥrī Mamlūks, 662/1264–789/1387* (Leiden: Nederlands Histoirisch-Archaeologisch Institut te Istanbul, 1985). And, building on an insight from Marshall Hodgson, Frank Vogel writes of the period 950–1500 CE, "[T]he ruler and the ʿulamā, siyāsah and the fiqh, understood themselves as opposed in a way somewhat similar to western experiences of opposition of church and state." See his *Islamic Law*, 201.
25. See, e.g., Schacht, *Introduction*, 54, where he contrasts "*sharīʿa*, the religious law of Islam" with *siyāsah* as the "secular law" of the sultans.
26. See Vogel, *Islamic Law*, 172.
27. Vogel, *Islamic Law*, 172.
28. K. Fahmy, *In Quest of Justice: Islamic Law and Forensic Medicine in Modern Egypt* (Oakland: University of California Press, 2018), 81–2.

29. Fahmy writes, "[A]s with Asad, I take issue with Hallaq, not only with his preference of the paradigmatic over the historical but also with his *fiqhī* understanding of *sharīʿa*." See Fahmy, *Quest*, 27.
30. Fahmy, *Quest*, 37.
31. Fahmy, *Quest*, 120.
32. Lest I be seen as applying a double standard, we might recall that the Islamic Secular's "secular," which *is* included in the Islamic "religious," is a "religious secular."
33. Up to this point I have used "Islamic law" in accordance with scholarly convention as a synonym for *sharīʿah*. Hence forth "Islamic law" should be understood as I describe it here, as both including and going beyond *sharīʿah*.
34. See, however, Zysow, *The Economy of Certainty*, 259–77.
35. See the discussions in Chapter 2, sections "Ibn al-Qayyim" and "Ibn Taymīyah." See also Stilt, *Islamic Law in Action*, 10; Y. Rapaport, "Royal Justice and Religious Law: *Siyāsah* and Shariʿah Under the Mamluks," *Mamlūk Studies Review 16* (2012): 71–102 at 102.
36. ʿAbū al-Faraj Abd al-Raḥmān Ibn al-Jawzī, *Talbīs iblīs* (Cairo: Idārat al-Ṭibāʿah al-Munīrīyah, 1368/1948), 132: "*fa muddaʿī al-siyāsah muddaʿī al-khalal fī al-sharīʿah*." See also the Shāfiʿī jurist, Tāj al-Dīn ʿAbd al-Wahhāb al-Subkī, *Muʿīd al-niʿam wa mubīd al-niqam* (Beirut: Muʾassasat al-Kutub al-Thaqāfīyah, 1407/1986), 38–9, for a similar attitude toward *siyāsah*, though the examples he gives seem to point to the abuse of *siyāsah*.
37. U. F. A. Wymann-Landgraf, *Mālik and Medina: Islamic Legal Reasoning in the Formative Period* (Leiden: E. J. Brill, 2013), 8–11.
38. See M. Fadel, "'*Istiḥsān* Is Nine-Tenths of the Law': The Puzzling Relationship of *Uṣūl* to *Furūʿ* in the Mālikī *Madhhab*," in B. Weiss, ed., *Studies in Islamic Legal Theory* (Leiden: E. J. Brill, 2002), 161–76 at 164.
39. Fadel bases his conclusions on a study of pledges (*ruhūn*/sg. *rahn*). He cites among the rules for which there is no revelatory evidence "the principle right the pledgee obtains by virtue of his agreement with the pledgor is the right to retain possession of the pledge until the pledgor repays his debt to the pledgee." Fadel, "'*Istiḥsān*,'" 165.
40. Fadel, "'*Istiḥsān*,'" 163.
41. A rule's transgenerational incumbency may blur the distinction between its *sharʿī* and non-*sharʿī* elements. This is what we see, for example, with expressions listed in early manuals as formulae for divorce, which al-Qarāfī goes to great lengths to isolate as essentially non-*sharʿī*, customary derivatives that are subject to challenge and change. See, e.g., my *Islamic Law and the State*, 130–3.
42. According to Samy Ayoub, "In the 17th and 18th centuries Ottoman state edicts and sulṭānic orders were consistently incorporated, *for the first time*, in authoritative Ḥanafī legal commentaries, treatises, and *fatwās*." See his "'The Sulṭān Says': State Authority in the Late Ḥanafī Tradition," *Islamic Law and Society*, *23* (2016): 239–78 at 241. Emphasis mine. While some may see this as collapsing the *sharīʿah-siyāsah* distinction, Ayoub notes (p. 248): "Ottoman state interventions in juristic discourse were legitimated and sustained *by Ḥanafī jurists* themselves—who were attempting to create a legal order in which state policies are taken into consideration." Emphasis

mine. In other words, it was not state-authority but juristic authority that ratified this inclusion, and the fact that this was theretofore unprecedented points to where the actual *shar'ī* authority and jurisdiction resided. If I understand him correctly, Ayoub ultimately confirms the idea that *siyāsah* does not collapse into *sharī'ah* when he states that, even for late Ottoman Ḥanafism, "In my view, the idea of a 'state *madhhab*' is a contradiction in terms." (p. 248)

43. For such instances in the nineteenth and early twentieth centuries, see Vogel, *Islamic Law*, 211–21.
44. I discuss this further in Chapter 4 in the context of what al-Qarāfī refers to as the "*taṣarruf*," or "discretionary action." See the section "The Promise and Threat of Discretionary Authority" in Chapter 4.
45. See, e.g., Ahmed, *What is Islam?* 475–7; Stilt, *Islamic Law in Action*, 10; Rapaport, "Royal Justice," 102; N. Hurvitz, "The Contribution of Early Islamic Rulers to Adjudication and Legislation: The Case of the *Maẓālim* Tribunals," in *Law and Empire: Ideas, Practices, Actors*, eds. J. Duindam et al. (Leiden: E. J. Brill, 2013), 135–56 at 138–9, where he attributes this view to Vogel and appears to agree with it. See also Emon, *Religious Pluralism and Islamic Law*, 12 where his concept of "Rule of Law" is explained in terms that might be taken to include *siyāsah* as part of *sharī'ah*: "To view Sharīa as Rule of Law forces a reconsideration of the near monopoly of authority granted to pre-modern jurists and their corpus in defining the content and intelligibility of Sharī'a."
46. See Fahmy, *Quest*, 28.
47. Fahmy, *Quest*, 25.
48. As a child growing up in Philadelphia, I heard a police officer speak to his partner with no hesitation of threatening to "punch a man in the mouth and then locking him up for assault and battery on a police officer." If and when this came to pass, the official record would obviously not reflect how the law had actually been applied. More recently, it has come to light that Chicago police officers kept "street files" containing information about events that they did not want to enter into the official record, some of which established the innocence of those eventually convicted of crimes. Amateur videos have also pointed to critical discrepancies between police reports and what really happened on the ground. Meanwhile, in its attempt to break the back of the notorious *al-Gamā'ah al-Islāmīyah* back in the 1980s and 90s, the Egyptian government routinely resorted to the practice of "re-arresting" incarcerated *Gamā'ah* members "on paper" in order to extend their prison sentences, a practice obviously not reflected in the official record. Or we might consider the practice of prison administrations in Egypt officially recording prisoners who had died under torture as "exited upon release" (*khurūj li al-ifrāj 'anhu*). My point here is that, while archives and official records tell us something, what they tell us is neither always clear nor necessarily what actually happened. On the *Gamā'ah*, see my *Initiative to Stop the Violence: Sadat's Assassins and the Renunciation of Political Violence* (New Haven: Yale University Press, 2014), 131, note. 37. On recording dead prisoners as released, see Ḥ. al-Shāfi'ī, *Ḥayātī fī ḥikāyātī* (My Life Through My Stories) (Tunis: Dār al-Gharb al-Islāmī, 1436/2015), 147–8.

49. See, e.g. 'Alā' al-Dīn Abū al-Ḥasan b. Khalīl al-Ṭarābulisī, *Mu'īn al-ḥukkām fīmā yataraddad bayna al-khaṣmayn min al-aḥkām*, 2nd ed. (Cairo: Muṣṭafā al-Bābī al-Ḥalabī and Sons, 1393/1973), 173; Burhān al-Dīn Ibrāhīm b. 'Alī b. Abī al-Qāsim b. Muḥammad b. Farḥūn, *Tabṣirat al-ḥukkām fī uṣūl al-aqḍiyah wa manāhij al-aḥkām*, 2 vols. ed. Ṭ. 'A. Sa'd (Cairo: Maktabat al-Kullīyāt al-Azharīyah, 1406/1986), 2: 146. Meanwhile, al-Qarāfī registers an almost identical view. See *al-Dhakhīrah*, 10: 58.
50. Stilt, *Islamic Law in Action*, 37. I do not agree unqualifiedly with Stilt when she adds, "[T]he writings that do attempt to define the power of rulers were written by jurists, whose goal was typically to circumscribe it." Even the *sharī'ah*-maximalists Ibn Taymīyah and Ibn al-Qayyim in *al-Ṭuruq al-ḥukmīyah* and Ibn Taymīyah alone in *al-Siyāsah al-shar'īyah* encourage the ruler to take a more active role in using his discretion to uphold the law.
51. The Mālikī al-Qarāfī appears to be the odd exception. In *al-Dhakhīrah*, 10: 38–58, he discusses *maẓālim* and *ḥisbah* and alludes to *siyāsah*. He also mentions *maẓālim, ḥisbah*, and *siyāsah* in *Tamyīz*, 162–5 and 167–70. In *al-Furūq*, meanwhile (on legal canons, or *qawā'id*) he discusses *ta'zir* (4: 177–83) and alludes to *siyāsah* (4: 39). Nielsen seems to take this as the basis of his claim that "Malikites allow maẓālim a role in the general discussion of qaḍā,'" a position that Mālikī *fiqh* works in general do not bear out. See Nielsen, *Secular Justice in an Islamic* State, 31. Meanwhile, Fahmy refers to al-Māwardī's (and, one would assume, Abū Ya'lā's) *al-Aḥkām al-sulṭānīyah* as a "*fiqh* text." See Fahmy, *Quest*, 188.
52. See Hurvitz, "The Contribution of Early Rulers," 139.
53. H.A. R. Gibb, "Constitutional Organization," in *Law in the Middle East*, eds. M. Khaddury and H. J. Liebesney (Washington, DC: Middle East Institute, 1995), 1. See also the view of J. N. D. Anderson "Law as a Social Force in Islamic Culture and History," in *The Law of the Near and Middle East: Readings, Cases & Materials*, ed. H. J. Liebesny (Albany: State University of New York Press, 1975), 3–5 at 4: "[H]e (the ruler) had executive and judicial powers, but was—in the classical theory—denied any true legislative authority." See also, however, F. Vogel, "Tracing Nuance in al-Māwardī's *al-Aḥkām al-Sulṭānīyah*: Implicit Framing of Constitutional Authority," in *Islamic Law Theory: Studies on Jurisprudence in Honor of Bernard Weiss*, eds. A. K. Reinhart and R. Gleave (Leiden: E. J. Brill, 2014), 331–59, for a critical engagement with Gibb.
54. See, e.g., Gibb, "Al-Mawardi's Theory of the Caliphate," 162: "Sunni political theory was, in fact, only the rationalization of the history of the community. Without precedents, no theory; and all the imposing fabric of interpretation of the sources is merely the *post eventum* justification of the precedents which have been ratified by *ijma*."
55. Abū Ya'lā, *al-Aḥkām al-sulṭānīyah*, ed. M. H. al-Fiqi (Beirut: Dār al-Kutub al-'Ilmīyah, 1403/1983), 83; Abū al-Ḥasan 'Alī b. Ḥabīb al-Māwardī, *al-Aḥkām al-sulṭānīyah wa al-wilāyāt al-dīnīyah*, ed. A. M. al-Baghdādī (Kuwait: Maktabat Dār Ibn Qutaybah, 1409/1989), 117.

56. Al-Māwardī, *al-Aḥkām al-sulṭānīyah*, 91; Abū Ya'lā, *al-Aḥkām al-sulṭānīyah*, 260, where he distinguishes between the interventions of government officials (*umarā'*/sg. *amīr*) as *siyāsah* and the rulings of judges (*aḥkām*/sg. *ḥukm*).
57. Abū Ya'lā, *al-Aḥkām al-sulṭānīyah*, 73; al-Māwardī, *al-Aḥkām al-sulṭānīyah*, 103, 111.
58. Ibn Farḥūn, *Tabṣirat*, 2: 137.
59. Al-Ṭarābulisī, *Mu'īn al-ḥukkām*, 169.
60. Al-Ṭarābulisī, *Mu'īn al-ḥukkām*, 170.
61. See Rapaport, "Royal Justice," 77.
62. Al-Māwardī, *al-Aḥkām al-sulṭānīyah*, 91.
63. We should be clear on the difference between "violating" and "differing from." Mālikī rules often differ from Shāfi'ī rules, while neither violates *sharī'ah*. What is being claimed in the present cases is that these rules of *siyāsah* violate *sharī'ah* in the sense that they go against the explicit or implicit consensus of the jurists.
64. See the point made by Sami Ayoub, "The Sultan Says," 248. See also note 42 of this chapter.
65. Abū Ya'lā, *al-Aḥkām al-sulṭānīyah*, 34, 36; al-Mawardī, *al-Aḥkām al-sulṭānīyah*, 40, 43.
66. As far back as the *Mudawwanah* we read of Ibn Abbās's recollection of Alī's dispatching him to negotiate with the Ḥarūrīyah Kharijites. When they raised their battle cry, "There is no ruling but God's," implying that no rules other than those dictated by scripture have any legitimacy, Ibn 'Abbas tacitly agreed but responded that God had granted ordinary men discretionary powers to settle disputes between spouses [4:35] as well as the transgressions of pilgrims who hunt during the Ḥājj [5:95]. He then asked if God is more likely to be interested in settling private matters among couples and pilgrims than in settling political disputes that engulf the *ummah* in bloodshed. See Saḥnūn b. Sa'īd al-Tanūkhī, *al-Mudawwanah al-kubrā* 4 vols. (Beirut: Dār al-Fikr, 1406/1986), 4: 409.
67. Abū Ya'lā, *al-Aḥkām al-sulṭānīyah*, 36; al-Mawardī, *al-Aḥkām al-sulṭānīyah*, 43.
68. As we will see in a moment, Professor Baber Johansen traces the jurists' acceptance of state-owned discretion in the form of *siyāsah* as far back as the second/eighth century.
69. See the discussion on evidence and *maẓālim* below.
70. See, e.g., Rapaport, "Royal Justice," 71–102, where *siyāsah* is depicted as a rather cynical attempt by the Mamlūk state to encroach upon *sharī'ah* and bend it to the state's advantage. In a similar vein, Shahab Ahmed claimed, "[T]he acceptance by Muslims of ruler's law emerges as a purely pragmatic stratagem without a normative basis *in terms of Islam*." *What Is Islam?* 461. Emphasis original. He went on to imply that recognizing a Muslim rulers' law-making powers, in terms of Islam, was a preserve of philosophical-Sufi thought. Ahmed, *What Is Islam?* 505.
71. See al-Qarāfī, *al-Dhakhīrah*, 10:45–47.
72. Shihāb al-Dīn al-Qarāfī, *Kitāb al-iḥkām fī tamyīz al-fatāwā 'an al-aḥkām wa taṣarrufāt al-qāḍī wa al-imām*, ed. A. Abū Ghuddah (Aleppo: Maktabat al-Maṭbū'āt al-Islāmīyah, 1387/1967), 26.
73. Al-Qarāfī, *Tamyîz*, 26–28.

74. This was an integral part of his "pure-law doctrine" which I lay out in detail in my *Islamic Law and the State*, esp. Chapters 3–5, and which I discussed in Chapter 2.
75. Al-Qarāfī, *Tamyīz*, 93–4. On the distinction between the judge's discretion and his authority to issue *shar'ī* rules (*aḥkām*), see the discussion of the *taṣarruf* in Chapter 4.
76. Al-Qarāfī, *Tamyīz*, 41.
77. B. Johansen, "Secular and Religious Elements in Hanafite Law. Function and Limits of the Absolute Character of Government Authority," in *Contingency in a Sacred Law: Legal and Ethical Norms in the Muslim* Fiqh (Leiden: E. J. Brill, 1999), 216.
78. Johansen, "Secular and Religious Elements," 216.
79. Johansen, "Secular and Religious Elements," 216–17.
80. Johansen, "Secular and Religious Elements," 217.
81. Burhān al-Dīn Abū al-Ḥasan 'Alī b. Abī Bakr b. 'Abd al-Jalīl al-Rushdānī al-Marghīnānī, *al-Hidāyah sharḥ bidāyat al-mubtadi'*, 4 vols. (Cairo: Muṣṭafā al-Bābī al-Ḥalabī wa Awlāduh, N.d.), 2: 99.
82. Ibn 'Ābidīn, *Radd al-muḥtār*, 6: 20.
83. Ibn 'Ābidīn, *Radd al-muḥtār*, 6: 20. See also Ibn Nujaym (d. 969–70/1562–63), *Baḥr al-rā'iq sharḥ kanz al-daqā'iq*, 9 vols., ed. T. al-Hindī (Beirut: Dār al-Kutub al-'Ilmīyah, 1434/2013), 5: 17–18, where he equates *ta'zīr* with *siyāsah* and then goes on to say that *siyāsah* (in this context) is "for the ruler (*ḥākim*) to carry out an action based on some interest (*maṣlaḥah*) he sees, even if there are no specific textual indicants (*dalīl juz'ī*) to back this."
84. Ibn 'Ābidīn, *Radd al-muḥtār*, 6: 20.
85. Ibn 'Ābidīn, *Radd al-muḥtār*, 6: 19.
86. Al-'Aynī, *al-Bināyah*, 6: 291.
87. Al-Qarāfī, *al-Furūq*, 4: 180. See also, 'Izz al-Dīn b. 'Abd al-Salām, *Qawā'id al-aḥkām fī maṣāliḥ al-anām*, 2 vols., ed. Ṭ. 'A. Sa'd (Beirut: Dār al-Jīl, 1400/1980), 1: 178, and 1: 186. Incidentally, the Ḥanafī position on *nabīdh* evolved over the centuries. See N. Haider, "Contesting Intoxication: Early Juristic Debates over the Lawfulness of Alcoholic Beverages," *Islamic Law and Society*, *20*:1–2 (2013): 48–89.
88. I say "necessarily" here because the ruler *may* intervene, as a matter of *siyāsah*, to insist on the application of a particular rule of *sharī'ah*. See, e.g., Ayoub, " 'The Sultan Says,' " 254ff. See the "*Siyāsah*" section of this chapter for a discussion of whether discretionary acts by the ruler necessarily constitute *shar'ī* rules.
89. Beyond this, the rules that come of *siyāsah* are applied in a much more individualized manner than those of *sharī'ah*. According to both al-Māwardī and Abū Ya'lā, e.g., *ta'zīr* punishments contrast with *ḥudūd* punishments in that they may be levied according to the offender's station in society, from shunning (*i'rāḍ*) for elites, to imprisonment (*ḥabs*) for common delinquents. See Al-Māwardī, *al-Ahkām al-sulṭānīyah*, 310. See also Abū Ya'lā, *al-Ahkām al-sulṭānīyah*, 279–80.
90. Ibn Taymīyah, *Majmū'at al-fatāwā*, 19: 19.
91. Ibn Farḥūn, e.g., cites as an example of *siyāsah* 'Alī's slapping a young maiden to get her to reveal what she knew about 'Ā'ishah's character in the face of the slanderous charges made against her. Obviously, Ibn Farḥūn would not consider 'Alī's action to be consistent with the *rules* of *sharī'ah*, but he counts it a valid act of *siyāsah*, because

its aim was consistent with the aims of *sharīʿah*—as he put it, "to get her to tell what she knew" (*li tuqirr bimā ʿindahā*). See Ibn Farḥūn, *Tabṣirat*, 2: 142. See also 2: 144, where he explicitly describes Alī's threatening to strip naked a woman who refused to hand over a treasonous note from the Companion Ḥāṭib b. Abī Balṭaʿah to Quraysh as an example of *al-siyāsah al-sharʿīyah*. Again, clearly, stripping a woman naked would not be consistent with the rules of *sharīʿah*. For al-Ṭarābulisī, see *Muʿīn al-ḥukkām*, 170–3.

92. See the discussion in the section "'*Sharīʿah*' and 'Islamic Law'" in this chapter.
93. See the discussion in the section "*Siyāsah*" in this chapter.
94. Ibn Farḥūn, *Tabṣirat*, 2: 146–55; al-Ṭarābulisī, *Muʿīn al-ḥukkām*, 173. We will see in the treatment of discretionary actions in Chapter 4 that he acknowledges the legitimacy of judges' reliance on *siyāsah*. But see also al-Qarāfī, *Tamyīz*, 162, where his wording might be taken to confirm the attribution of Ibn Farḥūn and al-Ṭarābulisī.
95. In fact, Ibn Farḥūn insists strenuously that, "[w]hat al-Qarāfī related in *al-Dhakhīrah* is not the *madhhab* of Mālik." See Ibn Farḥūn, *Tabṣirat*, 2: 149.
96. Rappaport insightfully points to the threat posed to the reputation and integrity of *siyāsah* (including *maẓālim*) as an institution by the rough-and-tumble justice meted out by Mamlūk junior *amīrs*. See his "Royal Justice," 96.
97. Ibn Farḥūn, *Tabṣirat*, 2: 137; al-Ṭarābulisī, *Muʿīn al-ḥukkām*, 169.
98. Nielsen, e.g., seems to misrecognize this when he has al-Maqrīzī say of *siyāsah*, "It is part of the Sharīʿa; they have in common what it recognizes and ignores." Nielsen, *Secular Justice*, 33. What al-Maqrīzī actually argues is that "good *siyāsah*" (*siyāsah ʿādilah*) is *sharīʿah*-compliant (*min al-aḥkām al-sharʿīyah*) and deserves recognition by *sharīʿah*, while "bad *siyāsah*" (*siyāsah ẓālimah*) is not compliant and does not deserve recognition. He then adds, "Those who know this know it, and those who do not do not." Al-Maqrīzī, *Kitāb al-mawāʿiẓ wa al-iʿtibār bi dhikr al-khiṭaṭ wa al-āthār*, 2 vols. (Cairo: Maktabat al-Thaqāfah al-Dīnīyah, 1987), 2: 220. Nielsen apparently reads al-Maqrīzī's "*ʿalimahā man ʿalimahā wa jahilahā man jahilahā*" as "they have in common what it recognizes and ignores." Part of the problem with this rendering is that the whole point of *siyāsah* is to address what *sharīʿah* 'ignores'.
99. See Nielsen, "Maẓālim," *EI2*, 6: 933–5 at 933.
100. "Maẓālim," *EI2*, 6: 934. Nielsen might be seen as somewhat contradicting this statement when he notes in the same paragraph that it was Abū Yūsuf, a judge and prominent jurist, who suggested to Hārūn al-Rashīd that the latter take charge.
101. Taqī al-Dīn al-Maqrīzī, *al-Khiṭaṭ*, 2: 208.
102. Al-Ṭarābulisī, *Muʿīn al-ḥukkām*, 174. See also Ibn Farūn, *Tabṣirat*, 2: 146, where he interprets al-Qarāfī as including *maẓālim* as part of *al-wilāyah al-siyāsīyah*, or "discretionary authority." This is simply a mistake. The passage in al-Qarāfī's *al-Dhakhīrah*, 10: 38, from which this is taken, read "*al-wilāyat al-sādisah wilāyat al-kashf ʿan al-maẓālim*." Al-Ṭarābulisī and Ibn Farḥūn reads this as "*al-wilāyah al-siyāsīyah wa hiya wilāyat al-kashf ʿan al-maẓālim*." Ultimately, at any rate, it is clear that al-Ṭarābulisī, like al- Maqrīzī, saw *maẓālim* as a constituent of *siyāsah*.
103. Abū Yaʿlā, *al-Aḥkām al-sulṭānīyah*, 78; al-Māwardī, *al-Aḥkām al-sulṭānīyah*, 102.
104. Al-Māwardī, *al-Aḥkām al-sulṭānīyah*, 316; Abū Yaʿlā, *al-Aḥkām al-sulṭānīyah*, 285.

105. Al-Māwardī, *al-Aḥkām al-sulṭānīyah*, 310; Abū Ya'lā, *al-Aḥkām al-sulṭānīyah*, 284.
106. See the previous discussion of the views cited by Johansen and Ibn 'Ābidīn.
107. See 'Abd al-Raḥmān b. Naṣr al-Shayzarī, *Nihāyat al-rutbah fī ṭalab al-ḥisbah* (Cairo: Maṭba'at Lajnat al-Ta'līf wa al-Tarjamah wa al-Nashr, 1365/1946), 6: "The *muḥtasib* must be a jurist, knowledgeable of the rules of *sharī'ah*, so that he can know what to command and what to forbid. For 'good' is what the religious law defines as 'good,' and 'bad' is what the religious law defines as 'bad.' And there is no place for reason in distinguishing the decent (*ma'rūf*) from the indecent (*munkar*) except on the basis of the Book of God and the *sunnah* of His Prophet." We will see momentarily, however, how the *muḥtasib* routinely, indeed, necessarily, goes beyond these sources.
108. Al-Māwardī, *al-Ahkām al-sulṭānīyah*, 115; Abū Ya'lā, *al-Ahkām al-sulṭānīyah*, 81. See also al-Māwardī, *al-Ahkām al-sulṭānīyah*, 111, and Abū Ya'lā, *al-Ahkām al-sulṭānīyah*, 79, where it is stated that the *maẓālim* magistrate can resolve disputes only in a manner consistent with the ruling a judge would give. Al-Māwardī: "*lā yasūgh an yaḥkum baynahum illā bimā yaḥkum bihi al-ḥukkām wa al-quḍāh*." Abū Ya'lā: "*lā yajūz an yaḥkum baynahum bimā lā yaḥkum bihi al-ḥukkām wa al-quḍāh*."
109. See al-Māwardī, *al-Aḥkām al-sulṭānīyah*, 114–22; Abū Ya'lā, *al-Aḥkām al-sulṭānīyah*, 80–7. In both texts, incidentally, this comes under the subheading, "The Difference between the Jurisdiction of *Maẓālim* and That of Judges" (*al-farq bayna naẓar al-maẓālim wa naẓar al-quḍāh* and *al-farq bayna naẓar al-quḍāh wa naẓar nāẓir al-maẓālim*, respectively).
110. Interestingly, though he generally equates Islamic law with *sharī'ah*, Wael Hallaq insightfully points out in his earlier work that "mediation is not only integral to the legal system and the legal process but also accorded precedence over court litigation, which was usually seen as the last resort." See Hallaq, "What Is Shari'a?" *Yearbook of Islamic and Middle Eastern Law Online, 12*:1 (2005): 151–80 at 159. doi:https://doi.org/10.1163/22112987-91000130
111. See al-Māwardī, *al-Aḥkām al-sulṭānīyah*, 114–22; Abū Ya'lā, *al-Aḥkām al-sulṭānīyah*, 80–7.
112. See al-Māwardī, *al-Aḥkām al-sulṭānīyah*, 122 (see also 114, 115, 116, and 118 for a similar depiction). See also Abū Ya'lā, *al-Aḥkām al-sulṭānīyah*, 86–7 for the same basic depiction as al-Māwardī as above though with a slightly different wording.
113. Al-Māwardī, *al-Aḥkām al-sulṭānīyah*, 109. See also Abū Ya'lā, *al-Aḥkām al-sulṭānīyah*, 77. The text is garbled but seems to support the same conclusion.
114. See Abū al-Ḥasan 'Alī b. Ḥabīb al-Māwardī, *al-Ḥāwī al-kabīr fī fiqh madhhab al-imām al-shāfi'ī raḍī Allāh 'anhu wa huwa sharḥ mukhtaṣar al-muzanī*, 18 vols., eds. 'A. M. Mu'awwaḍ and 'A. M. 'Abd al-Mawjūd (Beirut: Dār al-Kutub al-'Ilmīyah, 1414/1994), 17: 301.
115. On the definition of *ghaṣb* in *fiqh*, see al-Māwardī, *al-Ḥāwī al-kabīr*, 7: 133–5.
116. Nielsen, *Secular Justice*, 27.
117. Al-Māwardī, *al-Aḥkām al-sulṭānīyah*, 102; Abū Ya'lā, *al-Aḥkām al-sulṭānīyah*, 73.
118. Al-Māwardī, *al-Aḥkām al-sulṭānīyah*, 106; Abū Ya'lā, *al-Aḥkām al-sulṭānīyah*, 76. It seems that *maẓālim* magistrates were not strictly held to the views of the jurists. See, e.g., al-Māwardī, *al-Aḥkām al-sulṭānīyah*, 115–16, where he states that the *fuqahā'*

agreed that a case could not be decided solely based on a document's being written in the hand of one of the litigants though some *maẓālim* magistrates did so.

119. Al-Māwardī, *al-Aḥkām al-sulṭānīyah*, 107–11; Abū Ya'lā, *al-Aḥkām al-sulṭānīyah*, 76–9.
120. Al-Māwardī, *al-Aḥkām al-sulṭānīyah*, 102; Abū Ya'lā, *al-Aḥkām al-sulṭānīyah*, 73–4.
121. See also al-Qarāfī, *Tamyīz*, 162–5.
122. Al-Māwardī, *al-Aḥkām al-sulṭānīyah*, 40; Abū Ya'lā, *al-Aḥkām al-sulṭānīyah*, 34.
123. Al-Māwardī, *al-Aḥkām al-sulṭānīyah*, 102; Abū Ya'lā, *al-Aḥkām al-sulṭānīyah*, 73. The judiciousness here relates to the judge's acumen in weighing facts or applying rules not in interpreting texts.
124. Al-Māwardī, *al-Aḥkām al-sulṭānīyah*, 102, 318; Abū Ya'lā, *al-Aḥkām al-sulṭānīyah*, 287. Cf., al-Qarāfī, *al-Dhakhīrah*, 10: 48–9, where he notes that there are ways in which the judge is above the *maẓālim* magistrate, e.g., in being authorized to hear cases involving civil disputes, and ways that he is below him, i.e., in not having the same coercive powers. Meanwhile, N. Hurvitz, in "The Contributions of Early Rulers," 154, and 155, categorically counts *maẓālim* tribunals as "inferior," because, according to him, they were "not based on Qur'an and *hadith.*"
125. Al-Māwardī, *al-Aḥkām al-sulṭānīyah*, 111; Abū Ya'lā, *al-Aḥkām al-sulṭānīyah*, 79. See also al-Qarāfī, *Tamyīz*, 164.
126. Professor Christopher Melchert has also endorsed this view. See his "Māwardī, Abū Ya'lá and the Sunni Revival," in *Prosperity and Stagnation: Some Cultural and Social Aspects of the Abbasid Period (750–1258)*, ed. K. Kościelniak (Cracow: UNUM, 2010), 37–1 at 38 note 6. I suspect that a certain anti-Traditionalist/Ḥanbalite bias in the field has delayed Abū Ya'lā's rightful recognition to date.
127. The reverse is also true, albeit to a lesser degree.
128. We also have Abū Ya'lā's *al-Jāmi' al-ṣaghir* on *fiqh*, but this monograph is nowhere near as detailed as al-Māwardī's compendium.
129. Al-Māwardī, *al-Aḥkām al-sulṭānīyah*, 285.
130. Al-Māwardī, *al-Aḥkām al-sulṭānīyah*, 286–7. Al-Māwardī seems to suggest that, if a suspect confesses under torture to such facts as his whereabouts at the time of the crime, his confession to these facts is accepted. But if he is tortured with the expressed purpose of getting him to confess to the crime itself, his confession is not accepted unless he voluntary offers it after the fact.
131. Al-Māwardī, *al-Aḥkām al-sulṭānīyah*, 286–87.
132. Al-Māwardī, *al-Aḥkām al-sulṭānīyah*, 285–6.
133. Al-Māwardī, *al-Aḥkām al-sulṭānīyah*, 286–7. In his section on *jarā'im*, Abū Ya'lā's presentation is basically identical to that of al-Māwardī, though he attributes to Ibn Ḥanbal the position that judges *may* jail persons accused of offenses in order to investigate the charges. See Abū Ya'lā, *al-Aḥkām al-sulṭānīyah*, 257–8.
134. Al-Māwardī, *al-Aḥkām al-sulṭānīyah*, 287: "These are nine ways in which the difference between the jurisdiction of judges and that of *amīrs* is established with regard to criminal matters during the fact-finding stage and before the application of punishment, based on the fact that *amīrs* rely on *siyāsah* and judges rely on *sharī'ah*-rules" (*fa hādhihi tis'at awjuh*^{in} *yaqa'u bihā al-farq fī al-jarā'im bayna naẓar al-umarā' wa*

al-qudāh fī ḥāl al-istibrā' wa qabla al-ḥadd li ikhtiṣāṣ al-amīr bi al-siyāsah wa ikhtiṣāṣ al-qudāh bi al-aḥkām).

135. Al-Māwardī, *al-Aḥkām al-sulṭānīyah*, 288.
136. Al-Māwardī, *al-Aḥkām al-sulṭānīyah*, 288. This does not appear to be entirely consistent with what al-Māwardī stated at *al-Aḥkām al-sulṭānīyah*, 43 (see above). Both statements, however, confirm the existence of a condominium or bicameral system and the reliance upon *shar'ī* and non-*shar'ī* tools and offices of adjudication.
137. Al-Māwardī, *al-Aḥkām al-sulṭānīyah*, 291–309.
138. Al-Māwardī, *al-Ḥāwī al-*kabīr, 16: 19–20.
139. Al-Māwardī, *al-Ḥawī al-kabīr*, 13: 184–450.
140. Al-Māwardī, *al-Ḥawī al-kabīr*, 12: 3–209.
141. Al-Māwardī, *al-Ḥawī al-kabīr*, vol. 16.
142. N. Hurvitz, "The Contributions of Early Rulers," 150–1.
143. Al-Māwardī, *al-Aḥkām al-sulṭānīyah*, 285–7.
144. Schacht, as we have seen, depicted all of this as a concession that the jurists grudgingly made to the ruler, as the simple result of being overpowered by the latter and/or overwhelmed by circumstances on the ground, a depiction that gives no sense of the jurists' free and positive recognition of any of this as a part of "Islamic law." As Schacht put it, clearly pointing not only to the limits but also to the limitations of Islamic law, "[T]he laws which rule the lives of the Muslim peoples have never been coextensive with pure Islamic law." See his *Introduction*, 85, and also 54 and 76ff.
145. Al-Māwardī, *al-Aḥkām al-sulṭānīyah*, 339.
146. Stilt, *Islamic Law in Action*, 3.
147. Stilt, *Islamic Law in Action*, 10.
148. Stilt, *Islamic Law in Action*, 207.
149. Al-Māwardī, *al-Aḥkām al-sulṭānīyah*, 315, 335–6, 337, and 338, esp. 315, where he states that the *muḥtasib* "may exert his independent discretion in matters connected with custom, not those connected to the identity of a *sharī'ah* rule" (*lahu an yajtahid ra'yah fīmā ta'allaqa bi al-'urf dūna al-shar'*). See also Abū Ya'lā, *al-Aḥkām al-sulṭānīyah*, 305: "because even if this requires *ijtihād*, it is *'urfī* and reclines upon the habits and customs of the people; it is not *ijtihād shar'ī*."
150. Al-Māwardī, *al-Aḥkām al-sulṭānīyah*, 338. This particular passage does not appear in Abū Ya'lā. But see the latter's *al-Aḥkām al-sulṭānīyah*, 303, 305, and 306 for references to and distinctions between *ijtihād 'urfī* and *ijtihād ḥukmī* or *shar'ī*. Interestingly, the later Shāfi'ī jurist, Ibn Ḥajar al-Haytamī (d. 974/1566) recognizes a distinction between "*fuqahā' al-shar'*" and "*fuqahā' al-ḥarth*" (those knowledgeable of farming). See his *al-Fatāwā al-kubrā al-fiqhīyah 'alā madhhab al-imām al-Shāfi'ī*, 4 vols. (Beirut: Dār al-Kutub al-'Ilmīyah, 1417/1997), 1: 437.
151. Stilt, *Islamic Law in Action*, 67, 150. See also Fahmy, *Quest*, 196, where, building on Jonathan Berkey's work, he notes that, in contrast to the early period when *ḥisbah* was thought of as a religious post and was generally filled by persons from the ranks of the *fuqahā'*, "by the mid- to late fifteenth century [9th AH] . . . the military elite had effectively monopolized the post."

152. Al-Māwardī, *al-Aḥkām al-sulṭānīyah*, 316. Al-Māwardī cites the lone Shāfiʿī jurist, al-Istakhrī, who allows *muḥtasib*s to exercise *ijtihād sharʿī*, though one imagines that there must have been others. Meanwhile, drawing on his Ḥanbalī heritage, Abū Yaʿlā speaks in terms that might seem to agree. He argues, e.g., that where there is disagreement among the schools as to whether a particular group fulfills the conditions for being obligated to hold the Friday prayer, the *muḥtasib* may order them to hold it, based on his own discretionary view of the practical consequences of not holding it. Closely examined, however, this turns out to be more an exercise in *ijtihād ʿurfī*; for, it is based on the *muḥtasib*'s assessment of the broader implications of not holding the prayer and whether this will develop into a tradition that leads later generations to assume that they are under no obligation to establish it. See Abū Yaʿlā, *al-Aḥkām al-sulṭānīyah*, 287–8.
153. Al-Māwardī, *al-Aḥkām al-sulṭānīyah*, 316. See also Stilt, *Islamic Law in Action*, 44, where she identifies al-Māwardī's view as the "majority opinion" in the Shāfiʿī school.
154. Al-Māwardī, *al-Aḥkām al-sulṭānīyah*, 337; Abū Yaʿlā, *al-Aḥkām al-sulṭānīyah*, 305–06.
155. See the discussion in the section "The Bounded *Ḥukm Sharʿī*," in Chapter 2.
156. Al-Qarāfī, *al-Dhakhīrah*, 10: 53 (basically copying al-Māwardī). See also, al-Qarāfī, *al-Dhakhīrah*, 10: 47–8, where he notes regarding the *muḥtasib* that, "He may perform *ijtihād* regarding matters of customary practice (*awāʾid*/sg. *ādah*), such as the arrangements of seats and awnings in the market." Elsewhere, however, he states, "Our statement, 'juristic,' is to avoid confusion with the determination of what is customary" (*fa qawlunā sharʿan iḥtirāzan ʿan taḥdīd al-ʿurf*). See al-Qarāfī, *Nafāʾis*, 1: 123. It seems clear that he recognizes much of what the *muḥtasib* deliberates as not amounting to *ijtihād sharʿī*.
157. Stilt, *Islamic Law in Action*, 166–7. See also al-Maqrīzī, *al-Sulūk*, 3/1: 232–9.
158. Again, *sharīʿah*'s role in all of this is not to determine the policy but to ensure that it remains within prescribed moral, ethical, or prudential parameters. This would seem to be al-Shayzarī's meaning when he writes: "The standard (*ḍābit*) regarding matters of *ḥisbah* is the purified *sharīʿah*. Everything *sharīʿah* prohibits is proscribed, and the *muḥtasib* must prevent and curtail its occurrence. And what *sharīʿah* permits, he is to confirm its allowance as such." See al-Shayzarī, *Niyāyat al-rutbah*, 118. Of course, al-Shayzarī is assuming here a formal reality in which things function as they should. Where this proves not to be the case, it is precisely the discretionary role of the *muḥtasib* to require or forbid what might otherwise be simply allowed. This "requiring" or "forbidding," however, is not *sharʿī*, as it says nothing about the status of these actions outside the circumstances at hand. In other words, while many arrangements may be *prima facie* permissible, the *muḥtasib*, under this or that particular circumstance, is bound to favor some over others.
159. Stilt points out that the *muḥtasib* was often caught between the competing interests of lower bread prices for the populace and higher prices at which the *amīr*s could sell the wheat they received from the sultan as payment for their military service. See Stilt, *Islamic Law in Practice*, 157.
160. See the discussion in the section "Shahab Ahmed" in Chapter 1.

161. See Ibn al-Qayyim, *al-Ṭuruq al-ḥukmīyah*, 344, 345. In a similar vein, Sohaira Siddiqui notes that al-Juwaynī recognized the importance of the Community as a whole in upholding the law: "[I]t is the members of the community who embody the law through their adherence to it." See her *Law and Politics*, 250–1.
162. See Ibn 'Abd al-Salām, *Qawā'id al-aḥkām*, 1: 24.
163. Ibn 'Abd al-Salām, *Qawā'id al-aḥkām*, 1: 43.
164. Ibn 'Abd al-Salām, *Qawā'id al-aḥkām*, 1: 43.
165. See Hallaq, "What Is Shari'a?" 159.
166. Ibn 'Abd al-Salām, *Qawā'id al-aḥkām*, 1: 79.
167. See Berger, *Sacred Canopy*, 3–28. See the discussion in the section " 'Islamic' and My Evolutionary Turn" in Chapter 1.
168. Berger, *Sacred Canopy*, 19.
169. Berger, *Sacred Canopy*, 22.
170. Berger, *Sacred Canopy*, 24.
171. See R. Cover, "Nomos and Narrative," in *Narrative, Violence, and the Law: The Essays of Robert Cover*, eds. M. Minow, M. Ryan, and A. Sarat (Ann Arbor: University of Michigan Press, 1995), 95–172. S. Siddiqui also draws on Cover in her insightful study of al-Juwaynī. She and I have different understandings, however, of Cover's thesis. She seems to think that law produces its *nomos*, whereas I see the *nomos* as coming from elsewhere and as largely defining and sustaining the law. See her *Law and Politics*, 279–82.
172. Cover, "Nomos and Narrative," 95–6.
173. Cover, "Nomos and Narrative," 96.
174. Cover, "Nomos and Narrative," 97.
175. Cover, "Nomos and Narrative," 103.
176. I should note that sound narrations of this interpretation go back to the Companions Ibn Mas'ūd and Ibn 'Abbās. See, e.g., Muḥammad b. 'Alī al-Shawkānī, *Nayl al-awṭār sharḥ muntaqā al-akhbār*, 10 vols. eds. Ṭ 'A. Sa'd and M.M. al-Hawarī (Cairo: Maktabat al-Kullīyāt al-Azharīyah, 1398/1978), 9: 28–40, esp. 32, 38. My point, however, is that if this less obvious interpretation can sustain a negative attitude towards music and singing, seemingly more obvious interpretations of Qur'ānic verses should cast aspersions on poetry.
177. Berger, *Sacred Canopy*, 45.
178. Berger, *Sacred Canopy*, 48. There are resonances in all of this with Anver Emon's notion of "Rule of Law." Again, however, the *shar'ī*/non-*shar'ī* distinction and the idea that this extra-*shar'ī* activity may be micro-secular in nature appears to play no role in his theory. .
179. Scholars (myself included) have traditionally assumed that al-Māwardī was the target of this invective. But al-Juwaynī never mentions al-Māwardī by name, only "the author of the book entitled *al-Aḥkām al-sulṭānīyah*." See al-Juwaynī, *Ghiyāth al-umam*, 155. Not only did Abū Ya'lā also author a book by the same title, the view on which al-Juwaynī takes this author to task (allowing *dhimmī*s to serve as *wazīr al-tanfīdh*) is shared by Abū Ya'lā. See the latter's *al-Aḥkām al-sulṭānīyah*, 32. In his informative study *Friends of the Emir: Non-Muslim State Officials in Premodern*

Islamic Thought (Cambridge: Cambridge University Press, 2019), 132–3, Luke Yarbrough argues that Abū Yaʿlā dissented from al-Māwardī on this question. On my reading of Abū Yaʿlā, however, he is simply offering a vindication of Ibn Ḥanbal's contradicting what would later become the going opinion of the *madhhab*. He takes a similar approach to vindicating Aḥmad's dissent on whether the Imām had to be just and knowledgeable, without abandoning the later position of the *madhhab*, which held these characteristics to be legal prerequisites (*shurūṭ*/sg. *sharṭ*) for the occupant of this office. See Abu Yaʿlā, *al-Aḥkām al-sulṭānīyah*, 20.

180. See al-Juwaynī, *Giyāth al-umam*, 155–7. He also mentions the basic untrustworthiness of *dhimmī*s, as reflected in the fact that their courtroom testimony is not accepted.
181. I say "almost" because in his contemplation of the possibility of *sharīʿah*'s disappearance, I assume that his position might change. For al-Juwaynī on the disappearance of *sharīʿah*, see A. A. Ahmad, *Fatique of Sharīʿah*; S. Siddiqui, *Law under the Abbasids*, 256–83.
182. In their critique of ISIS, e.g., one member and one former member of Egypt's notorious *al-Gamāʿah al-Islāmīyah*, who were involved in President Anwar Sadat's assassination in 1981 but renounced political violence beginning in 1997, point to radical *jihādism*'s 's tendency to rely more on interpretive presuppositions gleaned from an idealized reading of the past than on scripture itself. They write: "Turning certain chapters of Muslim history into proofs that can be invoked in a manner that rivals the religion and the religious law (*ḥujjah ʿalā al-sharʿ wa al-dīn*) is among the major crises of our time." In other words, it is these readings of history and their elevation to an interpretive prism, rather than scripture itself, that holds radical *jihādīst* meanings in place. See N. Ibrāhīm and H. al-Najjār, *Dāʿish: al-sikkīn allatī tadhbaḥ al-islām*, 2nd ed. (Cairo: Dār al-Shurūq, 2015), 79. See also my *Initiative to Stop the Violence*.
183. See I. Berlin, *Three Critics of the Enlightenment: Vico, Hamann, Herder*, ed. H. Hardy (Princeton: Princeton University Press, 2000), 131.
184. See A. Watts, *The Way of Zen* (New York: Vintage Books, 1957), 8.
185. Alasdair MacIntyre, *Three Rival Versions of Moral Inquiry* (Notre Dame: Notre Dame University Press, 1990), 82.
186. See E. Moosa, *Ghazālī and the Poetics of Imagination* (Chapel Hill The University of North Carolina Press, 2005), 237–60; Hallaq, *Impossible State*, 13, 135–8, 218, and passim.
187. On "legitimate prejudices," see Hans-Georg Gadamer, *Truth and Method*, 2nd ed., trans. J. Weinsheimer and D. G. Marshall (New York: Continuum, 1998), 278.
188. Rorty, *Contingency*, 97.
189. See E. Bernays, *Propaganda* (New York: Ig Publishing, 2005), 37.
190. This may be the context in which to understand the position reached by the modern jurist Shaykh Yūsuf al-Qaraḍāwī when he states that, rather than violent *jihādī*s, what Islam needs today is "a massive army of preachers, teachers and competently trained journalists who are able to address today's public in the language of the age and the style of the times, through voice, image, spoken word, physical gesture, books, pamphlets, magazines, newspapers, dialogue, documentaries, drama,

motion pictures and everything that ties people to Islam. This peaceful *jihād*, which is an absolute necessity (*al-jihād al-silmī al-ḍarūrī*), we have not undertaken by one thousandth of what is required of us." See his *Fiqh al-jihād*, 2 vols. (Cairo: Maktabat Wahba, 1430/2009), 1: 402–03.

191. See al-Ghazālī, *Tahāfut al-falāsifah*, 7th ed., ed. S. Dunyā (Cairo: Dār al-Ma'ārif, 1392/1972), 74.
192. Ibn Taymīyah, *Iqtiḍā' ṣirāṭ al-mustaqīm wa mukhālafat aṣḥāb al-jaḥīm*, ed. M. 'A. al-Ṣābūnī (Mecca: Maṭābi' al-Majd 1390/1970), 16.
193. This perspective is explicitly confirmed by the modern Arab legal scholar Ṭāriq Al-Bishrī in his *al-Waḍ' al-qānūnī bayna al-sharī'ah al-islāmīyah wa al-qānūn al-waḍ'ī*, 2nd ed. (Cairo: Dār al-Shurūq, 1426/2005),143.
194. In fact, it may be less reasonable to expect this from them today than it was in the past, given how difficult it is today to master one discipline or calling, let alone several.
195. See his *Slavery and Islam* (London: Oneworld Publications, 2019), 206–18.
196. Brown, *Slavery and Islam*, 275. See also, however, B. Ware, *The Walking Qur'ān: Islamic Education, Embodied Knowledge, and History in West Africa* (Chapel Hill: University of North Carolina Press, 2014), 114, where he challenges the notion of the West preceding Muslims to the abolition of slavery.
197. Speaking of these developments, Brown notes: "A major ubiquitous and previously unquestioned component of humanity's economy of labor came under fierce and convincing moral attack during precisely the era in which the introduction of new technologies of agriculture, the use of fossil fuels, and the resulting steel-based technologies enabled society to break from the millennia-old reliance on human and animal labor." Brown, *Slavery and Islam*, 190.
198. Al-Qaraḍāwī, *Thaqāfatunā*, 21. As noted earlier, this could be understood to mean that the Islamic culture aspired to consists of *shar'ī* (or what al-Qaraḍāwī calls here "religious") and non-*shar'ī* (or what he calls 'secular') elements. See note 166 in Chapter 1.
199. As we will see in greater detail in Chapter 4, my claim here is not that efficiency is not valued in Islam or even in *sharī'ah* but rather that the *fuqahā' qua-fuqahā'* are not the authorities by whom authoritative assessments of efficiency are made.
200. Ibn Taymīyah, *Majmū'at al- fatāwa*, 29: 25.
201. See al-Qarāfī, *al-Furūq*, 1: 122. Meanwhile, both al-Māwardī and Abū Ya'lā are speaking of norms when they note that such otherwise perfectly permissible acts as intimately engaging with one's spouse can be banned if carried out in public. See al-Māwardī, *al-Aḥkām al-sulṭānīyah*, 329; Abū Ya'lā, *al-Aḥkām al-sulṭānīyah*, 295.
202. The size of the community in question will affect how effectively it can reach enough of a social consensus to establish and sustain norms. This takes us back to some of MacIntyre's insights and his focus on the *polis* as the optimal site of moral and ethical discourse.
203. Al-Qarāfī, *Al-Furūq*, 2:51, but see also the discussion at 2: 50–5.
204. Ahmed, *What Is Islam?*" 93.
205. Ibn Taymīyah, *Majmū'at al-fatāwā*, 21: 179.
206. Ibn Taymīyah, *Majmū'at al-fatāwā*, 21: 179.

207. Ibn Taymīyah, *Majmūʿat al-fatāwā*, 21: 180.
208. Ibn Taymīyah, *Majmūʿat al-fatāwā*, 21: 181. Going back to the discussion in Chapter 2 on Traditionalism and the scope of scripture, we see here that, even as a staunch Traditionalist, Ibn Taymīyah was willing to indulge extra-scriptural considerations in law in a manner that he would never accept in theology.
209. See the discussion in the section "The Islamic Secular's Religion" in Chapter 1.
210. See al-Qarāfī, *al-Istibṣār fīmā tudrikuhu al-abṣār* (Madrid: Escorial, MS. No. 707), 1 recto. See also, incidentally, A. M. Sayili, "Al-Qarāfī and His Explanation of the Rainbow," *Isis 32*:1 (Jul. 1940): 16–26 at 25, where he suggests that al-Qarāfī's understanding of certain scientific subjects, e.g., the reflection of light, was superior to that of Ibn Sīnā (though the latter, along with Aristotle, was clearly among his sources).
211. See Hallaq, "What Is Shariʿa?" 177, confirming the insight of Nicholas Dirks.
212. See T. Ramadan, *Radical Reform: Islamic Ethics and Liberation* (New York: Oxford University Press, 2009), 30. Ramadan recognizes the difference between what he refers to as the "scholars of the text" and the "scholars of the context," a clear indication of the need to go beyond the *sharʿī* realm. The ultimate goal, however, seems, still, to be establishing the appropriate *ḥukm sharʿī*, as the sole properly Islamic metric of assessment. Moreover, his text/context distinction does not explain how all this extra-*sharʿī* activity is or can be Islamic.
213. Muḥammad ʿAbduh, "*al-Zawāj*," in *al-Aʿmāl al-kāmilah li ʿl-imām muḥammad ʿabduh*, 5 vols., ed. M. ʿUmārah (Cairo: Dār al-Shurūq, 1427/2006), 2: 70 (the essay runs from 2: 70–5).
214. M. H. Katz, "Ethics, Gender, and the Islamic Legal Project," *Yale Law School Occasional Papers* (2015): 10. Later noting al-Māwardī's acknowledgment that a man may marry for three reasons, she quotes him: "[S]exual enjoyment (istimtaʿ) . . . is the most blameworthy of the three cases and the one that most diminishes the manly virtues (muruwwa) because [a man who pursues this objective] is being led by his animalistic characteristics and pursuing his blameworthy lust (shahwa)." "Ethics," 11.
215. ʿAbduh, "*al-Zawāj*," 73. Incidentally, it is not my intention to imply that ʿAbduh failed to recognize the Islamic secular *tout court* as a matter of principle. At one point, for example, he insists adamantly on the distinction between law and fact, pointing to how misrecognition thereof leads to lamentable claims in the name of *sharīʿah*. See his *al-Islām dīn al-ʿilm wa al-madanīyah* (Cairo: Sīnā li al-Nashr, 1986), 145. Nor should I be understood as dismissing ʿAbduh's prescription in its entirety, as some of what ails women (and men) in marriage is undoubtedly their husbands' (or wives') violation of certain rules of *sharīʿah*.
216. It seems, incidentally, that the famed Shāfiʿī jurist Jalāl al-Dīn al-Ṣuyūṭī received the memo on this: his book on "erotic education," which is some 140 pages of text proper, contains only one marginally relevant Prophetic *ḥadīth*, itself not traced to any of the canonical collections. See his *Nawāḍir al-ayk fī maʿrifat al-nayk*, ed. Ṭ. Ḥ. ʿAbd al-Qawī (Damascus: Dār al-Kitāb al-ʿArabī, n. d.).
217. Riḍā, *Majallat al-Manār*, 34 vols. (Cairo: Dār al-Manār, 1315–1352 A. H.), 23: 543.
218. For Riḍā's overall depiction, see, e.g., *al-Manār*, 23: 539–48; 21: 73–80.
219. See, e.g., Riḍā, *al-Manār*, 4: 860.

220. Riḍā, *al-Manār*, 4: 689.
221. Cited in J. J. Owen, "Church and State in Stanley Fish's Antiliberalism," *American Political Science Review* 93:4 (1999): 922.
222. Even if the religious is counted *shar'ī* in the sense of being *mubāḥ*, the very nature of the *mubāḥ* is that it does not bind a Muslim to any concrete action or inaction.
223. Hunter, *To Change the World*, 28.
224. Following the insight of Stanley Tambiah, I am inclined to dub this tendency "religionized magic." Tambiah described magic as "ritual action that is held to be automatically effective, and ritual action that dabbles with forces and objects that are outside the scope, or independent, of the gods." In other words, divine will ceases to be a factor in human destiny, the latter being seen as ensured entirely by simple adherence to right acts and rituals. See Tambiah, *Magic*, 7. This is the cautionary prism through which I read such statements as, "It was the common understanding that the Sharī'a constitutes the path to the good life, a path that claimed to guarantee well-being in this world and in the hereafter." See Hallaq, *Impossible State*, 112. As the late Yugoslavian Muslim intellectual 'Alija Izetbegovic (d. 1423/2003) put the matter: "We can follow all Islamic rules which, in their ultimate result, should provide us with the 'happiness in both worlds' . . . but, because of the terrific entanglement of destinies, desires and accidents, we can still suffer in body and soul. What can console a mother who has lost her only son? Is there any solace for a man who has been disabled in an accident?. . . Islam does not get its name from its laws, orders, or prohibitions, nor from the efforts of the body and soul it claims, but from something that encompasses and surmounts all that: from a moment of cognition, from the strength of the soul to face the times, from the readiness to endure everything that an existence can offer, from the truth of submission to God." See A. A. Izetbegovic, *Islam between East and West*, 3rd ed. (Oak Brook, IL: American Trust Publications, 1993), 290, 292.
225. See, e.g., Asad, *Formations*, 209: "The separation [of state-administered from religious law] presupposes a very different conception of ethics from the one embedded in the classical *sharī'a*. That is why my reading of [Aḥmad] Safwat's texts is followed by a discussion of the relation between law and ethics in classical Islamic jurisprudence (*fiqh*)."
226. Asad, *Formations*, 16. See also *Formations*, 180, and his summation at *Formations*, 256: "In order to understand 'secularism' I therefore did not begin with an a priori definition of the concept." Regarding religion, he writes, "My argument is that there cannot be a universal definition of religion, not only because its constituent elements and relationships are historically specific, but because that definition itself is the historical product of discursive processes." See his *Genealogies of Religion*, 29.
227. See 'Abd al-Jabbār, *Sharḥ al-uṣūl al-khamsah*, ed. 'A. 'Uthmān (Cairo: Maktabat Wahbah, 1416/1996), 432.
228. Asad, *Formations*, 3.
229. Asad, *Formations*, 5, 15–16.
230. Asad, *Formations*, 8.
231. Asad, *Formations*, 52, 135.
232. Asad, *Formations*, 94.
233. Asad, *Formations*, 106.

234. Asad, *Formations*, 111.
235. Asad, *Formations*, 147.
236. Asad, *Formations*, 206.
237. Asad, *Formations*, 208. I agree, incidentally, with Asad's implied critique here. Contrary to the insinuation of some reformists, Muslim secular engagements in the past went nowhere near the notion of proceeding "*as if* God did not exist."
238. Asad, *Genealogies*, 229.
239. Asad, *Formations*, 208.
240. Asad, *Formations*, 211–12.
241. Asad, *Formations*, 215.
242. Asad, *Formations*, 218
243. Asad, *Formations*, 222.
244. Asad, *Formations*, 228.
245. Asad, *Formations*, 231.
246. Asad, *Formations*, 238.
247. Asad, *Formations*, 253.
248. Asad, *Formations*, 227–32.
249. Asad, *Formations*, 232–5.
250. Asad seems to assume in his analysis of Ṣafwat a connection between a focus on family law and the advocacy of privatization as a general trend among reformists. If we take another text from this same period, however, such as Muḥammad 'Abd al-Hādī al-Jundī's *al-Tashrī' wa wājib al-musharri'* (?Cairo: Maṭba'at al-Iṣlāḥ, 1921), this assumption might be challenged. Al-Jundī is also a Western-trained reformist lawyer and judge. But while the bulk of his concern is with "family law," he also criticizes the public law. For example, he complains bitterly that Article 346 of the Criminal Code, which criminalizes marrying girls under the age of twelve, violates *sharī'ah*, arguing that the foreign sources of this law failed to recognize the distinction in Islamic law between *nikāḥ* as entering a marriage contract and *nikāḥ* as consummation. Al-Jundī, *al-Tashrī'*, 59–64. Meanwhile, al-Jundī also criticizes the criminal law for "effectively legalizing and allowing illicit sex and protecting female fornicators/adulterers in an Islamic country" (*li annahu yadullu alā taḥlīl al-zinā wa ibāḥatih fī balad islāmī*). Al-Jundī, *al-Tashrī'*, 69. In fact, even as a reformer, he sees people imputing outsized *qadāsah* not to *sharī'ah* but more so to Western (particularly French) codes. Al-Jundī, *al-Tashrī'*, 2.
251. Asad, *Formations*, 237.
252. For more on this point, see, e.g., B. M. 'Abd al-Lāwī, *Sulṭat walī al-amr fī taqyīd al-mubāḥ* (Beirut: Dār Maktabat al-Ma'ārif, 1432/2011).
253. See Ṣafwat, *Baḥth fī qā'idat iṣlāḥ qānūn al-aḥwāl al-shakhṣīyah* (Alexandria: Maṭba'at Jurjī Gharzūzī, 1917), 32–8. This is the same text and edition that Asad uses.
254. Ṣafwat, *Baḥth*, 27, 29.
255. Asad, *Formations*, 238.
256. Asad, *Formations*, 208.
257. Asad, *Formations*, 25. It is not my understanding that Asad sees the Western, macro-secular as either the exclusive or the normative understanding of the secular. It is,

rather, that this is the understanding he places in conversation with Islam. Later, he notes that in the Islamic tradition, "[T]he life of this world doesn't clearly separate 'religion' from 'nonreligion.' It is precisely an achievement of [modern, Western] secularism that makes 'religion' an autonomous domain and 'religious discourse' a technical language." See his *Secular Translations: Nation-State, Modern Self and Calculative Reason* (New York: Columbia University Press, 2018), 69.

258. See above, p. 155–56.
259. See above, p. 142–43.
260. See above, p. 139–41.
261. As S. D. Goitein observed, "[W]ith the exception of some local statutes promulgated and abrogated from time to time, the [Muslim] state as such did not possess any law." On this understanding, there would be little basis for zero-sum competition between *sharīʿah* and state law as a free-standing system of non-Islamic rules. See Goitein, *A Mediterranean Society*, 4 vols. (Berkeley: University of California Press, 1967) 1: 66.
262. In some of my popular writing, I have suggested that, in the context of America, those aspects of *sharīʿah* to which Muslims would attach the most importance are those related to family law. I see now, however, that, taking Asad's thesis as their point of departure, some may have seen this as an endorsement of the privatization of *sharīʿah* and, with it, the privatization of Islam as *dīn*. This was not at all my meaning. I simply took seriously the concrete realities of Muslims as a powerless minority in America, and I contemplated these realities in light of the way that scholars such as Ibn Taymīyah analyzed, e.g., the Abyssinian king al-Najāshī's inability to adhere fully to *sharīʿah* following his conversion to Islam, even as king, or the prophet Yūsuf's inability to apply *sharīʿah* fully during his time in Egypt. See Ibn Taymīya, *Majmūʿat al-fatāwā*, 19: 116–17ff. In each case, choices had to be made within specific circumstances, and none of them had anything to do with a commitment to secularization or the privatization of religion. I also took seriously the question of whether or how various aspects of *sharīʿah* even apply to non-Muslims (a point I discuss in Chapter 5). Most important, even if *sharīʿah* were restricted to family law, this would not necessarily imply secularization in the sense of the full privatization of religion, i.e., proceeding in the public sphere "*as if* God did not exist." For, as I have argued at length in this book, Islam as religion, or *dīn*, does *not* equal *sharīʿah*.
263. Ṣafwat, *Baḥth*, 18. Similarly, his use of "*qadāsah*" rather than "*ḥurmah*" reflects an affinity for a Christian over an Islamic vocabulary.
264. At one point, Ṣafwat even cites Ibn al-Qayyim in support of his approach. See *Baḥth*, 40. My point here is that Muslim jurists routinely addressed the historically contingent aspects of the law.
265. See the discussion in the section "The Emergence of the Theoretical Foundations of a Bounded *Sharīʿah*" in Chapter 2. See also my *Islamic Law and the State*, 123–39.
266. See the previous discussion in the section "*Siyāsah*" in this chapter.
267. See the discussion in the section "Differentiation" in Chapter 1.
268. See above; see also my discussion of this issue in Chapter 4.
269. Chadwick, *Secularization*, 16.

270. See my "*Sharīʿah*, Democracy, and the Modern Nation-State: Some Reflections on Islam, Popular Rule, and Pluralism," *Fordham International Law Journal, 27*:1 (2003): 88–107 at 96–7.
271. Batnitzky, *How Judaism Became a Religion*, 1–2.
272. Al-Bishrī, *al-Ḥiwār*, 7–49, esp. 38–42. But see the entire discussion, pp. 7–49.
273. Ahmed, *What Is Islam?* 318. Emphasis original. See also the discussion in the section "Shahab Ahmed" in Chapter 1.
274. Asad, *Formations*, 235.
275. Asad, *Formations*, 235.
276. Al-Bishrī, *al-Ḥiwār*, 48–9.
277. Al-Bishrī, *al-Ḥiwār*, 16.
278. Al-Bishrī, *al-Ḥiwār*, 49.
279. See above.
280. Asad, *Formations*, 212–13; al-Bishrī, *al-Ḥiwār*, 9, 13, 16, 23, 24.
281. See above, p. 168.
282. See above, p. 163.
283. Asad, *Formations*, 182.
284. Lewis, "The Roots of Muslim Rage," 56.
285. One might add gender. But that subject is beyond the scope of the present project and could perhaps only build on the latter.

Chapter 4

1. F. Ajami, "The Summoning: 'But They Said, We Will Not Hearken,'" *Foreign Affairs*, *72*:4 (Sept.–Oct. 1993): 2–9, at 9.
2. Hallaq, *Impossible State*, ix. For Hallaq, the contradiction between the Islamic State and the modern state is unqualified and complete. To clear up any doubt in this regard, he states a bit later in the Introduction: "The argument of this book, as we have already mentioned, is that *any* conception of a modern Islamic state is *inherently self-contradictory*." Hallaq, *Impossible State*, xi. Emphasis original.
3. Hallaq, *Impossible State*, 7, 16, 82. Elsewhere, however, Hallaq writes of the modern state: "Its educational and cultural institutions are designed to manufacture the 'good citizen' who is respectful of the law, submissive to notions of order and discipline, industrious, and productive." See "What Is Shariʿa?" 170.
4. See MacIntyre, *After Virtue*, 255: "Modern systematic politics, whether liberal, conservative, radical or socialist, simply has to be rejected from a standpoint that owes genuine allegiance to the tradition of the virtues; for modern politics itself expresses in its institutional forms a systematic rejection of that tradition." See also Hallaq, *Impossible State*, 6.
5. See Hallaq, *Impossible State*, 7–18. C.f., P. Crone, *Pre-Industrial Societies*, 222: "[A]s long as cognitive and economic growth remain supreme values, neither God nor traditional morality can be allowed to shape the quest for knowledge and wealth."

6. "We . . . argue that modern forms of globalization and the position of the state in the ever increasing intensity of these forms are sufficient to render any brand of Islamic governance either impossible or, if possible, incapable of survival in the long run. . . . Islamic governance is unsustainable, given the conditions prevailing in the modern world." Hallaq, *Impossible State*, xiii.
7. Hallaq, *Impossible State*, 49.
8. As the Arabs say, "*mā lā yudrak kulluh lā yutrak kulluh*," i.e., "The inability to realize a thing in its entirety does not justify abandoning it in its entirety."
9. See, e.g., Hallaq, *Impossible State*, 2–5.
10. "The present book may therefore be regarded as a continuation of and expansion upon *Sharīʿa*'s [i.e., the book's] interest in the state, in *both empirical substance and theoretical direction.*" Hallaq, *Impossible State*, vii. Emphasis original.
11. On jurispathy and the conception of the modern state as a "jurispathic" entity, see Cover, "Nomos and Narrative," 138–44. I will have more to say about the state's legal monism and jurispathic tendencies in Chapter 5.
12. Thus, e.g., when Egypt's Supreme Constitutional Court (SCC) declares itself to be the highest authority in the land and the instance of last resort, not only in determining the *application* of *sharīʿah* (or the law of Coptic Christians) but also regarding the definition of its *substance* and principles, it arguably apotheosizes the state. See, e.g., B. Johansen, "The Relationship between the Constitution, the *Sharīʿa* and the *Fiqh*: The Jurisprudence of Egypt's Supreme Constitutional Court," *Zeitschrift für Ausländisches Öffenliches Recht und Völkerrecht*, 64:4 (2004): 881–96.
13. Thus, the First Amendment of the US Constitution would bar the American state, at least in theory, from assuming the powers to determine religious doctrine, which Egypt's SCC explicitly arrogates to itself.
14. See my *Islamic Law and the State*, xiv.
15. Hallaq, *Impossible State*, 51–2: "The Sharīʿa . . . is the 'legislative power' par excellence." See also pp. 66–70 where Hallaq acknowledges the discretionary powers of the Muslim ruler in principle but then makes every effort to force them back into subservience to *sharīʿah*. I will discuss this further below.
16. At Hallaq, *Impossible State*, 12, there is a passing allusion to the tendency on the part of some modern Muslims to secularize or reduce Islam to "a nominal religious affiliation" with "no system of practices and obligations," in response to the growing hegemony of the modern state, a move that ultimately fails. But this is basically it.
17. Hallaq, *Sharīʿa*, 5.
18. See Cavanaugh, "The City: Beyond Secular Parodies," 188. See also his *The Myth of Religious Violence*, 123–80.
19. See, e.g., Hallaq, *Impossible State*, 156: "[N]one of this should mean that the modern state is an immutable phenomenon, that it does not and cannot change, that it has not adapted or could not adjust to an ever-changing world. For it is hardly deniable that the state of the nineteenth century had noticeably evolved by the middle of the twentieth."
20. In *Impossible State*, 172, note 15, Hallaq writes: "Thus it must be stated once and for all that the argument of this book rests on the premise that a creative reformulation of

Sharī'a and Islamic governance may be one of the most *relevant* and constructive ways to reshape the modern project." Emphasis original. This is not part of the text itself but appears in an endnote appended to a sentence on p. xi.

21. See below, in the section "Is vs. Ought" of this chapter.
22. I.e., the obligatory, automatic shares outlined in the Qur'ān, not the bequest of up to one-third that a Muslim may bequeath to anyone, regardless of religion. On this problem, see Ibn al-Qayyim, *Aḥkām ahl al-dhimmah*, 2: 853–60.
23. Hallaq, *Impossible State*, 57, 64.
24. Hallaq, *Impossible State*, ix. One should not misread his statement at *Impossible State*, 48: "There never was an Islamic state." His point there is that Muslims never organized themselves politically along the lines of what would constitute a modern state.
25. On these form-properties, see the discussion in the section, "Hallaq and the Modern State," below.
26. Interestingly, according to Brian Nelson, American political theorists are known to downplay the importance of the state as an analytical category. See his *The Making of the Modern State*, 1–6. Hallaq seems more interested in the European perspective.
27. Hallaq, *Impossible State*, 20.
28. Hallaq, *Impossible State*, 21. Emphasis original.
29. See M. Foucault, *Power/Knowledge: Selected Interviews and Other Writings, 1972–1977*, trans. C. Gordon, L. Marshall, J. Mepham, and K. Soper (New York: Pantheon books, 1980), 121.
30. See, e.g., K. Morrison, *Marx, Durkheim, Weber: Formations of Modern Social Thought*, 2nd ed. (London: Sage Publications Ltd., 2006), 386: "[H]e [Weber] states that as soon as bureaucracy develops the governed tend to accept the authority of bureaucratic decision making without question and in doing so they give up the right to accountable government. . . . A second consequence of bureaucracy is the tendency to develop secrecy. . . . This leads to the exclusion of the public from decision making and from participation in the production of consensus. Bureaucratic institutions thus become closed, and this entails a loss of democracy."
31. The opening line of Schmitt's classic text, *Political Theology*, reads: "Sovereign is he who decides on the exception." See C. Schmitt, *Political Theology: Four Chapters on the Concept of Sovereignty*, trans. and ed., G. Schwab (Chicago: University of Chicago Press, 2003), 5.
32. See, e.g., Hallaq, *Sharī'a: Theory, Practice, Transformations*, 455, 469, 485, 488, 510. See also below, in the section "Provenance."
33. See, e.g., W. B. Hallaq, "Was the Gate of Ijtihad Closed?" *International Journal of Middle East Studies, 16* (1984): 3–41; "On the Origins of the Controversy about the Existence of Mujtahids and the Gate of Ijtihad," *Studia Islamica, 63* (1986): 129–41.
34. It is interesting that Schmitt should rise to such primacy in Hallaq's theory, given his marginality in the general literature on the state, compared to the likes of Hobbes, Locke, Kant, Hegel, and Rawls, for example. Indeed, whole books are written on the state, including some that Hallaq cites, that make no mention of Schmitt. See, e.g., J. Hall and J. Ikenberry, *The State* (Princeton: Princeton University Press, 1989);

Nelson, *Making of the Modern State*; M. Van Creveld, *The Rise and Decline of the State* (Cambridge: Cambridge University Press, 1999).

35. Hallaq, *Impossible State*, 25.
36. Hallaq, *Impossible State*, 3: "[T]he modern state's genealogy is exclusively European. For given the geographic, systemic, and epistemic genealogy of the modern state, then, it could not have, ipso facto, been Islamic." See also, Hallaq, *Impossible State*, 23–5 and passim.
37. In fact, see, e.g., Ṭaha ʿAbd al-Raḥmān, *Fī uṣūl al-ḥiwār wa tajdīd ʿilm al-kalām* (Beirut: al-Markaz al-Thaqāfī al-ʿArabī, 2014), 19, where he criticizes the tendency of some to exaggerate Islam's debt to the Greeks.
38. See G. Hourani, "Islamic and Non-Islamic Origins of Muʿtazilite Ethical Rationalism," *International Journal of Middle East Studies* 7:1 (1976): 59–87.
39. Al-Māwardī, *al-Aḥkām al-sulṭānīyah*, 189–200, 224–30; Abū Yaʿlā, *al-Aḥkām al-sulṭānīyah*, 165–75.
40. See his view in the section "Efficient Decision-Making" in Chapter 3, on bathhouses and the like. As I stated there, none of this is to impute to Ibn Taymīyah a laissez-faire attitude toward borrowing. In the end, however, he too is clear that provenance alone is not the sole consideration.
41. See the discussion on Ibn Taymīyah in the subsection, "*Efficient Decision-Making*," in Chapter 3 and the discussion of al-Ghazālī in the section, "Beyond the *Ḥukm Sharʿī*" in Chapter 2.
42. See ʿIzz al-Dīn Ibn ʿAbd al-Salām, *Fatāwā sulṭān al-ʿulamāʾ al-ʿizz ibn ʿabd al-salām* (Cairo: Maktabat al-Qurʾān, n.d.), 112. For an identical view, see Khayr al-Dīn al-Tūnisī, *Muqaddimat aqwam al-masālik fī maʿrifat aḥwāl al-mamālik* (appended to Badr al-Dīn Ibn Jamāʿah's *Taḥrīr al-aḥkām fī tadbīr ahl al-islām*) (Beirut: Dār al-Kutub al-ʿIlmīyah, 1424/2003) 10. Again, this is not to suggest that Ibn ʿAbd al-Salām or other jurists would limit their considerations to the simple question of lawfulness. If the act or institution to be borrowed is deemed to violate norms or weaken the plausibility structure or to result in other undue, disproportionate hardship, they may rule that it should not or must not be borrowed.
43. Hallaq, *Impossible State*, 25. Emphasis original.
44. See, e.g., Nelson, *Making of the Modern State*, 66–72.
45. Hallaq, *Impossible State*, 38.
46. See "Law Without Nations: An Introduction," *Law Without Nations*, eds. A. Sarat, L. Douglass and M. M. Humphrey (Stanford: Stanford University Press, 2011), 7. One gets a clear sense of the difference between "the people" and *das Volk* from two inscriptions on the German Reichstag or parliament building. The first, going back to 1916 reads, "*Dem Deutschen Volke*" (To the German People); the second, from the post-War period after the Reichstag had been restored, reads, "*Der Bevölkerung*" (To the Population). Jews (and others) were clearly included in the latter, whereas they could be excluded from the former. See "Law Without Nations," 6–8. The connection between this and Schmitt's all-important distinction between "friend and enemy" and his resulting opposition to pluralism is obvious.

47. To understand the difficulty Schmitt had with popular sovereignty as commonly understood and how he theoretically solved it, see, e.g., L. Vinx, "Carl Schmitt," *The Stanford Encyclopedia of Philosophy* (Fall 2019 Edition), ed., Edward N. Zalta, 4–5. <https://plato.stanford.edu/archives/fall2019/entries/schmitt/>.
48. See, e.g., G. Poggi, *The Development of the Modern State: A Sociological Introduction* (London: Hutchinson of London, 1978), 8, where he notes that in Schmitt's view, "Ultimately a single individual must make each properly political decision, since only a single mind can effectively weigh the momentous contingencies involved in deciding the paramount question of who are the collectivity's friends and foes."
49. "For Schmitt, the very definition of sovereignty is the capacity to declare exceptions to the norm (of civil liberties, human rights, the rule of law, and so on)." See Neal, "Cutting Off the King's Head," 374. Neal points out that this notion of the "exception" caught fire in the aftermath of 9/11, as an analytical construct for both justifying and critiquing practices undertaken as part of the so-called war on terror, including Guantanamo Bay, the extrajudicial killing of terrorists (including American citizens abroad), the pre-emptive war in Iraq, the tightening of immigration policies, and so on.
50. Hallaq, *Impossible State*, 28.
51. See the longish quote from Kahn at Hallaq, *Impossible State*, 27. (The quote is actually found on p. 268 of Kahn's text, not p. 267.)
52. Hallaq, *Impossible State*, 89.
53. Hallaq, *Impossible State*, 178 note 44.
54. Hallaq, *Impossible State*, 152–3. In seeking to understand why Hallaq confers such prominence upon Schmitt, the insights of Seyla Benhabib may prove useful. According to her, "Schmitt . . . offers those who 'obstinately' wish to resist the 'West' a theoretical foothold." In this capacity he has become "the indispensable reference point for all those who want to unveil the hypocrisies, inadequacies, and maybe even bankruptcy, of liberal democratic politics at home and abroad." See her "Carl Schmitt's Critique of Kant: Sovereignty and International Law," *Political Theory*, *40*:6 (2012): 688–713 at 690–1. Benhabib adds, however, that "Schmitt is no innocent defender of multiculturalism resisting the Western hegemon." "Carl Schmitt's Critique," 691.
55. Hallaq, *Impossible State*, 29.
56. Hallaq, *Impossible State*, 29.
57. Hallaq, *Impossible State*, 30.
58. Hallaq, *Impossible State*, 30.
59. Hallaq, *Impossible State*, 30.
60. Hallaq, *Impossible State*, 25. See also the discussion above, in the section "Sovereignty and Law."
61. Counterevidence from Islamic tradition makes it difficult to sustain such a position. Even in the area of *'ibādāt*, where it is generally conceded that *qiyās* (analogy) has no role, there are instances where the Prophet confirms human discretion. For example, when a man praying behind the Prophet came out of the bowing position and unilaterally added the words "*hamd*^{an} *kathīr*^{an} *ṭayyib*^{an} *mubārak*^{an} *fīh*" (bounteous, felicitous,

blessed praises), the Prophet is reported to have praised his action, confirming that the angels rushed to write it down, despite the man's receiving no prior instruction from the Prophet to utter these words in prayer. See al-Bukhārī, *Ṣaḥīḥ al-bukhārī*, 1: 375. Or one may consider the story of how the *adhān*, or Call to Prayer, reportedly came about as the result of a dream by one of the Companions. See, e.g., Ibn Kathīr, *al-Sīrah al-nabawīyah*, 4 vols., ed. M. 'Abd al-Wāḥid (Cairo: 'Īsā al-Bābī al-Ḥalabī, 1384/1964), 2: 334–7. See also *al-Sīrah al-nabawīyah*, 2: 336, for Bilāl's uninstructed, unilateral addition of "Prayer is better than sleep" (*al-ṣalātu khayr*[un] *min al-nawm*) to the Call for the morning prayer, of which it remains a part to this day.

62. This is not a commitment to blind statism. It *is* to say, however, that (beyond the gift of divine facilitation) the integrity of Islam in actual practice, in any place or time, is a function of the quality of commitment and execution on the part of Muslim men and women. The state simply consists of the Muslim men and women who happen to discharge the community's public affairs.
63. Also, recall my earlier reference to al-Qarāfī regarding oaths (*nadhr*). See the discussion in the subsection, "*Siyāsah*," in Chapter 3.
64. See the section "*Siyāsah*" in Chapter 3 on Ibn al-Qayyim. For al-Qarāfī's take on the matter, see his *Tamyīz*.
65. See, e.g., http://www.servat.unibe.ch/dfr/bv006032.html p. 4, section c, lines 6–7 and 9–12. Accessed January 5, 2020.
66. See, e.g., M. Mutua, *Human Rights: A Political and Cultural Critique* (Philadelphia, PA: University of Pennsylvania Press, 2002).
67. See A. Marmor, *Law in the Age of Pluralism* (New York: Oxford University Press, 2007), 90.
68. See Cavanaugh, *Migrations of the Holy: God, State, and the Political Meaning of the Church* (Grand Rapids: William B. Eerdmans Publishing Company, 2011), 26–7, 36, 42, 92, 96, and passim; see also his *The Myth of Religious Violence*, 10, 15–56. Among the manifestations of this migration, Cavanaugh notes, is the sense today that only in the name of the state are we authorized to take human life. Where the death penalty exists, it exists for crimes against "the state" (e.g., treason) or "the people" as the embodiment of the state (murder, terrorism, etc.), not offenses against God (e.g., blasphemy, apostasy).
69. Al-Qarāfī, *Tamyīz*, 148.
70. Hallaq, *Impossible State*, 23.
71. Hallaq, *Impossible State*, 92.
72. Hallaq, *Impossible State*, 28.
73. Hallaq, *Impossible State*, 26–7.
74. Rosa Parks was a Blackamerican woman known for her courageous refusal to give up her seat to a White passenger on a legally segregated Alabama bus in December of 1955. Almost a year earlier, a fifteen-year-old Blackamerican girl, Claudette Colvin, preceded Parks in a similar action, refusing to give up her seat on a legally segregated bus in Alabama to a White woman.
75. See, e.g., M. C. Dawson, *Black Visions: The Roots of Contemporary African-American Political Ideologies* (Chicago: University of Chicago Press, 2001), 23–43.

76. Long, "Theologies Opaque," 207: "[T]he opaque ones deny the authority of the white world to define their reality, and deny the methodological and philosophical meaning of transparency as a metaphor for a theory of knowledge." See also his "Civil Rights–Civil Religion: Visible People and Invisible Religion," in *American Civil Religion*, eds. R. E. Richey and D. G. Jones (New York: Harper Forum Books, 1974), 211–221.
77. According to Long in "Civil Rights," 219, Blackamericans and White Americans simply relate to the state differently: "In the telling of the story of America and American cultural reality we have been dominated by one tradition, the tradition of the 'mighty saga of the outward acts told and retold' in such a manner, 'until it overshadowed and suppressed the equally vital but more somber story of *the inner experience*.'" (Emphasis original.) Included in this "inner experience" is an episteme of "transparency" that predisposes White Americans to assimilate state propaganda as an extension of the "mighty deeds of the white conquerors," whereas the opacity of Blackamericans predisposes them to resist, if not reject, these very efforts.
78. Hallaq, *Impossible State*, 32.
79. Hallaq, *Impossible State*, 31.
80. Hallaq, *Impossible State*, 33.
81. Hallaq, *Impossible State*, 33.
82. See Tāj al-Dīn al-Subkī, *Mu'īd al-ni'am wa mubīd al-niqam*, 35, 36. In fact, al-Subkī considers this latter office a vile innovation.
83. See my "The Primacy of Domestic Politics: Ibn Bint Al-A'azz and the Establishment of Four Chief Judgeships in Mamlūk Egypt," *Journal of the American Oriental Society*, *115*:1 (1995): 52–65. We might recall, meanwhile, some of al-Māwardī's descriptions of the bureaucratic role of Mamlūk *amīr*s in the administration of justice.
84. Hallaq, *Impossible State*, 31 and the footnote reference at 179, note 55.
85. R. Euben and M. Q. Zaman, eds., *Princeton Readings in Islamist Thought: Texts and Contexts from al-Banna to Bin Laden* (Princeton: Princeton University Press, 2009), 176.
86. "When the juridical methods of Islam were applied, the shari'a judge in each town, assisted only by two bailiffs and with only a pen and an inkpot at his disposal, would swiftly resolve disputes among people and send them about their business." Euben and Zaman, *Princeton Readings*, 176.
87. We should recall, however, the positive attitude that Fahmy displayed towards bureaucracy. See the discussion in the subsection, "'Sharī'ah and *Islamic Law*'" in Chapter 3 above.
88. See note 152 in the subsection, "*Ḥisbah*" in Chapter 3.
89. See below, in the section "Reason and Islamic Law." Of course, we could also go back to Ibn al-Muqaffa' (d. 139/756) and his *Risālat al-ṣaḥābah*, with its attempt to persuade the Caliph to codify *sharī'ah* in order to bolster the state's image as upholder of justice.
90. On the *miḥnah*, see below, in the section "Reason and Islamic Law."
91. See, e.g., Stilt, *Islamic Law in Practice*, 101–48, 194–202.
92. In the year 700/1300, e.g., in response to the Muslim populace's undue public fawning over a Christian notable, the Sultan is reported to have issued a discretionary decree imposing all kinds of restrictions on non-Muslims, clearly for the purpose of reversing this

inclination to venerate them. See al-Maqrīzī, *Kitāb al-Sulūk*, 1/3:909–11. See also the discussion in the section, "*The Empire-State between* Sharī'ah *and the Islamic Secular*," in Chapter 5 on whether these were *shar'ī* or non-*shar'ī* stipulations.

93. A. Bilgrami, "Secularism, Nationalism, and Modernity," in R. Bhargava, ed., *Secularism and Its Critics*, 380-417 at 412. Bilgrami, incidentally, is not a proponent of an Islamic State.
94. Bilgrami, "Secularism," 417.
95. See the section "Non-Muslims: Islam-cum-*Sharī'ah* between the Modern State and the Empire-State" in Chapter 5.
96. Note the incessance with which the Qur'ān chides those who refuse to follow reason, suggesting that, if they did, they would follow the message brought by Muḥammad. Of course, it may be argued that "reason" in the Qur'ān did not mean what it generally does today, namely, disembodied, transcendent Kantian reason. But this is precisely the point: there are multiple modes or systems of reasoning, and to defy any one of them is not necessarily to defy reason itself.
97. See, e.g., K. Sorensen, "Revelation and Reason in Leo Strauss," *The Review of Politics*, 65:3 (2003): 383–408.
98. Mariña, "Kant, Schleiermacher and the Study of Theology," 7.
99. See A. El Shamsy, *The Canonization of Islamic Law: A Social and Intellectual History* (Cambridge: Cambridge University Press, 2013), 57–8.
100. This is one of the reasons it has been so easy to dismiss Traditionalism as crass fideism. In fact, Traditionalists are routinely excluded from the construct "theology/theologians" when scholars speak or write about Islam. Because they oppose the interpretations of Greek-inspired Rationalist thought, Traditionalists have been cast as opposing reason, period. The idea that Traditionalist views might be just as reasonable as Rationalist views but simply based on a different, i.e., non-Greek-inspired, system of reasoning is rarely contemplated.
101. A. J. Arberry traces the origins of the reason/revelation complex in general to the encounter between Greek philosophy and revealed Semitic religion—as he put it, "between Greece and Israel." He claims that no such conflict was perceived among the carriers of the "Old Testament," and it was hardly an issue for the early recipients of the New Testament. It was the apologetics of the Jewish thinker Philo of Alexandria (d. first century BCE), however, that put forth the thesis that "Scripture was a divine revelation and that Greek philosophy was [also] true," as a result of which Philo found himself "faced with the problem of effecting 'the reconciliation of philosophy with the Law, Plato with Moses.'" See A. J. Arberry, *Revelation and Reason in Islam*, 2nd impression (London: George Allen and Unwin Ltd., 1965), 9–10.
102. W. B. Hallaq, *The Origins and Evolution of Islamic Law* (Cambridge: Cambridge University Press, 2005), 75.
103. Hallaq, *Sharī'a*, 43.
104. Hallaq, *Sharī'a*, 57. See also Hallaq, *Sharī'a*, 49–50, where he describes various forms of *ra'y*.

105. According to Schacht, "[E]verything that is not based on a tradition from the Prophet is in the last resort *ra'y* for al-Shāfiʿī." See his *Origins of Muhammadan Jurisprudence*, 113.
106. Hallaq, *Sharīʿa*, 49.
107. Hallaq, *Impossible State*, 166. See also Hallaq, *Sharīʿa*, 59.
108. Abū Dā'ūd al-Sijistānī, *Risālat al-imām abī dā'ūd al-sijistānī ilā ahl makka wa waṣf sunanih*, ed. ʿA. Abū Ghuddah (Aleppo: Maktab al-Maṭbūʿāt al-Islāmīyah, 1417/ 1997), 32–3.
109. See Ibn Rushd, *Bidāyat al-mujtahid*, 2: 31–5. According to Ibn Rushd, the Ḥanafīs were not the only ones to hold this view in the early period.
110. See the section, "*Sharīʿah* between Hallaq and the Islamic Secular," above, p.217–18.
111. On this conflict, see A. El Shamsy, *Canonization*, 55–6.
112. For example, Ibn al-Nadīm counts Abū Ḥanīfa and his Irāqī partisans (including Abū Yūsuf) among the *aṣḥāb al-ra'y*, while placing al-Awzāʿī among the *aṣḥāb al-ḥadīth*. See his *al-Fihrist*, ed. Y.ʿA. Ṭawīl (Beirut: Dār al-Kutub al-ʿIlmīyah, 1416/ 1996), 344, 376. In Abū Yūsuf's polemic against al-Awzāʿī, however, he systematically deploys *ḥadīth* against al-Awzāʿī and adduces *ḥadīth* to back his attitude toward and approach *to ḥadīth*. See Abū Yūsuf, *al-Radd ʿalā siyar al-awzāʿī*, ed. Abū al-Wafā' al-Afghānī (Cairo: Lajnat Iḥyā' al-Maʿārif al-Nuʿmānīyah,?1358/ 1939), 24–33.
113. See al-Qāḍī ʿIyāḍ, *Tartīb al-madārik wa taqrīb al-masālik*, 2 vols., ed. M. S. Hāshim (Beirut: Dār al-Kutub al-ʿIlmīyah, 1418/1998), 1: 273. Two points. First, this is too early to have been part of a "Great Synthesis." Second, Asad's point is that the boundary between what is *ra'y* and what is *athar* is not as rigid as is sometimes assumed. In fact, immediately after the statement cited, he notes that sometimes, when he asked Ibn al-Qāsim about Mālik's doctrine, Ibn al-Qāsim would relate the latter through such phrases as "I suppose" (*akhāl*) or "I think" (*arā*), clearly blurring the boundary between *ra'y* and *athar*.
114. Qādi Iyāḍ, *Tartīb al-madārik*, 1: 102.
115. See his *The Origins of Islamic Jurisprudence: Meccan* Fiqh *before the Classical Schools*, trans. M. Katz (Leiden: E. J. Brill, 2002), 90–1.
116. Abū Dā'ūd al-Sijistānī, *Risālat al-imām abī dā'ūd al-sijistānī ilā ahl makka wa waṣf sunanih*, 32–3.
117. See Ibn Qutaybah, *Ta'wīl mukhtalaf al-ḥadīth*, 2nd ed., ed. A. S. al-Hilālī (Riyadh: Dār Ibn al-Qayyim, 1430/2009), 131.
118. Hallaq, *Sharīʿa*, 57.
119. We saw in Chapter 2 Ibn Taymīyah's attempt to break the Rationalist claim over "reason." See the subsection, "Ibn Taymīyah," in Chapter 2 above, p116–17.
120. *Qiyās*, e.g., or *al-barā'ah al-aṣlīyah* (presumption of former status) would be admitted in law but not in Traditionalist theology.
121. See Ibn Qudāmah, *Rawḍat al-nāẓir*, 4–15. For Ibn Qudāmah's staunchly Traditionalist credentials, see his *Taḥrīm al-naẓar fī kutub ahl al-kalām*, ed. and trans. G. Makdisi, as *Ibn Qudāma's Censure of Speculative Theology* (Cambridge: E. J. W. Gibb Memorial Trust, 1985). Meanwhile, Hallaq insists that Ibn Taymīyah

rejected "elements of Greek logic." *Sharīʿa*, 81. It is unclear in this depiction whether Ibn Taymīyah rejected these as theological/philosophical tools or as juristic ones.

122. Abū Yaʿlā, *al-ʿUddah*, 1: 22–39.
123. See, e.g., ʿAbd Allāh b. Aḥmad b. Ḥanbal, *Masāʾil al-imām aḥmad bin ḥanbal*, ed. A. al-Miṣrī (Manṣūrah: Dār al-Mawaddah, 1429/2008), 75. See also *Masāʾil*, 151, where he responds to his son ʿAbd Allāh's question about whether to pay *zakāt al-fiṭr* (at the end of Ramadan) to a single individual or to distribute it among several, by stating that one should distribute it among several and that "That would be most preferable to me (*aʿjabu lī*)." Also, at *Masāʾil*, 151, in response to whether one may pay *zakāt al-fiṭr* in cash instead of food, he states, "I fear that that might not retire his obligation (*lā yujziʾuh*)." Meanwhile, the Shāfiʿī jurist Taqī al-Dīn al-Subkī (d. 756/1355) notes that al-Shāfiʿī, "did not proceed on the basis of many *ḥadīth* whose soundness he accepted but in the face of which he recognized some other indicant that detracted from its probative value, or which he saw as abrogated, or whose general scope he saw as restricted or whose meaning he took to be figurative." See Taqī al-Dīn ʿAlī b. ʿAbd al-Kāfi al-Subkī, *Maʿnā qawl al-imām al-muṭṭalabī idhā ṣaḥḥa al-ḥadīth fa huwa madhhabī*, ed. ʿA. N. Biqāʾī (Beirut: Dār al-Bashāʾir, 1413/1993), 108.
124. Abū Yaʿlā, *Ṭabaqāt al-ḥanābilah*, 2 vols. (Beirut: Dār al-Maʿrifah, n.d.), 1: 171.
125. Wymann-Landgraff, *Mālik and Medina*, 9.
126. C.f., however, S. A. Spectorsky, "Aḥmad Ibn Ḥanbal's *Fiqh*," *Journal of the American Oriental Society*, *102*:3 (1982): 461–5 at 462 note 7: "Abū Dāwūd reports him (Aḥmad) saying, 'I don't like Malik's' or anyone else's *raʾy* (*lā yuʿjibunī raʾy mālik wa lā raʾy aḥad*[in])." Even taking Aḥmad (or Abū Dāʾūd) at his word, this *raʾy* is not necessarily the same as "human reason." Indeed, Ahmad El Shamsy's description of *raʾy* suggests that it was a very particular style of human reason. Noting that the Companions engaged in legal reasoning, he adds, "[T]here was an equally clear recognition among second/eighth century observers that they were witnessing the emergence of a new kind of reasoning." See his *Canonization*, 22.
127. Wymann-Landgraff, *Malik in Medina*, 508. See also S. Lucas, "Principles of Traditionist Jurisprudence Reconsidered," *The Muslim World*, *100*:1 (2010): 145–56, where he challenges the notion that early Traditionalists relied on scriptural/textual authority alone. C.f., however, C. Melchert, *The Formation of the Sunni Schools of Law, 9th–10th Centuries C.E.* (Leiden: E. J. Brill, 1997), 1: "From the later eighth century to the beginning of the tenth, there raged fierce controversy between those who would found their jurisprudence exclusively on hadith, *aṣḥāb al-ḥadīth*, or traditionalists, and those who reserved a leading place for common sense, *aṣḥāb al-raʾy*"; and C. Melchert, "Traditionist-Jurisprudents and the Framing of Islamic Law," *Islamic Law and Society* 3:3 (2001): 383–406, esp., 385: "In sum, the distinction between rationalist jurisprudents and traditionist jurisprudents is no mere modern projection on the past."
128. Hallaq, *Sharīʿa*, 542.
129. "Unlike the modern state, in Islamic governance the Sharīʿa is unrivaled in this domain, and no power other than it can truly legislate." Hallaq, *Impossible State*, 52.

130. Hallaq, *Impossible State*, 57.
131. See also Hallaq, *Impossible State*, 58–9.
132. See Hallaq, *Authority, Continuity and Change in Islamic Law* (Cambridge: Cambridge University Press, 2001), 103.
133. Hallaq, *Authority, Continuity and Change*, 103. This was a reversal (unacknowledged) of his earlier views on *taqlīd*. See my "*Ijtihād* and *Taqlīd*: Between the Islamic Legal Tradition and Autonomous Western Reason," in *Routledge Handbook of Islamic Law*, eds. K. Abou El Fadl, A. A. Atif, and S. F. Hassan (London and New York: Routledge, 2019), 255–72.
134. Hallaq, *Sharīʿa*, 455.
135. Hallaq, *Impossible State*, 469.
136. Hallaq, *Sharīʿa*, 485.
137. See the subsection, "*The Standard View*" and note 68 in Chapter 2 above, p. 412.
138. Hallaq, *Sharīʿa*, 503–04. He goes on to conduct similar dissections of Riḍā and Khallāf.
139. See, e.g., Ibn al-Qayyim, *Aḥkām ahl al-dhimmah*, 2: 853–72. Again, the issue is the automatic shares (*mīrāth*) outlined in the Qurʾān, not bequests (*waṣīyah*). On the Ḥanafīs, see the subsection "*Differentiation*" in Chapter 1.
140. See the subsection, "*The Secular: Macro- and Micro-Modes*," in Chapter 1, p. 38.
141. Hallaq, *Sharīʿa*, 503. In fairness, Hallaq is merely echoing here a view commonly held and long maintained in the field, a view under whose influence I have also ocassionally fallen. See, e.g., my "The Alchemy of Domination: Some Ashʿarite Responses to Muʿtazilite Ethics," *International Journal of Middle East Studies,* 3 (1999): 185-201 at 195, 197; *Islam and the Problem of Black Suffering*, 84, 114 and passim. Thus articulated, this view fails to distinguish between 1) morality as what is good or bad and morality as what God rewards or punishes; and 2) morality as an extra-mental ontological reality and morality as human preference and perspective. *Mea culpa*.
142. See A. Zysow, *The Economy of Certainty*, 203, note 269. Scholars generally attributed to early Muslim theologians, especially Ashʿarites, a commitment to what George Hourani called "theistic subjectivism," i.e., "the idea that 'good,' 'right,' and similar terms have no other meaning than that which God wills; thus God makes things good or right for us by His decision that they should be so." See G. Hourani, "Two Theories of Value in Early Islam," in his *Reason and Tradition in Islamic Ethics* (Cambridge: Cambridge University Press, 1985), 59. This article was originally published in 1960. In a footnote at the beginning of its republished version (p. 57) Hourani states that the article needs to be updated in light of more recent studies, though he believes it still holds valid for the formative period. I note, again, that my claim here is simply that this view was popularized at the hands of al-Rāzī, not that he was its innovator. We find this perspective at least over a century earlier in the views of al-Ghazālī and even al-Juwaynī. Meanwhile, such earlier characterizations of mine of al-Rāzī as "removing morality from the realm of reason and establishing scripture as the only legitimate source of value" are simply wrong. See my "Alchemy,"

187. There are similar misstatements in this article regarding Ash'arite doctrine as well. *Mea culpa*.

143. Al-Qarāfī, *Sharḥ tanqīḥ*, 108. We find similar language in al-Ghazālī, absent the explicit *'aqlī/shar'ī* distinction. See his *al-Iqtiṣād*, 80–6. This is distinct, of course, from al-Ghazālī's discussion of the *ḥukm shar'ī*.

144. Al-Qarāfī, *Sharḥ tanqīḥ*, 109. This perspective is not limited to Ash'arites among the Rationalists. See, e.g., Ibn al-Humām, *al-Musāmarah*, 2: 35–6, where he confirms the same for the Māturīdīs.

145. Al-Qarāfī, *Sharḥ tanqīḥ l*, 109.

146. Al-Shāṭibī, *al-Muwāfaqāt*, 1: 35.

147. Ibn 'Abd al-Salām, *Qawā'id al-aḥkām*, 1: 5. He adds at 1: 8 that it is simply otherworldly interests and liabilities that are known by revelation only.

148. Al-Shahrastānī *Nihāyat al-iqdām 'alā 'ilm al-kalām*, ed. A. Guillaume (n.p.: n.d.), 371.

149. Al-Zarkashī, *Al-Baḥr al-muḥīt*, 1: 146.

150. They remain uncomfortable, however, with the Ash'arite response to the Mu'tazilites. The latter argued that acts are good or bad because they are the repository of an inherently good or bad essence (*ṣifah dhātīyah*). The Ash'arites denied this and argued that acts are good or bad either by divine designation or by individual preference or social convention; they are not the repository of any good or bad essence. Ibn Taymīyah and Ibn al-Qayyim believed that there is inherent good and bad in acts, which is why God commands or forbids them, but on God's own accord, not because the goodness or badness of the acts compel God to do so. While they do not completely confirm the Mu'tazilites' realist moral ontology, they remain opposed to what they see as the Ash'arites' complete denial of all inherent good or bad traits in acts. See, e.g., Ibn Taymīyah, *Majmū' at al-fatāwā*, 8: 256–9. See also Ibn al-Qayyim, *Madārij al-sālikīn bayna manāzil iyyāka na'budu wa iyyāka nasta'īn*, 3 vols., ed. B. M 'Uyūn (Beirut: Maktabat Dār Lubnān, 1420/1999), 1: 237: "Actions are good or evil in themselves, just as they are beneficial or harmful, the difference among them being as that among various smells or objects of sight. Nevertheless, no reward or punishment accrues to them except on the basis of a command or prohibition, prior to which an act's evil does not oblige punishment, despite its being absolutely evil in and of itself. God simply does not mete out punishment for such evil except after God sends messengers."

151. Speaking of the efforts of 'Abduh, Hallaq states that he "instigated a relative break from the pre-modern Ash'arite conception of causality and rationality. A chief postulate of this ['Abduh's] theology, considerably influenced by Mu'tazilite thought (and no doubt reflecting an indirect Kantian influence), was that sound human reason is, on its own, capable of distinguishing right from wrong." *Sharī'a*, 503. Clearly, however, 'Abduh did not necessarily borrow from Mu'tazilism or Kant here nor depart from (especially later) Ash'arism.

152. In its essential features, the Baghdādī school paralleled the pre-Enlightenment doctrine of "intelligible essences," according to which a stone is distinguishable from a plant because it is the repository of an objectively intelligible "stoneness." The Baṣrian position, meanwhile, anticipated Kant's "a priori concepts of understanding"

or "categories of the mind," according to which the mind apprehends reality according to preset schemas. See, e.g., R. Scruton, *Kant: A Very Short Introduction* (New York: Oxford University Press, 2001), 36–7. On the Muʿtazilite doctrine more generally, see G. Hourani, "Two Theories of Value"; S. Vasalou, *Moral Agents and Their Deserts: The Character of Muʿtazilite Ethics* (Princeton: Princeton University Press, 2008), 1–11.

153. See Qāḍī al-Qudāh ʿAbd al-Jabbār b. Aḥmad, *Sharḥ al-uṣūl al-khamsah*, 41.

154. Ibn Taymīyah continues to portray the Ashʿarites as denying the idea that benefits or harms accrue to acts and that this is why God commands or prohibits them. He complains that, on the Ashʿarite understanding, where the Qurʾān speaks of the Prophet's "commanding good and forbidding evil," this does not refer to any good or evil that accrues to these acts prior to the command itself; it simply means that "he commands them to do what he commands them to do and forbids them to do what he forbids them to do." Ibn Taymīyah, *Majmūʿat al-fatāwā*, 8: 257. This is strange on Ibn Taymīyah's part, as he is writing in the period *after* al-Rāzī and al-Qarāfī, both of whose works he knew.

155. Al-Qarāfī, *al-Furūq*, 4: 122–3: "*fa al-istiqrāʾ dalla ʿalā anna al-mafāsid wa al-maṣāliḥ sābiqah ʿalā al-awāmir wa al-nawāhī wa al-thawāb wa al-ʿiqāb tābiʿ*[un] *li al-awāmir wa al-nawāhī.*" See also, al-Qarāfī, *Nafāʾis al-uṣūl*, 1: 150, where he notes that the Ashʿarites acknowledge that God issues rulings pursuant to harms and benefits and that they only disagree with the Muʿtazilites in that the latter hold God to be bound to do so.

156. Opwis, *Maṣlaḥa and the Purpose of the Law*, 1.

157. See, e.g., the father-and-son team Taqī al-Dīn and Tāj al-Dīn al-Subkī, *al-Ibhāj fī sharḥ al-minhāj*, 3 vols., ed. M. A. al-Sayyid (Beirut: Dār al-Kutub al-ʿIlmīyah, 1424/2004), 3: 46. This work is particularly pertinent, given that Tāj al-Dīn was a highly partisan Ashʿarite, in whose theology reason, according to Hallaq, was not supposed to be able to penetrate the aims and objectives behind God's law.

158. Ibn ʿAbd al-Salām, *Qawāʿid al-aḥkām*, 1: 11–12. For an almost identical view, see Ibn Taymīyah, "*al-Iḥtijāj bi al-qadar*," *Majmūʿ al-rasāʾil*, 2: 103.

159. On this point, see, e.g., Ibn Taymīyah, *Majmūʿ at al-fatāwā*, 20: 30–6, esp. 20: 33: "Thus, it becomes clear that evil may be tolerated in two instances: where tolerating it repels an evil that is greater and there is no other way to avoid the latter; and where it occurs as the result of doing an act that entails a greater good that would not obtain were this act abandoned" (*fa tabayyana anna 's-sayyiʾah tuḥtamal fī mawḍiʿayn dafʿ mā huwa aswaʾ minhā idhā lam tudfaʿ illā bihā wa taḥṣul bimā huwa anfaʿ min tarkihā idhā lam taḥṣul illā bihā*). Of course, the point here is that there is often tension between the morally good and the practically good, and juristic discourse cannot (or should not) ignore this.

160. Al-Qarāfī, *al-Furūq*, 4: 180. See also al-ʿIzz, *Qawāʿid al-aḥkām*, 1: 178, 1: 186.

161. See also the discussion in the subsection, "*Siyāsah*" and note 87 in Chapter 3, Incidentally, he cites al-Shāfiʿī as agreeing with this premise.

162. Hallaq, *Impossible State*, 1.

163. Hallaq, *Impossible State*, 50. Emphasis original.

164. Hallaq, *Impossible State*, 49.
165. Hallaq, *Impossible State*, 159. At *Impossible State*, 88, he adds: "*Īmān* must be proven, and only good works can be the effectual means." I beg to differ with Professor Hallaq here. While morality, or "doing good," is highly valued in Islam, it is *not* the core and kernel of Islam. The core and kernel is *tawḥīd*, the refusal to absolutize, supernaturalize, or worship any power, value, authority, or relationship save as these are located in God. Morality, or doing good, may—and should—follow this; but there is no mechanical relationship between the two, such that lapses in morality absolutely spoil *tawḥīd*. In fact, *tawḥīd* implies a moral humility born of a recognition of ultimate dependence on God, even for the ability to act morally. In other words, not only does the oft-repeated principle *lā ḥawla wa lā quwwata illā billāh*, "There is no capacity and no power except by God," extend to moral behavior, it is prior to it. Thus, whatever value doing good devoid of *tawḥīd* may have, it falls short of constituting the core of Islam. We simply do not need Islam (or religion in general) to make us act morally: gulags, shock treatments, Big Brother and now cancel culture can do that on their own. Indeed, among the complaints of the morally "puritanical" Ibn Taymīyah against the philosophers (*falāsifah*) was that they took the goal of *'ibādāt* (religious observances) to be nothing more than the cultivation of good morals (*tahdhīb al-akhlāq*), *sharī'ah* becoming thus little more than a "civic code" (*siyāsah madanīyah*). This, he implied, was a naïve and sinister corruption of *tawḥīd* and the true meaning of *'ibādah*. See his *al-Nubūwāt*, ed. M.Ḥ al-Fiqī (Cairo: Maktabat al-Sunnah, N.d.), 81. Meanwhile, it is well known that Sunnism rejected the Khārijite perspective on faith (*īmān*), according to which faith could only be expressed by good deeds, those who committed major sins being excommunicated.
166. Hallaq, *Impossible State*, 160.
167. Hallaq, *Impossible State*, 75–89.
168. Ibn Taymīyah, *al-Siyāsah al-shar'īyah fī iṣlāḥ al-rā'ī wa al-ra'īyah*, 4th ed. (Egypt: Dār al-Kitāb al-'Arabī, 1969), 16. Incidentally, I am not sure what would distinguish Aḥmad's opinion here from *ra'y*.
169. Hallaq, *Impossible State*, 82. Emphasis original. To my mind, the Qur'ān might be read as yielding a different conclusion. For example, where the pagan Arabians protest that there is no difference between mark-ups in sale (*bay'*) and charging interest on loaned money after the passing of an agreed-upon due date (*ribā*), the Qur'ān responds defiantly: "But God made sale lawful and charging interest unlawful." [2: 275] In his famous exegesis, al-Ṭabarī (d. 310/922) confirms that the Arabians were technically right—there is no ontological distinction between sale and *riba*, between increasing the price of a commodity before the sale and increasing it after the originally agreed-upon due date had passed, both being simply mark-ups. He affirms, however, that God simply posited the ban on *ribā* by divine fiat: "God the Exalted is saying, 'The increase in sale is not like the increase in *ribā*, because I have permitted sale and forbidden *ribā*. The command is My command and the creation My creation. And I adjudicate among them as I please.'" In other words, God, not the ontological Is, determines the Ought. See his *Jāmi' al-bayān 'an tafsīr al-qur'ān*,

30 vols. (Cairo: Muṣṭafā al-Bābī al-Ḥalabī wa Awlāduh, 1388/1968), 3: 103–04 esp. 3: 104 for the quoted segment.

170. See his *Knowledge and Politics* (New York: The Free Press, 1975), 32–43. It is interesting that the Muʿtazilites, whose "moral objectivism" echoes this position, have long enjoyed an image in Western scholarship as rationalists par excellence and thus more likely to promote the kind of liberty we now value. But their ontology arguably goes further than that of their opponents in facilitating theocracy, since human assessments of good and evil can be attributed to God in a manner that is direct and non-negotiable. In other words, according to them, we can know—and police—good and evil in the same way that we know and police mathematics.

171. As I see it, there are two problems with mapping MacIntyre onto Islam. First, as Christopher Lutz puts it, "MacIntyre's catastrophe is not the Protestant Reformation, nor is it Protestantism combined with Jansenism, rather it is the whole process of that turn from natural teleology to theological voluntarism and nominalism." And, further, "MacIntyre's criticism of modern voluntarism and nominalism indicates the shortcomings of non-realist approaches to philosophy." See C. S. Lutz, *Reading Alasdair MacIntyre's After Virtue* (New York: Continuum International Publishing Group, 2012), 46 and 51. As we will see, the position of both Islamic Rationalism (excepting Muʿtazilites) and Traditionalism challenges the notion that moral chaos and dislocation flow inevitably from nominalism. Second, whereas MacIntyre's teleology is a "natural teleology," Islam's is essentially a "religious teleology" (to the extent that we can justifiably speak of such). This makes for an important distinction between "morality," on the one hand, and "*ʿibādah*," or acceptance of psycho-dynamic dependence on and commitment to God, on the other. In explaining, e.g., how the Is implies the Ought, MacIntyre writes: "From such factual premises as 'He gets a better yield for this crop per acre than any other farmer in the district,' 'He has the most effective programme of soil renewal yet known' and 'His dairy herd wins all the first prizes at the agricultural shows,' the evaluative conclusion validly follows that 'He is a good farmer.'" *After Virtue*, 58. This would presumably map onto Islam as follows: "He performs all of his prayers, gives regularly in charity, honors his parents, and avoids illicit sex. The evaluative conclusion validly follows that 'He is a good Muslim.'" Without categorically denying this conclusion, one would be hard pressed to explain on its basis such things as the Prophet's references to a man who repeatedly drank wine as "loving God and loving God's Messenger," or to the prostitute who was granted entry to Paradise for rescuing a dog dying of thirst. In sum, while morality, or living in accordance with divine dictates, is an inextricable constituent of the Islamic *telos*, it does not exhaust the latter. The moral Is—in terms of rule-following—simply cannot be assumed to encompass all the Islamic Ought. As the famed Ibn ʿAṭāʾ Allāh al-Sakandari (d. 709/1309) put it: "Disobedience in a state of humiliation and recognizing one's need for guidance is better than obedience in a state of vaingloriousness and arrogance." See my *Sufism for Non-Sufis? Ibn ʿAta' Allāh al-Sakandarī's* Tāj al-ʿArūs (New York: Oxford University Press, 2012), 46.

172. According to Charles Taylor, nominalism has been linked to the rise of secularization and "the development of a clear distinction between nature and supernature, immanent order and transcendent reality, which as we have seen has been an essential intellectual background of modern secularity." See Taylor, *A Secular Age*, 773. See also S. White, "Weak Ontology: General and Critical Issues," *Hedgehog Review* 7:2 (2005): 11–25, esp. 16, where it is noted that religious monotheists have a particular affinity for strong, realist ontologies: "It is perhaps the case that religions with an omnipotent creator-god have the most difficulty avoiding strong ontological formulations. Creation by a subject entails intentionality, and the *created* are presumed bound in some way to conform to those intentions. What then could provide a more powerful sense of affirmation and self-righteousness than to know and feel that your words and will have tapped directly into divine intentionality." Emphasis original. I have no interest in contesting any of these as statements of fact. My point is simply that Islam suggests that there is no *necessary* connection between religiosity and realist ontology, a position supported even in the West. For example, Isaiah Berlin describes the deeply religious German thinker and frequent sparring partner of Kant, J. G. Hamann (d. 1788), as a "genuine nominalist." See I. Berlin, *The Magus of the North: J. G. Hamann and the Origins of Modern Irrationalism* (New York: Farrar, Straus, and Giroux, 1993), 45. This book was reprinted in Berlin's *Three Critics of the Enlightenment: Vico, Hamann, Herder*, ed. H. Hardy (Princeton: Princeton University Press, 2000).
173. See al-Ghazālī, *al-Iqtiṣād*, 79.
174. Hallaq, *Impossible State*, 89. Bracketed segments mine.
175. C. Taylor, "Justice After Virtue," in *After MacIntyre: Critical Perspectives on the Work of Alasdair MacIntyre*, eds. J. Horton and S. Mendus (Notre Dame: University of Notre Dame Press, 1994), 16–43 at 18.
176. "Justice After Virtue," 18. Hallaq cites this source but depicts Taylor as presenting only one side of the conflict. He writes: "As Charles Taylor has cogently argued, 'the fact/value split' has become 'a dominant theme in our [twentieth] century' and has undergirded 'a new understanding and valuation of freedom and dignity.'" Hallaq, *Impossible State*, 80.
177. See her *Pre-Industrial Societies*, 224.
178. Hallaq, *Sharīʿa*, 362.
179. Hallaq, *Sharīʿa*, 362.
180. Ibn ʿAbd al-Salām, *Qawāʿid al-aḥkām*, 1: 10.
181. Hallaq, *Impossible State*, 51–2. Emphasis original.
182. Hallaq, *Impossible State,* 67. One notices that Hallaq consistently capitalizes "*Sharʿīyya*" in this construct.
183. Hallaq, *Impossible State*, 69.
184. Hallaq, *Sharīʿa*, 502.
185. Hallaq, *Sharīʿa*, 503.
186. As Aron Zysow points out, apparently with *early* Ashʿarism in mind, Ashʿarites *as theologians* appear to deny the ethical cognition that would enable humans to locate any good in acts outside the fact that God commanded them. Taken seriously,

this would deny the whole basis of analogy, at the heart of which is identifying the benefits and harms that mark certain traits as the reason (*'illah*) for scripture commanding or forbidding acts. Precisely because of this, when it came to law, Ash'arites *as jurists* "were led to acknowledge not merely that God's actions are purposeful, a proposition that the Qur'ān itself supports, but, much the more significant, to claim that these purposes could be recognized by the human mind." See A. Zysow, *The Economy of Certainty*, 199–203, esp. 203 for the quoted segment. See also al-Ghazālī, *al-Mustaṣfā*, 2: 280: "The legal *'illah* (*al-'illah al-shar'īyah*) is simply a sign and an indicator which does not by its essence necessitate (*tūjib*) any ruling." In other words, while the philosophical *'illah* is assumed to produce its product by its essence, the legal *'illah* is not. This does not mean, however, that the latter is impervious to rational analysis or apprehension.

187. See, e.g., al-Qarāfī, *al-Furūq*, 1:48.

188. See the discussion in the section, "Beyond the *Ḥukm Shar'ī*," in Chapter 2 above, p. 77–80.

189. See the section, "The Theoretical Consummation of a Bounded *Sharī'ah*" in Chapter 2.

190. A house in seventh-century Arabia, e.g., would have no indoor plumbing or electricity. Could such a structure satisfy a husband's obligation to provide "housing" in America today?

191. Professor Baber Johansen seems to think that I have misinterpreted al-Qarāfī in imputing such a central role to this distinction between law and fact. Johansen, however, whose focus throughout his career has been Ḥanafī law, may not have been sufficiently sensitive to this feature of al-Qarāfī's thought, i.e., *mashrū'īyah/sababīyah* versus *wuqū'* and the sources for determining each. Drawing on Hans Kelsen's *Pure Theory of Law*, Johansen writes: "Th[e] individual norm establishes the facts of the case." But this misses al-Qarāfī's point. He would agree that a judge may accept as an established legal norm that divorce is executed through verbal formulae and, on this basis, settle disputes by bringing them under this norm. But al-Qarāfī's point is that the substance of such norms (i.e., the actual formulae themselves) are not scripturally determined and, therefore, this judge could be legitimately challenged (and in fact might be wrong) in holding that a particular verbal formula, e.g., "go back to your family," came under this norm. Such formulae, according to al-Qarāfī, are only customary, and the question of whether and when a custom obtains is one of fact, not law—*wuqū'* not *mashrū'īyah/sababīyah*. As such, in any particular instance, the presumed norm may *not* establish the determinative facts of the case, and judges are not free to "force" facts under such norms. See B. Johansen, "Can the Law Decide That Egypt Is Conquered by Force? A Thirteenth-Century Debate on History as an Object of Law," in *Studies in Islamic Law: A Festschrift for Colin Imber*, eds. A. Christmann and R. Gleave (New York: Oxford University Press, 2007), 143–63, esp. 157 for the quoted segment.

192. See my *Islamic Law and the State*, 113–41, esp. 123–39, where I discuss the problem of "proper" versus "improper" *taqlīd*, the latter consisting of instances where jurists are followed on questions of fact rather than law.
193. This is clarified in al-Qarāfī, *Tamyīz*, 201: "Know that when we follow individual jurists by way of *taqlīd* in their pronouncements regarding legal causes, we follow them only regarding what they say about their status as legal causes, not their occurrence" (*i'lam annā idhā qalladnā aḥād al-'ulamā' fī al-asbāb innamā nuqalliduhum fī kawnihā asbāb*[an] *lā fī wuqū'ihā*).
194. Al-Qarāfī, *al-Furūq*, 1: 11. By the law applying to humanity at large, al-Qarāfī means that the whole of humanity, *mutatis mutandis*, will be held to this law on the Day of Judgment, not that all of humanity is bound by the details (*furū'*) of Islamic law in the Here and Now. Christians and Jews, e.g., would not be held to the ban on alcohol.
195. Even when a judge rules based on courtroom evidence, only the form that that evidence must assume, e.g., two or four eyewitnesses, is determined by scripture, not the substance of that evidence.
196. Al-Qarāfī, *al-Furūq*, 4: 11.
197. Recall the comments of al-'Izz b. 'Abd al-Salām regarding the difficulty that rulers and other officials face in determining what is in the best interest of the Community. See the discussion at the end of the subsection, "*Ḥisbah*," in Chapter 3 above, p. 155–56. Recall also the view of Ibn Taymīyah that it is impossible for revelation to address every contingency directly. See the subsection, "*The Islamic Secular's Religion*," in Chapter 1 above, p. 53.
198. Al-Qarāfī, *Tamyīz*, 41. See also the section "*Siyāsah*" in Chapter 3.
199. Al-Qarāfī lays this out under the subject heading: "The Principle Establishing the Difference between Those Discretionary Actions of Officials and Judges that Are to Be Implemented and Those that Are Not." See *al-Furūq*, 4: 39–48.
200. Indeed, the fifth-/eleventh-century Mālikī judge and jurist Abū al-Asbagh b. Sahl (d. 486/1093) states: "Had it not been for my routine attendance at the royal consultative sessions with other judges, I would not have known how to respond to the governor, Sulaymān b. Aswad, at the first session in which he sought my advice, despite the fact that, at that time, I had both *al-Mudawwanah* and *al-Mustakhrajah* memorized cold." See Ibn Farḥūn, *Tabsirah*, 1: 2.
201. Opwis, *Maṣlaḥa*, 44.
202. Al-Qarāfī, *Sharḥ tanqīḥ*, 435.
203. In his commentary on al-Qarāfī's *Tanqīḥ al-fuṣūl fī 'ilm al-uṣūl*, the ninth-/fifteenth-century Mālikī al-Shūshāwī (d. 899/1494) writes: "This was simply called *maṣlaḥah mursalah* because the *shar'* omitted it, neither validating nor invalidating it; rather, it was silent regarding it. And this (i.e., *mursalah*) is taken from the idea of "setting free" (*irsāl*), which is to leave alone." See al-Ḥusayn b. 'Alī b. Ṭalḥah al-Rajrājī al-Shūshāwī, *Raf' al-niqāb 'an tanqīḥ al-shihāb*, 4 vols., ed. N. al-Suwayd (Beirut: Dār al-Kutub al-'Ilmīyah, 1436/2015), 4: 139.
204. See my *Islamic Law and the State*, 133–9. Professor Johansen thinks that this term "does not seem to be very felicitous." He bases this on the definition of "paralegal" in *Black's Law Dictionary*. See his "Can the Law Decide," 150. I do not wish to quibble

over minutiae, but Johansen equates *Black's* "paralegal" with my hyphenated phrase, "para-legal." For the prefix, "para-," *Webster's Third New International Dictionary* gives the following: "beside; alongside of; parallel; parasitic; associated in a subsidiary or accessory capacity; closely resembling the true form; almost. . . ." There is a difference, in other words, between "paralegal" and "para-legal," and it is the basic sense of "beside," "alongside," and, especially, "associated in a subsidiary or accessory capacity" that I aim to capture with "para-legal."

205. On the *taṣarruf* and "non-legal," discretionary aspects of rulings, see my *Islamic Law and the State*, 133–9. This protected status assumes that the ruling does not violate a univocal text of scripture (*naṣṣ*), a clear analogy (*qiyās jalī*), unanimous consensus, or standard legal precepts or canons (*qawā'id*). See also al-Qarāfī, *Tamyīz*, 128–32.

206. It is this *shar'ī* dimension of the judge's ruling, which is assumed to represent the corporate authority of the *madhhab* as a whole, that the juristic tradition is referring to when it insists that "a judge's ruling cannot be overturned" (*ḥukm al-qāḍī lā yunqaḍ*).

207. See, e.g., Khaled Abou El Fadl's important work, *Rebellion and Violence in Islamic Law* (Cambridge: Cambridge University Press, 2001), esp. 321–42.

208. Ibn Taymīyah makes the problem clear when he notes that, even though reason alone may guide us to the good or bad (*ḥusn* or *qubḥ*) of an action, "[i]t does not follow that one who engages in such a bad action will be punished in the Hereafter, if *sharī'ah* contains no indication to that effect" (*lā yalzam min ḥuṣūl hādhā al-qabīḥ an yakūn fā'iluhu mu'āqab*^{an} *fī al-ākhirah idhā lam yarid al-shar' bi dhālika*). Ibn Taymīyah, *Majmū'at al-fatāwā*, 8: 258.

209. The basis of this position appears at least as early as al-Māwardī and Abū Ya'lā, both of whom confirm that obedience is owed to the Imām who fulfills his basic responsibilities. See al-Māwardī, *al-Aḥkām al-sulṭānīyah*, 24; Abū Ya'lā, *al-Aḥkām al-sulṭānīyah*, 28. See also, however, Rashīd Riḍā, *al-Manār*, 4: 859, where he insists that the ruler must be an authority in both religious and 'secular' (*shar'ī* and non-*shar'ī*) knowledge, i.e., "*mujtahid fī 'ulūm al-dīn wa al-dunyā*."

210. Riḍā, *al-Manār*, 20: 435–6. The examples Riḍā cites relate to questions of justice rather than, say, questions of efficiency and the like. At *al-Manār*, 4: 852–66 (esp. 4: 860) he binds to ruler to "consult" (*mushāwarah*). But it is still not entirely clear what status this would confer upon the ruler's economic, education, or immigration policy.

211. See, e.g., the critique of Ibn Ḥazm. *Al-Iḥkām fī uṣūl al-aḥkām*, 4: 128–238. In a modern context, assuming that one could canvas the opinions of the global or national *ahl al-ḥall wa al-'aqd*, one would probably not find a unanimous consensus or even a reliable majority agreement. Moreover, if the issue is one of majority consensus, the question becomes how much of a majority and how firmly this could bind the Community. I admit that my suggestion (below) is no less theoretically assailable. It has the advantage, however, of being up front about this vulnerability and of empowering the Community to negotiate its limitations, on the understanding that *no* legal theory can be completely devoid of fictions or limitations.

212. See the section "'*Sharī'ah* and 'Islamic Law'" in Chapter 3.

213. Muslims do all kinds of things out of a sense of amoral compulsion, duty or interest, just because they recognize such acts as preferable, prudent, or beneficial, and this in the absence of any binding *ḥukm sharʿī*. Such acts can range from buying the cheaper rather than the more expensive item, to avoiding calorie-rich deserts, to exercising regularly at the gym (wink, wink).
214. See, e.g., al-Qarāfī, *al-Furūq*, 2: 33. Al-Qarāfī points to the Qurʾānic verse, 9:120, which speaks of those who come forth to fight in the path of God being rewarded for the hunger, thirst, and fatigue they suffer, even though God did not command this suffering and they themselves did not intentionally bring it about. They are rewarded, rather, because this suffering served a desired end by simple entailment.
215. See, e.g., 2: 180, 2: 228, 2: 232, 3: 104, 4: 6, 60: 14, and passim for references to the obligation to act in accordance with the *maʿrūf*, i.e., that which is *conventionally* recognized as fair, just, and appropriate.
216. Again, there seems to be a conflation of law and theology here. Whatever "elitist" reason may have been deployed in law, it was not particularly "Ashʿarite" but was used by jurists of all theological persuasions, including Traditionalist Ḥanbalites, as is evident from even a perfunctory perusal of their books on *fiqh* and *uṣūl al-fiqh*. While some of the vocabulary of *kalām* came into jurisprudence, the overall function of *kalām* was not the same in law as it was in theology. Indeed, *kalām* would impose none of the *taʾwīl* (figurative interpretation) on law that it imposed on theology. My overall point here is that, in contradistinction to Rationalist theology, law, even as conceived by Ashʿarites, would not have been as resistant to *fiṭrah* as Anjum seems to imply.
217. Ovamir Anjum, *Politics, Law and Community in Islamic Thought: The Taymiyyan Moment* (Cambridge: Cambridge University Press, 2012), 237, 249. If I have understood him correctly, I'm not sure Anjum is entirely consistent here. He argues that the Community co-owns only that part of *sharīʿah* that is the object of unanimous consensus, the *fuqahāʾ* owning the disputed, *mukhtalaf fih* realm. But if this is so, there would seem to be little on which the Community's view amounted to much, since it would be considered only in that area of *sharīʿah* where they already agreed with the jurists.
218. See Anjum, *Politics*, 197–275.
219. Al-Qarāfī, *Tamyīz*, 183. He adds importantly, ". . . unless the Imām invites one to condemn an act and one's refusal to comply will amount to an act of sedition (*shiqāq*). Then it becomes incumbent upon him to comply." Clearly, however, this relates to matters of public policy for the public good, not in deference to the Imām per se.
220. Anjum, *Politics*, 273.
221. Ṭ. J. al-ʿAlwānī, *al-Taʿlīm al-dīnī bayna al-tajdīd wa al-tajmīd* (Cairo: Dār al-Salām li al-Ṭibāʿah wa al-Nashr wa al-Tawzīʿ wa al-Tarjamah, 1430/2009), 41–4, esp. 43 for the quoted segment.
222. See Hallaq, *Impossible State*, 153.
223. Hallaq, *Impossible State*, 110–35.
224. See, e.g., Riḍā, *al-Manār*, 4: 429; 23: 539.

225. One does not have to go as far as the Muslim world to ask this question. As Cornel West perceptively observes in the case of Blackamericans: "The paradox of Afro-American history is that Afro-Americans fully enter the modern world precisely when the postmodern period commences." See his *Prophecy Deliverance: An Afro-American Revolutionary Christianity* (Philadelphia: The Westminster Press, 1982), 44.
226. Referencing fieldwork at al-Azhar, conducted as late as 2009–2011, A. Nakissa describes a British woman's frustration at her Azharī boyfriend's willingness to engage in every intimate act except actual sex! " 'It doesn't make sense,' she said. 'How can you do all of these other things but not sex?' He had difficulty explaining to her that even though he was not scrupulous in his religious practice, there were still certain lines that he could not cross." See A. Nakissa, *The Anthropology of Islamic Law: Education, Ethics, and Legal Interpretation at Egypt's al-Azhar* (New York: Oxford University Press, 2019), 84.
227. It is not my aim here to exaggerate in the key of apology the role of women in this clearly male-dominated tradition. But their role should also not be minimized or denied. See, e.g., M. A. Nadwi, *al-Muḥaddithāt: The Women Scholars in Islam* (Oxford: Interface Publications, 2002); A. Sayeed, *Women and the Transmission of Religious Knowledge in Islam* (Cambridge: Cambridge University Press, 2015); M. Fadel, "Two Woman, One Man: Knowledge, Power, and Gender in Medieval Sunni Legal Thought," *International Journal of Middle East Studies, 29* (1997): 185–204 at 90–2. As for "Islamic law" beyond *sharīʿah*, one could mention the famous Thumal who, probably at the behest of the mother of the Caliph al-Muqtadir, was appointed to the position of *naẓar al-maẓālim*. For a brief description of her, see Hurvitz, "The Contribution of Early Islamic Rulers," 145–6.
228. See the end of the discussion in the subsection, "*Violence, Sacrifice, Bureaucracy, Culture*, above.
229. I discuss this concept of "empire-state" in Chapter 5.

Chapter 5

1. An-Naʿim, *Secular State*, 1.
2. An-Naʿim, *Secular State*, 232.
3. An-Naʿim, *Secular State*, 101.
4. An-Naʿim, *Secular State*, 102.
5. An-Naʿim, *Secular State*, 112. An-Naʿim offers a caveat: "This view does not uphold human rights as the standard by which Islam itself is judged, but only proposes that these rights constitute the framework for *human* understanding of Islam and interpretation of Shariʿa." Emphasis original. It seems to me, however, that if human rights provide the prism though which we can determine and evaluate the meaning of Islam-cum-*sharīʿah*, then it *is* the standard to which the latter is held, since, on this

approach, there can be no legitimately constituted Islam-cum-*sharīʿah* outside what is understood through the prism of human rights.

6. An-Naʿim, *Secular State*, 126.
7. An-Naʿim, *Secular State*, 127.
8. An-Naʿim, *Secular State*, 72–3, 177.
9. An-Naʿim, *Secular State*, 18, 31, 224–5.
10. An-Naʿim, *Secular State*, 4.
11. An-Naʿim, *Secular State*, 247.
12. See An-Naʿim, *Secular State*, 7–8: "By civic reason, I mean that the rationale and the purpose of public policy or legislation must be based on the sort of reasoning that most citizens can accept or reject. Citizens must be able to make counterproposals through public debate without being open to charges about their religious piety." See also An-Naʿim, *Secular State*, 100: "[C]ivic reason [i]s the requirement that the rationale and purpose of public policy or legislation be based on the sort of reasoning that most citizens can accept or reject and use to make counterproposals through public debate without reference to religious belief as such." At 97–101, An-Naʿim explains the difference between Rawls's more famous "public reason" and his own "civic reason." I am not sure I captured the distinction. On Rawls's "public reason," see my discussion of it in Chapter 6.
13. An-Naʿim, *Secular State*, 4.
14. An-Naʿim, *Secular State*, 276.
15. An-Naʿim, *Secular State*, 45, 55.
16. An-Naʿim, *Secular State*, 254.
17. An-Naʿim, *Secular State*, 263.
18. An-Naʿim, *Secular State*, 211.
19. An-Naʿim, *Secular State*, 208.
20. The question of wearing wigs is controversial, going all the way back to early times. I am taking here, for the sake of argument, the position of those who allow the practice or allow it with qualifications. For an early discussion on wigs (or, more precisely, hair extensions), see Abū Jaʿfar al-Ṭaḥāwī, *Mushkil al-āthār*, 4 vols., ed. M.ʿA. Shāhīn (Beirut: Dār al-Kutub al-ʿIlmīyah, 1415/1995), 2: 29–30.
21. See, e.g., An-Naʿim, *Secular State*, 4, 268, 277, 282, 291 and passim.
22. An-Naʿim, *Secular State*, 282.
23. Indeed, given the evidentiary burden of proving fornication or adultery, i.e., four male eye-witnesses to the actual act of penetration (and according to some jurists pregnancy), one might ask if any Muslims avoid this sin purely out of fear of sanctions imposed by a Muslim state.
24. An-Naʿim, *Secular State*, 103.
25. His comment on India in this regard is welcomingly transparent: "Indian secularism has been limited in several ways. For example, it tends to give higher regard to collective claims in the name of the community than to those of individual members of those communities." *Secular State*, 177. Similarly, "[T]he state should promote an understanding and practice of secularism that gives higher priority to *citizenship* than to vague notions of *collective group identity* that are vulnerable to abuse and manipulation

by some elite in the name of the community." *Secular State*, 178. Emphasis original. He also speaks of certain issues becoming "communalized" to the point that "the state feels obliged to sacrifice the constitutional principles of secularism for the sake of a political compromise that keeps the peace among communities." *Secular State*, 176.

26. M. Nussbaum, "The Feminist Critique of Liberalism," *Political Philosophy: The Essential Texts*, 3rd ed., ed. S. M. Cahn (New York: Oxford University Press, 2015), 1033. Nussbaum's essay is taken from her book *Sex and Social Justice*. She is defending liberalism here against criticisms by such feminists as Alison Jager, Catherine MacKinnon, and Andrea Dworkin.
27. See F. Copleston, *A History of Philosophy*, 9 vols. (New York: Image Books, 1962–77), 9:1: 213.
28. This is not to say that all acts of coercion are justifiable, moral, or devoid of harmful effects. My point is simply that, depending on what one is being coerced to do—let's use the example of piano lessons—the act of coercion itself does not negate the benefit potentially derived from the forced act, in this case, learning how to play the piano. Of course, this is very different from forcing someone into a sexual act.
29. An-Na'im, *Secular State*, 282: "[T]here is simply no human or religious value in coerced religious belief *or practice*." Emphasis mine.
30. See Paul Kahn, *Putting Liberalism in Its Place* (Princeton: Princeton University Press, 2005), 231.
31. See, e.g., al-Qarāfī, *al-Dhakhīrah*, 3: 145–6, where he discusses the Mālikī, Shāfi'ī, and Ḥanafī positions on this issue.
32. See my *Islamic Law and the State*, 197–203. I should note here, incidentally, that al-Qarāfī's presentation does not appear to be entirely consistent, given his recognition of the punishment for abandoning prayer altogether as well as the Imām's duty to collect *zakāh* from unwilling donors. Moreover, there is disagreement over what he saw fit to regulate. Talal Asad, e.g., read my earlier work as indicating that al-Qarāfī's focus was not on intention as a subjective phenomenon to which the state has no access but on the fact that "the absence of an established consensus on matters of worship among the learned limits the ability of government to define true worship." See T. Asad, *Secular Translations*, 82. Asad's overall argument suggests that a re-examination of al-Qarāfī's views on intention might reveal nuances that escaped me twenty-five years ago. I hesitate, however, to endorse the view Asad cites here (if I understand him correctly) as it would apply to most of *sharī'ah*, which is not a point of consensus, and would ultimately justify separating *sharī'ah* from the state altogether, a position I do not think he intends to take. I also disagree, incidentally, with those who equate the *'ibādāt* with *dīn* (as religious) and the *mu'āmalāt* with *dunyā* (as secular). For both are equal in their provenenance and status as religious.
33. See Chapter 4. Meanwhile, the *sharī'ah*-maximalist Ibn Taymīyah seeks to limit state intervention in theological disputes on similar grounds: "If the Community disputes the meaning of the verse '*The All-Merciful mounted the Throne*', some saying that God in God's essence is above the Throne, the meaning of 'mounting' being known while its modality is unknown, others saying that there is no Lord above the Throne and

that there is nothing at all there, the meaning of the verse being that 'God seized control over the Throne' or something like this, there would be no benefit in a judge's issuing a ruling that held one of these views to be correct and the other incorrect." See his *Majmū'at al- fatāwā*, 3: 152. Again, however, Ibn Taymīyah would never advocate removing *sharī'ah* from the state.

34. See Reinhold Neibuhr, *Moral Man in Immoral Society: A Study in Ethics and Politics* (New York: Charles Scribner's Sons, 1960), xii. The book first appeared in 1932.
35. Niebuhr, *Moral Man*, 231.
36. Niebuhr, *Moral Man*, 233.
37. Niebuhr, *Moral Man*, 233.
38. C.f., however, Rabb, *Doubt*, 320–1, where she suggests that lack of familiarity with the intellectual history of Islam, including Islamic jurisprudence, leaves modern activists with only the crudest methods of applying the law.
39. Ibn Taymīyah, "*al-Iḥtijāj bi al-qadar*," *Majmū'at al-rasā'il al-kubrā*, 2: 108. This may appear to support the view of those who distinguish between *fiqh* and *sharī'ah*. Ultimately, however, the view of a just and knowledgeable judge, according to Ibn Taymīyah, *would* constitute *sharī'ah*, once again, collapsing the practical distinction between the two.
40. See Michael Ignatieff, *Human Rights as Politics and Idolatry* (Princeton: Princeton University Press, 2001), 58.
41. An-Na'im, *Secular State*, 111.
42. An-Na'im, *Secular State*, 111.
43. Ignatieff, *Human Rights*, xxv–xxvi, 53.
44. See al-Qarāfī, *al-Furūq*, 1: 141. See also my "Domestic Terrorism in the Islamic Legal Tradition," *The Muslim World*, *91* (Fall, 2001): 293–310, esp. 297–9, on the implications of violating the public space.
45. I should clarify the distinction between "formal equality" in a socio-political as opposed to a purely theological context. In a theological context, Islam recognizes and indeed insists upon the inherent equality of all humans as humans, i.e., the repository of the "soul" or "*nafs*" that "God has rendered inviolable, except for just cause" (*an-nafs allatī ḥarrama Allāh illā bi al-ḥaqq*) [6: 151, 17: 33, 25: 68]. This *nafs* is neither male nor female, Black, White, Muslim, nor non-Muslim. All are equally human in this regard.
46. See, e.g., the US State Department's recent *Report of the Commission on Unalienable Rights*, p. 20, available at https://www.state.gov/wp-content/uploads/2020/07/Draft-Report-of-the-Commission-on-Unalienable-Rights.pdf
47. "What Are Human Rights? Four Schools of Thought," *Human Rights Quarterly*, *32*:1 (February, 2010): 1–20.
48. See e.g., C. Brenna, "The Transfiguration of Rights: A Proposal for Orthodoxy's Appropriation of Rights Language," *Logos: A Journal of Eastern Christian Studies*, 55:1–2 (2014): 15–40; A. Yannoulatos, "Eastern Orthodoxy and Human Rights," *International Review of Mission*, *73*:292 (1984): 454–6; A. Papanikolaou, *The Mystical as Political: Democracy and Non-Radical Orthodoxy* (Notre Dame: Notre Dame University Press, 2014), esp. 87–130. See also, however, A. Pollis, "Eastern Orthodoxy

and Human Rights," *Human Rights Quarterly*, 15:2 (May, 1993): 339–56, where she insists explicitly that Eastern Orthodoxy is simply incompatible with human rights.

49. We might also consider the limits of human rights and how, based on local assessments of interests and harms, other concerns might assume priority. As Talal Asad points out, the economic dislocation caused by Western monetary and financial policies often breed economic suffering and other socio-political problems of massive proportions. "But these interventions themselves cannot be regarded as instances of human rights violations; they are presented as the promotion of economic restructuring necessary for development." See Asad, *Formations*, 128. Asad also points to ways in which human rights, much like colonial constructions of what is "repugnant to civilized sensibilities," can be weaponized against local populations, especially minorities. See Asad, *Formations*, 135–6, esp. note 16.
50. For example, Article 9 of the 1990 OIC Declaration guarantees the right to education and says that the state shall "ensure the availability of ways and means to acquire education and shall guarantee educational diversity in the interest of society." Of course, this entails many Islamic Secular deliberations, from how to ensure access to education to how much variety the curriculum must or should contain and what this looks like. Available at https://www.oic-iphrc.org/en/data/docs/legal_instruments/OIC_HRRIT/571230.pdf

    It is not my contention, incidentally, that these articulations are ideal or even satisfactory articulations of human rights. For a general critique of Muslim articulations of human rights grounded in Islamic tradition, see, e.g., A. Sachedina, *Islam and the Challenge of Human Rights* (New York: Oxford University Press, 2009), 42–3. Here too, however, one notices that the concept of human rights is apparently conceived as an exclusively *shar'ī* enterprise.
51. An-Na'im, *Secular State*, 131.
52. An-Na'im, *Secular State*, 85: "To be clear on the point, I am not suggesting that any conception of Shari'a is inherently or necessarily incompatible with these modern principles [of constitutionalism, human rights, and citizenship]. Rather, I am referring specifically to certain aspects of the traditional interpretations of Shari'a, especially those regarding women and non-Muslims."
53. See An-Na'im, *What Is an American Muslim: Embracing Faith and Citizenship* (New York: Oxford University Press, 2014), 20. Emphasis original. He goes on to affirm, "In historical fact, the notion of an 'Islamic state' that will enforce Sharia emerged for the first time in the late colonial period (1930s–1940s)."
54. An-Na'im, *Secular State*, 45.
55. An-Na'im, *Secular State*, 46.
56. An-Na'im, *Secular State*, 45. Emphasis mine.
57. An-Na'im, *Secular State*, 46–7.
58. An-Na'im, *Secular State*, 47–8.
59. An-Na'im, *Secular State*, 283.
60. An-Na'im, *Secular State*, 280.
61. This to my mind, appears to be a manifestation of what Stephen Toulmin refers to as the modern replacement of the standard of reasonableness with that of certainty. See

his *Cosmopolis: The Hidden Agenda of Modernity* (New York: The Free Press, 1990), 75, 80, 198–201. See also T. Bauer, *Ambiguity*, esp. 259–79, where he identifies the obsession with certainty with the European desire to eliminate ambiguity, which entered the Muslim world as a by-product of colonialism. Meanwhile, sticking with the reasonableness criterion, none other than Ibn Taymīyah states openly, "The Inner Essence of the Creator is unknowable to humans" (*kunh al-bārī ghayru maʿlūm li al-bashar*). Yet, he would hardly take this as a critique of belief in God. See his *al-Munāẓarah fī al-ʿaqīdah al-wāsiṭīyah*, in *Majmūʿat al-rasāʾil al-kubrā*, 2 vols. (Cairo: Muṣṭafā al-Bābī al-Ḥalabī wa Awlāduh, n.d), 1: 416; *al-ʿAqīdah al-ḥamawīyah al-kubrā* in *Majmūʿat al-rasāʾil al-kubrā*, 1: 474.

62. See Khaled Abou El Fadl, "Islam and the Challenge of Democratic Commitment," *Fordham International Law Journal, 27*:4 (2003): 4–71 at 16. Abou El Fadl is not alone here. See, e.g., An-Naʿim, *Secular State*, 252, where An-Naʿim cites Indonesian scholars who invoke the same argument.
63. Abou El Fadl, "Democratic Commitment," 17.
64. Abou El Fadl, "Democratic Commitment," 62.
65. Abou El Fadl, "Democratic Commitment," 62. Nowhere in this article, I should note, does Abou El Fadl endorse secularism per se, and I do not attribute that to him here. For an almost identical statement from An-Naʿim, see *Secular State*, 283.
66. Abou El Fadl, "Democratic Commitment," 69. In a footnote to this passage, Abou El Fadl adds that "embarrassing apologetics could be avoided if Muslims would abandon the incoherent idea of Shariʿah State law." One wonders, however, if *sharīʿah* iself survives this analysis, as non-state interpreters cannot be assumed to have any more a direct access to the divine mind than do state actors. On another note, I do not know what to make in all instances of the notion of the law "failing." Does a wife's decision not to work (though the husband insists that they need the income), or a husband's decision to divorce for no known reason constitute a "failure" of Islamic *law*? Or do such instances reflect failures in human decision-making? Once again, we see how non-recognition of the Islamic Secular can lead to Manichaean judgments.
67. See An-Naʿim, *Secular State*, 280–4. An-Naʿim might (rightly) respond that his point was that these "problematic" provisions should be dealt with through programs of interpretive reform *by Muslims*, not by the state. Yet, he states in this very context at *Secular State*, 280, "No state can successfully operate on the totality of what Muslims accept as Shariʿa principles." In other words, without the "right" reforms, the state will have to intervene.
68. An-Naʿim, *Secular State*, 29.
69. An-Naʿim, *Secular State*, 261, 290.
70. Schacht, *Introduction*, 76. Note that Schacht also writes: "As regards constitutional law, the state as envisaged by the theory of Islamic law is a fiction which has never existed in reality." *Introduction*, 76. While An-Naʿim might take this as a confirmation of his view that there never was an Islamic State, all Schacht is actually saying here is that the state did not conform perfectly to the theoretical blueprint laid out by the doctors of *sharīʿah*.

71. See the section "Siyāsah" in Chapter 3, citing Gibb, "Constitutional Organization," 1.
72. Rabb, *Doubt*, 48.
73. Imber, *Ebu 's-su'ud*, 24.
74. See my *Islamic Law and the State*, 49–68.
75. See my "The Primacy of Domestic Politics," 54.
76. Jackson, "Primacy," 54.
77. Incidentally, Muslims were not alone in their appreciation of reasonableness in the absence of absolute certainty. On the dialectical relationship between the two in the West, see again S. Toulmin, *Cosmopolis*.
78. An-Na'im, *Secular State*, 28. Bracketed segment mine.
79. In their reformist critique of *al-Qā'idah*, Egypt's notorious *al-Gamā'ah al-Islāmīyah* explicitly targeted the tendency to transcendentalize Muslim history wherein violence was assumed to be the only medium of exchange between Muslims and non-Muslims, an assumption that held certain violent readings of scripture in place. This led the group's one-time leader, Karam Zuhdī, to declare, "[Post-Prophetic] Islamic history is not a source for deriving law" (*al-tārīkh al-islāmī laysa maṣdar*^{an} *li al-tashrī'*). See *al-Multaqā al-Dawlī* no. 561 (June, 2004): 7. In a later critique of ISIS, one present and one former member warn: "Turning certain chapters of Muslim history into proofs that can be invoked in a manner that rivals the religion and the religious law (*ḥujjah 'alā al-shar' wa al-dīn*) is among the major crises of our time." See Ibrāhīm and al-Najjār, *Dā'ish*, 79.
80. An-Na'im, *Secular State*, 108.
81. See my *State*, 103–12, where, following the insights of Professor George Makdisi, I describe the "corporate" status of the *madhhabs*, i.e., that disallowing individual members to follow their schools' dictates violated the status of the *madhhab* as a "corporate entity."
82. Al-Qarāfī, *Tamyīz*, 66–7.
83. Ibn Taymīyah, *Majmū'at al-fatāwā*, 27: 162–3.
84. Ibn Taymīyah, *Majmū'at al-fatāwā*, 33: 79.
85. See, e.g., Ibn Amīr al-Ḥājj, *al-Taqrīr wa al-taḥbīr*, 3 vols. (Beirut: Dār al-Kutub al-'Ilmīyah, 1403/1983), 3: 106, where he notes that the silence of jurists in the face of *fatwās* from other *madhhabs* does not signal agreement but simply their recognition of the authority and legitimacy of the sister schools.
86. See, e.g., al-Qarāfī, *Tamyīz*, 96. Of course, al-Qarāfī is operating with a more communitarian mindset, wherein the individual choices made in the name of *sui juris* are mediated by unchosen aspects of the self that attach one to community.
87. Al-Qarāfī, *Tamyīz*, 151.
88. On this point, see my "From Prophetic Actions to Constitutional Theory: A Novel Chapter in Medieval Muslim Jurisprudence," *International Journal of Middle East Studies*, *25* (1993): 71–90.
89. Al-Qarāfī, *Tamyīz*, 96. See also on this point al-Qarāfī's discussion in *al-Furūq*, 1: 205–09, esp. 206.
90. Al-Qarāfī, *Tamyīz*, 146–50.
91. See Alan Watson, *The Nature of Law* (Edinburgh: Edinburgh University Press, 1997).

92. I have alluded to this point several times in passing. Islamic Secular deliberations whose source is non-*shar'ī* can be sublated into the *shar'ī* dimension of the law. This is what we find, e.g., with the discretionary decision of Umar I to double the penalty for wine-drinking from forty lashes, as had been the practice of the Prophet, to eighty lashes, when he perceived that forty had become an insufficient deterrent. The Mālikī school cites eighty lashes as the standard penalty for wine-drinking as a matter of *fiqh*.
93. I am reminded here of an important insight I gained years ago from a presentation by Dr. Ingrid Mattson in which she suggested that the problem of what Catholic thinkers refer to as "subsidiarity" was a major lacuna in Muslim juridical thought. I see now, that, while subsidiarity remains an issue, it is perhaps more an issue for Muslim *fikr* than for *fiqh*.
94. See, e.g., al-Qarāfī, *Tamyīz*, 44, 85, 235 and passim; al-Qarāfī, *al-Furūq*, 2: 106. See also, e.g., al-Qarāfī, *al-Furūq*, 2: 102, where *ḥukm Allāh* is applied to the *fatwā*s of *muftī*s as well, even though the *fatwā*s of some *muftī*s contradict those of others.
95. See, e.g., al-Ghazālī, *al-Mustaṣfā*, 2: 373.
96. See the section "The Theoretical Consummation of a Bounded *Sharī'ah*" in Chapter 2.
97. An-Na'im, *Secular State*, 51.
98. An-Na'im, *Secular State*, 52.
99. An-Na'im, *Secular State*, 49–50. An-Na'im imputes to Ibn Taymīyah and Ibn al-Qayyim "the necessity of separating the religious dimension of any individual from his function or role in the state, which must be entrusted to those who are best qualified to accomplish the task." An-Na'im, *Secular State*, 50.
100. Al-Bishrī, *al-Ḥiwār*, 57.
101. There is also a reverse-benefit to more explicit recognition of the Islamic Secular's *shar'ī*/non-*shar'ī* distinction. The non-*shar'ī* proposals of pious Muslims could be rejected on their merits without necessarily implying any anti-*sharī'ah* bias or prejudice against them as pious Muslims. For, the activity in question would be explicitly identified as non-*shar'ī* and could thus be assessed based on such metrics.
102. An-Na'im, *Secular State*, 4.
103. The non-*shar'ī* would be "non-religious" from An-Na'im's perspective, not from the perspective of the Islamic Secular.
104. See the discussion in section "The Basic Aim of the Present Analysis and Critique" in this chapter. According to An-Na'im, the European Court of Human Rights unanimously upheld the ban on head-scarves on grounds that the state was "primarily pursuing the legitimate aims of protecting the rights and freedoms of others and of protecting the public order." An-Na'im, *Secular State*, 211.
105. An-Na'im, *Secular State*, 219.
106. See An-Na'im, *Secular State*, 211–14.
107. An-Na'im, *Secular State*,177. See also An-Na'im, *Secular State*, 181.
108. An-Na'im, *Secular State*, 178.
109. An-Na'im, *Secular State*, 283. Bracketed segment mine.
110. An-Na'im, *Secular State*, 283–4.

111. An-Naʿim, *Secular State*, 178. In fact, early on An-Naʿim acknowledges that one should not assume that "the state can or should be completely neutral, because it is a political institution that is supposed to be influenced by the interests and concerns of its citizens." See An-Naʿim, *Secular State*, 3.
112. An-Naʿim, *Secular State*, 281.
113. An-Naʿim, *Secular State*, 179.
114. S. L. Carter, *God's Name in Vain: The Wrongs and Rights of Religion in Politics* (New York: Basic Books, 2000), 160.
115. I assume that he is speaking here about the *modality* of women's dress, not women's dress in the absolute. For, not just Islam but all but a very few societies regulate women's (and men's) dress to some degree, e.g., by banning nudity.
116. J. Burbank and F. Cooper, *Empires in World History: Power and the Politics of Difference* (Princeton: Princeton University Press, 2010), 8.
117. Burbank and Cooper, *Empires*, 8.
118. S. A. Ayoub, *Law, Empire, and the Sultan: Ottoman Imperial Authority and Late Ḥanafī Jurisprudence* (New York: Oxford University Press, 2020), 2. Bracketed segment mine.
119. Burbank and Cooper, *Empires*, 9. In fact, one could argue that early modern European states acted like modern states at home but as empire-states abroad, often (though not always) recognizing a degree of legal pluralism that they would not recognize in Europe.
120. Muhammad b. Idrīs al-Shāfiʿī, *al-Umm*, 9 vols. (Beirut: Dār al-Kutub al-ʿIlmīyah, 1413/1993), 6: 193–4. Later jurists would refer to such persons as "*ahl al-ʿahd*," i.e., those with whom there is an agreement of non-aggression. Meanwhile, Ibn Rushd confirms the view that it was the Jewish community who *voluntarily* brought this couple to the Prophet and asked him to rule in their case. See *Bidāyat al-mujtahid*, 2: 637.
121. Al-Shāfiʿī, *al-Umm*, 6: 194–5.
122. Al-Shāfiʿī, *al-Umm*, 6: 195.
123. Al-Shāfiʿī, *al-Umm*, 6: 192.
124. Al-Shāfiʿī, *al-Umm*, 6: 195.
125. Al-Shāfiʿī, *al-Umm*, 6: 198.
126. Al-Shāfiʿī, *al-Umm*, 6: 195. Al-Shāfiʿī also notes that where there are rights disputed between a Muslim and a non-Muslim, the Imām is obligated both to rule and to do so based on Islamic law. See al-Shāfiʿī, *al-Umm*, 6: 192.
127. See, e.g., R. al-Sayyid, "Dār al-Ḥarb and Dār al-Islām: Traditions and Interpretations," in *Religion between Violence and Reconciliation* (*Beiruter Texts und Studien*, 76), ed. T. Scheiffler (Beirut: Orient-Institute der Deutschen Morgenlandischen Gesellschaft, 2002), 123–33 at p. 126.
128. Al-Shāfiʿī, *al-Umm*, 6: 195.
129. Al-Shāfiʿī, *al-Umm*, 6: 195. Incidentally, this would appear to be an exercise in *raʾy*, to which al-Shāfiʿī (as we saw in Chapter 4) was supposed to be categorically opposed.
130. Al-Shāfiʿī, *al-Umm*, 6: 192: "He [al-Shāfiʿī's interlocutor] said, 'What are the circumstances in which the Muslim ruler is obligated to adjudicate non-Muslims'

cases, either for or against them?' I [al-Shāfiʿī] said; 'Whenever there is business (*tibāʿah*) between a non-Muslim and a Muslim . . . it is not permissible for anyone other than a Muslim to rule for or against the Muslim.'" Interestingly, according to Burbank and Cooper, "This question led Romans to produce theories that distinguished the civil laws of different nations—laws that were understood to be different for different peoples—from the law of all nations (a single set of rules) to be applied to foreigners in the Romain empire by the praetor or to disputes between Romans and non-Romans." See Burbank and Cooper, *Empires*, 31.

131. Saḥnūn, *al-Mudawwanah*, 4: 384. One could cite other examples. For instance, in *al-Mudawwanah*, Saḥnūn asks about a *dhimmī* man who divorces his *dhimmī* wife thrice but refuses to release her, as a result of which she presents her case to a Muslim judge. Ibn al-Qāsim responds: "Mālik said, 'He should not intervene in anything of this nature.' And Mālik said, 'He should not judge between them unless they both agree. If they agree, the judge has a choice to rule or not; and if he rules, he must do so on the basis of Islam. But my preference would be (*aḥabbu ilayya*) that he not rule.'" See *al-Mudawwanah*, 2: 219. Similarly, Saḥnūn asks if *dhimmī*s should be allowed to marry their mothers or sisters if their religion permits this. Ibn al-Qāsim responds that they should be left to their religious teachings. When Saḥnūn then asks if they should be allowed to engage in illicit sex (*zinā*), Ibn al-Qāsim responds: "In Mālik's view, they should be prohibited from doing so and disciplined (*yuʾaddabū*) if they make an open display of it (*in aʿlanū bih*)." See *al-Mudawwanah*, 2: 219.

132. Abū Bakr ʿAbd al-Razzāq al-Ṣanʿānī, *al-Muṣannaf*, 12 vols., ed. A. al-Azharī (Beirut: Dār al-Kutub al-ʿIlmīyah, 2010), 7: 273.

133. On this point more generally, see Mohammad Fadel, "'*Istisḥsān* Is Nine-Tenths of the Law,'" where he perceptively suggests that, if it had been the aim of Muslims to produce *hadīth*s to back every ruling, they surely did a poor job of it, as countless questions in the law remain outstanding with no *hadīth* to resolve them.

134. *Kitāb al-aṣl*, 12 vols., ed. M. Buyukalin (Beirut: Dār Ibn Ḥazm 1433/2012), 7: 163, 7: 183.

135. See Baber Johansen, "Muslim *Fiqh*," 71. Johansen expresses surprise at Western scholars who held that Islamic law did not apply to non-Muslims.

136. Al-Shaybānī, *Kitāb al-aṣl*, 7: 144–5. I should note here that the Ḥanafī position on *zinā* is mildly misstated in my "Islamic Reform between Islamic Law and the Nation-State," in J. L. Esposito and E. Shahin, eds., *The Oxford Handbook of Islam and Politics* (New York: Oxford University Press, 2013), 42–55 at 45. *Mea culpa*.

137. Al-Rāzī, *al-Maḥṣūl*, 2: 237. For a fuller discussion of the doctrine, see A. K. Reinhart, "Failures of Practice or Failures of Faith: Are Non-Muslims Subject to the Sharia?" in M. H. Khalil, *Between Heaven and Hell: Islam, Salvation, and the Fate of Others* (New York: Oxford University Press, 2013), 13–34.

138. Emon, *Religious Pluralism*, 150.

139. Emon, *Religious Pluralism*, 161.

140. Emon, *Religious Pluralism*, 76.

141. See Reinhart, "Failures of Practice," 19. Reinhart speaks of "the categorical illegitimacy of non-Muslim practices and the unrestrained inclusiveness of the Muslim *shar'*."
142. M. Fadel, "No Salvation Outside Islam: Muslim Modernists, Democratic Politics, and Islamic Theological Exclusivism," in M. H. Khalil, ed., *Between Heaven and Hell: Islam, Salvation and the Fate of Others* (New York: Oxford University Press, 2013), 53.
143. For more on this point, see my discussion of Rawls and March in Chapter 6.
144. Emon, *Religious Pluralism and Islamic Law*, 12. See, however, the discussion in the section "'*Sharī'ah*' and 'Islamic Law'" in Chapter 3, esp. note 45, where he appears to include all of this as part of *sharī'ah*.
145. There does appear to be wide agreement on the application of the "rules of Islam" (*aḥkām al-islām*), though, as we will see, the phrase can carry more than one meaning.
146. Al-Māwardī, *al-Ḥāwī al-kabīr*, 13: 250.
147. Al-Māwardī, *al-Ḥāwī al-kabīr*, 13: 251.
148. Al-Māwardī, *al-Ḥāwī al-kabīr*, 13: 251. Al-Māwardī explains that they are liable for violating the rights of other humans because the Muslim state is bound to protect people's property rights, etc. But having been allowed to reject God (*kufr*), they have already been allowed to violate God's right.
149. On these two forms of *jizyah*, see, e.g., Ibn Rush, *Bidāyat al-mujtahid*, 1: 610; Wahbah al-Zuḥaylī, *Mawsū'at al-fiqh al-islāmī wa al-qaḍāyā al-mu'āṣirah*, 14 vols. (Damascus: Dār al-Fikr, 2010), 3: 746.
150. See, e.g., al-Sarakhsī, *al-Mabsūṭ*, 10: 85, 86; al-Sarakhsī, *Uṣūl al-sarakhsī*, 1: 89; al-Kāsānī, *Badā'i' al-ṣanā'i' fī tartīb al-sharā'i'*, 10 vols., eds. 'A. Mu'awwaḍ and 'A. 'Abd al-Mawjūd (Beirut: Dār al-Kutub al-'Ilīmyah, 1418/1997), 9: 189; Ibn Qayyim, *Aḥkām ahl al-dhimmah*, 1: 121, 2: 873–4. See also the modern jurist W. al-Zuḥaylī, *Mawsū'at al-fiqh al-islāmī*, 3: 848: "The jurists agree that non-Muslims are bound to abide by the civil and criminal rules of Islam."
151. Al-Māwardī, *al-Ḥāwī al-kabīr*, 14: 317; Al-Māwardī, *al-Aḥkām al-sulṭānīyah*, 184–5.
152. Al-Māwardī, *al-Ḥāwī al-kabīr*, 14: 298–9. Elsewhere this is expressed alternatively as "*aḥkām al-muslimīn*" (the rules of the Muslims). See, e.g., al-Kishnāwī, *Ashal al-madārik*, 2:6.
153. Al-Māwardī, *al-Ḥāwī al-kabīr*, 14: 317; *al-Aḥkām al-sulṭānīyah* 184–5.
154. Al-Māwardī, *al-Aḥkām al-sulṭānīyah*, 185. Al-Māwardī's list here differs somewhat from his list in *al-Ḥāwī al-kabīr*, 14: 17–18.
155. Al-Māwardī, *al-Aḥkām al-sulṭānīyah*, 185.
156. Al-Qarāfī, *al-Dhakhīrah*, 10:11–12.
157. Al-Māwardī, *al-Ḥāwī al-kabīr*, 14: 316.
158. Abū al-Ḥasan 'Alī b. Muḥammad al-Lakhmī, *al-Tabṣirah*, 14 vols. (Beirut: Dār Ibn Ḥazm, 1433/2012), 13: 6163. Al-Lakhmī explicitly exempts *dhimmī*s from Islamic laws governing illicit sex (*al-zinā*). I might add that, according to al-Qāḍī 'Abd al-Wahhāb, the going opinion in the Mālikī and Ḥanafī schools (and in one narration from al-Shāfi'ī) is that *poor* non-Muslims are *exempt* from the *jizyah*. See, e.g.,

al-Qāḍī ʿAbd al-Wahhāb, *ʿUyūn al-majālis*, 6 vols., ed. A. K. Kāh (Riyadh: Maktabat al-Rushd, 1421/2000), 2: 756.

159. See the discussion in section "*Al-Shāfiʿī, Mālik, Ḥanafīs*, and the Early Period" in this chapter.
160. See the section "'*Sharīʿah*' and 'Islamic Law'" in Chapter 3.
161. See, e.g., An-Naʿim, *Secular State*, 260: "Although advocates of this view often make the point that Shariʿa will apply only to Muslim citizens, the recent experiences of countries like Sudan and Nigeria clearly show this to be both unworkable in a modern state in its global context and necessarily discriminatory against non-Muslim citizens."
162. See *al-Ahrām*, June 10, 2010, p. 3. See also my "Islamic Reform between Islamic Law and the Nation-State," 42–55. Cf., meanwhile, An-Naʿim, *Secular State*, 263, where An-Naʿim cites approvingly the commitment of Indonesia's Sukarno to separating Islam from the state out of fear that not doing so "would undermine the solidarity between Muslims and non-Muslims, the latter being opposed to the implementation of Shariʿa."
163. One might ask, incidentally, how An-Naʿim's Secular State would adjudicate this impasse. Would it allow no-fault divorces to all citizens, including Coptic Christians, in which case it would appear to favor a Muslim perspective? Or would it ban them across the board, except in cases of adultery or apostasy, which would reflect a bias in favor of Christians? Indeed, one might ask if "civic reason" can ever provide a thick enough consensus to retire such disputes and the social divisions they entail.
164. An-Naʿim, *Secular State*, 38–9. This would apply as well to such issues as women being allowed to drive.
165. See J. M. Barry, *Roger Williams and the Making of the American Soul: Church, State and the Birth of Liberty* (New York: Penguin Books, 2012), 12.
166. Barry, *Roger Williams*, 17.
167. Chadwick, *Secularization*, 23.
168. Cavanaugh, *The Myth of Religious Violence*, 131.
169. Chadwick, *Secularization*, 50–1.
170. On al-Ḥākim's eccentric policies, see, e.g., *EI2*, 3: 77–81.
171. On the Qādirī Creed, see Makdisi, *Rise of Humanism*, 7–9.
172. See the Introduction to Ibn Maḍāʾ, *Kitāb al-radd ʿalā al-nuḥāt*, ed. S. Ḍayf (Cairo: Dār al-Fikr al-ʿArabī, 1366/1947), 8.
173. See Samuel P. Huntington, *Who Are We? The Challenges to America's National Identity* (New York: Simon & Schuster, 2004), 16.
174. See, e.g., Y. Sezgin, "Muslim Family Laws in Israel and Greece: Can Non-Muslim Courts Bring About Change in Sharīʿa?" *Islamic Law and Society*, *25* (2018): 235–73 at 237. My use of "empire-state" is intended solely as I have discussed it above; it has nothing to do with the substance of a state's foreign or domestic policies per se.
175. An-Naʿim, *Secular State*, 168.
176. Carter, *God's Name in Vain*, 158.

177. On "equality of respect," see my "Sharī'ah, Democracy, and the Modern Nation-State," 102–06.
178. An-Na'im, *Secular State*, 270.
179. Al-Qarāfī, *al-Furūq*, 3:125.
180. See Y. al-Qaraḍāwī, *al-Aqallīyāt al-dīnīyah wa al-ḥall al-islāmī* (Cairo: Maktabat Wahba, 1999/1420), 15–16. Of course, al-Qaraḍāwī has in mind commercial and civil rules in general, e.g., basic banking procedures, not specific rules such as *sharī'ah*'s ban on *ribā*.
181. See, e.g., N. Feldman, *The Arab Winter: A Tragedy* (Princeton: Princeton University Press, 2020), 137–42.
182. For an insightful discussion on the participation of non-Muslims in pre-modern Muslim government, see Yarborough, *Friends of the Emir*, 113–63.
183. See section "Morality vs. *Shar*'" in Chapter 4.
184. This is not to suggest that everyone would be open to such participation. As Yarborough's work makes clear, Muslim jurists often expressed deep distrust of non-Muslims, which drove many to ban their participation in government, *shar'an*, i.e., as a *ḥukm shar'ī*. Such rulings, however, routinely entailed non-*shar'ī*, factual assessments regarding such things as non-Muslim loyalty, etc., which, as we have seen, opened them to legitimate challenge and further adjudication.
185. https://www.constituteproject.org/constitution/Sudan_2005.pdf?lang=en
The 2019 Constitution, meanwhile, is a very different document. It does not mention *sharī'ah*.
186. An-Na'im, *Secular State*, 291.
187. An-Na'im, *Secular State*, 46. See also An-Na'im, *Secular State*, 147, where he contrasts the "Mogul Indian state" with the "European state."
188. An-Na'im, *Secular State*, 19–20.
189. Abou El Fadl also wants to preempt this ability to *sharī*'atize bad state policies, which is why he too wants to distance "state law" from "God's law," lest the latter be identified with the failures and miscarriages of the former. See section "The Islamic State, Secularism, and An-Na'im's Secular State" in this chapter.
190. See the discussion at the end of the section "*Ḥisbah*" in Chapter 3.
191. See Chapter 3.
192. This is the argument of Anthea Butler in her *White Evangelical Racism: The Politics of Morality in America* (Chapel Hill: The University of North Carolina Press, 2021).

Chapter 6

1. March, *Liberal Citizenship*, 7. Italics original. See also March, *Liberal Citizenship*, 80: "In this study, my main focus is on the tradition of Islamic jurisprudence (*fiqh*), both classical and contemporary, and the answers that it contains to the specific questions posed by this book."

2. March, *Liberal Citizenship*, 263. On "overlapping consensus," see the section "Rawls" in this chapter.
3. March, *Liberal Citizenship*, 6.
4. See, e.g., Charles W. Mills, "Rawls on Race/Race in Rawls," *The Southern Journal of Philosophy*, *47* (2009): 18. Drawing on Thomas Nagel, Mills notes, "Ideal theory enables you to say when a society is unjust because it falls short of the ideal. But it does not tell you what to do if, as is almost always the case, you find yourself in an unjust society, and want to correct that injustice."
5. See K. Morrison, "Karl Marx," *Marx, Durkheim, Weber*, 38. The quoted segment is from Marx's *The Holy Family*.
6. See Makdisi, *The Rise of Humanism*, esp. 339–43. I should note that alongside the likes of al-Farābī, Miskawayh, and even al-Ghazālī (though obviously wearing a different hat), Makdisi includes such works as al-Māwardī's *al-Aḥkām al-sulṭānīyah* and Ibn Taymīyah's *al-Siyāsah al-shar'īyah* as part of this literature. Neither of these latter works deals in abstract, ideal moral theory in the sense intended by March.
7. See, e.g., Makdisi, *Rise of Humanism*, 339–43.
8. See the section "Efficient Decision-Making" in Chapter 3.
9. See, e.g., the discussion by Wahbah al-Zuḥaylī, *Mawsū'at al-fiqh al-islāmī*, 7: 212–13, where he notes that it was not scripture but circumstances on the ground in the second/eighth century that produced this construct.
10. Al-Qarāfī, *al-Furūq*, 1: 176–7. See also my *Islamic Law and the State*, 123–39, on his distinction between proper and improper *taqlīd*.
11. Al-Qarāfī, *Tamyīz*, 231.
12. See the section "Ibn al-Qayyim" in Chapter 2.
13. Ibn Taymīyah, *Majmū'at al-fatāwā*, 20: 33. See section "Morality vs. *Shar'*" in Chapter 4, note 159, where he speaks of instances where evil may be tolerated in the interest of a greater good or lesser evil.
14. March, *Liberal Citizenship*, 7. Emphasis original.
15. Pointing to Utilitarianism as an example, Rawls defines "comprehensive doctrines" as systems of belief that "hold for all kinds of subjects ranging from the conduct of individuals and personal relations to the organization of society as a whole, as well as the law of peoples." Rawls, *Political Liberalism*, 13.
16. March, *Liberal Citizenship*, 94.
17. That March privileges this demographic is reflected in his centering of the so-called *fiqh al-aqallīyāt* literature. See March, *Liberal Citizenship*, 80: "In particular I focus on the growing body of 'jurisprudence of Muslim minorities' (*fiqh al-aqallīyāt al-muslima*), which addresses directly the ethical aspects of Muslims living in non-Muslim states." This literature tends almost exclusively to address the plight of immigrant Muslims.
18. See the Pew Study, "Black Muslims Account for a Fifth of All US Muslims, and About Half Are Converts to Islam," https://www.pewresearch.org/fact-tank/2019/01/17/black-muslims-account-for-a-fifth-of-all-u-s-muslims-and-about-half-are-converts-to-islam/

There is some ambiguity in the assertion that "about half are converts to Islam," as it is not clear if the children of converts are also considered converts. Moreover, Pew's methodology basically relied on data derived from names, i.e., Muslim or Muslim-sounding names. On this approach, neither I, Keith Ellison, Andre Carson, nor countless other Blackamerican, White American, Native American, or Latino Muslims would be counted.

19. March, *Liberal Citizenship*, 156.
20. March, *Liberal Citizenship*, 154.
21. See, e.g., M. F. Jacobson, *Whiteness of a Different Color: European Immigration and the Alchemy of Race* (Cambridge, MA: Harvard University Press, 1998); N. Ignatiev, *How the Irish Became White* (New York: Routledge, 1995); E. L. Goldstein, *The Price of Whiteness: Jews, Race, and American Identity* (Princeton: Princeton University Press, 2006); W. P. Reeve, *Religion of a Different Color: Race and the Mormon Struggle for Whiteness* (New York: Oxford University Press, 2015); S. M. A. Gualtieri, *Between Arab and White: Race and Ethnicity in the Early Syrian American Diaspora* (Los Angeles: University of California Press, 2009).
22. Again, "[T]he present study is, rather, a work of political theory that seeks to analyze Islamic as opposed to Muslim attitudes towards shared citizenship through a method of comparative political ethics." March, *Liberal Citizenship*, 4.
23. See the discussion in sections "The Bounded *Ḥukm Sharʿī*" in Chapter 2 and "*Sharʿī* vs. Non-*Sharʿī*: Law vs. Fact" in Chapter 4 . See also my "The Second Education of the *Muftī*: Notes on Shihāb al-Dīn al-Qarāfī's Tips to the Jurisconsult," *The Muslim World, 82*: 3–4 (1992): 201–17 at 209, where I discuss al-Qarāfī's instructions to junior *muftīs* on how to field suspicious questions. For example, if a Mamlūk soldier asks if it is permissible to take money by way of loans, the *muftī* should not allow himself to be used. Mamlūk soldiers routinely confiscated people's property on the argument that they would later return it, which they claimed rendered their action a loan. In light of this, al-Qarāfī advised the *muftī* to respond as follows: "If he takes it (i.e., the money) with the owner's permission, according to the provisions of the law, without force and without coercion, it is permissible; if not, it is not."
24. As I have stated elsewhere, I do not believe that Muslims, even Ẓāhirīs, ever embraced a literalist hermeneutic like that which we find in Christian fundamentalism. See my "Literalism, Empiricism, and Induction: Apprehending and Concretizing Islamic Law's *Maqāṣid al-Sharīʿah* in the Modern World," *Michigan State Law Review*, Special Issue 6 (2006):1469–86 at 1469–76. See also A. Sabra, "Ibn Ḥazm's Literalism: A Critique of Islamic Legal Theory (I)," *al-Qantara* (2007): 7–40, esp. 22–3: "It would be incorrect, however, to characterize Ibn Ḥazm as a 'fundamentalist.' As we have seen, he clearly had little sympathy for those who insisted on the literal meaning of every passage, regardless of the plausibility of such a narrow understanding of the canon of sacred texts." See, however, R. Gleave, *Islam and Literalism: Literal Meaning and Interpretation in Islamic Legal Theory* (Edinburgh: Edinburgh University Press, 2013), for an alternate view.

25. As we saw with al-Ghazālī and others above, some jurists went so far as to draw a formal distinction between a *dalīl*, or apodictic indicant, and an *amārah*, or probable indicant. See the Introduction to this text, especially note 30.
26. For example, 'Fundamentalists' tend to read the legal monism of the modern state seamlessly into the Muslim past and then derive *from the latter* the duty to impose one-size-fits-all *sharīʿah*-based legal orders. One is reminded, incidentally, of the insight of N. J. Coulson: "The Muslim jurist of today cannot afford to be a bad historian." See his *A History of Islamic Law*, 7.
27. On "blocking the means," see Chapter 2. "Opening the means" refers to the opposite, i.e., rendering *prima facie* forbidden acts permissible, such as paying a customary bribe (*bakhshīsh*) to gain one's ailing relative admittance to a hospital. On opening the means, see, e.g., al-Qarāfī, *Sharḥ tanqīḥ al-fuṣūl*, 437–8, and al-Qarāfī, *al-Furūq*, 2: 33.
28. March, *Liberal Citizenship*, 103.
29. This is hardly unique to Islam as far as legal traditions go. When I studied American constitutional law at my university's law school, we spent virtually the entire course on Supreme Court opinions, rarely if ever directly engaging with the Constitution. This did not mean, however, that the Constitution had been demoted or ignored. Rather, it was assumed that the precedents of the Supreme Court included, even as they refined, the dictates of the Constitution. In a similar example, the tenth-/sixteenth-century Mālikī judge and jurist Badr al-Dīn al-Qarāfī (d. 1008/1599) (not to be confused with Shihāb al-Dīn) wrote a *fatwā* of some seventy pages in which he cited not a single Qurʾānic verse or Prophetic *ḥadīth*. See my "Kramer Versus Kramer in a Tenth/Sixteenth Century Egyptian Court: Post-Formative Jurisprudence between Exigency and Law," *Islamic Law and Society*, 8:1 (2001): 27–51. Clearly, al-Qarāfī did not expect his colleagues to discount his effort for lack of evidence.
30. John Rawls, *Political Liberalism* (New York: Columbia University Press, 2005), 14. This is an "expanded edition" of the original 1993 publication.
31. Kahn, *Putting Liberalism in Its Place*, 29. I interpret Kahn as alluding to the fact that, even without our agreeing on their meaning or even without giving them a second thought, buzzwords such as "fairness," "equality," "reason," "freedom," "justice," "tolerance," "democracy," and the like inform all public conversations and frequently our interpersonal relationships, whether we are self-proclaimed liberals, conservatives, or other.
32. March himself appears to recognize this distinction. See *Liberal Citizenship*, 12.
33. March, *Liberal Citizenship*, 3. Alternatively, "The purpose of this book is to examine the possibilities for an Islamic *full justification* of liberal citizenship." March, *Liberal Citizenship*, 28. Italics original.
34. March, *Liberal Citizenship*, 13.
35. Rawls, *Political Liberalism*, 40–3.
36. March, *Liberal Citizenship*, 29. Italics original.
37. I am ignoring the distributive (or economic) side of Rawls's theory because it does not play a significant role in March's thesis. This includes Rawls so-called "difference principle," according to which unequal treatment can be countenanced if, and only if, it operates in the interest of the least fortunate.

38. Rawls, *Political Liberalism*, xxxviii.
39. Rawls, *Political Liberalism*, 11–12.
40. A partial list of sources for this synopsis includes J. Rawls, *Political Liberalism*; A. F. March, *Liberal Citizenship*; D. Bell, "A Communitarian Critique of Liberalism," *Analyse and Kritik, 27*(2005): 215–38; I. Berlin, "Two Concepts of Liberty," *Liberty*, ed. H. Hardy (New York: Oxford University Press, 1995), 166–217; M. Fadel, "The True, the Good and the Reasonable: The Theological and Ethical Roots of Public Reason in Islamic Law," *Canadian Journal of Law and Jurisprudence, 21*:1 (2008): 5–69; M. Fadel, "Public Reason as a Strategy for Principled Reconciliation: The Case of Islamic Law and International Human Rights Law," *Chicago Journal of International Law, 8*:1 (Summer 2007): 1–20; S. Fish, *The Trouble with Principle* (Cambridge, MA: Harvard University Press, 1999); S. Fish; S. Fish, "Liberalism Doesn't Exist," *Duke Law Journal* (1987): 997–1001; W. Galston: *The Practice of Liberal Pluralism* (Cambridge: Cambridge University Press, 2005); A. Gutman, "Communitarian Critics of Liberalism," *Philosophy and Public Affairs, 14*:3 (1985): 308–22; S. Macedo, "Hauerwas, Liberalism, and Public Reason: Terms of Engagement?" *Law and Contemporary Problems, 75*:161, no. 4 (2012): 161–80; P. Kahn, *Putting Liberalism in Its Place*; C. W. Mills, "Rawls on Race/Race in Rawls," 161–84; C.W. Mills, "Racial Liberalism," *Modern Language Association of America, 123*:5 (2008):1380–97; C.W. Mills, *Black Rights/White Wrongs: The Critique of Racial Liberalism* (New York: Oxford University Press, 2017); S. Muhall and A. Swift, *Liberals and Communitarians,* 2nd ed. (Oxford: Blackwell Publishing, 1996); M. Nussbaum, "The Feminist Critique of Liberalism," 1028–53; M. Sandel, *Liberalism and Its Critics*, ed. M. Sandel (New York: New York University Press, 1984); M. Sandel, *Justice: What's the Right Thing to Do?* (New York: Farrar, Straus and Giroux, 2009); B. A. Shain, "Liberalism: A Religious-Dependent Faith," *Campbell Law Review 33*:3 (2011): 559–67; M. Walzer, "The Communitarian Critique of Liberalism," *Political Theory 18*:1 (1990): 6–23; S. Wolin, *Politics and Vision*; L. Zerilli, "Value Pluralism and the Problem of Judgment: Farewell to Public Reason," *Political Theory, 40*:1 (2012):6–32.
41. March, *Liberal Citizenship*, 42–64.
42. Rawls, *Political Liberalism*, 11; March, *Liberal Citizenship*, 41–2.
43. March, *Liberal Citizenship*, 98. See also March, *Liberal Citizenship*, 18, where March is explicit in affirming that liberal democracy protects individual Muslims not simply from state authority but also from "communal authority." This is in tension with how he describes Rawls's view: "Rawls and others quite clearly restrict the duty of civility (the duty to give only 'public' reasons to one another) to debates over coercive legislation, not to every matter of nonprivate concern." March, *Liberal Citizenship*, 41.
44. Rawls, *Political Liberalism*, 13. Rawls notes, "I assume that the basic structure is that of a closed society: that is, we are to regard it as self-contained and as having no relations with other societies. Its members enter it only by birth and leave it only by death." Rawls, *Political Liberalism*, 12. One seems to notice here lingering influences of Europe on Rawls.
45. In fact, in March, *Liberal Citizenship*, 54 and 67, March speaks of "religion's inherent inclination to authority and tradition." One might recall in this context the insight of

Karl Popper, that Enlightenment thinkers did not free themselves from authority per se but simply replaced one authority, i.e., The Bible or Aristotle, with another, namely, Enlightenment reason. See K. R. Popper, *Conjectures and the Refutations: The Growth of Scientific Knowledge*, 5th ed. Reprinted (New York: Routledge, 1992), 15–16. Meanwhile, at present, liberalism itself is some three hundred years old, and one wonders when, if ever, it will recognize itself as a "tradition."

46. March, *Liberal Citizenship,* 10.
47. March, *Liberal Citizenship*, 10.
48. March, *Liberal Citizenship*, 10.
49. See note 155 in Chapter 1.
50. See, e.g., the section "Beyond the *Ḥukm Sharʿī*" in Chapter 2, on al-Ghazālī's "ignorant friends of Islam." For Ibn Taymīyah's view, see, e.g., Ibn Taymīyah, *Dar'*, 4: 146; Ibn Taymīyah, *Juhd*, 91–2.
51. March, *Liberal Citizenship*, 10–11.
52. March, *Liberal Citizenship*, 136.
53. March, *Liberal Citizenship*, 138. As with An-Naʿim's categorical indictment of coercion, one senses a subtle double-standard here. Public reason sees no boundaries to its right to convert people to its cause, and "unreasonableness" is not tolerated precisely because it inoculates individuals against liberal arguments. As Paul Kahn puts it, from the liberal perspective, "No one, we believe, is beyond conversion to our values. When we dream of a global order, we project our own values onto it. We do not imagine that the global community of the future will be led by an Islamic cleric." Kahn, *Putting Liberalism in Its Place*, 7.
54. March, *Liberal Citizenship*, 12.
55. See A. Mazrui, "Islam and the End of History," *The American Journal of Islamic Social Sciences, 10*:4 (1993): 512–35 at 516.
56. March, *Liberal Citizenship*, 136.
57. Rawls, *Political Liberalism*, 460. In fact, Rawls insisted that political liberalism, "[e]mphatically . . . does not aim to replace comprehensive doctrines, religious or nonreligious." Rawls, *Political Liberalism*, xxxviii.
58. Again, "Liberalism not only requires that the state not be used to impose a vision of the good life but also imposes constraints on what we can do individually or severally to coerce others privately toward acting in concert with a conception of the good." March, *Liberal Citizenship*, 98.
59. March, *Liberal Citizenship*, 21. See also March, *Liberal Citizenship*, 56, where March cites the equally explicit view of Stephen Macedo: "[L]iberalism needs the support of private beliefs and practices that are at least congruent with liberal politics. Liberalism depends, after all, on a certain ordering of the soul." Whether one agrees with the overall program of Barry or Macedo, their logic is sound. One cannot require people to speak in some third language that does not reflect their true beliefs and feelings, without at some point making an effort to ensure that those beliefs and feelings sufficiently match their public declarations. Otherwise, the resulting "consensus" will be counterfeit and unstable, if not volatile, as those whose acquiescence has been (mis) taken for agreement seethe with resentment and possibly explode.

60. March, *Liberal Citizenship*, 136.
61. March notes, e.g., that while groups such as the Amish, Dukhobors, or Haredim do not violate the demands of justice, "this book argues that an overlapping consensus can be sought not only on requirements of justice but also on conceptions of citizenship." Moreover, the need to address questions of belonging and membership, beyond the simple demands of justice, "is particularly strong in the case of communities that—unlike the Amish, Dukhobors, or Haredim [read: Islam]—see themselves as adhering to a universal, proselytizing faith." See March, *Liberal Citizenship*, 139.
62. Fadel, "Public Reason as a Strategy for Principled Reconciliation," 5. My focus here is on the liberal logic on display not on the extent to which Fadel may or may not hold these views today.
63. Fadel, "Public Reason," 3.
64. Fadel, "Public Reason," 11, note 34.
65. Of course, three or four generations of this kind of normalized avoidance will inexorably normalize this reordering beyond recognition and critique.
66. Rawls, *Political Liberalism*, 461, note 46.
67. Rawls, *Political Liberalism*, 461, note 46.
68. Rawls, *Political Liberalism*, 461, note 46.
69. In fact, elsewhere, without mentioning Fadel, March mounts a public-reason defense of polygamy wherein he explicitly refutes the harm-to-women-and-children argument. See his "Is There a Right to Polygamy? Marriage, Equality and Subsidizing Families in Liberal Public Justification," *Journal of Moral Philosophy* 8:2 (2011): 246–72, esp. 258–62. March makes it clear, however, that this is not the "public-reason" position of most liberals. Moreover, the extension of some of the public-reason arguments he adduces in favor of polygyny might require Muslims to approve of Muslim women marrying non-Muslim men or to abolish the exclusive obligation upon Muslim men to pay *mahr* (bridal gift) or *nafaqah* (maintenance).
70. Thus, March writes: "The Muslim may assert no wish for his society to be conquered . . . but is in fact wishing for this *less* than he wishes to obey God, as he imagines God requires. Here he joins the class of partial citizens or semialiens, along with all committed pacifists." March, *Liberal Citizenship*, 150. Emphasis original. In other words, the ideal liberal citizen is one who is willing to disobey God in the interest of liberal commitments produced by "public reason."
71. March, *Liberal Citizenship*, 60. Emphasis added.
72. March, *Liberal Citizenship*, 65.
73. March, *Liberal Citizenship*, 83.
74. March, *Liberal Citizenship*, 68.
75. March, *Liberal Citizenship*, 119.
76. March states that "in the modern period Islamic jurisprudence has given way to some new genres of Islamic theorizing, and old genres (like exegesis and *fatwa*-issuing) have been appropriated by persons who would not traditionally be considered qualified. I have included some of these thinkers, such as the Muslim Brotherhood ideologue Sayyid Quṭb and Swiss Muslim reformer Tariq Ramadan, within my survey." March, *Liberal Citizenship*, 83.

77. March, *Liberal Citizenship*, 73.
78. See, e.g., I. Lapidus, *A History of Islamic Societies* (Cambridge: Cambridge University Press, 1988), 389.
79. March, *Liberal Citizenship*, 108, 112.
80. March does not treat these as factual claims but rather (apparently) as *sharʿī* justifications. He takes a similar approach with other classical jurists, writing, e.g., that the fifth-/eleventh-century Ḥanafī jurist al-Sarakhsī "argued that a primary reason for not settling in *dār al-ḥarb* is that one's 'children might acquire the morals of non-Muslims.'" March, *Liberal Citizenship*, 113. Both al-Wansharīsī (above) and al-Sarakhsī may be right about these factual claims. But a jurist or thinker who dissented on these factual assessments, based on changes in times and circumstances or on his or her concrete knowledge thereof, could clearly arrive at a different conclusion without being accused of going against Islam-cum-*sharīʿah,* or Islamic "doctrine."
81. Aḥmad b. Yaḥyā al-Wansharīsī, *al-Miʿyār al-muʿrib wa al-jāmiʿ al-mughrib ʿan fatāwā ʿulamāʾ ifriqīyah wa al-andalus wa al-maghrib*, 13 vols., ed. M. Ḥajjī et al. (Beirut: Dār al-Gharb al-Islāmī, 1401/1981), 2: 119–20.
82. Al-Wansharīsī, *al-Miʿyār*, 2:121.
83. Al-Wansharīsī, *al-Miʿyār*, 10: 108. Al-Māzarī was among those jurists March cites in support of the rejectionist position of al-Wansharīsī. But see S. Davis-Secord, "Muslims in Norman Sicily: The Evidence of Imām al-Māzarī's Fatwās," *Mediterranean Studies, 16* (2007): 46–66 at 47, where she describes al-Māzarī's *fatwās* as reflecting "leniency toward the Muslims remaining in Sicily following the Norman conquest." Similarly, while March presents al-Wansharīsī's opposition to non-Muslims' appointing Muslim judges as an unqualified *sharʿī* statement of law, al-Wansharīsī cites approvingly the position of al-Māzarī when the latter argues that there may be circumstances that warrant accepting such appointments as well as the rulings of Muslim judges so appointed. See al-Wansharīsī, *al-Miʿyār*, 10: 108–09.
84. ʿAbd al-Qādir, *al-Aqallīyāt al-muslimah*, 684.
85. March, *Liberal Citizenship*, 62. March mildly misrepresents me on this point.
86. March, *Liberal Citizenship*, 74.
87. See March, *Liberal Citizenship*, 304, note 2 (attached to material on p. 166). This comes after he has presented the obligation (*wujūb*) to migrate (*hijrah*) from non-Muslim lands to an Islamic State as a veritable point of consensus backed by his own interpretation of Prophetic biography (*sīrah*), Qur'ān, and *ḥadīth*, and then the views of al-Jarbūʿ, al-Wansharīsī, ʿAbd al-Qādir, and Quṭb (March, *Liberal Citizenship*, 103–07).
88. March, *Liberal Citizenship*, 232. March translates this as "secularism and neutrality." Incidentally, I suspect that Bin Bayyah is struggling here with the "nemesis of language," using *ʿalmānīyah* because that term is what he sees as available in the contemporary Arabic lexicon. Otherwise, I doubt that he supports the strict separation of *sharīʿah* from the state as commonly connoted by the commitment to *ʿalmānīyah* in the Muslim world.

89. On this point, see Carter, *God's Name in Vain*, 160: "[W]hat we are bold to call neutrality means in practice that big religions win and small religions lose." See also my discussion in the section "The Nemesis of Neutrality" in Chapter 5.
90. In his conclusion, March writes, "[T]here was surprisingly strong support from classical, conservative jurisprudence, particularly on questions relating to the terms of residence, loyalty to the state of residence, recognition of religious difference, and contribution to non-Muslim welfare." March, *Liberal Citizenship*, 263. One wonders how surprising all of this would have been had March begun with these scholars instead of leading with the likes of Quṭb and al-Jarbūʿ.
91. March, *Liberal Citizenship*, 103–13.
92. March, *Liberal Citizenship*, 113–27.
93. March, *Liberal Citizenship*, 127–33.
94. March, *Liberal Citizenship*, 207–36.
95. Rawls, *Political Liberalism*, xxviii; Wolin, *Vision*, 541.
96. Wolin, *Vision*, 540.
97. Wolin, *Vision*, 540.
98. See Wolin, *Vision*, 538–56.
99. See S. Wolin, "The Liberal/Democratic Divide: On Rawls's *Political Liberalism*," *Political Theory* (Feb. 1996): 98–119 at 98.
100. March, *Liberal Citizenship*, 178, but see also 165–79.
101. March, *Liberal Citizenship*, 294, note 5.
102. Al-Qaraḍāwī, *Fī fiqh al-aqallīyāt al-muslimah*, 33. This should not be dismissed as a cynical display of pragmatism in the face of modernity. Pre-modern jurists were also pragmatic. For example, the eighth-/fourteenth-century Ḥanbalī jurist Ibn al-Laḥḥām cites numerous practical considerations informing discussions on whether a non-Muslim or a Muslim traveler should be allowed to eat openly in public during the fast of Ramaḍān, despite the fact that, as a matter of doctrine, it was permissible for both to do so. See Ibn al-Laḥḥām, *al-Qawāʿid wa al-fawāʾid*, 60–1.
103. March, *Liberal Citizenship*, 140–1.
104. March, *Liberal Citizenship*, 181.
105. March, *Liberal Citizenship*, 181.
106. March, *Liberal Citizenship*, 182. I should be clear here that March does *not* categorically deny the right of Muslims to refuse to participate in unjust wars based on conscientious objection. There may be considerations that justify, *prima facie* at least, such a position. But, "[t]he concern in the case of Islam as a comprehensive doctrine is that because it commands believers to defend their Muslim-majority political community, their unwillingness to fight for their non-Muslim political community may reflect indifference, lack of commitment, or, in the worst case, contempt for that community's legitimate interests." March, *Liberal Citizenship*, 146–7.
107. March, *Liberal Citizenship*, 140.
108. March, *Liberal Citizenship*, 141. One wonders in this context what would be "un-Islamic" about a building-occupancy code or the requirement to register one's car, even though no explicit basis for such can be found in Islamic doctrine. One might also interrogate the assumption that the Imām will order Muslims in a non-Muslim

domicile to fight rather than not to fight, based on his assessment of their or the *ummah*'s interests or of their *shar'ī* obligations to this non-Muslim domicile in their capacity as a protected group (*musta'man*).

109. March, *Liberal Citizenship*, 141. This is simply not what we find in the juristic tradition. Take, for example, Rashīd Riḍā's exegesis on Qur'ān 8:72: "*And if they [fellow Muslims] seek your aid in resisting a threat to their religion, you must provide them with aid, except against a people between whom and you there is a covenant.*" Riḍā states explicitly that even if Muslims are attacked for their religion, their co-religionists' covenant with non-Muslim others would bar them from coming to these Muslims' aid. While the question of whether one's status as an American citizen constitutes a "covenant" may not be settled, it is certainly worthy of consideration. See *Tafsīr al-qur'ān al-ḥakīm al-mashhūr bi tafsīr al-manār*, 12 vols., ed. A. Shams al-Dīn (Beirut: Dār al-Kutub al-'Ilmīyah, 1420/1999),10: 95. For similar or identical views before Riḍā, see Muḥammad b. 'Alī al-Shawkānī (d. 1250/1834), *Fatḥ al-qadīr al-jāmi' bayna fann al-riwāyah wa al-dirāyah min 'ilm al-tafsīr*, 5 vols. (Beirut: Dār Iḥyā' al-Turāth al-'Arabī, n.d.), 2: 330; Ibn Kathīr (d. 774/1372), *Tafsīr al-qur'ān al-'aẓīm*, 4 vols. (Cairo: al-Maktab al-Thaqāfī, 2001), 2:332; Abū Ja'far Muḥammad b. Jarīr al-Ṭabarī (d. 310/922), *Jāmi' al-bayān*, 10: 53–4. Of course, these doctrines would also have to be analyzed in light of the facts on the ground.

110. Again, this may make perfect post-colonial, 'Fundamentalist' sense, but it does not reflect the Islamic juristic tradition. Al-Māwardī, for example, states explicitly that "the contract of protection (*'aqd al-dhimmah*) obligates us to defend them (non-Muslims) against everyone who attacks them, be they Muslims or non-Muslims." See his *al-Ḥāwī al-kabīr*, 14: 298. See also the discussion in sections "*Al-Shāfi'ī, Mālik, Ḥanafīs*, and the Early Period" and "The Post-Formative Scene" in Chapter 5.

111. March, *Liberal Citizenship*, 184–5, 197. Of course, the Qur'ān is relevant to juristic deliberation. But in cases where non-jurists put forth even plausible interpretations of the Qur'ān, this cannot be automatically assumed to represent the "Islamic juristic tradition."

112. Banū Hāshim, e.g., were the Prophet's clan, who, though predominantly pagan, refused to abandon him in Mecca. Banū Khuzā'ah were a predominantly pagan tribe with whom the Prophet formed an alliance while in Medina and on whom he relied for intelligence in his confrontations with Quraysh.

113. March, *Liberal Citizenship*, 141, 182.

114. March, *Liberal Citizenship*, 142, 183 . (P. 183 reads"... her Muslim state.")

115. March, *Liberal Citizenship*, 151, 183.

116. March, *Liberal Citizenship*, 151.

117. March, *Liberal Citizenship*, 183.

118. March, *Liberal Citizenship*, 183, 185 and passim. The basis for this principle is routinely Qur'ān 5:1: "*O you who believe, uphold your covenants.*"

119. March, *Liberal Citizenship*, 190.

120. March, *Liberal Citizenship*, 183.

121. Ibn al-Qayyim, *Aḥkām ahl al-dhimmah*, 2: 874. To be clear, it is not my claim that this was a matter of consensus across the schools. It clarifies, however, that the view

that March is putting forth has no basis in such a would-be consensus, as he clearly implies.

122. See, e.g., al-Sarakhsī, *al-Mabsūṭ*, 10: 93, 95.
123. See, e.g., Saḥnūn, *al-Mudawwanah*, 2: 218; al-Sarakhsī, *al-Mabsūṭ*, 5: 38–41; Ibn al-Qayyim, *Aḥkām ahl al-dhimmah*, 2: 614–39.
124. In fact, al-Qarāfī even problematizes the notion that the purpose of *jihād* is to eradicate Unbelief (*kufr*), noting the unanimous consensus against killing Unbelievers who are women, children, farmers, monks, the terminally ill, and the like. See his *al-Dhakhīrah*, 3: 387.
125. March, *Liberal Citizenship*, 196–7. Interestingly, according to Rashīd Riḍā, imposing the *jizyah* was not a cause (*ʿillah*) *for* fighting but the *terminus ad quem* (*ghāyah*) *of* fighting. In other words, Muslims were not obligated to wage war on the world in order to impose the *jizyah*; they were obligated to impose the *jizyah* as the means of terminating wars that had been dictated by material circumstances on the ground. See Riḍā, *Tafsīr al-manār*, 11: 247.
126. March, *Liberal Citizenship*, 197.
127. March, *Liberal Citizenship*, 197.
128. March, *Liberal Citizenship*, 310, notes 37, 39.
129. March, *Liberal Citizenship*, 236.
130. This presumption is clearly overturned in Yūsuf al-Qaraḍāwī's *Fiqh al-jihād*, esp., 1: 255–371.
131. March, *Liberal Citizenship*, 200.
132. March, *Liberal Citizenship*, 201. Emphasis original. Curiously, March ignores the explicit testimony of as influential an authority in the pre-modern juristic tradition as Ibn Rushd the Grandfather (d. 520/1122) cited on p. 17 of my "Jihād and the Modern World": "So, whenever we are placed beyond the reach of the enemy and the outlying districts of the Muslim lands are secured and the gaps in their fortifications are filled, the obligation to wage jihad falls from all the rest of the Muslims." See my "Jihad and the Modern World," *The Journal of Islamic Law and Culture*, 7:1 (2002). For this quote in the Arabic source, see Ibn Rushd, *al-Muqaddimāt*, 4 vols. (Beirut: Dār al-Fikr, n.d.), 1: 374 at the bottom of Saḥnūn, *al-Mudawwanah al-kubrā*), which was provided in the original citation. Clearly, Ibn Rushd could not have been capitulating to modern pressures. Nor do we find in him any obsession with toppling regimes or systems of unbelief per se.
133. C.f., however, Hallaq, *Impossible State*, 49: "Generally, in whichever territory the Sharīʿa is applied as the paradigmatic law, the territory is deemed an Islamic domain, Dār al-Islām. Wherever the Sharīʿa does not operate, or in whichever territory it is relegated to a secondary, inferior status, the territory is deemed Dār al-Ḥarb, a territory that is subject to conversion by peace or by war. The ultimate purpose of this conversion is to bring non-Muslims to accept Islam's law, which is primarily a set of moral principles sustained by legal concepts." Hallaq's reference here is the Ḥanafī jurist Ibn al-Saʿātī.
134. See the section "*Al-Shāfiʿī, Mālik, Ḥanafīs and the Early Period*" in Chapter 5. In fact, the full quote from al-Shāfiʿī reads: "If a hostile enemy attacks them [*ahl*

al-dhimmah], seizes them and prevents them from engaging in polytheistic practices (*shirk*), drinking wine, and eating pork, would I [as Muslim ruler or official] with whom they had a contract of *dhimmah* be required to rescue them if I was able?" Al-Shāfiʿī's answer is "Yes." See al-Shāfiʿī, *al-Umm*, 6:195.

135. Al-Shāfiʿī, *al-Umm*, 6: 195.
136. See the section "*The Empire-State Between Sharīʿah and the Islamic Secular*" in Chapter 5.
137. See, e.g., the lengthy discussion on *jizyah* in Ibn Rushd I, *Muqaddimāt ibn rushd* (at the bottom of Saḥnūn's *al-Mudawwwanah*), 1: 393–402.
138. Al-Qarāfī, *al-Furūq*, 3:15.
139. Even the Muslim Caliph was technically bound to fulfill certain duties and serve certain interests before he could command loyalty. See al-Māwardī, *al-Aḥkām al-sulṭānīyah*, 24; Abū Yaʿlā, *al-Aḥkām al-sulṭānīyah*, 28.
140. Cited in M. Walzer, "Welfare, Membership and Need," in M. Sandel, ed., *Liberalism and its Critics*, 200–18 at 200.
141. March, *Liberal Citizenship*, 146.
142. March, *Liberal Citizenship*, 208.
143. March, *Liberal Citizenship*, 238.
144. See J.J. Rousseau, *The Social Contract* (London: Penguin Books, 1968), 186–7.
145. March, *Liberal Citizenship*, 214.
146. See the section "*Siyāsah*" in Chapter 3.
147. In fact, I recall Shaykh Yūsuf al-Qaraḍāwī, during some of his visits to America decades ago, encouraging inter-marriage with non-Muslim women in order to strengthen Muslim-non-Muslim bonds.
148. March, *Liberal Citizenship*, 218.
149. March, *Liberal Citizenship*, 217.
150. March, *Liberal Citizenship*, 220.
151. For more on *maʿrūf*, see the discussion below in this chapter.
152. See the discussion in section "*Al-Ḥusn wa al-Qubḥ al-ʿAqlīyān*" in Chapter 4.
153. See the section "The Secular State and the Islamic Secular" in Chapter 5. See also al-Qaraḍāwī, *al-Aqallīyāt al-dīnīyah wa al-ḥall al-islāmī*, 15–16.
154. March, *Liberal Citizenship*, 238.
155. The full *ḥadīth* reads, "The Prophet stated, 'Help your brother whether he is an oppressor or is oppressed.' A man asked, 'O Messenger of God, I will help him when he is oppressed. But what about when he is the oppressor? How shall I help him?' He responded, 'You stop or prevent him from oppressing. That is helping him.' " See al-Bukhārī, *Ṣaḥīḥ al-bukhārī*, 9: 635.
156. James Baldwin, *The Fire Next Time* (New York: Dell, 1963), 40.
157. James Baldwin, "How One Black Man Came to be an American," in *Baldwin: Collected Essays* (New York: Literary Classics of the United States, Ind., 1998), 762–5 at 762.
158. See his "Interpretations of Black Religion in America," *Significations*, 152–3. Emphasis original. See also Charles Mills, "Rawls on Race/Race on Rawls," 161–84 at 177, where he speaks of Blackamericans as an "ineluctably Western" people.

159. See, e.g., R. Mottahedeh, "The Shu'ūbīyah Controversy and the Social History of Early Islamic Iran," *International Journal of Middle East Studies*, 7 (1976): 161–82. See also my *Islam and the Blackamerican*, 103–04.
160. Cited in Ahmed, *What Is Islam?* 496.
161. See, e.g., S. Marmon, "Black Slaves in Mamlūk Narratives: Representations of Transgressions, *al-Qantara*, 28:2 (2007): 435–64.
162. See Muḥammad 'Alī Ḥusayn al-Makkī al-Mālikī, *Tahdhīb al-furūq wa al-qawā'id al-sanīyah fī al-asrār al-fiqhīyah*, 4 vols., 1: 3 (on the margin of al-Qarāfī's *al-Furūq*, note 1 at the bottom of the page).
163. See, e.g., Shāfi'ī b. 'Alī, *Ḥusn al-manāqib al-sirrīyah al-muntaza'ah min al-sīrah al-ẓāhirīyah*, 2nd ed., ed. 'A. Khowaytar (Riyadh, 1410/1989), 79; Shams al-Dīn al-Dhahabī, *Duwal al-islām*, 2 vols., eds. F. M. Shaltūt and M. M. Ibrāhīm (Cairo: al-Hay'ah al-Miṣrīyah al-'Āmmah li al-Kitāb, 1974), 2: 165.
164. Thus, Bernard Lewis writes, "[A]t no time did the Islamic world ever practice the kind of racial exclusivism . . . which has existed until very recently in the United States." See his *Race and Color in Islam* (New York: Harper and Row, 1971), 102. Some may point to the so-called Zanj rebellion of black slaves in southern Iraq in the third/ninth century as a reflection of institutionalized racism. But it seems that the Zanj rebels were not all black (nor slaves); and sectarianism, economics, politics, and charismatic leadership also contributed to the saga. For a quick, critical summary of the event and the scholarly controversy surrounding it, see G. H. Talhami, "The Zanj Rebellion Reconsidered," *The International Journal of African Historical Studies*, *10*:3 (1977): 443–61.
165. By analogy, while we may speak of homosexual activity in the pre-modern Muslim world, it might be inaccurate to speak of "homosexuals" or "homosexuality." As Khaled Rouayheb observes, those who engaged in homosexual acts were simply placed on a par with people who were "lazy or cowardly or frivolous or irascible." In short, there was no such thing as a "homosexual." See K. Rouayheb, *Before Homosexuality in the Arab-Islamic World, 1500-1800* (Chicago: University of Chicago Press, 2009), 1–51, esp. 48. Drawing on the work of M. McIntosh, Rouayheb implies that homosexuality is a thoroughly modern category: "[S]uch a homosexual 'role' or stereotype only emerged in England in the late seventeenth century. Prior to that time, and in most contemporary non-Western societies, 'there may be much homosexual behavior, but there are no homosexuals.'" *Before Homosexuality*, 44.
166. This is essentially what Edward Curtis describes as bedeviling the efforts of Malcolm X, i.e., that, being limited to the cognitive frame of his Sunni teachers, he never developed an *Islamic* approach to the problem of race in America and resorted instead to Pan-Africanism. See E. E. Curtis IV, "Why Malcolm X Never Developed an Islamic Approach to Civil Rights," *Religion*, 32:3 (2002): 227–42, esp. 239: "[Said] Ramadan, [Mahmoud] Shawarbi, [Omar] Azzam, and even Prince Faysal had made it clear to Malcolm that Islam paid no heed to race. If Malcolm were to practice the 'real' Islam, they said, he could not appropriate Islam in an explicitly black struggle."
167. See the section "The Authority of the Islamic Secular" in Chapter 4.

168. Cited in F. Esack, *Qur'ān, Liberation and Pluralism: An Islamic Perspective of Interreligious Solidarity against Oppression* (Oxford: Oneworld Press, 1997), 31. For a more nuanced perspective on the MJC, see E. Moosa, "Muslim Conservatism in South Africa," *Journal of Theology for Southern Africa*, *69* (1989); 73–81.
169. See S. Bangstad and A. Fataar, "Ambiguous Accommodation: Cape Muslims and Post-Apartheid Politics," *Journal of Southern African Studies*, *36*:4 (2010): 817–31 at 819. We should note that the MJC was not a strict monolith, and other factors, e.g., class, economics, broader political interests, informed the various positions assumed. As Bangstad and Fataar note (p. 820): "[A] small number of MJC members did declare their opposition to the doctrine of apartheid during the 1960s." More recently, the MJC has evolved to the point of admitting that it is now "compelled to give guidance on more than religious issues." Bangstad and Fataar, "Ambiguous Accommodation," 829. Finally, my critical assessment of the MJC's position should not be taken as a wholesale endorsement of the views of its opponents.
170. See, e.g., J. S. Mbiti, *African Religions and Philosophy*, 2nd ed. (Oxford: Heinemann Educational Publishers, 1997), 1–5, esp., 4: "[T]here is no conversion from one traditional religion to another." The book first appeared in 1969.
171. R. W. Bulliet, *Conversion to Islam in the Medieval Period: An Essay in Quantitative History* (Cambridge: Harvard University Press, 1979).
172. Jacobson, *Whiteness of a Different Color*, 143.
173. Jacobson, *Whiteness of a Different Color*, 109–35. See also the discussion in the section "March's Framing and Its Implications" and note 21 in this chapter. America's Naturalization Act of 1790, however, limited citizenship to "free White persons."
174. Jacobson, *Whiteness of a Different Color*, 215.
175. When the US congress in 1790 limited eligibility for citizenship to "free white persons," Muslims were overwhelmingly excluded not as Muslims but as non-Whites—not along doctrinal lines, in other words, but along racial lines.
176. See especially Mills, *Black Rights/White Wrongs*. See also, Mills, "Rawls on Race" and "Racial Liberalism."
177. Mills, "Rawls on Race," 161. Emphasis mine.
178. Mills, *Black Rights*, 28–48.
179. Mills, *Black Rights*, 200–15.
180. Bell, "A Communitarian Critique of Liberalism," 225. The Blackamerican political theorist Michael Dawson identifies an important communitarian strain among Blackamericans: "[N]onliberal theoretical perspectives which emphasize the primacy of community are prominent in the black counterpublic." See M. C. Dawson, *Black Visions*, 30.
181. Kahn, *Putting Liberalism in Its Place*, 144.
182. See Ibn Khaldūn, *al-Muqaddimah*, 91, 92, 96, 107, and passim. Ibn Khaldūn notes, incidentally, that, while biology was the default basis of *'aṣabīyah*, it can also come as a result of sustained historical narratives that have no basis in biology, constituting what we would call today a "social construct" or "imagined community," as we see in the case of "Blacks" and "Whites" in America. See Ibn Khaldūn, *al-Muqaddimah*, 89.
183. Cited in Unger, *Knowledge and Politics*, 37–8.

184. Al-Ghazālī, *al-Mustaṣfā*, 1: 61.
185. J. Williams, *White Working Class: Overcoming Class Cluelessness in America* (Boston: Harvard Business Review Press, 2017), 5.
186. This is not inalterably the case. Matthew Frey Jacobson describes the effort and partial success of the "white ethnic movement" to "displace . . . Plymouth Rock by Ellis Island in our national myth of origins." See his *Roots Too: White Ethnic Revival in Post-Civil Rights America* (Cambridge, MA: Harvard University Press, 2006), 9. Even here, however, the anti-Black impulse persists: "England out of Ireland—Niggers out of South Boston"; "I'm not white; I'm Italian." Jacobson, *Roots Too*, 7. One can imagine a similar attitude toward Muslims.
187. Williams, *White Working Class*, 70.
188. On America as a racial caste system, see Isabel Wilkerson, *Caste: The Origins of Our Discontents* (New York: Random House, 2020). Meanwhile, I tend to agree with Alasdair MacIntyre on the hegemonic influence of liberalism in American life: "So-called conservatism and so-called radicalism in these contemporary guises are in general mere stalking horses for liberalism: the contemporary debates within modern political systems are almost exclusively between conservative liberals, liberal liberals, and radical liberals. There is little place in such political systems for the criticism of the system itself, that is, for putting liberalism in question." See A. MacIntyre, *Whose Justice? Which Rationality* (Notre Dame, IN: University of Notre Dame Press, 1988), 392.
189. See R. Balmer, *Bad Faith: Race and the Rise of the Religious Right* (Grand Rapids, MI: William B. Eerdmans Publishing Co., 2021). Balmer is careful not to be overinclusive, noting that there have been and are White Evangelicals for whom anti-racism is a major constituent of their religious vision. See Balmer, *Bad Faith*, 22–3, 32, 79.
190. On this point, see, e.g., Theodore Allen, *The Invention of the White Race*, vol. 1: *Racial Oppression and Social Control*, 3rd ed. (New York: Verso, 1994), esp. 1–33, where he suggests that part of the whole point of "inventing" American Whiteness was to grant poor and working-class Whites a "social promotion" that would bring them into a common identity with the White establishment, assuaging and pacifying them, even as it enlisted them in the effort to control Blacks.
191. This was the chant of right-wing White nationalists in a rally in Charlottesville, VA, in August 2017. I am reminded here of an experiment we were shown in an undergraduate psychology course demonstrating the effects of external affliction. A rat and a raccoon were placed in a metal cage. The latter simply ignored the former, until an electric current was run through the floor of the cage. In two seconds, the rat was in the raccoon's mouth, innocent though that rat was of what had afflicted the raccoon!
192. See Roy Mottahedeh's insightful, "The Shuʿūbīyah Controversy," 169–70, where it is noted that, according to some Qurʾān commentators, a *shaʿb* is "a people related by a common place of residence or birth," while a *qabīlah* is "a people related through a common ancestor." This is not a point of consensus among Muslim scholars, and Mottahedeh does not make that claim. See, however, al-Māwardī, *al-Aḥkām al-sulṭānīyah*, 49, for a different set of distinctions.

193. See, e.g., al-Rāghib al-Iṣfahānī, *al-Mufradāt fī gharīb al-qur'ān*, ed. M. S. Kīlānī (Beirut: Dār al-Maʿrifah, n.d.), 418–19, where he ties *qawm* to lineage.
194. This phrase appeared in the famous footnote number 4 of the 1938 US Supreme Court case, *United States v. Carolene Products Company*.
195. See J. Joffe, "A Canvas, Not a Country: How Europe Sees America," in *Understanding America: The Anatomy of an Exceptional Nation*, eds. P. Schuck and J. O. Wilson (New York: Public Affairs, 2008), 602.
196. See A. de Tocqueville, *Democracy in America*, 2 vols. (New York: Vintage Books, 1990), 1: 358: "It is difficult for us, who have had the good fortune to be born among men like ourselves by nature and our equals by law, to conceive of the irreconcilable differences that separate the Negro from the European in America." He continues: "If it be so difficult to root out an inequality that originates solely in the law, how are those distinctions to be destroyed which seem to be based upon the immutable laws of Nature herself?"
197. Numerous Muslims, e.g., from the Middle East, are legally classified as White. But, since 9/11, many legally White Muslims have experienced a social non-Whiteness, what many of them now refer to as "racialization."
198. Rorty, *Contingency*, 67. Bracketed segment original.
199. This explains, to my mind, the Prophet's response to those who cursed the Companion who consistently drank wine: "Do not curse him; for I have only known him to love God and God's Messenger." In other words, the Prophet recognized that the primacy of the proper want was still alive in this man. See the section "*The Secular in Historical Perspective*" in Chapter 1.
200. See, e.g., B. R. Ashford, "Wittgenstein's Theologians: A Survey of Ludwig Wittgenstein's Impact on Theology," *Journal of the Evangelical Theological Society*, *50*:2 (2007): 357–75, esp. 360–1.
201. See S. Hauerwas, "On Keeping Theological Ethics Theological," *The Hauerwas Reader*, eds. J. Berkman and M. Cartwright (Durham: Duke University Press, 2001): 51–74 at 72.
202. Hauerwas, "On Keeping Theological Ethics Theological," 71.
203. In fact, elsewhere, in a manner reminiscent of Brian Barry, March indicates that liberalism may need to pre-empt communities, especially religious communities, not only from carrying out certain public or private practices but even from inculcating in its members attitudes that conflict with the liberal vision of justice. See his "Is There a Right to Polygamy?" 271.
204. Compare this with its use in a standard text on Mālikī *fiqh* still used at al-Azhar today. Speaking of the Muslim duty to be good to parents, we read, *inter alia*: "And s/he must guide the blind parent to church, even though the latter is a *kāfir*, delivering him or her there and providing him or her with money to spend during their holidays, though not to donate to the church or priest." See Aḥmad al-Dardīr, *al-Sharḥ al-ṣaghīr*, on the margins of Aḥmad b. Muḥammad al-Ṣāwī, *Bulghat al-sālik li aqrab al-masālik ilā madhhab al-imām mālik*, 2 vols. (Cairo: Muṣṭafā al-Bābī al-Ḥalabī, n.d.), 2: 523.
205. March, *Liberal Citizenship*, 10.
206. "Is There a Right to Polygamy?" 249. Emphasis mine.

207. See the section "*Nomos* and Plausibility Structure" in Chapter 3.
208. March, *Liberal Citizenship*, 98.
209. March, *Liberal Citizenship*, 56.
210. Albert Murray, *The Omni-Americans: Black Experience and American Culture* (New York: Da Capo Press, Inc., 1970), 36.
211. A society's *maʿrūf* as a presumptive norm for Muslims is not necessarily the exclusive product of Muslims themselves. The Qur'ān repeatedly commands Muslims to settle various disputes in accordance with the *maʿrūf* of pagan Arabia, which *maʿrūf* was not put in place by Muslims. See Qur'ān 2: 178, 2: 180, 2: 228, 2: 229, 2: 331, 3: 104, 3: 114, 4: 25, 9: 71, 22: 41, 60: 12, and passim. See further the insightful article by A.K. Reinhart, "What We Know about Maʿrūf," in *Journal of Islamic Ethics* 1 (2017): 51–82. I would assign perhaps a less negative role to *taqlīd*, however, and see the *maʿrūf* as being "known" more through convention than through thought, that is, as something closer to Hegel's *Sittlichkeit* than to Kant's *Moralität*. On this latter distinction, see Charles Taylor, "Hegel: History and Politics," in M. Sandel, ed., *Liberalism and Its Critics*, 177–99.
212. See Aḥmad al-Raysūnī, *Fiqh al-thawrah: murājaʿāt fī fiqh al-siyāsī al-islāmī* (Cairo: Dār al-Kalimah, 2013), 12–13, note 1. Al-Raysūnī is of the view that only *taʿaruf*, as opposed to *maʿrūf/ʿurf*, is probative as a source in politics. I am not sure I share al-Raysūnī's view that *taʿāruf* is less susceptible than *ʿurf* to government manipulation.
213. V. J. Cornell, "Reasons Public and Divine: Liberal Democracy, Shariʿa Fundamentalism and the Epistemological Crisis of Islam," in C. Ernst and R. C. Martin, eds., *Rethinking Islamic Studies*, 23–51 at 38–9.
214. S. Jackson, "Soft Shariʿa Fundamentalism and the Totalitarian Epistemology of Vincent Cornell," *The Religion and Culture Forum, University of Chicago Divinity School*, 2011. Now available at http://www.marcmanley.com/media/pdfs/jackson-response-to-cornell.pdf
215. For example, if individuals left Mecca to join Muḥammad in Medina without the permission of one who had authority over them, Muḥammad had to send them back. But if individuals left Medina to rejoin the Meccans, even without Muḥammad's permission, the Meccans would not be bound to send them back.
216. Indeed, the "manifest victory" mentioned in *Surat al-Fatḥ*, "The Victory," is often identified not as the Conquest of Mecca but as the Treaty of Ḥudaybīyah, which occurred two years earlier. See, e.g., Ibn Kathīr, *Tafsīr al-qur'ān al-ʿaẓīm*, 4: 182.
217. See my *Islam and the Blackamerican*, 148. Notice how firmly shackled my own examples were to Islam's *sharʿīyāt*.
218. See also my "Not Truth But Tolerance: A (Much Belated) Response to Atif Khalil," *The American Journal of Islamic Social Sciences, 28*:4 (2011): 146–61.
219. See the section "*Al-Shāfiʿī, Mālik, Ḥanafīs and the Early Period*" in Chapter 5.
220. From M. Walzer, *What It Means to Be an American: Essays on the American Experience* (New York: Marsilio Publishers Corp., 1992), 21–49. It is not my contention that Walzer would agree with my reading of his argument. Nor should it be assumed that my invoking him here implies an acceptance of other aspects of his thought, particularly regarding religion, and more particularly regarding Islam and Muslims.

221. Walzer, "What Does It Mean to Be an American?" 45. As intimated in the Introduction (note 1), Blackamericans complicate this scheme in ways that I cannot elaborate further here. For present purposes, one may think of Blackamericans as African-Americans.
222. This remains a challenge for Muslim-Americans as well, given their ethnic, racial, class, and cultural diversity, i.e., whether Islam, as a higher form of love or commitment, can domesticate the myriad parochial regimes of love among them.
223. M. J. Sandel, "Religious Liberty: Freedom of Choice or Freedom of Conscience," in R. Bhargava, ed., *Secularism and Its Critics*, 73–93, at 87.
224. See, e.g., my *Islam and the Blackamerican*, 144–5. In fact, with *tawḥīd* as the center of their analytical apparatus, they did not see such practices as the biggest problem that Zoroastrians (and other non-Muslims) presented. Thus, in response to an incredulous student who asked how such practices could be allowed, an early Mālikī scholar responded: "The terms of *dhimmah* allow them to do more than marry their mothers and daughters; it allows them to invent lies against God and worship other than the All-Merciful." See Saḥnūn, *al-Mudawwanah*, 2: 219.
225. Al-Sarakhsī, *al-Mabsūṭ*, 5: 39. He also cites a minority opinion from Abū Yūsuf (though the latter seems to have had other opinions too) that bans the practice. See also Ibn al-Qayyim, *Aḥkām ahl al-dhimmah*, 2: 764–69, where the practice is also allowed. We should note, meanwhile, that the analogy in question would be severely weakened by the fact that it could only extend to same-sex marriage among non-Muslims, not to homosexual acts, as Ḥanafīs ban and punish the latter. See al-Sarakhsī, *al-Mabsūṭ*, 9: 85..
226. See, e.g., Wolin: "Agreement is therefore seen [by liberalism] as the critical political problem and disagreement as the major evil." *Vision*, 545. Earlier he wrote, "Liberalism has always been accused of seeking to dissolve the solidarities of social ties and relationships to replace them by the unfettered, independent individual, the masterless man. In reality, the charge is almost without foundation and completely misses the liberal addiction towards social conformity." Wolin, *Vision*, 307.
227. Personally, I prefer a nomenclature other than "people of color" as a catch-all for non-Whites, as it reinforces the notion that Whiteness, as a racial identity, is not a color but the natural, original constitution of humanity, color being a distinguishing additive, which tends to make Whiteness as a color invisible, especially to Whites. As Richard Dyer notes, "[T]he position of speaking as a white person is one that white people now almost never acknowledge and this is part of the condition and power of whiteness; white people claim and achieve authority for what they say by not admitting, indeed not realising, that for most of the time they speak only for whiteness." See R. Dyer, *White* (New York: Routledge, 1997), xiv.
228. See S. Hauerwas and D. Bourns, "Marriage and the Family," *Quaker Religious Thought*, *56*:3 (1984): 4–24 at 23–4.
229. On Vico's understanding of *sensus communis*, see T. I. Bayer, "Vico's Principle of *Sensus Communis* and Forensic Eloquence," *Chicago-Kent Law Review*, *83*:3 (2008): 1131–55.
230. C. Mouffe, *The Return of the Political* (London: Verso, 1993), 4. This is the heart of the approach that Mouffe refers to as "Agonism."

Conclusion

1. See Berlin, *The Magus of the North*, 40. Emphasis original. The words are Berlin's, describing the position of Hamann.
2. Kant, *Groundwork*, 15.
3. Kant, *Groundwork*, 17. Ṭāriq al-Bishrī registers a similar critique of the approach of many modern Muslims: "Many of those who defended the 'Islamic System' (*al-niẓām al-islāmī*) simply viewed the latter as a free-standing, pre-fabricated system with clear-cut features, which could be mechanically implemented, as one would implement architectural plans or designs (*al-rusūm wa al-taṣmīmāt al-handasīyah*) that had been drawn up on paper, with nothing left but to transfer them onto the plane of quotidian reality." See his *al-Ḥiwār al-islāmī al-ʿalmānī*, 31.
4. Berlin, *Magus*, 38. The words are Berlin's.
5. Berlin, *Magus*, 35. Again, the words are Berlin's depicting the position of Hamann.
6. See the section "*Efficient Decision-Making*" in Chapter 3.
7. See the section "Beyond the *Ḥukm Sharʿī*" in Chapter 2.
8. See K. Zuhdī et al., *Mubādarat waqf al-ʿunf,: ruʾyah wāqiʿīyah wa naẓrah sharʿīyah* (Cairo: Maktabat al-Turāth al-Islāmī, 2002), 35. They add that this is "in addition to the external enemy who lies in wait for us, our religion and our nation." For a full English translation of this text, see my *Initiative to Stop the Violence*.
9. Berlin, *Magus*, 47. Again, the words are Berlin's depicting the position of Hamann.
10. See the section "March's Framing and Its Implications" in Chapter 6, where Ibn Taymīyah points out the difference between knowing what is good or bad and knowing what is better or worse, clearly invoking the context of real life on the ground as the difference-maker.
11. Ebrahim Moosa deploys this trope in his insightful *Ghazālī and the Poetics of Imagination*. My use of the concept, however, is slightly different. For Moosa, the primary domain of Islam's *poiesis* appears to be that of ethics. While ethics is not alien to the Islamic Secular's *poiesis*, its value resides as much in its practical and aesthetic as it does in its ethical work.
12. In summarizing the Aristotelian concept of *phronesis*, Chantal Mouffe writes: "This 'ethical knowledge', distinct from the knowledge specific to the sciences (*episteme*), is dependent on the ethos, the cultural and historical conditions current in the community, and implies a renunciation of all pretence to universality." See her *Return of the Political*, 14. Again, I appeal to phronesis for its utility beyond the realm of ethics alone.
13. The *qāfiyah* of a poem is the rhyme-cluster on which each line successively ends, the heart of classical Arabic poetry.
14. Asad, *Secular Translations*, 69. Bracketed segment mine.
15. I am using "Western" here in its conventional sense of referring to Europeans and their descendants. As pointed out in Chapter 6 and intimated elsewhere in this book, however, I do not subscribe to that monolithic understanding of "the West."

Bibliography

Abbasi, Rushain, "Did Premodern Muslims Distinguish the Religious and the Secular? The *Dīn-Dunyā* Binary in Medieval Islamic Thought," *Journal of Islamic Studies*, *3*:2 (2020):185-225.

Abbasi, Rushain, *Beyond the Realm of Religion: The Idea of the Secular in Premodern Islam*, PhD dissertation, Harvard University, 2021.

ʿAbd al-Jabbār, al-Qāḍī Abū al-Ḥasan, *Sharḥ al-uṣūl al-khamsah*, ed. ʿA. ʿUthmān. Cairo: Maktabat Wahbah, 1416/1996.

ʿAbd al-Lāwī, al-Bashīr M. *Sulṭat walī al-amr fī taqyīd al-mubāḥ*. Beirut: Dār Maktabat al-Maʿārif, 1432/2011.

ʿAbd al-Raḥmān, Ṭaha, *Rūḥ al-ḥadāthah: al-madkhal ilā taʾsīs al-ḥadāthah al-islāmīyah*, 4th ed. Casablanca: al-Markaz al-Thaqāfī al-ʿArabī, 2016.

ʿAbd al-Raḥmān, Ṭaha, *Fī uṣūl al-ḥiwār wa tajdīd ʿilm al-kalām*. Beirut: al-Markaz al-Thaqāfī al-ʿArabī, 2014.

ʿAbd al-Wahhāb, al-Qāḍī (ʿAbd al-Wahhāb b. ʿAlī b. Naṣr), *ʿUyūn al-majālis*, 6 vols., ed. A. K. Kāh. Riyadh: Maktabat al-Rushd, 1421/2000.

ʿAbduh, Muḥammad, "*al-Zawāj*," in *al-Aʿmāl al-kāmilah li ʾl-imām muḥammad ʿabduh*, 5 vols., ed. M. ʿUmārah. Cairo: Dār al-Shurūq, 1427/2006, 2:70-5.

ʿAbduh, Muḥammad, *al-Islām dīn al-ʿilm wa al-madanīyah*. Cairo: Sīnā li al-Nashr, 1986.

ʿAbduh, Muḥammad, *Majallat al-manār*, 34 vols. Cairo. Dār al-Manār, 1315–1352/ 1898–1935 [*sic*].

Abou El -Fadl, Khaled, "Islam and the Challenge of Democratic Commitment," *Fordham International Law Journal*, *27*:4 (2003):4-71.

Abou El -Fadl, Khaled, *Reasoning with God: Reclaiming Shariʿah in the Modern Age*. Lanham, MD: Rowman and Littlefield, 2014.

Abou El -Fadl, Khaled, "What Type of Law Is Islamic Law," in *Routledge Handbook of Islamic Law*, eds. K. Abou El Fadl, A. A. Ahmad, and S. F. Hassan. London and New York: Routledge, 2019, 11-39.

Abou El -Fadl, Khaled, *Rebellion and Violence in Islamic Law*. Cambridge: Cambridge University Press, 2001.

Abu Lughod, Janet, "The Islamic City—Historic Myth, Islamic Essence, and Contemporary Relevance," *International Journal of Middle East Studies 19*:2 (1987):15-76.

Abū Yaʿlā, Muḥammad b. al-Ḥusayn al-Farrāʾ, *al-ʿUddah fī uṣūl al-fiqh*, 2 vols. ed. M.ʿA. A. ʿAṭā. Beirut: Dār al-Kutub al-ʿIlmīyah, 1423/2002.

Abū Yaʿlā, Muḥammad b. al-Ḥusayn al-Farrāʾ, *al-Aḥkām al-sulṭānīyah*, ed. M. Ḥ. al-Fiqi Beirut: Dār al-Kutub al-ʿIlmīyah, 1403/1983.

Abū Yaʿlā, Muḥammad b. al-Ḥusayn al-Farrāʾ, *Ṭabaqāt al-ḥanābilah*, 2 vols. Beirut: Dār al-Maʿrifah, n.d.

Abū Yūsuf (Yaʿqūb b. Ibrāhīm), *al-Radd ʿalā siyar al-awzāʿī*, ed. Abū al-Wafāʾ al-Afghānī. Cairo: Lajnat Iḥyāʾ al-Maʿārif al-Nuʿmānīyah,?1358/1939.

Abū Zahra, Muḥammad, *Uṣūl al-fiqh*. Cairo: Dār al-Fikr al-ʿArabī, n.d.

Adams, Charles, "The History of Religions and the Study of Islam," in *The History of Religions: Essays on the Problem of Understanding*, 2nd impression, eds. J. M. Kitagawa, M. Eliade, and C. H. Long. Chicago: University of Chicago Press, 1969, 177-93.

Adams, Nicholas, "Shapers of Protestantism: F. D. E. Schleiermacher," *The Blackwell Companion to Protestantism*, eds. A. McGrath and D. C. Marks. London: Blackwell Publishers, 2004,66-82.

Ahmad, Ahmad A., *The Fatigue of the Shari'a*. New York: Palgrave Macmillan, 2012.

Ahmed, Shahab, *What Is Islam? The Importance of Being Islamic*. Princeton: Princeton University Press, 2016.

Ajami, Fouad, "The Summoning: 'But They Said, We Will Not Hearken,'" *Foreign Affairs*, *72*:4 (Sept.–Oct. 1993): 2-9.

Al-Albānī, Nāṣir al-Dīn, *Ṣaḥīḥ sunan al-nasā'ī bi ikhtiṣār al-sanad*, 3 vols. Riyādh: Maktab al-Tarbīyah al-'Arabī li Duwal al-Khalīj, 1408/1988.

'Alī, Shāfi'ī b., *Ḥusn al-manāqib al-sirrīyah al-muntaza'ah min al-sīrah al-ẓāhirīyah*, 2nd ed., ed. 'A. Khowaytar. Riyadh, 1410/1989.

Allen, Theodore, *The Invention of the White Race*, vol. 1: *Racial Oppression and Social Control*, 3rd ed. New York: Verso, 1994.

Allouche, Adel, *Mamluk Economics: A Study and Translation of al-Maqrīzī's* Ighāthah. University of Utah Press. Salt Lake City, 1994.

Al-'Alwānī, Ṭāhā Jābir, *al-Ta'līm al-dīnī bayna al-tajdīd wa al-tajmīd*. Cairo: Dār al-Salām li al-Ṭibā'ah wa al-Nashr wa al-Tawzī' wa al-Tarjamah, 1430/2009.

Al-Āmidī, Sayf al-Dīn, *al-Iḥkām fī uṣūl al-aḥkām*, 4 vols. Riyadh: Dār al-Ṣumay'ī li al-Nashr wa al-Tawzī', 1424/2003.

Anderson, J.N.D., "Law as a Social Force in Islamic Culture and History," in *Law of the Near and Middle East: Readings, Cases and and Materials*, ed. H. J. Liebesny. Albany, N.Y.: State University of New York Press, 1975, 3-5.

Anjum, Ovamir, *Politics, Law and Community in Islamic Thought: The Taymiyyan Moment*. Cambridge: Cambridge University Press, 2012.

An-Na'im, Abdullahi, A. An-Na'im, *Islam and the Secular State: Negotiating the Future of Shari'a*. Cambridge, Mass: Harvard University Press, 2008.

An-Na'im, Abdullahi, A. An-Na'im, *What Is an American Muslim: Embracing Faith and Citizenship*. New York: Oxford University Press, 2014.

Al-Anṣārī, Abū Yaḥyā Zakarīyah, *Asnā al-maṭālib sharḥ rawḍ al-ṭālib*, 9 vols. ed. M. M. Tāmir Beirut: Dār al-Kutub al-'ilmīyah, 1434/2013.

Arberry, A. J., *Revelation and Reason in Islam*, 2nd impression. London: George Allen and Unwin Ltd., 1965.

Asad, Talal, *Genealogies of Religion: Discipline and Reasons of Power in Christianity and Islam*. Baltimore: The Johns Hopkins University Press, 1993.

Asad, Talal, *Formations of the Secular: Christianity, Islam, Modernity*. Stanford: Stanford University Press, 2003.

Asad, Talal, *Secular Translations: Nation-State, Modern Self and Calculative Reason*. New York: Columbia University Press, 2018.

Al-Ash'arī, Abū al-Ḥasan 'Alī b. Ismā'īl, *Maqālāt al-islāmīyīn wa ikhtilāf al-muṣallīn* 2 vols., ed. M. M. 'Abd al-Ḥamīd. Cairo: Maktabat al-Nahḍah al-Miṣrīyah, 1389/1969.

Ashford, B. R., "Wittgenstein's Theologians: A Survey of Ludwig Wittgenstein's Impact on Theology," *Journal of the Evangelical Theological Society*, *50*:2 (2007):357-75.

Al-Attas, Syed Muhammad Naquib, *Islām and Secularism*. Kuala Lumpur: International Institute of Islamic Thought and Civilization, 1993.

Ayalon, David, "The System of Payment in Mamluk Military Society I," *Journal of the Economic and Social History of the Orient, 1*:1 (1957): 37-65.

Ayalon, David, "System of Payment II," *Journal of the Economic and Social History of the Orient, 1*:3 (1958):257-96.

Al-'Aynī, Badr al-Dīn, *al-Bināyah sharḥ al-hidāyah*, 13 vols. ed., A. Ṣ. Sha'bān. Beirut: Dār al-Kutub al-'Ilmīyah, 1433/2012.

Ayoub, Samy A., "'The Sulṭān Says': State Authority in the Late Ḥanafī Tradition," *Islamic Law and Society, 23* (2016): 239-78.

Ayoub, Samy A., *Law, Empire, and the Sultan: Ottoman Imperial Authority and Late Ḥanafī Jurisprudence*. New York: Oxford University Press, 2020.

Azam, Hina, *Sexual Violation in Islamic Law: Substance, Evidence, and Procedure*. Cambridge: Cambridge University Press, 2017.

Al-Azami, Mustafa, M., *On Schacht's Origins of Muhammadan Jurisprudence*. Oxford: The Oxford Centre for Islamic Studies and The Islamic Texts Society, 1996.

Al-Baghdādī, Abū Bakr Aḥmad b. Thābit al-Khaṭīb, *al-Taṭfīl wa ḥikāyāt al-ṭufaylīyīn wa akhbāruhim wa nawādir kalāmihim wa ash'ārihim*, ed. B.'A. al-Jābī. Beirut: Dār Ibn Ḥazm, n.d.

Al-Baghdādī, Abū Manṣūr 'Abd al-Qāhir al-Tamīmī, *Kitāb uṣūl al-dīn*. Beirut: Dār al-Kutub al-'Ilmīyah, n.d.

Al-Bājī, Abū al-Walīd, Iḥkām al-fuṣūl fī aḥkām al-uṣūl, ed. 'Abd al-Majīd Turkī. Beirut: Dār al-Gharb al-Islāmī, 1407/1986.

Baldwin, James, *The Fire Next Time*. New York: Dell, 1963.

Baldwin, James, "How One Black Man Came to be an American," in *Baldwin: Collected Essays*. New York: Literary Classics of the United States, Ind., 1998, 762-65.

Balmer, Randall, *Bad Faith: Race and the Rise of the Religious Right*. Grand Rapids, MI: William B. Eerdmans Publishing Co., 2021.

Bangstad Sindre and Fataar, Aslam, "Ambiguous Accommodation: Cape Muslims and Post-Apartheid Politics," *Journal of Southern African Studies, 36*:4 (2010):817-31.

Al-Bāqillānī, *al-Taqrīb wa al-irshād (al-ṣaghīr)* 3 vols., ed. 'A. Abū Zayd. Beirut: Mu'assasat al-Risālah, 1418/1998.

Barry, John M., *Roger Williams and the Making of the American Soul: Church, State and the Birth of Liberty*. New York: Penguin Books, 2012.

Al-Baṣrī, Abū al-Ḥusayn, *al-Mu'tamad fī uṣūl al-fiqh*, 2 vols., ed. K. al-Mays. Beirut: Dār al-Kutub al-'Ilmīyah, 1403/1983.

Batnitzky, Leora, *How Judaism Became a Religion: An Introduction to Modern Jewish Thought*. Princeton: Princeton University Press, 2011.

Bauer, Thomas, *A Culture of Ambiguity: An Alternative History of Islam*, transl. H. Biesterfeldt and T. Tunstall. New York: Columbia University Press, 2021.

Bayer, Thora I., "Vico's Principle of *Sensus Communis* and Forensic Eloquence," *Chicago-Kent Law Review, 83*:3 (2008):1131-55.

Al-Bazdawī, Fakhr al-Islām 'Alī b. Muḥammad, *Uṣūl al-bazdawī*, ed. S. Bakdāsh. Beirut: Sharikat Dār al-Bashā'ir al-Islāmīyah, 1436/2014.

Bell, Daniel, "A Communitarian Critique of Liberalism," *Analyse and Kritik, 27* (2005):215-38.

Benhabib, Seyla, "Carl Schmitt's Critique of Kant: Sovereignty and International Law," *Political Theory, 40*:6 (2012):688-713.

Berger, Peter, *The Sacred Canopy: Elements of a Sociological Theory of Religion*. New York: Anchor Books, 1990.

Berger, Peter (ed.), *The Desecularization of the World: Resurgent Religion and World Politics*. Grand Rapids: Eerdmanns Publishing Company, 1999.

Berlin, Isaiah, *Three Critics of the Enlightenment: Vico, Hamann, Herder*, ed. H. Hardy. Princeton: Princeton University Press, 2000.

Berlin, Isaiah, *The Magus of the North: J. G. Hamaan and the Origins of Modern Irrationalism*. New York: Farrar, Straus and Giroux, 1993.

Berlin, Isaiah, "Two Concepts of Liberty," *Liberty*, ed. H. Hardy. New York: Oxford University Press, 1995, 166-217.

Bernays, Edward, *Propaganda*. New York: Ig Publishing, 2005.

Bharghava, Rajeev (ed.), *Secularism and Its Critics*, 6th ed. New Delhi: Oxford University Press, 2007.

Bilgrami, Akeel, "Secularism, Nationalism, and Modernity," in R. Bhargava, ed., *Secularism and Its Critics* 6th ed., ed. R. Bhargava. New Delhi: Oxford University Press, 2007, 380-417.

Al-Bishrī, Ṭāriq, *al-Ḥiwār al-islāmī al-ʿalmānī*. Cairo: Dār al-Shurūq, 1417/1996.

Al-Bishrī, Ṭāriq, *al-Waḍʿ al-qānūnī bayna al-sharīʿah al-islāmīyah wa al-qānūn al-waḍʿī*, 2nd ed. Cairo: Dār al-Shurūq, 1426/2005.

Brenna, C., "The Transfiguration of Rights: A Proposal for Orthodoxy's Appropriation of Rights Language," *Logos: A Journal of Eastern Christian Studies*, *55*:1–2 (2014):15-40.

Brown, Jonathan A. C., *Slavery and Islam*. London: Oneworld Publications, 2019.

Brunschvig, Robert, "Conceptions monétaires chez les jurists musulmans (VIIe-XIIIe siècles)," *Arabica 14* (1967):113-43.

Al-Bukhārī, Abū ʿAbd Allāh Muḥammad b. Ismāʿīl, *Ṣaḥīḥ al-bukhārī*, 9 vols., ed. Q. S. al-Rifāʿī. Beirut: Dār al-Arqam b. Abī al-Arqam, n.d.

Bulliet, Richard W., *Conversion to Islam in the Medieval Period: An Essay in Quantitative History*. Cambridge: Harvard University Press, 1979.

Burbank, Jane and Cooper, Frederick, *Empires in World History: Power and the Politics of Difference*. Princeton: Princeton University Press, 2010.

Butler, Anthea, *White Evangelical Racism: The Politics of Morality in America*. Chapel Hill: The University of North Carolina Press, 2021.

Calder, Norman, "*Sharīʿa*," *Encyclopedia of Islam*, 2nd ed., 12 vols., ed. P. J. Bearman et al. Leiden: E. J. Brill, 1960–2005, IX: 323-26..

Calhoun, Craig, "Rethinking Secularism," *Hedgehog Review*, *19*:3 (2010):1-7.

Carter, Stephen L., *God's Name in Vain: The Wrongs and Rights of Religion in Politics* (New York: Basic Books, 2000.

Casanova, José, *Public Religions in the Modern World*. Chicago: University of Chicago Press, 1994.

Casanova, José, "Secularization Revisited: A Reply to Talal Asad," in *Powers of the Secular Modern: Talal Asad and His Interlocutors*, eds. D. Scott and C. Hirschkind. Stanford, CA: Stanford University Press, 2006, 12-30.

Casanova, José, "The Secular and Secularisms," *Social Research*, *76*:4 (2009): 1049-66.

Cavanaugh, William T., *The Myth of Religious Violence: Secular Ideology and the Roots of Modern Conflict*. New York: Oxford University Press, 2009.

Cavanaugh, William T., *Migrations of the Holy: God, State, and the Political Meaning of the Church*. Grand Rapids: William B. Eerdmans Publishing Company, 2011.

Cavanaugh, William T., "The City: Beyond Secular Parodies," in *Radical Orthodoxy: A New Theology*, eds. J. Milbank, C. Pickstock, and G. Ward. London and New York: 1999, 182-200.

Chadwick, O., *The Secularization of the European Mind in the 19th Century* (Cambridge: Cambridge University Press, 1975.

Cipriani, Roberto, *Sociology of Religion: An Historical Introduction*, trans. L. Ferrarotti. New Brunswick: Transaction Publishers, 2000.

Cook, Michael, *Commanding Right and Forbidding Wrong in Islamic Thought*. Cambridge: Cambridge University Press, 2000.

Cornell, Vincent J., "Reasons Public and Divine: Liberal Democracy, Shari'a Fundamentalism and the Epistemological Crisis of Islam," in C. Ernst and R. C. Martin, eds., *Rethinking Islamic Studies: From Orientalism to Cosmopolitanism*. Columbia, S.C.: University of South Carolina Press, 2010, 23–51.

Cover, Robert, "Nomos and Narrative," in *Narrative, Violence, and the Law: The Essays of Robert Cover*, eds. M. Minow, M. Ryan, and A. Sarat. Ann Arbor: University of Michigan Press, 1995,95-172.

Coulson, Noel J., *A History of Islamic Law*. Edinburgh: Edinburgh University Press, 1964.

Coulson, Noel J., "The State and the Individual in Islamic Law," *International and Comparative Law Quarterly*, 6:1 (1957): 49-60.

Crone, Patricia, Crone's *God's Rule: Government and Islam: Six Centuries of Medieval Islamic Political Thought*. New York: Columbia University Press, 2004.

Crone, Patricia, *Pre-Industrial Societies: Anatomy of the Pre-Modern World*. London: Oneworld, 2020.

Curtis IV, Edward E., "Why Malcolm X Never Developed an Islamic Approach to Civil Rights," *Religion*, *32*:3 (2002): 227-42.

Al-Dabūsī, Abū Zayd, *Taqwīm al-adillah*, ed. K. M. al-Mays. Beirut: Dār al-Kutub al-'Ilmīyah, 1421/2001.

Al-Dardīr, Muḥammad b. Aḥmad, *al-Sharḥ al-ṣaghīr*, 2 vols. Cairo: Muṣṭafā al-Bābī al-Ḥalabī, 1372/1952 (on the margin of Aḥmad al-Ṣāwī's *Bulghat al-sālik*).

Davis-Secord, Sarah, "Muslims in Norman Sicily: The Evidence of Imām al-Māzarī's Fatwās," *Mediterranean Studies*, *16* (2007): 46-66.

Dawson, Michael C., *Black Visions: The Roots of Contemporary African-American Political Ideologies*. Chicago: University of Chicago Press, 2001.

Dembour, Marie-Bénédicte, "What Are Human Rights? Four Schools of Thought," *Human Rights Quarterly*, *32*:1 (February, 2010): 1-20.

Al-Dhahabī, Shams al-Dīn, *Duwal al-islām*, 2 vols., eds. F. M. Shaltūt and M. M. Ibrāhīm. Cairo: al-Hay'ah al-Miṣrīyah al-'Āmmah li al-Kitāb, 1974.

Donner, Fred, *Muhammad and the Believers: At the Origins of Islam*. Cambridge, MA: The Belknap Press of Harvard University Press, 2010.

DuBois, W. E. B., *The Souls of Black Folk* (reprint). Greenwich, CN: Fawcett Publications, Inc., 1961.

DuBois, W. E. B., "Strivings of the Negro People," in *The Atlantic*, *80* (Aug. 1897): 1-10.

Durkheim, Emile, *The Elementary Forms of Religious Life*, trans. C. Cosman. New York: Oxford University Press, 2001.

Dyer, Richard, *White*. New York: Routledge, 1997.

Eliade, Mircea, *The Sacred and the Profane: The Nature of Religion*. Orlando: Harcourt, Inc., 1987.

El-Rouayheb, Khaled, *Before Homosexuality in the Arab-Islamic World, 1500-1800*. Chicago: University of Chicago Press, 2009.

El-Shamsy, Ahmed, *The Canonization of Islamic Law: A Social and Intellectual History*. Cambridge: Cambridge University Press, 2013.

El Shamsy, Ahmed, *Rediscovering the Islamic Classics: How Editors and Print Culture Transformed an Intellectual Tradition*. Princeton: Princeton University Press, 2020,

El-Shamsy, Ahmed, "Rethinking *Taqlīd* in the Early Shāfiʿī School," *Journal of the American Oriental Society, 128*:1 (2008):1-24.

El-Shamsy, Ahmed, "Bridging the Gap: Two Early Texts of Islamic Legal Theory," *Journal of the American Oriental Society, 137*:3 (2017):505-36.

El-Tobgui, Carl S., "Ibn Taymiyyya on the Incoherence of the Theologians' Universal Law: Reframing the Debate Between Reason and Revelation in Medieval Islam," *Journal of Arabic and Islamic Studies, 18* (2018): 63-85.

Emon, Anver, *Islamic Natural Law Theories*. New York: Oxford University Press, 2010.

Emon, Anver, *Religious Pluralism and Islamic Law:* Dhimmīs *and Others in the Empire of Law*. New York: Oxford University Press, 2012.

Engler, Steven, "'Religion,' 'the Secular' and the Critical Study of Religion," *Studies in Religion, 43*:1 (2014): 419-42.

Esack, Farid, *Qurʾān, Liberation and Pluralism: An Islamic Perspective of Inter-religious Solidarity against Oppression*. Oxford: Oneworld Press, 1997.

Euben, Roxanne, and Zaman, Muhammad Q., eds., *Princeton Readings in Islamist Thought: Texts and Contexts from al-Banna to Bin Laden*. Princeton: Princeton University Press, 2009.

Fackenheim, Emil L., "Immanuel Kant," *Nineteenth Century Religious Thought in the West*, vol. 1, eds. Ninian Smart et al. Cambridge: Cambridge University Press, 1985, 17-40.

Fadel, Mohammad, *The Criterion for Distinguishing Legal Opinions from Judicial Rulings and the Administrative Acts of Judges and Rulers: al-Ihkam fi Tamyiz al-Fatawa 'An al-Ahkām wa Tasarrufat al-Qadi wa'l-Imam*. New Haven: Yale University Press, 2017.

Fadel, Mohammad, "'*Istiḥsān* Is Nine-Tenths of the Law': The Puzzling Relationship of *Uṣūl* to *Furūʿ* in the Mālikī *Madhhab*," in B. Weiss, ed., *Studies in Islamic Legal Theory*. Leiden: E. J. Brill, 2002, 161-76.

Fadel, Mohammad, "Two Woman, One Man: Knowledge, Power, and Gender in Medieval Sunni Legal Thought," *International Journal of Middle East Studies, 29* (1997): 185-204.

Fadel, Mohammad, "No Salvation Outside Islam: Muslim Modernists, Democratic Politics, and Islamic Theological Exclusivism," in M. H. Khalil, ed., *Between Heaven and Hell: Islam, Salvation and the Fate of Others*. New York: Oxford University Press, 2013, 35-61.

Fadel, Mohammad, "The True, the Good and the Reasonable: The Theological and Ethical Roots of Public Reason in Islamic Law," *Canadian Journal of Law and Jurisprudence, 21*:1 (2008), 5-69.

Fadel, Mohammad, "Public Reason as a Strategy for Principled Reconciliation: The Case of Islamic Law and International Human Rights Law," *Chicago Journal of International Law, 8*:1 (Summer 2007):1-20.

Fahmy, Khaled, *In Quest of Justice: Islamic Law and Forensic Medicine in Modern Egypt*. Oakland: University of California Press, 2018.

Fakhry, Majid, *A History of Islamic Philosophy*, 3rd ed. New York: Columbia University Press, 2004.

Al-Fārūqī, Ismail, R "Islamization of Knowledge: Problems, Principles and Prospective," 15-63. https://www.academia.edu/5737422/Islamisation_of_Knowledge_Problems_Principles_and_Prospective_Ismail_al_Faruqi

Feldman, Noah, *The Arab Winter: A Tragedy*. Princeton: Princeton University Press, 2020.

Fish, Stanley, *The Trouble with Principle*. Cambridge, MA: Harvard University Press, 1999.

Fish, Stanley, "Liberalism Doesn't Exist," *Duke Law Journal* (1987): 997-1001. Available at https://scholarship.law.duke.edu/cgi/viewcontent.cgi?article=3010&context=dlj

Fitzgerald, T., *The Ideology of Religious Studies*. New York: Oxford University Press, 2000.

Fitzgerald, T., "Critical Religion and Critical Research on Religion: Religion and Politics As Modern Fictions," *Critical Research on Religion*, *3*:3 (2015):303-19.

Fitzgerald, T., "Bruce Lincoln's 'Theses on Method': Antithesis," *Method and Theory in the Study of Religion*, *18*:1 (2006): 392-423.

Foucault, Michel, *Power/Knowledge: Selected Interviews and Other Writings, 1972–1977*, trans. C. Gordon, L. Marshall, J. Mepham, and K. Soper. New York: Pantheon books, 1980.

Gadamer, Hans-Georg, *Truth and Method*, 2nd ed., trans. J. Weinsheimer and D. G. Marshall. New York: Continuum, 1998.

Galston, William, *The Practice of Liberal Pluralism*. Cambridge: Cambridge University Press, 2005.

Gane, E. R., "Luther's Views of Church and State," *Andrews University Seminary Studies (AUSS)*, *8*:2 (1970): 120-43.

Gardet, Louis, "*Dīn*," *Encyclopedia of Islam*, 2nd ed., 12 vols., ed. P. J. Bearman et al. Leiden: E. J. Brill, 1960–2005, II: 293-96.

Gauchet, Marcel, *The Disenchantment of the World: A Political History of Religion*, transl. O. Barge. Princeton: Princeton University Press, 1997.

Gerish, B. A., "Friedrich Schleiermacher," *Nineteenth Century Religious Thought in the West*, eds. N. Smart et al., vol. 1. Cambridge: Cambridge University Press, 1985, 123-56.

GhaneaBassiri, Kambiz, *A History of Islam in America*. Cambridge: Cambridge University Press, 2010.

Al-Ghazālī, Abū Ḥāmid, *al-Mustaṣfā min 'ilm al-uṣūl*, 2 vols. Būlāq: al-Maṭba'ah al-Amīrīyah, 1324 AH.

Al-Ghazālī, Abū Ḥāmid, *Iḥyā 'ulūm al-dīn*, 4 vols. Cairo: Dār Iḥyā' al-Kutub al-'Arabīyah, 1377/1967.

Al-Ghazālī, Abū Ḥāmid, *al-Iqtiṣād fī al-i'tiqād*. Cairo: Muṣṭafā al-Bābī al-Ḥalabī wa Awlāduh, n.d.

Al-Ghazālī, Abū Ḥāmid, *al-Munqidh min al-ḍalāl wa al-muwaṣṣil ilā dhi al-'izzah wa al-jalāl*, eds. J. Ṣalība and K. Iyāḍ. Beirut: Dār Maktabat al-Hilāl li al-Ṭibā'ah wal al-Nashr, 1986.

Al-Ghazālī, Abū Ḥāmid, *Tahāfut al-falāsifah* 7th ed., ed. S. Dunyā. Cairo: Dār al-Ma'ārif, 1392/1972.

Ghobazadeh, Naser, *Religious Secularity: A Theological Challenge to the Islamic State*. New York: Oxford University Press, 2017.

Gibb, Hamilton A. R., "Al-Mawardi's Theory of the Caliphate," in *Studies on the Civilization of Islam*, eds. S. J. Shaw and W. Polk. Boston: Beacon Press, 1962, 151-65.

Gibb, Hamilton A. R., "Constitutional Organization," in *Law in the Middle East*, eds. M. Khaddury and H. J. Liebesney. Washington, DC: Middle East Institute, 1995, 3-27.

Gleave, Robert, Islam *and Literalism: Literal Meaning and Interpretation in Islamic Legal Theory*. Edinburgh: Edinburgh University Press, 2013.

Goitein, S. D., *A Mediterranean Society*, 4 vols. Berkeley: University of California Press, 1967.

Goldstein, Eric L., *The Price of Whiteness: Jews, Race, and American Identity*. Princeton: Princeton University Press, 2006.

Gothóni, Rene, "Religio and Superstitio Reconsidered," *Archiv Für Religionspsychologie/ Archive for the Psychology of Religion, 21*:1 (1994):37-46.
Grewal, Zareena, *Islam Is a Foreign Country: American Muslims and the Crisis of Global Authority*. New York: New York University Press, 2014.
Gualtieri, Sarah M. A., *Between Arab and White: Race and Ethnicity in the Early Syrian American Diaspora*. Los Angeles: University of California Press, 2009.
Gutman, Amy, "Communitarian Critics of Liberalism," *Philosophy and Public Affairs, 14*:3 (1985): 308-22.
Haider, Najam, "Contesting Intoxication: Early Juristic Debates over the Lawfulness of Alcoholic Beverages," *Islamic Law and Society, 20*:1–2 (2013): 48-89.
Hall, John A., and Ikenberry, G. John, *The State*. Princeton: Princeton University Press, 1989.
Hallaq, Wael, *The Impossible State: Islam, Politics and Modernity's Moral Predicament*. New York: Columbia University Press, 2013.
Hallaq, Wael, *Ibn Taymiyya Against the Greek Logicians*. New York: Oxford University Press, 1993.
Hallaq, Wael, *Sharīʿa: Theory, Practice, Transformations*. Cambridge: Cambridge University Press, 2009.
Hallaq, Wael, "Juristic Authority vs. State Power: The Legal Crisis of Modern Islam," *Journal of Law and Religion, 19*:2 (2003–2004): 101-16.
Hallaq, Wael, "Review of Islamic Law and the State: The Constitutional Jurisprudence of Shihāb al-Dīn al-Qarāfī," *Islamic Law and Society*, 5:1 (1998):127-30.
Hallaq, Wael, "What Is Shariʿa?" *Yearbook of Islamic and Middle Eastern Law Online, 12*:1 (2005): 151-80.
Hallaq, Wael, "Was the Gate of Ijtihad Closed?" *International Journal of Middle East Studies, 16* (1984): 3-41.
Hallaq, Wael, "On the Origins of the Controversy about the Existence of Mujtahids and the Gate of Ijtihad," *Studia Islamica, 63* (1986): 129-41.
Hallaq, Wael, *The Origins and Evolution of Islamic Law*. Cambridge: Cambridge University Press, 2005.
Hallaq, Wael, *Authority, Continuity and Change in Islamic Law*. Cambridge: Cambridge University Press, 2001.
Hamdan, Omar, "The Second *Maṣāhif* Project: A Step Towards the Canonization of the Qur'anic Text," in *The Qur'ān in Context*, eds. A. Neuwirth, N. Sinai, and M. Marx. Leiden: E. J. Brill, 2011, 795-835.
Haneef, M. A. and Barakat, E. R., "Must Money Be Limited to Only Gold and Silver? A Survey of *Fiqhi* Opinions and Some Implications," *Journal of King Abdulaziz University: Islamic Economics, 19*:1 (2006): 21-34.
Hashemi, Nader, N. Islam, *Secularism and Liberal Democracy: Toward a Democratic Theory for Muslim Societies*. New York: Oxford University Press, 2012.
Hauerwas, Stanley, "On Keeping Theological Ethics Theological," *The Hauerwas Reader*, eds. J. Berkman and M. Cartwright. Durham: Duke University Press, 2001, 51-74.
Hauerwas, Stanley, and Bourns, D., "Marriage and the Family," *Quaker Religious Thought, 56*:3 (1984): 4-24.
Hayes, C., *What's Divine About Divine Law? Early Perspectives*. Princeton: Princeton University Press, 2015.
Haykal, Bernard, "On the Nature of Salafi Thought and Action," in *Global Salafism: Islam's New Religious Movement*, ed. R. Meijer. New York: Columbia University Press, 2009, 33-57.

Al-Haytamī, Ibn Ḥajar, *al-Fatāwā al-kubrā al-fiqhīyah 'alā madhhab al-imām al-Shāfi'ī*, 4 vols. Beirut: Dār al-Kutub al-'Ilmīyah, 1417/1997.

Al-Hindī, Aḥmad b. Sa'īd b. 'Ubayd Allāh b. 'Abd al-Razzāq (aka Mullā Jīwan), *Nūr al-anwār fī sharḥ al-manār*, 2 vols., ed. M. A. 'Abd al-'Azīz. Beirut: Dār al-Kutub al-'Ilmīyah, 2018.

Hodgson, Marshall G. S., *The Venture of Islam: Conscience and History in World Civilization*, 3 vols. Chicago: University of Chicago Press, 1974.

Hoover, Jon, *Ibn Taymiyya's Theodicy of Perpetual Optimism*. Leiden: E. J. Brill, 2007.

Hourani, George, "Islamic and Non-Islamic Origins of Mu'tazilite Ethical Rationalism," *International Journal of Middle East Studies*, 7:1 (1976): 59-87.

Hourani, George, *Reason and Tradition in Islamic Ethics*. Cambridge: Cambridge University Press, 1985.

Hoyt, Sarah F., "The Etymology of Religion," *Journal of the American Oriental Society*, 32:2 (1912): 126-9.

Hughes, Aaron, *Islam and the Tyranny of Authenticity: An Inquiry into Disciplinary Apologetics and Self-Deception*. Sheffield, UK: Equinox Press, 2015.

Hunter, James Davison, *To Change the World: The Irony, Tragedy and Possibility of Christianity in the Late Modern World*. New York: Oxford University Press, 2010.

Huntington, Samuel P., *The Clash of Civilizations and the Remaking of the World Order*. New York: Simon and Schuster, 2011.

Huntington, Samuel P., *Who Are We? The Challenges to America's National Identity*. New York: Simon & Schuster, 2004.

Hurd, Elizabeth S. *The Politics of Secularism in International Relations*. Princeton: Princeton University Press, 2008.

Hurvitz, Nimrod, "The Contribution of Early Islamic Rulers to Adjudication and Legislation: The Case of the *Maẓālim* Tribunals," in *Law and Empire: Ideas, Practices, Actors*, eds. J. Duindam, , et al. Leiden: E. J. Brill, 2013, 133-56.

Husayn, Ṭaha, *Ḥadīth al-arbi'ā'*, 3 vols., 15th ed. Cairo: Dār al-Ma'ārif, n.d.

Ibn 'Abd al-Salām, 'Izz al-Dīn, *Qawā'id al-aḥkām fī maṣāliḥ al-anām*, 2 vols., ed. Ṭ. 'A. Sa'd. Beirut: Dār al-Jīl, 1400/1980.

Ibn 'Abd al-Salām, 'Izz al-Dīn, *Fatāwā sulṭān al-'ulamā' al-'izz ibn 'abd al-salām*. Cairo: Maktabat al-Qur'ān, n.d.

Ibn 'Ābidīn, Muḥammad Amīn, *Radd al-muḥtār 'alā al-durr al-mukhtār sharḥ tanwīr al-abṣār*, 12 vols., ed. A. 'Abd al-Mawjūd and A. Mu'awwaḍ. Beirut: Dār al-Kutub al-'Ilmīyah, 1415/1994.

Ibn Amīr al-Ḥājj, Abū 'Abd Allāh Shams al-Dīn Muḥammad, *al-Taqrīr wa al-taḥbīr*, 3 vols. Beirut: Dār al-Kutub al-'Ilmīyah, 1403/1983.

Ibn 'Aqīl, Abū al-Wafā' 'Alī, *al-Wāḍiḥ fī uṣūl al-fiqh*, 5 vols., ed. G. Makdisi. Beirut: al-Sharikah al-Muttaḥidah li al-Tawzī', in a commission by Franz Steiner, Stuttgart, 1417/1996.

Ibn Āshir, Abū Muḥammad 'Abd al-Wāḥid, *al-Murshid al-mu'īn 'alā al-ḍarūrī min 'ulūm al-dīn*. Beirut: Dār al-Fikr, 1416/1996.

Ibn 'Āshūr, Muḥammd al-Ṭāhir, *Tafsīr al-taḥrīr wa al-tanwīr*, 30 vols. Beirut: Mu'assasat al-Tārīkh, 1420/2000.

Ibn 'Āshūr, Muḥammd al-Ṭāhir, *al-Tawḍīḥ wa al-taṣḥīḥ li mushkilāt kitāb al-tanqīḥ*, 2 vols. Tunis: Maṭba'at Nahḍah Nahj al-Jazīrah, 1341/1923.

Ibn Baṭṭa, Abū 'Abd Allāh 'Ubayd al-Dīn Muḥammad, *al-Ibānah 'an sharī'at al-firqat al-nājiyah wa mujānabat al-firaq al-madhmūmah*, 4 vols., ed. S. 'Imrān. Cairo: Dār al-Ḥadīth, 1427/2006.

Ibn Farḥūn, Burhān al-Dīn Ibrāhīm b. ʿAlī b. Abī al-Qāsim b. Muḥammad, *Tabṣirat al-ḥukkām fī uṣūl al-aqḍiyah wa manāhij al-aḥkām*, 2 vols., ed. Ṭ. ʿA. Saʿd. Cairo: Maktabat al-Kullīyāt al-Azharīyah, 1406/1986.

Ibn al-Ḥājib, Jamāl al-Dīn Abū ʿUmar ʿUthmān, *Muntahā al-wuṣūl wa al-amal ilā ʾilmay al-uṣūl wa al-jadal*. Beirut: Dār al-Kutub al-ʿIlmīyah, 1405/1985.

Ibn al-Ḥajj, *al-Madkhal*, 4 vols. Cairo: Dār al-Fikr, n.d.

Ibn Ḥanbal, ʿAbd Allāh b. Aḥmad, *Masāʾil al-imām aḥmad bin ḥanbal*, ed. A. al-Miṣrī. Manṣūrah: Dār al-Mawaddah, 1429/2008.

Ibn Ḥazm, Abū Muḥammad ʿAlī b. Aḥmad b. Saʿīd, *al-Iḥkām fī uṣūl al-aḥkām*, 8 vols. Beirut: Manshūrāt Dār al-Āfāq al-Jadīdah, 1403/1983.

Ibn Ḥazm, Abū Muḥammad ʿAlī b. Aḥmad b. Saʿīd,*Marātib al-ʿulūm* in *Rasāʾil ibn ḥazm al-andalūsī*, 4 vols., ed. I. ʿAbbās. Beirut: al-Muʾassasah al-ʿArabīyah li al-Dirāsah wa al-Nashr, 1983.

Ibn al-Humām, Kamāl al-Dīn, *al-Musāmarah sharḥ al-musāyarah*, 2 vols. Cairo: al-Maktabah al-Azharīyah li al-Turāth, 2006.

Ibn al-Jawzī, Jamāl al-Dīn Abū al-Faraj ʿAbd al-Raḥmān b. ʿAlī, *Akhbār al-adhkiyāʾ*, ed. B. ʿA. al-Jābī. Beirut: Dār Ibn Ḥazm, 1424/2003.

Ibn al-Jawzī, Jamāl al-Dīn Abū al-Faraj ʿAbd al-Raḥmān b. ʿAlī, *Talbīs iblīs*. Cairo: Idārat al-Ṭibāʿah al-Munīrīyah, 1368/1948.

Ibn Kathīr, Abū al-Fidāʾ Ismāʿīl, *al-Sīrah al-nabawīyah*, 4 vols., ed. M. ʿAbd al-Wāḥid. Cairo: ʿĪsā al-Bābī al-Ḥalabī, 1384/1964.

Ibn Kathīr, Abū al-Fidāʾ Ismāʿīl, *Tafsīr al-qurʾān al-ʿaẓīm*, 4 vols. Cairo: al-Maktab al-Thaqāfī, 2001.

Ibn Khaldūn, ʿAbd al-Raḥmān, *al-Muqaddimah*, ed. Ḥ. ʿĀṣī. Beirut: Dār Maktabat al-Hilāl li al-Ṭibāʿah wa al-Nashr, 1986.

Ibn Khalikān, Abū al-ʿAbbās Shams al-Dīn Aḥmad b. Muḥammad, *Wafāyāt al-aʿyān wa anbāʾ abnāʾ al-zamān*, 8 vols. ed. I. ʿAbbās. Beirut: Dār al-Maʿrifah, n.d.

Ibn al-Laḥḥām, Abū al-Ḥasan ʿAlāʾ al-Dīn Muḥammad b. ʿAbbās, *al-Qawāʿid wa al-fawāʾid al-uṣūlīyah wa mā yataʿallaq bihā min al-aḥkām al-farʿīyah*, ed. A. Faḍīlī. Beirut: al-Maktabah al-ʿAṣrīyah, 1418/1998.

Ibn Maḍā, Abū al-ʿAbbas Aḥmad b. ʿAbd al-Raḥmān b. Muḥammad, *Kitāb al-radd ʿalā al-nuḥāt*, ed. S. Ḍayf. Cairo: Dār al-Fikr al-ʿArabī, 1366/1947.

Ibn Manẓūr, *Lisān al-ʿarab*, 6 vols., eds. ʿA. ʿA. ʿA. al-Kabīr, M. A. Ḥasab Allāh, and H. M. al-Shādhilī. Cairo: Dār al-Maʿārif, n.d.

Ibn al-Nadīm, *al-Fihrist*, ed. Y.ʿA. Ṭawīl. Beirut: Dār al-Kutub al-ʿIlmīyah, 1416/1996.

Ibn Nujaym, Zayn al-Dīn b. Ibrāhīm b. Muḥammad, *Baḥr al-rāʾiq sharḥ kanz al-daqāʾiq*, 9 vols., ed. T. al-Hindī. Beirut: Dār al-Kutub al-ʿIlmīyah, 1434/2013.

Ibn al-Qaṣṣār, Abū al-Ḥasan ʿAlī b. ʿUmar, *al-Muqaddimah fī uṣūl al-fiqh*, ed. M. al-Sulaymānī. Beirut: Dār al-Gharb al-Islāmī, 1417/1996.

Ibn Qayyim al-Jawzīyah, Shams al-Dīn Abū ʿAbd Allāh Muḥammad b. Abī Bakr, *Aḥkām ahl al-dhimmah*, 3 vols., eds. A. al-Bakrī and A. al-ʿArūrī. Dammām: al-Ramadī li al-Nashr, 1418/1998.

Ibn Qayyim al-Jawzīyah, Shams al-Dīn Abū ʿAbd Allāh Muḥammad b. Abī Bakr, *Iʿlām al-muwaqqiʿīn ʿan rabb al-ʿālamīn*, 4 vols., ed. M. M. ʿAbd al-Ḥamīd. Mecca: Dār al-Bāz, n.d.

Ibn Qayyim al-Jawzīyah, Shams al-Dīn Abū ʿAbd Allāh Muḥammad b. Abī Bakr, *al-Ṭuruq al-ḥukmīyah fī al-siyāsah al-sharʿīyah*, ed. M. J. Ghāzī. Cairo: Maṭbaʿat al-Madanī, n.d.

Ibn Qayyim al-Jawzīyah, Shams al-Dīn Abū ʻAbd Allāh Muḥammad b. Abī Bakr, *Madārij al-sālikīn bayna manāzil iyyāka naʻbudu wa iyyāka nastaʻīn*, 3 vols., ed. B. M ʻUyūn. Beirut: Maktabat Dār Lubnān, 1420/1999.

Ibn Qudāmah, Muwaffaq al-Dīn, *Rawḍat al-nāẓir wa junnat al-munāẓir*. Beirut: Dār al-Kutub al-ʻIlmīyah, 1401/1981.

Ibn Qudāmah, Muwaffaq al-Dīn, *Taḥrīm al-naẓar fī kutub ahl al-kalām*, ed. and trans. G. Makdisi, as *Ibn Qudāma's Censure of Speculative Theology*. Cambridge: E. J. W. Gibb Memorial Trust, 1985.

Ibn Qutaybah, Abū Muḥammad Abd Allāh b. Muslim, *ʻUyūn al-akhbār*, 4 vols. Beirut: Dār al-Kutub al-ʻIlmīyah, 1418/1998.

Ibn Qutaybah, Abū Muḥammad Abd Allāh b. Muslim, *Taʼwīl mukhtalaf al-ḥadīth*, 2nd ed., ed. A. S. al-Hilālī. Riyadh: Dār Ibn al-Qayyim, 1430/2009.

Ibn Rushd, Abū al-Walīd Muḥammad b. Aḥmad b. Muḥammad (the Grandson), *Bidāyat al-mujtahid wa nihāyat al-muqtaṣid*, 2 vols., ed. ʻA. M. Muʻawwaḍ and ʻA. A. ʻAbd al-Mawjūd. Beirut: Dār al-Kutub al-ʻIlmīyah, 1418/1997.

Ibn Rushd, Abū al-Walīd Muḥammad b. Aḥmad (the Grandfather), *al-Muqaddimāt*, 4 vols. Beirut: Dār al-Fikr, n.d. (at the bottom of Ṣaḥnūn, *al-Mudawwanah al-kubrā*).

Ibn Saʻātī, Aḥmad b. ʻAlī b. Taghlib, *Nihāyat al-wuṣūl ilā ʻilm al-uṣūl*, ed. S. al-Sulamī. Mecca: Maʻhad al-Buḥūth al-ʻIlmīyah wa Iḥyāʼ al-Turāth al-Islāmī, 1418/1998.

Ibn Taymīyah, Taqī al-Dīn, *al-Tuḥfah al-ʻirāqīyah fī al-aʻmāl al-qalbīyah*. Cairo: al-Maktabah al-Salafīyah, 1386/1967.

Ibn Taymīyah, Taqī al-Dīn, *al-Īmān*. Damascus: al-Maktab al-Islāmī, n.d.

Ibn Taymīyah, Taqī al-Dīn, *Amrāḍ al-qulūb wa shifāʼuhā*. Cairo: al-Maṭbaʻah al-Salafīyah wa Maktabatuhā, 1386/1966.

Ibn Taymīyah, Taqī al-Dīn, *Majmūʻat al-rasāʼil wa al-masāʼil*, 5 vols. Beirut: Dār al-Kutub al-ʻIlmīyah, 1421/2001.

Ibn Taymīyah, Taqī al-Dīn, *Majmūʻat al- fatāwā*, 4th ed., 37 vols. (in 20 books) ed. ʻA. al-Jazzār and A. al-Bāz. Al-Manṣūrah: Dār al-Wafāʼ li al-Ṭibāʻah wa al-Nashr wa al-Tawzīʻ, 1432/2011.

Ibn Taymīyah, Taqī al-Dīn, *Minhāj al-sunnah al-nabawīyah fī naqḍ kalām al-shīʻah al-qadarīyah*, 9 vols., ed. M. R. Sālim. n.p., 1406/1986.

Ibn Taymīyah, Taqī al-Dīn, *Darʼ taʻāruḍ al-ʻaql wa al-naql*, 11 vols., ed. M. R. Sālim. Cairo: Dār al-Kutub, 1391/1971.

Ibn Taymīyah, Taqī al-Dīn, "*al-Kalām ʻalā al-fiṭrah*," in *Majmūʻat al-rasāʼil al-kubrā*, 2 vols. Cairo: Muḥammad ʻAlī Ṣubayḥ wa Awlāduh, n.d.

Ibn Taymīyah, Taqī al-Dīn, *al-Ḥisbah fī al-islām*. Beirut: Dāral-Fikr al-ʻIlmīyah, n.d.

Ibn Taymīyah, Taqī al-Dīn, *Iqtiḍāʼ ṣirāṭ al-mustaqīm wa mukhālafat aṣḥāb al-jaḥīm* ed. M. ʻA. al-Ṣābūnī. Mecca: Maṭābiʻ al-Majd, 1390/1970.

Ibn Taymīyah, Taqī al-Dīn, *al-Nubūwāt*, ed. M. Ḥ al-Fiqī. Cairo: Maktabat al-Sunnah, n.d.

Ibn Taymīyah, Taqī al-Dīn, "*al-Iḥtijāj bi al-qadar*," in *Majmūʻat al-rasāʼil al-kubrā*, 2 vols. Cairo: Muḥammad ʻAlī Ṣubayḥ wa Awlāduh, n.d., 2: 99-155.

Ibn Taymīyah, Taqī al-Dīn, *al-Siyāsah al-sharʻīyah fī iṣlāḥ al-rāʻī wa al-raʻīyah*, 4th ed. Egypt: Dār al-Kitāb al-ʻArabī, 1969.

Ibn Taymīyah, Taqī al-Dīn, "*al-Munāẓarah fī alʻaqīdah al-wāsiṭīyah*," in *Majmūʻat al-rasāʼil al-kubrā*, 2 vols. Cairo: Muṣṭafā al-Bābī al-Ḥalabī wa Awlāduh, n.d., 1: 413-21.

Ibn Taymīyah, Taqī al-Dīn, *al-ʻAqīdah al-ḥamawīyah al-kubrā in Majmūʻat al-rasāʼil al-kubrā* , 2 vols. Cairo: Muṣṭafā al-Bābī al-Ḥalabī wa Awlāduh, n.d, 1: 423-78.

Ibrāhīm, Nājiḥ and al-Najjār, Ḥisham, *Dā'ish: al-sikkīn allatī tadhbaḥ al-islām*, 2nd ed. Cairo: Dār al-Shurūq, 2015.

Ignatieff, Michael, *Human Rights as Politics and Idolatry*. Princeton: Princeton University Press, 2001.

Ignatiev, Noel, *How the Irish Became White*. New York: Routledge, 1995.

Imber, Colin, *Ebu's-su'ud: The Islamic Legal Tradition*. Stanford: Stanford University Press, 1997.

Iqtidar, Humaira, Comment on "The Islamic Secular," *American Journal of Islamic Social Sciences, 34*:2 (2017): 35-8.

Al-Iṣfahānī, al-Rāghib, *al-Mufradāt fī gharīb al-qur'ān*, ed. M. S. Kīlānī. Beirut: Dār al-Ma'rifah, n.d.

'Iyāḍ, al-Qāḍī Abū al-Faḍl, *Tartīb al-madārik wa taqrīb al-masālik*, 2 vols., ed. M. S. Hāshim. Beirut: Dār al-Kutub al-'Ilmīyah, 1418/1998.

Izetbegovic, Alija A., *Islam between East and West*, 3rd ed. Oak Brook, IL: American Trust Publications, 1993.

Izutsu, Toshihiko, *God and Man in the Koran: Semantics of the Koranic Weltanschauung*. Tokyo: The Keio Institute of Cultural and Linguistic Studies, 1964.

Jackson, Sherman, *Islamic Law and the State: The Constitutional Jurisprudence of Shihāb al-Dīn al-Qarāfī*. Leiden: E. J. Brill, 1996.

Jackson, Sherman, *Islam and the Blackamerican: Looking Towards the Third Resurrection*. New York: Oxford University Press, 2005.

Jackson, Sherman, *Islam and the Problem of Black Suffering*. New York: Oxford University Press, 2009.

Jackson, Sherman, *On the Boundaries of Theological Tolerance in Islam: Abū Ḥāmid al-Ghazālī's Fayṣal al-Tafriqa*. Karachi: Oxford University Press, 2002.

Jackson, Sherman, *Initiative to Stop the Violence: Sadat's Assassins and the Renunciation of Political Violence*. New Haven: Yale University Press, 2014.

Jackson, Sherman, "*Sharī'ah*, Democracy, and the Modern Nation-State: Some Reflections on Islam, Popular Rule, and Pluralism," *Fordham International Law Journal, 27*:1 (2003):88-107.

Jackson, Sherman, "The Primacy of Domestic Politics: Ibn Bint Al-A'azz and the Establishment of Four Chief Judgeships in Mamlūk Egypt," *Journal of the American Oriental Society, 115*:1 (1995):52-65.

Jackson, Sherman, "*Ijtihād* and *Taqlīd*: Between the Islamic Legal Tradition and Autonomous Western Reason," in *Routledge Handbook of Islamic Law*, eds. K. Abou El Fadl, A. A. Ahmad, and S. F. Hassan. London and New York: Routledge, 2019, 255-72.

Jackson, Sherman, "Domestic Terrorism in the Islamic Legal Tradition," *The Muslim World, 91* (Fall, 2001): 293-310.

Jackson, Sherman, "From Prophetic Actions to Constitutional Theory: A Novel Chapter in Medieval Muslim Jurisprudence," *International Journal of Middle East Studies, 25* (1993): 71-90.

Jackson, Sherman, "Islamic Reform between Islamic Law and the Nation-State," in J. L. Esposito and E. Shahin, eds., *The Oxford Handbook of Islam and Politics*. New York: Oxford University Press, 2013, 42-55.

Jackson, Sherman, "The Second Education of the *Muftī*: Notes on Shihāb al-Dīn al-Qarāfī's Tips to the Jurisconsult," *The Muslim World, 82*:3–4 (1992): 201-17.

Jackson, Sherman, "Literalism, Empiricism, and Induction: Apprehending and Concretizing Islamic Law's *Maqāṣid al-Sharī'ah* in the Modern World," *Michigan State Law Review*, Special Issue 6 (2006): 1469-86.

Jackson, Sherman, "The Alchemy of Domination: some Ash'arite Responses to Mu'tazilite Ethics," *International Journal of Middle East Studies*, 3 (1999): 185-201.

Jackson, Sherman, "Kramer Versus Kramer in a 10th/16th Century Egyptian Court: Post-Formative Jurisprudence between Exigency and Law," *Islamic Law and Society*, *8*:1 (2001): 27-51.

Jackson, Sherman, "Jihad and the Modern World," *The Journal of Islamic Law and Culture*, *7*:1 (2002):1-26.

Jackson, Sherman, "Not Truth But Tolerance: A (Much Belated) Response to Atif Khalil," *The American Journal of Islamic Social Sciences*, *28*:4 (2011): 146-61.

Jackson, Sherman, "Soft Sharī'ah Fundamentalism and the Totalitarian Epistemology of Vincent Cornell," *The Religion and Culture Forum, University of Chicago Divinity School*, 2011, now available at http://www.marcmanley.com/media/pdfs/jackson-response-to-cornell.pdf

Jacobson, Matthew F., *Whiteness of a Different Color: European Immigration and the Alchemy of Race*. Cambridge, MA: Harvard University Press, 1998.

Jacobson, Matthew F., *Roots Too: White Ethnic Revival in Post-Civil Rights America*. Cambridge, MA: Harvard University Press, 2006.

Al-Jaṣṣāṣ, Abū Bakr Aḥmad b. 'Alī, *Aḥkām al-qur'ān*, 3 vols., ed. 'A. M. 'A. Shāhīn. Beirut: Dār al-Kutub al-'Ilmīyah, 1415/1994.

Al-Jaṣṣāṣ, *Uṣūl al-jaṣṣāṣ* (a.k.a. *al-Fuṣūl fī al-uṣūl*) 2 vols., ed. M. M. Tāmir. Beirut: Dār al-Kutub al-'Ilmīyah1420/2000.

Al-Jawharī, Ismā'īl b. Ḥammād, *al-Ṣiḥāḥ tāj al-lughah wa ṣiḥāḥ al-'arabīyah*, 6 vols., ed. A.'A. 'Aṭṭār. Beirut: Dār al-'Ilm li al-Malāyīn, 1376/1965.

Joffe, Josef, "A Canvas, Not a Country: How Europe Sees America," in *Understanding America: The Anatomy of an Exceptional Nation*, eds. P. Schuck and J. O. Wilson. New York: Public Affairs, 2008, 597-626.

Johansen, Baber, *Contingency in a Sacred Law: Legal and Ethical Norms in the Muslim Fiqh*. Leiden: E. J. Brill, 1999.

Johansen, Baber, "The Relationship between the Constitution, the *Sharī'a* and the *Fiqh*: The Jurisprudence of Egypt's Supreme Constitutional Court," *Zeitschrift für Ausländisches Öffenliches Recht und Völkerrecht*, *64*:4 (2004):881-96.

Johansen, Baber, "Can the Law Decide that Egypt Is Conquered by Force? A Thirteenth-Century Debate on History as an Object of Law," in *Studies in Islamic Law: A Festschrift for Colin Imber*, eds. A. Christmann and R. Gleave. New York: Oxford University Press, 2007, 143-63.

Al-Jundī, Muḥammad 'Abd al-Hādī, *al-Tashrī' wa wājib al-musharri'*.? Cairo: Maṭba'at al-Iṣlāḥ, 1921.

Al-Juwaynī, Abū al-Ma'ālī 'Abd al-Malik b. Abd Allāh b. Yūsuf, *al-Burhān fī uṣūl al-fiqh*, 2 vols. ed. 'A. M al-Dīb. Al-Manṣūrah: Dār al-Wafā', 1418/1997.

Al-Juwaynī, Abū al-Ma'ālī 'Abd al-Malik, *al-Talkhīs fī uṣūl al-fiqh*, 3 vols., ed. 'A. J. al-Niyābī and S. A. al-'Amrī. Beirut: Dār al-Bashā'ir al-Islāmīyah, 1417/1996.

Al-Juwaynī, Abū al-Ma'ālī 'Abd al-Malik, *al-Ghiyāthī, ghiyāth al-umam fī iltiyāth al-ẓulam*, 2nd ed., ed. 'A. al-Dīb. Cairo: Maṭba'at Nahḍat Miṣr, 1401/1981.

Kahn, Paul, *Putting Liberalism in Its Place*. Princeton: Princeton University Press, 2005.

Kant, Immanuel, *Religion Within the Limits of Reason Alone*, trans. T. M. Greene and H. H. Hudson. New York: Harper One, 1960.

Kant, Immanuel, *Religion within the Boundaries of Mere Reason and Other Writings*, 17th printing, transl. and ed. A. Wood and G. Di Giovanni. Cambridge: Cambridge University Press, 2016.

Kant, Immanuel, *Groundwork of the Metaphysic of Morals*, trans. T. K. Abbott. San Bernardino: Digireads.com Publishing), 2017.

Al-Karāmastī, Yūsuf b. Ḥusayn, *Zubdat al-wuṣūl ilā ʿumdat al-uṣūl*, ed. ʿA. Ḥajqalī. Beirut: Dār Ṣādir, 1428/2008.

Al-Kāsānī, ʿAlāʾ al-Dīn Abū Bakr b. Masʿūd, *Badāʾiʿ al-ṣanāʾiʿ fī tartīb al-sharāʾiʿ*, 10 vols., eds. ʿA. Muʿawwaḍ and ʿA. ʿAbd al-Mawjūd. Beirut: Dār al-Kutub al-ʿIlīmyah, 1418/1997.

Kato, H., "Reconsidering al-Maqrīzī's View on Money in Medieval Egypt," *Mediterranean World, 21* (2012):33-44.

Katz, Marion H., "Ethics, Gender, and the Islamic Legal Project," *Yale Law School Occasional Papers* (2015): 3-29.

Keddie, Nikki, "Secularism and Its Discontents," *Daedalus* (Summer, 2003): 14-30.

Khalīfah, Ḥajjī, *Kashf al-ẓunūn ʿan asāmī al-kutub wa al-funūn*, 3 vols. Beirut: Dār al-Kutub al-ʿIlmīyah, 1413/1992.

Khalil, Mohammad H. *Between Heaven and Hell: Islam, Salvation and the Fate of Others*. New York: Oxford University Press, 2013.

Khallaf, ʿAbd al-Wahhāb, *al-Siyāsah al-sharʿīyah aw niẓām al-dawlah al-islāmīyah fī al-shuʾūn al-dustūrīyah wa al-khārijīyah wa al-mālīyah*. Cairo: Maṭ baʿat al-Taqaddum, 1397/1977.

Al-Kishnāwī, Abū Bakr Ḥasan, *Ashal al-madārik sharḥ irshād al-sālik fī fiqh imām al-aʾimmah mālik*, 3 vols. Beirut: Dār al-Fikr, 1420/2000.

Kloppenberg, J. T., *Uncertain Victory: Social Democracy and Progressivism in European and American Thought, 1870–1920*. New York: Oxford University Press, 1988.

Kronman, Anthony T., *Confessions of a Born-Again Pagan*. New Haven: Yale University Press, 2016.

Kuhn, Thomas S., *The Structure of Scientific Revolutions*, 2nd ed. Chicago: The University of Chicago Press, 1970.

Al-Lakhmī, Abū al-Ḥasan ʿAlī b. Muḥammad, *al-Tabṣirah*, 14 vols. Beirut: Dār Ibn Ḥazm, 1433/2012.

Al-Lāmishī, Abū Thanāʾ Maḥmūd b. Zayd, *Kitāb al-tamhīd fī qawāʿid al-tawḥīd*. Beirut: Dār al-Gharb al-Islāmī, 1995.

Al-Lāmishī, Abū Thanāʾ Maḥmūd, *Kitāb fī uṣūl al-fiqh*, ed. ʿA. Turkī. Beirut: Dār al-Gharb al-Islāmī, 1995.

Lane, F. C., and Mueller, R. C., *Money and Banking in Medieval and Renaissance Venice*. Baltimore and London: The Johns Hopkins University Press, 1985.

Lapidus, Ira, "The Separation of State and Religion in the Development of Early Islamic Society," *International Journal of Middle East Studies 6:4* (1975): 363-85.

Lapidus, Ira, *A History of Islamic Societies*. Cambridge: Cambridge University Press, 1988.

Lawrence, Bruce, "Afterword: Competing Genealogies of Muslim Cosmopolitanism" in C. Ernst and R. C. Martin, eds., *Rethinking Islamic Studies: From Orientalism to Cosmopolitanism*. Columbia, SC: University of South Carolina Press, 2010, 302-23.

Lewis, Bernard, "The Roots of Muslim Rage," *The Atlantic 266*:3 (1990): 47-60.

Lincoln, Bruce, "Thesis on Method," *Method and Theory in the Study of Religion, 17*:1 (2005): 8-10.

Lindberg, D. L., "Galileo, the Church and the Cosmos," in *When Science and Christianity Meet*, eds. D. L. Lindberg and R. L. Numbers. Chicago: University of Chicago Press, 2003, 33-60.

Long, Charles H., *Significations: Signs, Symbols, and Images in the Interpretation of Religion*. Aurora, CO: The Davies Group, 1995.

Long, Charles H., "African American Religion in the United States of America: An Interpretive Essay," in C. H. Long, *Ellipsis: The Collected Writings of Charles H. Long*. London: Bloomsbury, 2018, 199-211.

Long, Charles H., "Civil Rights– Civil Religion: Visible People and Invisible Religion," in *American Civil Religion*, eds. R. E. Richey and D. G. Jones. New York: Harper Forum Books, 1974, 211-21.

Lucas, Scott, "Principles of Traditionist Jurisprudence Reconsidered," *The Muslim World, 100*:1 (2010): 145-56.

Lutz, C. S., *Reading Alasdair MacIntyre's After Virtue*. New York: Continuum International Publishing Group, 2012.

Macedo, Stephen, "Hauerwas, Liberalism, and Public Reason: Terms of Engagement?" *Law and Contemporary Problems 75*:161, no. 4 (2012): 161-80.

MacIntyre, Alasdair, *After Virtue*, 2nd ed. Notre Dame, IN: University of Notre Dame Press, 2003.

MacIntyre, Alasdair, *A Short History of Ethics: A History of Moral Philosophy from the Homeric Age to the Twentieth Century*, 2nd ed. Notre Dame, IN: University of Notre Dame Press, 2009.

MacIntyre, Alasdair, *Three Rival Versions of Moral Inquiry*. Notre Dame, IN: Universtiy of Notre Dame Press, 1990.

MacIntyre, Alasdair, *Whose Justice? Which Rationality*. Notre Dame, IN: University of Notre Dame Press, 1988.

Madan, T. N., "Secularism in its Place," in *Secularism and Its Critics*, 6th ed., ed. R. Bhargava. New Delhi: Oxford University Press, 2007, 297-320.

Al-Maḥallī, Jalāl al-Dīn Muḥammad b. *Aḥmad, Sharḥ al-waraqāt fī uṣūl al-fiqh*. Beirut: al-Maktabah al-ʿAṣrīyah, 1434/3013.

Mahmood, Saba, "Can Secularism Be Otherwise," in *Varieties of Secularism in a Secular Age*, eds. M. Warner, J. Vanantwerpen, and C. Calhoun. Cambridge, MA: Harvard University Press, 2010, 282-99.

Makdisi, George, *The Rise of Humanism in Islam and the Christian West*. Edinburgh: Edinburgh University Press, 1990.

Al-Maqrīzī, Taqī al-Dīn, *Kitāb al-sulūk li maʿrifat duwal al-mulūk*, 12 vols. in four parts. Cairo: Maṭbaʿat Dār al-Kutub wa al-Wathāʾiq al-Qawmīyah, 1435/2014.

Al-Maqrīzī, Taqī al-Dīn, *Igāthat al-ummah bi kashf al-ghummah*, ed. K. H. Farhāt. Giza: ʿAyn li al-Dirāsāt wa al-Buḥūth al-Insānīyah wa al-Ijtimāʿīyah, 2007/1427.

Al-Maqrīzī, Taqī al-Dīn, *al-Nuqūd al-islāmīyah* (aka, *Shudhūr al-uqūd fī dhikr al-nuqūd*), in *Thalath Rasāʾil*. Constantine, Algeria: Maṭbaʿat al-Jawāʾib, 1298/1881.

Al-Maqrīzī, Taqī al-Dīn, *Kitāb al-mawāʿiẓ wa al-iʿtibār bi dhikr al-khiṭaṭ wa al-āthār*, 2 vols. Cairo: Maktabat al-Thaqāfah al-Dīnīyah, 1987.

March, Andrew, *Islam and Liberal Citizenship: The Search for an Overlapping Consensus*. New York: Oxford University Press, 2009.

March, Andrew, "Is There a Right to Polygamy? Marriage, Equality and Subsidizing Families in Liberal Public Justification," *Journal of Moral Philosophy* 8:2 (2011): 246-72.

Al-Marghīnānī, Burhān al-Dīn Abū al-Ḥasan 'Alī b. Abī Bakr b. 'Abd al-Jalīl al-Rushdānī, *al-Hidāyah sharḥ bidāyat al-mubtadi'*, 4 vols. Cairo: Muṣṭafā al-Bābī al-Ḥalabī wa Awlāduh, n.d.

Mariña, Jacqueline, "Kant, Schleiermacher, and the Study of Theology," in *Theology, History and the Modern German University*, eds. K.M. Vander Schel and M.P. DeJonge. Tübingen: Mohr Siebeck, 2021. Available in pdf with pagination 1-24 at https://www.academia.edu/38954292/Kant_Schleiermacher_and_the_Study_of_Theology

Marmor, Andrei, *Law in the Age of Pluralism*. New York: Oxford University Press, 2007.

Marty, Martin, "Our Religions-Secular World," *Daedalus*, *132*:3 (2003): 42-8.

Masud, Khalid, "The Doctrine of *Siyāsa* in Islamic Law," *Recht van de Islam 18* (2001):1-29.

Al-Māwardī, Abū al-Ḥasan 'Alī b. Ḥabīb, *al-Aḥkām al-sulṭānīyah wa al-wilāyāt al-dīnīyah*, ed. A. M. al-Baghdādī. Kuwait: Maktabat Dār Ibn Qutaybah, 1409/1989.

Al-Māwardī, Abū al-Ḥasan 'Alī b. Ḥabīb, *al-Ḥāwī al-kabīr fī fiqh madhhab al-imām al-shāfi'ī raḍi Allāh 'anhu wa huwa sharḥ mukhtaṣar al-muzanī*, 18 vols., eds. 'A. M. Mu'awwaḍ and 'A. M. 'Abd al-Mawjūd. Beirut: Dār al-Kutub al-'Ilmīyah, 1414/1994.

Mazrui, Ali, "Liberal Islam versus Moderate Islam: Elusive Moderates and the Siege Mentality," *American Journal of Islamic Social Sciences*, *22*:3 (2005):83-89.

Mazrui, Ali, "Islam and the End of History," *The American Journal of Islamic Social Sciences 10*:4 (1993): 512-35.

Mbiti, John S., *African Religions and Philosophy*, 2nd ed. Oxford: Heinemann Educational Publishers, 1997.

McCutcheon, Russell T., "The Category 'Religion' in Recent Publications: A Critical Survey," *Numen 42*:3 (1995): 284-309.

McCutcheon, Russell T., "What Is the Academic Study of Religion?" 2017, at http://religion.ua.edu/wp-content/uploads/2017/07/mccutchintrohandout.pdf

McGrath, Alister, *The Twilight of Atheism*. New York: Galilee Doubleday, 2006.

Melchert, Christopher, *The Formation of the Sunni Schools of Law, 9th–10th Centuries C.E.* Leiden: E. J. Brill, 1997.

Melchert, Christopher, "Māwardī, Abū Ya'lá and the Sunni Revival," in *Prosperity and Stagnation: Some Cultural and Social Aspects of the Abbasid Period (750–1258)*, ed. K. Kościelniak. Cracow: UNUM, 2010, 37-61.

Melchert, Christopher, "Traditionist-Jurisprudents and the Framing of Islamic Law," *Islamic Law and Society* 3:3 (2001): 383-406.

Milbank, John (ed., with C. Pickstock and G. Ward), *Radical Orthodoxy: A New Theology*. London: Routledge, 1999.

Miller, James, "What Secular Age?" *International Journal of Politics, Culture and Society*, *21*:1/4 (2008).

Mills, Charles W. "Rawls on Race/Race in Rawls," *The Southern Journal of Philosophy*, *47* (2009): 161-84.

Mills, Charles W., "Racial Liberalism," *Modern Language Association of America*, *123*:5 (2008): 1380-97.

Mills, Charles W., *Black Rights/White Wrongs: The Critique of Racial Liberalism*. New York: Oxford University Press, 2017.

Molnár, Attila K., "The Construction of the Notion of Religion in Early Modern Europe, *Method and Theory in the Study of Religion*, *14*:1 (2002): 47-60.

Moosa, Ebrahim, "Allegory of the Rule (*Ḥukm*): Law as Simulacrum in Islam?" *History of Religions*, *38*:1 (1998): 1-24.
Moosa, Ebrahim, "Muslim Conservatism in South Africa," *Journal of Theology for Southern Africa*, *69* (1989): 73-81.
Moosa, Ebrahim, *Ghazālī and the Poetics of Imagination*. Chapel Hill, NC: The University of North Carolina Press, 2005.
Morrison, Ken, *Marx, Durkheim, Weber: Formations of Modern Social Thought*, 2nd ed. London: Sage Publications Ltd., 2006.
Mottahedeh, Roy, *Lessons in Islamic Jurisprudence*. Oxford: Oneworld, 2003.
Mottahedeh, Roy, "The Shuʿūbīyah Controversy and the Social History of Early Islamic Iran," *International Journal of Middle East Studies*, *7* (1976): 161-82.
Motzki, Harald, *The Origins of Islamic Jurisprudence: Meccan* Fiqh *before the Classical Schools*, trans. M. Katz. Leiden: E. J. Brill, 2002.
Mouffe, Chantal, *The Return of the Political*. London: Verso, 1993.
Muhall, Stephen, and Swift, Adam, *Liberals and Communitarians*, 2nd ed. Oxford: Blackwell Publishing, 1996.
Murray, Albert, *The Omni-Americans: Black Experience and American Culture*. New York: Da Capo Press, Inc., 1970.
Muslim b. Ḥajjāj, *Ṣaḥīḥ muslim*, 5 vols. Beirut: Dār Ibn Ḥazm, 1416/1995.
Mustafa, Abdul Rahman, "Innovation in Premodern Islam: Between Non-Religion, Irreligion and the Secular," *Journal of Islamic Studies* 34: 1 (2023): 1-41 at https//doi.org/10.1093/jis/rtac029
Mutua, Makau, *Human Rights: A Political and Cultural Critique*. Philadelphia, PA: University of Pennsylvania Press, 2002.
Nadwi, M. A., *al-Muḥaddithāt: The Women Scholars in Islam*. Oxford: Interface Publications, 2002.
Nakissa, Aria, *The Anthropology of Islamic Law: Education, Ethics, and Legal Interpretation at Egypt's al-Azhar*. New York: Oxford University Press, 2019.
Nandy, Ashis, "An Anti-secularist Manifesto," *India International Centre Quarterly*, *22*:1 (1995): 35-64.
Al-Nasafī, Abū al-Barakāt ʿAbd Allāh b. Aḥmad, *Al-Manār*, ed. I. Qabalāt. Beirut: Dār al-Kutub al-ʿIlmīyah, 1437/2016.
Al-Nawawī, Abū Zakarīyah Yaḥyā b. Sharaf, *Kitāb al-majmūʿ*, 23 vols., ed. M. N. al-Muṭīʿī. Cairo: Dār Iḥyāʾ al-Turāth alʿArabī, 1415/1995.
Nelsen, Brian, *The Making of the Modern State: A Theoretical Evolution*. New York: Palgrave Macmillan, 2006.
Niebuhr, H. Richard, *Christ and Culture*. New York: HarperSanFrancisco, 2001.
Niebuhr, Reinhold *Moral Man in Immoral Society: A Study in Ethics and Politics*. New York: Charles Scribner's Sons, 1960.
Nielsen, Jørgen, "*Maẓālim* and *Dār al-ʿAdl* under the Early Mamluks," *The Muslim World* *66*:2 (1976): 114-32.
Nielsen, Jørgen, *Secular Justice in an Islamic State: Maẓālim under the Baḥrī Mamlūks, 662/1264–789/1387*. Leiden: Nederlands Histoirisch-Archaeologisch Institut te Istanbul, 1985.
Nielsen, Jørgen, "*Maẓālim*," *Encyclopedia of Islam*, 2nd ed., 12 vols., ed. P. J. Bearman et al. Leiden: E. J. Brill, 1960–2005, VI: 933-35.
Nietzsche, Friedrich, *Beyond Good and Evil*. San Bernardino, CA: Millennium Publications, 2014.

Nongbri, Brent, *Before Religion: A History of a Modern* Concept. New Haven: Yale University Press, 2013.

Nussbaum, Martha, "The Feminist Critique of Liberalism," *Political Philosophy: The Essential Texts*, 3rd ed., ed. S. M. Cahn. New York: Oxford University Press, 2015, 1028-53.

Opwis, Felicitas, Maṣlaḥa *and the Purpose of the Law: Islamic Discourse on Legal Change from the 4th/10th to 8th/14th* Century. Leiden: E. J. Brill, 2010.

O'Sulllivan, J. M., "Church and State According to Luther," *Studies: An Irish Quarterly Review*, *3*:10 (1914): 1-12.

Otto, Rudolph, *The Idea of the Holy*, trans. J. W. Harvey. Mansfield, CT: Martino Publishing, 2010.

Owen, J. J., "Church and State in Stanley Fish's Antiliberalism," *American Political Science Review 93*:4 (1999): 911-24.

Pals, Daniel L., *Eight Theories of Religion*. New York: Oxford University Press, 2006.

Papanikolaou, A., *The Mystical as Political: Democracy and Non-Radical Orthodoxy*. Notre Dame, IN: University of Notre Dame Press, 2014.

Peters, Ruud, "Murder on the Nile: Homicide Trials in 19th Century Egyptian Sharī'a Courts," *Die Welt des Islams*, *30* (1990): 98-116.

Poggi, G., *The Development of the Modern State: A Sociological Introduction*. London: Hutchinson of London, 1978.

Pollis, A. "Eastern Orthodoxy and Human Rights," *Human Rights Quarterly*, *15*:2 (May, 1993): 339-56.

Popper, Karl R., *Conjectures and the Refutations: The Growth of Scientific Knowledge*, 5th ed. New York: Routledge, 1992.

Powers, David S., *Law, Society and Culture in the Maghrib, 1300–1500*. Cambridge: Cambridge University Press, 2002.

Al-Qaraḍāwī, Yūsuf, *al-Ḥurrīyah al-dīnīyah wa al-ta'addudīyah fī naẓar al-islām*. Beirut: al-Maktab al-Islāmī, 1428/2007.

Al-Qaraḍāwī, Yūsuf, *Thaqāfatunā bayna al-infitāḥ wa al-inghilāq*. Cairo: Dār al-Shurūq, 2005.

Al-Qaraḍāwī, Yūsuf, *Fiqh al-jihād*, 2 vols. Cairo: Maktabat Wahba, 1430/2009.

Al-Qaraḍāwī, Yūsuf, *Al-aqallīyāt al-dīnīyah wa al-ḥall al-islāmī*. Cairo: Maktabat Wahba, 1999/1420.

Al-Qaraḍāwī, Yūsuf, *Fī fiqh al-aqallīyāt al-muslimah: ḥayāt al-muslimīn wasaṭ al-mujtama'āt al-ukhrā*. Cairo: Dār al-Shurūq, 1422/2001.

Al-Qarāfi, Shihāb al-Dīn, *Sharḥ tanqīḥ al-fuṣūl fī ikhtiṣār al-maḥṣūl fī al-uṣūl*, ed. A. F. al-Mazīdī. Beirut: Dār al-Kutub al-'Ilmīyah, 1428/2007.

Al-Qarāfi, Shihāb al-Dīn, *al-Furūq* (a.k.a. *Anwār al-burūq fī anwā' al-furūq*) 4 vols. Beirut. 'Ālam al-Kitāb, n.d.

Al-Qarāfi, Shihāb al-Dīn, *Nafā'is al-uṣūl fī sharḥ al-maḥṣūl*, 4 vols., ed. M.'A. 'Aṭā. Beirut: Dār al-Kutub al-'Ilmīyah, 1421/2000.

Al-Qarāfi, Shihāb al-Dīn, *al-Dhakhīrah*, 14 vols. Beirut: Dār al-Gharb al-Islāmī, 1994.

Al-Qarāfi, Shihāb al-Dīn, *Kitāb al-iḥkām fī tamyīz al-fatāwā 'an al-aḥkām wa taṣarrufāt al-qāḍī wa al-imam*, ed. A. Abū Ghuddah. Aleppo: Maktabat al-Maṭbū'āt al-Islāmīyah, 1387/1967.

Al-Qarāfi, Shihāb al-Dīn, *al-Istibṣār fīmā tudrikuhu al-abṣār*. Madrid: Escorial, MS. no. 707.

Rabb, Intisar, *Doubt in Islamic Law: A History of Legal Maxims, Interpretation, and Islamic Criminal Law*. Cambridge: Cambridge University Press, 2015.

Rabbat, Nasser, "Who Was al-Maqrīzī? A Biographical Sketch," *Mamlūk Studies Review* 7:2 (2003): 1-19.

Rahman, Fazlur, *Major Themes of the Qur'ān*. Chicago: University of Chicago Press, 2009.

Ramadan, Tariq, Ramadan, *Radical Reform: Islamic Ethics and Liberation*. New York: Oxford University Press, 2009.

Rapaport, Yossef, "Royal Justice and Religious Law: *Siyāsah* and Shari'ah Under the Mamluks," *Mamlūk Studies Review 16* (2012): 71-102.

Rawls, John, *Political Liberalism*. New York: Columbia University Press, 2005.

Al-Raysūnī, Aḥmad, *Fiqh al-thawrah: murāja'āt fī fiqh al-siyāsī al-islāmī*. Cairo: Dār al-Kalimah, 2013.

Al-Rāzī, Fakhr al-Dīn, *al-Maḥṣūl fī 'ilm uṣūl al-fiqh*, 6 vols., ed. Ṭ. J. al-'Alwānī. Beirut: Mu'assasat al-Risālah, 1418/1997.

Reeve, W. Paul, *Religion of a Different Color: Race and the Mormon Struggle for Whiteness*. New York: Oxford University Press, 2015.

Reinhart, A. Kevin, "Islamic Law as Islamic Ethics," *The Journal of Religious Ethics, 11*:2 (1983): 186-203.

Reinhart, A. Kevin, *Before Revelation: The Boundaries of Muslim Moral Thought*. New York: State University of New York Press, 1995.

Reinhart, A. Kevin, "Failures of Practice or Failures of Faith: Are Non-Muslims Subject to the Sharia?" in M. H. Khalil, *Between Heaven and Hell: Islam, Salvation, and the Fate of Others*. New York: Oxford University Press, 2013, 13-34.

Reinhart, A. Kevin, "What We Know about Ma'rūf," *Journal of Islamic Ethics, 1* (2017): 51-82.

Riḍā, Rashīd, *Tafsīr al-qur'ān al-ḥakīm al-mashhūr bi tafsīr al-manār,* 12 vols., ed. A. Shams al-Dīn. Beirut: Dār al-Kutub al-'Ilmīyah, 1420/1999.

Rommen, Heinrich A., *The State in Catholic Thought: A Treatise on Political Philosophy*, transl. B.P. Frohnen. Providence, R.I.: Cluny Media, 2016.

Rorty, Richard, *Contingency, Irony and Solidarity*. Cambridge: Cambridge University Press, 1989.

Rousseau, Jean-Jacques, *The Social Contract*. London: Penguin Books, 1968.

Roy, Olivier, *Secularism Confronts Islam*. New York: Columbia University Press, 2009.

Sabra, Adam, "Review of Islamic Law and the State: The Constitutional Jurisprudence of Shihāb al-Dīn al-Qarāfī," *Journal of Law and Religion 15*:1/2 (2000): 413-16.

Sabra, Adam, A. Sabra, "Ibn Ḥazm's Literalism: A Critique of Islamic Legal Theory (I)," *Al-Qantara* (2007): 7-40.

Sachedina, Abdulaziz, *Islam and the Challenge of Human Rights*. New York: Oxford University Press, 2009.

Ṣafwat, Aḥmad, *Baḥth fī qā'idat iṣlāḥ qānūn al-aḥwāl al-shakhṣīyah*. Alexandria: Maṭba'at Jurjī Gharzūzī, 1917.

Saḥnūn (Saḥnūn b. Sa'īd al-Tanūkhī), *al-Mudawwanah al-kubrā* 4 vols. Beirut: Dār al-Fikr, 1406/1986.

Salaymeh, Lena, *The Beginnings of Islamic Law: Late Antique Islamicate Legal Traditions*. Cambridge: Cambridge University Press, 2016.

Saler, B. "Religio and the Definition of Religion," *Cultural Anthropology 2*:3 (1987): 395-99.

Al-Samarqandī, 'Alā' al-Dīn, *Mizān al-uṣūl fī natā'ij al-'uqūl,* 2nd ed., ed. M. Z. 'Abd al-Barr. Cairo: Maktabat al-Turāth, 1418/1997.

Al-Ṣanʿānī, Abū Bakr ʿAbd al-Razzāq, *al-Muṣannaf*, 12 vols., ed. A. al-Azharī. Beirut: Dār al-Kutub al-ʿIlmīyah, 2010.

Sandel, Michael, *Justice: What's the Right Thing to Do?* New York: Farrar, Straus and Giroux, 2009.

Sandel, Michael (ed.), *Liberalism and Its Critics*. New York: New York University Press, 1984.

Sandel, Michael, "Religious Liberty: Freedom of Choice or Freedom of Conscience," in R. Bhargava, ed., *Secularism and Its Critics*, 6th ed. New Delhi: Oxford University Press, 2007, 73-93.

Al-Sarakhsī, Abū Bakr Muḥammad b. Aḥmad b. Abī Sahl *Uṣūl al-sarakhsī*, 2 vols., ed. R. al-ʿAjam. Beirut:Dār al-Maʿrifah,1418/1997.

Sarat, A. "Law Without Nations: An Introduction," in *Law Without Nations*, eds. A. Sarat, L. Douglass, and M. M. Humphrey. Stanford: Stanford University Press, 2011, 1-21.

Al-Ṣāwī, Aḥmad b. Muḥammad, *Bulghat al-sālik li aqrab al-masālik ilā madhhab al-imām mālik*, 2 vols. Cairo: Muṣṭafā al-Bābī al-Ḥalabī, 1372/1952.

Sayeed, Asma, *Women and the Transmission of Religious Knowledge in Islam*. Cambridge: Cambridge University Press, 2015.

Sayili, Aydin M., "Al-Qarāfī and His Explanation of the Rainbow," *Isis 32*:1 (Jul. 1940): 16-26.

Al-Sayyid, Riḍwān, "Dār al-Ḥarb and Dār al-Islām: Traditions and Interpretations," in *Religion between Violence and Reconciliation* (*Beiruter Texts und Studien,* 76) ed. T. Scheiffler. Beirut: Orient-Institute der Deutschen Morgenlandischen Gesellschaft, 2002): 123-33.

Schacht, Joseph, *The Origins of Muhammadan Jurisprudence*. Oxford: The Clarendon Press, 1950.

Schacht, Joseph, "Problems in Modern Islamic Legislation," *Studia Islamica, 12* (1960): 99-129.

Schacht, Joseph, *An Introduction to Islamic Law*. Oxford: Clarendon Press, 1964.

Schacht, Joseph, "*Fiḳh*," *Encyclopedia of Islam*, 2nd ed., 12 vols., ed. P. J. Bearman et al. Leiden: E. J. Brill, 1960–2005, II: 886-91.

Schleiermacher, Friedrich, *On Religion: Speeches to its Cultured Despisers*, trans. and ed. R. Crouter. Cambridge: Cambridge University Press, 1996.

Schmidtke, Sabine, "The Muʿtazilite Movement (III)," *The Oxford Handbook of Islamic Theology*, ed. S. Schmidtke. New York: Oxford University Press, 2016, 159-80.

Schmitt, Carl, *Political Theology: Four Chapters on the Concept of Sovereignty*, transl. and ed., G. Schwab. Chicago: University of Chicago Press, 2003.

Schultz, Warren C., "'It Has No Root Among Any Community That Believes in Revealed Religion, Nor Legal Foundation for Its Implementation': Placing al-Maqrīzī's Comments on Money in a Wider Context," *Mamlūk Studies Review*, *7*:2 (2003): 169-81.

Scruton, Roger, *Kant: A Very Short Introduction* (New York: Oxford University Press, 2001).

Sezgin, Yüksel, "Muslim Family Laws in Israel and Greece: Can Non-Muslim Courts Bring About Change in Sharīʿa?," *Islamic Law and Society*, *25*:3 (2018): 235-73.

Al-Shāfiʿī, Ḥasan, *Ḥayātī fī ḥikāyātī*. Tunis: Dār al-Gharb al-Islāmī, 1436/2015.

Al-Shāfiʿī, Muḥammad b. Idrīs, *al-Risālah*, ed. A. M. Shākir. Beirut: al-Maktabah al-ʿIlmīyah, n.d.

Al-Shāfiʿī, Muḥammad b. Idrīs, , *al-Umm,* 9 vols. Beirut: Dār al-Fikr al-ʿIlmīyah, 1413/ 1993.

al-Shahrastānī, Muḥammad b. 'Abd al-Karīm, *al-Milal wa al-niḥal*, 2 vols., ed. A. A. Mahnā and A. H. Fā'ūr. Beirut: Dār al-Ma'rifah, 1417/1997.

al-Shahrastānī, Muḥammad b. 'Abd al-Karīm *Niyāyat al-iqdām 'alā 'ilm al-kalām*, ed. A. Guillaume. N.p., n.d.

Shain, Barry A., "Liberalism: A Religious-Dependent Faith," *Campbell Law Review 33:3* (2011): 559-67.

Shannon, Christopher, *Conspicuous Criticism: Tradition, The Individual, and Culture in Modern American Social Thought*. Scranton, PA: University of Scranton Press, 2006.

Sharif, M. M. (ed.), *A History of Muslim Philosophy*, 2 vols. (reprint). Karachi: Royal Book Company, 2018.

Al-Shāṭibī, Ibrāhim b. Mūsā, *al-Muwāfaqāt fī uṣūl al-sharī'ah*, 4 vols., ed. M. 'A. Drāz. Cairo: al-Maktabah al-Tijārīyah al-Kubrā, n.d.

Al-Shawkānī, Muḥammad b. 'Alī, *Fatḥ al-qadīr al-jāmi' bayna fann al-riwāyah wa al-dirāyah min 'ilm al-tafsīr*, 5 vols. Beirut: Dār Iḥyā' al-Turāth al-'Arabī, n.d.

Al-Shawkānī, Muḥammad b. 'Alī, *Nayl al-awṭār sharḥ muntaqā al-akhbār*, 10 vols. eds. Ṭ 'A. Sa'd and M.M. al-Hawarī. Cairo: Maktabat al-Kullīyāt al-Azharīyah, 1398/1978.

Al-Shaybānī, Muḥammad b. al-Ḥasan, *Kitāb al-aṣl*, 12 vols., ed. M. Buyukalin. Beirut: Dār Ibn Ḥazm 1433/2012.

Al-Shayzarī, 'Abd al-Raḥmān b. Naṣr, *Nihāyat al-rutbah fī ṭalab al-ḥisbah*. Cairo: Maṭba'at Lajnat al-Ta'līf wa al-Tarjamah wa al-Nashr, 1365/1946.

Shihadeh, Ayman, *The Teleological Ethics of Fakhr al-Dīn al-Rāzī*. Leiden: E. J. Brill, 2006.

Al-Shirāzī, Abū Isḥāq, *al-Luma' fī uṣūl al-fiqh*, ed. 'A. al-Khaṭīb al-Ḥasanī. Bahrain: Maktabat al-Niẓām al-Ya'qūbī al-Khāssah, 1434/2013.

Al-Shirbīnī, Shams al-Dīn Muḥammad b. Aḥmad, *al-Iqnā' fī ḥall alfāẓ abī shujā'*, 2 vols. Cairo: Muṣṭafā Bābī al-Ḥalabī, 1359/1940.

Al-Shūshāwī, al-Ḥusayn b. 'Alī b. Ṭalḥah al-Rajrājī, *Raf' al-niqāb 'an tanqīḥ al-shihāb*, 4 vols., ed. N. al-Suwayd. Beirut: Dār al-Kutub al-'Ilmīyah, 1436/2015.

Sibler, J. R., "The Ethical Significance of Kant's Religion," in Kant's *Religion Within the Limits of Reason Alone*, trans. T. M. Greene and H. H. Hudson. New York: Harper One, 1960, lxxix-cxxxiv.

Siddiqui, Sohaira, *Law and Politics under the Abbasids: An Intellectual Portrait of al-Juwayni*. Cambridge: Cambridge University Press, 2019.

Al-Sijistānī, Abū Dā'ūd, *Risālat al-imām abī dā'ūd al-sijistānī ilā ahl makka wa waṣf sunanih*, ed. 'A. Abū Ghuddah. Aleppo: Maktab al-Maṭbū'āt al-Islāmīyah, 1417/1997.

Smart, Ninian (et al., eds.) *Nineteenth Century Religious Thought in the West*, vol. 1. Cambridge: Cambridge University Press, 1985.

Smith, James K. A., *How (Not) to Be Secular: Reading Charles Taylor*. Grand Rapids: William B. Eerdmans Publishing Company, 2014.

Smith, Jonathan Z., "'Religion' and 'Religious Studies': No Difference at All,"" in *On Teaching Religion: Essays by Jonathan Z. Smith*, ed. C. I. Lehrich. New York: Oxford University Press, 2013, 77-90.

Smith, Jonathan Z., "Religion, Religions, Religious," in *Critical Terms for Religious Studies*, ed. M. C. Taylor. Chicago: University of Chicago Press, 1998, 269-84.

Smith, Wilfred Cantwell, *The Meaning and End of Religion*. Minneapolis: Fortress Press, 1991.

Sorensen, Kim, "Revelation and Reason in Leo Strauss," *The Review of Politics*, 65:3 (2003): 383-408.

Spectorsky, Susan A., "Aḥmad Ibn Ḥanbal's *Fiqh*," *Journal of the American Oriental Society, 102*:3 (1982): 461-65.

Stewart, Devin, "Muḥammad b. Dā'ūd al-Ẓāhirī's Manual of Jurisprudence, *Al-Wuṣūl Ilā Ma'rifat al-Uṣūl*," in B. Weiss, ed., *Studies in Islamic Legal Theory*. Leiden: E. J. Brill, 2002, 99-158.

Stolzenberg, Nomi, "The Profanity of the Law," in *Law and the Sacred*, eds. A. Sarat, L. Douglas, and M. M. Umphrey. Stanford: Stanford University Press, 2007, 29-90.

Stout, Jeffrey, *The Flight from Authority: Religion, Morality and the Quest for Autonomy*. Notre Dame, IN: University of Notre Dame Press, 1981.

Al-Subkī, Tāj al-Dīn 'Abd al-Wahhāb, *Mu'īd al-ni'am wa mubīd al-niqam*. Beirut: Mu'assasat al-Kutub al-Thaqāfiyah, 1407/1986.

Al-Subkī, Taqī al-Dīn 'Abd al-Kāfī, *Ma'nā qawl al-imām al-muṭṭalabī idhā ṣaḥḥa al-ḥadīth fa huwa madhhabī*, ed. 'A. N. Biqā'ī. Beirut: Dār al-Bashā'ir, 1413/1993.

Al-Subkī, Taqī al-Dīn, and al-Subkī, Tāj al-Dīn, *al-Ibhāj fī sharḥ al-minhāj*, 3 vols., ed. M. A. al-Sayyid Beirut: Dār al-Kutub al-'Ilmīyah, 1424/2004.

Al-Sulamī, Iyāḍ, *Uṣūl a-fiqh alladhī lā yasa'u al-faqīh jahlah*. Riyadh: Dār al-Tadmurīyah, 1429/2008.

Al-Suyūṭī, Jalāl al-Dīn, *Juhd al-qarīḥah fī tajrīd al-naṣīḥa*. Beirut: al-Maktabah al-'Aṣrīyah, 1430/2009.

Al-Suyūṭī, Jalāl al-Dīn, *al-Ḥāwī li al-fatāwī*, 2 vols. Beirut: Dār al-Kutub al-'Ilmīyah, 1408/1988.

Al-Suyūṭī, Jalāl al-Dīn, *Nawāḍir al-ayk fī ma'rifat al-nayk*, ed. Ṭ. Ḥ. 'Abd al-Qawī. Damascus: Dār al-Kitāb al-'Arabī, n.d.

Al-Ṭabarī, Muḥammad b. Jarīr, *Jāmi' al-bayān 'an tafsīr al-qur'ān*, 3rd ed., 30 vols. Cairo: Muṣṭafā al-Bābī al-Ḥalabī wa Awlāduh, 1388/ 1968.

Al-Taftazānī, Sa'd al-Dīn, *Sharḥ al-talwīḥ 'alā al-tawḍīḥ*, 2 vols. Cairo: Muḥammad 'Alī Ṣubayḥ wa Awlāduh, n.d.

Al-Ṭaḥāwī, Abū Ja'far, *Mushkil al-āthār*, 4 vols., ed. M.'A. Shāhīn. Beirut: Dār al-Kutub al-'ilmīyah, 1415/1995.

Talhami, G. H., "The Zanj Rebellion Reconsidered," *The International Journal of African Historical Studies, 10*:3 (1977): 443-61.

Tambiah, Stanley J., *Magic, Science, Religion, and the Scope of Rationality*. Cambridge: Cambridge University Press, 1990.

Tanner, Kathryn, *Theories of Culture: A New Agenda for Theology*. Minneapolis: Fortress Press, 1997.

Al-Ṭarābulisī, 'Alā' al-Dīn Abū al-Ḥasan b. Khalīl, *Mu'īn al-ḥukkām fīmā yataraddad bayna al-khaṣmayn min al-aḥkām*, 2nd ed. Cairo: Muṣṭafā al-Bābī al-Ḥalabī wa Awlāduh, 1393/1973.

Tarnas, Richard, *The Passion of the Western Mind: Understanding the Ideas that Have Shaped Our World View*. New York: Ballantine Books, 1991.

Taylor, Charles, *A Secular Age*. Cambridge, MA: The Belknap Press of Harvard University Press, 2007.

Taylor, Charles, "Modes of Secularism," in *Secularism and Its Critics*, ed. R. Bharghava, 6th ed. New Delhi: Oxford University Press, 2007, 31-53.

Taylor, Charles, "Justice After Virtue," in *After MacIntyre: Critical Perspectives on the Work of Alasdair MacIntyre*, eds. J. Horton and S. Mendus. Notre Dame: University of Notre Dame Press, 1994, 16-43.

Taylor, Charles, "Hegel: History and Politics," in M. Sandel, ed., *Liberalism and Its Critics*. New York: New York University Press, 1984. 177-99.

Tocqueville, Alexis de, *Democracy in America*, 2 vols. New York: Vintage Books, 1990.

Toulmin, Stephen, *Cosmopolis: The Hidden Agenda of Modernity*. New York: The Free Press, 1990.

Al-Ṭūfī, Najm al-Dīn, *Sharḥ mukhtaṣar al-rawḍah*, 3 vols., ed. A. al-Turkī. Damascus: Mu'assasat al-Risālah, 1435/2014.

Al-Tūnisī, Khayr al-Dīn, *Muqaddimat aqwam al-masālik fī maf'rifat aḥwāl al-mamālik* (appended to Badr al-Dīn Ibn Jamā'ah's *Taḥrīr al-aḥkām fī tadbīr ahl al-islām*). Beirut: Dār al-Kutub al-'Ilmīyah, 1424/2003.

Turner, Brian, *Weber and Islam: A Critical Study*. London: Routledge and Kegan Paul, 1974.

Unger, Roberto M., *Knowledge and Politics*. New York: The Free Press, 1975.

Van Creveld, Martin, *The Rise and Decline of the State*. Cambridge: Cambridge University Press, 1999.

Vasalou, Sophia, *Moral Agents and Their Deserts: The Character of Mu'tazilite Ethics*. Princeton: Princeton University Press, 2008.

Vinx, L., "Carl Schmitt," *The Stanford Encyclopedia of Philosophy* (Fall 2019), ed. Edward N. Zalta. https://plato.stanford.edu/archives/fall2019/entries/schmitt/≥

Vogel, Frank, *Islamic Law and Legal System: Studies of Saudi Arabia*. Leiden: E. J. Brill, 2000.

Vogel, Frank, "Tracing Nuance in al-Māwardī's *al-Aḥkām al-Sulṭānīyah*: Implicit Framing of Constitutional Authority," in *Islamic Law Theory: Studies on Jurisprudence in Honor of Bernard Weiss*, eds. A. K. Reinhart and R. Gleave. Leiden: E. J. Brill, 2014, 331-59.

Wach, Joachim, "Introduction: The Meaning and Task of the History of Religions (Religionswissenschaft)," *The History of Religions: Essays on the Problem of Understanding*, 2nd impression, eds. J. M. Kitagawa, M. Eliade, and C. H. Long. Chicago: University of Chicago Press, 1969, 1-19.

Walzer, Michael, "The Communitarian Critique of Liberalism," *Political Theory 18*:1 (1990): 6-23.

Walzer, M., *What It Means to Be an American: Essays on the American Experience*. New York: Marsilio Publishers Corp., 1992.

Walzer, Michael, "Welfare, Membership and Need," in M. Sandel, ed., *Liberalism and Its Critics*. New York: New York University Press, 1984.

Al-Wansharīsī, Aḥmad b. Yaḥyā, *al-Mi'yār al-mu'rib wa al-jāmi' al-mughrib 'an fatāwā 'ulamā' ifriqīyah wa al-andalus wa al-maghrib*, 13 vols. ed. M. Ḥajjī et al. Beirut: Dār al-Gharb al-Islāmī, 1401/1981.

Ware, Rudolph, *The Walking Qur'ān: Islamic Education, Embodied Knowledge, and History in West Africa*. Chapel Hill: University of North Carolina Press, 2014.

Watson, Alan, *The Nature of Law*. Edinburgh: Edinburgh University Press, 1997.

Watt, W. Montgomery, *Muhammad at Mecca*. Oxford: Clarendon Press, 1953.

Watt, W. Montgomery, *Muhammad at Medina*. Oxford: Clarendon Press, 1956.

Watt, W. Montgomery, *Islamic Fundamentalism and Modernity*. London and New York: Routledge, 1988.

Watts, Alan, *The Way of Zen*. New York: Vintage Books, 1957.

Weber, Max. *From Max Weber: Essays in Sociology*, eds. H. H. Gerth and C. Wright Mills. New York: Oxford University Press, 1946.

Wehr, Hans, *A Dictionary of Modern Written Arabic*, 3rd ed., ed. J. M. Cowan. Ithaca, NY: Spoken Language Services, Inc., 1976.

Weiss, Bernard, *The Search for God's Law: Islamic Jurisprudence in the Writings of Sayf al-Dīn al-Āmidī*. Salt Lake City: University of Utah Press, 1992.

Weiss, Bernard (ed.), *Studies in Islamic Legal Theory*. Leiden: E. J. Brill, 2002.

West, Cornell, *Prophecy Deliverance: An Afro-American Revolutionary Christianity*. Philadelphia: The Westminster Press, 1982.

Wilkerson, Isabel, *Caste: The Origins of Our Discontents*. New York: Random House, 2020.

Williams, Joan, *White Working Class: Overcoming Class Cluelessness in America*. Boston: Harvard Business Review Press, 2017.

White, S., "Weak Ontology: General and Critical Issues," *Hedgehog Review 7*:2 (2005):11-25.

Wolin, Sheldon, *Politics and Vision: Politics and Change in Western Political Thought*. Princeton: Princeton University Press, 2006.

Wolin, Sheldon, "The Liberal/Democratic Divide: On Rawls's *Political Liberalism*," *Political Theory* (Feb. 1996): 97-142.

Wymann-Landgraff, Umar R. A., *Mālik and Medina: Islamic Legal Reasoning in the Formative Period*. Leiden: E. J. Brill, 2013.

Yannoulatos, A., "Eastern Orthodoxy and Human Rights," *International Review of Mission*, *73*:292 (1984): 454-56.

Yarbrough, Luke, *Friends of the Emir: Non-Muslim State Officials in Premodern Islamic Thought*. Cambridge: Cambridge University Press, 2019.

Al-Zarkashī, Badr al-Dīn, *al-Baḥr al-muḥīṭ*, 6 vols., eds. 'A. 'A. 'A. al-'Ānī, S. al-Ashqar and 'A. Abū Ghuddah. Kuwait: Wizārat al-Awqāf wa al-Shu'ūn al-Islāmīyah, 1413/1992.

Al-Zarqā, Muṣṭafā, *Fatāwā muṣṭafā al-zarqā*. Damascus: Dār al-Qalam, 1420/1990.

Zaydān, 'Abd al-Karīm, *al-Wajīz fī uṣūl al-fiqh*. Beirut: Mu'assasat al-Risālah, 1980.

Zerilli, Linda, "Value Pluralism and the Problem of Judgment: Farewell to Public Reason," *Political Theory*, *40*:1 (2012): 6-32.

Al-Zubaydī, Muḥibb al-Dīn Abū Fayḍ al-Sayyid Muḥammad Murtaḍā al-Ḥusaynī al-Wāsiṭī *Tāj al-'arūs min jawāhir al-qāmūs*, 10 vols. Cairo: Dār al-Fikr, n`.d.

Al-Zuḥaylī, Wahbah, *Uṣūl al-fiqh al-islāmī*, 2 vols. Damascus: Dār al-Fikr, 1406/1986.

Al-Zuḥaylī, Wahbah, *Mawsū'at al-fiqh al-islāmī wa al-qaḍāyā al-mu'āṣirah*, 14 vols. Damascus: Dār al-Fikr, 2010.

Zuhdī, Karam, et al., *Mubādarat waqf al-'unf: ru'yah wāqi'īyah wa naẓrah shar'īyah*. Cairo: Maktabat al-Turāth al-Islāmī, 2002.

Zysow, Aron, *The Economy of Certainty: An Introduction to the Typology of Islamic Legal Theory*. Atlanta, GA: Lockwood Press, 2013.

Zysow, Aron, "Mu'tazilism and Māturīdism in Ḥanafī Legal Theory," in B. Weiss, ed., *Studies in Islamic Legal Theory*. Leiden: E. J. Brill, 2002, 235-65.

Index

For the benefit of digital users, indexed terms that span two pages (e.g., 52–53) may, on occasion, appear on only one of those pages.

Abbasi, Rushain, xii, 391–92n.58
'Abd al-Jabbār, al-Qāḍī, 176–77, 226
'Abd al-Qādir, Khālid, 324
'Abd al-Raḥmān, Ṭaha, 1, 3, 16, 446n.37
'Abd al-Wahhab, al-Qāḍī, 103–4
'Abduh, Muḥammad, 48, 169–73, 223–24, 246–47
Abou El Fadl, Khaled, 8–9, 266–67, 461n.207, 468nn.65–66
Abū Dā'ūd (al-Sijistānī), 219
Abū Ḥanīfa, 218–19, 220–22, 225, 402n.200
Abu Lughod, Janet, 55, 56–57
Abū Nuwās, 32–33, 389n.33
Abū Ya'lā, Muḥammad b. al-Ḥusayn al-Farrā', 97, 118, 136–38, 139–40, 144–45, 146–47, 152–53, 159, 203–4, 215, 221
Abū Zahrah, Muḥammad, 107
Adams, Charles, 45, 396n.96
Adams, Henry, 349
Adams, John Quincy, 349
Adams, Nicholas, 398n.131
Adonis ('Alī Aḥmad Sa'īd), 86
Afghanī, Jamāl al-Dīn al-, 48
"aggregates of love", 351, 362
aḥkām al-islām, 288, 289
Ahmad, Ahmad A., xii, 126–27
Ahmed, Shahab, 63, 83, 121, 184–85, 352, 424n.1, 429n.70
  on "Islamic," 66
  on Pre-Text, 68
  on Context, 66–67
Ajami, Fouad, 193
'Alī (Ibn Abī Ṭālib), 282–83, 284
Ali, Muhammad, 340
Allen, Theodore, 489n.190
Allouche, Adel, xii, 406n.3, 406n.6, 406nn.7–8, 406n.9, 406n.10, 406n.11, 407n.16, 407n.20
'almāni, 124, 125–26
al-'almānī al-islāmī, 1–2, 124, 125–26
'Alwānī, Ṭaha Jābir al-, 245, 348
amārah (probable indicant), 9, 383n.30
Āmidī, Sayf al-Dīn al-, 89, 98–99, 100, 106
Amīn, Qāsim, 178
Anjum, Ovamir, xii, 244–45
An-Na'im, Abdullahi, 15–16, 21, 86, 375
  on the Islamic State, 250, 251, 253
  on *sharī'ah*, 251–54, 268, 463–64n.5, 464n.12, 464–65n.25, 467n.52, 468n.67, 470n.99
  on secularism, 252–54
  and non-Muslims, 250, 251–53, 254, 267, 278, 474n.161, 474n.162
  and women, 253, 267, 278
  on citizenship, 252
  on constitutionalism, 252, 322
  on "civic reason", 252–53, 254, 464n.12
  and "politics", 252–53, 254
  on state neutrality, 252, 277–79, 471n.111
  on religion, 253
  on his Secular State, 251, 254
  on purity of religion, 257–62
  on human rights, 252, 262–64
  on "non-religious state", 265, 266
  and equality, 263, 295–96
Anṣārī, Abū Yaḥyā Zakarīyah al-, 75–76, 77
'aql, 19, 95, 116, 219–20, 379–80
'aqlī, 91–92, 95, 96, 97–98, 115, 117, 119, 134, 228, 237–39, 245, 341
Arberry, Arthur J., 450n.101
Area Studies, xi, 13–14, 44–45
Arendt, Hannah, 358–59
Aristotle, 67, 71–72, 164, 379–80
'aṣabīyah, 351, 367
Asad, Talal, 4–5, 20, 27–28, 86, 130, 175, 380, 390n.45, 440n.225, 440n.226, 441–42n.257, 465n.32
  and "religious law", 178, 179, 180
  and family law, 178–79, 180–81
  and foreign codes, 182–83
aṣḥāb al-ḥadīth, 218–19
aṣḥāb al-ra'y, 218–19
Ash'ari, Abū al-Ḥasan al-, 71–72, 225, 231
Ash'arites/ Ash'arism, 94, 96, 97, 99, 224, 225, 230–31, 233, 244, 340, 341, 382n.23, 382–83n.24

Ashford, B.R., 490n.200
'Asqalānī, Ibn Ḥajar al-, 78
Ataturk, Mustafa Kemal, 252–53, 254–55
Attas, Syed Muhammad Naquib al-, 86
Awzā'ī, 'Abd al-Raḥmān al-, 220–21
Ayalon, David, 78, 406n.4, 408n.27
'Aynī, Badr al-Dīn al-, 75–76, 142
Ayoub, Samy, xii, 280–81, 426–27n.42
Azam, Hina, 86
Azami, Mustafa, 86

Baghdādī, Khaṭīb al-, 65–66
Bājī, Abū al-Walīd al-, 82
Baldwin, James, 1, 3, 16, 345–46
Balmer, Randall, 352–53, 489n.189
Bangstad, Sindre (and Faatir, Aslam), 488n.169
Bannā, Ḥassan al-, 48
Bāqillānī, Abū Bakr al-, 89, 95–96, 231
Baṣrī, Abū al-Ḥusayn al-, 91–92, 97–99
Batnitzky, Leora, 184–85, 399–400n.146
Bauer, Thomas, 405n.236
Baybars, Rukn al-Dīn, 213–14, 269
bayyinah, 129, 146, 149
Bazdawī, Fakhr al-Islām 'Ali al-, 97–98, 105, 106, 138
Bell, Daniel, 350
Benhabib, Seyla, 447n.54
Berger, Peter, 35–36, 51–52, 56–57, 156–57, 158, 388n.16
Bergson, Henri, 258–59
Bergsträsser, Gotthelf, 83
Bernays, Edward, 162
Béteile, Andre, 38, 188, 224
"beyond the law", 156–73, 215, 216–17, 235
Bilgrami, Akeel, 216, 248
Bin Bayyah, 'Abd Allah, 327–28, 482n.88
Binder, Leonard, 13
Bin Lādin, Usāmah, 360
Bishrī, Ṭāriq al-, 184–85, 186, 277, 493n.3
Brenna, C., 466n. 48–67
Brown, John, 339
Brown, Jonathan A. C., 164, 438n.197
Budhhism, 125
Bulliet, Richard, 349
Burbank, Jane, 280–81
Burke, Edmund, 338–39
Buyids, 293

Calder, Norman, 425n.18
Calhoun, Craig, 4–5, 27–28
"Cannon First", 325, 327
Carter, Stephen, 278–79, 296, 430n.89
Casanova, José, 28–29, 31–32, 39–40, 41, 49–50, 187, 382n.16, 387n.5, 390n.45
Cavanaugh, William, 210, 396n.111, 444n.18, 448n.68
Chadwick, Owen, 5, 182, 382n.14
Christianity, 30–31, 32, 42–43, 44–45, 47, 56–57, 59, 72–73, 80–81, 182, 232, 302–3, 356, 394–95n.84, 401n.165
Cicero, 46–47, 50, 349
civic reason, 252–53, 254, 277–78, 297, 464n.12
Clifford, William K., 391n.51
Colvin, Claudette, 211
Communism, 5
complementarity (theory of), 42–43
Cooper, Frederick, 280–81
Coptic Christians, 277, 290–91, 297
Cornell, Vincent, 360, 361
Coulson, Noel, 14–15, 45–46, 84, 127–28, 411n.57, 478n.26
counterpublic, 212, 488n.180
Cover, Robert, 157, 158, 281, 444n.11
Crone, Patricia, 80–81, 232, 385n.52, 443n.5
culture, 3, 56, 57–58, 60
Curtis IV, Edward, 487n.166

Dabūsī, Abū Zayd al-, 91–92
dahrī, 32–33
dalīl, 9, 89, 333, 383n.30
Damīrī, Shams al-Dīn al-, 153, 154
dār al-ḥarb, 307
dār al-islām, 334–35
Dardīr, Aḥmad al-, 490n.204
Davis-Secord, Sarah, 482n.83
da'wah, 319
Dawson, Michael, 488n.180
Dembour, Marie-Bénédicte, 263–64
dhimmi/ dhimmah, 267, 278–79, 282–84, 285–86, 287–88, 333, 337, 365
differentiation/ differentiated, 3, 17, 39–40, 41, 80–81, 82–83, 104–5, 118, 165, 187–88, 232, 242, 245, 254–55, 287, 294, 374
dīn, 3, 41, 48–50, 51, 52–53, 65–66, 79, 172, 180–81, 183, 184, 187–88, 243–44, 354–55, 367, 442n.262
disenchantment, 35–36
'divine mind', 8–9
Donner, Fred, 385n.52, 395n.95
Douglas, Mary, 33–34
DuBois, W.E.B., 34–35, 390n.47
dunyā, 37–38, 52, 391–92n.58
dunyawī/dunyawīyah, 19–20, 49–50, 126
Durkheim, Emile, 43–44, 121
Dworkin, Ronald, 305

Dyer, Richard, 492n.227
dystopian narrative, 127–28

Ebu's s-su'ud, 127–28
Eliade, Mircea, 44–45, 51–52, 395n.90
Elizabeth I (Queen), 292
Emon, Anver, 285, 383n.27
empire-state, 248, 280–81, 353–54
Engels, Friedrich, 5
Enlightenment, 31, 39–40, 43–45, 63, 73, 275–76
Esack, Fareed, 488n.168
Euben, Roxanne (and Zaman, Muhammad Qasim), 449n.85
European codes, 178, 182–83

Fadel, Mohammad, xii, 108–9, 131, 286, 321–22, 463n.227, 472n.133
Fahmy, Khaled, 129, 130, 131–32, 133, 150–51
Fakhry, Majid, 389n.32
falāsifah/*falsafah*, 36, 64, 68, 116–17, 187, 391n.54
fantasia, 160–62
farḍ kifāyah, 355
Faruqi (al-Fārūqī), Ismā'īl al-, 23–24, 55, 400n.158
Fāṭimids, 293
fikr, 245, 299, 345
fikr 'almānī, 1–2, 184–85
fiqh 6, 8–10, 79, 89, 90, 95, 97, 108, 115, 118–19, 130, 131, 133–34, 146, 151–52, 183, 235–36, 379
  as *sharī'ah*, 130, 237, 304–5, 307–8, 348
  See also sharī'ah
fiṭrah, 36, 48, 51, 244, 441n.235
Fitzgerald, Timothy, 4–5, 13, 381n.11
Five Juristic Statuses, 54–55, 87, 90–91, 228–29
Foucault, Michel, 162, 201–2, 216, 248
Frank, Jerome, 7
Freud, Sigmund, 43–44, 354
fulūs/*fals*, 74–77

Galileo, 80, 409n.37
Gamā'ah al-Islāmīyah al-, 376, 425n.28, 469n.79
Gane, E. R., 409n.40
Gardet, Louis, 396n.112
Gauchet, Marcel, 35–36
GhaneaBassiri, Kambiz, 400n.152
Ghannouchi, Rached El-, 298
Ghazālī, Abū Ḥāmid al-, 9, 37–38, 49, 60–61, 81–82, 95–96, 98–99, 163, 187, 230–31, 351, 391–92n.58, 392n.60
  and "ignorant friends of Islam", 81–82, 188
Ghobadzadeh, Naser, 386n.59
Gibb, Hamilton A. R., 127–28, 135–36
Gleave, Robert, 477n.24
Goitein, S.D., 442n.261
Goldziher, Ignaz, 14–15
Gothóni, Rene, 397n.115
Gramsci, Antonio, 57, 201, 318
Grewal, Zareena, 400n.158, 404n.228
Grotius, Hugo, 29

Hacking, Ian, 4
ḥadīth, 13–14, 52, 71, 219, 283–84, 304–5, 343, 404–5n.229, 408–9n.33, 451n.112, 452n.123, 472n.133, 478n.29, 486n.155, 490n.199
Haider, Najam, 430n.87
Hallaq, Wael, 14–16, 20, 108–9, 127–28, 130, 162, 245, 375, 405n.231, 432n.110, 443n.2, 443n.3, 443–44nn.5–6, 444n.10, 444n.15, 444n.16, 444n.19, 444–45n.20, 445n.24, 454n.151, 456n.165, 458n.176, 485n.133
  on morality, 84–86, 199, 228–29
  on the modern state, 194–96, 198–200, 201–16
  on provenance of the modern state, 203–4, 466n.36
  on state sovereignty, 204–10
  on state violence, 210–11
  on sacrifice for the state, 211–13
  on state bureaucracy, 213–15
  on the state and culture, 215
  on the Islamic State, 194, 198
  and Carl Schmitt, 203–4, 206, 447n.54
  on divine authority, 207
  on *ijtihād*, 223
  and *sharī'ah*, 216–34
  on Is vs. Ought, 229–32
  on reason and revelation, 216–23
  and *siyāsah shar'īyah*, 232–33
  on Ash'arite rationality, 224, 233
  on reason, 196, 222–23, 232–34
Hamann, J.G., 372–73, 378–79, 458n.172
Hamdan, Omar, 389n.34
Ḥanafī school, 18, 91–92, 93, 94, 97–98, 100–1, 105, 106–7, 119, 365, 382n.23, 426–27n.42
Hauerwas, Stanley, 305, 356, 367
Hayes, Christine, 6, 7–8, 68–69
Hill, W.E., 23
ḥisbah, 19–20, 151–55
History of Religions, 43–44, 45
  See also Religionswissenschaft
Hitler, Adolph, 71, 203, 209
Hobbes, Thomas, 204–5, 230, 282, 351, 361–62
Hodgson, Marshall, 55, 57, 59–63, 401n.180, 402n.189
  on "Islamic", 60

Hoover, Jon, 115–16, 422n.236
Hourani, George, 14–15, 203–4, 453–54n.142
Hughes, Aaron, 12–15, 384n.42, 385n.45, 385n.50
ḥukm Allāh, 9, 274
ḥukm shar'ī, 17, 77, 87–89, 94, 97, 100, 104–5, 108–9, 165, 169, 328, 347, 348, 368
ḥukm taklīfī, 87–88
ḥukm waḍ'ī, 87–89
Hume, David, 40
Hunter, James Davison, 56, 174, 390n.38
Huntington, Samuel P., 193, 293–94, 396–97n.113
Hurgronje, Christiaan Snouck, 6
Hurvitz, Nimrod, 135, 150–51
Ḥusayn, Ṭaha, 389n.33
ḥusn wa al-qubḥ 'aqlīyān al-, 224, 228, 230–31, 453n.141, 453–54n.142

'ibādah/ 'ibādāt, 2, 48, 226–27, 260, 284–85, 341–42, 357
Ibn 'Abd al-Salām 'Izz al-Dīn, 142, 155–56, 180, 203, 302
Ibn Abī Rabāḥ, 'Aṭā', 220–21
Ibn 'Adī, Yaḥyā, 67
Ibn al-Furāt, Asad, 220–21
Ibn al-Ḥājib, Jamāl al-Dīn, 103, 105
Ibn al-Ḥājj, 420–21n.212
Ibn al-Humām, Kamāl al-Dīn, 15, 382n.23
Ibn al-Jawzī, 'Abd al-Raḥmān, 65–66, 130, 402n.200, 409n.36
Ibn al-Laḥḥām, Abū al-Ḥasan 'Alā' al-Dīn Muḥammad, 118
Ibn al-Nafīs, 242
Ibn al-Qāsim, 451n.113
Ibn al-Qaṣṣār, Abū al-Ḥasan 'Ali, 18, 94–95, 247
Ibn al-Qayyim (al-Jawzīyah), 19, 94, 112, 119–20, 154–55, 208, 225, 230–31, 276–77, 307–8, 454n.150
Ibn al-Rawandī, 32–33, 389n.32
Ibn Amīr al-Ḥājj, 469n.85
Ibn 'Aqīl, 97, 114, 118
Ibn 'Āshir, 'Abd al-Wāḥid, 423n.243
Ibn 'Āshūr, Muḥammad al-Ṭāhir, 404n.224, 416n.145
Ibn Bint al-A'azz, Tāj al-Dīn, 213–14
Ibn Farḥūn, Burhān al-Dīn Ibrāhīm, 136–37, 143, 144–45, 208, 430–31n.91
Ibn Ḥanbal, Aḥmad, 218–19, 221–22, 229, 452n.123
Ibn Ḥazm, 110–11
Ibn Isḥāq, Ḥunayn, 67
Ibn Jurayj, 220–21
Ibn Kathīr, Abū al-Fidā' Ismā'īl, 447–48n.61
Ibn Khaldūn, 'Abd al-Raḥmān, 98–99, 106, 351, 488n.182
Ibn Khalikān, 98–99
Ibn Qudāmah, Muwaffaq al-Dīn al-, 221
Ibn Qurah, Abū Bakr Thābit, 67
Ibn Qutaybah, 64, 65, 154, 220–21
Ibn Rushd (the Grandson), 393–94n.76
Ibn Sa'ātī, 106
Ibn Sahl, Abū al-Asbagh, 460n.200
Ibn Surayj, 90–91
Ibn Taymīyah, Taqī al-Dīn, 19, 32–33, 42–43, 71–72, 80, 94, 115, 225, 229, 230–31, 261–62, 276–77, 307–8, 423n.241, 455n.154, 455n.159, 461n.208, 465–66n.33, 467–68n.61, 493n.10
  on sunna, 167–68
  against *falāsifah*, 456n.165
Ibn 'Ulayya, Abū Bishr Ismā'īl, 220
Ibn Yūsuf, al-Ḥajjāj, 32–33
Ibrāhīm, Nājiḥ (and al-Najjār, Hishām), 437n.182
ideal theory, 306–8
ijmā', 75–76, 97, 103–4, 110–11, 119, 242, 265–66, 270, 271–72
ijtihād (shar'ī), 9, 91, 109, 134, 147, 152–53, 164, 169, 170, 171, 186–87, 202, 223, 235, 299, 370–71, 374–75, 434n.149, 434n.150, 435n.152
  definition of, 137, 152
ijtihād 'urfī, 153, 154, 171, 434n.149, 434n.150, 435n.152
  definition of, 137, 152
  'illah in philosophy, 233–34
  in law, 226–27, 233–34, 458–59n.186
  See also ratio essendi
'ilm al-kalām/ kalām, 60–61, 94, 99, 116–17
'ilmānī, 125–26
Imber, Colin, 127–28, 268–69
Iqtidar, Humaira, 386n.57
irādah kawnīyah, 101–2, 117, 418n.168
irādah shar'īyah, 101–2, 117
ISIS, 71
islāmī, 66, 124, 125–26
islāmī al-'almānī al-, 124, 125
"Islamic", 3–4, 10–11, 17, 35, 54, 60, 66, 70, 184–85, 242, 253, 373, 378
  my change regarding, 58–59
Islamic law, 19–20, 83–84
  as *fiqh/sharī'ah* plus *siyāsah*, 130–33, 426n.33
Islamic Secular, 1–2, 3–4, 19–20, 23, 122
  Arabic translation of, 123–27
Islamic State, 194, 196, 198

Islamic Studies 1.0, 14–15, 306
Islamic Studies 2.0, 14–15, 306
Islamization of Knowledge, 23–24
islām khārij al-ḥukm al-shar'ī, 124, 126–27
islām mā warā' al-ḥukm al-shar'ī, 124, 126, 172
Is/Ought, 54, 127–28, 229
istiḥsān, 40–41, 208, 311–12
Izetbegovic, Alija, 440n.224
Izutsu, Toshihiko, 48–49, 399n.144

Jacobson, Matthew Frey, 352, 489n.186
Jāḥiẓ, Abū 'Uthmān 'Amr, 346
James (King), 292
jarā'im, 147–50
Jarbū', 'Abd al-'Azīz b. Ṣāliḥ al-, 324, 325, 327
Jaṣṣāṣ, Abū Bakr al-, 91, 97–98, 404n.224
jihād, 212–13, 267, 278–79, 283–84, 328–29, 334, 335–37
jizyah, 287–88, 335–36, 337, 485n.125
Joffe, Josef, 490n.195
Johansen, Baber, 1–2, 141, 142, 143, 284–85, 383n.27, 449n.91
Judaism, 6, 125, 182–83, 184–85
jurispathic/jurispathy, 197, 281, 294, 296, 444n.11
Juwaynī, Abū al-Ma'ālī (Imām al-Ḥaramayn) al-, 96–97, 98–99, 138, 159, 231, 239

Kahn, Paul, 259–60, 305, 480n.53
  on liberal background culture, 313
  on love, 351
Kant, Immanuel, 17, 40, 59, 85, 152–53, 181, 217, 243–44, 317, 372, 373, 379–80, 393n.69, 401n.164, 411n.67
  and *Sapere aude*, 356
Karāmastī, Yūsuf b. Ḥusayn al-, 106–7
kashf, 6–7, 145
Katz, Marion, 170, 439n.214
Keddie, Nikki, 4–5, 34
Kelsen, Hans, 201
Khalīfah, Ḥājjī, 98–99, 100, 106
Khallāf, 'Abd al-Wahhāb, 86, 107, 223
Khārijites/ Khārijism, 13
khilāf, 272, 275, 294
Khomeini, Ayatolla, 214
Kierkegaard, Søren, 43–44
Kuhn, Thomas, 22–23
kullu mujtahid muṣīb, 9

Lactantius, 46
Lakhmī, Abū al-Ḥasan 'Alī al-, 289
Lāmishī, Abū al-Thanā' Maḥmūd b. Zayd al-, 97–98
Lane, F.C. and Mueller, R.C., 406n.5
Lapidus, Ira, 425 n.24
Lawrence, Bruce, 400n.154
law versus fact, 88–89, 104, 235–36, 275, 290, 460n.193
legal monism, 197, 281, 291, 294
Leuba, J.H., 46
Lewis, Bernard, 48, 189, 293, 487n.164
liberalism, 21–22, 304–5, 308, 313, 316, 317, 320, 322, 344–45, 349, 351, 352, 353, 354–55, 359–60, 363, 366, 367, 370
Lincoln, Bruce, 13, 318, 400n.155
Llewelyn, Karl, 7
Locke, John, 204–5, 329–30
Long, Charles H., xi, 43–44, 50–52, 212, 391n.52, 449nn.76–77
Lucas, Scott, 452n.127
Lutz, Christopher, 457n.171

Macedo, Stephen, 480n.59
MacIntyre, Alasdair, 78, 194, 230, 246, 443n.4, 489n.188
Madan, T.N., 386n.61
madhhab, 89, 90, 94, 111, 142, 188, 239, 240–41, 246, 293, 365
Mahmood, Saba, 20, 388n.16
Makdisi, George, xi, 14–15, 92–93
Mālik (b. Anas), 218–19, 220–21, 222–23, 284–85, 286
māni', 87, 100–1
Mankdīm, Aḥmad b. al-Ḥusayn, 226
man-made law, 311
manṭinqat al-farāgh, 22
Maqdisī, Kamāl al-Dīn al-, 15, 382n.23
Maqrīzī, Taqī al-Dīn al-, 74, 77, 85, 144–45, 154, 276–77
maraḍ al-ifranjī, 186
March, Andrew, 15–16, 21–22, 375, 476n.17, 477n.22, 478n.33, 479n.43, 479–80n.45, 480n.58, 481nn.69–70, 481n.76, 483n.90, 483n.106, 485n.132, 490n.203
  and ideal theory, 306–8
  on comprehensive doctrine, 309, 319–20
  and 'Fundamentalist' imaginary, 311
  on "conjecture", 323–24
  on residence in non-Muslim lands, 331–32
  on loyalty to non-Muslim states, 332–34
  on *jihād*, 334–37
  on pluralism and solidarity, 339–43
  and race, 344, 345–54
  and religion, 354–58
  and politics, 358
  on *fiqh*, 306–8, 311–12, 327–28, 475n.1
  and overlapping consensus, 304–5, 316, 318–19, 320, 481n.61

Marghinānī, Burhān al-Dīn Abū al-Ḥasan ʿAlī al-, 141
Mariña, Jacqueline, 242
Marīsī, Bishr al-, 217–18, 220
Marmor, Andrei, 448n.67
Martin Luther, 40, 80–81, 409n.40
maʿrūf, 243–44, 359–60, 432n.107, 491n.211
Marxism, 35, 201, 204
Marx, Karl, 5, 292–93, 306
mashrūʿīyat al-sabab, 104, 235–36, 275
See also sababīyat al-sabab
maṣlaḥah/ maṣāliḥ, 9–10, 40–41, 76–77, 111, 155–56, 208, 224, 226–27, 238, 239, 330–31, 338, 342–43, 358, 365
maṣlaḥah mursalah, 239, 311–12, 460n.203
Masud, Khalid, 114
Mattson, Ingrid, 470n.93
Māturīdī, Abū Manṣūr al-, 384n.34
Māturīdites, 382n.23
Māwardī, Abū al-Ḥasan ʿAlī al-, 136–40, 144–50, 152–53, 159, 170, 203–4, 287–88
Mawdūdī, Abū al-Aʿlā al-, 48
Mawlawī Fayṣal al-, 328
maẓālim, 19–20, 144–51
Māzarī, Muḥammad b. ʿAlī al-, 326, 482n.83
Mazrui, Ali, 319, 403n.212
Mbiti, John, 488n.170
McCutcheon, Russell T., 48, 395nn.90–91
"meaning", 4, 5
Melchert, Christopher, 452n.127
Michelangelo, 2
miḥnah, 218–19, 293
Millbank, John, 388n.23
Mills, Charles W., 305, 349–50
and Racial Liberalism, 350, 476n.4
Montesquieu, 173–74
Moosa, Ebrahim, xii, 108–9, 162, 405n.234, 420n.209, 493n.11
morality, 40, 59, 61, 84–86, 87–88, 121, 195–96, 199–200, 227, 228–29, 287, 379
moral objectivism, 6–7
Morrison, Ken, 445n.30
Mottahedeh, Roy, 489n.192
Motzki, Harald, 220–21
Mouffe, Chantal, 369–70, 493n.12
muʿāmalāt, 226–27, 260
mubāḥ, 77, 164–65, 166–67, 178–79, 228–29, 237–38, 340, 362, 379
Muḥammad (Prophet), 36, 38–39, 175
muḥtasib, 144–45, 152–38
mujaddid, 346–47
mujtahid, 9
mukhaṭṭiʾah, 9
Müller, F. Max, 43–44
Murray, Albert, 358–59
murūwah, 166–67
Muslim Judicial Council (MJC), 347–48
Mustafa, Abdul Rahman, 391–92n.58
Mustanṣir, al (Black Caliph), 346–47
Muʿtazilites/ Muʿtazilism, 6–7, 13, 97–98, 181, 203–4, 226, 230–31, 382n.23
Mutua, Makau, 448n.66

nabīdh, 142, 181, 228, 430n.87
nadhr, 139–40
Nadwi, A.M., 463n.227
Nakissa, Aria, 463n.226
Nandy, Ashis, 34, 388n.16
Naqshuwānī, Najm al-Dīn al-, 101–2
Nasafī, Abū al-Barakāt al-, 106–7
Nation of Islam, 70–71, 358
natural law, 8, 209–10
Nawawī, Yaḥyā b. Sharaf al-, 75–76
Niebuhr, H. Richard, 57
Niebuhr, Reinhold, 260–61
Nielsen, Jørgen, 144, 146–47, 431n.98
Nietzsche, Fredrich, 71, 168–69, 403n.221
nominalism/nominalist, 7–8, 70, 188, 230, 232, 382–83n.24
nomos, 157–59, 160, 161–62, 164, 174, 186–87, 235, 278, 302, 348, 364, 365–66
Nongbri, Brent, 31
Non-Muslims, 279, 326, 328–29, 339–43, 475nn.182–84, 482n.83, 484n.110, 485n.124
non-religious, 1–2, 10–11, 23, 31, 32, 37–38, 39, 41, 42, 46, 80–82, 121, 122, 180, 247–48, 265, 277, 373, 374, 378–79
non-*sharʿī*, 3, 10–11, 17, 19–20, 41, 42–43, 76–77, 80, 88, 95, 108, 110, 115, 134, 135, 165, 172, 173, 180, 186, 202, 213–14, 235, 237, 240–41, 242–43, 255–56, 264, 291, 297–98, 300, 301, 340, 341, 342, 362, 377, 380, 419n.197

obeisance, 52–53, 54, 210, 243–44
See also ṭāʿah
oppugnancy, 51–52, 70, 167–68
Opwis, Felicitas, 226–27, 239
O'Sullivan, J.M., 40–41
Ottomans, 22, 171–72, 426–27n.42
Otto, Rudolph, 43–44, 51
over-*sharīʿ*atization, 183, 185, 300, 301

Papanikolaou, A., 466–67n.48
Parks, Rosa, 211

peripheral vision, 160–61
Peters, Ruud, 424–25n.14
Philo (of Alexandria), 450n.101
Pickstock, Catherine, 388n.23
Plato (Platonic), 9, 67, 70
plausibility structure, 156–57, 158, 174, 186, 348, 364, 365–66, *See also nomos*
Poggi, G., 447n.48
poiesis, 379–80, 493n.11
Pollis, A., 466–67n.48
Pope Shenouda III, 290–91
Popper, Karl, 375–76, 479–80n.45
Powers, David S., 424n.13
Protestantism, 45–46
public reason, 315–16, 319–20, 321–23, 343–44, 366–68, 480n.53

Qādirī Creed, 293
qānūn, 171–35
Qaraḍāwī, Yūsuf al-, 58–59, 164, 297–98, 328, 332, 342, 437–38n.190
Qarāfī, Badr al-Dīn al-, 478n.29
Qarāfī, Shihāb al-Dīn al-, xi, 18, 49–50, 78, 79, 82, 98–99, 101–5, 109–10, 139–41, 143–44, 153, 166–67, 168, 180, 181–82, 208, 224, 234, 235–36, 245, 260, 272–74, 297–98, 307, 336, 337, 378, 460n.193, 462n.214, 462n.219, 477n.23
qawā'id, 40–41, 79, 237–38, 311–12
qiwāmah, 267, 268, 278–79
qiyās, 7, 18–19, 93, 97, 110–11, 112, 219–20, 447–48n.61
Qur'ān, 13–14, 33, 36–37, 52, 53, 55, 64, 66, 83–84, 92, 112–13, 138, 159, 163, 170, 171, 175, 219, 235, 243–44, 246, 257–58, 304–5, 309, 321–22, 336–37, 359–60, 362, 450n.96, 456–57n.169, 478n.29, 484n.111, 484n.118, 491n.211
qurbah, 52, 54, 70, 167, 210, 243–44, 247
Quṭb, Sayyid, 48, 324, 325, 327, 335–37, 481n.76

Rabb, Intisar, xii, 268–69, 412–13n.80, 466n.38
Rabbat, Nasser, 406n.12
Rahman, Fazlur, 36, 403–4n.222
Ramadan, Tariq, 169, 439n.212, 481n.76
Ramlī, Abū al-'Abbās b. Aḥmad al-, 75–76, 77
Rappaport, Yossef, 429n.70, 431n.96
ratio essendi, 93, 226–27, 233–34
Rationalism, 92–93, 218–19
Rawls, John, 21, 304–5, 314–17, 322, 329–30, 351, 364, 476n.15, 479n.44, 480n.57
ra'y, 218–19
Raysūnī, Aḥmad al-, 359–60, 491n.212
Rāzī, Fakhr al-Dīn al-, 18, 98–101, 104–5, 106
Rāzi, Muḥammad b. Zakarīyah al-, 32–33
realism/realist, 7, 188, 230, 232, 382–83n.24
reason, 6, 16–17, 20, 68, 84–85, 196, 223, 225, 233–34, 237, 244, 317–18, 372–73, 432n.107, *see also 'aql*
  versus "system of reason" 116–17, 422n.234, 422n.236, 422–23nn.240–41
  versus revelation, 217–23
Reinhart, A. Kevin, 108–9, 110–11, 285–86, 420n.209, 473n.141, 491n.211
relegere, 46, 397n.115
religare, 46, 397n.115
religio, 46–47, 48, 397n.115
religion, 1, 2, 3–5, 11, 17, 43–50, 60–61, 63, 65, 73, 129, 183, 230, 255, 275–78, 372–73
  Islamic Secular's 50–53
  as-concrete-doctrine-and-practice, 48–49, 50, 52–53, 64
  as psychodynamic orientation, 48–49, 51, 52–53, 62
  in the proper, the religious sense, 59, 60, 62, 186–87, 253, 277–78, 365–66, 373, 374–75
  as *sharī'ah*, 253, 254, 256
Religionswissenschaft, 43–44
  See also History of Religion
religious secular, 1–2, 41, 374
Religious Studies, xi, 43–46
Riḍā, Muḥammad Rashīd, 48, 171–73, 223, 246–47, 328, 485n.125
Rorty, Richard, 16–17, 162, 305, 354–55, 358
Rouayheb, Khaled, 487n.165
Rousseau, Jean-Jacques, 292–93, 339–40
Roy, Olivier, 388n.16

sabab, 87, 94–95
sababīyat al-sabab, 104, 181, 235–36, 240–41
  See also mashrū'īyat al-sabab
Sabra, Adam, 108–9, 477n.24
sadd al-dharā'i', 79, 208, 243–44, 478n.27
Sa'dī, 346
Ṣadr al-Sharī'ah, 'Ubayd Allāh b. Mas'ūd, 105
saeculum, 4–5
Ṣafwat, Aḥmad, 178, 181
Saḥnūn (Ibn Sa'īd al-Tanūkhī), 284, 472n.131
Said, Edward, 45–46
Sakandarī, Ibn 'Aṭā' Allāh al-, 457n.171
Salafī(s), 55, 57, 301
Salaymeh, Lena, 412–13n.80
Ṣāliḥ, Ḥasan Salīm Ḥasan, xi
Samarqandī, 'Alā' al-Dīn al-, 97–98, 416n.130
same-sex marriage, 299–300, 357, 365–66

Ṣanʿānī, ʿAbd al-Razzāq al-, 284
Sandel, Michael, 364–65
Sarakhsī, Abū Bakr Muḥammad al-, 91–92, 365, 492n.225
Sayeed, Asma, 463n.227
Sayyid, Riḍwān al-, 471n.127
Sayili, Aydin M., 439n.210
Schacht, Joseph, 6, 14–15, 45–46, 83–84, 127–28, 410–11n.54, 468n.70
Schimmel, Annemarie, 14–15
Schleiermacher, Fredrich, 43–44, 51, 53, 399–400n.146
Schmidtke, Sabine, 99
Schmitt, Carl, 71, 201–2, 203–4, 445n.31
  and *das Volk*, 205, 351, 447nn.47–49, 447n.54
  Schultz, Warren C., 406n.3, 407n.17, 407n.20
Science of Religion, 43–44
  See also Religionswissenschaft
Scruton, Roger, 454–55n.152
Secular, 1, 2, 3–4, 30–35
  macro-, 35, 37–38, 41
  micro-, 38–39, 41, 188
  political, 20, 176–79
  Western, 1–2, 17, 19–20, 29–30, 41, 42
secularism/secularization, 21, 28–29, 252–53
September 11, 2001, 12, 324, 338, 361–62, 447n.49
Sezgin, Yüksel, 474n.174
Shāfiʿī, Muḥammad b. Idris al-, 75–76, 90–91, 92, 93, 217–18, 219, 220, 362, 407n.20
  on non-Muslims, 282, 471n.126, 471–72n.130, 485–86n.134
Shahrastānī, Muḥammad b. ʿAbd al-Karīm, al-, 67, 225
Shakman Hurd, Elizabeth, 393n.71, 396n.106
Shamsy, Ahmad El, 10, 413n.92, 413n.95, 450n.99, 451n.111, 452n.126
Shannon, Christopher, 70
sharʿī, 3, 21, 65–66, 76–77, 80, 88, 95, 96, 97–98, 101–2, 108, 110, 113–15, 165, 186, 204–5, 228, 235, 240–41, 242, 254–55, 256, 261–62, 264, 267, 275, 364–65, 380
sharīʿah, 3, 6, 7, 8–10, 17, 20, 21–22, 23–24, 33, 41, 42, 73, 83–86, 87–89, 94–95, 103, 108–9, 114–15, 116–17, 122–23, 127–28, 142, 151, 174–75, 178–79, 180–81, 182–83, 184, 186, 187, 189, 195, 198–200, 207, 209, 210, 216–17, 222–23, 224, 228, 231, 232, 234, 235, 236, 237–38, 240, 244, 246, 247, 248–49, 251, 253, 254–56, 257, 259–62, 266, 267, 268–69, 271, 275–76, 279–80, 281–82, 300, 301, 302, 305, 341–42, 344–45, 348, 362, 373, 374–76, 379–80
  and *siyāsah*, 128–29, 130, 131–35, 136, 137–38, 139–41
  and non-Muslims, 280, 297–99
  and pluralism, 294–95
  and equality, 295–96
  and lapsed Muslims, 298
  and constitutionalism, 298–99
  and the US Constitution, 360–62
  and ideal theory, 306–8
  as a comprehensive doctrine, 308–9, 319–21
  and public reason, 321–22
sharīʿah-maximalism, 19, 112–98, 172
sharīʿah-minimalism, 18–19, 110–11
sharʿī/non-*sharʿī*, 18, 94, 95–96, 97–98, 100, 103–4, 106–7, 108, 112, 119, 131, 136, 185, 188, 189, 210, 247–48, 254, 255–56, 275, 291, 301–2, 323, 329, 374
sharṭ, 87, 100–1
Shāṭibī, Abū Isḥāq Ibrāhīm b. Mūsā al-, 22, 49, 225, 239
Shaybānī, Muḥammad b. al-Ḥasan al-, 284–85, 327
Shayzarī, ʿAbd al-Raḥmān b. Naṣr al-, 144–45, 432n.107, 435n.158
Shīʿism, 22
Shirāzī, Abū Isḥāq al-, 383n.30
Shūshāwī, al-Ḥusayn b. ʿAlī al-, 460n.203
Siddiqui, Sohaira, 126–27, 421n.216, 436n.171
Sinan, 2, 186–87
siyāsah, 19–20, 22, 112, 114–15, 128–44, 151–52, 156, 291
  as distinct from *sharīʿah*, 130–33
siyāsah sharʿīyah, 113–14, 141, 142–43, 235
Smart, Ninian, 44–45
Smith, Jonathan Z., 43, 45–46
Smith, Wilfred Cantwell, 47
sola scriptura, 80–81, 184, 217
Sorensen, Kim, 450n.97
Sourdel, Dominique, 100
Spectorsky, Susan A., 452n.126
speculative jurisprudence (see *ṭarīqat al-mutakallimīn*)
Stewart, Devin, 414n.96
Stilt, Kristen, 151, 153, 215
Stolzenberg, Nomi, 40
Stout, Jeffrey, 4, 40
Subkī, Tāj al-Dīn al-, 213–14, 449n.82, 452n.123
Subkī, Taqī al-Dīn al-, 452n.123
Sufism, 48
sui juris, 272, 275
Sukarno, 254–55
Sulamī, Iyāḍ al-, 107–8, 419–20n.204

Sunna, 53, 55, 92, 167–68, 170, 171, 246, 321–22, 324
superstitio, 46
Suyūṭī, Jalāl al-Dīn al-, 76, 439n.216

ṭā'ah, 52–53
 See also obeisance
Ṭabarī, Ibn Jarīr al-, 456–57n.169
Taftazānī, Sa'd al-Dīn al-, 105
Ṭahāwī, Abū Ja'far al-, 464n.20
Ṭā'ir, Ya'qūb al-, 293
taklīf, 38, 87–88
ta'līq, 139–40
Tambiah, Stanley, 68–69, 397n.122, 440n.224
taqlīd, 94–95, 109, 134, 223, 235, 491n.211
 improper, 181, 188
taqwā, 50–51, 52–53, 54, 70, 210, 243–44, 247, 367
Ṭarābulisī, 'Alā' al-Dīn al-, 136–37, 143, 144–45, 208
ṭarīqat al-fuqahā', 18, 91–93, 106–7
ṭarīqat al-mutakallimīn, 91–93, 100, 373
 See also speculative jurisprudence
Tarnas, Richard, 32
taṣarruf, 240–41, 245
ta'wīl, 161
Taylor, Charles, 4–5, 27–28, 31, 35–36, 40, 42, 51–52, 231–32, 387n.4, 391n.51
ta'zīr, 141, 142, 148
technologies of the self, 162, 375
Thawrī, Sufyān al-, 39–40
theology, 6–7, 12, 47, 54, 94, 99, 306–7, 322
Timbuktī, Aḥmad Bābā al-, 346–47
Tīmūr Lenk, 197–98
Tocqueville, Alexis de, 354, 490n.196
Tönnies, Ferdinand, 392–93n.66
Topolyak, Sulaymān, 324
Toulmin, Stephen, 467–68n.61
tradition, 46
Traditionalism, 92–93, 94, 218–19
Troeltsch, Ernst, 57–58
Ṭūfī, Najm al-Dīn al-, 118

Ulugh Beg (Muḥammad b. Taraghay b. Shāhrukh b. Tīmūr), 2, 186, 242
'Umar (I) (Ibn al-Khaṭṭāb), 208, 282–83, 470n.92
'Umar (II) (Ibn 'Abd al-'Azīz), 242
Unger, Roberto M., 230
U.S. Constitution, 326–27, 358–62, 385n.50
uṣūl al-fiqh, 1, 5–6, 17, 18, 79, 89, 90, 92–93, 101, 132–33, 304–5, 306–7, 336

Van Ess, Josef, 14–15
Vico, Giambattista, 160–61
 (and *sensus communis*), 368
Vogel, Frank, 129, 425n.24
von Harnack, Adolph, 43–44, 394–95n.84

Wach, Joachim, 45
waḍ', 6–7
Walzer, Michael, 305, 363, 491n.220
Wansbrough, John, 13–14
Wansharīsī, Aḥmad b. Yaḥyā al-, 324, 325, 326, 327, 482n.83
Ward, Graham, 388n.23
Watson, Alan, 273
Watt, W. Montgomery, 14–15, 38-39, 66–67
Watts, Alan, 160–61
Weber, Max, 35, 39, 85, 201–2, 392–93n.66, 445n.30
Weiss, Bernard, 87–88, 93, 101, 413n.88
West, Cornel, 463n.225
Westphalia, 292–93
White, Stephen, 458n.172
Wilkerson, Isabel, 489n.188
Williams, Joan, 352
Wittgenstein, Ludwig, 4, 356
Wolin, Sheldon, 40–41, 329–31, 492n.226
wulāt al-aḥdāth, 148–49
wulāt al-ma'āwin, 148–50
wuqū' al-sabab, 104, 181, 235–36, 240–41, 460n.193
Wymann-Landgraff, Umar F. Abd-Allah, 131, 221–22

X, Malcolm, 340

Yannoulatos, A., 466–67n.48
Yarbrough, Luke, 475n.182, 475n.184

Ẓāhirī school, 18–19, 40–41, 110–11, 221–22, 477n.24
Zanj, 487n.164
Zarkashī, Badr al-Dīn al-, 90–91, 98–99, 225, 383n.30, 384n.33
Zoroastrians, 203–4, 365, 492n.224
Zuḥaylī, Wahbah al-, 108, 247
Zuhdī, Karam, 469n.79
Zysow, Aron, 93, 458–59n.186